THE BIRTH OF
PURGATORY

Jacques Le Goff
THE BIRTH OF
PURGATORY

Translated by Arthur Goldhammer

The University of Chicago Press • Chicago

Originally published as *La naissance du Purgatoire*,
© 1981, Editions Gallimard
The University of Chicago Press, Chicago 60637
Scolar Press
90/91 Great Russell Street, London WC1B 3PY
© 1984 by The University of Chicago
All rights reserved. Published 1984
Paperback edition 1986
Printed in the United States of America
05 04 03 02 01 00   5 6 7 8

LIBRARY OF CONGRESS CATALOGING IN PUBLICATION DATA
Le Goff, Jacques, 1924–
The birth of purgatory.

Translation of: La naissance du purgatoire.
Includes bibliographical references and index.
1. Purgatory—History of doctrines. I. Title.
BT842.L413   1983   236'.5'09   83-1108
ISBN: 0-226-47083-0 (ppbk.)

♾ The paper used in this publication meets the minimum
requirements of the American National Standard for
Information Sciences—Permanence of Paper for Printed
Library Materials, ANSI Z39.48–1984.

Purgatory—what a grand thing!
Saint Catherine of Genoa

Purgatory surpasses heaven and hell in poetry, because it
represents a future and the others do not.
Chateaubriand

Contents

A group of illustrations follows p. 208

Acknowledgments

THIS research has been helped by many people. To begin with I want to mention the members of the Historical Anthropology Group of the Ecole des Hautes Etudes en sciences sociales: Andrée Duby, Marie-Claire Gasnault, Georgette Lagarde, Colette Ribaucourt, Jean-Claude Schmitt, and my friend and colleague Anne Lombard-Jourdan.

Also in Paris, at the Institut de Recherche et d'Histoire des Textes of the Centre National de Recherche Scientifique, François Dolbeau and Monique-Cécile Garand; at the Comité Du Cange, Anne-Marie Bautier; at the Lexique du Latin philosophique médiéval, Annie Cazenave; and the staff of the Bibliothèque du Saulchoir, whose competence and kindness were enjoyed in equal measure.

In Rome, my friends Girolamo Arnaldi and Raoul Manselli gave me the benefit of their learning and their attention. I received incomparable assistance at the Bibliothèque de l'Ecole française from Nöelle de La Blanchardière, Pascale Koch, and the entire staff. Jean-Claude Maire-Vigueur, director of medieval studies at the school, and Jacques Chiffoleau of its faculty, assisted me in many ways. The school's director, Georges Vallet, and André Hartmann provided me at the Piazza Navona with the perfect surroundings for accomplishing the bulk of the writing. At the Vatican Library, Agostino Paravicini-Bagliani above all, but also Louis Duval-Arnould and Msgr. Joseph Sauset, did not stint in either learning or kindness. I also enjoyed excellent working conditions at the Library of the Pontifical Gregorian University. Professor Reinhard Elze, director of the German Historical Institute, and Dr. Goldbrünner, the Institute's librarian, anticipated all of my needs and desires.

To three friends who, at various stages of this work, especially in intelligent criticism of the manuscript, provided invaluable assistance, I wish to express my special thanks: Father Pierre-Marie Gy, Jean-Claude Schmitt, and especially Jacques Revel.

Christine Bonnefoy, assisted from time to time by Simone Brochereau, devoted much effort and kind consideration to the material task of assembling this book.

To all of these people I express my heartfelt thanks.

The Third Place

I N THE bitter disputes that pitted Protestants against Catholics in the
sixteenth century, the former severely reproached the latter for their
belief in Purgatory, to which Luther referred as "the third place."[1]
This "invented" world—the "other world"—is not mentioned in the
Bible.

The aim of this book is to trace the formation of the idea of this third
place through time, from its roots in Judeo-Christian antiquity to its final
emergence with the flowering of medieval civilization in the second half of
the twelfth century, when the idea of Purgatory finally took hold in the
West, and beyond, into the next century. I shall try to explain why the idea
of Purgatory is intimately bound up with this important moment in the
history of Christendom and to show, further, the crucial role that Purgatory played in persuading people to accept (or, in the case of the heretics, to
reject) the new society that was the result of two and one-half centuries of
prodigious growth following the year 1000.

WHAT WAS AT STAKE?

It is rare that we can follow the historical development of a belief, even
if—as is the case with Purgatory—it is made up of many very ancient
elements, whose origins often seem to be lost in the depths of time. But
belief in Purgatory is no mere adjunct, no minor addition to the great
edifice whose foundations were first laid by primitive Christianity and
which eventually developed into the medieval Church. Ideas about the
other world are among the more prominent features of any religion or
society. The life of the believer undergoes a change when he becomes
convinced that life does not end with death.

The gradual emergence—or perhaps one should say, the lengthy construction—of the doctrine of Purgatory at once required and entailed a
substantial modification in the spatial and temporal framework of the
Christian imagination. Such mental structures are the framework within
which society lives and thinks. In a society as thoroughly permeated with
religion as was the Christian West from the end of antiquity down to the
industrial revolution—an epoch to which I refer, with some license, as the

"Middle Ages" in the broad sense—to change the geography of the other world and hence of the universe, to alter time in the afterlife and hence the link between earthly, historical time and eschatological time, between the time of existence and the time of anticipation—to do these things was to bring about a gradual but nonetheless crucial intellectual revolution. It was, literally, to change life itself.

Clearly, the emergence of such a belief is associated with far-reaching social change. The new way of thinking about the other world was related to specific changes in this one. What were these changes? What ideological role did Purgatory play? The fact that the Church exerted tight control over the new doctrine, going so far as to divide power over the other world between itself and God, shows that the stakes were high. Why not leave the dead to wander as they will, or to rest in peace?

Before Purgatory

Purgatory did indeed come to prominence as a "third place." Christianity inherited from earlier religions and civilizations a geography of the other world. Two models were set before it: Christianity might well have followed Judaism in choosing a monistic other world—*sheol*—rather than a dualistic one like the Roman Hades and Elysian Fields, the former a place of terror, the latter of happiness. But it adopted the dualistic model and even accentuated some of its features. Rather than send all the dead, good and bad alike, to repose underground for some portion of the interval between Creation and the Day of Judgment, Christianity decided that the just would reside in Heaven from the moment of their death. That is, at least some of them would—namely, the best: the martyrs and later the saints. Christianity even identified a place on the surface of the earth as the location of the Earthly Paradise. Thus Christianity took the ancient myth of a Golden Age and assigned it a place and not, as the ancients had been content to do, just a time, a nostalgic memory of the good old days. The Earthly Paradise figures on medieval maps in the Far East, beyond the great wall and the fearsome inhabitants of Gog and Magog. Through it flowed a four-branched river created by Yahweh "to water the garden" (Gen. 2:10). What is more, Christianity pushed the contrast between Heaven and Hell to the limit, drawing an analogy between Heaven and Hell on the one hand and earth and sky on the other. Though underground, Hell was still identified with earth, and in the Christian mind the infernal world contrasted with the celestial world, just as in the Greek mind the chthonic world contrasted with the uranian. Despite occasional impulses to look heavenward, the Ancients—Babylonians and Egyptians, Jews and Greeks, Romans and pagan barbarians—had been more afraid of the depths of the earth than drawn to the vastness of the sky, which in any case was often inhabited by angry gods. Christianity, in the first few centuries at any rate and subsequently during the medieval barbarization, did not try to focus attention exclusively on Hell. Rather, it lifted up man's eyes toward Heaven. Jesus himself had shown the way: after descending into Hell, he went up to Heaven. Whereas the Greeks and Romans had emphasized the contrast between right and left in their spatial symbolism, Christianity, while not abandoning a distinction mentioned in both the Old and New Testaments,[2] nevertheless quickly accorded pride of place to the opposition between high and low. Throughout the Middle Ages it was the latter that oriented the inner dialectic of Christian values whenever thought was translated into spatial terms.

To ascend, to raise oneself, to move higher—the direction in which the compass of moral and spiritual life pointed was up, whereas in social life the norm was to stay in one's proper place, where God had placed one on this earth, guarding against ambition to escape one's condition while at the same time taking pains not to lower oneself, not to fail.[3]

When, between the second and fourth centuries, Christianity set itself to thinking about the situation in which souls find themselves between the death of the individual and the Last Judgment, and when, in the fourth century, the greatest Fathers of the Church conceived of the idea (shared, with minor differences as we shall see, by Ambrose, Jerome, and Augustine) that certain sinners might be saved, most probably by being subjected to a trial of some sort, a new belief was born, a belief that gradually matured until in the twelfth century it became the belief in Purgatory; but the place where these souls were to reside and where this trial was to take place was not yet specified. Until the end of the twelfth century the noun *purgatorium* did not exist: *the* Purgatory had not yet been born.[4]

It is a remarkable fact that the first appearance of the word *purgatorium*, expressing a newly acquired awareness of Purgatory as a place and thus the birth of Purgatory per se, has been neglected by historians, and in the first place by historians of theology and spirituality.[5] Historians doubtless do not yet attach sufficient importance to words. The clerics of the Middle Ages knew better: whether realists or nominalists, they knew that words and things are as closely connected as soul and body. For historians of ideas and of *mentalités*, historians of the *longue durée*, historians of the deeply rooted and the slowly changing, words—certain words—offer the advantage of making their appearance at specific points in time. Their introduction can be dated with reasonable accuracy, thus providing the historian with valuable chronological evidence, without which no true history is possible. Of course a belief cannot be dated in the same way as an event, but the idea that the history of the *longue durée* is a history without dates is to be firmly rejected. A slowly developing phenomenon such as the belief in Purgatory may lie stagnant for centuries, or slowly ebb and flow, only to burst forth suddenly—or so it seems—in a kind of tidal wave that does not engulf the original belief but rather testifies to its presence and power. Anyone, however erudite, who uses the word purgatory in speaking of the period between the fall of the Roman Empire and the thirteenth century is missing an important point, perhaps the crucial point in the history of the idea: its spatialization, which first found expression in the appearance of the substantive sometime between 1150 and 1200. Worse still, he is missing an opportunity to shed some light on certain far-reaching social changes associated with a critical era in the history of medieval Christendom. And he is missing an opportunity to touch on one of the most important episodes in the whole history of ideas and *mentalités*: what I shall call the "spatialization" of thought.

SPACE: "GOOD TO THINK"

The idea that space plays an important part in scientific thought is a familiar one. Recent work on the history of this idea has done much to revitalize such disciplines as "geographical history," geography, and urban history. The potency of the idea of space manifests itself above all in symbolism. Following the zoologists, anthropologists have demonstrated the fundamental importance of territoriality.[6] In *The Hidden Dimension*, Edward T. Hall has shown that for humans and animals territory is an extension of the organism itself and, further, that the perceptions of space depends in large part on culture (indeed, on this point he may be too much of a "culturalist") and that the idea of "territory" is an internalization of space, organized by thought.[7] The way in which different societies organize "space"—geographic space, economic space, political space, and ideological space—has an important bearing on their history. Organizing the space of the other world had lasting consequences for Christianity. If one is looking forward to the resurrection of the dead, the geography of the other world is of no small moment. Indeed, it seems reasonable to suppose that there is a connection between the way Christian society lays out the other world and the way it organizes this one, since the two are related by the ties that bind the society of the living to the society of the dead. Between 1150 and 1300, Christendom gave itself over to a wholesale revision of the maps of both this world and the other. To Christians it seemed that things lived and moved here below as in the hereafter, more or less at the same pace.

THE LOGIC AND THE GENESIS OF PURGATORY

What exactly was Purgatory when, between 1150 and 1200 or so, it installed itself firmly in the mind of Western Christendom? Briefly, it was an intermediary other world in which some of the dead were subjected to a trial that could be shortened by the prayers, by the spiritual aid, of the living. But before the concept achieved this degree of specificity, a long

4

prior history was necessary, a history of ideas and images, of beliefs and deeds, of theological debates and, as seems probable, of profound, hard-to-grasp social change.

The first part of this book will be devoted to the formation of the various elements that would finally be assembled in the twelfth century into what we know as Purgatory. It may be regarded as a reflection on the originality of the religious thought of Latin Christendom, a reflection on the traditions, discontinuities, and conflicts both internal and external out of which the theology of the Christian West was constructed.

Belief in Purgatory implies, in the first instance, belief in immortality and resurrection, since something new may happen to a human being between his death and resurrection. It offers a second chance to attain eternal life. Finally, belief in Purgatory entails the belief that immortality can be achieved in the life of a single individual. Thus religions such as Hinduism and Catharism, which believe in perpetual reincarnation and metempsychosis, cannot accommodate the idea of a Purgatory.

The existence of a Purgatory also depends on the idea that the dead are judged, an idea shared by any number of religions, though, to be sure, "the forms of judgment have varied widely from one civilization to another."[8] The particular form of judgment that allows for the existence of a Purgatory is quite a novel one. In fact, two judgments are involved: one at the time of death and a second at the end of time. In between—in the eschatological interlude, as it were—every human soul becomes involved in complex judicial proceedings concerning the possible mitigation of penalties, the possible commutation of sentences, subject to the influence of a variety of factors. Belief in Purgatory therefore requires the projection into the afterlife of a highly sophisticated legal and penal system.

Furthermore, belief in Purgatory is associated with the idea of individual responsibility and free will. Though guilty by nature because of original sin, man is judged for the sins he himself is responsible for committing. There is a close connection between Purgatory, the "intermediary hereafter," and a type of sin that falls between the purity of the saints and the saved on the one hand and the unpardonable culpability of criminal sinners on the other. For a long time there had been a rather vague notion of "slight," "routine," or "habitual" sins, as Augustine and Gregory the Great were well aware, but it was not until shortly before the emergence of Purgatory that this idea finally gave rise to the category of sin known as "venial"—indeed, this was a prerequisite for the emergence of the doctrine of Purgatory. Broadly speaking, Purgatory developed as the place where venial sins might be expurgated—though in reality things were a bit more complicated, as we shall see.

In order to believe in Purgatory—a place of punishment—one must have a clear understanding of the relation between the soul and the body. From very early times Church doctrine on this point was as follows: the immortal soul separates from the body at death and is rejoined with it only at the end of time, when the body is resurrected. As I see it, however, the question whether the soul is corporeal or incorporeal seems not to have posed a problem for the development of Purgatory or its forerunners. Once separated from the body, the soul was endowed with a materiality *sui generis*, and punishment could then be inflicted upon it in Purgatory as though it were corporeal.[9]

THE IDEA OF THE INTERMEDIATE

Purgatory is situated in a position that is intermediate in more than one sense. In respect of time it falls between the death of the individual and the Last Judgment. But before settling in this location, as it were, Purgatory had first to pass through a period of uncertainty. Though Augustine played a crucial role in locating the time of purgation, he himself never moored Purgatory firmly to any berth in the beyond. Whether the time of Purgatory was earthly time or eschatological time long remained a matter of controversy: Purgatory might begin here below in the form of penitence, only to be completed in the hereafter with a definitive purification at the time of the Last Judgment. But, later, Purgatory began to encroach on eschatological time, and Judgment Day, once a mere moment, swelled to fill a large expanse of time.

Spatially, Purgatory is also in an in-between position, between Hell and Paradise. Yet for a long time it tended to be confused with one or the other pole. Before it could begin to exist in its own right, Purgatory had to supersede both the *refrigerium*, that antechamber to Paradise invented by the early Christians, and the "bosom of Abraham" mentioned in the story of Lazarus and the wicked rich man in the New Testament (Luke 16:19–26). Above all it had to detach itself from Hell, of which it long remained a relatively undistinguished department, a sort of upper Gehenna. This wrangling between Hell and Paradise suggests that to Christians Purgatory was no minor issue. Before Dante could map the other world's three realms in his incomparable poem, the soil had to be prepared by long and arduous effort. Purgatory was not ultimately a true intermediary. Reserved for the purification of the future elect, it stood closer to Heaven than to Hell. No longer in the center, Purgatory was situated above rather than below the true middle. In other words, Purgatory was a part of one of those not quite balanced systems that are so characteristic of the feudal mentality. The feudal mind had a predilection for symbols of inequality within equality: consider, for example, the symbolism of vassalage and marriage. Everyone is equal, and yet the vassal is subordinate to the lord, the wife to the husband. It is therefore illusory to think of Purgatory as lying midway between the Hell escaped and the Heaven desired by the soul, all the more so because the soul's stay in Purgatory is merely temporary, ephemeral, not everlasting like its term in Heaven or Hell. And yet space and time in Purgatory were different from space and time here below, governed by different rules—rules that make Purgatory a part of the imagination to which the men of the Middle Ages referred as "marvelous."

At the heart of the matter, perhaps, was a question of logic. In order for Purgatory to be born, the notion of "intermediacy" had to take on some substance, had to become "good to think"* for the men of the Middle Ages. Purgatory was one component of a system—the system of the hereafter—and is meaningless unless viewed in conjunction with the other elements of that system. I ask the reader to keep this in mind. But since, of the three principal zones of the other world, Purgatory took longest to define, and since its role proved the most problematic, I have thought it possible and desirable to treat Purgatory without going into detail about Heaven and Hell.

A logical, mathematical concept, "intermediacy" is an idea whose significance is closely bound up with profound changes in the social and intellectual reality of the Middle Ages. We see other signs of the increased importance attached to intermediate categories in the attempts made to introduce "middle classes" or third orders between the powerful and the poor, the clergy and the laity. To move from binary to tertiary schemes was to cross a dividing line in the organization of social thought, a step the importance of which Claude Lévi-Strauss has pointed out.[10]

Penal Imagery: Fire

Unlike the Jewish *sheol*—a sad, disturbing place but one devoid of punishments—Purgatory is a place where the dead are subjected to one or more trials. As we shall see, these may resemble the tortures to which the damned are subjected in Hell. Of these, fire and ice are the most common, and trial by fire played a role of fundamental importance in the history of Purgatory.

Anthropologists, folklorists, and historians of religion are all familiar with fire as a sacred symbol. In medieval Purgatory and its precursors we find almost all the forms of fire symbolism that have been identified by anthropologists or religion: circles of fire, lakes and seas of fire, rings of fire, walls and moats of fire, fire-breathing monsters, burning coals, souls in the form of sparks, rivers of fire, and burning mountains and valleys.

What is sacred fire? "In initiation rites," G. Van der Leeuw tells us, "fire wipes out the past period of existence and makes a new period possible."[11] Fire, then, is part of a rite of passage, quite appropriate to this place of

*As Lévi-Strauss would say.—Trans.

transition. Purgatory is one of what Van Gennep calls "liminal rites," whose importance has sometimes been overlooked by anthropologists intent on the phases of "separation" and "incorporation" that open and close rites of passage.

But there is still more to the significance of fire. Using fairy tales, legends, and popular plays of both medieval and modern times, Carl-Martin Edsmann has clearly demonstrated the presence of regenerative fires analogous to those found in Greek and Roman mythology, and even earlier, in Iranian and Indian mythology, where the concept of a divine fire—*Ignis divinus*—seems to have originated.[12] Accordingly, it may be that the rise of Purgatory is related to the resurgence of Indo-European folklore that seems to have taken place in Christendom between the eleventh and the thirteenth century. Roughly contemporary with that rise is the emergence (or reemergence?) of the trifunctional schema recently brought to light by Georges Duby and others. Fire was associated with oven, forge, and stake, and it is alongside these elements of popular culture that we must set the fire of Purgatory, upon which folklore also seized.

Fire rejuvenates and renders immortal: the legend of the phoenix is the most famous embodiment of this idea, a commonplace of medieval thought from the time of Tertullian on. The phoenix became the symbol of mankind waiting to be reborn. One text, erroneously attributed to Ambrose, applies to this legend the remark of Saint Paul, that "the fire shall try every man's work of what sort it is" (1 Cor. 3:13), which was destined to serve, throughout the Middle Ages, as the biblical basis for Purgatory.

This tradition helps to clarify, I think, three important characteristics of the idea of purgatory fire as it figures in the doctrine that interests us here. The first of these is that the fire that rejuvenates and renders immortal is a fire "through which one passes." Again it was Paul, in the same celebrated passage (1 Cor. 3:15), who said "he himself shall be saved; yet so as by fire." Purgatory is a transitory location (or state), and imaginary voyages in Purgatory, it is worth pointing out explicitly, may have been symbolic in intent. The more the passage through Purgatory came to be modeled after a judicial proceeding, the more trial by fire was emphasized. Trial by fire was an ordeal: an ordeal for the souls in Purgatory themselves, and also for the living souls allowed to pass through Purgatory not as mere tourists but at their own risk and peril. It is easy to see how this rite might have appealed to men who combined ancient Indo-European traditions of divine fire, handed down through Greece and Rome, with barbarian beliefs and practices. It is not hard to understand why one bit of natural geography attracted particular attention when it came to locating the site of Purgatory, or at least the mouths of Purgatory, on earth: volcanoes. As mountains that spit fire from a crater or pit at the center, these had the advantage of combining three key physical and symbolic ingredients of

Purgatory's structure. We shall see presently how men roamed Sicily between Stromboli and Etna hoping to compile a map of Purgatory. But in Sicily there was no group capable of taking advantage of the opportunity offered by the local geography; by contrast, the Irish, their English neighbors, and the Cistercians who organized carefully controlled pilgrimages to the site of Saint Patrick's Purgatory were able to do this. The problem with Frederick II's Sicily was that it had a sovereign suspected of heresy, Greek monks, and Moslem inhabitants and so was thought to be insufficiently "catholic" to be the site of one of Purgatory's main portals. Mount Etna, moreover, had a long association with Hell, which proved difficult to overcome.

If fire came to occupy a place of paramount importance in the symbolic system of Purgatory and ultimately became the symbol of the doctrine par excellence, it generally figured in a symbolic pair, coupled with water. In texts properly belonging to the prehistory of the Middle Ages, we commonly find a pair of sites, one fiery, the other damp, one hot, the other cold, one in flames, the other frozen. The fundamental trial to which the dead are subjected in Purgatory is not merely to pass through fire but to pass in succession first through fire and then through water—through a probative sauna, as it were.

Carl-Martin Edsmann has discerningly pointed to certain texts dating from classical Rome in which one finds Caucasian ascetics described as living nude, now in flames, now in ice. Cicero speaks of "sages who live nude and withstand the snows of the Caucasus and the rigors of winter without pain and then hurl themselves into the fire and burn without a moan."[13] Valerius Maximus also refers to "men who spend their whole lives in the nude, now hardening their bodies by throwing themselves into the harsh ice of the Caucasus, now exposing themselves to flame without uttering a cry."[14]

The symbolic coupling of fire and water (or cold) recurs in a rite of early Christian times which must have played a part in the prehistory of Purgatory: baptism by fire. Christians were made familiar with this rite by the Gospels of Matthew and Luke, where they discuss John the Baptist. Matthew (3:11) puts the following words into the mouth of Christ's forerunner: "I indeed baptize you with water unto repentance: but he that cometh after me is mightier than I, whose shoes I am not worthy to bear: he shall baptize you with the Holy Ghost, and with fire." A similar speech is attributed to John the Baptist in Luke 3:16.

The idea of baptism by fire, which stems from ancient Indo-European myths about fire, took concrete shape in Judeo-Christian apocalyptic writings. The earliest Christian theologians, especially the Greeks, were aware of it. Commenting on Luke 3:16, Origen tells us that "baptism by fire and the spirit is necessary so that, when he who has been baptized comes to the river of fire, he can show that he has preserved the vessels of water and spirit and is therefore worthy of receiving baptism by fire in Jesus Christ as well" (*In Lucam*, Homily 24). Edsmann sees the pearls mentioned in Matthew 13:45–46 ("Again, the kingdom of heaven is like unto a merchant man, seeking goodly pearls, who, when he had found one pearl of great price, went and sold all that he had, and bought it") as a symbol of Christ, who had joined fire and water. In "orthodox" Christianity baptism by fire remained metaphorical. This was not true of certain sects (Baptists, Messalians, and some Egyptian ascetics, for example) or, for that matter, of the Cathari, who in the twelfth century were accused by Ecbert, an "orthodox" apologist, of not really practicing baptism "in fire" but rather "alongside" the fire.

In ancient mythology and religion the nature of fire is manifold and varied. We find great variety, for example, in Judeo-Christian fire symbolism and in particular in the many different functions and meanings attributed to the fire of Purgatory. In these various aspects of fire, "at once deifying and vivifying, punitive and destructive," Edsmann sees "the different sides of divinity's very being," and he consequently reduces fire's many faces to unity in the godhead. This explanation helps us to understand the variety of interpretations of purgatorial fire put forward by Christians from the earliest days of the religion until the thirteenth century. Although it may seem that a different kind of fire is being talked about, the apparent diversity can be traced to the polysemy of "divine fire" as it was understood in the ancient world. At times it was seen as purifying, at other times as punitive or probative. Sometimes it seems to exist in the present, sometimes in the future. Usually it is real but occasionally spiritual. Sometimes it affects only certain people, sometimes everyone. But the fire is always one and the same, the fire of Purgatory, whose complexity can be traced back to its origins in the Indo-European notion of a divine or sacred fire.

Augustine apparently understood this continuity, which, despite certain fundamental changes of meaning, links ancient and Christian concepts of fire: "The Stoics," he wrote in the *City of God* (book 8, chap. 5), "believed that fire, one of the four elements that constitute the visible universe, is endowed with life and wisdom, and is the creator of the universe and of all its contents; that fire, in fact, is actually God." To be sure, in Christianity, fire, as Francis of Assisi magnificently put it, is merely a creature. But as Edsmann rightly says, "all the complexity of the fire of the hereafter in either its general or special forms—for example the river of fire—can be understood as so many functions of one and the same divine fire." This assertion holds good for the fire of Purgatory. However, neither the men of the Middle Ages nor the bulk of medieval clerics had any idea of the rich past history of purgatorial fire, apart from a few passages in the Bible, which for medieval man constituted a necessary and sufficient guarantee of the authenticity of this sacred tradition. Nevertheless, I have felt the need to make mention of this lengthy heritage. It casts a revealing light on some disconcerting aspects of the history of Purgatory in the Middle Ages. It enables us to understand the reasons behind certain hesitations in regard to Purgatory, certain debates, and certain choices: a tradition proposes as much as it imposes. And above all it explains in part, I think, why the doctrine of Purgatory proved so successful: because it incorporated certain very ancient symbolic traditions. What is rooted in tradition is more likely to succeed than what is not. Though new to Christianity, Purgatory borrowed much of its baggage from earlier religions. When incorporated into the Christian tradition, divine fire underwent a change in meaning to which the historian must of course be sensitive. Yet, however dramatic the changes that history may bring, we must nevertheless remain attentive to a certain persistence of certain fundamental elements over the long term. Revolutions rarely create anything that is new. Rather, they change the meaning of what already exists. Christianity was, if not a revolution, then at least a key element in a revolution. From the past it took over the idea of a divine fire that rejuvenates man and renders him immortal; it made this idea, not into a belief coupled with a ritual, but rather into an attribute of God, the use of which is determined by human behavior in two ways: by the behavior of the dead while they were still on earth, which determines whether or not they will be subjected to purgatorial fire, and by the behavior of the living, which can modify the length of time a dead soul must remain in Purgatory. The fire of Purgatory, while remaining a symbol imbued with meaning and signifying salvation through purification, became an instrument to be wielded by a complex system of justice associated with a society quite different from those that believed in the regenerative power of fire.

THE SOLIDARITY OF THE DEAD AND THE LIVING

The last important characteristic of Purgatory to be mentioned is this: Purgatory is an intermediary other world in which the trial to be endured by the dead may be abridged by the intercessory prayers, the "suffrages," of the living. That the early Christians were persuaded of the efficacy of their prayers for the dead we know from funerary inscriptions, liturgical formulas, and the *Passion of Perpetua*, which dates from the early third century and is the first in a long line of spatial representations of what would one day be Purgatory. This belief in the efficacy of prayer began a movement of piety that culminated in the creation of Purgatory. It is significant that Augustine, in the *Confessions*, broaches for the first time the line of thought that would lead him toward the idea of Purgatory when he describes his feelings after the death of his mother Monica.

Christian confidence in the efficacy of prayer was not immediately linked to a belief in the possibility of postmortem purification. As Joseph Ntedika has clearly shown in the case of Augustine, the two beliefs were elaborated separately and had virtually nothing to do with one another. Before the idea of the suffrage or prayer in behalf of the dead could be evolved, solidarity had to be established between the living and the dead: institutions were required to finance intercessory prayer, namely, wills, and to execute it, namely, the confraternities, which took prayer for the dead as one of their daily obligations. Beyond that, it took time for the necessary links to be established.

What an enhancement of the power of the living there was in this hold over the dead! Meanwhile, here below, the extension of communal ties into the other world enhanced the solidarity of families, religious organizations, and confraternities. And for the Church, what a marvelous instrument of power! The souls in Purgatory were considered to be members of the Church militant. Hence, the Church argued, it ought to have (partial) jurisdiction over them, even though God was nominally the sovereign judge in the other world. Purgatory brought to the Church not only new spiritual power but also, to put it bluntly, considerable profit, as we shall see. Much of this profit went to the mendicant orders, ardent propagandists of the new doctrine. And finally, the "infernal" system of indulgences found powerful support in the idea of Purgatory.

PURGATORY: THE EVIDENCE

I invite the reader to examine along with me the evidence I have gathered concerning the history of Purgatory. I can think of no more cogent support for my interpretation than to put the reader in contact with the texts: the writings of great theologians as well as of obscure, sometimes anonymous compilers. Some of these texts are of great literary merit, others are mere instruments of communication, but many are translated here for the first time and most are imbued, in one degree or another, with the charm of imagination, the warmth of evangelical zeal, and the excitement of discovering a world within as well as a world without. There is no better way to get at the nature of the place called Purgatory, and the belief in that place, than to watch it being built up, piece by piece, slowly but not always surely and without leaving out any of history's complex texture.

These texts often repeat one another, for it is by repetition that a corpus is constituted and a history perpetuated. The echoes that reverberate through this book reflect reality. To have eliminated repetitions that actually occurred would have been to distort and falsify the past.

We shall see what happened to the geography of the other world as the first chapter of the Middle Ages unfolds, as the foundations of our Western world are being laid. This period of slow change, which extends from the third through the seventh century, used to be referred to as the Late Empire and the early Middle Ages. Now that it is much better known than it used to be, it is more properly called "late antiquity." This was a period when ancient traditions were being decanted, Christianity was shaping new habits, and mankind was struggling to survive physically and spiritually. Caught between Hell and Paradise, anticipating an imminent end to the world, men had no time for Purgatory, a superfluous luxury that remained hidden in the depths of their consciousness. Later, between the eighth and eleventh century, various precursors of Purgatory were proposed only to be left in suspense as progress in theology and religious practice came to a virtual standstill with the birth of feudalism, though the monastic imagination did depict the hidden recesses of the next world in chiaroscuro canvases slashed across by shafts of light. The great century of creation, the twelfth, was also the century in which Purgatory was born, and this birth can only be understood when set against the context of the feudal system then being given its definitive shape. The time that followed was one of restoration of order. The domestication of the next world that paved the way for Purgatory also made it possible to include the dead among the ranks of the social order. Purgatory gave this society a new lease on eternal life, as it were, a second chance at salvation, and this change entailed other modifications in the social system.

Theology and Popular Culture

Two points remain to be cleared up. The first concerns the place of theology in this work. I am neither a theologian nor a historian of theology. Clearly, theology has an important part in the discussion of a belief that became a dogma. I hope to do justice to the theological aspects of the question. But the belief in Purgatory took hold, I think, for reasons that go beyond theology, and it is these other reasons that particularly interest me, because they tell us more than theology does about the relation between belief and society, about mental structures, and about the historical role of imagination. I am not unaware of the fact that, in modern Catholic theology, Purgatory is not a place but a "state." The Tridentine Fathers, anxious in this respect as in all others to avoid contamination of the faith by "superstition," expunged the idea of Purgatory from dogma. Accordingly, Church dogma specifies neither the location of Purgatory nor the penalties to which souls are there subjected, these being matters left up to individual opinion.

Nevertheless, I hope to show in this book that the idea of Purgatory as a place and the imagery associated with that idea had a very important part in Purgatory's success.[15] This is true of the idea's success not only with the masses of the faithful but also with theologians and ecclesiastical authorities in the twelfth and thirteenth centuries. When there arose among the laity a man of genius who also happened to be highly learned, he, better than anyone else, gave voice to what the idea of Purgatory meant to the men of the later Middle Ages, after 1150. The theologian who gave the best account of the history of Purgatory was Dante.

The second point I wish to clear up has to do with the place of popular culture in the birth of Purgatory. This was undoubtedly important, and we shall have several occasions to point this out. Behind a number of key elements that went into the structure of Purgatory we can make out the active presence of popular tradition, not in the vulgar sense of "mass culture" but in the more useful sense of specific folkloric traditions. As Carl-Martin Edsmann has shown, the notion of purgatorial fire partakes of rites and beliefs that can be understood with the help of popular tales, legends, and spectacles. Voyages through the other world belong to a genre that tightly interweaves strands of scholarly culture with strands of folklore.[16] *Exempla* of Purgatory frequently derive from popular tales or are related to them. In conjunction with a number of colleagues and friends, I have for a number of years now been pursuing the question of relations between high and popular culture in my seminar at the Ecole des Hautes Etudes en sciences sociales. In this book, however, I have chosen not to pursue this particular path very far. With this kind of subject there is too much uncertainty to permit any accurate assessment or interpretation of the undeniable role played by popular culture. But it should be kept constantly in mind that popular culture did indeed play a role in the birth of Purgatory. The century in which this occurred was also the century in which the influence of folklore on the culture of the learned was at its height and the Church was most receptive to traditions that in earlier years it had rooted out, covered up, or ignored.[17] The rise of this new influence also contributed to the birth of Purgatory.

PART ONE

THE HEREAFTER BEFORE PURGATORY

ONE

Ancient Imaginings

MEDIEVAL Purgatory reused motifs that had gained currency in very early times: darkness, fire, torture, the bridge as ordeal and passageway, mountains, rivers, and so on. Certain other motifs, such as the idea of souls wandering or in repose, were very nearly included but in the end rejected. And still others, such as the idea of metempsychosis and reincarnation, were rejected out of hand. I shall therefore begin by describing some of the elements that were taken over from other times and places, some of them very remote indeed.

To include discussion of ancient religions in a study of Purgatory is to view Purgatory as one particular response to a problem faced by many religious systems: What is the structure of the other world? How is the hereafter to be imagined in order to display its function? In some cases to refer to another religion's solution to this problem is to indicate a genuine historical tradition, which actually influenced the way Purgatory was conceived in the West. The fire motif, for example, was one that circulated from ancient India to Western Christendom, though it should be said that the fire of Purgatory was the result of a mingling of many different fires ignited in various places over the ages. And Egyptian ideas of the other-world seem to have weighed heavily on subsequent visions of Hell. But in other cases the comparison with other religions has only a theoretical and not a historical significance. That is, it serves only to show how other religions conceived of the hereafter rather than to provide a demonstrable historical link. What does it mean when another religion gives a solution to the problem of the hereafter similar to the Christian solution? We cannot be sure of any direct influence. To take one concrete example, consider the Gnostic Hell. For the Gnostics, the time spent in Hell was essentially a time of anguish. For the Christians, the time spent in Purgatory was certainly an anxious time but also one tinged with hope. Is it possible that both systems of thought incorporate a similar sensitivity to time but do so in different ways?

In the final analysis, to describe what selections were made at one time or another from various extant traditions is to make clear that the relationship between the Christian Purgatory and earlier imaginings of the hereafter is a historical rather than a genealogical one. Purgatory did not emerge automatically from a "diachronic" series of beliefs and images. Rather, it was the result of history, of a history in which chance and necessity both played a part.

THE HINDU "THREE WAYS"

In ancient India, at the end of the Vedic age when the first of the Upanishads appeared (in the sixth century B.C.), it was believed that the dead followed one of three paths according to their deserts, though no formal judgment was handed down. Each of these paths began in fire, since the dead were burned on pyres. Those who were saved passed "from the flame into the light of day, from daylight into the light of the waxing moon (the first two weeks of the lunar month), from the light of the waxing moon into the six months of the rising sun, from these six months into the world of the gods, from the world of the gods into the sun, and from the sun into the world of lightning. From the world of lightning those (who know) are led to the worlds of the brahman by a spiritual being (who comes to find them). In these worlds of the brahman they live in places infinitely remote (from this world). For them there is no return."

Those who are reasonably deserving but less pure than the purest "enter into the smoke, from the smoke into the night, from the night into the phase of the waning moon, from the phase of the waning moon into the six months of the falling sun, from these six months into the world of the Manes, and from the world of the Manes into the moon." There they are eaten by the gods and then return to earth, beginning a cycle of reincarnations that lead by stages of greater and greater perfection to Paradise.

The incorrigibly wicked are also reincarnated but only in order to be punished. They come back to earth in the form of "worms, insects, and animals" until finally they fall into Hell.[1]

The Isha Upanishad evokes this stay in Hell, "in the worlds called sunless, blanketed as they are with the darkest shadows: here after death go those who have killed their souls." But other texts suggest that the fate of these souls is not settled once and for all. It depends, we are told, on whether or not they cross a threshhold guarded by two dogs. If they cross, they are admitted to a fairly pleasant place, reminiscent of the Romans' Elysian Fields or the Germanic Valhalla: "a meadow that is theirs forever," where they may share in the banquet of Yama, the first man, the Adam of Indo-Iranian tradition, who has become the king of the infernal regions. If the dogs do not allow them to pass, they are either cast down into the shadows of Hell or sent back to earth to wander in misery in the form of a ghost.[2]

Some elements from these diverse traditions recur in Purgatory: the idea of a "middle way" of salvation, for example, as well as the passage through fire, the dialectic of light and darkness, the gradual improvement in the state of a soul between death and ultimate salvation, and the function of the hereafter as a place of welcome for souls that would otherwise be condemned to wander as ghosts. But the absence of any form of judgment and the central role of metempsychosis set this system apart from the Christian.

IRAN: THE FIRE AND THE BRIDGE

In Iran what is especially striking in the doctrines of the hereafter and their associated imagery is the ubiquity of fire. But certain features of Zoroastrian eschatology are reminiscent of Christian conceptions that led to Purgatory, even if there was most likely no direct influence.[3] First of all there was the hesitation between "infernal" and "paradisiacal" interpretations of the state of the dead prior to judgment. In the Veda the dead awaiting judgment pass their time in the kingdom of Yama, described sometimes as a paradise of light, sometimes as a sinister subterranean world, an abyss into which one descends along a sloping path. The bridge motif is also present—it is found in India as well: a bridge leads from earth to heaven, and on this bridge the dead are subjected to tests of strength and skill, which also have a moral connotation.[4]

Finally, for souls whose bad actions precisely balance the good, there is an intermediary place of sojourn. Specialists warn, however, that this is not to be confused with the Christian Purgatory, which is more comparable, they say, to the Mazdean Hell in that the soul's stay in the latter is temporary, as in the case of Purgatory.[5]

EGYPT: HELL IMAGINED

The history of ancient Egypt is too long to permit brief summary of Egyptian beliefs regarding the judgment of the dead, which changed over the centuries and appear to have varied from one social group to another. That the dead are judged is a belief that was held in Egypt from a very early date. "Inventions of the ancient Egyptians, the idea, the fear, the hope of Judgment," Jean Yoyotte tells us, "survived long after they were gone."[6]

The Egyptian Hell was particularly impressive and highly refined. It was an immense region filled with walls and gates, with muddy marshes and lakes of fire surrounding mysterious chambers. Maspero reports that the Egyptian dead were required to climb sheer cliffs. The geography of the hereafter was so well developed in the Egyptian imagination that some sarcophagi bear maps of the other world. In this other world the dead were subjected to many forms of drastic punishment, directed at their bodies as well as their souls. The penalties were physical as well as moral, accentuating remoteness from the gods. Confinement and imprisonment played an important role. The tortures were bloody, and punishment by fire was frequent and terrifying. Even the most infernal versions of the Christian Purgatory do not come close to some of the tortures inflicted on the dead in the Egyptian Hell: the loss of the sensory organs, for example, or the disintegration of the individual personality. When it came to the topography of Hell, the Egyptian imagination knew no limits: the dead were lodged in a bewildering variety of houses, chambers, niches, and various other places.[7] But not in Purgatory—the ancient Egyptians conceived of no such place. Erik Hornung has shown clearly that, despite the abundance of terms used to describe human beings residing in the other world, all the terminology may be subsumed under two starkly contrasting heads: the "blessed" and the "damned." "Intermediate states or phases in the other-wordly process of purification" did not exist.

Not until some time between the first century B.C. and the second century A.D., when a tale was written describing a voyage in another world called Si-Osiris, do we encounter a division of the dead into three groups: those whose good actions outweigh the bad, those whose bad actions outweigh the good, and those in whom the good precisely balances the bad. Still, however, there is no process of purification. There are no Egyptian precedents for the slight differentiation of individual fates that first appeared in the Coptic apocalypses (such as those of Peter and Paul) in the second century A.D.[8]

Nevertheless, it is important to discuss the Egyptian background, because it was in Egypt, particularly in Alexandria, both before and after the birth of Christ, and in Christian monasteries, that Jewish, Greek, and Coptic writers enriched the imagery of the other world and especially of Hell. The characteristic features of the infernal tradition have been summarized by Budge: "We find, in all books about the Other World, pits of fire, abysses of darkness, deadly knives, rivers of boiling water, fetid exhalations, fire-breathing dragons, frightful monsters, and creatures with the heads of animals, cruel and murderous creatures of various aspect . . . similar to those familiar to us from early medieval literature. It is almost certain that modern nations owe much of their concept of hell to Egypt."[9] The "infernalized" Purgatory that we sometimes encounter in medieval Christendom undoubtedly drew some of its inspiration from this Egyptian heritage.

GREECE AND ROME: THE DESCENT INTO HELL

The theme of the descent into the underworld is virtually the only contribution to Christian imagery of the hereafter made by the ancient Greeks and Romans. Long before Christ himself descended into Hell, the theme was common in ancient Greece: Orpheus, Pollux, Theseus, and Herakles all went down into the shadowy realm. One of the most famous of these catabases is that of Ulysses in book 11 of the Odyssey. But it is known that many interpolations were added to the original text, which made no mention of either the judgment of the dead, moral sanctions, or penal torment. Compared with the underworlds of the Orient, Homer's seems a poor thing indeed. It is worth singling out a few of its features, however, for these recur in the birth of Purgatory: an island (that of Circe), a mountain, which rises vertically out of the sea and is punctuated with caves, a descent into Hades, where the atmosphere is truly infernal, and a description of the dead—this last feature was not taken over by official Christianity, since only God was supposed to have the power to make the dead in Purgatory visible to certain of the living.[10] By comparison, Hesiod's description of Tartarus is superficial (*Theogony*, 695–700, 726–33).

In the long run the most important Greek contributions to the idea of the hereafter came in the form of two works of the intellect, whose influence on Christian thought is difficult to estimate.

A Philosophy of Reincarnation: Plato

It is a risky thing to try to summarize Plato's ideas on the fate of the soul after death in the context of a discussion of Purgatory. Here, Victor Goldschmidt is my guide.[11] Plato's doctrine is dominated by the idea that sin is due in part to the will, and is hence a matter of individual responsibility, and in part to ignorance, which can be eliminated only by a complex process. Thus the fate of the soul depends both on individual will and on a judgment of the gods.

Normally the dead individual can choose more or less freely the form in which he or she wishes to be incarnated, but this choice can be altered or hindered by the intervention of the gods. The wicked may be subjected by the gods either to degrading metamorphosis, by having their souls placed in the bodies of men of base condition or in the bodies of disgusting animals, or to infernal punishments. These punishments are described in the *Republic* (10:615e): blazing men bind tyrants hand and foot, flay them, and drag them along the ground. This calls to mind a passage of the Apocalypse of Peter (5:30). Those who achieve the Platonic ideal of practicing philosophy "in purity and justice" are rewarded by being sent to rest in a place perfect for contemplation, usually a "blessed isle": note the constant need to be explicit about where the soul resides, the need for "spatial concreteness" in the other world.

For various reasons Plato thought it wise to provide for intermediary conditions in which souls might be placed after death. One of these reasons was the idea that the penalty must be proportioned to the crime, which is forcefully expressed in the *Republic* (10:615a–b). Another was the idea that souls of middling virtue should have a specific fate of their own: though still caught up in the cycle of reincarnations, they enjoy interludes during which they are allowed to partake of unspecified rewards: "set free from confinement in these regions of the earth (Tartarus), and passing upward to their pure abode, [they] make their dwelling upon the earth's surface" (*Phaedo* 114c, 1–2).

Like the Old Testament's, Plato's thinking about the afterlife remained fundamentally dualist. Through metempsychosis a soul might enter another soul either better or worse than itself. No man is exempt from the judgment of the gods, as Plato warns his fellows: "This doom of heaven be sure neither thyself nor any other that has fallen on ill ways shall ever claim to have escaped. . . . Though thou make thyself never so small and creep into the depths of earth, or exalt thyself and mount up to heaven, yet shalt thou pay them the due penalty" (Laws 10:905a), which is reminiscent of Psalm 139:9–12: "If I take the wings of the morning, and dwell in the uttermost parts of the sea, even there shall thy hand lead me. . . . If I say, Surely the darkness shall cover me, even the night shall be light about me. Yea, the darkness hideth not from thee; but the night shineth as the day; the darkness and the light are both alike to thee." As Plato says, "Yet shalt thou pay them the due penalty, either while thou art still here among us, or after thy departure in Hades, or, it may be, by translation to some yet grimmer region" (*Laws* 10:905a). In the celebrated myth of Er, those who meet in the marvelous meadow can only have come from one of two places: either from Heaven or from the bowels of the earth where they have been consigned to wander for a thousand years.

Influenced by the idea that the penalty must be proportioned to the crime, which is related not only to Plato's philosophy but doubtless also to the Athenian system of justice (in all religions in which the dead are judged there is a link between earthly justice and the divine justice meted out in the hereafter), Plato fashioned a conception of man's fate in which the soul may find itself in one of several possible situations: "If their [i.e., the souls'] changes of character are unimportant and few, they are transferred over the surface of the soil; if they are more and in the direction of grave wickedness, they fall into the depths and the so-called underworld, the region known by the name of Hades and the like appelations, which fill the fancy of quick and departed alike with dreams of dismay. If a soul have drunk still deeper of vice or virtue, by reason of its own volition and the potent influence of past converse with others, when near contact with divine goodness has made it especially godlike, so surely is it removed to a special place of utter holiness, and translated to another and a better world, or, in the contrary case, transported to the opposite realm" (*Laws* 10.904c–905a).

It was mainly the belief in metempsychosis that made it possible to establish a scale of punishments, a range of intermediate penalties. This was also characteristic of Orphism, "which from the beginning seems to have accepted the belief that between successive periods of earthly existence there comes a period of expiation in Hades."[12] The influence of Orphism on Christianity has often been stressed. Since there is no evidence of a belief in an intermediate state between celestial happiness and the torments of Hell in ancient Judaism, and since the precursors of Purgatory first appear among Christian Greeks, it has been suggested that the Christian idea of a "purgatory" in which souls not sufficiently guilty to deserve eternal torment might be purified of their sins derives from beliefs of the pagan Greeks and specifically from Orphic doctrine.[13] If such an influence did exist, it must, I think, have affected segments of the Jewish community first. For it is in the apocalyptic writings of the Jews, particularly rabbinical teaching dating from around the time of Christ's birth, that one finds the earliest true forerunner of what was to become the Christian Purgatory. Now, it is true that the Jewish and, later, Christian communities in Palestine and Egypt were in fact immersed in a Greek environment in which mystery religions flourished.

Pindar is often taken as an exemplar of this Orphic influence. In a fragment cited by Plato in the *Meno* (81b), Pindar estimates that the period of purification in the underworld lasts eight years, and in an ode dealing with a Sicilian mystery religion, probably related to Orphism, dating from the early part of the sixty century B.C., he says the following:

> [Opulence coupled with merit] is the glittering star, the true splendor of a human life. Oh! Especially if he who possesses it can foretell the future! If he knows that when death strikes the guilty in this world, their spirits are at once subjected to punishment: beneath the earth, a judge hands down inexorable decrees against crimes committed in this, Zeus's kingdom.[14]

A Precursor: Aeneas in the Underworld

The time has come to devote particular attention to the descent of Aeneas into the underworld as described in Vergil's *Aeneid*. Here, the description of the topography of the underworld aims at greater precision than is usual in most ancient accounts, apart from the Egyptian. In fact, Brooks Otis has recently sketched a map from Vergil's description. The descent takes one through a vestibule, a feature commonly associated with the image of the underworld or Purgatory as a pit. Then there is the field of the tombless dead, the River Styx, the fields of tears, and the final meadows before the fork in the path, the left branch of which leads to Tartarus (Hell) and the right beyond the walls of Dis (Pluto, the king of the underworld) to the Elysian Fields, a paradise of repose, and beyond that the enclosed sacred wood and Lethe, the river of forgetfulness.[15]

Eduard Norden, in his celebrated commentary on Vergil,[16] has called attention not only to Dante's borrowings in the *Divine Comedy*—hardly surprising since Dante took Vergil as his poetic model as well as his guide to the underworld—but also to features of the medieval imagination of Purgatory that are also present in earlier accounts. When Aeneas enters the vestibule, for example, he hears, "from within," deep groans and the savage crack of whips and the rattle of metal from dragging shackles. Aeneas stopped, horrified with this din. . . . [17]

A similar episode may be found not only in the *Visio Wettini* (ninth century) and the *Visio Tnugdali* (mid-twelfth century, in which Purgatory is not yet distinct) but also in the *Purgatory of Saint Patrick* (late twelfth century), in which the idea of Purgatory is born, and of course in Dante, where we find echoes of Vergil in the *Inferno* (3.22–30), while in the *Purgatorio* (12.112–14), if there are yet sighs, still

> . . . what a difference between these trails
> and those of Hell: here every entrance fills
> with joyous song, and there with savage wails.[18]

Similarly, Aeneas, in the underworld, points from below to the brilliant fields above.[19] His upward glance from the lower depths and his gesture toward the light above are typical. We find them in the apocalypses (the Apocalypse of John, i.e., Revelation 21:10, and the [apocryphal] Apocalypse of Peter 5:4ff), in various medieval "visions" that predate Purgatory (*Visio Fursei*, *Visio Wettini*, and *Visio Tnugdali*), and above all in the episode in the Gospel (Luke 16:23) involving Lazarus and the wicked rich man, where it is said of the latter that "in hell he lift up his eyes, being in torments, and seeth Abraham afar off, and Lazarus in his bosom." This passage was to play an important role in the early history of the Christian Purgatory.

Perceptively, Norden also remarks that, while both Vergil and Dante are occasionally capricious in their recording of time, both poets do have in mind a fixed period for the duration of the voyage to the other world, on the order of one day (twenty-four hours) and particularly one night. In the *Aeneid* the ascent back from the underworld must be completed before midnight, when the real shades come out (v. 893ff.), and in the *Divine Comedy* the voyage is supposed to last twenty-four hours (*Inferno*, 34.68ff.). In the apocalypses and the medieval visions the journey to the hereafter must generally be completed before dawn and the first crow of the cock. This is true of the *Purgatory of Saint Patrick*, where the time requirement is part of the ordeal.

As far as Christianity and the Middle Ages are concerned, the crucial passage of book 6 of the *Aeneid* is the following:

> From these [the "corrupting flesh," "earthly habiliments," "limbs imbued with death"] derive our fears and our desires, our grief and joy, nor can we compass the whole aura of heaven shut as we are in the prison of the unseeing flesh. And furthermore when on the last day we are lost to the light we do not shed away all evil or all the ills the body has bequeathed to us

poor wretches, for many flaws cannot but be ingrained and must have grown hard through all our length of days. Therefore we souls are trained with punishment and pay with suffering for old felonies—some are hung up helpless to the winds; the stain of sin is cleansed for others of us in the trough of a huge whirlpool; or with fire burned out of us—each one of us we suffer the afterworld we deserve.[20]

In this passage we find a number of themes that would later figure in Purgatory: the mixture of pleasure and pain, the dim perception of Heaven's light, the references to imprisonment, the detailing of penalties, the combination of expiation and purification, and the idea of purification by fire.

Still, we cannot be sure that there was any direct historical link in this instance. But between Babylonian and Judeo-Christian traditions the historical link is demonstrable. It is to this question that we turn next.

GILGAMESH IN THE UNDERWORLD

One of the liveliest and most haunting descriptions of the otherworld derives from Babylon, the source of several startling stories of travels in the underworld. The oldest known such travelogue of European–Middle Eastern origin dates from the eighth century B.C. and concerns the descent into the underworld of one Our-Nammou, the prince of Our. The hero is judged by Nergal, king of the underworld; allusion is made to a fire; a river flows in the vicinity of a mountain; and the otherworld is shrouded in "darkness."[21]

In the well-known epic of Gilgamesh the underworld is mentioned twice. One occasion concerns Gilgamesh himself. Since he has not attained immortality, the gods offer him a choice spot in the underworld. This favor is apparently not due to his merits, however. Gilgamesh owes it, rather, to his rank and to an arbitrary decision of the gods.[22] We get a more detailed account of the underworld when Gilgamesh's friend Enkidou pays it a visit prior to his death. The underworld, we are told, is a realm of dust and darkness—"the great land," "the land of no return," "the land from which no traveler returns," a place to which one descends and from which certain of the dead "rise" when called. It is a place to which one goes when one is caught in the snares of the gods, a prison. Perhaps the most troubling feature is that the living and the "normal" among the dead are tormented by their "embittered" confrères, known as *ekimmu*. These are shades who have been left unburied and uncared for by the living (here we find the appeal to the solicitude of the living that was to play such an important role in the symbolic system of Purgatory), in consequence of which they either return to earth as ghosts to haunt the living or torture others of the dead in the underworld.

THE JEWISH *SHEOL*: A PLACE OF DARKNESS

Various writers have called attention to the kinship between these Babylonian beliefs and certain Jewish beliefs mentioned in the old Testament. This should come as no surprise, given the close relations between the Babylonians and the Hebrews, particularly at the time of the Exile.[23]

The *arallu*, or Syrian underworld, is similar to the Hebrew *sheol* and the Greek Hades, though the latter two seem rather pale by comparison. The resemblance of *arallu* and *sheol* is particularly striking. The location of *sheol* is below: Jacob, believing Joseph dead, says, "I will go down into the grave unto my son mourning" (Gen. 37:35). Hannah, the mother of Samuel, declares that "the Lord killeth and maketh alive; he bringeth down to the grave, and bringeth up" (1 Sam. 2:6). Finally, when Saul asks the witch of En-dor to call forth Samuel from the dead, she says, "I saw gods ascending out of the earth," and "An old man cometh up" (1 Sam. 28:13–14). The image of the trap or snare recurs in the Psalms: "The sorrows of hell [*sheol*] compassed me about: the snares of death prevented me" (Ps. 18:5), and "The sorrows of death compassed me, and the pains of hell gat hold upon me" (Ps. 116:3).[24] So does the image of the pit: "O Lord, thou hast brought up my soul from the grave: thou hast kept me alive, that I should not go down to the pit" (Ps. 30:3), and "Thou hast laid me in the lowest pit, in darkness, in the deeps" (Ps. 88:6). In Psalm 40:2 the image of the pit is associated with a mire: "He brought me up also out of an horrible pit, out of the miry clay, and set my feet upon a rock, and established my goings." According to Nicholas J. Tromp, the word *bor* meant first "well," then "prison," and finally both "tomb" and "underground pit." The "pit of destruction" mentioned in Psalm 55:24 has been compared with the pit that stands at the entrance to the otherworld in Grimm's tale *Frau Hölle* (*Hölle* is German for Hell). Dust, generally associated with worms, also figures in the Old Testament: "They shall go down to the bars of the pit, when our rest together is in the dust" (Job 17:16), and "They shall lie down alike in the dust, and the worms shall cover them" (Job 21:26).

Sheol, the Hebrew word for the infernal otherworld, occurs frequently in the Old Testament.[25] Some of its connotations belong specifically to Hell and do not pertain to the Christian Purgatory: *sheol* is sometimes identified with a devouring monster, for example—an idea that may have been taken over from the Egyptians.[26] Or again, *sheol* is sometimes described as a city, an idea which was presented earlier in Ugaritic documents and which prefigures Dante ("Inferno" 3.1). Among *sheol*'s other connotations are some quite typical of Hebrew thought. There is a close connection, for example, between *sheol* and the symbolism of chaos, sometimes embodied in the desert, sometimes in the ocean. Closer attention should perhaps be paid to the possible links between the medieval Purgatory and certain saints or anchorites who wander the oceans or live in solitude in the forest or desert.

Sheol bequeathed to Purgatory (and to Hell) its characteristic darkness (from which souls in Purgatory eventually emerge into the light), a darkness that penetrates every recess of the subterranean world of the dead. This theme is repeatedly hammered home in the Book of Job. Consider, for example, this passage, from Job 10:21–22:

> Before I go whence I shall not return, even to the land of darkness and the shadow of death. A land of darkness, as darkness itself, and of the shadow of death, without any order, and where the light is as darkness.[27]

As for the landscape of *sheol*, two features also found in the Christian Purgatory and Hell should be noted: the mountain and the river. Some versions of Psalm 42:6 refer to a "mountain of torment," "Mount Mizar," and the Book of Job twice mentions the river that must be crossed to enter *sheol*:*

> He keeps back his soul from the pit, and his life from drowning in the Canal (Job 33:18).
> But if they do not hearken they shall fall into the Canal and die without knowledge (Job 36:12).

Tromp is convincing when he argues, against other Old Testament exegetes, that the terms used to describe *sheol* are indeed descriptive of a place and not metaphors, but he believes that the word evolved toward a more "literary" and "moralistic" usage which was taken up by the New Testament.

Be that as it may, the world *sheol*, as it is used in the Old Testament, stands in sharp contrast to the word for Heaven in a clearly dualistic system. For example, Psalm 139:8 says, "If I ascend up into heaven, thou art there; if I make my bed in hell, behold, thou art there." And in Isaiah 44:24, the Lord says, "I am the Lord that maketh all things; that stretcheth forth the heavens alone; that spreadeth abroad the earth by myself." Here "the earth" means the world of both the living and the dead, the underground abode as much as the surface where the living reside.

Rarely is a tripartite system mentioned (such as the one later proposed by Dante, with Hell underground, Purgatory on earth, and Paradise above). In Jeremiah 10:11–12, however, where the exile of the Jews and the power of the Lord are recalled, we do find this: "The gods that have not made the heavens and the earth, even they shall perish from the earth and

---

*Here, Le Goff cites in French variant readings of Job 33:18 and 36:12 not translated in either the King James or Revised Standard Version; I translate from his French.—Trans.

from under these heavens. He hath made the earth by his power, he hath established the world by his wisdom, and hath stretched out the heavens by his discretion." Thus the prophet here distinguishes between Heaven, the world beneath Heaven, and earth (beneath the world), just as Paul does (Phil. 2:10): "That at the name of Jesus every knee should bow, of things in heaven, and things in earth, and things under the earth."

Redoubtable as *sheol* may be, it was not viewed as a place of torture. Three special punishments were associated with it, however: the bed of vermin, which is not found in the Christian Hell or Purgatory (unless these vermin be regarded as the ancestors of the serpents of Hell, which seems to me incorrect), thirst, and fire. Fire has already been mentioned, and I shall defer further discussion of it until later. Thirst is mentioned, for example, in Jeremiah 17:13: "They that depart from me shall be written in the earth, because they have forsaken the Lord, the fountain of living waters." It also figures in two Christian texts important in the prehistory of Purgatory. One of these is the story of Lazarus and the wicked rich man, who from the depths of Hell cries out to Father Abraham, "Have mercy on me, and send Lazarus, that he may dip the tip of his finger in water and cool my tongue" (Luke 16:24). Even more important is a text that may be the first to present a vision of Purgatory as a place, the *Passion of Perpetua* from the early third century, in which thirst plays a crucial role.

It has been observed that, although *sheol* is frequently mentioned in the Old Testament, few precise details are provided. The reason for this, we are told, is that Yahweh is the god of the living, reminding us of the words of Ecclesiastes 9:4: "For him that is joined to all the living there is hope, for a living dog is better than a dead lion."

Jesus puts it even more directly (Matt. 22:31–32): "But as touching the resurrection of the dead, have ye not read that which was spoken unto you by God, saying, "I am the God of Abraham, and the God of Isaac, and the God of Jacob? God is not the God of the dead, but of the living.' " That the Lord's omnipotence extends even to *sheol* is repeated many times in the Old Testament, but it is never stated that he intends to deliver a soul prematurely from captivity there, or that he intends to pardon a soul that has gone down to Hell or to shorten its stay there.

Thus, apart from the imagery of Hell that was carried over into Purgatory, there is very little in the Old Testament that prefigures the Christian Purgatory except for one highly singular passage in the Second Book of Maccabees, which I shall discuss below.

There are, however, certain indications in the Old Testament that distinctions were indeed made between one region of *sheol* and another and that souls might be plucked from *sheol* by the hand of God. In the first place, we are told that the lowest depths of *sheol* are reserved for souls in particular disgrace: the souls of the uncircumcised, of victims of murder, and of the unburied. But note that these are souls not so much guilty as impure. Second, certain of the Psalms suggest the possibility of liberation from *sheol*:

> Return O Lord, deliver my soul: oh save me for thy mercies' sake. For in death there is no remembrance of thee: in the grave who shall give thee thanks? (Ps. 6:4–5).

> Like sheep they are laid in the grave; death shall feed on them; and the upright shall have dominion over them in the morning; and their beauty shall consume in the grave from their dwelling. But God will redeem my soul from the power of the grave: for he shall receive me. Selah (Ps. 49:14–15).

> For thou wilt not leave my soul in hell; neither wilt thou suffer thine Holy One to see corruption. Thou wilt shew me the path of life: in thy presence is fullness of joy; at thy right hand there are pleasures for evermore (Ps. 16:10–11).

JUDEO-CHRISTIAN VISIONS OF THE APOCALYPSE

The conception and representation of the hereafter were significantly enriched by a number of texts that originated in the Middle East, particularly Egypt and Palestine, between the second century B.C. and the third century A.D. (and even later, as Greek and, above all, Latin versions of these Hebrew, Syrian, Coptic, Ethiopian, and Arabic writings made their tardy appearance). Most of these texts have not been accepted by the various official churches as so-called "authentic documents" of doctrine and faith. They belong to the corpus of texts called "apocryphal" by the "Latin" Church (Protestants refer to noncanonical Old Testament texts as "pseudo-epigraphic"). Some of these texts were not labeled "apocryphal" until rather late in the day, in 397 by the council dominated by Augustine or even as late as the sixteenth century by the Council of Trent. Accordingly, many of these writings remained influential during the Middle Ages, either because they had not yet been judged apocryphal, so that their use did not call down the wrath of the Church, or because, even though expunged from the canon, they continued to circulate clandestinely by various routes. An extraordinary case in point is that of the Apocalypse of Saint John (i.e., the Book of Revelation), which was finally accepted into the canonical Latin Bible after lengthy controversy, though it did not differ substantially from other texts of its genre.

Among the Judeo-Christian apocrypha I am interested particularly in texts whose Latin versions or whose influence on Latin Christianity affected representations of the hereafter in the medieval West. I have in mind not so much the apocryphal gospels as the accounts of visions of, or imaginary voyages in, the hereafter (some bearing the title "Apocalypse," i.e., "revelation," some not), particularly those that played a role in the inception of Purgatory. I shall not here inquire as to the social and historical context surrounding the preparation and circulation of these texts, preferring to confine historical and sociological analysis to the specific period during which the doctrine of Purgatory came into being and gained currency, thta is, the twelfth and thirteenth centuries. For this earlier period I shall content myself with indicating the relevant intellectual, literary, and artistic traditions. In this apocalyptic literature one element was particularly important, namely, the belief that Jesus himself had descended into Hell. The luster of this episode reflected, as it were, on the whole body of apocalyptic writings. I shall adduce evidence drawn mainly from Christian and New Testament sources. It is worthy of note that most of the "apocalypses" tell of a journey to Heaven rather than a descent into Hell, typical of the hopeful, expectant climate of the period during which Christianity emerged.

Of the Jewish apocalypses I shall use the Book of Enoch and the Fourth Book of Ezra, and of the Christian, the Apocalypse of Peter, the Apocalypse of Ezra, and especially the Apocalypse of Paul.

Of the Book of Enoch the only extant Latin version is a very short abridgement contained in a single manuscript dating from the eighth century. The most complete version that has come down to us is in Ethiopian, based on a Greek original.[28] The text was originally written in a Semitic language, probably Hebrew, during the second or first century B.C. and bears marks of Egyptian influence. It is a composite text, the oldest portion of which very probably dates from the period when apocalyptic writings first began to appear, slightly before 170 B.C. Thus the Book of Enoch is one of the earliest examples we have of apocalyptic literature.

The portion of the text concerned with the hereafter is contained mainly in the first part, which tells the story of Enoch's assumption. Guided by angels, Enoch is wafted away to "a place (a house) whose inhabitants are like a blazing fire" and then to the place where storms, thunder, and the waters of life reside. "And I came upon a river of fire, where the fire flows like water and empties into the vastness of the oceans. . . . And I reached a place of utter darkness. . . . I saw the mountains of the shadows of winter . . . and the mouth of the abyss" (chap. 17). He next comes to the pit of Hell: "Then I saw a deep pit near the heavenly columns of fire, and I saw between them descending columns of fire, columns whose height and depth were immeasurable" (chap. 18). Enoch then asks the angel Raphael, who is accompanying him, where the souls of the dead reside prior to judgment. The first mention of the idea that there are different regions in the hereafter and various categories of souls awaiting judgment occurs in chapter 22. Unlike the Babylonians and the Jews, who situated *arallu* and *sheol* beneath the surface of the earth, but like most Egyptian writers, the author of this chapter apparently situates these waiting souls in a very remote corner of the earth's surface. "From there I went to another place, and in the west he pointed to a great, high mountain and rocky cliffs. There were four very deep cavities, very broad and smooth, three of which were dark and one light with a wellspring in its midst." Raphael explains to Enoch that these "are for the children of the souls of the dead to gather in . . . and to remain until the day of judgment, until their time has come, and that time shall be until the great judgment (is handed down)." Enoch continues: "I saw the spirits of the children of men who were dead; their pleading voice reached the ears of heaven."

Each of these four "cavities" was filled with one of four categories of souls, grouped according to their relative degree of guilt or innocence and according to the suffering that they either did or did not endure on earth. The cavity filled with light contains the martyred saints, allowed to reside close to the luminous wellspring. Other "just" souls reside in the second cavity in the dark, awaiting the eternal reward that will be theirs at the Last Judgment. In the third cavity are the sinners who have not been punished or tried on earth and who will be condemned to eternal punishment at the Last Judgment. Finally, the fourth category consists of sinners who were persecuted in this world, particularly those put to death by other sinners. They are to be punished less than other sinners.

Continuing his journey, Enoch encounters Hell one more time, but in a new guise. "Then I said, 'Why is this land blessed and filled with trees, while that gorge in the middle (of the mountains) is damned?' " Enoch's guide is now Uriel, who answers, "This accursed valley is for the eternally damned" (chap. 28).

Thus the Book of Enoch contains the images of Hell as a pit or narrow valley and of a mountain on earth where souls reside prior to the last judgment; it also features the idea of an intermediate state between death and judgment as well as the notion of graduated penalties for the dead. The latter depend only in part on the soul's merit, however.

Since the Book of Enoch is a composite of sections composed at different times, it contains a number of contradictions, particularly in regard to the hereafter. In chapter 22 of part 1 the souls of martyred saints cry for vengeance, whereas in part 5 the souls of the just are all as in a long sleep, watched over by angels, awaiting the last judgment. In part 2, the Book of Parables, Enoch has quite a different vision of the "place of waiting": he sees the just bedded down on the outskirts of Heaven or perhaps even inside Heaven itself, amid the angels and by the side of the Messiah (chap. 35). The idea of a prolonged period of waiting recurs in certain forerunners of the medieval Purgatory, e.g., in regard to Arthur at Etna. Finally, in chapter 39, the souls of the dead intervene with the gods on behalf of the living: "They intercede and they pray for the children of men." It was a long time before the Middle Ages accepted the idea that the soul's deserts could be altered in the hereafter. Only then were souls in Purgatory granted the privilege once and for all.

The Fourth Book of Ezra also consists of a number of segments, probably linked together by a zealous Jew around 120 A.D., that is, toward the end of the apocalyptic period in Jewish thought. Several versions have come down to us, in Syriac, Arabic, and Armenian, though the Greek original has been lost. A Latin version is preserved in a number of manuscripts, the oldest of which dates from the ninth century. Here I shall refer to the Latin version.[29]

Ezra puts the following question to the Lord: "If I have found grace in your eyes, O Lord, show thy servant if, now or at the hour of our death, when each of us gives thee back his soul, we thereafter rest in peace until thou redeemest us, or are we punished?"[30] The answer is that "those who have scorned the path of the Most High, those who have scorned his law and hated whosoever feared God, shall not enter into the dwelling places but first shall wander and then be punished, in everlasting sadness and tears, by seven ways."[31] The fifth of these "ways" is to be shown the sight "of other (souls) kept by angels in dwelling places in a deep silence."[32] Here the idea is the same as the one that occurs in the fifth part of the Book of Enoch.

By contrast, seven "orders" (*ordines*) of souls are fated to dwell in "safe and secure" places.[33] After being separated from their bodies, these souls "shall have seven days of freedom in which to see the reality of what had been foretold, and then they shall gather in their dwelling places."[34] This "spatial conception" of the other world is reinforced and broadened by the following passage. The "order" consisting of those who have followed in the paths of the Most High shall repose in seven different "ranks," or *ordines*. Of the fifth of these, it is said that they shall "exult upon seeing that now they have escaped the corruptible (flesh) and are in possession of the bequest to come, still in view of the narrow world of sorrow from which they have been set free and beginning to catch sight of the spacious, blessed, and immortal world they are to receive."[35]

Here we find expression of that feeling of "spatial liberation," that concern for space in the other world, that I think was of fundamental importance in the inception of Purgatory. Purgatory, when it finally evolves, is a dwelling place or a series of dwelling places: an enclosed place but a spacious one. As one moves from Hell to Purgatory and from Purgatory to Paradise the boundaries are pushed back, space expands. This effect Dante was capable of rendering in splendid language.

The Fourth Book of Ezra captured the attention of early Christian writers. The earliest citation of which we can be certain occurs in the *Stromata* (3.16) of Clement of Alexandria, one of the "fathers" of Purgatory, but somewhat later, in the fourth century, the passage I have just cited was commented on by Saint Ambrose.

In his treatise *De bono mortis* (On the Good of Death) Ambrose is at pains to prove that the soul is immortal and to combat the Roman predilection for extravagant burials. "Our soul," says Ambrose, "is not buried with our body in the tomb. . . . It is pure waste that men build sumptuous tombs as though they were receptacles [*receptacula*] of the soul and not merely of the body. . . . The dwelling place of the soul is on high."[36] He then quotes at length from the Book of Ezra, arguing that the *habitacula* mentioned there are the same as the dwelling places (*habitationes*) referred to by Jesus in John 14:2: "In my Father's house are many mansions [*mansiones*]." Ambrose excuses himself for citing Ezra, whom he numbers among the pagan philosophers, on the grounds that Ezra's words may well be impressive to pagans. After expatiating on the "dwelling places of the soul," still citing from Ezra, he goes on to mention the classification of the souls of the saved into seven ranks or orders. In fact he confuses the seven "ways" with the seven "orders" and speaks of "dwelling places in which a great tranquility reigns" (*in habitaculis suis cum magna tranquillitate*). He points out that, according to Ezra, the souls of the just have begun to discover the vastness of space along with happiness and immortality.[37] Ambrose concludes his lengthy commentary on the Fourth Book of Ezra by congratulating Ezra for having ended his account with a description of the souls of the just at the end of their seven days' liberty, returning to their dwelling places: it is better, Ambrose tells us, to go on about the happiness of the just than about the misfortune of the wicked.

The Christain apocalypses are both continuous with and sharply differentiated from the Jewish apocalypses. Continuous because they draw extensively from the same environment—indeed, for the first two centuries of the "Christian" era it is frequently more correct to speak of a "Judeo-Christian religion" than of two separate religions. But at the same time sharply differentiated, because gradually the differences between the two religions were accentuated by the presence of Jesus in one and his absence in the other, in consequence of which the adherents of each sect took different attitudes toward the Messiah and hence toward doctrine in general. Socially, moreover, the two groups became increasingly differentiated.[38] Here, I shall discuss the Apocalypse of Peter, probably the oldest and certainly the most popular in the first few centuries of the Christian era; the Apocalypse of Ezra, because interesting medieval versions have survived; and finally, the Apocalypse of Paul, because it exerted the greatest influence in the Middle Ages and because it was an important point of reference not only for *Saint Patrick's Purgatory*, a late twelfth-century document that played a crucial role in the birth of Purgatory, but also for Dante.

The Apocalypse of Peter was probably composed at the end of the first century or the beginning of the second century in the Christian community of Alexandria by a converted Jew influenced both by the Jewish apocalypses and by Greek popular eschatology.[39] It figures in a catalogue of canonical works compiled by the Church of Rome in the second century, but it was stricken from the canon by the Council of Carthage in 397. The apocalypse lays particular stress on the punishments meted out to sinners in Hell, punishments which are depicted with much gusto, largely by means of imagery transmitted through Judaism and Hellenism from the Mazdaism of Iran. Medieval literature concerned with the afterlife would retain Mazdaism's classification of penalties according to the category of sin and sinner. Since usurers were among the first to profit from Purgatory in the thirteenth century, it is worth pausing to note that in the Apocalypse of Peter it is reported that they are punished by being submerged in a lake of boiling blood and pus.

The description of Hell follows along traditional lines. Among the major themes darkness and ubiquitous fire are prominent, as usual. For example, (chap. 21): "I saw another place, totally dark. This was the place of punishment." As for fire, we have the following examples. "And certain sinners were hanging by their tongues: these were the slanderers, and beneath them was a blazing fire, which tortured them" (chap. 22). Or again (chap. 27): "And other men and women were standing in flames up to their waists." And again (chap. 29): "Facing them were men and women who bit their tongues and in whose mouths a fire raged. They had borne false witness."

The Apocalypse of Peter is based on a firmly dualistic vision and delights in the infernal side of things. This dualistic vision also influenced other early Christian texts, such as *De laude martyrii* (In Praise of the Martyr), which was once attributed to Saint Cyprian and is probably by Novatian. "The cruel place called Gehenna reverberates with loud, plaintive moans. Amid tongues of flame, in a horrid night of thick smoke, paths of hot coal emit undying flames. The flame will compress itself into a compact ball and then lash out with a variety of tortures. . . . Those who refused to obey the voice of the Lord and who scorned his orders are punished by tortures appropriate to the crime. The Lord judges each man on his merits, awarding salvation or meting out punishment. . . . Those who have constantly sought and known God are assigned to the place of Christ where grace resides, where the luxuriant earth is covered with green, flowering meadows."[40] And yet, from this dualism, this portrait in somber shades, there emerges an appeal to justice. "Justice," say the angels, "is the justice of God; God's justice is good."

By contrast, the Apocalypse of Ezra, much read and much invoked in the Middle Ages, contains no adumbration of Purgatory, though it does include a number of elements that later went into the construction of Purgatory, such as the fire and the bridge. There are steps that the souls must climb. Above all, Ezra's apocalypse tells of the presence in the underworld of many of the great of this world, in passages intended as political polemic, whose significance was not lost on Dante.

Three versions of the Apocalypse of Ezra are known: the Apocalypse of

Ezra properly so called, the Apocalypse of Sedrach, and the Vision of the Blessed Ezra. The latter is the oldest. It is the Latin version of a Hebrew original and two manuscripts have survived, one dating from the tenth or eleventh century, the other from the twelfth century.[41]

Guided by seven infernal angels, Ezra goes down to Hell by a staircase that has seventy steps. He then encounters a fiery portal guarded by two lions spitting searing flames from their mouths, nostrils, and eyes. As he watches, a number of robust men pass through the flame without being touched by it. These, the angels explain, are the souls of the just, whose renown has reached as far as Heaven. When others try to pass through the portal, they are torn by dogs and consumed by the fire. Ezra asks the Lord to pardon the sinners, but his appeal is not heard. The angels tell him that these unfortunates have denied God and sinned with their wives on Sunday before mass. Descending further along the staircase, Ezra sees men being tortured. A giant caldron is filled with a fiery liquid, across the surface of which the saved walk without difficulty, while sinners are being pushed in by devils. He encounters Herod on a throne of fire, flanked by counselors standing in fire. In the east there is a broad, fiery path, down which numerous kings and princes of this world are sent. Ezra then moves on to Paradise, where all is "light, joy, and salvation." He says a prayer for the damned, but the Lord says to him, "Ezra, I shaped man in my own image and I commanded him not to sin, but he has sinned, and that is why he must suffer torment."

A Source: The Apocalypse of Paul

Of all the apocalypses the one that had the greatest influence on medieval literature concerned with the afterlife in general and with Purgatory in particular was the Apocalypse of Paul. It is one of the latest of the apocalyptic writings, having been composed in Greek around the middle of the third century A.D., somewhere in Egypt. There are extant versions in Armenian, Coptic, Greek, Old Slavic, and Syriac as well as eight different Latin versions. The oldest of these Latin versions dates perhaps from the end of the fourth century, in any case no later than the sixth century. This is the longest of the eight versions. Shorter versions were prepared in the ninth century. Of these the one known as Number 4 was the most popular. Thirty-seven manuscripts have survived. Among the novel features incorporated in this version were the image of the bridge, which comes from Gregory the Great, and the wheel of fire, which comes from the Apocalypse of Peter and the sibylline oracles. This was generally the version that was translated into various vernacular languages in the late Middle Ages. Version 5 is the most interesting for the history of Purgatory, for it was the first to introduce the distinction between an upper and a lower Hell, due originally to Augustine and later repeated by Gregory the Great. Between the sixth and the twelfth centuries this became the cornerstone of the idea that there is another place above Hell in the other world, a place which by the end of the twelfth century would become Purgatory.[42]

It is remarkable that the Apocalypse of Paul proved so popular in the Middle Ages after it was severely condemned by Augustine. Doubtless the reason for this censure, apart from Augustine's distate for apocalyptic ideas, was that the work contradicts Paul's Second Epistle to the Corinthians on which it pretends to be based. In 2 Corinthians 12:2–4, Paul actually says: "I knew a man in Christ above fourteen years ago (whether in the body, I cannot tell; or whether out of the body, I cannot tell: God knoweth) such an one caught up to the third heaven. And I knew such a man (whether in the body, or out of the body, I cannot tell; God knoweth). How that he was caught up into paradise and heard unspeakable words, which it is not lawful for a man to utter." Here is Augustine's commentary: "Some presumptuous men, some very stupid men, have invented the Apocalypse of Paul, which the Church rightly does not recognize and which is full of I know not what fables. They say that this is the story of his being carried off to the third heaven and the revelation of the ineffable words he heard there, which it is not lawful for a man to utter. Is their audacity tolerable? When Paul says that he heard what it is not lawful for a man to utter, would he then have said what it is not lawful for a man to utter? Who are they who dare to speak with such impudence and indecency?"[43]

Here I shall refer to Version 5 of the Apocalypse of Paul. After a brief introduction, where the question of two Hells is discussed (about which I shall have more to say later on), Paul comes to the upper Hell, the future Purgatory, about which nothing is said except that "souls live there awaiting the mercy of God."

The bulk of this short tale is devoted to the description of infernal tortures, in which two concerns are paramount: to be as detailed as possible and to identify and classify the damned. Paul sees trees of fire from which sinners are hanged and then a flaming, seven-colored oven in which others are tortured. He sees the seven punishments that the souls of the damned must undergo each day, to say nothing of the innumerable supplementary tortures such as thirst, cold, heat, worms, stench, and smoke. He "views" (the Latin word is *vidit*, which recurs constantly and which is typical of the whole apocalyptic genre, in which what is normally hidden from view, invisible, can now be seen) the wheel of fire on which a thousand souls are burned, one at a time. He sees a horrible river traversed by a bridge across which all the souls must pass: the damned are thrown into the water and sink in up to the knees, or the navel, or the lips, or the eyebrows. He sees a dark place where usurers (men and women) eat their tongues. He sees a place where young girls, black from head to toe, are delivered to dragons and serpents: these are girls who have sinned against chastity and caused their infant children to die. He views naked men and women, persecutors of widows and orphans, in an icy place where they are half roasted, half frozen. Finally (to abridge the account somewhat), when the souls of the damned see one saved soul pass by, wafted by the archangel Michael to Paradise, they beg him to intercede on their behalf with the Lord. The archangel invites the damned, along with Paul and the angels who accompany him, to beg God in tears for a modicum of "refreshment" (*refrigerium*). This sets off a tremendous concert of tears, which causes the Son of God to descend from heaven to remind the sinners of his passion and their sins. Swayed by the prayers of Michael and Paul, Christ grants respite (*requies*) from Saturday night to Monday morning (*ab hora nona sabbati usque in prima secunde ferie*). The author of the apocalypse eulogizes Sunday. Paul asks the angel how many infernal tortures there are, and the angel replies that the number is 144,000, adding that if one hundred men, each equipped with four iron tongues, had begun to pronounce the names of these tortures when the world was created, they still would not have come to the end of the list. The author then invites the witnesses to his revelation to intone the *Veni creator*.

This, then, is the basic outline of one twelfth-century version of the vision of the hereafter that was most popular in the Middle Ages prior to the inception of Purgatory. The description of infernal tortures found here is in large part carried over into Purgatory when this comes to be defined as a temporary Hell. Above all, we sense in the distinction between an upper and a lower Hell and in the idea of a Sabbath rest in Hell a felt need to mitigate the tortures inflicted in the other world, a need for a more discriminating and more clement divine justice.[44]

I shall say little about Manichaeanism and Gnosticism, which, despite their complex relations with Christianity, seem to me to have been quite different religions and to have subscribed to quite different philosophies. Still, one cannot avoid saying a word or two on this score, if only because there was contact, in the early centuries of the Christian era, between Manichaeans and Gnostics on the one hand and Christians on the other. Hence it is important to mention those Manichaean and Gnostic doctrines that may have influenced Christianity, primarily Greek Christianity but possibly Latin Christianity as well.

Although the Gnostics, like the Christians, did conceive of Hell as a prison, a dark night, a sewer, or a desert, the fact that they also tended to identify the world with Hell prevents our carrying the parallel between Gnosticism and Christianity too far. Even when contempt for the world (*contemptus mundi*) was at its height in the medieval West, Christians did not go to such lengths. Nor, I think, does the Mandaean and Manichaean division of Hell into five regions bear any relation to the Christian geography of the hereafter. There remains the obsession with darkness, which had both a negative, infernal significance and a positive, mystical significance. But darkness is such a general feature of sacred imagery that I cannot see it as grounds for drawing a parallel between Gnosticism or Manichaeanism and Christianity. As for the "anguish of time," which was perceived as a primary evil and which led to the view that Hell is the terrifying incarnation of pure duration, this too, I think, separates the Gnostic and Manichaeans from the Christians.[45]

This lengthy if superficial journey through the other worlds of antiquity has not been a quest for lost origins. Historical phenomena do not emerge from the past as a child does from the womb of its mother. Each society, each period makes choices from its past heritage. My aim has been simply to make clear what choices Latin Christianity made in two different periods: first between the third and the seventh century, at which time the logic implicit in the choices made was not followed out to the end, and then again between the mid-twelfth and mid-thirteenth century, when Purgatory was introduced as a full-fledged intermediary zone between Heaven and Hell, a place where certain souls reside between the time of death and the time of final judgment.

This brief glance backward in time has shed light on our subject in two ways. First, it has enabled us to identify certain ideas and images that Christians would later choose to incorporate into their Purgatory. These features will take on certain accents and colors later in our story, and it is easier to understand why this was so if we know their likely sources, even if the new system into which they have been incorporated is of a different nature from the various systems from which they were drawn originally. Furthermore, these early precursors of Purgatory, which might have developed in a variety of ways, provide information about the historical and logical conditions in which an idea such as that of Purgatory may be born, and also about what conditions may cut short the development of such an idea. The notion of justice and responsibility that underlies all these early attempts to describe the other world proved incapable of development into a scale of graduated penalties related to existing social and mental structures: only the idea of metempsychosis seems to have been able to satisfy this need at the time. The gods were not lacking in subtlety, but they saved it for other problems, such as that of sacrifice. To have spent much time on the fate of the good as compared to the fate of the less good, the wicked as compared to the less wicked, would have been a luxury in an age when the pressing need was for rough-and-ready selection and when subtlety was useless ornament. Beyond that, even if, as Pierre Vidal-Naquet has shown, the importance of ideas such as "circular time" and "eternal recurrence" has been exaggerated, still it is true that the way in which time was conceived in these ancient societies made it difficult to find solid moorings for the doubtful period between death and eternity. Where was there room, between heaven and earth, between, as the Greeks said, the uranian and the chthonic, for a third afterworld? Surely not on this earth, which ever since the end of the Golden Age had been forsaken by the imagination as a suitable setting for eternal happiness.

THE JEWS DISCOVER AN INTERMEDIATE OTHER WORLD

As the Christian era began, in a time of great changes, there was a development in Jewish religious thought which was, I think, decisive for the subsequent history of the idea of Purgatory. Evidence of this development is contained in rabbinical writings from the first two centuries of the Christian era.

The change manifests itself first of all in more detailed descriptions of the geography of the other world. As far as the majority of the texts is concerned, there is little change in substance. At the moment of death the soul goes either to an intermediate locale, *sheol*, or directly to eternal punishment in Gehenna or eternal reward in Eden. Heaven is for the most part the abode of God, though certain rabbis also make it the abode of the just. The souls of the saved, these writers hold, reside in the seventh heaven, that is, the highest of the seven firmaments. The new element is this: people are beginning to ask questions about the size and location of the afterworld in relation to earth. *Sheol* is still dark and underground: it is the world of graves and tombs, the world of the dead.

Gehenna is beneath the abyss or beneath the earth, which serves as its cover. It can be reached from the bottom of the ocean, or by digging in the desert, or beyond the dark mountains. It connects with earth through a small hole, through which the fire of Gehenna passes to heat the surface of the earth. Some writers place this hole near Jerusalem, in the valley of Hinnom, where the gateways to Gehenna, numbering either three or seven, are situated between two palm trees.

Gehenna is huge: sixty times larger than Eden. For some writers it is beyond measure: built to accommodate two to three hundred myriad of the wicked, it must grow every day to make room for new guests.

The Garden of Eden is of course the garden of the Creation story. There is no distinction between the terrestrial paradise of Adam and the celestial paradise of the just. Some place it opposite Gehenna, others alongside. For some it is nearby, for others far away—but in any case an unbreachable gulf separates the two. According to some writers Eden is sixty times the size of the world, while others see it as beyond all measure. It has gates, generally three in number. Some rabbis have visited it, but Alexander tried in vain to gain entry via one of its portals. Among the saved souls is that of Abraham, who receives his children into Eden.[46]

Of particular importance is the tripartite conception of the soul's fate in the hereafter which now begins to make its appearance in the teaching of certain rabbinical schools: witness two treatises from the period between the destruction of the Second Temple (A.D. 70) and the revolt of Bar-

Kochba (A.D. 132–35), one concerning the New Year (Rosh Hashanah), the other concerning the courts of law (the Sanhedrin). In the first we read the following:

> Rabbi Sammai teaches this: that there will be three groups at the judgment: one of the truly holy, another of the truly wicked, and a third in between. It is immediately written and sealed that the truly holy shall live until the end of time, and it is likewise written and sealed that the truly wicked shall remain in Gehenna, as it is written (Dan. 12:2). As for the third group, they shall go down to Gehenna for a time and then come up again, as it is written (Zech. 13:9 and 1 Sam. 2:6). But the Hillelites say: He who is abundant in mercy inclines toward mercy, and it is of them that David speaks (Ps. 116:1) unto God, who hears him, and responds in these terms: . . . Sinners, Jew and Gentile alike, having sinned in their body, (shall be) punished in Gehenna for twelve months, and then reduced to nothingness.

The second citation is taken from a treatise on the courts (Sanhedrin). Its tenor is practically the same:

> The Sammaites say this: there are three groups. One shall live until the end of time, the other shall remain forever in shame and contempt. These are the completely wicked, of whom the least wicked shall go down to Gehenna to be punished and come back up cured, according to Zechariah 13:9; it is of them that it is written (1 Sam. 2:6): the Lord giveth and the Lord taketh away. The Hillelites say (Ex. 34:6) that God abounds in mercy; he inclines toward mercy; and of them David says this passage (Ps. 116:1): The sinners of Israel, guilty in their body, and the sinners of the nations of the world, guilty in their body, go down to Gehenna to be punished there for twelve months, then their souls are reduced to nothing and their bodies are burned and Gehenna vomits them up; they become ash and the wind disperses them to be trodden underfoot by the holy (Mal. 4, 3, 3, 21).

Finally, Rabbi Akiba, one of the leading scholars of the Mishnah, who died while being tortured after the failure of Bar-Kochba's revolt (135), taught the same doctrine. He "also said that five things last twelve months: the judgment of the generation of the flood, the judgment of Job, the judgment of the Egyptians, the judgment of Gog and Magog in the future yet to come, and the judgment of the wicked in Gehenna, as it is written (Is. 46:23): from month to month."[47]

Thus, there exists an intermediate category, consisting of men who are neither entirely good nor entirely bad, who will punished for a time after their death and then go to Eden. But this expiation will occur only after the

Last Judgment, not in a special place but in Gehenna itself. This view leads to the drawing of a distinction between a lower and an upper part of Gehenna, the later being the place in which temporary punishments are meted out.

What we see, then, is a tendency to elaborate the spatial characteristics of the afterworld coupled with a tendency to establish an intermediate category of souls condemned for a fixed length of time. Now, we know that the inception of Purgatory in the twelfth century coincides with the development of urban schools whose masters created scholastic philosophy. It seems reasonable to suppose that in the first few centuries after the birth of Christ, as the social structure and intellectual framework of the Jewish community evolved, the Jews too moved toward developing their own idea of something rather similar to the Christian Purgatory.[48]

Is Purgatory Prefigured in the Bible?

The Christian doctrine of Purgatory was not finally worked out until the sixteenth century by the Council of Trent. Rejected by Protestants, it was an exclusively Catholic doctrine. After Trent, Bellarmine and Suarez, who were responsible for Purgatory, put forth several biblical references in support of the newly approved doctrine. Of these I will mention only the ones that actually played a role in the inception of Purgatory during the Middle Ages, up to the beginning of the fourteenth century.

From the Old Testament, a single passage, taken from the Second Book of the Maccabees (which Protestants do not consider to be canonical) was pointed to by Christian theologians between the time of Augustine and the time of Thomas Aquinas as proving the existence of a belief in Purgatory. The passage describes a battle in which a number of Jewish soldiers, who are supposed to have committed a mysterious sin, are killed, after which Judas Maccabeus orders prayers on their behalf:

> All men therefore praising the Lord, the righteous judge, who had opened the things that were hid, betook themselves unto prayer, and besought him that the sin committed might wholly be put out of remembrance. Besides, that noble Judas exhorted the people to keep themselves from sin, forsomuch as they saw before their eyes the things that came to pass for sins of those that were slain. And when he had made a gathering throughout the company to the sum of two thousand drachmas of silver, he sent it to Jerusalem to offer a sin offering, doing therein very well and honestly, in that he was mindful of the resurrection; For if he had not hoped that they were slain should have risen again, it had been superfluous and vain to pray for the dead. And also in that he perceived that there was great favour laid up for those that died godly, it was an holy and good thought. Whereupon he made a reconciliation for the dead, that they might be delivered from sin (2 Macc. 12:41–46).

This is a difficult passage, concerning which there is disagreement among experts on ancient Judaism and biblical exegesis. It alludes to beliefs and practices not mentioned elsewhere in the Bible. I will not here enter into this debate. For my purposes the essential point is that, in accordance with the Fathers of the Church, medieval Christians looked upon this text as confirming two things: that sins can be redeemed after death and that the prayers of the living are an effective way of accomplishing this. These two beliefs were of course fundamental ingredients of what was to become the doctrine of Purgatory. For the medieval mind, such a passage was, I should add, a necessity: for the men of the Middle Ages believed that all reality and, a fortiori, all doctrinal truth could be traced to a two-fold source in Scripture: according to the doctrine of typological symbolism, every truth in the New Testament is prefigured by a passage in the Old.

What New Testament passages are at issue here? Three texts played a particularly important role. The first of these is Matthew 12:31–32:

> Wherefore I say unto you, All manner of sin and blasphemy shall be forgiven unto men: but the blasphemy against the Holy Ghost shall not be forgiven unto men. And whosoever speaketh a word against the Son of man, it shall be forgiven him: but whosoever speaketh against the Holy Ghost, it shall not be forgiven him, neither in this world, neither in the world to come.

This is a very important passage. Indirectly, it involves the assumption that sins can be redeemed in the other world. But it is customary in Christian exegesis to bring out the unstated assumptions in a passage, a problem that I for one regard as logical and perfectly legitimate.

A second text is the story[49] of poor Lazarus and the wicked rich man, as told in the Gospel of Luke 16:19–26:

> There was a certain rich man, which was clothed in purple and fine linen and fared sumptuously every day; and there was a certain beggar named Lazarus, which was laid at his gate, full of sores, and desiring to be fed with the crumbs which fell from the rich man's table: moreover the dogs came and licked his sores. And it came to pass, that the beggar died, and was carried by the angels into Abraham's bosom: the rich man also died, and was buried; and in hell he lift up his eyes, being in torments, and seeth Abraham afar off, and Lazarus in his bosom. And he cried and said, Father Abraham, have mercy on me, and send Lazarus, that he may dip the tip of his finger in water, and cool my tongue; for I am tormented in this flame. But Abraham said, Son, remember that thou in thy lifetime receivedst thy good things, and likewise Lazarus evil things: but now he is comforted, and thou art tormented. And beside

all this, between us and you there is a great gulf fixed: so that they which would pass from hence to you cannot; neither can they pass to us, that would come from thence.

This passage adds three new details concerning the hereafter. Hell (Hades) is located close to the place where the saved await the Last Judgment, since it is possible to see one from the other. Hell is dominated by the characteristic thirst that Mircea Eliade calls "the thirst of the dead" and that is fundamental to the idea of *refrigerium*.[50] Finally, the waiting place of saved souls is named: the bosom of Abraham.

The last of the three passages I want to cite is the one that has aroused the most commentary. It is a passage from 1 Corinthians 3:11–15:

For other foundation can no man lay than that is laid which is Jesus Christ. Now if any man build upon this foundation gold, silver, precious stones, wood, hay, stubble; Every man's work shall be made manifest: for the day shall declare it, because it shall be revealed by fire; and the fire shall try every man's work of what sort it is. If any man's work shall be burned, he shall suffer loss: but he himself shall be saved; yet so as by fire.

This is a very difficult passage, but one which played a crucial role in the development of Purgatory in the Middle Ages, a development whose progress we can follow simply by attending to the successive exegeses of this text from Paul.[51] Speaking generally, we can say that, at a very early date, the idea emerged that a man's fate in the hereafter depends on his quality as a man, and that there is a certain proportionality between a man's merits and demerits and the rewards and punishments meted out to him in the hereafter. In the afterworld, each man must undergo a trial, which determines what his ultimate fate will be. But the time of trial here seems to be the time of the Last Judgment. In this respect Paul's ideas are still very close to Jewish thinking on the question. The other feature of Paul's thought that was destined to exert considerable influence in the Middle Ages was that of fire. The expression "yet so as by fire" (*quasi per ignem*) was taken to warrant certain metaphorical interpretations of purgatorial fire, but by and large the passage was invoked to justify belief in a real fire.

Before being considered a place, Purgatory was first conceived as a kind of fire, whose location was not easy to specify but which embodied the doctrine from which the later doctrine of Purgatory was to develop. Indeed, since fire symbolism played an important role in that development, it is worth pausing to say a word or two about it. The nature of purgatorial fire was much discussed from patristic times onward. Was it punitive, purifying, or probative? Modern Catholic theology distinguishes between the fire of Hell, which is punitive, the fire of Purgatory, which is expiatory and purifying, and the fire of judgment, which is probative. But this is a late rationalization. In the Middle Ages all three were more or less confounded. Purgatorial fire was considered akin to hellfire: though not eternal, it burned just as fiercely while it lasted. When, later, the fire of judgment was reduced to an individual judgment that followed closely after death, purgatorial fire and the fire of judgment were, in practice, usually identified. Theologians may stress one aspect of Purgatory or another; medieval preachers did the same, and the ordinary faithful must have had similar attitudes, after their own fashion. Purgatorial fire was at once a punishment, a purification, and an ordeal, which accords well with the ambivalent nature that fire has in Indo-European mythology, as C. -M. Edsmann has shown.

There is another episode from the New Testament, which, if did not play a direct role in the history of Purgatory, then at least played an important indirect role by influencing the general conception of the afterworld in Christian thought: I am thinking of Christ's descent into Hell. Three passages of the New Testament treat this episode. First, there is Matthew 12:40: "For as Jonas was three days and three nights in the whale's belly, so shall the Son of man be three days and three nights in the heart of the earth." The Acts of the Apostles 2:31 speaks of the event in the past: "He [David] seeing this before spake of the resurrection of Christ, that his soul was not left in hell, neither his flesh did see corruption." Finally, in Paul's Epistle to the Romans 10:6–7, which contrasts the "righteousness which is of faith" with the "righteousness which is of law," we read the following: "But the righteousness which is of faith speaketh on this wise, Say not in thine heart, Who shall ascend into heaven, (that is to bring Christ down from above), or Who shall descend into the deep? (that is, to bring up Christ again from the dead)."

CHRIST'S DESCENT INTO HELL

Apart from the obvious Christian meaning of this passage—which offers proof of the divinity of Christ and promise of future resurrection—the episode relates to an old oriental tradition, which has been studied extensively by Joseph Kroll.[52] The theme is one of a struggle between God/the sun and the forces of darkness, in which the kingdom of darkness is identified with the abode of the dead. This was a popular theme of medieval liturgy: it figures in exorcistic formulas, hymns, lauds, and tropes as well as in the dramatic games of the late Middle Ages. But the episode really became popular thanks to the wealth of detail contained in the apocryphal Gospel of Nicodemus. There we learn that Christ went down to Hell and retrieved from its clutches righteous souls who had not been baptized because they were born prior to his coming. For the most part these are the souls of patriarchs and prophets. Those souls left behind by Christ are doomed to remain in Hell until the end of time, for Jesus seals

Hell forever with seven seals. With respect to Purgatory this episode is important in three ways. First, it demonstrates that the fate of certain men is susceptible to amelioration after death, if only in exceptional circumstances. At the same time it excludes the souls in Hell from the possibility of improvement in their condition, by sealing Hell until the end of time. Finally, it helps to create yet another world, Limbo, which came into being at roughly the same time as Purgatory, in the great reworking of the geography of the hereafter that occurred in the twelfth century.

Prayers for the Dead

Christians seem to have acquired the habit of praying for their dead at a very early date. This was an innovation, as Salomon Reinach nicely observes: "Pagans prayed to the dead, Christians prayed for the dead."[53] Now, it is of course true that beliefs and mentalities do not change overnight, so it should come as no surprise that we do find instances, particularly in the domain of popular belief, in which non-Christians prayed for the suffering dead in the other world. Orphism is a case in point:

> Orpheus said: Men . . . perform holy works in order to obtain deliverance for their wicked ancestors. You who have power over them . . . you deliver them from great pain and extreme torture.[54]

These practices developed around the beginning of the Christian era. They were a phenomenon of the times, particularly noticeable in Egypt, the great meeting ground for peoples and religions. Traveling in Egypt around 50 B.C., Diodorus of Sicily was struck by the funerary customs: "As soon as the casket containing the corpse is placed on the bark, the survivors call upon the infernal gods and beseech them to admit the soul to the place received for pious men. The crowd adds its own cheers, together with pleas that the deceased be allowed to enjoy eternal life in Hades, in the society of the good."[55]

The passage cited earlier from the Second Book of Maccabees, which was composed by an Alexandrian Jew during the half-century preceding Diodorus's journey, should no doubt be seen against this background.[56] It then becomes clear that at the time of Judas Maccabeus—around 170 B.C., a surprisingly innovative period—prayer for the dead was not practiced, but that a century later it was practiced by certain Jews. No doubt it is in relation to beliefs of this type that we should think of the strange custom described by Paul in 1 Corinthians 15:29–30: "Else what should they do which are baptized for the dead, if the dead rise not at all? Why are they then baptized for the dead?" This baptism for the dead was not the Christian baptism but rather the baptism received by Greek proselytes who converted to Judaism.

The abundant epigraphic and liturgical evidence available for the first few centuries of the Christian era has often been used to prove that belief in Purgatory is very ancient indeed.[57] But it seems to me that the interpretation goes beyond the evidence. The favors that God is urged to grant the dead essentially involve the pleasures of Paradise, or at any rate a state defined by *pax et lux*, peace and light. Not until the end of the fifth century (or the beginning of the sixth) do we find an inscription that speaks of the "redemption of the soul" of one who is deceased. The soul in question is that of a Gallo-Roman woman from Briord, whose epitaph includes the phrase *pro redemptionem animae suae*.[58] Furthermore, the inscriptions and prayers make no mention of a specific place of redemption or waiting other than the one traditional since the time of the Gospels, the "bosom of Abraham." But in order for the idea of Purgatory to develop, it was essential that the living be concerned about the fate of their dead, that the living maintain contacts with the dead, not in order to call on them for protection, but rather in order to improve their condition through prayer.

A Place of Refreshment: *Refrigerium*

Finally, some of these texts describe a place which, though quite similar to the "bosom of Abraham," is not always identical with it: the *refrigerium*. A number of funerary inscriptions bear the words *refrigerium* or *refrigerare* (refreshment, to refresh), either alone or in conjunction with the word *pax* (peace): *in pace et refrigerium, esto in refrigerio* (may he be in *refrigerium*), *in refrigerio anima sua* (may his soul be in *refrigerium*), *deus refrigeret spiritum tuum* (may God refresh his spirit).[59]

An excellent philological study by Christine Mohrmann has clearly traced the semantic evolution of *refrigerium* from classical to Christian Latin: "Alongside these rather vague and shifting definitions, the words *refrigerare* and *refrigerium* took on, in Christian idiom, a very definite technical meaning: heavenly happiness. We find *refrigerium* used in this sense as early as Tertullian, in whose writing it denotes both the temporary happiness of souls awaiting the return of Christ in the bosom of Abraham, according to Tertullian's own conception of the matter, and the everlasting good fortune of Paradise, which is enjoyed by martyrs from the time they die and which is promised to the elect after the final divine verdict. . . . Among later Christian writers *refrigerium* is used in a general way to denote the joys of the world beyond the grave, promised by God to the elect."[60]

Refrigerium has a special place in the prehistory of Purgatory only because of the personal conception of Tertullian, to which Mohrmann alludes in the above paragraph. Indeed, as we have seen, *refrigerium* denotes a quasi-paradisaical state of happiness and not a place. But Tertullian imagined a special kind of *refrigerium*, the *refrigerium interim* or "interim refreshment" reserved for certain of the dead, singled out by

God as worthy of special treatment during the period between their death and the time of final judgment.

An African who died sometime after 220, Tertullian wrote a brief treatise, now lost, in which he argued "that every soul was confined in Hell until the Lord's [judgment] day" (*De anima* 55.5). This was an adaptation of the Old Testament idea of *sheol*. This other world was located underground, and it was here that Christ descended for three days (*De anima* 54.4).

In *Against Marcion* and *On Monogamy* Tertullian goes into detail about the other world and presents his concept of *refrigerium*. Marcion argued that not only martyrs but ordinary righteous people were admitted into Heaven or Paradise immediately after their death. Tertullian, on the other hand, basing his contention on the story of Lazarus and the rich man, maintains that, while awaiting resurrection, ordinary righteous souls reside not in heaven but in a *refrigerium interim*, the bosom of Abraham: "This place, the bosom of Abraham, though not in heaven, and yet above hell, offers the souls of the righteous an interim refreshment [*refrigerium interim*] until the end of all things brings about the general resurrection and the final reward" (*Adversus Marcionem* 4.34).[61] Until the end of time the bosom of Abraham shall serve as "the temporary receptacle of faithful souls."[62]

Tertullian's thought in fact remains highly dualistic. In his view there are two contrasting fates: punishment, which is conveyed by such words as torment (*tormentum*), agony (*supplicium*), and torture (*cruciatus*), and reward, denoted by the term refreshment (*refrigerium*). In two places it is stated that both of these destinies are eternal.[63]

On the other hand, Tertullian lays great stress on offerings for the dead on the anniversary of their death and asserts that pious practices may be based on tradition and faith even if there is no foundation for them in Scripture. (Broadly speaking, with the exception of Matthew 12:32 and Paul's 1 Corinthians 3:10–15, textual underpinnings are almost entirely lacking for the doctrine of Purgatory.) Tertullian writes: "We make oblations for the deceased on the anniversary of their death. . . . If you look in Scripture for a formal law governing these and similar practices, you will find none. It is tradition that justifies them, custom that confirms them, and faith that observes them" (*De corona militis* 3.2–3).[64]

With regard to the prehistory of Purgatory, Tertullian's innovation, if it was an innovation, was to have the righteous spend a period of time in *refrigerium interim* before coming to reside in eternal *refrigerium*. But there is nothing really new about the place of refreshment, which is still the bosom of Abraham. Between Tertullian's *refrigerium interim* and Purgatory there is a difference not only of kind—for Tertullian it is a matter of a restful wait until the Last Judgment, whereas with Purgatory it is a question of a trial that purifies because it is punitive and expiatory—but also of duration: souls remain in *refrigerium* until the resurrection but in Purgatory only as long as it takes to expiate their sins.

Much ink has been spilled over the *refrigerium interim*. The most enlightening debate involves Alfred Stuiber, the historian of early Christian art, and various of his critics, most notably L. de Bruyne.[65] De Bruyne sums up his objections to Stuiber's theory as follows: "According to this theory . . . a decisive role in the choice of themes for sepulchral art is supposed to have been played by the doubts that the first generations of Christians entertained with regard to the fate of the soul immediately after death. It is argued that Christians believed that, when a near relative died, his or her soul must await the final resurrection in unsettled surroundings, the underworld of Hades. No one can fail to see that there is something improbable in such an assertion in light of the optimism and lightness of spirit that are among the most prominent characteristics of the art of the catacombs."[66]

The phrase "no one can fail to see" is unfortunate. It expresses the naiveté of the specialist who assumes that his readers share the views of a small group of experts; worse still, it puts gratuitous assertion in the place of needed proof.

When the question is examined closely, however, it seems to me that de Bruyne is right on two important points. First, the funerary art on which Stuiber rests his case does not allow one to assert that there was an uncertain belief in a *refrigerium interim*. As the specialist de Bruyne maintains, the art of the catacombs expresses certainty more than uncertainty. Furthermore, an idea as subtle as that of *refrigerium interim* was very difficult to represent in material images. I shall have more to say about this kind of difficulty later on, when I discuss it in connection with medieval representations of Purgatory. On the other hand, this "optimism," undoubtedly reinforced if not imposed by the ecclesiastical authorities, already quite coercive, should not be allowed to obscure the doubts that most Christians very probably felt with regard to their fate in the other world prior to the time of judgment and resurrection. For these doubts there were at least two reasons: one doctrinal, since the Bible and Christian theology were far from clear on this score, the other existential, in that, countering the militant optimism of the early Christians was a deep "anxiety" that they shared with the pagans of late antiquity, as E. R. Dodds has so masterfully demonstrated.[67]

THE EARLIEST IMAGES OF PURGATORY: PERPETUA'S VISION

With all this said, it remains true that the idea and the image of "refreshment" inspired—in the very circles in which Tertullian developed his thinking—the earliest document we have in which it is possible to catch a glimpse of Purgatory.

This is a text extraordinary both by its nature and by its content: *The Passion of Perpetua and Felicitas.* [68] When Septimius Severus persecuted the Christians of Africa in 203, it happened that two women, Perpetua and Felicitas, and three men, Saturus, Saturninus, and Revocatus, were put to death near Carthage. While being held in prison prior to her martyrdom, Perpetua, aided by Saturus, either wrote or dictated her memoirs to other Christians, one of whom edited the text and added an epilogue recounting the death of the martyrs. The authenticity of this text, both as to its form and the gist of its content, is not doubted by even the severest critics. The circumstances in which this brief work was written and the simplicity and sincerity of its tone make it one of the most moving examples we have of Christian literature, indeed of literature in general. During her imprisonment, Perpetua has a dream in which she sees her dead younger brother, Dinocratus:

> A few days later, while we were all at prayer, a voice came to me suddenly and the name of Dinocratus escaped from my lips. I was stupefied, because before that moment I had never thought about him. With pain I remembered his death. I knew at once that I was worthy to ask a favor in his behalf, and that I must do so. I began a long prayer, addressing my lamentations to the Lord. On the following night I had this vision: I saw Dinocratus coming out of a place of darkness, where he found himself in the midst of many others, all burning and parched with thirst, filthy and clad in rags, bearing on his face the sore that he had when he died. Dinocratus was my own brother. He died of illness at age seven, his face eaten away by a malignant canker, and his death repulsed everyone. I prayed for him: and between me and him the distance was so great that we could not touch. In the place where Dinocratus was there was a basin full of water, whose lip was too high for a small child. And Dinocratus stood on the tips of his toes, as though he wanted to drink. It caused me pain to see that there was water in the basin but that he could not drink because the lip was so high. I woke up with the knowledge that my brother was being tried. But I had no doubt that I could relieve him in his trial. I prayed for him every day until we were taken to the prison in the Imperial Palace. We were to be forced to fight in the games that were to be held at the Palace for the birthday of Caesar Geta. And I prayed for him night and day, wailing and crying that my prayers be granted. [69]

A few days later Perpetua has another vision:

> The day we were put in irons, this is what I saw: I saw the place that I had seen before, and Dinocratus, his body clean, well

dressed, refreshed [*refrigerantem*], and where the sore had been I saw a scar; and the lip of the basin that I had seen had been lowered to the height of the child's navel, and water flowed out of it continuously. And above the lip there was a golden cup filled with water. Dinocratus drew near and began to drink from it, and the cup never emptied. Then, his thirst quenched, he began playing happily with the water, as children do. I awoke and I understood that his penalty had been lifted.[70]

The important word here is *refrigerantem*, which clearly refers to the notion of *refrigerium*. Not everything in this extraordinary text was entirely novel; similar works were not unheard of in the early third century. A Greek apocryphal work from the late second century, *The Acts of Paul and Thekla*,[71] speaks of prayers for a dead young girl. The pagan queen Tryphena asks her adopted daughter, the Christian virgin Thekla, to pray for her real daughter Phalconilla, who has died. Thekla prays to God for eternal salvation for Phalconilla.

Tertullian, who is sometimes named (surely in error) as the editor of the *Passion of Perpetua and Felicitas* and who did live in Carthage at the time of their martyrdom, knew the *Acts of Paul and Thekla*, which he cites in his work *De baptismo* (17.5). Elsewhere he remarks that a Christian widow should pray for her dead husband and ask that he be granted *refrigerium interim*.[72]

The importance of the *Passion of Perpetua and Felicitas* in the prehistory of Purgatory should neither be exaggerated nor minimized. It is not Purgatory as such that is being discussed here, and none of the images contained in Perpetua's two visions recur in medieval imagery associated with Purgatory. The garden in which Dinocratus finds himself is almost paradisaical in nature; it is neither a valley nor a plain nor a mountain. The thirst and feebleness from which he suffers are described as psychological rather than moral defects. He suffers psychic and physical pain rather than the pain of punishment for a wrong, *labor* rather than *poena*, whereas the texts that foreshadow Purgatory or that concern Purgatory per se prefer the latter term to the former. The *Passion* makes no mention of either judgment or punishment.

And yet, from the time of Augustine onward, this text would be used and commented upon in works that contributed to what ultimately became Purgatory. It contains a discussion of a place which is neither *sheol* nor Hades nor the bosom of Abraham. In this place, a creature, who in spite of his youth must have been a sinner (for the sore or ulcer on his face, the *vulnus* or *facie cancerata*, which disappears by the time of the second vision, cannot in the Christian scheme of things be anything other than a visible sign of sin), suffers from thirst, a typical affliction of those being punished in the other world.[73] He is saved thanks to the prayers of a person worthy of obtaining his pardon. Perpetua is in a position to do this first of all because of the blood ties between her and Dinocratus but even more because of her merits: about to be martyred, she has acquired the right to intercede with God on behalf of her close relatives.[74]

Now that the Catholic Church has embarked upon a drastic revision of its calendar of saints, I would not want to gamble on the actions of those responsible for making and unmaking patronesses. But it is impressive that a still hesitant account of what would one day become Purgatory occurs in this admirable document, under the auspices of so moving a saint.

T W O

The Fathers of Purgatory

ALEXANDRIA: TWO GREEK "FOUNDERS" OF PURGATORY

THE real history of Purgatory begins with a paradox, a twofold paradox. Those who have rightly been called the "founders" of the doctrine of Purgatory were Greek theologians. Although their ideas were not without impact on Greek Christianity, the Greek Church never developed the notion of Purgatory as such. Indeed, during the Middle Ages, Purgatory was one of the principal bones of contention between Greek Christians and Latin Christians. What is more, the theory on which the Greek theologians based their version of Purgatory was plainly heretical in the eyes of the Greek as well as the Latin Church. Thus the doctrine of Purgatory commences with one of history's ironies.

In this book I shall take no notice of Greek ideas concerning the other world except insofar as they came into conflict with Latin ideas of Purgatory in 1274 at the Second Council of Lyons and later—in 1438 and 1439, beyond the chronological limits of this study—at the Council of Florence. Because of this divergence of views between the two churches and for that matter between two worlds—a divergence whose roots can be traced back to late antiquity—the history of Purgatory is an affair of the Latin West. Nevertheless, it is important, in considering the very beginnings of the doctrine, to say a few words about the two Greek "inventors" of Purgatory, Clement of Alexandria (d. prior to 215) and Origen (d. 253/254). Clement and Origen were the two greatest exponents of Christian theology in Alexandria during the period when that port was, in H.-I. Marrou's words, "the center of Christian culture," and in particular a melting pot in which Christianity and Hellenism mingled and fused.

The foundations of the doctrine elaborated by Clement and Origen drew in part on certain pagan Greek philosophical and religious traditions and in part on their own original reflection on the Bible and on Judeo-Christian eschatology.[1] The two theologians were indebted to ancient Greece for the idea that the chastisement inflicted by the gods is not punishment but rather a means of education and salvation, part of a process of purification. In Plato's view this chastisement is a boon offered by the gods.[2] Clement and Origen deduce from this the idea that "to punish" is synonymous with "to educate"[3] and that any chastisement by God contributes to man's salvation.[4]

Plato's idea was vulgarized by Orphism and transmitted by Pythagoreanism. The notion that infernal suffering serves to purify can be found, for example, in the sixth book of Vergil's *Aeneid* (vv. 741–42, 745–47):

> Therefore we souls are trained with punishment
> And pay with suffering for old felonies—
> some are hung up helpless to the winds;
> The stain of sin is cleansed for others of us
> In the trough of a huge whirlpool or with fire
> Burned out of us—each one of us we suffer
> The afterworld we deserve.[5]

From the Old Testament, Clement and Origen took the notion that fire is a divine instrument, and from the New Testament the idea of baptism by fire (from the Gospels) and the idea of a purificatory trial after death (from Paul).

The notion of fire as a divine instrument comes from commonly cited interpretations of Old Testament passages. Their Platonic idea of Christianity led Clement and Origen to take a comforting view of the matter. Clement, for example, argued that God could not be vindictive: "God does not wreak vengeance, for vengeance is to return evil with evil, and God punishes only with an eye to the good" (*Stromata* 7.26). In keeping with this attitude, the two theologians give a soothing interpretation of the Old Testament passages in which God explicitly uses fire as an instrument of his wrath. Consider Leviticus 10:1–2: "And Nadab and Abihu, the sons of Aaron, took either of them his censer, and put fire therein, and put incense thereon, and offered strange fire before the Lord, which he commanded them not. And there went out fire from the Lord, and devoured them, and they died before the Lord." Or Deuteronomy 32:22: "For a fire is kindled in mine anger, and shall burn unto the lowest hell, and shall consume the earth with her increase, and set on fire the foundations of the mountains." Origen, in his *Commentary on Leviticus*, sees these passages as exemplifying God's concern to punish man for his own good. Similarly, he interprets those passages in which God describes himself as a fire not as expressions of a God of wrath but rather of a God who, by consuming and devouring, acts as an instrument of purification. One example of this is the sixteenth homily in Origen's *Commentary on Jeremiah*, which deals with Jeremiah 15:14: "A fire is kindled in mine anger, which shall burn upon you." Another is his treatise *Contra Celsum* 15.13.

The idea of a baptism by fire is based on what John the Baptist says in Luke 3:16: "I indeed baptize you with water; but one mightier than I cometh, the latchet of whose shoes I am not worthy to unloose: he shall baptize you with the Holy Ghost and with fire." Origen, in the Twenty-fourth Homily of his *Commentary on Luke*, gives the following gloss:

As John stood near the Jordan among those who came to be baptized, accepting those who confessed their vices and their sins and rejecting the rest, calling them "rotten vipers" and the like, so will the lord Jesus Christ stand in a river of fire [*in igneo flumine*] next to a flaming sword [*flammea rompea*] and baptize all those who should go to paradise after they die but who lack purgation [*purgatione indiget*], causing them to enter into the place they wish to go. But those who do not bear the mark of the first baptism will not be baptized in the bath of fire. One must first be baptized in water and spirit so that, when the river of fire is reached, the marks of the baths of water and spirit will remain as signs that one is worthy of receiving the baptism of fire in Jesus Christ.

Finally, in the Third Homily on Psalm 36, which contrasts the fate of the wicked man, the victim of God's wrath, with that of the righteous man, the beneficiary of God's protection, Origen gives the following gloss on the passage in Paul's First Epistle to the Corinthians in which Paul describes the final purification by fire:

I think that we all must come to this fire. Whoever we may be, be it Peter or Paul, we come to this fire . . . as before the Red Sea if we are Egyptians we shall be swallowed up in this river or lake of fire, for sins will be found in us . . . or else we too shall enter into the river of fire but, just as the waters formed a wall to the right and to the left of the Jews, so shall the fire form a wall for us . . . and we shall follow the pillar of fire and the pillar of smoke.

Clement of Alexandria was the first to distinguish two categories of sinners and two categories of punishments in this life and in the life to come. In this life, for sinners subject to correction, punishment is "educational" (*didaskalikos*), while for the incorrigible it is "punitive" (*kolastikos*).[6] In the other life there will be two fires, a "devouring and consuming" one for the incorrigible, and for the rest, a fire that "sanctifies" and "does not consume, like the fire of the forge," a "prudent," "intelligent" (*phronimon*) fire "which penetrates the soul that passes through it."[7]

Origen's conceptions were more detailed and far-reaching than Clement's. As we have seen, Origen thought that all men, even the righteous, must be tried by fire, since no one is absolutely pure. Every soul is tainted by the mere fact of its union with the flesh. In the Eighth Homily of the *Commentary on Leviticus*, Origen invokes a passage from the Book of Job (14:4): "Who can bring a clean thing out of an unclean?" For the righteous, however, the trial by fire is a kind of baptism, which, by melting the lead that weighs down the soul, transforms it into pure gold.[8]

Origen and Clement agree that there are two kinds of sinners, or, rather, that there are the righteous, whose only taint is that inherent in human nature (*rupos*, later translated into Latin as *sordes*), and the sinners properly so called, who bear the extra burden of sins that in theory are mortal (*pros thanaton amartia*, or *peccata* in Latin).

The peculiar notion that made a heretic of Origen was this: that there is no sinner so wicked, so inveterate, and so essentially incorrigible that he cannot ultimately be completely purified and allowed to enter into Paradise. Even Hell is only a temporary abode. G. Anrich has put it nicely: "Origen thinks of Hell as a kind of Purgatory." Origen develops to the full the theory of purification, *catharsis*, which came to him from Plato, the Orphics, and the Pythagoreans. The pagan Greek idea of metempsychosis was too un-Christian for Origen to accept, so he replaced it with a theory he thought would be compatible with Christianity, namely, that the soul steadily improves after death and, no matter how sinful it may have been at the outset, eventually makes sufficient progress to be allowed to return to the eternal contemplation of God, which Origen called *apokatastasis*.

Now, to souls of each type—those merely tainted by the flesh and those truly besmirched by sin—there corresponds a different kind of purifying fire. Those tainted by the flesh simply "pass through" the "spirit of judgment," which lasts only an instant. Those besmirched by sin, on the other hand, remain for a more or less extended period in the "spirit of combustion." Though horribly painful, this punishment is not incompatible with Origen's optimism: the more drastic the punishment, the more certain the salvation. In Origen's thought there is a feeling for the redemptive value of suffering that we do not encounter until the end of the Middle Ages, in the fifteenth century.

For Clement of Alexandria, the "intelligent" fire that enters into the sinner's soul was not a material thing (as A. Michel has observed), but neither was it a mere metaphor: it was a "spiritual" fire (*Stromata* 7.6 and 5.14). Some commentators have attempted to draw a distinction between the two kinds of fire described by Origen along the following lines: the fire through which souls merely tainted by association with the flesh must pass is a real fire, we are told, whereas the "fire of combustion" that the really sinful souls must endure is only a "metaphorical" blaze, since these wicked souls, which are ultimately to be saved, are not consumed by it. But this interpretation is not, I think, supported by the texts invoked to justify it (*De principiis* 2.10, *Contra Celsum* 4.13 and 6.71, etc.). In both cases what is involved is a purificatory fire, which, though immaterial, is not merely a metaphor: it is real but spiritual, subtle. When does this purification by fire take place? On this point Origen is quite clear: after the Resurrection, at the time of the Last Judgment.[9] Surely what we have here is nothing other than the fire associated with the end of the world in age-old beliefs known to us from Indo-European, Iranian, and Egyptian sources and subsumed by the Stoics under the head of *ekpurosis*.

In the Jewish apocalyptic literature the most important text concerning the fire associated with the end of the world is found in the vision recounted in the Book of Daniel 7:9–12: "His throne was like the fiery flame, and his wheels as burning fire. A fiery stream issued and came forth from him. . . . the beast was slain, and his body destroyed, and given to the burning flame."

But Origen's eschatological notions were highly personal and not based directly on this kind of text. He believed that the souls of the righteous would pass through the fire of judgment in an instant and would reach Paradise on the eighth day after Judgment Day. The souls of the wicked, on the other hand, would continue to burn after Judgment Day for a "century of centuries." But this does not mean for eternity, since sooner or later all souls go to Paradise. It is just a long time (*In Lucam*, Homily 24). Elsewhere Origen is even more specific: using a curious arithmetic, he calculates that, just as the real world lasts for one week prior to the eighth day, so too will the souls of sinners undergo purification in the "fire of combustion" for one or two weeks, that is, for a very long time, at the end of which, with the beginning of the third week, they will be purified (Seventh Homily in the *Commentary on Leviticus*). It should be noted that this calculation is merely symbolic, whereas in the thirteenth century calculations concerning Purgatory involved real quantities of time. But already we see a system of purgatorial bookkeeping taking shape.

Concerning the fate of the soul between the time of death and the time of the Last Judgment, Origen is quite vague. He assures his readers that the righteous go to Paradise the moment they die, but this Paradise, he says, is different from Heaven, in which the soul arrives only after the Last Judgment and trial by fire, a trial that may last for a shorter or longer period.[10] This preliminary Paradise seems rather like the bosom of Abraham, although as far as I am aware, Origen never mentions this by name. Nor does Origen ever speak of the fate of the sinner in the period between death and the Last Judgment. The reason is that, like many of his contemporaries—indeed, probably more than most—Origen believed that the end of the world was near: "The consumption of the world by fire is imminent. . . . The world and all its elements are going to be consumed in the heat of fire by the end of this century" (Sixth Homily of the *Commentary on Genesis*, PG 12.191). And further: "Christ came in the last days, when the end of the world was already near" (*De principiis* 3.5–6). The period between death and the Last Judgment is so brief that it is not worth thinking about. Trial by fire "awaits us at the end of life" (*In Lucam*, Homily 24).

Thus, if Origen glimpsed the future Purgatory, still his idea of Purgatory was so overshadowed by his eschatology and by his idea of Hell as a temporary abode that ultimately it vanishes from view. Nevertheless, it was Origen who clearly stated for the first time the idea that the soul can be purified in the other world after death. For the first time a distinction was drawn between mortal and lesser sins. We even see three categories beginning to take shape: the righteous, who pass through the fire of judgment and go directly to heaven; those guilty of the lesser sins only, whose sojourn in the "fire of combustion" is brief; and "mortal sinners," who remain in the flames for an extended period. Origen actually develops the metaphor introduced by Paul in 1 Corinthians 3:10–15. He divides the substances mentioned by Paul into two categories. Gold, silver, and the precious gems are associated with the righteous; wood, hay, and straw indicate the "lesser" sinners. And Origen adds a third category: iron, lead, and bronze are associated with those guilty of worse sins.

We also find a rudimentary "arithmetic of purgation" in the work of both Clement and Origen, who are at pains to emphasize what they see as a close link between penitence and the fate of the soul in the hereafter. For Clement of Alexandria, the corrigible sinners are those who repent at the moment of death and reconcile themselves with God, but who do not have the time to do penance. And Origen ultimately sees *apokatastasis* as a process of gradual purification through penitence.[11]

In this vision of the other world a number of ingredients of the true Purgatory are lacking, however. No clear distinction is made between time in Purgatory and the time of the Last Judgment. This confusion is so troublesome that Origen is forced both to expand the end of the world and to collapse it into a single moment, while at the same time making its prospect imminent. Purgatory is not really distinguished from Hell, and there is no clear awareness that Purgatory is a temporary and provisional abode. The responsibility for postmortem purification is shared by the dead, with their weight of sin, and God, the benevolent judge of salvation; the living play no part. Finally, no place is designated as the place of purgatory. By making the purifying fire not only "spiritual" but also "invisible," Origen prevented the imagination of the faithful from gaining a purchase on it.

LATIN CHRISTIANITY: PROGRESS AND INDECISION CONCERNING THE HEREAFTER

We must wait until the very end of the fourth century and the beginning of the fifth for the next major event in the prehistory of Purgatory, an event associated with the name of Augustine and hence with Latin Christianity.

Some writers have credited Cyprian with making an important doctrinal contribution to Purgatory as early as the mid-third century. In his *Letter to Antonian* Cyprian distinguishes between two kinds of Christians: "It is one thing to await forgiveness and another thing to arrive in glory; it is one thing to be sent to prison [*in carcere*] to be let out only when the last farthing has been paid and another thing to receive immediately the reward of faith and virtue; it is one thing to be relieved and purified of one's sins through a long suffering in fire and another thing to have all of one's faults wiped out by martyrdom; and it is one thing to be hanged by the Lord on Judgment Day and another to be crowned by him at once."[12] This passage has been glossed as follows: "This purificatory suffering, this fire beyond the grave, can only be Purgatory. Though Cyprian has not yet achieved the clarity of expression that we find in later periods, he has already advanced beyond Tertullian."[13] This interpretation is typical of an evolutionary view of Purgatory, according to which Christian doctrine made slow but steady progress toward a belief which we are told was present in Christian dogma, in embryo, from the beginning. In my view nothing could be farther from the historical truth. Faced with bouts of millenarianism, with belief in a thundering apocalypse that would save some and annihilate others more or less arbitrarily, the Church, acting in accordance with historical circumstances, with the structure of society, and with a tradition that it gradually transformed into an orthodoxy, began to assemble the elements of a doctrine which, in the twelfth century, culminated in a systematic account of the other world, in which Purgatory played a primary role. But this development was neither uniform nor inevitable. It might easily have gone awry. Changes came more rapidly in some periods than in others: the pace picked up at the beginning of the fifth century, again between the end of the sixth and the beginning of the eighth century, and finally in the twelfth century. But in between there were long periods of stagnation which might have spelled an end for the doctrine once and for all. Jay's refutation of the notion that Cyprian put forth a doctrine akin to that of Purgatory seems to me well founded. According to Jay, what is being discussed in the letter to Antonian is the difference between Christians who did not stand up to persecution (the *lapsi* and apostates) and the martyrs. It is not a question of "purgatory" in the hereafter but of penitence here below. The reference to imprisonment has to do not with Purgatory, which in any case did not yet exist, but rather with the penitential discipline of the Church.[14]

The writings of the Church Fathers and other ecclesiastical authors of the fourth century form a coherent whole in spite of their diversity. This was a time when the persecution of the Christians ended and Christianity became the official religion of the Roman Empire. In this period Christian thought concerning the fate of the soul after death was based mainly on the vision of Daniel (Dan. 7:9) and on a passage from Paul (1 Cor. 3:10–15), and less frequently on Tertullian's idea of *refrigerium* and Origen's concept of a purifying fire. In particular, Origen's ideas had an influence on the Christian portion of the sibylline oracles, and this influence insured that the oracles would not go unnoticed by posterity.

Lactantius (d. after 317) believed that all who died, including the righteous, would be tried by fire, but not until the Last Judgment: "When God examines the righteous, he will also do so by means of fire. Those whose sins prevail by weight or number will be enveloped by fire and purified, while those made ready by unblemished justice or fullness of virtue will not feel this flame, indeed, there is in them something that will repel the flame and turn it back" (*Institutiones* 7.21, *PL* 6.800).

Hilary of Poitiers (d. 367), Ambrose (d. 397), Jerome (d. 419/420), and the unidentified writer known as Ambrosiaster, who lived in the second half of the fourth century, all had ideas on the fate of the soul after death that make them heirs of Origen.

As Hilary of Poitiers saw it, the righteous await the Last Judgment in the bosom of Abraham, while sinners are tormented by fire. At the Last Judgment the righteous go directly to Heaven, the wicked and infidels directly to Hell, and the rest, the bulk of Christian sinners, are submitted to judgment: the unrepentant must pay heavy penalties in Hell. In his commentary on the Forty-fourth psalm, Hilary speaks of "the purification that burns us by the fire of judgment,"[15] but it is not clear whether this fire purifies all sinners or only some of them.

Though more precise on certain matters, Ambrose is on the whole even more ambiguous than Hilary. To begin with, he believed, as we saw earlier, that the souls of the dead await judgment in different "dwelling places," as in the Fourth Book of Ezra. Furthermore, he held that at the final resurrection the righteous would go directly to Paradise and the wicked directly to Hell. Only sinners would be examined and judged. They would be tried by fire (that is, subjected to the baptism of fire mentioned by John the Baptist in Matthew 3:11): "Before the resurrected lies a fire, which all of them must cross. This is the baptism of fire foretold by John the Baptist, in the Holy Ghost and the fire, it is the burning sword of the cherub who guards the gate of heaven, before which everyone must pass: all shall be subjected to examination by fire; for all who want to return to heaven must be tried by fire."[16] Ambrose points out that even Jesus, the apostles, and the saints first had to pass through the fire before entering Heaven. How is this assertion to be reconciled with the contention that the righteous go to Heaven without being judged? Ambrose wavered; his ideas were not very clear. He seems to have held that there are three kinds of fire. For the righteous, who are like pure silver, the fire is refreshing, like a cooling dew (the same idea lies behind the pearl as a symbol of Christ—the pearl is the union of heat and cold). For the wicked, the apostate, and the sacrilegious, who are like lead, the fire is punishment and torture. And for those sinners who are like a mixture of silver and lead, the fire is a purifying instrument, whose painful consequences will last only as long as their sins are heavy, as long as it takes to melt away the admixture of lead in their souls. Is this fire "spiritual" or "real" in nature? Though much influenced by Origen, Ambrose wavered on this point too. Ultimately more a follower of Paul than of Origen, Ambrose believed that all sinners would be saved by passing through fire because, despite their faults, they had the faith: "And if the Lord saves his servants, we will be saved by the faith, but we will be saved as by fire."[17] He also clearly stated that the prayers of the living could help to relieve the suffering of the dead, that suffrages could be of use in mitigating the penalties meted out in the other world. In particular, in regard to the Emperor Theodosius, with whom Ambrose's relations were mixed, he had this to say: "Grant, O Lord, that thy servant Theodosius may rest in peace, in that rest thou hast made ready for thy saints. . . . I loved him, and that is why I want to accompany him in the sojourn of life: I shall never leave him as long as my prayers and lamentations are not heard on high, on the holy mountain of the Lord, where those he has lost call out to him."[18]

When his brother Satyrus dies, Ambrose expresses the hope that the tears and prayers of the unfortunate people he has helped during his life will obtain God's forgiveness and eternal salvation.[19]

These two instances in which Ambrose discusses the fate of the dead in the other world are interesting for another reason, one that will come up again later in the history of Purgatory: the Church was able to use its portrayal of great laymen—emperors and kings—in the afterworld as a powerful political weapon. Later on we will see how this weapon was used in the cases of Theodoric, Charles Martel, and Charlemagne. The possibilities were not lost on Dante. What better means did the Church have to make sovereign rulers obedient to its will—spiritual or temporal—than to point to the punishments awaiting them in the hereafter if they disobeyed, while also making it clear that the suffrages of the Church carried great weight in determining whether or not a soul would ultimately be delivered from perdition and saved? Given what we know about the relations between Ambrose and Theodosius, we can hardly avoid mentioning the political background to Ambrose's remarks. In the case of his brother Satyrus, another aspect of the relations between the living and the dead comes into view. Ambrose is praying for his brother: families formed a rescue service to relatives in the other world. The family becomes even more important in the Middle Ages, when Purgatory is fully developed. Ambrose speaks primarily of the suffrages of those whom Satyrus has helped. Here we see evidence of a phenomenon of social history: the Roman clientele relations, transposed into a Christian key. Other bonds—aristocratic, monastic, lay-monastic, and fraternal—would later supplant the (more or less compulsory) postmortem support offered to the patron by his clients. Finally, as we shall see presently, Ambrose subscribed to the notion that there are two resurrections.

Saint Jerome, though an enemy of Origen, was, when it came to salvation, more of an Origenist than Ambrose. He believed that all sinners, all mortal beings, with the exception of Satan, atheists, and the ungodly, would be saved: "Just as we believe that the torments of the Devil, of all the deniers of God, of the ungodly who have said in their hearts, 'there is no God,' will be eternal, so too do we believe that the judgment of Christian sinners, whose works will be tried and purged in fire will be moderate and mixed with clemency."[20] Furthermore, "He who with all his spirit has placed his faith in Christ, even if he die in sin, shall by his faith live forever."[21]

Ambrosiaster, if he adds little to what Ambrose has already said, is important because he is the author of the first real exegesis of 1 Corinthians 3:10–15. As such he had considerable influence on the medieval commentators on this passage, which played a key role in the inception of Purgatory, and in particular on the early scholastics of the twelfth century. Like Hilary and Ambrose, Ambrosiaster distinguishes three categories: the saints and the righteous, who will go directly to heaven at the time of the resurrection; the ungodly, apostates, infidels, and atheists, who will go directly into the fiery torments of Hell; and the ordinary Christians, who, though sinners, will first pay their debt and for a time be purified by fire but then go to Paradise because they had the faith. Commenting on Paul, Ambrosiaster writes: "He [Paul] said: 'yet so as by fire,' because this salvation exists not without pain; for he did not say, 'he shall be saved by fire,' but when he says, 'yet so as by fire,' he wants to show that this salvation is to come, but that he must suffer the pains of fire; so that, purged by fire, he may be saved and not, like the infidels [*perfidi*], tormented forever by eternal fire; if for a portion of his works he has some value, it is because he believed in Christ."[22]

Paulinus of Nola (d. 431) also speaks in a letter of the "knowing" or "intelligent" (*sapiens*) fire through which we must pass as a trial, the idea for which comes from Origen. Combining the notions of heat and cold, fire and water, and *refrigerium*, he writes: "We passed through fire and water and he led us to refreshment."[23] In a poem he refers to the "judgmental fire" (*ignis arbiter*) that will play over the work of every man, "the flame that will test but not burn," that will eat away the wicked part, consume the flesh, so that man, his body gone, might flee the flames and hasten to his eternal reward, life everlasting.[24]

THE TRUE FATHER OF PURGATORY: AUGUSTINE

It was the role of Augustine, who left so deep an imprint on Christianity and who, in the Middle Ages, was regarded as probably the greatest of all the Christian "authorities," to have been the first to introduce a number of ingredients that later went to make up the doctrine of Purgatory.

Joseph Ntedika, in his excellent essay on the *Evolution of the Doctrine of Purgatory in Saint Augustine* (1966), has collected all Augustinian writings with a bearing on the question. Ntedika has in large part been able to show just what Augustine's role in the prehistory of Purgatory was, and he has put his finger on a key point, showing not only that Augustine's position evolved over the years, which was to be expected, but that it underwent a marked change at a specific point in time, which Ntedika places in the year 413. The cause of this change, Ntedika tells us, was the battle against the *misericordes* (the "merciful"), the laxists in regard to beliefs about the other world—a battle into which Augustine threw himself with great fervor in 413. Here, I shall be satisfied merely to present, situate, and comment on the main Augustinian texts concerning "pre-Purgatory." I want to look at these texts from two angles: first in relation to Augustine's thought and action in general and, second, in a broader perspective, in relation to the inception of Purgatory.

To begin with, I want to call attention to a paradox. Augustine's importance in shaping the doctrine of Purgatory has often been stressed, and rightly so, not only by modern historians and theologians reconstructing the history of that doctrine but also by the medieval clerics responsible for composing it in the first place. Yet it seems clear to me that the question did not really excite Augustine and that, if he alludes to it frequently, the reason is that it was of great interest to his contemporaries and touched on (not to say overwhelmed) issues that Augustine considered fundamental: faith and works; man's place in God's plan; relations between the living and the dead; the concern for order, for a meaningful series of stages ascending from the terrestrial social order to the supernatural order; the distinction between the essential and the accessory; and the requirement that man make an effort to achieve spiritual progress and eternal salvation.

In my view, one reason for Augustine's indecision is his comparative lack of interest in the fate of the soul between death and the Last Judgment. But there are also deeper reasons, which have to do with the period in which he lived. Roman society was in the throes of a profound crisis. There were enormous problems connected not only with the barbarian challenge but also with the establishment of a new dominant ideology, which, in regard to the afterlife, revolved around the belief in resurrection and the choice to be made between damnation and eternal salvation. Thoroughly imbued with millenarian thought and believing, more or less confusedly, that the Last Judgment was imminent, late Roman society was little inclined to refine its thinking about the interval between death and eternity. The men and women of late antiquity, it seems to me, based their hopes for the hereafter not so much on the ambiguous idea of salvation as on the notion of compensation in the other world for injustices suffered in this one—it has always been so, I think, and in any case Paul Veyne has shown that this was the case in his studies of public giving in antiquity. Now, the demand for equity after death could be satisfied, in a sophisticated way, by justice in the form of redemption after death. But this was a luxury. By the twelfth century society had changed so much that this luxury had become a necessity, and it was this change that paved the way for the inception of Purgatory.

Furthermore, it also seems to me that Augustine had personal reasons for expressing doubts about certain aspects of a problem which, at the time, seemed marginal. These doubts will emerge from the texts I am about to cite.

Among the personal reasons for Augustine's doubts was, first of all, his discovery that the Bible was imprecise, not to say contradictory, on the subject of the hereafter. Admirable exegete that he was, Augustine does not hide the obscurities and difficulties he finds in the Bible. It has not been sufficiently remarked that when, in the twelfth century, Abelard introduced in *Sic et Non* what was then deemed a revolutionary method of exegesis, he was in fact harking back to techniques used earlier by Augustine. As a priest, a bishop, and a Christian intellectual, Augustine was convinced that the Bible was the "foundation" of all religious teachings (the term "foundation," borrowed from 1 Corinthians 3:10–15, pleased him enormously). Wherever the Bible is unclear, nothing definite can be asserted, though of course Augustine believed deeply that one might do one's utmost to make the meaning of the text as clear as possible. Yet about questions touching on salvation it is even more difficult, Augustine believed, to say anything definite, because it is necessary to respect the secrecy, the mystery, in which certain aspects of these questions are shrouded. Some decisions, Augustine argued, are better left to God, who has spelled out, in the Bible and through the teachings of Jesus, the principles that guide his actions; within this framework, some decisions are reserved to God above, even aside from miracles.

Augustine's importance in the history of Purgatory stems first from the terminology he introduced, which remained current through much of the Middle Ages. There are three key terms, the adjectives *purgatorius, temporarius* or *temporalis*, and *transitorius*. "*Purgatorius*" figured in the phrase "*poenae purgatoriae*": I prefer to translate this as "purgatorial punishments" rather than "purificatory punishments," the latter being too precise for Augustine's way of thinking (the phrase occurs in *City of God*, 21.13 and 21.16). We also find *tormenta purgatoria*, purgatorial torments (in *City of God* 21.16), and *ignis purgatorius*, purgatorial fire (in *Enchiridion* 69).[25] *Temporarius* is used, for example, in the expression *poenae temporariae*, temporary punishments, which is contrasted with *poenae sempiternae*, eternal punishments (*City of God* 21.13). *Poenae temporales* is found in Erasmus's edition of the *City of God* (21.26).[26]

THE DEATH OF MONICA: PRAY FOR HER

Initially Augustine argued that suffrages for the dead are effective. He first did so in a moment of emotion, in the prayer* he wrote in 397–98 after the death of his mother, Monica (*Confessions* 9.13:34–37):

> Now that my soul has recovered from that wound, in which perhaps I was guilty of too much worldly affection, tears of another sort stream from my eyes. They are tears which I offer to you, my God, for your handmaid. They flow from a spirit which trembles at the thought of the dangers which await every soul that had died with Adam. For although she was alive in Christ even before her soul was parted from the body, and her faith and the good life she led resounded to the glory of your name, yet I cannot presume to say that from the time when she was reborn in baptism no word contrary to your commandments ever fell from her lips. Your Son, the Truth, has said: Any man who says to his brother, You fool, must answer for it in hell fire, and however praiseworthy a man's life may be, it will go hard with him if you lay aside your mercy when you come to examine it. But you do not search out our faults ruthlessly, and because of this we hope and believe that one day we shall find a place with you. Yet if any man makes a list of his deserts, what would it be but a list of your gifts? If only men would know themselves for what they are! If only they who boast would make their boast in the Lord!
>
> And so, my Glory and my Life, God of my heart, I will lay aside for a while all the good deeds which my mother did. For them I thank you, but now I pray to you for her sins. Hear me through your Son, who hung on the cross and now sits at your right hand and pleads for us, for he is the true medicine of our wounds. I know that my mother always acted with mercy and that she forgave others with all her heart when they trespassed against her. Forgive her too, O Lord, if ever she trespassed against you in all the long years of her life after baptism. Forgive her, I beseech you; do not call her to account. Let your mercy give your judgement an honorable welcome, for your words are true and you have promised mercy to the merciful. If they are merciful, it is by your gift; and you will show pity on those whom you pity; you will show mercy where you are merciful.
>
> I believe that you have already done what I ask of you, but Lord, accept these vows of mine. For on the day when she was so soon to be released from the flesh she had no care whether her body was to be buried in a rich shroud or embalmed with spices, nor did she wish to have a special monument or a grave

*Cited here after R. S. Pine-Coffin's English translation.—Trans.

in her own country. These were not the last wishes she passed on to us. All she wanted was that we should remember her at your altar, where she had been your servant day after day, without fail. For she knew that at your altar we receive the holy Victim, who cancelled the decree made to our prejudice, and in whom we hve triumphed over the enemy who reckons up our sins, trying to find some charge to bring against us, yet can find no fault in him whom we conquer. Who shall restore to him his innocent blood? Who shall take us from him by repaying him the price for which he bought us? By the strong ties of faith your handmaid had bound her soul to this sacrament of our redemption. Let no one tear her away from your protection. Let not the devil who is lion and serpent in one, bar her way by force or by guile. For she will not answer that she has no debt to pay, for fear that her cunning accuser should prove her wrong and win her for himself. Her reply will be that her debt has been paid by Christ, to whom none can repay the price which he paid for us, though the debt was not his to pay.

Let her rest in peace with her husband. He was her first husband and she married no other after him. She served him, yielding you a harvest, so that in the end she also won him for you. O my Lord, my God, inspire your servants my brothers— they are your sons and my masters, whom I serve with heart and voice and pen—inspire those of them who read this book to remember Monica, your servant, at your altar and with her Patricius, her husband, who died before her, by whose bodies you brought me into this life, though how it was I do not know. With pious hearts let them remember those who were not only my parents in this light that fails, but were also my brother and sister, subject to you, our Father, in our Catholic mother the Church, and will be my fellow citizens in the eternal Jerusalem for which your people sigh throughout their pilgrimage, from the time when they set out until the time when they return to you. So it shall be that the last request that my mother made to me shall be granted in the prayers of the many who read my confessions more fully than in mine alone.

This admirable passage is not a treatise on doctrine, but it is possible to draw from it important evidence concerning Augustine's views on the effectiveness of suffrages for the dead.

The decision whether Monica should or should not reside in Paradise, in the eternal Jerusalem, is God's alone to make. And yet Augustine is convinced that his prayers can reach God and influence his decision. Still, God's judgment is not arbitrary. Augustine's prayers are therefore neither absurd nor brazen, because Monica, despite her sins—every human being is a sinner—lived her life in such a way as to be worthy of God's mercy, thus allowing her son's prayers to have some effect. Without saying so in so many words, Augustine suggests that God's mercy and the suffrages of the living can hasten the day when the soul enters Heaven, but that suffrages alone cannot gain entry into Heaven for souls carrying an excessive burden of sin. Though not stated explicitly, it also seems likely that, since there is no Purgatory (and not a single sentence in any of Augustine's writings suggests a connection between suffrages and purgatorial fire), deserving sinners receive assistance from the living immediately after death, or in any case soon enough after death so that it is unnecessary to say precisely how long, much less to specify a place for the soul to wait prior to judgment.

The merits Augustine cites in Monica's behalf are worthy of note: baptism is taken for granted, and both faith and works are also mentioned. Following the traditional teaching, Monica's righteous acts include forgiveness of debts (and doubtless, since she was a wealthy aristocrat, we must assume that this is meant in a material as well as a moral sense), monogamy, renunciation of remarriage after her husband's death, and, above all, eucharistic piety. All these are tokens of salvation associated with Purgatory as well as with Heaven: merciful works, eucharistic devotion, respect for matrimony among the laity—all these count heavily in favor of the soul that wishes to avoid Hell, putting it in line to enter, if not Heaven, then at least Purgatory—thanks to God's mercy and to the suffrages of the living. Here, "the living" refers first and foremost to the person most closely related by blood to the dead woman, namely, her son, Augustine. But beyond him are also two communities of Christians who may be impelled to lift up their voices in prayer for the soul of the mother of the bishop and writer: his congregation and his readers.

Some years later, in his commentary on the Thirty-seventh Psalm, Augustine asks God to correct his behavior in this life so that he need not endure the "correctional fire" (*ignis emendatorius*) in the next. This not only reaffirms his belief, already apparent in the prayer for his mother, that the soul earns its salvation in this world, but also demonstrates another idea, which Augustine was to cherish as long as he lived: that the tribulations of this life are a kind of "purgatory."

Finally, in 426–27, in the *City of God* 21.24, Augustine once again took up the question of the efficacy of prayer for the dead. But this time his purpose was to set clear limits to what prayer could accomplish. The intercession of the living can do nothing for demons, for infidels, or for the godless: it cannot help the damned. Thus suffrages are worthwhile only for a certain category of sinners, a category which is not very clearly defined but which is characterized in a very particular way: sinners whose life in this world has been neither very good nor very bad. Augustine bases his argument on Matthew 12:31–32: "Wherefore I say unto you, All manner of sin and blasphemy shall be forgiven unto men: but the blasphemy against the Holy Ghost shall not be forgiven unto men. And whosoever speaketh a word against the Son of man, it shall be forgiven him: but whosoever speaketh against the Holy Ghost, it shall not be forgiven him, neither in this world, neither in the world to come." Augustine is also explicit about who may offer up efficacious prayer for those souls capable of being saved: those affiliated in an institutional capacity with the Church, either the Church itself or "a few pious men" (*quidam pii*).

> The reason then for not offering prayer at the time of judgment for those human beings who are consigned for punishment to the eternal fire is the same as the reason for not praying now for the evil angels. And likewise there is the same reason for praying at this time for human beings who are infidel and irreligious, and yet refusing to pray for them when they are departed. For the prayer of the Church itself, or even the prayer of devout individuals, is heard and answered on behalf of some of the departed, but only on behalf of those who have been reborn in Christ and whose life in the body has not been so evil that they are judged unworthy of such mercy, and yet not so good that they are seen to have no need of it.[27] Likewise, after the resurrection of the dead there will still be some on whom mercy will be bestowed, after punishment suffered by the souls of the dead, so that they will not be consigned to the eternal fire. For it could not truthfully be said of some people that they will be forgiven neither in this age nor in the age to come, unless there are were some who receive forgiveness in the age to come though not in this age. Nevertheless, this is what has been said by the Judge of the living and the dead: "Come, you that have my Father's blessing; take possession of the kingdom prepared for you from the foundation of the world"; and to the other, in contrast: "Out of my sight, you accursed ones, into the eternal fire, which is prepared for the Devil and his angels"; and "these will go to eternal punishment, while the righteous will go to eternal life."[28] In view of this, it is excessively presumptuous to assert that there will be eternal punishment for none of those who, so God has said, will go to punishment which will be eternal, and by the persuasion of this presumptuous notion to produce despair, or at least doubt, about the eternity of the future life itself.

Until 413 Augustine was content to add a few personal notes to the teachings of the third- and fourth-century fathers in regard to the fire of judgment and the abode of souls after death, particularly the bosom of Abraham. His views were based primarily on the exegesis of the story of Lazarus and the rich man (Luke 16:19–31) and Paul's First Epistle to the Corinthians (3:10–15). In the *Commentary on Genesis Against the Manichaeans*, written in 398, Augustine distinguishes between the fire of purgation and damnation: "and after this life there will be either the fire of purgation or eternal pain."[29] In the *Questions on the Gospels*, which dates from 399, he contrasts souls that cannot be saved, like that of the wicked rich man, with souls that paved the way for their own salvation by doing works of mercy, thus making it possible for suffrages to work their effects. But he asserts that he does not know whether the souls of the dead will be received immediately after death into the "everlasting habitations" mentioned in Luke 16:9 or at the end of time, on the Day of Judgment.[30]

In his *Commentaries on the Psalms*, probably written between 400 and 414, Augustine emphasizes the difficulties inherent in the idea of a purgatorial fire after death: the whole question, he says, is an obscure one (*obscura quaestio*). Yet in his *Commentary on Psalm 37* he makes a statement that would be widely quoted in medieval discussions of Purgatory: "Although some will be saved by fire, this fire will be more terrible than anything that a man can suffer in this life."[31]

AFTER 413: HARSH PENALTIES BETWEEN DEATH AND JUDGMENT FOR LESS THAN PERFECT SOULS

Starting in the year 413, Augustine's views on the fate of the soul after death and, in particular, on the possibility of redemption after death began to sharpen and narrow. Most specialists in Augustine's thought, especially Joseph Ntedika, think there is good reason to view this stiffening of Augustine's position as a reaction against the laxist ideas of the *misericordes*, whom Augustine regarded as dangerous adversaries. The change has also been seen as due in part to the influence of millenarian ideas that reached Augustine through Spanish Christians. For my part, I think it also reflects the impact of the great event of the year 410: the sack of Rome by Alaric and the Ostrogoths, which seemed not only to mark the end of the Roman Empire and the invulnerability of Rome but also, in the minds of some Christians, to presage the end of the world. Meanwhile, those cultivated Roman aristocrats who remained pagan accused the Christians of having undermined Rome's strength and of being responsible for a catastrophe which, if it was not the end of the world, at least marked the end of order and civilization. It was in response to this situation, to these ideas and accusations, that Augustine wrote the *City of God*.

What did the *misericordes*, about whom we know little more than what Augustine held against them, have to say?[32] Augustine describes them as heirs of Origen, who believed that, when the process of *paracatastasis* was complete, everyone would be saved, including Satan and the evil angels. Augustine does acknowledge, however, that the *misericordes* were concerned only with men and not with demons. Despite slight differences among themselves, all the *misericordes* believed that all, or most, inveterate sinners would be saved. Augustine distinguishes six different but closely related opinions. First, that all men will be saved but only after spending a period of time in Hell. Second, that the prayers of the saints will obtain salvation for everyone at the Last Judgment, without any passage through Hell. Third, that all Christians who have received the Eucharist will be saved, even schismatics and heretics. Fourth, that only Catholics will be saved, and not schismatics or heretics. Fifth, that all who keep the faith to the end will be saved, even if they have lived in sin. And sixth, that all who have given alms will be saved, no matter what else they may have done. Without going into detail, let it suffice to say that, however much these ideas may owe to Origen, all of them are based essentially on passages taken out of context from the bible and interpreted literally.

Against them Augustine argued that there are two fires, an everlasting fire in which the damned, for whom intercession is futile, burn forever—on which Augustine lays great stress—and a purgatorial fire, about which he is more hesitant. Thus what interests Augustine is not what would one day become Purgatory but rather Hell.

It is in order to establish Hell that he defines various categories of sinners and sins. Joseph Ntedika has identified three kinds of men, three kinds of sins, and three kinds of destiny. This does not do full justice, I think, to the complexity of Augustine's thought (this ternary division is really the work of twelfth- and thirteenth-century clerics). There are four kinds of men: the godless (infidels and perpetrators of criminal sins), who are consigned directly to Hell, with no possibility of a reprieve or second chance. At the other end of the scale are the martyrs, the saints, and the righteous, who, even if they have committed "slight" sins, go immediately, or at least very quickly, to Heaven. Between these two extremes are those who are neither altogether good nor altogether wicked. Those who are not altogether wicked are destined to go to Hell: the best that can be hoped for them is a "more tolerable" Hell, which may possibly, as we shall see later on, be obtained by suffrages. This leaves souls that are not altogether good. These can (perhaps) be saved by passing through a purgatorial fire. All in all, these souls are not very numerous. Though not entirely clear about whether this category of soul and this kind of fire actually exist or not, Augustine is more explicit about what they are like if they do exist. The purgatorial fire is extremely painful but not eternal, unlike the fire of Gehenna, and it acts not at the time of the Last Judgment but between the time of death and the time of resurrection. Furthermore, a mitigation of the pain may be obtained thanks to suffrages of certain of the living, those duly authorized to intercede with God, provided that the soul is worthy of salvation in spite of its sins. Worthiness is determined by one's having lived a generally good life and having made constant efforts to improve, by the performance of good works, and by the practice of penitence. The connection between penitence and "purgatory," which was to assume such great importance in the twelfth and thirteenth centuries, was clearly stated for the first time by Augustine. Explicitly, it may be true that Augustine situates the time of purgation prior to the Last Judgment, in the period between death and ultimate resurrection; but in the final analysis his deeper instinct is to situate it even earlier than that, in this world rather than the next. Underlying this instinct is the idea that earthly "tribulation" is the primary form of "purgatory." This accounts for Augustine's hesitation as to the true nature of purgatorial fire. If it burns after death there is no reason why it cannot be "real"; but if it burns on this earth, its nature must be essentially "moral."

As far as sins are concerned, Augustine distinguishes three classes of very serious sins, which he calls "crimes" (*crimina*)—*facinora, flagitia, scelara*—rather than sins and which condemn those who commit them to Hell. He also identifies various lesser sins, which he calls "slight," "minor," "petty," and, above all, "quotidian" (*levia, minuta, minutissima, minora, minima, modica, parva, brevia, quotidiana* are all words he uses in this connection): examples of this category are excessive attachment to one's family and excessive conjugal love (*City of God* 21.26). Joseph Ntedika points out that Augustine never discusses, either broadly or in detail, the so-called "intermediate" sins, namely, those that are supposed to disappear in purgatorial fire, and suggests that the reason for this is that Augustine was afraid that his ideas might be exploited by the *misericordes.* That may be. But it should be borne in mind that Augustine was more concerned with spiritual life in the broad sense, with the inner life of mankind as a whole, than with drawing up an inventory of moral acts that would serve to reify the life of the soul. The "crimes" of which he speaks are more criminal habits than specific misdeeds. The only sins that can be named are the "quotidian" ones, petty infractions committed in the course of everyday life. To name them entails no grave consequences for the quality of spiritual life, for they are the peccadilloes, the bagatelles, the inconsequential wrongs that are easily gotten rid of, provided they do not accumulate to the point where they begin to invade the spirit.

The conflict between Augustine and the *misericordes* and the change in his thinking about the fate of the dead first appear in his treatise *On Faith and Works* (*De fide et operibus*), which dates from 413, but they receive their fullest expression in the *Enchiridion* (421) and in Book 21 of the *City of God* (426–27). In the meantime, at the behest of his friends, he began to flesh out his thoughts. In the *Letter to Dardanus* (417) he sketches a geography of the otherworld which makes no place for Purgatory. Commenting on the story of Lazarus and the rich man, he says that there is a region of torment and a region of repose, but unlike some other writers he does not place both of these in the underworld, because the Bible says that Jesus went down to Hell but not that he visited the bosom of Abraham. The latter is none other than Paradise, a general term which does not, Augustine tells us, refer to the Earthly Paradise in which God placed Adam before the fall.[33]

In 419 a certain Vincentius Victor from Caesarea in Mauritania questions Augustine about the need to be baptized in order to be saved. Augustine answers him in the treatise *On the Nature and Origin of the Soul*, where he considers the example of Dinocratus in the *Passion of Perpetua and Felicitas*. The bishop of Hippo says that unbaptized children cannot enter Heaven or even, as the Pelagians thought, go to an intermediate place of rest and happiness (thus Augustine here denies the existence of what in the thirteenth century would be called the "children's limbo"). To go to Heaven one must be baptized: Dinocratus was baptized, but he must have committed some sin later on, perhaps the sin of apostasy under the influence of his father. Still, he is saved in the end thanks to the intercession of his sister.

At this point I want to cite at length important passages of the *Enchiridion*[34] and the *City of God*. First the *Enchiridion*:*

> So then if a wicked man is to be saved through fire for the sake of faith alone, and if that is the meaning of the blessed apostle Paul's statement, yet he himself shall be saved, yet so as through fire, in that case faith without works will have power to save, and the statement of his fellow-apostle James will be untrue. That also will be untrue which Paul himself has said: Be not misled: neither fornicators nor idolators nor adulterers nor effeminate nor abusers of themselves with men, nor thieves nor covetous nor revilers nor drunkards nor extortioners, shall obtain possession of the kingdom of God. If, however, while persisting in these crimes, they are for all that to be saved because of the faith of Christ, how can they fail to be in the kingdom of God? Seeing, however, that such clear and evident apostolic testimonies as these cannot be untrue, that other obscure statement made with reference to those who build, upon the foundation which is Christ, neither gold nor silver nor precious stones, but wood, hay and stubble (for it is of these that the statement is made that they will be saved through fire, because the goodness of the foundation will preclude their perishing) must be interpreted in such a manner as not to be found in contradiction with these statements that are not obscure. Wood and hay and stubble may without incongruity be taken as the sort of desires for the things of this world, things perfectly legitimate in themselves, which yet cannot be relinquished without regret. When, however, such regret is as a fire, yet in the man's heart Christ has his position as foundation (that is, so that nothing is given preference over him), and the man who is on fire with that regret would rather be deprived of the things he so loves than be deprived of Christ, he would be

---

*Cited here after Ernest Evans's English translation (London, 1953), pp. 59–60. Trans.

saved through fire. But if in time of temptation his preference has been to retain this kind of temporal and worldly thing rather than Christ, he has not had Christ at his foundation: for he has had these things in the prior place, though in a building there is nothing prior to the foundation. For the fire to which the apostle referred in that passage must be interpreted as of such a nature that both persons pass through it, the one who builds upon this foundation gold, silver, and precious stones, as well as he who builds wood, hay, and stubble. For the apostle continued: The fire shall try every man's work, of what kind it is: if any man's work shall abide, which he hath built thereupon, he shall receive a reward: but if any man's work shall be burned up, he shall suffer loss; but he himself shall be saved, yet so as through fire. It is not then the work of one of them, but of each one, that the fire shall try.

This excerpt from chapters 67 and 68 of the *Enchiridion* tells us about a number of aspects of Augustine's thought. To begin with we learn something about his method of exegesis. He takes an admittedly obscure passage from Paul (1 Cor. 3:13–15) and sets it against other passages in which Paul speaks more clearly. The principle is this: difficult passages are to be interpreted in the light of passages whose meaning is certain. Furthermore, he carefully distinguishes between men who have committed crimes (*homo sceleratus, crimina*) and men who have committed only minor sins, typified for Augustine by an excessive attachment to otherwise legitimate earthly goods. On Judgment Day both the criminals and the others will be tried by fire, but the criminals will be consumed and perish while the others will be saved. Augustine continues as follows:

It is not beyond belief that something of the sort takes place even after this life, and there is room for inquiry whether it is so, and the answer may be found (or not found) to be that a certain number of the faithful are the more belatedly or the more speedily saved, through a sort of fire, the more they have or the less they have set their affections on the good things that perish: not, however, those of whom the pronouncement was made that they shall not obtain possession of the kingdom of God, unless, on their doing appropriate penance, those crimes are forgiven them. By "appropriate" I mean that they be not unfruitful in almsgiving: for to it divine Scripture has assigned so high a value that our Lord declares that it is simply and solely with the fruit of it that he will credit those on his right hand, and simply and solely with unfruitfulness in it that he will discredit those on his left, when he says to the former, Come, ye blessed of my Father, receive the kingdom; and to the latter, Depart, ye cursed, into eternal fire. Of course we must take care that no one should think that those outrageous crimes, the commission of which excludes from possession of the kingdom of God, may be perpetrated every day, and every day bought off by almsgiving. Rather should there take place an amendment of life: and by means of almsgiving God should be brought to pardon sins past, and not in some sort of way bribed to allow them to be continually committed with impunity. For to no man hath he given licence to sin, albeit by showing mercy he blots out sins already committed, provided appropriate satisfaction be not neglected.

In the preceding passage Augustine emphasized that in order to be saved by fire one had to have lived a life in which faith and works were combined. Here (*Enchiridion* 69–70) he is even more explicit. It is not enough merely to have given alms; one's life must have "changed for the better" (*in melius quippe est vita mutanda*). In particular, one must have done an appropriate penance, one must have given satisfaction by performing a canonical penance. If this requirement was met, then remission could be obtained "after this life" (*post hanc vitam*) by means of "a certain purgatory fire" (*per ignem quemdam purgatorium*) to which Augustine does not pay close heed but which is in any case different from the eternal fire of Hell. In the *City of God* 21.26 Augustine again turns to the distinction between two kinds of fire, one which torments forever and one which purges and saves. Penitence, he says, can be so effective as to redeem even crimes (*crimina*), provided they are not infamous (*infanda*). Purgatorial fire is intended for those believers who have either not done the canonical penance or not had time to complete it. On the other hand, those who were subject to such penance but did not submit to it are not eligible to be purified by fire.

In chapters 109 and 110 of the *Enchiridion* Augustine refers to the "dwellings" into which the souls of the dead are welcomed between the time of death and the ultimate resurrection. There are both places of repose (the bosom of Abraham, not mentioned by name) and places of torment (Gehenna, also not mentioned), as in the Fourth Book of Ezra, which Ambrose cites explicitly. The souls of the dead may be aided by the suffrages of the living: eucharistic sacrifices and alms. This is where Augustine gives his fullest account of his concept of four types of men. The good have no need of suffrages, though these may be of use to the wicked. What about those who are neither entirely good nor entirely wicked? They have need of suffrages. Those who are almost entirely good will benefit from them. As for those who are almost entirely bad, the best they may hope for, it seems, is a "more tolerable damnation" (*tolerabilio damnatio*). Augustine does not explain what he means by this. We may assume that what he had in mind was either a Sabbath rest for those in Hell or less cruel torments. Here the idea of mitigating the suffering of the souls in Hell seems to encompass something other than what is usually meant by "Purgatory."

> But during the time which intervenes between a man's death and resurrection at the last, men's souls are reserved in secret storehouses, at rest or in tribulation according to each soul's deserts, according to its lot in the flesh during life. Nor is there room for denial that the souls of the deceased obtain relief through the dutiful service of the friends who are alive, when the Mediator's sacrifice is offered for them or almsgiving is done in the Church. Such acts, however, are of advantage to those who during their life have deserved that such acts should be of advantage to them. For there is a certain manner of living, neither good enough to dispense with the need for these after death, nor bad enough to preclude their being of advantage to it after death; and there is a certain manner of living which is so established in goodness as to dispense with the need for them, as again there is one so established in evil as to be incapable of benefiting even from these when it has passed on from this life. Therefore it is here and now that a man acquires any merit or demerit through which after this life he becomes capable of relief or depression. So let no man expect that after his death he can make up in the sight of God for his omissions while here. Thus these services which the Church repeatedly performs for the commendation of the departed are in no sense opposed to that apostolic statement which says: For we shall all stand before the judgment-seat of Christ, that each one may receive in accordance with the things he has done in the body, whether it be good or bad: because each of them, while living in the body, has acquired for himself even this merit, the possibility of their being of advantage to him. For they are not of advantage to everybody. And why are they not of advantage to everybody, unless because of the difference between the life which each one has lived in the body? At such times then as the sacrifices either of the altar or of any manner of alms are offered for all the baptized departed, on behalf of the very good they are thanksgivings, on behalf of the very bad they are propitiations, though they are no sort of consolation to the living. And in cases where they are of advantage, the advantage is either that they obtain complete remission, or at least that damnation itself becomes less intolerable.

Book 21 of the *City of God* is devoted to the question of punishment in Hell. Augustine's principal purpose is to argue that infernal punishments are everlasting. In addition to chapter 24, cited earlier to show for which categories of souls Augustine believed suffrages to be useful, I shall here be interested in chapter 13 and most of chapter 26.

In chapter 13 Augustine attacks those who believe that all punishment in this world and the next is merely purgatorial, that is, for the purpose of purification and therefore temporary. Once again he invokes the distinction between eternal punishments and purgatorial, or temporary punishments, but this time he is more clear in conceding that purgatorial punishments do exist, and he goes into greater detail about their nature:

Now the Platonists, while refusing to believe that any sins go unpunished, hold that all punishments are directed towards purification, whether they are punishments inflicted by human laws or those imposed by divine decree, and whether the latter are suffered in this life, or after death, when someone is spared in this life, or when his affliction does not result in his correction. This belief is expressed in the passage in Vergil, where he first speaks of earthly bodies and their mortal parts, and says of men's souls that "Hence come desire and fear, gladness and sorrow, they look not up to heaven, but lie confined in darkness and the sightless dungeon's gloom," and then goes on immediately: "Yet at their last light, when the life departs (that is when this mortal life leaves them at their last day) even then they are not freed from woe and pain; the body's plagues do not vanish utterly. For many evils, hardening deep within must needs grow rooted there in wondrous wise. Therefore they suffer chastisement of pain, paying the price of ancient sin. And some are hung suspended in the idle winds; others are washed from guilt beneath the surge of the vast deep; in others the infection is burned away by fire." Those who hold this view will have it that the only punishments after death are those intended to purify, so that souls may be cleansed from any infection contracted by contact with the earth by purifying pains inflicted by one of the elements superior to the earth, which are air, fire, and water. The air is meant by the phrase "suspended in the winds," the water, by "the vast deep," while the fire is expressly named in "is burned away by fire." On our part we acknowledge that even in this mortal life there are indeed some purificatory punishments; but penalties inflicted on those whose life is not improved thereby or is even made worse, are not purificatory. Punishments are a means of purification only to those who are disciplined and corrected by them. All other punishments, whether temporal or eternal, are imposed on every person in accordance with the treatment he is to receive from God's providence; they are imposed either in retribution for sins, whether past sins or sins in which the person so chastised is still living, or else they serve to exercise and to display the virtues of the good; and they are administered through the agency of men, or of angels, whether good or evil angels. It must be observed that when any man suffers any harm through the wickedness or the mistake of another, then that other human being commits a sin in doing some harm to another man either through ignorance or through ill-will; God commits no sin in allowing this wrong to happen by his decision, which is just, albeit inscrutable. As for temporal pains, some people suffer them in this life only, others after death, others both in this life and in the other; yet all this precedes that last and strictest judgment. However, not all men who endure temporal pains after death come into those eternal punishments, which are to come after that judgment. Some, in fact, will receive forgiveness in the world to come for what is not forgiven in this, as I have said above, so that they may not be punished with the eternal chastisement of the world to come.

These remarks are aimed not at Christian but rather at pagan authors, to whom Augustine refers as "Platonists" and among them he includes Vergil, thus recognizing the verses of the first book of the Aeneid that I have cited as a prefiguration of the Christian idea of the hereafter. He insists on the existence of "purgatorial punishments," also called "expiatory" punishments. He concedes that these can be endured either on this earth or after death. They are temporary punishments because they will cease on Judgment Day, at which time those who had been punished will enter Heaven. This last assertion is quite important: it will later become a major ingredient in the medieval system of Purgatory. Augustine concludes by reiterating that only those who have corrected themselves while on earth will be allowed to benefit from purgatorial punishments after death.

In the *City of God* 21.26 Augustine gives an exegesis of 1 Corinthians 3:13–15 more detailed and subtle than the one he gave earlier:

> Now listen to the Apostle describing a man who builds gold, silver, precious stones, on this foundation. "The unmarried man," he says, "gives his thoughts to the Lord's affairs; his aim is to please the Lord"; and then describing the builder in wood, hay, and straw, "The married man, in contrast, concentrates on worldly matters; his concern is how to please his wife," and so "The work of each builder will be revealed; for the day (the day of tribulation, of course) will show it up, since it will be revealed in fire." ("Fire" is his name for this tribulation, as in another place, where we read, "The furnace tests the vessels of the potter, and the trial of tribulation tests righteous men.") "And the fire will test the quality of each man's work. If a man's work on the foundation stands" (and it is a man's thoughts on the Lord's affairs, his aim to please God, that give this permanence) "he will get his wages" (that is, he will receive his reward from the object of his concern); "if anyone's work is burnt down, he will suffer loss" (since he will no longer have

what he was so fond of), "but the man himself will be saved" (because tribulation could never remove him from the firm base of that foundation) "but it will be as a man is saved from a fire" (for he must feel burning pain at the loss of what entranced him when he possessed it). There, then, you have this "fire," as it seems to me, which enriches the one and impoverishes the other; it tests both, while it condemns neither.

Thus Augustine distinguishes between two kinds of souls saved "by fire," a trial which must be endured both by those whose work survives and by those whose work is consumed. The former are rewarded by going directly to Paradise; the latter at first suffer loss, that is, expiation, but in the end they too are saved.

Finally, at the end of chapter 26, Augustine returns to the exegesis of the same passage from Paul, adding two further details. In the first place he states clearly that purgatorial fire will work its effects in "the interval of time" (*hoc temporis intervallo*) between bodily death and resurrection. Second, he specifies those human attitudes that lead to damnation and contrasts them with those that put the beneficial effects of purgatorial fire within reach. The criterion involved is the nature of the "foundation" on which each man builds his life. Christ is the only foundation that can bring salvation. He who chooses for his foundation the pleasures of the flesh rather than Christ goes straight to perdition. But he who merely indulges to excess the pleasures of the flesh, yet without putting those pleasures in Christ's place as the foundation of life itself, will be saved "by this kind of fire."

As for the interval between the death of this present body and the coming of that Day, the day of condemnation and reward which is to be after the general resurrection of the body, it may be alleged that during this interval the spirits of the departed suffer this sort of fire, though it is not felt by those whose ways of living and loving have not been such, in their life in the body, as to have produced "wood, hay, and straw" to be burnt down by the fire. Others, on this theory, feel that fire, because they carry about with them "buildings" of this sort; and such people experience the "fire" of transitory tribulation which reduces these "buildings" to ashes. For these structures belong to this world, although they receive pardon, and do not entail damnation; and the fire may be experienced perhaps only after this life, or both in this life and hereafter, or in this life only and not hereafter.

Now I am not concerned to refute this suggestion, because it may well be true. It is indeed possible that the actual death of the body may form part of this tribulation. This death came into being through the perpetration of the first sin; and it may be that the period which follows death brings to each one an experience suited to the "building" he has erected. The same is true of the persecutions in which the martyrs won their crowns, and which brought suffering to all Christian people; these attacks "test" both kinds of "structure," like a fire. Some "buildings" are destroyed, along with the builders, if Christ is not discovered to be their foundation; others are destroyed, but without the builders, if Christ is so discovered, for "the builders themselves will be saved" although "with loss." But other "buildings" are not destroyed, because they prove to be of such quality as to last forever. There will also be tribulation at the end of this world's history, in the time of Antichrist; and it will be such a tribulation as has never been before. How many buildings will there be then to be tested by that fire! Some will be of gold, some of straw, built upon the best of foundations, which is Christ Jesus, and so the fire will test both kinds of building, and to the one sort of people it will bring joy, to the others it will bring loss; but it will destroy neither sort in whom it finds those buildings, because of this stable foundation. But anyone who puts any loved objects before Christ does not have Christ for his foundation. I am not speaking only of man's wife, when he treats her as a means of sensual pleasure in carnal copulation; I am referring also to those relationships of natural affection where there is no question of such sensual indulgence. If a man loves any member of his family, with a human being's instinctive affection, in such a way as to put Christ second, then Christ is not his foundation, and for that reason such a man will not be "saved by fire," because it will be impossible for him to be with the Savior. Indeed Christ made a most explicit statement on this point when he said, "Anyone who loves his father or his mother more than me is not worthy of me; and anyone who loves a son or a daughter more than me is not worthy of me." On the other hand, anyone who loves those close relations in this instinctive way, without putting them in front of the Lord Christ, anyone who would prefer to be deprived of them rather than to lose Christ, if he were brought to the test of this dilemma, such a man will be "saved through fire," because the loss of those loved ones will cause him burning pain in proportion to the closeness of his attachment to them. But we may add that anyone who loves father or mother, sons or daughters according to the standards of Christ, so that he is concerned that they may inherit Christ's kingdom and be united to Christ, or anyone who loves them for the fact that they are members of Christ; it is impossible that such affection should prove to be something that has to be destroyed along with the "wood, hay, and straw." This will, beyond dispute, be reckoned as part of the structure of "gold, silver, and precious stone." For if a man loves others entirely for Christ's sake, how can he love them more than Christ?

AUGUSTINE AND GHOSTS

We cannot, I think, end our discussion of Augustine's ideas about the afterlife, which played so important a role in the inception of Purgatory, until we have discussed two related questions. The first of these comes up in the brief tract *On the Care to Be Given to the Dead*, which was dedicated to Paulinus of Nola sometime between 421 and 423. Here, Augustine returns to one of his favorite themes, one that figured earlier in his prayer for his mother Monica in book 9 of the *Confessions*: his strong distaste for the sumptuous funerary customs to which some Christians, following the habits of wealthy pagans, were inclined. The dead, Augustine argued, require only a minimum of care, and though he is willing to allow a certain decorum in funerals and cemeteries, it is simply out of respect for human life. The families of the dead derive some consolation from this, and there is no reason to deny them this much. But in the second part of *De cura pro mortuis gerenda*, Augustine turns to the question of ghosts. Ghosts, he says, are real, adducing examples from his own experience by way of proof:*

> Certain visions are reported which seem to bring into this discussion a question that should not be neglected. In fact some dead persons are reported to have appeared either in a dream or in some such fashion to the living, who were ignorant as to where their bodies were lying unburied. After pointing out these places to them, they admonished them to provide for them the burial which had been lacking. Now if we state that these things are false, we shall seem indifferently to go against the writings of certain of the faithful and against the senses of those who affirm that such things have happened to them. One must reply that it is not to be assumed that the dead have knowledge of these things merely because they seem to say them or to point them out or to seek them in dreams. The living often appear to the living while they are asleep, although they are entirely unaware of making any such appearance, and hear from them, as they speak, the things which they have dreamed, namely, that they saw them in their dreams doing or saying something. It is possible for someone to see me in his dreams indicating to him something that has happened, or predicting to him something that is to happen, when I am entirely ignorant of this and do not care what he may dream, or whether he is awake while I am sleeping, or he is asleep while I am awake, or whether we both are awake or asleep at one and the same time when he experiences the dream in which he sees me. Why then, is it so strange if the dead, without their knowledge and

*Cited here after the English translation in Augustine, *Treatises on Marriage and Other Subjects*, Roy J. Deferrari, ed., pp. 349–84. Trans.

not perceiving these things, are seen by the living in sleep and say something which, upon awaking, they realize to be true?

I might believe that this is done by the workings of angels. It may be permitted from above, or it may be ordered, that they may seem in their sleep to say something about the burying of their own bodies, when truly they whose the bodies are know nothing of this. Even this sometimes happens advantageously for some kind of solace for the living who are related to those dead whose images appear to them while dreaming, or that by these friendly admonitions to mankind the humanity of burial is commended. For, although burial may not help the dead, if one neglects it he may be considered irreligious. However, at times when false visions have been seen, men are led into great errors, which they ought to resist. Suppose someone should see in his dream what Aeneas by a false report of the poet is said to have seen among the dead, and then the image of someone not buried should appear to him and should say such things as Palinurus is said to have spoken to Aeneas. Then, on awaking, he should find the body in the very place where he heard that it was lying when he was dreaming. If then, on being admonished and requested to bury the body he had found and because he finds this to be true, he should believe that the dead are buried so that their souls may pass over to those places from which he dreamed that the souls of the unburied are prohibited by a wicked law, would he not by holding such a belief depart far from the path of Truth?

However, human weakness seems to be such that when anyone sees in his sleep one who is dead he thinks he sees the soul of the dead person. But, when he has dreamed of a living person, he feels confident that it is the likeness of the person and not his soul or body which has appeared to him. This amounts to the belief that the souls but not the likeness of the dead in the same manner without their knowledge may appear to those sleeping. Indeed, when we were at Milan, we heard of the following incident: Payment of a debt was demanded of a certain son, whose father, without the knowledge of the son, had made full settlement before his death, but had not received back the original note which was now produced. The son became very sad and was wondering why his father as he was dying had not told him what he owed, since he had made a will. Then the same father appeared to his son, who was now quite anxious. While the son was sleeping his father told him where he might find the receipt which would acknowledge full payment of his original note. And when the son found this and presented it, not only did he throw off the slander of the false claim but also recovered his father's signature, which the father had not recovered when he repaid the loan. Here, indeed, the mind of a man is thought to have exercised a care for his son and to have come to him sleeping, that he might inform his ignorance and so set him free from a great annoyance.

But, at almost the very same time at which we heard the above report, another story came to us at Milan from Eulogius, a rhetorician at Carthage. He was a disciple of mine in this art, and he himself told me the same story after we had returned to Africa. The story is as follows. When Eulogius was teaching the rhetorical works of Cicero to his pupils, as he was reviewing the lecture which he had intended to deliver the following day, he came upon an obscure passage, and, not being able to determine the exact meaning, could scarcely sleep. On that very night I expounded to him in his dream the passage which he did not understand. Indeed, not I, but my image, and without my knowledge, and so far across the sea, either doing or dreaming something else, and caring not at all for his worries! In what way such things happen I do not know, but in whatsoever way they do happen, why do we not believe that they happen in the same way, namely, as one in his sleep sees a dead person, so he sees a living person? In both instances it happens to those who neither know nor care who dreams of their images, or where, or when.

After discussing visions that may occur in periods of delirium or lethargy, Augustine concludes by advising his readers not to look too closely at these mysteries:

He might even reply using holy Scripture, and say: "Seek not the things that are too high for thee, and search not into things above thy ability; but the things that God hath commanded thee, think on them always" (Ecclesiastes 3:22). This I would gratefully accept, for it is a great gain if it should become clear that we should not even try to understand some obscure and uncertain facts which we were not able to understand, and if we should learn that it is of no disadvantage if we do not understand the things we wish to know, thinking that such knowledge is a gain when it is not.

The general conclusion of this tract is that suffrages for the dead are useful, though it is stipulated that only those worthy of salvation can benefit from them. But given the uncertainty surrounding the fate that God intends for any particular soul, it is better to err on the side of too much rather than too little. Augustine favors a trilogy of aids for the dead that we shall encounter again in connection with Purgatory: masses, prayers, and alms:

Since this is so, we should not think that any aid comes to the dead for whom we are providing care, except what we solemnly pray for in their behalf at the altars, either by sacrifices of prayers or of alms. Even this does not benefit all for whom it is done, but only those who while they lived made preparation that they might be aided. But, even though we do not know who these are, we ought none the less to do such works for all Christians, so that no one of them may be neglected for whom these aids can and ought to come. It is better that there be a superabundance of aids for those to whom these works are neither a hindrance nor a help, than that there be a lack for those who are thus aided. Yet, each one does this more diligently for his own friends and relatives, in order that a like service may be performed in his behalf by his friends and relatives.

I have cited these remarkable texts at some length because of the importance of Purgatory in relation to the question of ghosts: Purgatory would become the prison in which ghosts were normally incarcerated, though they might be allowed to escape now and then to briefly haunt those of the living whose zeal in their behalf was insufficient. It is of some importance that here too Augustine could figure as an authority. Always ready to denounce popular superstitions, that Christian intellectual shared the views of the common folk in regard to ghosts. It is clear, moreover, that he found himself at a loss when it came to interpreting dreams and visions. Christianity destroyed the learned oneiromancy of the ancient world and repressed or rejected popular methods of divination. With the path of dreams blocked, the way was open for nightmares. Medieval man would not reconquer the dream world for a long time to come.[35]

PURGATORIAL FIRE AND AUGUSTINIAN ESCHATOLOGY

Care should be taken, too, not to separate Augustine's concept of purgatorial fire from his general eschatological doctrine, and in particular his attitude toward millenarianism, even if he himself did not make the connection explicit.[36]

Inherited from Judaism, millenarianism was the belief of certain Christians that the end of time would begin with Christ's coming on earth, where he would reign in peace and happiness for a thousand years, or a millennium—metaphorically speaking, a very long time. Christian millenarians, especially numerous among the Greeks (which explains why the doctrine was first referred to as chiliasm, from the Greek word "chilia" meaning one thousand), based their belief primarily on a passage from the Book of Revelation (20:4–6), which some Christians opposed to millenarianism tried in vain to have expunged from the canonical compilation of Holy Scripture:

> And I saw thrones, and they sat upon them, and judgment was given unto them: and I saw the souls of them that were beheaded for the witness of Jesus, and for the word of God, and

which had not worshipped the beast, neither his image, neither had received his mark upon their foreheads, or in their hands; and they lived and reigned with Christ a thousand years. But the rest of the dead lived not again until the thousand years were finished. This is the first resurrection. Blessed and holy is he that hath part in the first resurrection: on such the second death hath no power, but they shall be priests of God and of Christ, and shall reign with him a thousand years.

The millenarian wave seems to have crested among the Christians in the second century and to have subsided thereafter. But millenarian beliefs did not die out altogether and flared up periodically during the Middle Ages. Doubtless the most important of these flare-ups occurred in the thirteenth century under the influence of the millenarian ideas of the abbot Joachim of Floris (in Calabria), who died in 1202.

Augustine devoted book 20 of the *City of God* to eschatology, to the end of time. While acknowledging that he himelf was a millenarian in his youth, he is harshly critical of millenarian thinking. The millennium, Augustine contends, began with the coming of Christ and continues with each baptism, the act of baptism representing the first resurrection, the resurrection of the soul. Belief in a future millennium is an error, at bottom the same error as that of the Jews, who still await the coming of the Messiah when in fact he has already come. Augustine interprets the millennium allegorically, moreover. The number one thousand is perfect, ten cubed, signifying the fullness of time. Augustine minimizes the significance of another event predicted by the Book of Revelation, the coming of the Antichrist, a demonic being who it is said will rule the earth just before the beginning of the millennium, when Satan, himself chained for a thousand years, will be released. According to Augustine, the reign of the Antichrist would be very brief, and during this time neither Christ nor the Church—which will not vanish—would abandon mankind. The denial of a resurrection of the righteous prior to the Last Judgment is connected with the claim that the souls of the dead will pass through a purgatorial fire in the time between death and resurrection, during which interval no other eschatological event is supposed to occur. Ambrose, by contrast, following Origen (who severely condemned chiliasm while putting forward his own theory of *apokatastasis*, according to which souls pass through several stages of purification), asserted that there was more than one resurrection to come and suggested that purgatorial fire would do its work mainly between the first and the second of these (Commentary on Psalm 1, n. 54).[37]

From Augustine onward what we find is that millenarianism was incompatible with a belief in Purgatory. It might be supposed that the Church put together the doctrine of Purgatory in response to the inroads made by millenarian thinkers. But it may be, too, that a residue of millenarian thinking in Augustine contributed to the lack of precision in his notions of purgatorial fire. As we saw earlier in the passage cited from the *City of God* 21.26, Augustine thought that the time of the Antichrist would witness an increase in the use of purgatorial fire. His belief that the millennium had already begun and that earthly tribulation constituted the first stage of purgation prevented him from conceiving of a special place in which the purgatorial fire might be located. Joseph Ntedika has, I think, given a very good account of what Augustine contributed to the future doctrine of Purgatory: "Posterity singled out for further development primarily two suggestions contained in Augustine's thought: the idea that that the purifying effects of fire work only on lesser sins, and the situation of the fire in the interval between death and resurrection" (p. 68).

These are indeed Augustine's two main contributions. To begin with he gave a very strict definition of purgatorial fire—strict in three respects. First, it would apply to a small number of sinners. Second, it would be very painful. And third, it would be a sort of temporary Hell (Augustine is among those most responsible for the "infernalization of Purgatory"), inflicting suffering far greater than any earthly pain. Furthermore, he defined when purgatorial fire would be applied: in the time between the death of the individual and the judgment of all. But Augustine left two major elements of the Purgatory system in the dark. While he specifies what kind of sinner can be purified (one who is neither altogether bad nor altogether good), he says nothing about what kind of sin can land the soul in Purgatory. He has no doctrine of "venial" sins. Beyond that, he says nothing about Purgatory as a place. Now we can see why Augustine refused to go this far. He specified the time of Purgatory in opposition to the millenarians and *misericordes*. He said nothing definite about the location or concrete content of Purgatory because in order to do so he would have had to echo more or less "popular" beliefs—beliefs embedded in the apocalyptic and apocryphal tradition that he rejected. As an intellectual aristocrat, Augustine was horrified by the "popular," which he identified with the "vulgar" and the "materialistic." When the Church Fathers institutionalized Purgatory at the Second Council of Lyons (1274), the Council of Florence (1438), and the Council of Trent (1563), they too tried to keep its imaginary furnishings separate from the verities of faith, the dogma of the Church; at Trent, at least, suspicion of the imagination was palpably in the air.

Augustine, despite his doubts and hesitations, did acknowledge the existence of purgatorial fire: in this, too, he made an important contribution to the prehistory of Purgatory. Sanctioned by the authority of Augustine, purgatorial fire remained, until the end of the twelfth century, the defining characteristic of "pre-Purgatory," and after that date, once Purgatory came to be defined as a distinctive place, fire continued to be one of its key elements. Once suspicion of popular imagery and beliefs had to

84

some extent subsided, as it did between 1150 and 1250, it became possible to set aside a distinctive location for Purgatory. In all of this history, Augustine's position is very illuminating in both positive and negative senses.[38]

Christian teaching gradually evolved toward its definitive position: that it is possible for some sinners to be redeemed after death. Because of the need to combat millenarianism, it was convenient to situate the time of this redemption in the period between the death of the individual and the Last Judgment. But the Church hierarchy remained cautious when it came to applying the new doctrine: it was best not to make accommodations in the new afterworld too ample, lest Hell be emptied out altogether. Above all, the Church worried about the danger of making the other world too material. There were risks involved in being too specific about the location in which purgation occurs and too concrete about the trials that it involves. Since Paul mentions fire or a passage through something like fire (*quasi per ignem*), the image of fire could be used: in any case the fire might be more or less immaterial and could eventually be reduced to a metaphor. But to concede any more than this to the "madwoman upstairs," as Malebranche called the imagination, threatened to give the devil a toehold, to open the way to devilish illusions in the form of pagan imaginings, Jewish follies, heretical fantasies—in short, to "popular" imagery. What Augustine bequeathed to the Middle Ages was this mixture of certainty and suspicion.

Caesarius of Arles (d. 542) has been credited with a milestone in the prehistory of Purgatory. This misinterpretation, which is based on two sermons delivered by the bishop of Arles, has been rectified by Pierre Jay, to whose careful reading of the evidence we now turn.[39]

Purgatory and Caesarius of Arles

Caesarius of Arles discusses purgatorial fire (*ignis purgatorius*) in two of his sermons, numbers 167 and 179.[40] Here is the purported text of the latter of these, a commentary on 1 Corinthians 3:10–15, based on the partial translation given by A. Michel in the *Dictionnaire de théologie catholique*:

> Those who understand this text improperly suffer from a false sense of security. They believe that, if they build on Christ's foundation an edifice of capital crimes, their sins may be purified by passing through fire (*per ignem transitorium*), and that they will then be able to enter into eternal life. Correct this manner of comprehending, my brothers: to comfort oneself with thoughts of such an end is sadly to mistake the truth. In this passing fire (*transitorio igne*), of which the Apostle has said, "he will be saved, yet as by fire," it is not capital sins but minor sins that will be purified. . . . Although these sins,

according to our belief, do not kill the soul, they disfigure it . . . and permit it to unite with its heavenly spouse only at the price of a great confusion. . . . Through continual prayer and frequent fasts we may redeem them . . . and what has not been redeemed by us must be purified in that fire of which the Apostle has said: (Every man's work) shall be made manifest by fire; and the fire shall try every man's work. (1 Cor. 3:13). . . . As long as we live in this world, therefore, let us mortify ourselves . . . so that these sins may be purified in this life, and so that in the other life the purgatorial fire will find in us little or nothing to devour. But if we do not give thanks to God in our afflictions, and if we do not redeem our wrongdoing by good works, we must remain in purgatorial fire long enough for our minor sins to be consumed like wood, hay, and straw.

Let no one say, What does it matter to me if I stay in purgatory if subsequently I am to enjoy eternal life! Ah! Do not speak that way, dear brothers, for this fire of purgatory will be more painful than any pain that we can conceive, suffer, and feel in this world.

But in fact Caesarius's original Latin text says something quite different. Where Michel has translated "fire of purgatory," the Latin reads "*ignis purgatorius*," purgatorial fire, and where he puts "in purgatory," there is nothing at all corresponding in Latin.[41]

In fact, Caesarius is merely repeating what the Church Fathers, especially Augustine, had said before him. Compared with Augustine, Caesarius has actually taken a step backward, because for Caesarius purgatorial fire is merely the fire of judgment and has nothing to do with the interval between death and resurrection. As Pierre Jay rightly observes, "Let us be careful, then, not to pay too much heed to the idea that there is constant progress in theology." Nevertheless, Caesarius does have his place in the prehistory of Purgatory, for misinterpreted texts have just as much historical importance as other texts. Caesarius's writings drew particular attention from medieval clerics because they were attributed to Augustine: as "Augustinian authorities" the words of the bishop of Arles would be passed down through the centuries and therefore be available for systematic exploitation by theologians whose concerns were entirely different from those of Caesarius. They would be scanned for answers to the questions, "Where is Purgatory?" and "How long does it last?"

In point of fact, Caesarius confirms two points made by Augustine and adds one detail not found in genuine Augustinian texts. Augustine, in his commentary on the Thirty-Seventh Pslam, had said that "purgatorial fire will be more terrible than anything a man can suffer in this life." As we have seen, Caesarius repeated this opinion and thereby helped to create the terrifying image of Purgatory that was held out to the men of the Middle Ages. Augustine also distinguished between grave sins, which he called *crimina*, and lesser sins, insignificant sins, with which it was not proper to be overly concerned. Caesarius borrows this distinction from Augustine and makes it even more explicit. He refers to the more serious sins as *crimina capitalia*: this is the origin of the notion of "capital sins" which Gregory the Great would later consolidate into a doctrine. Caesarius still refers to the lesser sins as *parva* (petty), *quotidiana* (routine), *minuta* (trifling), but adds that these are the sins that are expiated in purgatorial fire, a detail not mentioned by Augustine.

With Caesarius, finally, there was a change in the atmosphere surrounding the discussion of the fate of the dead and the nature of the hereafter. The Last Judgment was one of Caesarius's favorite themes, and he dwelt more readily on Hell than on Heaven. In one sermon he admits that his listeners have reproached him for speaking constantly about frightening subjects (*tam dura*). Even more than Augustine, his concern was to convince the faithful of the reality of eternal hellfire and of the painful quality of the temporary fire. He was obsessed, as one writer puts it, "with the image of his flock facing the eternal judge." His concern is essentially pastoral. His purpose was to provide the faithful with a ready supply of simple ideas and formulas. He therefore drew up lists of "capital" and "minor" sins, something Augustine never did. His attitude has been explained, correctly I think, as a result of the barbarization of society and religion. But this undeniable barbarization, which marks the beginning of the Middle Ages as such, was a more complex phenomenon than is often believed.

In the first place, the "responsibility" for the decline in the general cultural and spiritual level was not borne by the "barbarians" alone. The fact that the peasant masses, the "barbarians" within, took up the Christian religion was at least as important as the fact that invaders from outside the Roman world took up residence inside it. The "barbarization" of Roman society was in part a democratization. Here matters become still more complicated. Church leaders preached an egalitarian religion and tried to reach out to their congregations, to "get closer to the people." But the overwhelming majority of them were urban aristocrats who shared the prejudices of their class, which were closely tied to their worldly interests. Their contempt for the peasant and hatred of paganism, coupled with their lack of understanding of behavior informed by alien cultures, behavior they were quick to label "superstitious," led these ecclesiastical leaders to preach a religion of fear. Hell was better suited to this climate than was a process intended to bring about a reduction of punishment. For a long time the purgatorial fire discreetly lighted by the Church Fathers, particularly Augustine, smoldered in secret without finding the fuel that it needed to take hold in a world beset with insecurity and divided by fundamental conflict, a world illuminated by the brighter blaze of judgment, which was in large part confounded with the sinister light of the flames of Hell.

STORIES OF PURGATORY IN THIS WORLD
GREGORY THE GREAT, THE LAST FATHER OF PURGATORY

Yet it was in this eschatological atmosphere that one pontiff, moved by an ardent pastoral zeal in a dramatic earthly context, fanned the purgatorial flame back to life. After Clement of Alexandria and Origen, after Augustine, the last "founder" of Purgatory was Gregory the Great.

Gregory belonged to a great family of Roman aristocrats. Both before and after his "conversion," when he took vows and established a monastery in one of his family's villas in Rome, he occupied high office. He was for a time prefect of the city, in charge of feeding the population in a country ravaged by the Byzantines, the Goths, the Lombards, and the plague, and he later served as the pope's ambassador to the emperor in Constantinople. In 590 he was called to the throne of Saint Peter in dramatic circumstances: a terrible flood of the Tiber had inundated the city, whose population had been decimated by a horrible epidemic of plague (one of the worst outbreaks of the great pandemic, the first black plague, known as the plague of Justinian, which had been devastating the Middle East, the Byzantine Empire, North Africa, and Mediterranean Europe for nearly half a century). Like Caesarius, indeed more than Caesarius, given his position, his personality, and the historical moment, Gregory was an eschatological pastor. Convinced that the end of the world was at hand, he threw himself passionately into the great enterprise of saving the Christian people, in whose behalf he believed he would soon be called to plead at the bar of God's justice. To Christians living within the confines of the Roman world he issued repeated instructions on how to win salvation; he commented on the Bible, particularly the prophets; he addressed meditations on the Book of Job to his monks and a pastoral manual to the secular clergy; and he urged laymen to organize their lives with a view to ultimate salvation by taking part in disciplined liturgical ritual (Gregory was a great organizer of processions and ceremonies) and by paying heed to the moral teachings of the Church. To those living outside the Roman world he sent missionaries. The English had fallen back into paganism, so he sent to Canterbury a mission that began the reconquest of Britain for Christianity. To the Italians he gave a hagiography, and among the Italian Fathers he singled out a monk who had recently died, Benedict of Monte Cassino, whom he made one of the great saints of all Christendom. Among the Christians to be saved, why shouldn't there be some souls among the dead? Gregory's eschatological passion knew no bounds, extending beyond the threshhold of the grave.[42]

To the doctrine of Purgatory Gregory the Great made three important contributions. In the *Moralia in Job* he gives further details concerning the geography of the hereafter. In the *Dialogi*, along with observations on doctrine, he describes souls expiating their sins prior to the Last Judgment. Finally, although his story of the Gothic king Theodoric, who is carried off to Hell, makes no mention of a specific place called "Purgatory," it was later regarded as a very early clue to Purgatory's earthly location.

In *Moralia in Job* 12.13, Gregory comments on Job 14:13: "Quis mihi tribuat ut in inferno protegas me?" (translated in the Jerusalem Bible as, "O that thou wouldst defend me in *sheol*," the inferno in question being the Jewish Hell). The problem that Gregory is trying to resolve is the following: Before Christ's coming, it was usual for all who died to fall into Hell, because the coming of Christ was necessary to reopen the path to Heaven. But the righteous were not supposed to fall into that part of Hell where souls are tortured. There are in fact two parts of Hell, an upper part, where the righteous rest in peace, and a lower part, where the wicked are subjected to torment.

> *O that Thou wouldest defend me in hell!*
> That before the coming of the Mediator between God and man, every person, though he might have been of a pure and approved life, descended to the prisons of hell, there can be no doubt; in that man, who fell by his own act, was unable by his own act to return to the rest of Paradise, except that He should come, Who by the mystery of His Incarnation should open the way into that same Paradise. For hence after the sin of the first man it is recorded, that a flaming sword was placed at the entrance of Paradise, which is also called "moveable," in that the time should come one day, that it might even be removed. Nor yet do we maintain that the souls of the righteous did so go down into hell, that they were imprisoned in places of punishment; but it is to be believed that there are higher regions in hell, and that there are lower regions apart, so that both the righteous might be at rest in the upper regions, and the unrighteous be tormented in the lower ones. Hence the Psalmist, by reason of the grace of God preventing him, says, *Thou hast delivered my soul from the lowest hell.* Thus blessed Job before the coming of the Mediator, knowing of his going down into hell, implores the protecting hand of his Maker there, in order that he might be a stranger to the places of punishment; where, while he is brought to enjoy rest, he might be kept hidden from punishment.[43]

A little later on (*Moralia in Job* 13.53), Gregory again takes up this problem and goes into still further detail in discussing yet another passage from Job (17:16): "In profundissimum infernum descendent omnia mea." Here is what he says:

> *All of mine shall descend into the lowest hell.*
> Whereas it appears that among those below the righteous are held bound not in places of punishment, but in the bosom of tranquillity above, an important question springs up before us, why it is that blessed Job declares, saying, *All of mine shall*

descend into the lowest hell; who even if before the Advent of
the Mediator between God and man he had to descend into
hell, yet it is plain that into the "lowest hell" he had not to
descend. Does he call the very higher regions of hell, "the
lowest hell?" Plainly because in relation to the loftiness of
heaven, the region of this sky may not unappropriately be
called the lower region. Whence when the Apostate Angels
were plunged from the seats of heaven into this darksome
region of the air, the Apostle Peter says, *For if God spared not
the Angels that sinned, but delivered them, dragged down with
infernal chains, into hell, to be reserved for torments in the
Judgment.* If then relatively to the height of heaven this darksome air is infernal, relatively to the elevation of this air, the
earth which lies below may be taken both as infernal, and as
deep; and relatively to the height of that earth, even those parts
of hell which are higher than the other mansions of the place
below, may in this place not unsuitably be denoted by the
designation of the lowest hell; in that what the sky is to heaven,
and the earth to the sky, the same is that higher hollow of the
regions below to the earth.[44]

A concrete thinker, Gregory was interested in the geography of the
hereafter. The upper Hell of which he speaks may well have been the
Limbo of the Fathers, but when there came to be such a thing as Purgatory
and it became necessary, in the thirteenth century, to find early references
to justify it, the Old Testament passages that discuss the depths of Hell
would be interpreted in the light of Gregory the Great's exegesis.

In book 4 of the *Dialogues* Gregory the Great teaches some of the
fundamental truths of Christianity, especially the immortality of the soul,
the fate of the soul after death, and the doctrine of the Eucharist, with the
help of anecdotes—often visions—which he calls *exempla*, precursors of
the thirteenth-century *exempla* that popularized the belief in Purgatory.
The fate of certain souls after death is described in three stories distributed
over two chapters. These stories provide answers to two doctrinal questions, one concerning purgatorial fire and the other concerning the efficacy
of suffrages for the dead.

The deacon Peter, Gregory's interlocutor and foil, begins by asking,
"What I want to know is this—must we believe that there is a purgatorial
fire after death?"[45] To begin with, Gregory explains the dogma in terms of
passages from the Bible,[46] the most important of which is from Paul's First
Epistle to the Corinthians concerning the fate of the various materials out
of which the works of men may be constructed. The first references seem to
prove that men will come to the Last Judgment in whatever state they were
in when they died. But Paul's text seems to indicate "that we must believe
that for certain slight sins there will be a purgatorial fire prior to judgment." Gregory gives examples of this category of "petty and minor sins":

constant chattering, immoderate laughter, and attachment to private property, all sins which, whether committed knowingly or not, weigh, though lightly, on their authors after death, provided they have not been delivered from these sins in this life.[47] According to Gregory, Paul's meaning was as follows: he who builds out of iron, brass, or lead, i.e., he who commits "the major and hence the hardest sins," will not have his sins dissolved by fire, whereas the "very slight, minor sins," those built of wood or straw, will be dissolved. But the petty sins will be destroyed after death only if the good actions of the sinner in this life warrant such destruction.

Gregory's view, therefore, remains quite close to that of Augustine, but he places the accent on "slight, petty, minor" sins, which he specifies, and he clearly states that the action of the fire will take place only after death, omitting the earthly tribulation that Augustine tended to include as part of the process of purgation.

The novelty in Gregory's approach is mainly in his use of anecdotal illustration. "When I was still a young man," he says, "and in the lay estate, I heard (a story) told by men older and wiser than myself." Paschasius, deacon of the Holy See and the author of an admirable work on the Holy Spirit, which has survived, was a man whose life had been saintly, who dispensed alms, and who thought nothing of himself. But in the schism that began in 498 and pitted popes Symmachus and Laurentius against one other, Paschasius had been a stubborn supporter of the "false" pope, Laurentius. When Paschasius died, an exorcist touched his dalmatic, which had been placed on his coffin, and he was immediately saved. A good while after his death, Germanus, who was bishop of Capua (probably from 516 to 541) went to Abruzzi to take a cure at Augulum, near the present-day Città San Angelo. Imagine his surprise at finding Paschasius there in the capacity of a humble attendant at the baths! Germanus asked Paschasius what he was doing there. Paschasius answered, "The only reason for which I was sent to this place of punishment (*in hoc poenali loco*) is that I took the part of Laurentius against Symmachus. I beg you to pray to the Lord on my behalf. You will know that your prayers have been granted if, when you return, I am not here." Germanus prayed ardently and when he returned a few days later, Paschasius was nowhere to be found. But, Gregory adds, it was possible for Paschasius to be purged of his sin after death in the first place because he had sinned only out of ignorance and in the second place because he had given alms generously while he was alive, and this had made him worthy of forgiveness.

The second theoretical question that Peter puts to Gregory concerns suffrages for the dead: "What is the way to help the souls of the dead?" Gregory answers that if their sins are not of the sort ineffaceable after death, the sacred offering of the Host is generally of great help, and souls have even been seen to ask for it.

Here it what Bishop Felix tells me he knows about a priest who died two years ago after a holy life. He lived in the diocese of Centum Cellae and practiced his ministry at the Church of Saint John in Taurina. This priest was in the habit of washing himself, when necessary, at a place where much steam escapes from hot geysers; he was very careful about cleanliness and went frequently to the baths. One day, upon returning to them, he said to himself, "I must not seem ungrateful to the fellow who so assiduously helps me to clean myself. I must bring him a gift." He brought two loaves of bread. Upon arriving, he found the man who habitually waited on him. The priest washed and then, after dressing and as he was about to leave, he presented the man with the gift, by way of benediction, and asked him to accept it as a token of his affection. But the fellow answered sadly, "Father, why are you giving me this present? This bread is holy and I cannot eat it. In the form in which you see me now I used to be in charge of these baths and because of my sins I have been sent back here after my death. If you want to be of use to me, intercede on my behalf by giving this bread to Almighty God. You will know that your wish has been granted when you no longer see me in these parts." With these words he disappeared, thus revealing that he was really a spirit in the guise of a human being. For an entire week the priest cried for this man and every day offered the Host; when he returned to the baths, the fellow was nowhere to be found. This proves that sacred offerings can be useful to dead souls.[48]

Gregory immediately follows up this story with another. The event he recounts actually took place, he says, in his own monastery three years before. Living there was a monk named Justus, an expert in medicine. Justus fell hopelessly ill and was assisted by his brother, Copiosus, also a physician. Justus confided to his brother that he had hidden three pieces of gold, and Copiosus had no choice but to inform the monks of what he had been told.

The monks found the three pieces of gold hidden amid Justus's stock of medications. They took the matter up with Gregory, who reacted vehemently, because the rule of the monastery laid it down that all property was to be shared in common. Terribly upset, Gregory wondered what he might do that would serve both for the "purgation" of the dying man and for the edification of the monks. He forbade the monks to respond to Justus's appeal if he should call out to them from his deathbed, and he instructed Copiosus to tell his brother—so that he might repent at the moment of death—that the monks, having learned what he had done, were horrified by his act. Gregory further stipulated that when Justus died, his body would not be buried in the monks' cemetery but rather thrown in with the compost, and the monks would then throw his three gold coins after him, shouting "May your money follow you into perdition." And so it came to pass. Terrified, the monks avoided taking any reprehensible action. Thirty days after Justus's death, Gregory was saddened by the thought of the tortures that the dead monk would have to suffer and ordered that for the next thirty days a mass be celebrated daily in his behalf. At the end of this period the dead man appeared to his brother one night and said that until that day he had suffered but that now he had been admitted to the communion (of the elect). It was clear to all that Justus had escaped his torment thanks to the salutary offering.[49]

In his zeal as a pastor, Gregory the Great understood two psychological needs of the believers to whom he ministered: the need for authentic testimony delivered by witnesses worthy of belief and the need for details about the location of purgatorial punishments.

Gregory's stories are particularly important because they served as the model for anecdotes that the Church used to popularize the belief in Purgatory in the thirteenth century, once that belief was officially sanctioned and defined. Implicit in these stories is the notion that it is possible to check the truth of a historical assertion: the testimony is imputed to a credible witness and details are given as to time and place. More than that, though, the stories are told so as to enlist belief in quite different ways. There is, to begin with, the allure of a tale couched in an attractive narrative complete with plot, fascinating details, "suspense," and a striking ending. The tale is told, moreover, in a way that makes the supernatural palpable and believable: there are visions of the afterlife and evidence that the prayers of the living have actually achieved the desired end. All of these elements will figure in the doctrine of the true Purgatory, down to the nature of the bond between the living and the dead, the purpose of which is to snatch the dead from the purgatorial trials to which they are subjected. The living persons called upon to give help must be close relations, either by blood or by spirit, of the soul to be purged. Finally, the trilogy of suffrages is affirmed in these anecdotes: prayers, alms, and above all eucharistic sacrifice.

Gregory also shows his originality on another point: in two of the three stories cited he situates the place of expiation in this world. His choice of place was in fact a stroke of genius: this Roman aristocrat selected one of the most essential buildings of the surviving Roman civilization, that center of hygiene and sociability in the ancient world, the Roman bath. This Christian pontiff selected a place in which the alternation of heat and cold was a regular part of the treatment, an alternation characteristic of purgative locales in the older religions of which Christianity was the heir. And finally, he settled on a mixture of the supernatural and the quotidian in which bath attendants are ghosts and the vapors of the bath are effluvia of the other world. Gregory, it is clear, had a real imaginative flair.

Paradoxically, Gregory's most important contribution to Purgatory was the first to be sacrificed when the new doctrine was consolidated in the thirteenth century. Gregory had given credence to the idea that purgation could take place on this earth, in the places where sins had been committed, which became places of punishment: men were punished where they sinned, like the administrator of the baths who returned not to the scene of his crimes but rather to the place of his peccadilloes, transformed into a "penal place" (*in hoc loco poenali*). In view of Gregory's authority, the idea of a Purgatory on this earth was still mentioned from time to time after the inception of the "true" Purgatory, but as an improbable hypothesis, a curious remnant of the past. Thomas Aquinas and Jacobus da Voragine in *The Golden Legend* still speak of it. But by the thirteenth century the spectacle of Purgatory had been transferred to a special theater, not of this world but of the next. Only for the briefest of instants were the dead allowed to return to haunt the living. They were sternly forbidden to engage in activities in this world. Purgatory became a prison from which ghosts were not allowed to escape.

The last of Purgatory's founders, Gregory has only a peripheral interest in the doctrine. For him the main thing is still the Day of Judgment, a day on which there are only two kinds of souls: the chosen and the damned. For each kind of soul there are two possible ways to approach everlasting fate: either directly or indirectly after the Last Judgment, the moment of resurrection. "Some are judged and perish, others are not judged but perish (also immediately). Some are judged and reign, others are not judged but reign (also immediately)."

In the *Dialogues* 4.37 Gregory the Great gives another description of Purgatory, this time located not on earth but in the other world. A man, one Stephen, dies suddenly in Constantinople. His corpse, not yet embalmed, is left unburied overnight, and his soul is carried off to Hell, where it visits a number of places. But when the soul is brought before Satan, Satan announces that a mistake has been made. The Stephen expected in Hell is another Stephen, the blacksmith, and the first Stephen is returned to life as the second dies: the date is 590, during an epidemic of plague. Later, a wounded soldier dies for a brief period, during which he visits Hell. He is then revived and gives a detailed account of what he has seen, which is reported to Gregory. Among the sights of Hell is "a bridge beneath which a dark, black river was flowing, a river giving off smoke and an intolerable stench." Beyond the bridge lay charming meadows filled with flowers, men dressed in white wandering about in a sweet-scented atmosphere, and houses filled with light, some of them made of gold. A few dwellings stood on the banks of the river, some of them invaded by the fetid cloud from the river, while others were protected from the stench. The bridge is a trial: a wicked soul that tries to cross falls into the dark, malodorous river, while the righteous cross easily to reach the pleasanter spots. Stephen, too, had spoken of this bridge and told how, when he tried to cross it, he lost his footing and half slipped into the river. Horrid black creatures loomed up out of the stream and tried to pull him down by the thighs, while handsome white men lifted him up by the arms. During this battle he woke up. He understood the meaning of this vision as follows: on the one hand he frequently succumbed to the temptations of the flesh, but on the other hand he gave generous alms. Lasciviousness drew him down, benevolence lifted him up. From that moment on he lived a righteous life.

One final piece of evidence: in the *Dialogues* 4.31, Gregory tells a story which pertains to Hell but which will later play a role in the history of Purgatory. He relates what has been told to him by one Julian, a benevolent "defender" of the Roman Church who had died seven years earlier. In the time of King Theodoric (d. 526), a relative of Julian had gone to Sicily to collect taxes and been shipwrecked on the Isle of Lipari on the way back. He thereupon sought protection through the prayers of a hermit who lived there. "Do you know that King Theodoric is dead?" asked the hermit. To his listener's incredulous look the hermit responded, "Yesterday at noon, clad in a shirt and bare of foot, his hands bound, flanked by Pope John and the patrician Symmachus, he was taken to the neighboring isle of Vulcano and thrown into the mouth of its crater." Upon his return to Italy Julian's relative learned of Theodoric's death, and since Theodoric had had John and Symmachus put to death unjustly, the relative deemed it fitting that the defunct king should have been cast down into everlasting hellfire by those whom he had persecuted.

This legendary punishment of Theodoric is one more instance of the political usage made of the other world. Indeed, the threat of punishment in the hereafter was a powerful weapon in the hands of the Church. To show an illustrious soul being punished by fire tended to validate the threat and set it in incomparable relief. To imagine the other world was to wield a political weapon. But the only weapon available to Gregory was that of Hell, and this ultimate weapon could be used only in extreme cases. Purgatory made it possible to shape the threat to fit the case.

In the legend of Theodoric we see yet another precursor of Purgatory: the king who persecuted the Christians was delivered to the fires of Hell in Sicily, where he was cast into the mouth of a volcano. The lesson was not lost on the men of the Middle Ages, who remembered this fiery mouth and attempted to depict it as one of the portals of Purgatory.

The Early Middle Ages
Doctrinal Stagnation and the
Riot of Imagination

B ETWEEN Gregory the Great and the twelfth century—a period of five centuries—little progress was made in the construction of Purgatory. But the fire remained, and while there was nothing new in the theological aspect of the subject, there were visions of the other world and imaginary voyages in the hereafter aplenty, along with developments in the area of liturgy that helped to prepare the way for the notion of purgatorial fire and to cement relations between the living and the dead.

Why, then, should we bother to examine this period, in which men's conceptions of the other world changed only slightly? Not for the traditional reason of giving a continuous chronological account—quite the contrary. I should like to show that in history, unlike physics, motion is not uniformly accelerated; nor is there one goal toward which events are directed. As far as the other world is concerned, thinking seems to have been stagnant for these five centuries. But I feel bound to put the reader on guard against two possible misunderstandings.

One misunderstanding might result from the apparent confusion of texts cited. I shall be calling to witness not only some of the great names of Christian thought of the day—Alcuin, Johannes Scotus, Rabanus Maurus, Ratherius of Verona, Lanfranc—who, though they said little about our subject, are eloquent in their silence, but also writers of the second and third rank, who tell us more about the regular currents of intellectual life as well as its occasional periods of ferment and change. Each of these groups provides testimony of a different kind about the state of thinking in regard to the other world.

It might also seem that I am committing the very error I have denounced several times, that I am taking from this heterogeneous collection of texts only those features that seem to presage what ultimately became Purgatory, as though beneath the apparent immobility the inevitable end-result was already being prepared. Most of these texts are rather flat, without relief, and it seemed unnecessary to go into great detail about them. Still, from time to time they evoke the future Purgatory, either to herald its coming or to turn their back on it. This does not mean that these texts are simply precursors of Purgatory. Wetti's Vision, for example, is an astonishing document full of sound and fury, but it tells us little about the future Purgatory. What it does tell us is how men of the early Middle Ages thought about the other world, and I have therefore not hesitated to consider it at some length.

It would be wrong to assume that the early Middle Ages are of interest to our study only in a negative way. During this lengthy period we see the imagination at work, gathering and sifting its material. Even in a text of just a few lines, such as Sunniulf's vision as related by Gregory of Tours, we see new images embedding themselves in human memory: the image of the dead immersed to varying depths in a stream combined with the image of the narrow bridge that all souls must cross. Along with these is another image that proved less successful with posterity: that of the hereafter as a beehive, with the souls of the dead swarming around it.

We also see different imaginary features being combined into a comprehensive system. In Bede, for example, Fursy goes to the other world and brings back physical signs later used to prove that a Purgatory exists from which one can return. (In the nineteenth century the Museo del Purgatorio was established in Rome to house a collection of such tokens of Purgatory). Again in Bede, in the vision of Drythelm, various aspects of the geography of the hereafter are organized into an itinerary, a logical sequence of places to visit in the other world.

Early versions of various theological and moral definitions are also encountered. For example, we can trace the evolution of a typology of sins. We can also watch the virtually uninterrupted development of the scenic features of the other world. Influenced by apocalyptic literature, the new travelogues also bore the imprint of monastic concerns. Above all, they were destined for a new audience, an audience interested less in the illuminating than in the picturesque.

When we remember, moreover, that the Carolingian period was also the time of a great liturgical renaissance, it is natural to ask whether new ideas about the other world and the fate of the dead exerted an influence on liturgy. Bearing all these questions in mind, let us turn now to the actual texts.

THE AUGUSTINIAN OTHER WORLD IN THE WORK OF THREE SPANISH WRITERS

Exegetical and dogmatic works occasionally allude to suffrages for the dead, the end of time, and/or purgatorial fire, all of which later became features of the system of Purgatory. I should like to consider some of these works, beginning with the writings of three Spanish bishops who lived in the sixth and seventh centuries: Tajon of Saragossa, the celebrated Isidore of Seville, one of the fathers of medieval culture, and Julian of Toledo.

In chapter 21 of his fifth book of *Sententiae* (PL 80.975), Tajon of Saragossa, commenting on Paul's First Epistle to the Corinthians, devotes a few lines to summarizing the teachings of Augustine and Gregory the Great, without naming them: "Although it is possible to understand what the great preacher wrote as referring to the fire of tribulation in this life, his words can also be applied to the fire of the future purgation, if we mark well his meaning, that one can be saved by fire, not if on this foundation one has built of iron, brass, or lead, that is, major sins (*peccata majora*), but rather of wood, hay, or straw, that is, minor sins (*peccata minima*) and very slight sins (*peccata levissima*), which the fire easily consumes. But let it be known that, even in the case of minor sins, purgation will not be obtained unless it has been merited by good actions in this life."

Isidore of Seville deals with the problem primarily in his treatise *On Ecclesiastical Offices* (*De ecclesiasticis officiis*), where he deals with suffrages. Citing Matthew 12:32 on the subject of the remission of sins in the century to come, and Augustine's *City of God* 12.32 on the four kinds of men, Isidore asserts that the sins of some men will be remitted and "purged by a purgatorial fire."[1]

For our purposes Julian of Toledo is the most interesting of these three prelates. In the first place he is a genuine theologian. Furthermore, his *Prognosticon* is nothing less than a detailed treatise on eschatology. All of the second book is devoted to the state of the soul prior to the resurrection of the body. There is little in his thought that is new, however. For the most part it is based on the writings of Augustine.

Julian distinguishes two Heavens and two Hells. There is an earthly paradise as well as a celestial paradise, and the latter, as Ambrose, Augustine, and Gregory all believed, is the same thing as the bosom of Abraham. There are also, as Augustine taught, two Hells, but Augustine's teachings on this point varied (here Julian shows his critical and historical sense). He first believed that there was one Hell on earth and another under the earth, but later, in commenting on the story of Lazarus and the rich man, he saw that both Hells were beneath the earth, one on top of the other. "Therefore," Julian concludes, "there may be two Hells, one in which the souls of the saints have reposed, the other in which the souls of the godless are tortured." Then, still relying on Augustine for assistance, Julian explains, using philological and other kinds of arguments, why in his judgment both Hells are underground.

He then discusses various opinions as to whether the souls of saints (the perfectly righteous) go directly to Heaven or remain in certain "receptacles." Ever since Christ descended into Hell, these receptacles, or upper regions of Hell, have been closed, and the righteous now reside in, or upon death, go directly to, Heaven. By the same token, iniquitous souls go directly to Hell and never emerge. In a digression Julian makes it clear that, after death, the soul is not deprived of feeling and, again calling on Augustine for help (*De Genesi ad litteram* 12.33), he argues that the soul has "a bodily semblance" (*similitudo corporis*) that enables it to experience either peace or pain. Thus the soul can be tortured by corporeal fire. This is what occurs in Hell, but the damned do not all suffer in the same way: the torment of each soul is apportioned to the gravity of its sin, in much the same way as on this earth living persons suffer from the sun's heat in varying degrees. Finally, one must believe, as Paul, Augustine, and Gregory all have taught, that there is a purgatorial fire after death. Using the same words as Gregory the Great, Julian explains that this fire purges petty and minor sins such as constant gossiping, immoderate laughter, and excessive attachment to private property. More terrible than any earthly pain, this fire is such that only those made worthy by good actions in this world can benefit from it. Purgatorial fire is different from the eternal fire of Gehenna: it burns prior to the Last Judgment rather than afterward—and Augustine even thinks that it begins with early tribulation. Just as the torture of the damned is proportional to the gravity of their sins, so the length of time that a soul being purged must remain in the fire corresponds to the degree of the soul's imperfection. Here, the equivalence is expressed in terms not of intensity but rather of duration of the pain: "The more they have loved perishable goods, the longer it will take for them to be saved."

Julian's account of the future Purgatory, an account based on the Bible, especially the New Testament, and on patristic writings, is the fullest and clearest we have from the early Middle Ages.[2]

"BARBARIAN" OTHER WORLDS

Evidence from "barbarian" regions of the Christian world, which stems both from the ecclesiastical hierarchy and from the monasteries, shows that these newly Christianized territories took an interest in the hereafter without making any notably original contribution to its conception.

Ireland

It was long believed that the author of the *Book on the Order of Creatures* (*Liber de ordine creaturarum*) was Isidore of Seville. Manuel Diaz y Diaz has recently shown that it was in fact written by an anonymous Irish writer in the seventh century. Based on Genesis, the book deals with God, spiritual creatures, and corporeal creatures. The last four chapters are devoted to the nature of men (chap. 12), the various kinds of sinners and the place of punishment (chap. 13), purgatorial fire (chap. 14), and the future life (chap. 15).

This summary may give the impression that the writer of the treatise had a tripartite version of the hereafter: Hell, "Purgatory," Paradise. But this division is found only in certain manuscripts; it is less pronounced in the main body of the text.[3] What is more, the author's archaic conception of the hereafter all but rules out the possibility that he conceived of an other world having three parts. He sets forth his ideas starting with the chapter on the various conditions in which sinners find themselves. There are two major categories: sinners whose sins (*crimina*) can be purged by the fire of judgment and sinners who will be subjected to the pain of eternal fire. Of the latter group, some will be damned immediately, without judgment, while others will be damned after judgment. The fire is therefore the fire of judgment and is not applied prior to the time of judgment. This view is confirmed in chapter 14.

Those who will enjoy "eternal refreshment" (*refrigerium aeternum*) after purgation are those who will have performed what would later be called works of mercy. They will be baptized by fire, while the others will be consumed by inextinguishable fire. In giving an exegesis of Paul's First Epistle to the Corinthians, the author of the *Liber* is led to specify a type of sin which he characterizes exclusively in negative terms: "sins which are not very harmful, though little constructive." Included in this group are the following sins: "the idle use of legitimate marriage, overindulgence in eating, taking excessive pleasure in useless things, anger leading to abusive language, exaggerated interest in personal affairs, inattentiveness during prayers, late sleeping, undue bursts of laughter, overindulgence in sleep, holding back the truth, gossiping, sticking stubbornly to error, holding the false to be true in matters not involving the faith, neglect of duty, and disorderly attire."[4] It cannot be denied, we are told, that these sins can be purged by fire. To this is added one final observation: the purgatorial fire in question lasts longer and is more terrible than any imaginable earthly torment.

In the early seventh century the Irish Saint Columban (d. 615), a missionary who helped to carry the spirit of monasticism to the Continent, gave an abbreviated account of human existence from birth to eternity, in which a place was reserved for fire. Though not named, the fire in question was, if not a purgatorial fire then at least a probative one, for it was apparently situated in the period between resurrection and judgment:

> Here is the way the human being's miserable life runs: from the earth, on the earth, in the earth, from the earth into the fire, from the fire to judgment, from judgment either to Gehenna or to life (everlasting). You have been created from the earth, you tread the earth, you will be laid to rest in the earth, you will rise in the earth, you will be tried in fire, you will await the judgment, and then either torture or the kingdom of heaven will be yours forever.

Later on he adds that we "men, created out of the earth and making a brief sojourn on the earth return almost at once to the earth and then, a second time, on orders from God, are yielded up and put forth by the earth, and at the end of time tried by passing through the fire, which in some way will dissolve the earth and the mud; and if, after the counterfeit coin has melted, there remains gold or silver or some other useful matter from the earth, the fire will show it."[5]

Gaul

The famous Saint Eligius, bishop of Noyon (d. 659), recalled in a homily the distinction between mortal sins (*crimina capitalia*) and minor sins (*minuta peccata*) and observed that there was little likelihood that the giving of alms, even if they were generously dispensed on a daily basis, could redeem mortal sins. He then reminded his listeners of the two judgments and the purgatorial fire:

> We read in the Holy Scripture that there are two judgments: one by the water of the flood (Genesis 7) which prefigured the baptism by which we were cleansed of all our sins (1 Pet. 3) and the other, yet to come, by fire, when God will come for the Judgment, of which the Psalmist says: "Our God shall come and not keep silence. A fire shall devour before him, and it shall be very tempestuous round about him" (Ps. 50:3); like a tempest so that he may examine those whom the fire consumes. Cleanse us of all that fouls our flesh and spirit, and let us not be burned, neither by the eternal fire nor by this passing fire. Of this fire of God's judgment the Apostle says: "And the fire shall try every man's work of what sort it is" (1 Cor. 3:13). It is certain that here he spoke of purgatorial fire. Now, this fire will be felt in different ways by the godless, the saints, and the righteous. From the torment of this fire the godless will be cast into the flames of fire everlasting; the saints who will reawaken in their body without any stain of sin, for they will have built on the foundation which is Christ, in gold, in silver, and in precious gems, that is, the shining meaning of the faith, the resplendent word of salvation, and the precious works—they will triumph over this fire as easily as in this life they have been pure in faith and observed the commandments of Christ with love. This leaves the righteous guilty of minor sins who have built on the foundation which is Christ, of hay, of wood, or of straw, which denotes the diversity of minor sins of which they have not been properly purged and so are not yet found worthy of the glory of the celestial city. After having passed through this fire, when the day of the Last Judgment is complete, each one will be either damned or crowned, according to his merits. Therefore, my dear brothers, it is about this day that we must think intensely.[6]

This text is remarkable for its division of mankind into three categories rather than four as in the Augustinian tradition. Here, however, it interests us primarily because of its "archaic" conception of purgatorial fire, which it places at the time of the Last Judgment, a judgment that is drawn out to fill an entire day. More than that, Eligius seems to leave it up to the fire to separate the saints from the godless and the righteous; hence he does not guarantee that the righteous will go to Heaven after their trial. The "suspense" lasts right to the very end.

Germany

It is interesting to look at the instructions Pope Gregory III gave to Saint Boniface around the year 732 when the latter asked how he should behave with regard to Germans who remained pagans or had only recently converted: "You also ask me if one can give offerings for the dead. Here is the position of the Holy Church: each person may make offerings for his own dead if they are genuine Christians, and the priest may celebrate their memory. And even though all of us are subject to sin, it is proper that the priest celebrate the memory and intercede on behalf of none but those who have died Catholics; for the impious, even if they were Christians, these actions will not be allowed."[7]

Even though these instructions make no explicit mention of suffrages and do not allude to purgatorial fire, it is significant that a forceful distinction is being made, with respect to a country that is the object of a mission and in a missionary period, between the usefulness (and therefore the duty) of offerings for those of the dead who are "genuine Christians" and the futility (and therefore interdiction) of offerings in behalf of the "impious" dead, even if they are Christians.

Great Britain

In the same period, the celebrated monk Bede, who, as we shall see later on, played an important role in constructing the geography of the other world through his visions and imaginary travelogues, emphasized in his *Homilies* (written between 730 and 735) the importance of suffering for the dead. Bede makes explicit mention of purgatorial fire. Between death and resurrection, he tells us, apostles, martyrs, confessors, and the like go to the "bosom of the Father," which is to be understood as the "secret of the Father" (*secretum Patris*). He compares this *sinus Patris* to the *domus Patris* or "house of the Father" mentioned in the Gospel of John 14:2 and makes no mention of the bosom of Abraham. Then he continues:

> So the many righteous souls who are in the Church after the dissolution of the flesh are immediately received into the blessed repose of Paradise, where they wait in great joy, in vast choirs of joyous souls, for the moment when they will regain their bodies and appear before the face of God. But some who, because of their good works, are predestined to share the fate of the elect, but who, because of certain evil works have left the body in an unclean state, are taken after death by the flames of

purgatorial fire and severely punished. Either they are cleansed of the taint of their vices by a long trial [*longa examinatione*] in this fire, or thanks to the prayers, alms, fasting, tears, and eucharistic offerings of their faithful friends, they are delivered from punishment and allowed to enjoy the repose of the blessed.[8]

Thus Bede shows clearly how some souls are condemned to purgatorial fire. He makes a forceful case for the power of suffrages from the living and from faithful friends of the dead. Above all he shows the mechanism by which the time a soul must remain in "Purgatory" is decided: the maximum sentence is for the whole period from death to resurrection, but there is a possibility of reprieve by means of suffrages. He says nothing, however, about where the purgatorial fire is located and what kinds of penalties are meted out to souls sent there.

INDIFFERENCE AND TRADITIONALISM IN THE CAROLINGIAN PERIOD AND BEYOND

The Carolingian Church showed little interest in purgatorial fire and introduced no innovations. Alcuin, the great Anglo-Saxon ecclesiastic who inspired Charlemagne's cultural policy, commented on 1 Corinthians 3:13 in his treatise *On the Belief in the Holy Trinity* (*De fide Sanctae Trinitatis*), where he identifies purgatorial fire (*ignis purgatorius*) with the fire of judgment (*ignis diei judicii*). This, he tells us, is experienced in different ways by the impious, the saints, and the righteous. The impious will burn forever, while the saints, those who have built in gold, silver, and precious stones, will pass through the fire without injury, like the three young Jews in the furnace (Dan. 3). Finally, "certain of the righteous [are] guilty of certain minor sins, those who on the foundation which is Christ have built of hay, of wood, or of straw. They will be purged by the heat of this fire, purified of their sins, and made worthy by the glory of eternal happiness." All souls must pass through this transitory fire (*ignis transitorius*). Some will go to damnation, others to coronation. The former will be tormented either more or less, depending on the degree of their wickedness, while the latter will be rewarded more or less, depending on the degree of their sanctity. On this last point Alcuin is vague and confusing.[9]

Another important figure in the Carolingian Church and in Carolingian culture, Rabanus Maurus (d. 856), the abbot of Fulda and archbishop of Mainz and Germany's leading intellectual, has left us a sustained reflection on the theology of fire in his commentary on the Epistles of Paul. He, too, believes that the fire mentioned in 1 Corinthians is the fire of judgment. It does away with those illicit things (*illicita*), failures to abide by the rules, that a person can commit without ceasing to take Christ as his foundation, for example, indulgence in the pleasures of this world, in earthly love, which in the marital context is not cause for condemnation. All such sins are burned up in the fire of tribulation (*tribulationis ignis*). But for those who have built of wood, hay, and straw, "it is not incredible that after this life the following comes to pass, and it may be asked if it is not so: either overtly or covertly some of the faithful may be saved through a purgatorial fire, sooner or later according as they loved perishable goods to a lesser or greater degree."[10]

Here as in Bede we find the introduction of an element that was to play an important role in the system of Purgatory to come: the time of purgation is set between death and judgment, and the duration is allowed to vary.

Paschasius Radbertus (d. 860), the abbot of Corbia, based an even more fully developed theology of fire on the passage from the Gospel of Matthew that deals with baptism by fire. Paschasius examines the various aspects and functions of fire and ends with a description of the "fire of love" (*ignis charitatis*) and the "fire of divine love" (*ignis divini amoris*). He envisions a number of possible meanings for this:

> It may be, as some wish, that [the sentence], "He shall baptize you with the Holy Spirit and with fire," should be understood to mean that the Holy Spirit is identical with the fire, which we admit, because God is a consuming fire. But since there is a coordinating conjunction, it does not seem that one and the same thing is meant. This has led some to the opinion that the fire in question is purgatorial fire, which is presently purifying us by the Holy Ghost and then, if any stain of sin remains, makes us pure by combustion in the fire of conflagration (that is, of judgment). But if this be true, then it must be the lesser and more minor sins that are involved, for it is unthinkable that everyone should escape punishment. This is why the apostle says, "And the fire shall try every man's work of what sort it is."[11]

The most articulate discussion of purgatorial fire in the Carolingian era has been attributed to Haymo of Halberstadt (d. 853). He dealt with the subject on two occasions, first in the treatise *On the Diversity of Books* (*De varietate librorum*) and again in a commentary on the Epistles of Paul which some writers have attributed to Remy of Auxerre. Haymo's views are in fact an eclectic mix of what was written before him, strongly influenced by the ideas of Augustine and Gregory the Great (who are never mentioned by name). His writings often repeat word for word what Julian of Toledo had to say two centuries earlier. According to Haymo, we must believe that there is a purgatorial fire prior to judgment, which works on lesser, petty, or minor sins. There are two kinds of fire, one purgatorial (and temporary), the other eternal (and punitive). The duration of purgation by fire varies, depending on the strength of the soul's attachment to transitory ties. Some undergo purgatorial pains after death, others in this life. It is false that one can be saved by way of purgatorial fire if, in this life, one merely had the faith without doing good works. The Church can intervene effectively on behalf of those undergoing purgatorial pains. There are two categories of the saved: those who enjoy tranquillity in paradise immediately after death, and those who must be punished by the flames of Purgatory. Of the latter, some remain in the flames until Judgment Day, while others may be reprieved thanks to prayers, alms, fasting, tears, and offerings by the faithful who were their friends.[12] This note of solidarity between the dead and the living, probably inherited from Bede, is the only novelty—in form, not in substance, this being traditional—in the work of Haymo of Halberstadt.

In his commentary on the Epistles of Paul, Atto of Verceil (d. 921) gives a very traditional, very Augustinian interpretation of the First Epistle to the Corinthians (in which he cites Augustine several times). But there is one peculiarity in Atto's interpretation as well as one novelty. The peculiarity is this: what will be tried and judged (by purgatorial fire and, more generally, at the time of judgment) is, Atto tells us, essentially doctrinal orthodoxy, *doctrina*, rather than morals and feelings. What is more, the epithet *venialia*, venial, appears alongside the lesser sins and in contrast to capital sins, but it figures in a list of sins: the opposition between venial sins and mortal (or capital) sins did not become fully established until the twelfth century.[13]

Even Ratherius of Verona, a man with an original mind, trained in the Lotharingian schools and imbued with classical culture, has little to say about purgatorial fire. What little he does say carries a stringent message: merit cannot be acquired after death. As for the existence of purgatorial pains after death, no one should presume to rely on them, for they are good not for purging criminal sins but only for lesser sins, the ones likened to wood, hay, and straw.[14]

Even the great Lanfranc, who in the late eleventh century lent an incomparable luster to the abbey school at Bec-Hellouin (Normandy), where he became abbot before going on to become archbishop of Canterbury, was not inspired, in his commentary on the First Epistle to the Corinthians, by the passage concerning the trial by fire. For him, purgatorial fire was none other than the fire of judgment, and he implies accordingly that the fire of judgment will last as long as is necessary to purge those who are supposed to be saved.[15]

As for Johannes Scotus Erigena ("the Irishman"), despite his official functions in the palace school of Charles the Bald he remained an isolated intellect, virtually ignored by most medieval theologians even prior to his condemnation, two centuries after his death, by the Council of Paris (1210). He is much in favor today with historians of theology and philosophy. But he too wasted little time discussing purgatorial fire. The story of Lazarus and the rich man inspires in him the thought that the soul can turn to the saints, after as well as before it has been separated from the flesh, for help in gaining either release from punishment or a diminution in the intensity of its torment.[16] Elsewhere he says that eternal hellfire is corporeal, even though its subtle nature causes it to be spoken of as incorporeal.[17]

THE OTHER WORLD AND HERESY

Two texts from the early eleventh century are worthy of special mention, not because they contribute anything new in themselves but because the contexts in which they were produced were particularly significant for what was to come. The first of these texts consists of a long passage from what is called the *Decretum* of Burchard of Worms (d. 1025). This is a collection of authoritative texts on questions of dogma and discipline—a milestone in the compilation of the corpus of canon law. Burchard copies sections of the *Dialogues* of Gregory the Great and a passage from the *Moralia* devoted to the problem of purgation, as well as the passage from Augustine's *Enchiridion* (110) which deals with suffrages for the dead. The Augustinian text is preceded by the words "there are four kinds of offerings" (*quatuor genera sunt oblationis*), which would be used again, a century later, in the *Decretum* of Gratian, and which proved problematic for the scholastics because of the division into four kinds. A passage from the Bible cited here was to enjoy a great vogue, partly because Burchard mentions it: namely, John 14:2, which says, "In my father's house there are many mansions."[18]

In 1025 Bishop Gerard of Cambrai, in a synod held at Arras, effected a reconciliation between the Church and certain heretics who, among other "errors," had denied the efficacy of suffrages for the dead. In this connection the bishop requires them to recognize the following "truths":

> It is true, lest anyone believe that penitence is of use only to the living and not to the dead, that many of the dead have been rescued from punishment by the piety of their living [friends and relatives], according to Scripture, by means of the sacrificial offering of the Mediator [the mass], or alms, or by acquittance of the penance by a living friend of the deceased, in the case where an ill person has met death before being able to complete his penance and a living friend substitutes for him. You are not, contrary to what you assert, truly receptive to the Gospel. For the Truth there states: "Whoever speaketh against the Holy Ghost, it shall not be forgiven him, neither in this world, neither in the world to come" (Matt. 12:32). By this, as Saint Gregory says in his *Dialogue*, it is meant that some mistakes may be effaced in this world and others in the world to come. . . . But it must be believed, in regard to petty and minor sins like continual gossiping, immoderate laughter, excessive concern for one's patrimony, etc., things which are

inevitable in life but which are burdensome after death if they are not effaced beforehand, that, as he says, these sins may be purged after death by purgatorial fire, if in this life one has shown oneself to be worthy by good actions. Rightly, therefore, do the learned saints tell us that purgatorial fire exists by which certain sins are purged, provided that the living obtain (this purgation) by alms, by masses, or, as I have said, by a substitute penance. Thus it appears that for the price of these works the dead can be absolved of sin; otherwise we could not understand the apostle Paul, about whom you have lied in calling yourselves his auditors, who says that minor and very slight sins are easily consumed by purgatorial fire, whereas they would entail tortures not purgatorial but eternal if, by such offerings of the host, they had not deserved to be effaced by purgatorial fire."[19]

There is nothing new in this doctrinal concentrate. And yet this text, along with Burchard's *Decretum*, was to enjoy a singular fate: these two items formed the basis upon which Purgatory was erected, against opposition, in the twelfth century. The twelfth and thirteenth centuries were a time of heresy, and Saint Bernard, followed by other orthodox clerics, found the moment opportune for putting the finishing touches on Purgatory, which was thus in part the fruit of resistance to the heretical challenges to orthodox Christianity that began around the year 1000.

Travels in the Other World

While doctrine remained static, accounts of imaginary travels in the other world and other visionary writings were laying a firm basis for the future Purgatory.

Legacies

The genre was traditional. It was strongly influenced by Judeo-Christian apocalyptic writings. Specimens from the ancient world, particularly Greece, are known, though these constitute a minor seam, as it were, in the rich mine of ancient literature and were not readily accepted by more learned writers. Plutarch, in his *Moralia*, recounts the vision of Thespesios. Thespesios, after leading a life which, by all appearances, is one of debauchery, dies. Three days later he revives and thereafter leads a life of perfect virtue. Besieged with questions, he reveals that his spirit, after departing the body, traveled through space, amid wind-tossed spirits, some of them known to him. Several of these souls emitted terrible lamentations, while others seemed tranquil and happy. Some shone with a pure brilliance, others were bespattered, and still others were completely black. Those laden down by only a few sins had to endure only a slight punishment, but the godless were turned over to Justice, which, if she deemed them incurable, handed them over to the Erinnyes, who cast them down into a bottomless abyss. Thespesios is then taken into a vast plain full of flowers and pleasant scents, in which souls flutter about as happily as birds. Finally, he is taken to the place of the damned, where he witnesses their tortures. There he sees three lakes, one of boiling gold, another of frozen lead, and the third of molten iron, which is whipped up by a storm. Demons are constantly plucking souls out of one lake and plunging them into another. Finally, in another place blacksmiths are busy carelessly remolding souls destined for a second existence into a variety of shapes.[20] Later descriptions of Purgatory would retain from this vision the differences in color between one kind of soul and another and the idea that souls are transferred from one lake to another.

Plutarch also describes the vision of Timarchos. Timarchos goes down into a cave dedicated to Trophonios and performs the necessary ceremonies to obtain an oracle. He remains there two nights and one day in utter darkness, not knowing whether he is awake or dreaming. Then he is hit on the head and his soul takes flight. Soaring joyfully, it sees burning isles, whose flames in their changing colors make a pleasant sight. These isles are set in a multicolored sea in which souls are adrift. Two rivers flow into this sea, beneath which there is a dark, round pit out of which comes the sound of moans. Some souls are sucked into the hole, others are spit out. Here again, the description prefigures that contained in the work that would later create the vision of the genuine Purgatory, *The Purgatory of Saint Patrick*, which dates from the end of the twelfth century.

This visionary literature was strongly influenced by the Judeo-Christian apocalyptic treatises that I touched on earlier, especially the *Apocalypses* of Peter and Paul. It was also influenced by two traditions that I can do no more than mention here in passing: the Celtic and the Germanic, both of which include very old accounts of voyages in the other world.[21]

If I am neglecting these two components of medieval culture, which certainly contributed to the imaginary representation of Purgatory, the reason is that the amount of research that would have to be done in order to say anything useful would, I think, be out of proportion to the results that can be expected. In order to evaluate the contribution of these two cultures, even with the aid of the very fine work that has already been done on the subject, we would first have to resolve two difficult problems. To begin with, problems of dating. The written record obviously goes back no further than the time when these cultures first began to write, no earlier than the twelfth century. What the earliest written works in these languages express is certainly of much earlier date—but how much?

An even more important problem, as it seems to me, has to do with the fact that this ancient literature is a complex product, difficult to characterize. Here, the distinction between "high" and "popular" culture makes little sense. The oral sources of the immediately preceding period are, I think, learned: "orality" is no guarantee of "popular" origins. The written works that begin to be produced in the twelfth century are elaborations of the tales of learned oral artists. At the time when these "vulgar" works were being recited and sung and, later, written, the "barbarian" cultures had already enjoyed a fairly lengthy familiarity with the learned, ecclesiastical culture of Latin Christianity. This contamination only compounds the difficulty of identifying the true "barbarian" legacy. Far be it from me to dismiss the importance of that legacy: on the contrary, it seems to me that it exerted considerable influence on medieval culture, but we are not yet, I think, prepared to isolate that influence, much less to characterize or measure it. On the other hand, in regions where Latin had long since become the predominant language of learning, Latin scholars had more or less willingly, more or less wittingly, introduced, to one degree or another, elements of traditional "popular" culture into their works—and in this period popular culture means largely peasant culture: perhaps the least bad definition is "pre-Christian, rural folklore," which the Church characterized as "pagan." When it comes to pinning down this legacy, a method is available, though it is a method that is difficult to work with: we can use the thematic catalogues established by nineteenth- and twentieth-century folklorists and trace the themes listed there back through the centuries, cautiously and painstakingly comparing the catalogued themes with medieval documents whose dates are known or ascertainable. For all the uncertainty involved, when it comes to understanding the medieval imagination, I feel on safer ground using the information collected by the brothers Grimm, Pitre, Frazer, and van Gennep than I do speculating on Celtic *imramas* (stories devoted to the isles of the other world) or Scandinavian sagas.

That said, I will pause long enough to mention a few ways in which "barbarian" cultures did influence the development of Purgatory in the period prior to the twelfth century. A theme common among the Celts was that of the voyage to the islands of the blessed, the earliest example of which seems to be the voyage of Bran, which we are told can be traced back at least as far as the eighth century.[22] The other world is situated on an island, which can often be reached through a well but which has no holy mountain. The image of the bridge occurs frequently.

German and Scandinavian myths about the other world seem to be more coherent by the time they become accessible to us. After death souls can go, essentially, to one of two places: to the underworld, which is ruled by the goddess Hel and which is rather like the Jewish *sheol*, dark and depressing but devoid of torture, surrounded by a river that one crosses by means of a bridge; or else to Valhalla, a celestial site of tranquillity and relaxation, which is reserved for the deserving dead, particularly heroes who die on the field of battle. It may be that Valhalla, before being located in Heaven, was also underground, like the Elysian fields of the Romans. Whereas in Celtic mythology it is exceptional to find a mountain in the other world (the mountain being an essential element of Purgatory), German mythology has Mount Hecla in Iceland, a volcano which has both a pit and a realm of torture.[23]

Even more, perhaps, than the Celtic, the Germanic imagination of the hereafter, by the time it becomes accessible to us, already seems to have been subjected to strong influence from the high culture of Latin Christianity. This is true of the travels in the other world recounted by Saxo Grammaticus in his twelfth-century *History of the Danes*. The *Dialogues* of Gregory the Great were translated into Old Norse quite early and may have given the theme of the bridge to Scandinavian mythology, though it seems probable that the theme already existed, having come to Scandinavia, as it had come to the Mediterranean, from the East.

Doubtless the most important change was that the rather cheerful other worlds of primitive Celtic and German mythology turned somber, subterranean, and infernal under Christian influence. At the moment of Purgatory's inception, we shall see how the optimistic Celtic (and perhaps Germanic) conception of a place of waiting and purification gave way to the image of Purgatory as cruel, for a time, as Hell, an image that came from oriental apocalyptic sources and from official Christian tradition. The old conception did not disappear completely but was rather absorbed into visions of Paradise. These ambivalent other worlds of "folklore" were forced to gravitate toward either the positive or the negative pole, while Purgatory lingered for a time, occupying the middle ground.

In the period from the beginning of the eighth to the end of the twelfth century, three texts stand out from the run of Latin Christian literature concerning visions of the other world. One, the *Vision of Drythelm*, is the work of one of the greatest minds of the early Middle Ages, the Anglo-Saxon monk Bede. In it, for the first time, we find a specific place set apart for purgation in the other world through which the hero is traveling. The *Vision of Wetti* (Wetti was a monk from southern Germany) is a raving, infernal account of an other world which was used in part for political ends, against Charlemagne. The diversion to political ends of accounts of travels beyond the grave is fully developed in an anonymous work from the very end of the ninth century, the *Vision of Charles the Fat*, a pamphlet prepared to further the interests of a Carolingian pretender.

These three major texts were preceded by two shorter visions, one dating from the end of the sixth century, the other from the beginning of the eighth. These were recounted by two great ecclesiastical personages, the archbishops Gregory of Tours and Boniface of Mainz (an Anglo-Saxon also known as Winfrith). These describe the other world in terms more or less commonplace in monastic circles at the time.

Framing all of these in time were two poems influenced by the classical Roman literary tradition, one from the early sixth century, the other from the early eleventh century. The imaginary other worlds depicted in both are quite traditional and exerted little influence on Purgatory.

The two works we shall consider first are more important by dint of their author's personalities than for their content, the bulk of the imagery and ideas being derived from the *Apocalypse of Paul.*

Gregory of Tours, in the thirty-third chapter of book four of his *History of the Franks*, which dates from the late sixth century, recounts the vision of Sunniulf, the abbot of Randau:*

> He used himself to tell how once he was shown in a vision a certain river of fire, into which men, assembling together on one part of the bank, were plunging like so many bees entering a hive. Some were submerged up to the waist, some up to the armpits, some even up to the chin, and all were shouting out that they were being burned very severely. A bridge led over the river, so narrow that only one man could cross at a time, and on the other side there was a large house all painted white. Then Sunniulf asked those who were with him what they thought this meant. "From this bridge will be hurled headlong anyone who is discovered to have been lacking in authority over those committed to his charge," they answered. "Anyone who has kept good discipline may cross without danger and will be welcomed joyfully in the house which you see opposite." As he heard these words, Sunniulf awoke. From then on he was more severe with his monks.

At the beginning of the eighth century, Boniface, the apostle of the Germans, wrote (Epistle 10) to Eadburge, the abbess of Thanet, that a monk from Wenlock had had a vision. Angels had wafted him into the air, and he saw the whole world engulfed in flames. He saw an army of demons and a choir of angels representing his vices and virtues. He saw pits of fire belching flames and souls in the form of black birds crying and moaning and shouting with human voices. He saw a river of boiling fire across which a plank served as a makeshift bridge. Some souls made their away across this bridge, while others slipped and fell into Tartarus. Some were completely submerged in the waves, others immersed up to their knees, others to the waist, and still others to the elbows. Everyone emerged from the fire clean and shining. On the other side of the river stood thick, high, resplendent walls, the walls of the heavenly Jerusalem. The wicked spirits were cast down into the fiery pit.

Here, I think, is the proper place to consider a Latin poem from late antiquity, which, unlike Plutarch's writings, for example, has no relation either to apocalyptic visions as such or to the more or less "folkloric"

---

*Cited here after Lewis Thorpe's English translation.—Trans.

voyages of the subsequent period, but which, by its very uniqueness, commands our attention. The *Carmen ad Flavium Felicem* was written around 500 A.D. by a Christian in Africa. It concerns the resurrection of the dead and the judgment of God.[24] Its purpose is to describe Paradise and Hell (Gehenna) and to explain the omnipotence of God and the fall of Adam, which brought death in its wake. God keeps the souls of the dead in various places, awaiting the Last Judgment. The poem next gives proofs of the resurrection of the dead and describes that resurrection along with God's judgment. In a lengthy passage Paradise is described as a place abounding with flowers, precious gems, trees, gold, honey, and milk, where four rivers flow from a tranquil source in an eternal springtime, where the climate is moderate and the sun always shines, and where the chosen are free of care, sin, and illness and dwell in peace everlasting. The poem concludes with a brief account of the destruction of the world by fire, mentioning a river of fire, the wailing of the damned, and the need to repent before death, for it is too late to repent in Hell, where the damned can be seen calling out to God in vain.

Though nothing in this poem concerns the future Purgatory, except the vague allusion to the various abodes in which the dead reside, two points are worth mentioning. First, the accent is much more on Paradise than on Hell. The poem is still suffused with the optimism of the fourth and fifth centuries. Second, allusion is made to the prayers of the damned, though it is stated that these are without effect. This contrasts with the late medieval convention, which has it that the souls in Purgatory can be distinguished from those in Hell by the fact that the former pray, whereas the latter have given up on useless supplication.

Bede and Medieval Visions of the Hereafter

Bede, the great Anglo-Saxon churchman, in his *Ecclesiastical History of England*, written shortly before his death in 735 at the monastery of Yarrow, where he spent fifty years that were punctuated by numerous journeys including several to Rome, recounts a number of visions.[25] His purpose is to edify: he wants to prove to his readers that the other world is real and to inspire enough fear in the living to make them change their way of life in order to avoid torment after death. Bede's visions are less didactic, however, than the *exempla* of Gregory the Great. For our purposes the most interesting point about them is this: for the first time we find in one of these visions a special place set aside in the other world for souls undergoing purgation, a place which is more than just one of the receptacles described before this time by reference to the Gospel of John.

The first vision, that of Saint Fursey, need not detain us long. Fursey was an Irish monk who left Ireland for the Continent and who was buried around 650 at Peronne, where Erchinold, mayor of the palace of Clovis II, had a sanctuary built over his tomb. Bede bases his account on a life of

Saint Fursey which was written at Peronne shortly after his death. While he was living in East Anglia at the monastery of Cnobheresburg, which he had founded, Fursey fell ill and had a vision, in which his soul departed his body "from nightfall until the crow of the cock." Looking down from Heaven, he saw four fires beneath him: the fire of lying, the fire of greed, the fire of dissension, and the fire of impiety. Before long these had come together in a single huge blaze. Flying through this fire are demons as well as angels, and these fight for possession of the souls of the dead. Three angels protect Fursey from the fire and the demons: one clears the way and the other two protect his flanks. Nevertheless, one demon manages to seize Fursey and draw him close enough to the fire so that he is licked by its flames before the angels can intervene. Fursey is burned on the shoulder and chin. These burns are still visible when he returns to earth, and he shows them to others. An angel explains to him: "What you have set afire has burned in you." The angel then gives a discourse on penitence and salvation. After Fursey's soul has returned to earth, he remains so frightened by what he has seen that whenever he thinks about it he begins to sweat as though it were the height of summer, even if he is only lightly clad on a cold winter day.

The idea of purgatory in this story is vague. No details are given about the nature of the fire, and the character of Fursey's burn is ambiguous: does it represent an ordeal, a punishment for sins, or a purification? This ambiguity is implicit, however, in the definition of purgatorial fire, which is not mentioned here by name.[26]

The Vision of Drythelm: A Place Set Aside for Purgation

The vision of Drythelm (or Dryethelm), which constitutes the twelfth chapter of book five of the *Ecclesiastical History*, is far more important for our purposes. The hero of the story, Drythelm, is a pious layman, the father of a family, who lives in the region of Cunningham, near the Scottish border. One night he becomes gravely ill and dies. At dawn, however, he revives, causing those watching over his body to flee in terror, except for his wife, who, though terrified, is happy. Drythelm then divides his property into three portions, one for his wife, one for his children, and one for the poor, and withdraws to a hermitage attached to the isolated monastery of Melrose, located at a bend in the River Tweed. There he lives a life of repentance and, when the opportunity presents itself, tells of his adventure.

A person dressed in shining white leads him eastward through a very wide, deep, and infinitely long valley, flanked on the left by terrifying flames and on the right by horrible storms of hail and snow. Both slopes of the valley are filled with human souls, constantly tossed back and forth by the wind. Drythelm thinks that he must be in Hell. But his companion reads his mind and tells him that "this is not Hell as you imagine." As they continue it becomes increasingly dark and Drythelm can see nothing but the bright shape of his guide. Suddenly, masses of "dusky flame" shoot up out of a great pit and fall back into it. Drythelm finds himself alone. Human souls rise and fall like sparks in the midst of this flame. This spectacle is accompanied by inhuman cries and laughter, and the stench is terrible. Drythelm pays particular attention to the tortures inflicted on five souls, including a clergyman, recognizable by his tonsure, a layman, and a woman (we are in a world of binary oppositions: clerk/layman, man/ woman—these three figures represent all of human society, and the two others remain in a mysterious penumbra). Devils surround him and threaten to grab him with glowing tongs, and Drythelm thinks he is lost, but all at once a light appears, like a brilliant star that grows in size, and sends the devils fleeing. His companion has returned, and he now leads Drythelm off in another direction, toward the light. They come to a wall so long and high that his eye cannot take it in, but in some incomprehensible way they pass through it and Drythelm finds himself in a vast, green meadow, full of flowers, fragrant, and bathed in a brilliant light. Men in white are gathered there in happy groups. Drythelm thinks he has arrived in the Kingdom of Heaven, but again his companion reads his mind and tells him, "No, this is not the Kingdom of Heaven as you imagine." As Drythelm makes his away across this meadow, he sees an even more brilliant light ahead and hears the sweet sound of people singing; the fragrance he now smells makes the sweetness of the meadow that pleased him earlier seem a trifle. He is hoping to enter the marvelous place he has glimpsed when his guide forces him to turn back. When they reach the place where the white-clad souls were gathered, his companion asks him, "Do you know what all these things are that you have seen?" The answer is no. His companion then continues:

> "The valley that you saw, with its horrible burning flames and icy cold, is the place where souls are tried and punished who have delayed to confess and amend their wicked ways [*scelera*], and who at last had recourse to penitence at the hour of death, and so depart this life. Because they confessed and were penitent, although only at death, they will all be admitted into the Kingdom of Heaven on the Day of Judgment. But many are helped by the prayers, alms, and fasting of the living, and especially by the offering of Masses, and are therefore set free before the Day of Judgment. The fiery noisome pit that you saw is the mouth of Hell, and whosoever falls into it will never be delivered throughout eternity. This flowery place, where you see these fair young people so happy and resplendent, is where souls are received who die having done good, but are not so perfect as to merit immediate entry into the Kingdom of Heaven. But at the Day of Judgment they shall all see Christ and enter upon the joys of His heavenly Kingdom. And whoever are perfect in word, deed, and thought, enter the Kingdom

of Heaven as soon as they leave the body. The Kingdom is situated near the place where you heard the sound of sweet singing, with the sweet fragrance and glorious light. You must now return to your body and live among men once more; but, if you will weigh your actions with greater care and study to keep your words and ways virtuous and simple, then when you die you too will win a home among these happy spirits that you see. For, when I left you for a while, I did so in order to discover what your future would be."[27]

These words fill Drythelm with sadness at the thought of having to return to his body, and he eagerly contemplates the beauty and charm of the place he is in and the rest of the company there with him. But while he is wondering how he might ask his guide a question, and before he dares to do so, he finds himself back among the living.[28]

This text would be an important milestone on the road to Purgatory if it did not leave out a number of important elements of the future doctrine and if it had not been written at the dawn of an era that turned its attention away from the problems of purgation in the hereafter.

What it does contain is a place set aside especially for purgation. The nature of that place, moreover, is described in detail. Not only are the souls there punished alternately by heat and cold, to the point where Drythelm thinks he is in Hell, but we are also told that this place is one of examination and punishment, not of purification in the proper sense of the word. The kind of sin that brings a soul to this place is specified: it is a question of grave sins, *scelera*. The situation of the soul before death is also specified: the soul that goes to this place is the one that confesses and repents *in extremis*. We are told, further, that the souls here are guaranteed eternal salvation. We are told, too, what the various kinds of suffrage are: in ascending order of value, there are prayers, alms, fasts, and above all eucharistic sacrifices. The ultimate effect of these suffrages is to reduce the duration of purgation, which confirms that the time of purgation is set between death and resurrection and that the maximum term runs until Judgment Day.

What is lacking is the word "purgation" itself and, more generally, any word derived from "to purge." Doubtless Bede is here sacrificing to the exigencies of a literary genre, carefully omitting all canonical terms and even all references to authority, even though the presence of the Bible and Augustine can be felt between the lines. And yet a place that is not named does not quite exist in the full sense of the word.

Most important of all, perhaps, is that, in keeping with Augustine's views concerning the *non valde mali* and the *non valde boni*, the not-entirely-bad and the not-entirely-good, there is not one intermediary place but two—one of harsh punishment, the other of joyful anticipation, one practically an appendage of Hell, the other of Paradise. The system that underlies the vision of Drythelm is still a binary system: an apparently impenetrable wall separates an eternal Hell and a temporary Hell from Paradise everlasting and its antechamber. Before Purgatory can come into existence as such, a ternary system must be established. Even if, geographically speaking, Purgatory will remain cast down into the nether regions near Hell, it is not Purgatory until a better system of communications is installed between it and Paradise: the wall must come down.

Almost a century later, in southern Germany, a monk by the name of Wetti died at Reichenau on November 4, 824, after telling of a vision he had on the eve of his death. Subsequently the story was written down at the behest of the abbot of the monastery, Heito. Shortly thereafter, the poet Walahfrid Strabo, the abbot of Saint Gall, put it into verse.[29]

A Bizarre, Baroque Vision of the Other World: Wetti

Lying ill, Wetti is resting in his cell with his eyes closed though he is not asleep. Satan, disguised as a priest but with a black face so ugly that his eyes are swallowed by his flesh, appears to the monk and threatens him with instruments of torture. Meanwhile, an army of demons prepares to shut Wetti up inside a sort of torture chamber. But the Lord in his mercy sends a group of men, splendidly and decently clad in monastic garb and speaking Latin, to drive the demons away. An incredibly beautiful angel, clad in purple, then comes to Wetti's bedside and speaks affectionately to him. This ends the first part of the vision. The prior of the monastery and another brother come to help the sick monk. Wetti tells them what has just happened and asks them to intercede in order to obtain forgiveness for his sins, while he himself, making a familiar monastic gesture of penance, prostrates himself with his arms in the form of a cross. The two brothers sing the seven psalms of penance. Wetti returns to his bed and asks for the *Dialogues* of Gregory the Great. After reading nine or ten pages, he asks his visitors to go and rest and he prepares to do the same. The same angel that he had seen earlier clad in purple reappears, this time dressed in resplendent white and congratulates the monk for what he has just done. In particular he recommends that Wetti read and reread Psalm 118.[30]

The angel leads him down a pleasant road until they come to an immensely high and incredibly beautiful range of mountains, which seem to be made of marble and which are surrounded by a great river in which a multitude of the damned are being punished. Wetti recognizes many of them. In another place he views the many and varied tortures inflicted on numerous priests and the women they have seduced, who are immersed in fire up to their genitals. In a misshapen castle of wood and stone from which smoke is pouring he seeks monks who, the angel tells him, have been sent here for purgation (*ad purgationem suam*). He also sees a mountain, at the summit of which is an abbot who died a decade earlier and who has been placed there not for his eternal damnation but rather for his purgation. A bishop who should have prayed for this abbot is suffering infernal puishment on the other side of the mountain. Also living there is a prince who once ruled Italy and the Roman people, whose sexual parts are being torn by an animal, though the rest of his body is left untouched. Wetti is dumbfounded by the sight of this defender of the Catholic faith and Church (who is none other than Charlemagne, mentioned by name in Walahfrid Strabo's poem) being tortured in this way. The angel tells him that this person, many of whose actions were admirable and praiseworthy, had nonetheless given himself over to illicit loves. But ultimately he will number among the elect. Wetti sees many other judges, laymen, and monks, some in glory, some in pain. He then goes to a place of great beauty where he comes upon gold and silver arches. The King of Kings, the Lord of Lords, moves forward with a retinue of saints, and the splendor is too much for human eyes to behold. The angel urges the saints to intervene on Wetti's behalf, and they do so. From the throne a voice answers them: "His conduct should have been exemplary, and it was not." Wetti then sees the glory of the blessed martyrs, who also ask God to pardon his sins. The voice from the throne says that he should first have asked forgiveness of all those who had been led into sin by his bad example. They then go to a place where there is a host of holy virgins, who also intercede in Wetti's behalf. The Lord says that if the doctrine he taught was correct, if his example was good, and if he corrected those he led into evil, he will grant their request. The angel then explains that among all the horrible vices committed by men, one is particularly offensive to God: the sin against nature, sodomy. The angel then gives a long disquisition on sins to be shunned and particularly exhorts Wetti to invite the Germans and the Gauls to be humble and to live in voluntary poverty. In a digression he discusses the sins of feminine congregations. He then returns to the vice of sodomy and expatiates on the subject at length, explaining that epidemics befall men on account of their sins. He particularly recommends unfailing diligence in the service of God, the *opus Dei*. In passing he mentions that a certain count Geraud who governed Bavaria for Charlemagne and showed great zeal in the defense of the Church has been rewarded with eternal life. Then, after saying a good deal more besides, the angel takes his leave of Wetti, who, as dawn approaches, awakens and dictates his vision. A very realistic account of the monk's final moments concludes the story.

This extraordinary vision is worthy of detailed analysis. Here I shall concentrate entirely on three points of particular significance for the future Purgatory: the emphasis on purgation in the other world, the significance of the mountain as the site of temporary punishment (looking forward to the mountain of Dante's Purgatory, which makes its appearance at the end of our period), and the presence in this place of punishment of Charlemagne, for having succumbed to the temptations of the flesh. Indeed, this is one of the earliest instances of a legend that enjoyed wide currency in the

Middle Ages: the legend that Charlemagne had had illicit relations with his sister and that he was, therefore, the father of Roland. At a later date we will see Charlemagne's grandfather Charles Martel being tortured in the other world for having confiscated the Church's property. But Charles Martel would ultimately be damned along with Theodoric, while Charlemagne is "ultimately saved."[31]

If Charlemagne and his sin figure in Wetti's vision, it is the whole Carolingian dynasty that is featured in another astonishing vision, which dates from the late ninth century and which is probably the best example we have of that popular medieval pastime, the politicization of apocalyptic literature.[32]

The Politicization of the Other World: The Vision of Charles the Fat

Below is the complete text of the vision of Charles the Fat, probably composed shortly after his death in 888. It was intended to further the cause of Louis, the son of Boson and Hermegarde, the only daughter of Emperor Louis II the Younger, the son of Lothar and nephew of Charles the Fat. Louis III, known as "the Blind," was in fact proclaimed king in 890 and Holy Roman Emperor by Pope Benedict IV in 900. He was dethroned by his rival Berenger, who, following the Byzantine custom, had the deposed emperor's eyes put out. The text is the work of someone in the entourage of the archbishop of Rheims, and it affirms the intercessory power of Saint Rémi, the patron saint of the archiepiscopal see of that city. It runs as follows:

> An account of a vision of Charles, emperor, after his own statement:
>
> In the name of God, the sovereign king of kings, I, Charles, by the grace of God king of the Germans, patrician of the Romans, and emperor of the Franks, do hereby declare that, during the holy night of a Sunday, after celebrating the Lord's evening service, I went to lie down to rest, and I wanted to sleep and take a nap, whereupon a terrible voice spoke to me, saying: "Charles, thy spirit will soon leave thee and a vision reveal to thee the just judgment of God and certain signs regarding it; but subsequently thy spirit will return in a great time."
>
> Immediately afterward my spirit was abducted by a figure of great whiteness, and in his hand he held a ball of wool that gave off a ray of extremely clear light, as comets do when they appear. Then he began to unroll the ball and said to me: "Take a strand of shining wool and tie it firmly around the thumb of your right hand, because it will guide you through the labyrinth of infernal punishments." Saying this he went quickly before me, unrolling the shining thread as he went, and led me

into deep, blazing valleys full of pits in which pitch, sulphur, lead, wax, and soot were burning. There I came upon the prelates of my father and my uncles. When I asked them with terror why these painful torments were being inflicted on them, they answered: "We were the bishops of thy father and thy uncles. But rather than give them and their people counsel of peace and concord, we sowed discord and were the instigators of evil. That is why we are burning now and undergoing infernal tortures along with other lovers of murder and plunder. Thy bishops too shall come to this place along with the host of thy satellites who are pleased today to act in the same way."

As I listened, trembling, to these words, flying demons, black all over, tried to seize with iron hooks the shining thread that I held in my hand and draw me toward them, but the glare of the rays prevented them from getting close to the thread. Then they ran at me from behind and tried to hook me and throw me down into the pits of sulphur; but my guide, who held the glowing ball, cast a thread from it down on my shoulders and wrapped it round me and then pulled me forcefully along behind him, and thus we climbed very high mountains of fire from which there flowed forth burning swamps and rivers in which all sorts of metals were boiling. There I came upon countless souls of my father's and brothers' men and lords who had been thrown in, some up to their hair, others up to their chins, and yet others up to their navels, and they all shouted at me and screamed: "During our life we loved to do battle at thy side and at the side of thy father and brothers and uncles, and to commit murder and to plunder out of earthly greed; that is why we are undergoing torment in these boiling rivers in the midst of all sorts of metals."

As I listened timidly to these words, I heard behind me souls shouting, "These great men must endure a boiling river flowing from furnaces of pitch and sulphur and full of great dragons, scorpions, and serpents of many species." I also saw others of my father's lords and the lords of my uncles and brothers, as well as my own, who said to me: "Woe unto us. Charles, thou seest what painful torments we must endure in return for our wickedness and our pride as well as for the wicked counsel we gave out of greed to the king and thyself." While they made these protests to me, moaning all the while, dragons ran toward me, their mouths open and full of fire, sulphur, and pitch, and they would swallow me up. But my guide thrice wrapped the luminous thread around me more tightly still, and its bright rays outshone their fiery gullets as he pulled me along even more vigorously than before.

We then went down into a valley which on one side was dark but hot as an oven and on the other side more pleasant and charming than I can say. I turned toward the side that was in darkness and vomiting flames and saw there several kings from my family, who were undergoing great torture. And then I was gripped by a deep anguish, for I immediately imagined myself subjected to such tortures by the giants, black from head to toe, who roasted the valley in fire of every variety. Trembling, my way lighted before me by the radiant thread, I saw a momentary light on one side of the valley, and two wells from which liquid was flowing. One was boiling, but the other was clear and tepid, and there were two pools. As I approached the latter, guided by the thread, my gaze was fixed on the pool filled with boiling water, in which I saw Louis, my father,[33] standing up to his thighs.

He was suffering from extreme pain, which aggravated his anguish, and he said to me: "Monseigneur Charles, have no fear, I know that thy soul will return to thy body. God has permitted thee to come here in order to show thee the sins for which I and the others thou hast seen are undergoing such torments. One day I must stand in this pool of boiling water, but the next day I am transported to the other, where the water is very cool. This I owe to the prayers of Saint Peter and Saint Rémi, under whose patronage our royal race has reigned until now. But if thou comest quickly to my aid, thou and my liegemen, bishops, abbots, and clergy, by means of masses, offerings, psalmodies, vigils, and alms, I shall soon be delivered from this pool of boiling water, for my brother Lothar and his son Louis have already been reprieved from this punishment thanks to the prayers of Saint Peter and Saint Rémi, and they have already been led to the joy of God's paradise." Then he said to me: "Look to thy left." I looked and saw two deep pools. "Those," he added, "have been made ready for thee, if thou change not thy ways and do no penance for thy abominable crimes."

I then began to shiver terribly. Upon seeing the fright that had taken hold of my mind, my companion said to me: "Follow me to the right, toward the splendid valley of paradise." We moved on and I contemplated the sight of my uncle Lothar seated beside glorious kings in a bright light on a stone of topaz, which was extraordinary in size. He was crowned by a precious diadem, and near him he had his son Louis, wearing a similar crown. When he saw me draw near, he questioned me in a friendly way, and in a strong voice said, "Charles, my successor, who now reignest in security in the Empire of the Romans, come to me; I know that thou hast passed through a place of expiation where thy father, who is my brother, has been placed in a steam bath that was made ready for him. But the mercy of God will soon deliver him from these pains, just as we ourselves have been delivered from them by the merits of

Saint Peter and the prayers of Saint Rémi, upon whom God has conferred a supreme apostolate over the kings of the Francs and the whole Frankish race. If this saint had not given succor and aid to the survivors of our posterity, our family would already have ceased to reign and to wield the imperial power. Know therefore that this imperial power will soon be wrested from thy hands, and that thou shalt live but a short while thereafter." Then, turning toward me, Louis said to me: "The empire of the Romans that thou hast possessed until now as a hereditary title is to pass to Louis, the son of my daughter." With these words it seemed to me that Louis the child appeared before us.

Fixing him steadily, his grandfather said to me, "This little child is like the one whom the Lord set down in the midst of his disciples when he said: 'The kingdom of heaven belongs to these children; I say unto you that their angels always look upon the face of my Father, who art in heaven.' As for thee, transfer the power to this child by that thread that thou holdest in thy hand." Untying the thread from the thumb of my right hand, I gave him, through this thread, the whole of the imperial monarchy. Immediately the whole glowing ball was accumulated in his hand, as though it were a radiant sun. Thus it came to pass, that after having this miraculous vision, my spirit returned into my body, but I was very tired and filled with terror. To conclude, let it be known to all, whether they like it or not, that all of the empire of the Romans will come into his hands, in keeping with the will of God. But I am incapable of acting in his behalf, prevented as I am by the approach of the moment when the Lord will call me. God who rules the living and the dead will complete and confirm this work, for his eternal reign and his universal empire shall endure forever and ever.[34]

This text, which we know to have been read by Dante, shows how great was the need, even in the absence of theoretical reflection, to set apart from Hell, in which the grand personages of Charles's vision presumably reside, another place, a place from which it is theoretically possible to exit. The items of detail are also invaluable for our purposes. The theme, borrowed from folklore, of the glowing ball of wool which serves as a sort of Ariadne's thread occurs again in the work of Gervase of Tilbury, where it figures in the story of a witch who lived in Rheims in the late twelfth century. A prominent place is given to the themes of heat and cold and to the mitigation of punishments. And we glimpse one of the reasons why the punishment of sins in the other world was described: as a way of extorting favors from the living.

To conclude this discussion of some of the visions that enriched the ways in which the other world was imagined between the seventh and eleventh centuries, I should also mention a poem composed between 1010 and 1024 by Egbert of Liège, the *Fecunda Ratis*, which harks back to ancient literary forms and to the ancient concept of two fires, one purgatorial, the other eternal. Purgatorial fire is discussed in verses 231–40, where mention is made of rivers of fire and slight sins; the authorities invoked are John 2:3, Daniel 7:10, and Ezekiel 24:11. Verses 241–48 deal with eternal fire and mention an infernal lake, well, and abyss.[35]

THE LITURGY: PURGATORY NEAR AND FAR

The third avenue to explore along the road to Purgatory is that of liturgy. Paradoxically, this is at once perhaps the most abundant source of material for the new doctrine and the most disappointing. Even though we find few if any allusions to the remission of sins after death, the growing fervor of the living in praying for the dead helped to lay the groundwork for Purgatory.

Epitaphs have been read as one sign of the Christian concern for their dead. Other signs of this concern are also found in liturgy. What is requested in prayer is, if not immediate access to Paradise, then at least the promise of future life and tranquil repose in the meantime. *Refrigerium* (refreshment) and the bosom of Abraham were the terms in which this desire was most commonly couched. The most frequently used formula refers to a "place of refreshment, light, and peace."

It is possible to distinguish three versions of the prayer for the dead in the early Middle Ages: the "old Gelasian" prayer (that is, from the so-called Gelasian sacramentary); Alcuin's prayer, which in the ninth century became the most widely known version and which is still found in the Roman pontifical today; and the Gallican prayer, which comes from a sacramentary of Saint-Denis dating from the ninth century, and examples of which can be found as late as the sixteenth century.

Here is Alcuin's prayer:

> O God, for whom everything lives and for whom our bodies do not perish when they die but are changed into something better, we beg thee to order thy holy angels to take the soul of thy servant and lead it to the bosom of thy friend, the patriarch Abraham, to be revived on the last day of the great judgment; and whatever in the way of vice may have sullied thy servant's soul owing to the devil's deceit, by thy devotion, mercy, and indulgence, O Lord, wipe it clean, forever and ever.[36]

Broadly speaking, two things limit the importance of liturgical literature for a study of the inception of Purgatory. First, the liturgy deliberately avoids mention of punishment or expiation beyond the grave. When, as in the sacramentary of Hadrian, allusion is made to "purged souls" (*anima purgata*), remission of sin is meant. The eucharistic offering suggests the possibility of "final redemption and eternal salvation of the soul." According to certain sacramentaries, "the eucharistic offering breaks the chains of the empire of the dead and leads the soul into the abode of life and light."[37] The liturgical texts are deliberately euphemistic, optimistic. It is noteworthy that a preface in the Bobbio missal, for example, repeats verbatim the words of Augustine's prayer for his mother. Joseph Ntedika has shrewdly noted that, although Gregory the Great was "the first to explain the prayer for the dead in terms of the doctrine of Purgatory" and was followed in this by Isidore of Seville, Bede, and others, this way of looking at the matter had "no influence on the liturgical formularies." The relative autonomy of different spheres in history, of which this is one example, should give pause to all historians: we must resign ourselves to the fact that in history things do not all move at the same pace.

Second, liturgy, by its very function, is naturally conservative. The introduction to the memento for the dead in the canon of the mass probably dates back at least as far as Gregory the Great, but the text of which it forms a part remained unchanged until Vatican II: "From the beginning of the fifth century on, the portion of our Roman canon from the *Te igitur* to the words of the Institution has had substantially the same form that it has today."[38] Although this memento is omitted from the Gregorian sacramentary sent by Hadrian I to Charlemagne, the reason for this is simply that in Rome it was always omitted from Sunday masses and solemn services. This invocation, which was considered a mere gesture of respect toward the dead, was pronounced only in weekday masses.

Two further remarks are called for if we are to have a proper appreciation of the development of Purgatory in the general religious climate of the early Middle Ages. First, as Damien Sicard points out, religious ritual changed noticeably during the Carolingian era: "God was now deliberately represented as a judge. Appeal was made to his justice almost as much as to his mercy." The Last Judgment was evoked. The dying were "supposed to be purified, cleansed of their sins and errors." Concern about the sins of the deceased, which had been absent from the ancient liturgy, now began to make itself felt in expressions of fear and in "the first glimmerings of thought about the other world." But this other world consisted of only two places: Heaven and Hell. Carolingian liturgy introduced not the hope of Purgatory but growing fear of Hell, coupled with the more tenuous hope of Heaven. As early as the eighth century the Bobbio missal proposed a prayer to enable a dead soul to "escape the place of punishment, the fire of Gehenna, and the flames of Tartarus, and to reach the region of the living." Another ritual included these words: "Free him, O Lord, from the princes of darkness and the places of punishment, from all the perils of hell and the snares of punishment."

The second remark is this: throughout the early Middle Ages, the liturgy emphasized the idea of a first resurrection. Prayers for the dead accordingly figured in a millenarian context. The basis for this was Revelation 20:6: "Blessed and holy is he that hath part in the first resurrection." This passage was given currency by Origen and Ambrose, among others. Most liturgical texts included the words, "May he take part in the first resurrection" (*habeat partem in prima resurrectione*).

Damien Sicard has made use of Dom Botte's work in attempting to determine what problems were raised by this belief in a first resurrection. "This old liturgical formula," Sicard writes, "has a millenarian flavor which suggests that, during the time when the Gallican and Gelasian rituals were in use, people were not far from imagining that after death there is an intermediary place, a place of the first resurrection, where it is desirable and enviable to reign with Christ for a thousand years. . . . I wish, though, that our liturgical texts told us a little more than they do about what was meant by this intermediary place. Like the early Roman euchologion, they follow the Gospel of Luke in calling this place the bosom of Abraham, Heaven, or the Kingdom, terms that appear to have been used interchangeably." Change, he goes on, is in "the direction of belief in an intermediate place of tranquillity, a gentle paradise, in which the soul, redeemed from all its sins, waits in sweetness and light for the day of resurrection. But nothing in this conception suggests the purification, the punishment for already pardoned sins, that we associate with the current idea of Purgatory."[39]

It seems to me that this intermediate place of tranquillity is none other than the bosom of Abraham, or again, the meadow inhabited by souls clad in white in Bede's Vision of Drythelm. It is also the sabbath of souls awaiting the eighth day, that is, the resurrection described at length in many monastic documents.[40] But, just as Purgatory, after its inception, required the elimination of the class of souls that Augustine called the *non valde boni*, the not entirely good, and retained only the *non valde mali* or the *mediocriter boni et mali*, the average sinner, so too did it require the disappearance of that heavenly antechamber, the bosom of Abraham and its equivalents.

THE COMMEMORATION OF THE DEAD: CLUNY

The Christian liturgy showed its concern for the dead elsewhere than in the memento for the dead in the canon of the mass and in prayer for the dead. Roman sacramentaries attest that masses for the dead were celebrated not on the day of burial but on successive anniversaries of that day, as a commemoration. But the best evidence for the remembrance of the dead is undoubtedly provided by mortuary registers. During the Carolingian era registers were kept in certain monasteries on which were inscribed the names of persons both living and dead for mention during the canon of the mass. Known as Books of Life (*libri vitae*),[41] these registers took the place of the older diptychs, waxen tablets on which the names of those who had donated offerings were recorded. Later the dead and the living parted company. Monastic communities inscribed the names of their dead on "rolls," and these rolls were circulated so as to keep all the monasteries of the community informed.[42] This practice was in use as early as the seventh century in Ireland. Later the "necrologies" and "obituaries" made their appearance. Necrologies were lists of the dead kept in the margins of a calendar and read out at the office of prime, either in the choir or in the chapter. Obituaries were not normally read but were used as reminders of anniversary services provided for by certain persons before their death, requiring certain "services of mercy" (usually distribution of alms). K. Schmid and J. Wollash have called attention to the changes that took place between the Carolingian era (ninth and tenth centuries) and the time of the Gregorian reforms (end of the eleventh century). In particular, it became customary to mention the dead individually, by name, rather than as a group. The Carolingian *libri memoriales* contain from 15,000 to 40,000 names. The Cluniac necrologies mention no more than fifty to sixty names per calendar day. From this time forward "liturgical remembrance was guaranteed forever to the dead mentioned in these lists by name." This inaugurated the age of death as an individual phenomenon.[43] Schmid and Wollasch stress the role of the Cluniac order in this development. As W. Jorden has said, "when it came to the care of the dead, Cluny was original."[44]

Indeed, although Cluny generally devoted its attention to dead individuals from the ruling class and thus respected the elitist character of the new bonds between the dead and the living, once a year it solemnly extended the benefits of the liturgy to all the dead. In the eleventh century, probably between 1024 and 1033, Cluny began commemorating the dead on November 2, the day after All Saints' Day. The prestige of the Cluniac order was such that before long the "Day of the Dead" was being celebrated throughout Christendom. This solemn new bond between the living and the dead cleared the ground for the inception of Purgatory. But Cluny also cleared the ground in another, even more direct way. Shortly after the death of the abbot Odilo in 1049, the monk Jotsuald reported the following fact in the life of Saint Odilo that he was then writing:

> The lord bishop Richard told me of this vision, which I had heard spoken about but without remembering the slightest detail. One day, he told me, a monk from Rouergue was on his way back from Jerusalem. While on the high seas between Sicily and Thessalonika, he encountered a violent wind, which drove his ship onto a rocky islet inhabited by a hermit, a servant of God. When our man saw the seas calm, he chatted about one thing and another with this hermit. The man of God asked him what nationality he was, and he answered that he was Aquitanian. Then the man of God asked if he knew a

monastery which bears the name of Cluny, and the abbot of this place, Odilo. He answered: "I knew him, indeed knew him well, but I would like to know why you are asking me this question." And the other replied: "I am going to tell you, and I beg you to remember what you are about to hear. Not far from where we are there are places where, by the manifest will of God, a blazing fire spits with the utmost violence. For a fixed length of time the souls of sinners are purged there in various tortures. A host of demons are responsible for renewing these torments constantly: each day they inflict new pain and make the suffering more and more intolerable. I have often heard the lamentations of these men, who complain violently. God's mercy in fact allows these condemned souls to be delivered from their pains by the prayers of monks and by alms given to the poor in holy places. Their complaints are addressed above all to the community of Cluny and its abbot. By God I beg of you, therefore, if you have the good fortune to regain your home and family, to make known to this community what you have heard from my mouth, and to exhort the monks to multiply their prayers, vigils, and alms for the repose of souls enduring punishment, in order that there might be more joy in heaven, and that the devil might be vanquished and thwarted.

Upon returning to his country, our man faithfully conveyed this message to the holy father abbot and the brothers. When they heard him, the brothers, their hearts running over with joy, gave thanks to God in prayer after prayer, heaping alms upon alms, working tirelessly that the dead might rest in peace. The holy father abbot proposed to all the monasteries that the day after All Saints' Day, the first day of November, the memory of all the faithful should be celebrated everywhere in order to secure the repose of their souls, and that masses, with psalms and alms, be celebrated in public and in private, and that alms be distributed unstintingly to all the poor. Thus would hard blows be struck at the diabolical enemy and Christians suffering in Gehenna would cherish the hope of divine mercy.

A few years later the celebrated Italian monk and cardinal, Peter Damian, wrote another life of Odilo, almost all of which was copied from Jotsuald's life and which made this little story famous.[45] Jacopo da Varazze (Jacobus da Voragine) echoed it in his *Golden Legend* in the thirteenth century: "Saint Peter Damian recounts that Saint Odilo, abbot of Cluny, after learning that the cries and shrieks of demons were heard, in the vicinity of a volcano in Sicily, complaining that the souls of the dead were plucked from their hands by alms and prayers, ordered that the dead be commemorated in his monasteries on the day after All Saints' Day. Which was subsequently approved by all the Church." But this account is from the mid-thirteenth century: it interprets the episode in terms of Purgatory, which by that time existed in the full sense of the word. But when Jotsuald and Peter Damian were composing the *Life of Odilo*, Purgatory had not yet been born. Cluny marks an essential milestone along the way. The story gives us a definite spot: a mountain that spits fire. And the monastery established a crucial ritual of commemoration: the dead, especially those in need of suffrages, now had a day of their own in the calendar of the Church.

PART TWO

THE TWELFTH CENTURY
THE BIRTH OF PURGATORY

The Century of the
Great Advance

THE twelfth century was an explosive one for Latin Christendom. The system of social relations, having matured slowly, was no longer what it had been. Slavery had disappeared for good and the great estates of late antiquity and the early Middle Ages were profoundly altered. The seigneurial system took hold, bringing with it a twofold system of domination, a dual hierarchy. First there was the fundamental cleavage between the rulers, the lords, and the mass of peasants over whom they held dominion within the limits of the seigneury. By virtue of this dominion the lords confiscated a considerable share of the product of peasant labor, either as rent in kind or, increasingly, as money rent (also as labor services, though *corvées* were on the wane); these exactions constituted the so-called feudal rent. The lords ruled the peasants (including both the *manants*, or peasants who remained on the seigneury, and the morally contemptible *vilains*, or men of the old demesne) by means of various seigneurial rights, the most significant of which, apart from those related to the exaction of rent, involved powers of justice. Within the ruling class there grew up a second social division. The owners of the most important castles came to constitute an aristocracy which dominated the minor and middling nobility of knights, *chevaliers*, through relations of vassalage. In exchange for a range of services, primarily military but also including assistance and counsel, the seigneur extended his protection to the vassal and frequently gave him means of subsistence, generally in the form of a piece of land, a fief.

Taken together, these various elements constitute what is known as the feudal system. Although feudal relations were clearly defined in law only for the upper strata of feudal society, the lords and their vassals, that society could not have existed or functioned as such without the ties that linked lords and peasants, generally defined in rather vague terms by what were known as customs [coutumes].

I want to draw a distinction between this feudal system [*féodalité*] and feudalism [*féodalisme*] in general. The feudal system as it existed in medieval Europe was a specific historical embodiment of a more general phenomenon to which I shall refer as feudalism, which has existed (and still exists) in various parts of the world at various times. Though harsh for the subjugated masses, the feudal system did allow society as a whole to achieve an exceptional rate of growth—growth evident, to begin with, in population: between the beginning of the eleventh century and the middle of the thirteenth century, the population of Latin Christendom almost doubled. Other evidence of growth is apparent in the countryside: fields were expanded and yields increased thanks in part to technological progress, to an increase in the intensity of cultivation. Urban growth was spectacular in this period: the growth of the cities was based on exploitation of the agricultural surplus, on the availability of artisanal labor, and on the renewal of trade, all of which depended on the establishment of an urban society which, though linked to feudal structures, introduced a new element which, at least in part, worked against those structures—the free middle class of artisans and merchants out of which emerged the bourgeoisie, with a new system of values linked to labor, to calculation, to peace, and to a certain equality, to a horizontal as opposed to a vertical hierarchy, in which the most powerful were able to lead others without dominating them.

New ways of describing society and propounding social norms emerged. These were based on the old tripartite ideology, of remote Indo-European origins, revivified by historical developments. The clergy had a structural role to play in feudal society as a prop for seigneurial domination (and remember that ecclesiastical seigneuries were among the most powerful of all): the Church became the ideological guarantor of the social system, but its religious dimension transcended that system. The Church's sense of superiority was reinforced by the Gregorian reform, which made the clergy into a celibate society unsullied by sexuality and in direct contact with the sacred, which the Church administered according to the new theory of the seven sacraments. Reminding laymen of the equality of the faithful and of the superiority of ethical and religious values over social forms, the clergy was able to stake its claim to primacy among the three orders, as "that which prays." The nobles, whose specific function was military at a time when weaponry and the art of war were also changing (to take advantage of heavy armor, mounted combat, and fortified castles), constituted the second order, "that which fights." And finally, in an innovation worthy of note, a third order made its appearance: "that which works," the composition of which has been the subject of some dispute. Was it a rural elite engaged in bringing new land under the plow, or did it include the whole of the toiling masses, urban as well as rural? Be that as it may, we see here the outlines of a tripartite society as it was defined in the early eleventh century and amplified in the twelfth: the society whose three orders were referred to, respectively, as *oratores*, *bellatores*, and *laboratores*.[1]

What we have, then, is social growth sanctioned by a new system of social representations. But this is not all: the twelfth century was also an expansionist era, geographically as well as ideologically. It was the century of the great Crusades. And it was the time of spiritual and intellectual renewal, with the reform of the monasteries, led by the Carthusians, the Premonstratensians, and above all the Cistercians, and the inception of urban schools, which went hand in hand with the development of a new concept of knowledge and a new philosophical method, scholasticism.

Purgatory found its place as man's social imagination expanded to embrace the other world as well as this one. This was also a time of new religious certitude, which also affected Purgatory. In short, Purgatory was part of a comprehensive system involving both the social structure and the way it was conceived, and this new system was an achievement of the twelfth century.

At this point I propose to change my method somewhat. I want to look at the evidence in greater detail than I have done thus far, to delve more deeply into the matter at hand. This I propose to do systematically, following two lines of approach. The first is theological: I want to follow the development of the system of redemption, looking at the way this was related to the development of concepts of sin and penance and to an articulated doctrine of ultimate ends. Second, I propose to study the development of the medieval imagination: I want to look first at the nature of the functions ascribed to fire and then at how the various pieces of Purgatory were finally put together in the other world.

Until now I have tried to be comprehensive in my approach to cultural geography and sociology, looking at the whole of Christendom. From this point on, however, I shall concentrate on the places where the inception of Purgatory actually occurred, looking I trust at all the important evidence. I hope to identify where the final elaboration of the doctrine took place and to locate those regions of this world in which the geography of the next took root. Finally, since it is my contention that the inception of Purgatory is the expression of a profound social change, I shall analyze what part Purgatory played in the birth of the new society. These are the four main threads of the central portion of this work.

FOUR

The Fire of Purgatory
The Early Twelfth Century:
Certainty and Hesitation

THE Church's attitude toward the dead at the beginning of the twelfth century, so far as we are able to tell from documents of clerical origin, was this: After the Last Judgment men will be grouped for all eternity into two classes, the saved and the damned. A man's fate will be determined essentially by his behavior in life: faith and good works militate in favor of salvation, impiety and criminal sins consign the soul to Hell. About the period between death and resurrection Church doctrine had little of a precise nature to say. According to some writers, after death the deceased would await determination of their fate by the Last Judgment, either in the grave or in some dark but neutral region, such as the *sheol* of the Old Testament, which was not distinguished from the grave. Others, more numerous, believed that souls would reside in various dwelling places. Of these the most prominent was the bosom of Abraham, the abode of souls which, while waiting to be admitted to Heaven in the true sense of the word, bide their time in a place of refreshment and peace. Most believed—and this opinion seems to have been favored by ecclesiastical authorities—that a final decision was handed down immediately after death in the case of two categories: first, those who are entirely good, martyrs and saints, the fully righteous, who go to Heaven at once and enjoy the ultimate reward, the sight of God, the beatific vision; and second, those who are entirely bad, who go directly to Hell. Between the two there were one or two intermediate categories, depending on which authority we believe. According to Augustine, those who are not entirely good must undergo a trial before going to Heaven, and those who are not entirely bad must go to Hell but while there benefit from some moderation of their torment. Most of those who believed in the existence of an intermediate category held that the dead awaiting admission to Heaven would have to undergo some kind of purgation. Here opinions varied. Some held that this purification would take place at the moment of the Last Judgment. But again there were various positions among authorities committed to this view. Some argued that all the dead, including the righteous, the saints, the martyrs, the apostles, and even Jesus were required to undergo this trial. For the righteous it would amount to a mere formality, without consequences, for the godless it would lead to damnation, and for the almost perfect, to purgation. Others believed that only those who did not go immediately to Heaven would be subject to this examination.

What was the nature of this purgation? The overwhelming majority of writers held that it consisted of some sort of fire, largely on the authority of 1 Corinthians 3:10–15. But some held that there were various instruments of purgation and spoke of "purgatorial punishments" (*poenae purgatoriae*). Who was worthy of being subjected to such examination, which, however painful it might be, was an assurance of salvation? As we have seen, from the time of Augustine and Gregory the Great, it was believed that the only souls worthy of this "second chance" were those who had only "slight sins" to expiate or who, having repented, had not had time before dying to do penance on earth. When did purgation occur? After Augustine it was generally believed that it would take place in the period between death and resurrection. But it might extend beyond this period in one direction or the other. In Augustine's own view, trials endured here below, earthly tribulations, could be the first stages of purgation. Others believed that purgation took place at the moment of the Last Judgment and generally held that the "day" of judgment would last long enough so that purgation would be more than a mere formality.

Where was this purgation supposed to take place? Here opinions were not so much varied as ambiguous. Most authors said nothing in particular on the subject. Some thought that a dwelling place was set aside to receive souls for this purpose. Gregory the Great suggested in his anecdotes that purgation occurs in the place where the sin was committed. Authors of imaginary journeys to the other world were not sure where to locate the purgatorial fire. They were torn between situating it in the upper regions of Hell, hence in some sort of underground valley, and placing it, as Bede suggested, on a mountain.

All in all, there was much hesitation about the nature of this intermediary place. Although almost everyone agreed that some sort of fire, distinct from the eternal fire of Gehenna, played a role, few tried to locate that fire, or if they did were quite vague about it. From the Fathers to the final representatives of the Carolingian Church, the problem of the hereafter was essentially that of distinguishing between those who would be saved and go to Heaven and those who would be damned and sent to Hell. When all is said and done, the belief that gained the most ground between the fourth and the eleventh centuries and that helped to prepare the way for the inception of Purgatory was this: that the souls of the dead could be helped by prayer, and more particularly by suffrages. In these the faithful found what they needed both to satisfy their desire to support their relatives and friends beyond the grave and to sustain their own hopes of benefiting in turn from similar assistance. Augustine, a shrewd psychologist and attentive pastor, says as much in *De Cura pro mortuis gerenda*. This belief and its associated practices, which required the intervention of the Church, in particular for the eucharistic sacrifice, and which afforded the Church the benefits of alms and other gifts, helped to tighten its control over the living, who wished to avail themselves of its supposed power to intervene on behalf of the dead.

In this as in so many other areas, the twelfth century accelerated the pace of change. By the century's end Purgatory would exist as a distinct place. In the meantime pokers stirred the smoldering purgatorial fires. Before proceeding with the story, however, a preliminary remark is in order.

Handling twelfth-century sources is a delicate matter. The general growth alluded to above correlates with a marked increase in the number of written documents. Since the sixteenth century, scholars, especially nineteenth- and twentieth-century scholars, have been at pains to publish as many of these documents as possible, and yet many remain unpublished. The documents bear characteristic marks of the period. In order to make sure that a work would be successful, many twelfth-century clerics did not hesitate to attribute it to an illustrious or familiar author. Hence the literature of the twelfth century is rife with apocryphal material. In many cases questions of attribution and authenticity have not been resolved. The then new philosophy of scholasticism has left us many documents that are difficult to attribute to any author, assuming that the word "author" makes sense when speaking of *quaestiones, determinationes,* and *reportationes* that were often compilations of notes taken by a pupil of courses given by a master. It was not uncommon for the scribe to mix his own thoughts or the thoughts of other contemporary authors with the authentic words of the master. Finally, we possess few original manuscripts from the period. The manuscripts we do have were written later, between the thirteenth and the fifteenth century. In some cases the scribes have replaced a word of the original text with a word or expression current in their own time, either unconsciously or in the belief that they were thereby doing a good turn—for the men of the Middle Ages were inspired by the quest for eternal, not historical, truth.[1] In this essay I have been unable to resolve certain questions, in part because our knowledge of the Middle Ages is incomplete, but even more because of the very nature of twelfth-century religious literature, whose multifarious eloquence is too subtle for the classificatory grids of present-day history, concerned (and rightly so) mainly with questions of attribution and dating. Nevertheless, I am convinced by my research and textual analyses that Purgatory did not exist before 1170 at the earliest.

Purgatory did not exist, but the number of documents showing an interest in what goes on in the interval between death and the Last Judgment increased rapidly. The expositions may have been disorderly, but this merely reflects the state of work in progress, research under way. What is increasingly evident in these documents is the concern to specify the exact location where purgation occurs.

A Hesitant Author: Honorius Augustodunensis

A typical example of this early confusion may be found in the writings of the mysterious Honorius Augustodunensis, who was probably Irish by birth but who spent most of his religious life at Ratisbon. Honorius, who, according to M. Capuyns, was probably the only medieval disciple of Johannes Scotus Erigena, did indeed have original ideas about the other world. He believed, for one thing, that the other world did not exist "materially." It consisted, rather, of "spiritual places." What is meant here by "spiritual" is ambiguous. It may designate a certain corporeal quality, or it may mean a reality that is purely symbolic, metaphorical. Honorius hesitated between the two. In the *Scala coeli major*, in which he seems to lean toward the completely immaterial interpretation, he hedges by putting forward a theory of the seven hells (of which this world is the second). The degree to which these hells are material or immaterial varies from one to the next.[2] I am particularly interested in two features of Honorius's thought. First of all, he is harshly critical of a spatial conception of spiritual life. In the *Scala coeli major* he says the notion that Hell is underground is purely metaphorical, a way of conjoining the ideas of inferiority, heaviness, and sadness. He concludes with these words: "Every place has length, breadth, and height, but since the soul is deprived of these attributes, it cannot be shut up in any place."[3] The same idea occurs again in his *Liber de cognitione verae vitae*: "But it seems to me the height of absurdity to think that souls and spirits, since they are incorporeal, can be shut up in corporeal places, particularly since any place can be measured by its height, length, and breadth, whereas the spirit, as is well known, is deprived of all these attributes."[4] It seems reasonable to assume that if Honorius's way of thinking had triumphed, Purgatory, essentially defined as a place, would never have been born or would have remained of secondary importance, largely without influence.

Paradoxically, though, in another work, the *Elucidarium*, a treatise summarizing the main truths of the Christian faith, a sort of catechism, Honorius discusses purgatorial fire, and the passage in which he does so played a notable role in the gestation of Purgatory. In book three of this work, a dialogue, Honorius answers questions about the life to come. To a question about heaven he replies that it is not a corporeal place but the spiritual abode of the blessed, situated in the intellectual Heaven where they may contemplate God face to face. His interlocutor asks if this is where the souls of the just are taken. He answers that this is where the souls of the perfect are taken when they leave the body. Who are the perfect? Those who in this life were not content merely to do what was prescribed but attempted more: martyrs, monks, and virgins, for example. The just reside in other dwellings. And who are the just? Those who merely did gracefully what was prescribed. When they die, their souls are taken by angels to the earthly paradise; more precisely, they are transported into spiritual joy, since spirits do not live in corporeal places. There is, moreover, another category of the just known as the "imperfect." Though imperfect they are still inscribed in God's book. Among these, for example, are worthy married couples whose merits are such that they are received into very pleasant dwellings. Many of the imperfect are granted a greater glory even before the day of judgment, thanks to the prayers of saints and the alms of the living; all of them are reunited with the angels after judgment. Among the elect there are also some who are a long way from perfection and who delayed doing penance for their sins. These, like the wicked son who is turned over to a slave to be whipped, are, with the permission of the angels, handed over to demons to be purged. But the demons cannot torment them more than they deserve or than the angels permit.

The questioner next asks how the imperfect may be freed. The master, that is, Honorius, responds that masses, alms, prayers and other pious works are the proper means, particularly if the deceased person has accomplished such works on behalf of others while still alive. Some of the imperfect are set free on the seventh day, others on the ninth, others at the end of a year, still others even longer after being handed over to the demons. Using a mysterious symbolic arithmetic, Honorius then explains how the length of the sentence is determined.

Finally, he is asked a question that bears most directly on our subject:

DISCIPLE: What is purgatorial fire?

MASTER: Some undergo purgation in this life; it may come in the form of physical pain brought by various ills, or physical trials laid down by fasting, vigils, or other activities, or the loss of loved ones or treasured belongings, or pains or illness, or a want of food or clothing, or, finally, a cruel death. But after death purgation takes the form of excessive heat or excessive cold or any other kind of trial, but the least of these trials is greater than the greatest that one can imagine in this life. While they are there, angels sometimes appear to them, or saints in whose honor they did something during their lifetime, bringing air or a sweet fragrance or some other form of relief, until they are set free and allowed to enter into that court from which every taint is banned.

DISCIPLE: In what form do they live there?

MASTER: In the form of the bodies they wore in this world. And it is said of demons that they are given bodies made of air so that they feel their torments.

After explaining, not very clearly, the relations between the body and the soul, Honorius discusses Hell. Actually he thinks there are two hells. The upper one is the lower portion of the terrestrial world and is replete with torments: unbearable heat, biting cold, hunger, thirst, and various kinds of pain, some having physical causes, such as the pain caused by blows, some having spiritual causes, such as the pain caused by fear or shame. The lower hell is a spiritual place in which there is an inextinguishable fire; there the soul must endure nine special torments: a fire that burns without light, an unbearable cold, immortal worms, serpents, and dragons, a frightful stench, frightening noises such as hammers striking iron, thick darkness, the throng of sinners mingled without distinction, the horrible sight of demons and dragons glimpsed by the flickering light of the flames, the depressing din of wails and insults, and finally shackles of fire that bind all the limbs of the damned.[5]

This text does nothing more than recast the ideas of Augustine, including the idea that purgation begins on earth, with a trifle more insistence on the metaphorical character of the other world, which Augustine too sometimes thought more symbolic than material in nature. And yet Honorius, his imagination no doubt fired by the visionary tales he had read and heard, lets slip images that contradict his ideas. The reason why this text proved influential in the prehistory of purgatory was, I think, even more than the realistic descriptions of Hell, the role accorded to the angels and demons, which follows in the train of Gregory the Great and is more "medieval" than Augustinian.

FIRE AS SEEN FROM THE MONASTERIES

Up to the middle of the twelfth century, reflection on the purgation of sins usually occurred in the context of commentaries on Paul's First Epistle to the Corinthians and was limited to a traditional account of purgatorial fire. As a first example take Bruno the Carthusian (d. 1101), considered by some to have been one of the fathers of scholasticism along with the great Anselm of Canterbury (d. 1109). Bruno was the first to have a school in the true sense of the word. He prepared a scholastic *Commentary on the Epistles of Saint Paul*, revised and reworked many times after his death. Some writers attribute this work to a member of Bruno's entourage, generally named as Raoul of Laon (d. 1136), Anselm's brother and the best-known representative of the Laon school, the most brilliant of the early twelfth-century schools of theology. In any case, in this commentary on 1 Corinthians, it is stated, in line with Augustine, that even those who have loved the world will be saved provided they did not prefer the world to God, but that first they must be punished by fire. Those who built of wood will be punished for a long time, because wood is slow to burn; those who build of hay, which burns quickly, will escape fiery purgation more quickly; and finally, those built of straw, which burns even more quickly than hay, will pass most rapidly through the fire.[6]

Guerric of Igny, born in Tournai around 1087, was enticed by Saint Bernard to enter Clairvaux in about 1125. In 1138 he became the second abbot of the Cistercian abbey at Igny, between Reims and Soissons, which was founded by Bernard in 1128. There he died "in the fullness of days," in 1158. Fifty-four of his sermons to the monks have survived.[7] In the fourth and fifth sermons, in which he deals with the purification of the Virgin Mary, he also discusses purgatorial fire. Guerric, who seems to have been influenced by Origen, believed that purification must begin in this world, and he tends to identify the purgatorial fire of the next world with the fire of judgment. In his fourth sermon, for example, he has this to say about purification:

> How certain it is, my brothers, that it is sweeter to be purged by water than by fire! Make no mistake, those who have not been purged by water will have to be purged by fire if they are worthy of purgation at all, on the day when the judge shall sit in person like a fire ready to melt, to melt and purify silver, and he shall purge the sons of Levi (Mal. 3:2-3). . . . This I assert without hesitation, that if the fire that the Lord Jesus has sent down to earth burns in us with the ardor envisioned by him who sent it, the purgatorial fire that shall purge the sons of Levi on the day of judgment will find in us neither wood, nor hay, nor straw to consume. Each of them is a purgatorial fire, but of quite different kinds. One purifies by unction, the other by flame. This is a refreshing dew, the other an avenging wind [spiritus judicii], a burning blast. . . . And if this charity is not perfect enough to cover so many sins, and such sins, the refiner who purifies the sons of Levi will use his fire on them: all the rust is consumed by the fire of tribulations present and future, so that they may finally sing: "We went through fire and through water: but thou broughtest us out into a wealthy place [place of resfreshment]" (Ps. 66:12). And so it is with this world: first baptized by the water of the flood, then purged by the fire of judgment, it will pass into a new state, incorruptible.

The theme is again taken up, with Augustinian overtones, in the fifth sermon on purification:

> Woe unto us if we let these days [in this world] go by without completing our purgation and must later be purged by that most cruel [poenalius] of fires, quicker and more violent than any that one can imagine in this life! And who then, upon leaving this life, is so perfect and so holy that he owes nothing to this fire? . . . Yes a few are chosen, but among them there are, I think, very few perfect enough to have accomplished the

purgation of which the sage speaks: "Purge thyself of thy negligence with the small number" (Ecclus. 7:34).

Like Augustine, Guerric thinks that the population of the future purgatory will be small.

Greatly influenced by Hugh of Saint-Victor,[8] the *Deflorationes sanctorum Patrum*, or *Anthology of the Fathers*, of Werner II, the abbot of Saint-Blaise (d. 1174), mentions purgatorial fire in the context of a sermon on the fall of Adam:

> After death, too, we are told, there is a purgatorial fire [*ignis quidam purgatorius*] which purges and cleanses those who have begun to purify themselves in this life but who have not finished their work.... These tortures are hard to endure, even if they are but of minor degree. Thus it is better to finish here the work that one is supposed to do. But if one has not finished it, provided he has begun, he should not despair, because "he shall be saved, yet so as by fire" (1 Cor. 3:10–15). Your crimes will burn in you until they are consumed. But you will be saved because the love of God has remained in you as your foundation."[9]

THE URBAN THEOLOGIANS

I shall have several occasions to speak of the school begun by that original theologian Gilbert Porreta (d. 1154), also known as Gilbert de la Porrée, the bishop of Poitiers, who, like his contemporary Abelard, had his difficulties with the Church. His commentary on Saint Paul has not been published, but a fragment of a commentary on the First Epistle to the Corinthians, which dates from shortly after 1150 and which interprets Gilbert's commentary without always being faithful to it, also takes up the theme of a purgation in this world to be completed after death by a purgation "in fire." This purgatorial fire, it is expressly stated, comes before the Last Judgment.[10]

Purgatorial fire was also discussed in the celebrated abbey of the canons regular of Saint-Victor, by the gates of Paris at the foot of the Sainte-Geneviève. By way of example, I might mention, besides the great Hugh of Saint-Victor, whose work is one of the most important adumbrations of the future Purgatory, Achard, the abbot of Saint-Victor from 1155 to 1161 and bishop of Avranches from 1161 until his death in 1170 or 1171. On the occasion of the church dedication, Achard prepared two sermons, of which the second concerns purgatory fire. In discussing the symbolism of the hammer and chisel, tools used in the building of the church, he says that the former can be interpreted as "the terror of eternal fire" and the latter as "the terror of purgatorial fire."[11]

VERNACULAR LITERATURE

The questions of the fate of the soul after death and of the nature of purgatorial fire also drew attention from outside ecclesiastical circles. Not only were these matters discussed in urban schools and preached in the monasteries; they were given wider currency by sermons of which we generally possess only Latin versions but which we know to have been delivered in the vulgar tongue when clerics addressed themselves to the laity.[12] Indeed, I should like to turn next to two texts in Old French for evidence of the "popularity" of purgatorial fire in the twelfth century.

The first of these is none other than a French translation of Gregory the Great's *Dialogues: Li Dialoge Gregoire lo Pape*, written in the dialect of the Liège region. In chapters 40 and 41 of book 4, which were discussed earlier, we find the expressions "li fous purgatoires" and "lo fou purgatoire" (purgatorial fire), "(lo) fou de la tribulation", and "(lo) fou de la purgation." The question raised by Peter at the end of chapter 40 is rendered as follows: "Ge voldroie ke l'om moi enseniast, se li fous purgatoires après la mort doit estre crue estre" (I should like to be taught whether I must believe that purgatorial fire after death exists). Gregory gives his answer in chapter 41, whose title is "se li fous purgatoires est après la mort" (Whether Purgatorial Fire Exists after Death).[13]

In a verse version of the *Dialogues*, in which the word "purgatoire" (purgation, purgatory) appears, we are reminded of Gregory's opinion that there is no "determinate place" for purgation but that each soul is purged after death in the place where it sinned during its lifetime:

> *Par ces countes de seint Gregorie*
> *Deit houme entendre qi purgatorie*
> *N'est pas en une lieu determinez*
> *Ou les almes seint tout peinez.*

(According to Saint Gregory there is no definite place of purgation in which all souls are punished.[14])

The other vernacular text I wish to cite is the early thirteenth-century French translation (which reproduces the original twelfth-century translation) of the *History of the Crusades in the Holy Land (Historia rerum in partibus transmarinis gestarum)* by Guillaume de Tyr, who died between 1180 and 1184. Chapter 16 of book 1 describes how the lower orders, the *menu peuple*, departed for the crusade:

> *Tant avoit de pecheours el monde qui avoient eslongnie la grace de Nostre Seigneur, que bien covenoit que Dex leur monstrat un adrecoer par ou il alassent en paradis, et leur donast un travail qui fust aussiut comme feus purgatoires devant la mort.*

In other words: "There were so many sinners in the world who had refused the grace of Our Lord, that it was fitting that God show them the straight and narrow way to Heaven, and that he set them a trial which would be like purgatorial fire before death." This text invokes the idea that a crusade is like a penance, different from the original idea of the crusade as an eschatological expedition. It alludes, moreover, to the notion of purgation of sins in this world before, not after, death. The purpose is to "bypass" any possible stay in "Purgatory" and go straight to Heaven. This was a first step down the road that led to the purely metaphorical interpretation of "purgatory on earth" in the thirteenth century, as we shall see.[15]

FOUR GREAT THEOLOGIANS AND FIRE: THE ELEMENTS OF A TREATISE ON THE END OF TIME

At this point I should like to pause for a moment, in order to go into some detail about four important clerics of the mid-twelfth century, whose work is at once the culmination of a long tradition and a point of departure for further developments—in relation to Purgatory as well as other subjects.

A Parisian Canon: Hugh of Saint-Victor

The first of these four figures was a Parisian canon, Hugh of Saint-Victor, who died in 1141. The second was an Italian monk, a learned expert in canon law who lived in Bologna, where he compiled a collection of legal texts which bears his name, the *Decretum* of Gratian, the fountainhead of the corpus of canon law. The third was a Cistercian, a man famous in his own time, Bernard of Clairvaux, who died in 1153. The fourth was an Italian who became bishop of Paris, Peter Lombard, who died in 1159–60. In the thirteenth century his *Sententiae* became the great manual of the universities.

According to Jean Longère, it was in this period that "the outlines of *De novissimis* [i.e., a systematic account of the end of time] began to take shape" with Hugh of Saint-Victor and Peter Lombard. Various remarks and treatises on the end of the world, the resurrection of the dead, the Last Judgment, and the fate of the soul were collected and organized. It was natural to include in these collections opinions as to the fate of the soul between the time of death and the last days of mankind.

Hugh of Saint-Victor may have taught the first course of systematic theology not directly based on a *lectio* of the Bible, that is, on a commentary on the Holy Scriptures.[16] In particular, two passages of his work are devoted to purgatorial fire. The first concerns a question "on the purgatorial fire of the righteous," which takes the First Epistle to the Corinthians as its point of departure. Purgatorial fire, according to Hugh, is reserved for those who will be saved, the elect. Even the saints, those who build of gold, silver, and precious gems, must pass through the fire, but they will suffer no harm. Rather, they will emerge from the fire even stronger than when they went in, just as clay emerges from the oven stronger and more solid than it was originally. For them, "the passage through the fire is a part of resurrection." Some people, Hugh tells us, claim that this fire is a place of punishment (*quemdam poenalem locum*) in which the souls of those who have built of wood, hay, and straw are placed after death in order to complete the penance that they began here below. Once this penance is complete, they are sent to rest until the day of judgment, at which time they will pass through the fire unharmed, particularly since the fire is said to be purgatorial not for men but only for heaven and earth, which will be purged and renovated by a flood of fire, just as they were purged and renovated once before by another Flood. To this opinion Hugh is hostile, however, for he believes that the fire of judgment will last as long as is necessary to purge the elect. Others believe that the purgatorial fire is nothing more than earthly tribulation. As for the fire of judgment, the godless shall not pass through it; rather, they will be carried by it down into the (infernal) abyss.[17]

In his great work, the *Summa on the Sacraments of the Christian Faith* (*Summa de sacramentis christianae fidei*), the first great treatise on the theology of the sacraments that developed during the twelfth century (furnishing a background to the inception of Purgatory that we would do well to keep in mind, as we shall see when we come to discuss penance), Hugh grappled with the problems of the other world. *De sacramentis* is structured historically: it is a history of salvation. The first part runs "from the beginning of the world to the Incarnation of the Word." The second extends from the Incarnation to the end and consummation of all things. It is in this second part that Hugh speaks of purgatorial punishments in the context of a discussion "of the dying, or the end of man." This chapter is preceded by a chapter on "confession, penance, and remission of sins" and a very short chapter on extreme unction and followed by the two final chapters of the treatise, one concerned with the end of the world and the other with "the century to come." Thus the discussion of purgatorial punishments is contained in a history of salvation that is both individual and collective, a history in which a discussion of confession and penance figures prominently. In chapter 4 of part 16, book 2, Hugh discusses the "places of punishment" (*loca poenarum*), after making clear his view that souls can indeed receive corporeal punishments after leaving the body. Hell is the place where these torments are inflicted, in contrast to Heaven, a place of joy and pleasure. "Just as God has prepared corporeal punishments for sinners who must be tormented," Hugh tells us, "so he has set aside corporeal places for these corporeal punishments. It is right and proper that the place of torment is down below and the place of joy up above, because sin weighs the soul down, whereas justice raises it up." Hugh adds that the place below, Hell, is located in the depths of the earth, but about such matters nothing certain can be said. Some maintain that an inextinguishable fire rages in Hell. Be that as it may, those who leave this life purged of their sins go directly to Heaven.

Hugh then turns to the question of purgatorial punishment. "Finally, there is another punishment after death, which is called purgatorial punishment. Those who leave this life with certain sins, even though they be righteous and destined to eternal life, are tortured there for a time in order to be purged. The place where this pain is suffered is not definitely fixed, although many instances in which afflicted souls have appeared suggest that the pain is endured in this world, and probably in the places where the sin was committed, as an abundance of evidence proves. It is hard to know whether these pains are inflicted in other places."

Hugh of Saint-Victor also wonders if souls that are wicked, but less wicked than the godless and the worst criminals, are not held in places of punishment before being consigned to the worst torments of Gehenna, and further, if souls that are good but encumbered by certain sins are not kept in special dwelling places until they are promoted to the joys of Heaven. In Hugh's opinion, the perfectly good (boni perfecti) certainly go straight to Heaven and the very wicked (valde mali) go straight to Hell. As for the imperfectly good (boni imperfecti), it is certain that in the period between death and judgment they undergo certain pains before tasting the joys to come. And as for the imperfectly wicked or less wicked (imperfecti sive minus mali), nothing certain can be said about the place where they may be biding their time pending the day of resurrection, when they will be sent to Hell forever.

Finally, there are purgatorial punishments in this world, and those on whom they are inflicted are not made worse by their trials but better: they profit by their suffering and mend their ways. On the matter of suffrages for the dead, Hugh cites Gregory the Great to the effect that, if the sins a person has committed before dying are not indissoluble, and if he has led a good life and is thus worthy of assistance after death, the eucharistic sacrifice may be of great aid.[18]

Hugh of Saint-Victor made no substantial progress on the question beyond what had already been said by Augustine and Gregory the Great, and like those two writers he stresses his belief in the reality of ghosts. But his words do reflect the strong tendency of the times to find a place or places (locus or loca) in which purgatorial pain could be suffered. Even if, in the end, he expresses ignorance or skepticism as to the existence of such places and chooses, along with Gregory the Great, the answer that was ultimately rejected, namely, that purgation occurs on earth in the place where the sin was committed, he does question his beliefs and does recognize that others have put forward different answers, believing that purgation takes place in specific places in the other world in the time between death and final judgment.

A Cistercian: Saint Bernard

Saint Bernard's views on the purging of sins are, I believe, different from those that have been imputed to him. For I am convinced, and I believe that the following pages will substantiate my conviction, that the major text on this subject that has been attributed to him is not his work. Indeed, I believe that it was written considerably after his death in 1153 (at least twenty years later, in fact).[19]

Bernard lays out his position very clearly in two sermons: there are, he says, places of purgation (*loca purgatoria*) in the other world. In a sermon for Saint Andrew's Day on the three kinds of goods he states: "It is justly said that the souls that suffer in these purgatory places [*in locis purgatoriis*] run hither and yon in dark and dirty places, since in this life they were not afraid to inhabit these places in thought." Later he adds this: "We confess not only that we sympathize with the dead and pray for them but also that we wish them the joy of hope. For if we must feel sorry about their suffering in purgatorial places [*in locis purgatoriis*], we must also rejoice at the approach of the moment when 'God shall wipe away all tears from their eyes; and there shall be no more death, neither sorrow, nor crying, neither shall there be any more pain: for the former things are passed away' (Rev. 21:4)."[20]

In another sermon, delivered at the funeral of Humbert, a monk of Clairvaux, in 1148, less than five years before his own death, Bernard did not utter the word "purgatory": indeed, he could not have done so, for the place did not yet exist. Instead he issued the following warning: "Know that, after this life, whatever debts have not been paid here below must be repaid a hundredfold, to the 'uttermost farthing' (Matt. 5:26) in the places of purgation [*in purgabilibus locis*]."[21]

In a third sermon, for Advent, Bernard goes into rather complicated detail about the "three hells." My reading of the text is as follows:

> The first hell is obligatory [*obligatorius*], for there one is re-
> quired to pay the uttermost farthing and so the punishment is
> without end. The second is purgatorial. The third, being volun-
> tary [*voluntarius*], is remissive, for punishment and crime [*et
> poena et culpa*] are often both remitted. In the second [*purga-
> tory*], although the punishment is sometimes remitted, the
> crime never is, but is purged. Happy hell of poverty in which
> Christ was born and raised and in which he lived, so long as he
> remained incarnate! Into this hell he not only descended once
> to rescue his own but "gave himself for our sins, that he might
> deliver us from this present evil world" (Gal. 1:4), to set us
> apart from the mass of the damned and group us together until
> we are rescued. In this hell there were three new girls, very
> young, ghosts of souls, adolescents carrying dulcimers pre-
> ceded by angels playing cymbals and followed by other angels

playing the cymbals of jubilation. In two hells it is the men who are tormented but in this one it is the demons. They pass through dry and arid places in search of rest, and never find it. They hover about the spirits of the faithful but are everywhere driven off by holy thoughts and prayers. Thus they cry, with good reason: "Jesus, art thou come hither to torment us before the time?" (Matt. 8:29).[22]

It seems to me that Bernard is here drawing a distinction between a lower hell, properly speaking called Gehenna, an intermediate hell, in which purgation takes place, and an upper hell, on the surface of the earth, which corresponds to the future Limbo or to the traditional bosom of Abraham, in which innocent souls rest in peace even before the final judgment while demons, who had expected a reprieve until Judgment Day, are already being tormented.

What we find in Bernard, then, is an attempt to give the other world a spatial dimension and to assert the existence of either a "purgatorial hell" or of "purgatorial places" (*loca purgatoria* or *purgabilia*). But these places are not named, and the geography of the other world remains quite vague.

Gratian of Bologna: Monk and Expert in Canon Law

The *Decretum* of Gratian, which dates from about 1140, is a case apart. There would be nothing novel in this assemblage of texts were it not for the way they are arranged and selected. In any case, the fact that canon law later took on such great importance, at the end of the twelfth and throughout the thirteenth century, makes it essential that we pause to examine the *Decretum*, which inaugurates the medieval corpus of canon law. And we should, while we are at it, take a brief look at Bologna, which was not only the birthplace of the academic corporation but also, in the twelfth century, a bustling intellectual capital and the leading center for the study of law.

For our purposes two chapters of the *Decretum* are of particular importance, 22 and 23 of question 2, *casus* 13 of part 2.[23] The first consists of an interpretation of the (or of a) letter (dating from about 732) from Pope Gregory II to Boniface, the apostle of Germany, which has already been discussed. The *Decretum* repeats the list of suffrages that had been accepted since the time of Augustine and Gregory the Great: "The souls of the dead are delivered in four ways: by the sacrifices of the priests [masses], by the prayers of the saints, by the alms of dear friends, and by the fasting of relatives."

Placed as it is in the *Decretum*, this text carries a great deal of weight; it lends legitimacy to the actions of the living on behalf of the dead, it recalls the primacy of eucharistic sacrifice, it underscores the need to rely on the mediation of the Church (i.e., the priests), it encourages the worship of saints, it fosters the circulation of property (or its diversion into the coffers of the Church) through alms, and it sets in sharp relief the special role of those near and dear to the deceased—family and friends, spiritual as well as carnal.

Chapter 23 reproduces chapters 109 and 110 of Augustine's *Enchiridion* (with one minor omission) under the following title: "Prior to the day of judgment the dead are aided by sacrifices [i.e., masses] and alms." This important message reads as follows:

> But during the time which intervenes between a man's death and resurrection at the last, men's souls are reserved in secret storehouses, at rest or in tribulation according to each soul's deserts, according to its lot in the flesh during life. Nor is there room for denial that the souls of the deceased obtain relief through the dutiful service of the friends who are alive, when the Mediator's sacrifice is offered for them or almsgiving is done in the Church. Such acts, however, are of advantage to those who during their life have deserved that such acts should be of advantage to them. For there is a certain manner of living, neither good enough to dispense with the need for these after death, nor bad enough to preclude their being of advantage to it after death; and there is a certain manner of living which is so established in goodness as to dispense with the need for them, as again there is one so established in evil as to be incapable of benefiting even from these when it has passed on from this life. At such times, then, as the sacrifices either of the altar or of any manner of alms are offered for all the baptized departed, on behalf of the very good they are thanksgivings, on behalf of the very bad they are propitiations, though they are no sort of consolation to the living. And in cases where they are of advantage, the advantage is either that they obtain complete remission, or at least that damnation itself becomes less intolerable.

I ask the reader to recall that this passage contains two things that stood in the way of Purgatory's inception. First, although Augustine does speak of "places" for the dead between death and resurrection, these are like holes or dungeon cells, receptacles (*receptacula*), not an area or space in the full sense of the word, and what is more, they are hidden (*abdita*), in both a material and a spiritual sense. In the material sense what is meant is that the souls cannot be questioned; they are difficult if not impossible to find. In the spiritual sense they represent a mystery, which according to some it is illicit, if not sacrilegious, to wish to penetrate. For all these reasons it proved difficult for a long time to conceive of Purgatory as a genuine location with a definite geography.

Second, recall that for Augustine there were four categories of dead souls: the entirely good (*valde boni*), the entirely wicked (*valde mali*), the not entirely wicked (*non valde mali*), and, implicitly, the not entirely good (*non valde boni*). Now, there are two possibilities: either Purgatory is set aside for the last category, which is implicit in Augustine's classification, or, more likely, it requires combining into one category the not entirely good and the not entirely bad.

Hence this text, which ultimately served as one of the pillars of Purgatory, for a time delayed progress toward that end. The "impediment of authority" is probably one of the reasons why canon law played such a small role in the inception of Purgatory.

A Secular Parisian Master: Bishop Peter Lombard

On Purgatory as on so many other problems, Peter Lombard, a Parisian master of Italian birth who became bishop of Paris in 1159 only to die in the following year, looked both to the past and to the future. In his *Sententiarum Libri Quatuor*, or *Sententiae*, as the four books of judgments compiled between 1155 and 1157 are commonly known, Peter's achievement was in part to summarize with force, clarity, and a synthetic spirit the opinions of his predecessors, from the Fathers to the theologians and canonists of the first half of the twelfth century: Hugh of Saint-Victor, Abelard, Gilbert Porreta, Gratian, etc. Beyond that, it was to produce a work that became, despite its failure to make any significantly original contribution, a "classic for the following centuries." According to J. de Ghellinck, Peter Lombard's *Sententiae* constitute the "central focus" of twelfth-century theology.

Peter's most important opinions on the purgation of sins in the hereafter are found in two different places in his work, "distinctions" 21 and 45 of book 4 of the *Sententiae*. Distinction 21 figures in a discussion of the sacraments. After treating baptism, confirmation, and the Eucharist, Peter turns to a lengthy treatment of penance, which ends with a chapter on final penance and then (in chapter 21) with the distinction devoted to "the sins which are remitted after this life." At the very end of the work comes distinction 45, which deals with "the various receptacles of souls" as the end of time unfolds in the interval between the resurrection and the Last Judgment. Paradoxically, these texts, commentary on which shaped the doctrine of the great thirteenth-century scholastics, do not form a coherent whole. The future Purgatory would relate to both penance and individual death on the one hand and to the *novissima* ("last things") on the other hand. In space and time Purgatory would occupy the middle ground between the two. Peter Lombard etched, as it were, a negative image of the place that Purgatory was to occupy.

In distinction 21 he asks if some sins are remitted after death. After invoking the authority of Matthew 12:32 and 1 Corinthians 3:10–15 and discussing Augustine's hesitant interpretation of the passage from Paul (*City of God* 21.26), Peter gives his own opinion, which is clear-cut: the passage from Paul "insinuates overtly that those who build of wood, hay, and straw carry with them flammable structures, that is to say, venial sins, which must ultimately be consumed in purgatorial fire." Wood, hay, and straw stand in hierarchical order, representing venial sins of varying degrees of importance. Depending on the magnitude of the sin, the soul will be purged more or less quickly. Without adding anything new to what has gone before, Peter's comments help to clarify matters: some sins can be purged between death and judgment, namely, the venial sins, and the duration of purgatorial punishment (by fire) varies from one case to another.

Distinction 45 is even more important. It deals with the "receptacles of souls" and with suffrages for the dead. On the subject of receptacles Peter is content to cite from Augustine, particularly from the *Enchiridion*, where Augustine discusses "hidden receptacles." On the question of suffrages Peter also subscribes to Augustine's opinions. Masses and alms can be of service to the dead, but only if the persons have proved themselves worthy of such help in this life. He mentions Augustine's three categories, the entirely good (*valde boni*), the not entirely wicked (*non valde mali*), and the entirely wicked (*valde mali*). The corresponding suffrages of the Church are: thanksgiving, atonement, and mere consolation for the living relatives. But Peter also adds two additional categories derived from the Augustinian scheme: the medium good (*mediocriter boni*), for whom suffrages lead to full absolution, and the medium bad (*mediocriter mali*), for whom they lead to a mitigation of the punishment. He then gives two examples of the "medium good" (chapters 4 and 5 of distinction 45). Finally, Peter takes up a suggestion of Augustine concerning the entirely wicked: even here it is possible for God to distinguish between varying degrees of wickedness. Even though the wicked soul must remain in Hell for all eternity, God can choose to mitigate its suffering.[24] Peter thus takes a significant step: he sets the not entirely wicked apart from the entirely wicked and places them alongside the not entirely good, but still as a distinct category. What he begins is thus a move away from the extremes, a regrouping toward the center, the consequences of which we shall see shortly.

Lesser Contributors

Other works, some of them written after 1200 and thus after the introduction, between 1170 and 1200, of the word "purgatory" (*purgatorium*), even without using this word manifest the efforts of religious thinkers in the second half of the twelfth century to assign a place to purgation after death and to characterize the process of purgation in the other world. Here are a few examples.

Robert Pullus (or Pulleyn), who was a cardinal in 1134, became chancellor of the Roman Catholic Church in 1145, and died around 1146, considers the geography of the other world in book 4 of his *Sententiae*. After asserting that Hell is a place (*infernus . . . locus est*), he asks where purgatorial punishments take place. The ancients spent a certain period of time in the underworld and then went to the bosom of Abraham, "that is, to an upper region, in which tranquillity reigned." In our era, in other words, after the coming of Jesus Christ, those souls in which something remains that needs to be burned out after death are examined by purgatorial pains (*purgatoriis poenis*) and then go into the presence of Christ, i.e., to Paradise. These pains are inflicted by a fire, purgatorial fire (*ignis purgatorius*), which is fiercer than earthly tribulation but not as bad as infernal torment (*inter nostras et inferorum poenas medias*). But on this point Robert Pullus shows himself to have been quite perplexed:

> But where does this correction take place? Is it in Heaven? Is it in Hell? Heaven does not seem appropriate to tribulation, but torture does not seem appropriate to correction, particularly not in our time. For if Heaven is appropriate for the good alone, is not Hell appropriate only for the wicked? And if evil is entirely banished from Heaven, how is it that Hell can accept some good? Just as God made Heaven for the perfect only, so it seems that Gehenna is reserved for the godless alone; the latter is the prison of the guilty and the former the kingdom of souls. Where are those who are supposed to do penance after death? In purgatorial places. Where are those places? I do not yet know.[25] How long do they stay there? Until satisfaction is given [i.e., until their faults are expiated].

Robert Pullus offers the further opinion that, in our time, souls, once purged, leave the purgatorial places, which are located outside Hell, and go to Heaven, just as in ancient times purged souls left their purgatorial places, which were in Hell, to seek refreshment in the bosom of Abraham.[26] He concludes, moreover, with a discussion of the significance of Christ's descent into Hell.[27]

Pullus's treatment is a noteworthy attempt to introduce some semblance of order into the geography of the other world as well as to broaden eschatology to include historical and analogical dimensions. He is obsessed by the need to localize, to answer the question, "*Ubi sunt?* Where does it all happen?" But the upshot of all his curiosity is a respectful disclaimer of any knowledge of the secrets that shroud these places of mystery. Still, the discussion highlights the new expression "*in purgatoriis*," with "*locis*" understood: in purgatorial (places). All that was needed now was for the plural to be changed to the singular and the adjective to be changed to a noun, and Purgatory would be born.

The Italian Ugo of Pisa did not go this far in his book *On the Soul outside the Body (Liber de anima corpore exuta)*, written shortly after 1150. He cites Gregory the Great and the story of the bishop Felix encountering a ghost in the baths but draws no conclusions regarding the site of purgation. In a passage strikingly reminiscent of Hugh of Saint-

Victor, Ugo discusses the Last Judgment and the river of fire that will one day inundate heaven and earth and that he compares to the Flood. This fire will consume the wicked but the good will pass through it without harm. An exemplar of archaic modes of thought, Ugo also maintains that the offering of the consecrated host may be of service "to the sleeping."[28]

Robert of Melun (d. 1167), Abelard's successor at the School of Sainte-Geneviève in Paris, prepared his *Questions on the Epistles of Saint Paul* between 1145 and 1155. Following Augustine, he points out that purgatorial pains will be more terrible than any earthly pain, and he stresses that they will be felt in the future, that is, after this life.[29]

By contrast, Peter of Celle is much closer to Purgatory. First abbot of Saint-Pierre of Celle, near Troyes, then of Saint-Rémi of Reims, and finally John of Salisbury's successor as bishop of Chartres, where he died in 1182, Peter composed a treatise on monastic life entitled *The Cloister School (De disciplina claustrali)* in 1179. Here he asks the question, Where does the soul reside after death? "O soul separated from the body, where do you live? In Heaven? In Paradise? In purgatorial fire? In Hell? If it is in Heaven, you are blessed along with the angels. If it is in Paradise, you are safe, far from the miseries of this world. If it is in purgatorial fire, you are tormented by pains but in the meanwhile awaiting liberation. If it is in Hell, abandoning all hope, you are awaiting not mercy but truth and severity."[30] This passage is very clearly marked by the developments that would quickly lead to the invention of purgatory. Purgatorial fire is taken to be a place, just as Heaven, Paradise, and Hell are places.

But the expression *in purgatoriis*, in purgatorial (places understood) occurs most commonly at the end of the century, or perhaps even at the beginning of the next century, to indicate the search for a specific locale, a serach that has not yet found quite the right form or word. In a curious dialogue, which dates from some time between 1180 and 1195, the *Conflictus Helveticus de limbo Patrum*, an exchange of letters between Burchard of Saint-Johann, the first abbot of the Benedictine monastery St. Johann im Thurtale, and Hugo, the abbot of another Benedictine monastery, the All Saints Monastery at Schaffhouse, the two adversaries discuss the fate of the soul in the period prior to Christ's descent into Hell. Burchard argues that many souls went to Heaven even before Christ's descent, as attested by the New Testament's allusion to the bosom of Abraham (Luke 16:22), which is identified with peace (Wis. 3:3), repose (Augustine), and the "secret repose of the Father" (Gregory the Great). Hugo, together with most others who took part in the discussion, asserts that it was impossible, because of original sin, for any soul to go to the bosom of Abraham or to Paradise before Christ's descent into Hell.

In the course of the dialogue Burchard gives a good definition of Purgatory, which is still designated by the plural, *in purgatoriis*: "There are," he says, "three kinds of Church. One wages its battles on earth, another awaits its reward in purgatory [purgatories], and still another triumphs with the angels in the heavens."[31] Hell is forgotten in this remarkable account of a tripartite church, in which the church of the purged, defined as a church of waiting, is situated between heaven and earth. This passage contains two important bits of evidence: it shows not only that progress has been made toward a spatial conceptualization of Purgatory but also that a crucial stage in the evolution of the concept has been reached. Here we see a conception of Purgatory different from the one that eventually triumphed, a less infernal conception, but one that might have emerged victorious from the conflict. It is rather similar to the conception of Raoul Ardent, a twelfth-century author about whom little is known, not even the dates of his life. In his *Homilies*, which probably date from the end of the century, he speaks of souls in purgatory (purgatories): "If for a limited period of time they undergo correction in purgatory [purgatories], already they rest in the certain hope of repose to come."[32] Purgatory as hope—a theme we will meet again.

PARISIAN DEVELOPMENTS

To conclude this chapter I shall turn now to the work of two eminent Parisian masters and chancellors. Pierre de Poitiers (d. 1205), in the *Five Books of Judgments* (*Sententiae*) that he wrote prior to 1170, discusses the following question: "Suppose someone reasons as follows: Take two men. One is guilty of a mortal sin and a venial sin, while the other is guilty only of a venial sin equal to the venial sin of the other. They will be punished unequally, because one will be punished eternally and the other only in purgatory [*in purgatoriis*], and any purgatorial punishment [*poena purgatoria*] will be inferior to any eternal punishment. But the first man does not deserve to be punished more for his venial sin than the second for his. Hence the first man is being treated unjustly. This is false. Both of these men, who are guilty of equal venial sins, deserve to be punished equally for those sins, but one will be punished in this life, and the other in purgatorial fire [*in igne purgatorio*], and any pain suffered here below is inferior to any pain suffered in purgatorial fire (*ignis purgatorii*); thus the second man will be treated unjustly."[33]

This analysis is worthy of note: on the eve of Purgatory's inception, it gathers together all of the elements of the purgatorial lexicon, brings out the connection between purgatory and venial sins, uses the expression *in purgatoriis*, with its spatial connotations, and manifests, to an almost maniacal degree, a concern with penitential bookkeeping that is typical of thirteenth-century practices in regard to Purgatory.

In an undated sermon in commemoration of the dead, Praepositivus of Cremona (d. 1210), also chancellor of Paris, uses the expression *in purgatoriis*: "Since some people are cleansed in purgatory [purgatories], we must concern ourselves with those who are more unworthy today, by praying for them, and by making offerings and giving alms."[34] Here is evidence of the connection between the commemoration of the dead on November 2, inaugurated by Cluny in the previous century, and the newly emergent Purgatory: in Purgatory a liturgical chain was forged binding the dead to the living.

FIVE
"Locus Purgatorius"
A Place for Purgation

B ROADLY speaking, in the mid-twelfth century, fire not only evoked a place but was the spatial embodiment of the purgative phase through which certain souls passed after death. But this characterization of a place of purgation proved insufficient. Here I must beg the reader's indulgence, for it will be necessary to resolve certain technical problems before we can proceed, problems raised by the fact that our research will now focus on a number of specific places and groups where Christian doctrine was actively being elaborated in the twelfth century. Some detail is therefore necessary, but I shall try to avoid overwhelming those readers who are willing to bear with me.

Specifically, now that we have come to the moment in time when Purgatory is about to emerge as a specific place and when the noun *purgatorium*, purgatory, is about to enter the lexicon, it becomes necessary to deal with problems of authenticity and dating.[1]

1170–80: AUTHORS AND DATES

In the past, and in some cases even today, scholars have been misled by texts falsely attributed to ecclesiastical authors who died prior to 1170 and have thus been led to believe that Purgatory's inception occurred earlier than it actually did. I shall presently discuss a text attributed to Peter Damian, who died in 1072, and another attributed to Saint Bernard, who died in 1153. But first I want to consider an excerpt from a sermon which, until the end of the nineteenth century, was considered to be the work of Hildebert of Lavardin, bishop of Le Mans and one of the leading representatives of the "poetic renaissance" of the twelfth century in the Loire region, who died in 1133.

The sermon in question was prepared for the dedication of a church and takes for its theme a verse of Psalm 122:3 (i.e., Psalm 121:3 in the earlier numbering): "Jerusalem is builded as a city that is compact together." In a comparison that makes one feel the force of the extraordinary flourishing of architecture in the eleventh and twelfth centuries, the author of the sermon says the following:

In the building of a city three elements concur: first, with violence stones are drawn out of the quarry, with hammers and bars of iron and with much human sweat and labor; then with the burin, the double axe, and the rule they are polished, cut to measure, and squared; and third they are set in place by the artist's hand. In the same way, in the building of the heavenly Jerusalem three phases are to be distinguished: the separation, the cleansing, and the "setting." The separation is violent, the cleansing purgatorial, the setting eternal. In the first phase man is in anguish and affliction; in the second he is patient and expectant; in the third he is in glory and exultation. In the first phase man is sifted like grain, in the second examined like silver; in the third he is placed in the treasury.[2]

The rest of the sermon tries to clarify this image with the help of several passages from the Bible, the first of which is 1 Corinthians 3:10–15. The first phase is death, the separation of the soul from the body; the second is the passage through Purgatory; and the third is the entry into Paradise. In regard to the second phase, the author makes clear that it is those who pass through the fire with wood, hay, and straw who are cleansed in purgatory (*in purgatorio*)—"purgatory" figures as a noun in the text. Purgatory exists—it is the first of the places in which the elect reside temporarily before reaching the promised paradise. For the author of the sermon is concerned only with the itinerary of the elect; the damned, who go directly to Hell, are not discussed. He then develops an idea of great importance. The liturgical triduum of the vigil of All Saints, All Saints' Day, and the Commemoration of the Dead corresponds to the three phases of the itinerary of the elect after death. Now, it must be said that this analogy requires a certain chronological agility if it is to hold. For if Halloween, a fast day, corresponds to the first phase, separation, the order of the two remaining days must be inverted if the symbolism is to make sense. It is the third day, the commemoration of the dead, that corresponds to Purgatory: "The third day is the commemoration of the dead, whose purpose is to see that those who are cleansed in Purgatory obtain either complete absolution or else a mitigation of their penalty."[3] Again the expression "*in purgatorio*" is used. Finally, we learn that the second day is "the solemn day, the symbol of the superabundance of joy."

This sermon, once attributed to Hildebert of Lavardin, was restored in 1888 to its true author, known variously as Peter Comestor or Peter Manducator (or, in French, Pierre le Mangeur), that is, Peter the Eater, and this attribution has been upheld by recent research.[4] Peter Comestor, a disciple of Peter Lombard, owes his picturesque epithet to the fact that, according to his contemporaries, he was a great devourer of books. After becoming chancellor of the Church in Paris, he taught at the school of

Notre-Dame, after Peter Lombard was made a bishop in 1159, and died some twenty years later, probably in 1178 or 1179. He was one of the first, if not the first, to give a gloss or commentary on Peter Lombard's *Sententiae*. A considerable volume of his work has survived. His sermons are difficult to date, but a treatise *On the Sacraments* (*De sacramentis*) in which Purgatory is discussed has been assigned to the period 1165–70.

In this treatise Peter Comestor discusses the question of penance and notes first of all that the purgation of the elect takes place in purgatorial fire (*in igne purgatorio*) more or less quickly, depending on the sin and the penance. He invokes Augustine (*Enchiridion* 69) as his authority. He then turns to the question whether penance that has not been completed in this life can be completed in the next. Being merciful, God pardons sinners who do not deserve the cruelest of punishments, eternal pain. But since he is also just, he does not allow sin to go unpunished. Sin must be punished either by man or by God. But the contrition of the heart may be so great in some cases that, even though penance has not been completed here below, the soul can be spared by purgatorial fire (*immunis erit ab igne purgatorio*). On the other hand, whoever dies unrepentant must be punished eternally. Peter also considers the following question: if, owing to the priest's negligence or ignorance, the penance a man receives is insufficient for the gravity of his sins, is it enough if he completes this penance or can God inflict an additional penalty on him in purgatorial fire (*in igne purgatorio*)? Here again, according to Peter Comestor, the answer depends on contrition. With enough contrition, no additional punishment is necessary, but the judgment is God's to make. Then comes a question with a more direct bearing on Purgatory: "What is purgatorial fire and who must pass through it?" (*Quid est ignis purgatorius, et qui sint transituri per eum?*) Peter answers that, according to some authorities, it is a "material" fire, not an "elementary" fire or a fire for which wood serves as a fuel, but a fire existing in the sublunary world that will disappear along with other transitory things after the day of judgment. According to other authorities, the fire is nothing other than the pain itself and is called fire only because it burns like fire and lasts for a certain period of time. Furthermore, in order that it not be confused with the other kind of punishment, destructive and eternal, it is called "purgatorial" fire, i.e., a fire that does not destroy but rather purges through temporary rather than eternal suffering. In any case, whatever this fire may be, Peter adds, we must believe that some, though not all, of the faithful pass through it, namely, those who have not completed their penance in this life. But some suffer more than others, and some are delivered from the fire sooner than others, depending on the degree of sin and repentance and the intensity of contrition. According to some, only the perfectly good escape the fire of purgation, because, even though no one can be entirely free of venial sins, in the perfectly good these sins can be consumed by the fervor of love (*fervor caritatis*).[5]

The evidence of these texts admits of two possible explanations. Either the text of the first sermon was revised after the death of Peter Comestor by the scribes who prepared the manuscripts, or else Peter himself did not speak of purgatory in the nominative but rather used the traditional expression, "in purgatorial fire," *in igne purgatorio*. All that is needed is the addition of the short word *igne* (which might have been struck out in the preparation of the manuscript; see note 4 and appendix 2). In this case Peter would merely be one more precursor of the imminent emergence of Purgatory, and he would retain his importance as the man who established the direct link between what was soon to be Purgatory and the liturgy of early November. My own view, however, is that it is more likely that Peter did indeed employ the noun *purgatorium* and that he was therefore if not the inventor, then at least one of the earliest users, of a neologism related to what I consider to be a revolutionary change in ideas concerning the geography of the other world. Apart from the age of the manuscripts, there are two bits of evidence that tend to support this hypothesis. At the end of his life Peter Comestor occupied a central place in the Parisian intelligentsia. I am in no doubt whatever that this was the milieu in which Purgatory was born and, more specifically, that the birth took place at the school of Notre-Dame of Paris. Furthermore, Peter has been called "one of the most original minds" of his day (Hauréau). This intellectual, neglected by scholars and relatively obscure, may have played an innovative role in an area where his master, Peter Lombard, posed the problems in such a way as to allow new treatment. What I am suggesting is this: that before 1170 Peter used the then current expression of "purgatorial fire," and that, as his ideas developed between 1170 and his death in 1178 or 1179, he used the neologism "*purgatorium*," which, on this view of the matter, must have been introduced in the decade 1170–80. This would accord well with other evidence which, without being absolutely convincing, tends toward the same conclusion. Before turning to an examination of this evidence, I want to round out the discussion of Peter's ideas on the time between death and resurrection by mentioning a text in which he discusses the bosom of Abraham.

The text in question is drawn from the most celebrated of Peter's works, the one to which he owed his fame during his own lifetime and throughout the remainder of the Middle Ages: the *Historia Scholastica*. In chapter 113 of that work he recounts and comments on the story of Lazarus and the rich man (Luke 16): "Lazarus," Peter writes, "was placed in the bosom of Abraham. He was actually in the upper reaches of the infernal place [*in superiori margine inferni locus*], into which a little light penetrated and where there was no material suffering. Here the souls of the predestined remained until Christ's descent into the underworld. This place, because of the calm that reigned there, was called the bosom of Abraham, by analogy with the calm of the maternal bosom. It was named after Abraham because it was the first way of the faith [*prima credendi via*]."[6]

This is a "historical" definition of the bosom of Abraham, which situates it between the time of the patriarchs and the time of Christ's descent into Hell. Just as Christ had sealed off Hell, the men of the Middle Ages were preparing to seal off the bosom of Abraham, even though the New Testament had perpetuated its existence. From this time forward the intermediate space and time were to be occupied by Purgatory alone, and when the need was felt for something like the bosom of Abraham as a place set aside for righteous souls who predated Christ and for infants who died without benefit of baptism, men now turned to two ancillary regions of the other world: the Limbo of the fathers and the Limbo of infants.

The second (or, chronologically speaking, possibly the first) theologian to speak of Purgatory as such is properly known as Odo of Ourscamp (though he is sometimes still called Eudes de Soissons).[7] He was one of the most important masters of the period. Following in the wake of Peter Lombard, of whom he may have been either a disciple or, as some believe, an adversary, Odo had a very active school which continued to function after his death. He played a crucial role in advancing the *quaestio*, a typical scholastic form that he was the first to develop to the full: "a veritable dispute in which the kinds [*genres*] were divided between two distinct individuals" (Landgraf). After serving as master of theology at the school of Notre-Dame of Paris, Odo of Ourscamp retired at the end of his life to the Cistercian abbey at Ourscamp (in Aisne), where he died in 1171. His pupils published his *Quaestiones* as separate works.

It is in one of these anthologies attributed to Odo of Ourscamp that we encounter the noun "Purgatory" in a *quaestio On the Soul in Purgatory* (*De anima in Purgatorio*): "The soul separated from the body enters immediately into purgatory [*intrat purgatorium statim*]; there it is purged, and thus benefits. Contrary opinion: it undergoes this punishment against its will; there it does not benefit from it."

This is followed by arguments concerning the merits that may or may not be acquired by undergoing this punishment. Then comes the resolution: "It is true that certain souls, when they separate themselves from the body, enter immediately into a purgatorial fire [*statim intrant purgatorium quemdam ignem*], but they are not all purged there; only certain ones are purged. All that enter there are punished. Thus it would be better to call this fire punitive [*punitorius*] than purgatorial [*purgatorius*], but it has received the more noble name. Among the souls that enter there some are purged and punished, others merely punished."

The souls that are purged as well as punished are those that have brought with them wood, hay, and straw. The others are those that have not fully repented of their venial sins, whether voluntarily or involuntarily, and those who, surprised by death, have not confessed such sins. The souls that are merely punished are those that, after confessing and repenting of all their sins, have died without completing the penance prescribed by the priest. They are not purged, for none of their sins are remitted, unless the word "purged" is interpreted broadly as synonymous with being delivered from the punishment due. In the narrow sense "purged" applies only to someone whose sin is remitted. Hence those who are medium good also go immediately to Purgatory (*hi ergo qui sunt mediocriter boni, statim intrant purgatorium*).

The interlocutor revives the discussion by asking the following question: "If, to a dying man who repents of all his sins, the priest says: I absolve thee of all the penalty due, even that which thou shouldst undergo in Purgatory [*in purgatorio*], will he be punished in Purgatory anyway?"

The master answers as follows: "That is the kind of question which God can answer better [than I can]. All that I can say is that the priest should use good judgment." But he adds a very revealing sentence: "Since this fire is a material pain, it is in a place. But where this place is located is a question I shall leave unanswered."[8]

What is striking about this text is the incongruousness of the vocabulary, to say nothing of the ideas. Sometimes the discussion is about purgatory, other times about purgatorial fire. Purgatory is said to be a specific place, which is either named or adduced as the location in which the fire is found. And the whole discussion ends with a confession of ignorance as to the location of this place.

These findings confirm the view of A. M. Landgraf, that the *quaestiones* of this era, and particularly those attributed to Odo of Ourscamp, are in fact compilations of *quaestiones* from several authors, of which the attributions are in general "fantastic" and hard to verify.[9]

Let me suggest a plausible hypothesis: that the *quaestiones* attributed to Odo of Ourscamp were based on notes taken during courses given by him but that their form (and vocabulary) was subject to revision and that ideas not due to him were introduced when the manuscripts were prepared, probably between 1171, when Odo died, and 1190 or so, perhaps even in the decade 1171–80. Where Odo still speaks of purgatorial fire, his students are already speaking of Purgatory. That Purgatory is a place is taken for granted, but its location is still in doubt. The expression *mediocriter boni*, which probably comes from Peter Lombard, also reveals another aspect of the system.

A Counterfeit Purgatory

The time has now come to turn our attention to the two texts that pose the thorniest problems of attribution and dating. One of these was formerly attributed to Saint Peter Damian, the celebrated hermit and Italian cardinal of the first half of the eleventh century, but this untenable attribution has been recognized as false by recent students of Damian's life and works.[10] The other is a sermon that has been attributed to Saint Bernard, who died in 1153. But as Dom Jean Leclercq and Henri Rochais, the learned editors of the most recent edition of Bernard's complete works, candidly admit while standing by this attribution, the problems associated with the *Sermones de diversis*, the collection in which this particular text is found, make it impossible to be as certain about its authenticity as for other collections of Bernard's sermons. I am convinced that the sermon in question is not the work of Saint Bernard.[11] Even if the substance of the sermon is authentic, the form has certainly been altered in large part. Not only is it impossible, in my view, to speak of Purgatory as a place denoted by a noun before 1153; but I am even more dubious that, in the first half of the twelfth century, which as we have seen was a time of considerable uncertainty as to the structure of the other world, it would have been possible to advance a tripartite description of the other world as fully developed as the one found here: "There are three places to which the souls of the dead are destined, in accordance with their respective merits: hell, purgatory, and heaven."

Before speculating any further, let us examine the texts. The theme of these two sermons is that there are five regions in the natural and supernatural world. The first region is that of *dissimilitudio*, or dissimilarity between man and God, who made man in his image, like himself, though man then departed from that image through original sin. This region is of course the terrestrial world. The second region is the paradise of the cloister. "In truth, the cloister is a paradise" is one of many phrases repeated verbatim in both sermons. This exaltation of the monastic life makes the cloister a sort of appendage of the next world situated in this one.

The third region is that of expiation. Included within it are three different sites, each associated with souls of varying degrees of merit. These places are not designated by the same terms in both sermons, though it is the same places that are being discussed. In the sermon of the pseudo-Peter Damian they are called heaven, the infernal places, and the purgatorial places (*caelum*, *loca gehennalia*, *loca purgatoria*). In the sermon of the pseudo-Bernard, as we saw earlier, the three places, which are listed in a different order, are hell, purgatory, and heaven (*infernus*, *purgatorium*, and *caelum*).

The fourth region is Gehenna. What is the difference between this region and the lower part of the third region? This is not explained very clearly in either of the two sermons. But it would appear that the explanations that are given are contradictory. In the sermon of pseudo-Peter Damian, the infernal places of the third region are apparently intended for those sinners who died in a state of mortal sin, and the fourth infernal region is the dwelling place of the godless. In the sermon of pseudo-Bernard, on the other hand, the hell of the third region is explicitly said to be reserved for the godless, while the fourth region, also infernal, is intended for the devil and his (wicked) angels and for the men who resemble them, that is, the criminals and the vicious (*scelerati et vitiosi*).

The fifth and final region, according to pseudo-Bernard, is that of the supracelestial paradise in which the blessed gaze directly upon the Holy Trinity. According to pseudo-Peter Damian, it is the city of the Great King.

While the analogies between the two texts are substantial, the variations are also noteworthy. Rather than unduly tax the reader who has followed me this far, I shall confine my attention to the description of just one of the five regions, the third, that which contains our Purgatory, and compare the two texts side by side:

Pseudo-Peter Damian

Having left the world and the chosen way of life [the cloister], enter then into the third region, which is the region of expiation. In this region the benevolent Father examines his sons tarnished by corrosion, as one examines silver; he leads the way through fire and water toward refreshment [*refrigerium*, Psalm 65]. There are three different places, and souls are distributed among them according to their deserts. To heaven, immediately, fly those who have used the dwelling place of the body as a prison, who have preserved the human substance pure and free of taint. By contrast, those who until the moment of death committed acts worthy of death are sent without mercy to infernal places. Those who are neither one nor the other but between the two, who have committed mortal sins but who, as death drew near, began their penance but did not complete it, are not worthy of going immediately to the place of joy, nor do they deserve to burn forever, so they are assigned to purgatorial places, where they are scourged, but not to the point of

Pseudo-Bernard

The third region is the region of expiation. There are three places among which the souls of the dead are distributed according to their various deserts: hell, purgatory, heaven. Those who are in hell cannot be redeemed, for in hell there is no redemption. Those who are in purgatory are awaiting redemption but must first be tortured, whether by the heat of fire or by the rigors of cold or by some other harsh punishment. Those who are in heaven rejoice in the joyful vision of God, brothers of Christ in nature, co-inheritors in glory, alike one another in eternal happiness. As the first do not deserve to be redeemed and the third have no need of redemption, we have only to go among the middle group, out of compassion, having been joined to them by humanity. I shall go into that region and I shall see that great vision (Ex. 3:3) by which the pious Father, in order to glorify his sons, abandons them to the tempter, not to be killed but to be purged; not out of anger but out of mercy; not for their destruction but for their instruction, so that henceforth they insensibility [? *insipientia*], before being released and transferred to the kingdom. For those who are in heaven there is no need to pray, for it is to them that we pray, and not for them. For those who are in hell prayer is useless, because the gates of mercy are closed to them and the hope of salvation forbidden. On the other hand, for those who undergo correction in purgatorial places, we must be careful to pray and to help by sacrifice [i.e., in the mass, *sacrificio singulari*] so that the benevolent Father will soon transform their penance into satisfaction, and their satisfaction into glorification. Run to them, then, with an intimate feeling of piety and take compassion with thee as thy baggage.

may be not vessels of wrath fitted to destruction but vessels of mercy which he had already prepared unto glory (Rom. 9:22–23). I shall therefore rouse myself to help them: I shall question by my moans, I shall implore by my sighs, I shall intercede by my prayers, I shall satisfy by sacrifice [in the mass, *sacrificio singulari*] so that if by chance the Lord looks upon them and judges (Ex. 5:21) he shall change toil into rest, misery into glory, blows into crowns. By these devotions and others like them their penance shall be shortened, their toil ended, their pain destroyed. Go, then, faithful soul, and pass through the region of expiation; see what goes on there and in this commerce take compassion with thee as thy baggage.

What is most striking about these texts, despite certain differences between them, is the analogy of thought and structure, further reinforced by the occurrence of a number of identical expressions. One of the major differences is that pseudo-Peter Damian uses the phrase *loca purgatoria* (purgatorial places), whereas pseudo-Bernard uses the noun *purgatorium*.

One way to explain the similarity would of course be to assume that the texts were written by different authors but that both authors were inspired by the same source, or that one influenced the other (pseudo-Peter most likely influencing pseudo-Bernard in this case). This is not my view of the matter, however. The experts in the work of Peter Damian have suggested that the author of the sermon falsely attributed to him may have been Nicolas of Clairvaux, who was known as a "skillful forger" (*gerissen Fälscher*, in the words of F. Dressler). Now, Nicolas was Bernard's secretary, and he is known to have forged a number of texts imputed to Bernard. The nineteen sermons falsely attributed to Peter Damian were found originally in a manuscript in the Vatican Library, in which they appear alongside sermons by Bernard (or at least attributed to him). It is true that sermon 42 does not figure in this collection, but the coexistence of these two groups of sermons is disconcerting. I suspect that Nicolas of Clairvaux was the author of both sermons, and that, ingenious counterfeiter that he was, he made one a pastiche of Peter Damian, the other a pastiche of Saint Bernard.[12]

If the two sermons are not the work of the illustrious saints to whom they have been attributed, they are nevertheless excellent, and in this case trustworthy, evidence of the birth of Purgatory and the development of a tripartite division of the other world into Heaven, Purgatory, and Hell. It may be that the sermon by pseudo-Peter Damian was composed first and this is why the words *loca purgatoria* are used, whereas that by pseudo-Saint Bernard was written after Purgatory (*purgatorium*) had come into being. Or it may be, as I have suggested, that both sermons are the work of a single counterfeiter who probably took his inspiration from genuine works of the two authors he was imitating, perhaps even from one of Bernard's drafts, and that he used whatever vocabulary seemed to him most appropriate to the author he sought to counterfeit, even though *loca purgatoria* was not a phrase in use in the first half of the eleventh century, nor was *purgatorium* in use in the first half of the twelfth. That this forger was Nicolas of Clairvaux is well within the realm of possibility, chronologically speaking. The two earliest manuscripts in which pseudo-Bernard's sermon and the word *purgatorium* are found were probably copied at the end of the third quarter of the twelfth century.[13] Nicolas of Clairvaux died sometime after 1176. This again suggests that the first use of the term occurred in the decade 1170–80.

Whether the author of the sermon attributed to Bernard merely reworked one of the saint's genuine sermons or forged it from beginning to end, his work tends in the same direction as the great Cistercian's. For Bernard in fact did conceive of the other world largely in spatial terms. In the fourth sermon for the dedication of a church, "On the Threefold Dwelling," he offers this effusive passage on the subject of Paradise: "O marvelous Mansion, preferable to cherished tents, to desirable courts! . . . In the tents one moans in penance; in the courts one tastes joy; in thee one is heaped with glory."[14]

PURGATORY'S FIRST VISITORS: BERNARD

By an irony of history, Saint Bernard, Purgatory's putative father, may not have been its real "inventor," but he does seem to have been the first individual known to have benefited from belief in this new place. A letter from Nicolas of Saint-Alban to Peter of Celle, which must have been written prior to the latter's death in 1181, probably in 1180 or 1181, asserts that Saint Bernard passed briefly through Purgatory before entering Paradise. Why did this saint have to undergo purgation? Though greatly devoted to Mary, Bernard was hostile to the notion of her Immaculate Conception. The proponents of that doctrine appealed to the imagination of their audience and attempted to discredit their adversaries by maintaining that, for this mild error, the abbot of Clairvaux was (benignly) punished. In the thirteenth century the theme of celebrated men passing through Purgatory became commonplace. Bernard seems to have been the first of a long line. Philip Augustus, king of France from 1180 to 1223, was the first ruler of France to pass through Purgatory.

Saint Bernard, who was certainly connected in some way with the birth of Purgatory, figures again in an interesting Cistercian manuscript from the late twelfth century, one of the first collections of so-called *exempla*, or brief stories, which were inserted by preachers into their sermons and which were destined, as we shall see, to play a great role in the diffusion of Purgatory in the thirteenth century.[15] Chapter 34 treats the punishment of the soul after death (*De poenis animarum post mortem*) and begins with an excerpt from Bede's account of the vision of Saint Fursy. It goes on to present a number of other visions, after making the statement that "heavy punishments have been inflicted in Purgatory [*in purgatorio*] for misdeeds that we judge to have been quite minor." Here is still further evidence for the existence of Purgatory, both the word and the belief. One of the visions described is said to have been taken from the life of Bernard. Here is the story:

> A brother motivated by good intentions but unduly severe toward the other brothers and less compassionate than he should have been died at the monastery of Clairvaux. A few days after his death he appeared to the man of God [Bernard], looking mournful and disheveled, indicating that things were not going as he had wished. Bernard asked him what had happened to him, and he complained of being subjected to four tortures. At these words he was shoved from behind and precipitously whisked out of the sight of the man of God. The latter shouted after him with great moans, "I beg you in the name of the Lord to let me know soon what your situation is." He began to pray and asked the brother, whose holiness he knew, to aid him in prayer. And he did not let off until a few days later he was informed, as he had wished, by another revelation that the brother had been found worthy of the consolation of liberation.

This anecdote, along with others contained in the same manuscript, is the earliest example known to me of the kind of story that would popularize the belief in Purgatory in the thirteenth century, in which souls from Purgatory, mentioned by name, make an appearance. It is worth pointing out that, from this point on, the returning ghosts are of a very particular kind. They are closely watched from two vantage points: their torturers from the other world make sure that the number of apparitions is kept to a minimum, and their supporters in this world order them to report exactly what is happening to them.

The next section contains irrefutable evidence of the use of the word "purgatory" at the end of the twelfth century and the begining of the thirteenth, proving that, by this date, Purgatory existed. For the most part this evidence is drawn from the writings of theologians.

THE FIRST THEOLOGIANS OF PURGATORY
PETER THE CHANTER AND SIMON OF TOURNAI

In my view, the man who first integrated Purgatory into theological teaching was Peter the Chanter, whose importance as a founder of scholasticism is increasingly recognized. Peter, a master of the school of Notre-Dame of Paris who died in 1197 and who, when he looked about him, saw a world changing before his eyes, economically, socially, politically, and intellectually, was better able than anyone else to provide a theoretical account of the new urban world and monarchy as well as a new casuistry suited to the changed environment.[16]

Purgatory is again treated in relation to penance in Peter's *Summa* on the sacraments and on counsels for the soul (*Summa de Sacramentis et Animae Consiliis*). In discussing venial sin, Peter is led to assert that this kind of sin causes a determinate penalty to be inflicted in Purgatory (*in purgatorio*). He then attacks those who believe that the damned also pass through Purgatory (*per purgatorium*) before going to Hell and that they are purged and pardoned there. This, Peter the Chanter maintains, is absurd, because it would leave the elect no better off than the damned. He then comes to the crucial point of the argument: "We must distinguish between the places for the good and the places for the wicked after this life. The good either go at once to Paradise [*patria*] if they have nothing with them to burn, or they go first to Purgatory [*purgatorium*] and then to Paradise, as in the case of those who bring venial sins along with them. No special receptacle is set aside for the wicked, who, it is said, go immediately to Hell." The Chanter then asserts that only the predestined (the elect) are accepted into Purgatory and again reports that opinions vary. Some say, for example, that the wicked pass through Purgatory, but that for them it is not a true Purgatory but merely a vehicle that carries them into the eternal flames. Others say that venial sin is punished by eternal pain if there is no repentance at the moment of death. Against this, Peter argues that impenitence is the cause without which damnation would not occur, but it is not the cause because of which damnation does occur. In these few paragraphs the noun *purgatorium* occurs frequently, nine times to be exact. The word and the idea had clearly become commonplace, in Paris at any rate, by the end of the twelfth century, and it would seem that the tripartite system of Hell, Purgatory, and Paradise had been perfected.[17]

In another passage of *De sacramentis*, concerned with the remission of venial sins, Peter the Chanter points out that "our masters said that venial sin is remitted by purgatorial punishment (*per poenam purgatorii*), not by penitence." This is not Peter's opinion, however. He uses the noun Purgatory twice in the space of a few lines.[18] In part 3 of his work, an anthology of cases of conscience, Peter answers the question whether venial sins can be redeemed by alms. "There are two purgatories. One is in the future after death, and it can be diminished primarily by the celebration of masses and secondarily by other good works. The other purgatory is the penance imposed, and it can also be mitigated by the same things." Here, it is clear that even though Peter is taking Purgatory for granted, he does not conceive of it entirely in spatial terms: in this passage it is a state rather than a place.[19] In perhaps the best known of his works, the *Verbum abbreviatum*, the date of which has been put by some authorities at 1192, Peter asks what quantity and intensity of penance can equal purgatorial fire. He uses both the phrase "purgatorial fire" and the noun "purgatory," a common thing to do at this time and something we encounter also in the next century.[20]

Another well-known Parisian teacher, Simon of Tournai (d. 1201), a student of Odo of Ourscamp, has left us a collection of disputes (*Disputationes*), a genre which was made fashionable by Abelard and which, despite the opposition of conservatives like Bernard, Hugh of Saint-Victor (who does not discuss the question), John of Salisbury, and Stephen of Tournai, became a part of theological teaching in the second half of the twelfth century and was applied to biblical exegesis by Peter the Chanter. Simon of Tournai discusses Purgatory in three disputes.[21] In Dispute 40, he takes up the following question: Can one acquire merits after death? Some argue that merits can be acquired as a result of suffering endured in Purgatory. The expression used is *in purgatoriis*, "in purgatory (purgatories)," which we have encountered before. But in his answer Simon is opposed to this view. After asserting that there is no place where merits can be acquired after this life, he uses the word "purgatory" four times, twice to describe the suffering of Purgatory (*passio purgatorii*), once to speak of the pain of Purgatory (*poena purgatorii*), and once in alluding to a passage through Purgatory (*transeundo purgatorium*). In Dispute 55 there are two questions concerning Purgatory. One has to do with whether purgatorial fire can be an eternal punishment, and the other with whether the suffrages of the Church can exempt a soul from Purgatory altogether. Simon to some extent talks around the first question by stressing that the problem is not whether one has committed a venial or mortal sin but rather whether one has died unrepentant. To the second question he responds in the affirmative, indicating that, during a person's lifetime, he can win exemption from Purgatory through suffrages of the Church and can even become worthy not to enter into Purgatory (*ne intraret purgatorium*). As can be seen clearly in this dispute, Simon of Tournai distinguished very carefully between *purgatorium*, a noun designating a place, and purgatorial fire (*ignis purgatorius*), a phrase describing the punishment endured there.

Finally, in Dispute 73, Simon takes up the question whether souls are punished by a material fire in Purgatory or in Hell. Purgatory is denoted either by the noun *purgatorium* or by the older form, *in purgatoriis* (in purgatorial places, the final noun being understood). His answer is that a corporeal fire may exist in Hell, but that the fire in Purgatory must be a spiritual, metaphorical fire, a very severe punishment, since fire is the most painful form of bodily torment.

I should add that another celebrated Parisian teacher, Peter of Poitiers (d. 1205), who, as we saw earlier, used in his *Sententiae* the full arsenal of ancient terminology predating the introduction of the noun purgatory, also used the noun in the same work, unless the copyist somehow dropped the word *ignem* (fire): "They shall pass through purgatory" (*transibunt per purgatorium*).[22]

And finally, one further instance of the use of the noun *purgatorium* at the very end of the twelfth century, this time in a work not of theology but of hagiography. This occurs in a passage in a life of Saint Victor, the martyr of Mouzon, where Purgatory (*purgatorium*) is defined as a place of combustion, a prison of purgation.[23]

The significance of the inception of Purgatory remains to be explored. But before turning to that question, I want to summarize what we have found out thus far.

THE PARISIAN SPRING AND THE CISTERCIAN SUMMER

I have examined as many documents as I could from all over the Christian world. In particular, I have closely scrutinized works produced in the leading intellectual and cultural centers in the period around the turn of the thirteenth century. I think that I am on firm ground in asserting that the doctrine of Purgatory was developed and the word "Purgatory" first used in two different milieus. The first and most active of these was that of the Parisian intellectuals, especially those of the cathedral school—the school of the chapter of Notre-Dame—whose importance cannot be exaggerated in the period before the intellectual center shifted to the Left Bank and the new university where Dominican and Franciscan teachers predominated.

This feverish activity at Notre-Dame was preceded and fostered by another theological movement of the early twelfth century, which centered on the Left Bank abbeys of Saint-Victor and Sainte-Geneviève. One need only mention the illustrious names of Hugh of Saint-Victor and his school, and Abelard and his disciples at Sainte-Geneviève.

Still, it was from Notre-Dame that the new intellectual current surged forth. Building on the work of Peter Lombard, the masters and chancellors of the school of Notre-Dame led the way, with Odo of Ourscamp, Peter Comestor, and Peter the Chanter in the forefront. In the heart of the Paris of Louis VII and the young Philip Augustus, in contact with the money changers on the bridges, the shippers on the Seine, the artisans and workers who were traded as human commodities on the labor market in the place de Grève, Christianity's deepest truths were reworked and reshaped in a climate of intense creativity. It was a world of ideas in ferment, of torrents of discussion, of the peaceful clash of contradictory opinions. It was a feverish time in which masters and students wrote endlessly, turning out ream upon ream of *quaestiones, disputationes*, and *reportationes*, in which it is no longer possible to tell who was responsible for what idea, notwithstanding the authority of a few eminent masters. The positions that met in confrontation were of the most widely varied sort, sometimes pushed to absurd extremes: "Some say, . . . Others believe, . . . Still others maintain. . . ." It was the first great outpouring of scholastic thought, and it did not last long. As early as 1210 the Church and the monarchy moved to reassert their control. Pyres were raised to burn both books and men. This was just a warning. Scholasticism was yet to see great days and greater glories. But those cathedrals of the intellect, the great *Summas* of the century of Saint Louis, are decorous monuments from which all raving and enthusiasm have been expelled. Even this did not satisfy the censors of the day, for on two occasions, in 1270 and 1277, Etienne Tempier, the bishop of Paris, brought his crozier down on whatever seemed new and original, striking at Siger de Brabant, who was reproached for what he did not say, and at Thomas Aquinas, who was less audacious than is sometimes believed. Purgatory was born in this springtime of scholasticism, in this moment of exceptional creativity during which the intellectualism of the city joined for a brief moment with the idealism of the monastery.

Purgatory also grew up in another milieu, that of Cîteaux. The fact that Saint Bernard was not the inventor of Purgatory was of small importance. The special attention that the Cistercians devoted to the relations between the living and the dead and the new importance that they attached to the liturgy of early November—in this following Cluny despite the hostility between the two orders—led them to the brink of Purgatory. The ties they maintained with the urban intellectuals no doubt carried them over. Many urban academics, particularly the Parisians, ended their days in Cistercian monasteries: Odo of Ourscamp, Peter Comestor, Peter the Chanter, and Alan of Lille, to name a few. It was at the crossroads between these two worlds, that of the monasteries and that of the urban schools, that some time between 1170 and 1200—possibly as early as 1170–80 and surely by the last decade of the century—Purgatory first emerged.

PURGATORY AND THE BATTLE AGAINST HERESY

It is time now to enlarge our view to encompass the Church's battle against heresy. An important role in the inception of Purgatory was played by a number of ecclesiastical authors in the period around the turn of the thirteenth century. These authors have another characteristic in common: all were involved in the Church's battles against heretics and used the new doctrine of Purgatory as a weapon in this struggle. Like many beliefs, Purgatory owed its existence not merely to progress in philosophy and pressure from the masses but also to the need to do battle against those who would not accommodate themselves to the new belief. The fact that there was a battle shows that the stakes involved were sizeable. It was against the heretics of the twelfth and thirteenth centuries, the Greeks of the thirteenth to fifteenth centuries, and the Protestants of the fifteenth and sixteenth centuries, that the Roman Catholic Church honed the doctrine of Purgatory. The steadiness of the attacks on Purgatory by adversaries of the official Roman Church is impressive. All of the Church's enemies were agreed that a man's fate in the other world depended only on his merit and God's will. On this view, the game is up at death. After death (or after the last Judgment) the soul goes directly either to Heaven or to Hell; there is no redemption between death and resurrection. Hence there is no Purgatory and it is futile to pray for the dead. No admirers of the Church, heretics denied that the institution has any role in determining the fate of the soul after death and opposed its attempts to extend its power over men by claiming such a role.

We have already examined the case of the heretics of Arras brought to trial by Gerard of Cambrai at the beginning of the eleventh century. The problem of heresy crops up again in the twelfth century, sometimes with individual heretics, sometimes with whole heretical groups. One such was Pierre de Bruys, against whom Peter the Venerable, the celebrated abbot of Cluny, wrote a treatise. Even more flagrant was the case of Pierre's more radical disciple, Henri, first a monk and later a vagabond, who around 1116 preached ideas similar to those of the Arras heretics at Lausanne, Le Mans, and other unknown places, as a result of which he was arrested in 1134 and haled before the council of Pisa. An anonymous treatise composed in the first half of the twelfth century attempted to refute the teachings of Henri and his supporters. According to this treatise, these people believed that "nothing can help the dead, who are either damned or saved from the moment they die," a view characterized as "openly heretical" by the author of the treatise. Basing his argument on the texts traditionallly invoked by the Church (2 Macc. 12:41–45, Matt. 12:31, 1 Cor. 3:10–15, and Augustine's *De cura pro mortuis gerenda*), this writer contends that two kinds of fire exist, purgatorial fire and eternal fire. "There are," he claims, "some sins which will be erased in the future [in the other world] by the alms of friends and the prayers of the faithful or by purgatorial fire."[24]

The name of Saint Bernard again comes up in connection with the war on heresy. In a sermon on the Song of Songs which he wrote in 1135 and rewrote in the 1143–45 period, Bernard attacked heretics who "do not believe that purgatorial fire continues after death and who argue that the soul goes straightaway after death either to eternal rest or damnation." Bernard follows the tradition of the Church in branding these heretics perfidious beasts and, with the contempt of the noble cleric, alleges that "they are rustics, illiterates, people beneath contempt." Wishing to name this group, as was customary, by the name of their leader, he found that he could not, because they had none and impudently called themselves the "Apostolics." They were hostile to marriage, to baptism, to prayer for the dead, to the cult of the saints, and to the eating of meat (refusing to consume anything derived from sexual intercourse). Invoking Matthew 12:32, Bernard opposed their arguments by pointing, not to Purgatory, which did not yet exist, but rather to purgatorial fire and to the efficacy of suffrages for the dead.[25]

The "Arras line" is clear in the views of these heretics, even if there was no continuity of tradition or direct filiation. In the late twelfth and early thirteenth centuries Purgatory was also rejected by new groups of heretics, the Waldensians and the Cathari. Here, hostility to Purgatory was part of a different religious system, despite the presence of traditional heretical components. In regard to Purgatory the position of the new heretics was practically the same, however: the living can do nothing for the dead, and suffrages are useless. Among the Cathari the doctrine of metempsychosis very likely left no room for Purgatory, since it served the same function of purification "over time." The opening shot in this controversy was probably the *Book against the Waldensians* (*Liber contra Waldenses*) written by the Premonstratensian abbot Bernard of Fontcaude between 1190 and 1192. The word "purgatory" is not mentioned, but an other world consisting of three different regions is described with new clarity.[26]

In chapter 10 of this work Bernard of Fontcaude attacks those "who deny purgatorial fire and who say that the spirit [*spiritus*] goes immediately after its separation from the flesh to either heaven or hell." Against this view he holds up three authorities: Paul's First Epistle to the Corinthians, Augustine's *Enchiridion*, and chapter 14 of Ezekiel, in which Yahweh declares that the prayers of the righteous cannot set the infidel peoples free, but that they must deliver themselves from bondage. Bernard says that Paul's words apply "to the fire of the purgation to come." Augustine's words, in Bernard's view, mean that God purges sins either in baptism and in the temporary fire of tribulation (in this world) or else in the fire of purgation. And finally, he argues that Yahweh's words in Ezekiel are a command that the infidel people shall be placed in purgatorial fire.

The most interesting passage is found in chapter 11. Certain heretics claim that the spirits of the dead do not go to Heaven or Hell prior to the Last Judgment but are received instead into other receptacles. Bernard argues that they are mistaken: "There are in fact three places that receive spirits delivered from the flesh. Paradise receives the spirits of the perfect, hell the entirely wicked, and purgatorial fire those who are neither entirely good nor entirely wicked. In other words, an entirely good place receives the entirely good; an extremely bad place receives the entirely bad; and a place that is moderately bad receives the moderately bad: it is less harsh than hell but worse than the world."[27]

Thus Bernard of Fontcaude was not familiar with Purgatory but only with purgatorial fire. But this fire was now localized. Between the time of death and the Last Judgment, the other world, we are told, is divided into three parts. And for the first time, Purgatory is defined as a place that is intermediary in two senses: topographically and judicially.

Little is known about Ermangaud of Beziers (a name shared by several different individuals, moreover), but his treatise against the Waldensians (*Contra Waldenses*) probably dates from the final years of the twelfth century or the very beginning of the thirteenth. In chapter 17 of this work he attacks the perverse opinion of certain heretics that the prayers of saints are of no help to the living and that the dead are not relieved by the offerings and prayers of the living. Against this view Ermengaud asserts that there are three kinds of dead souls: the entirely good, who have no need of aid, the entirely wicked, for whom nothing can be done because in Hell there is no redemption, and a third category, those who are neither entirely good nor entirely bad, who have confessed but who have not completed their penance. Ermengaud does not use the word "purgatory" or any other derivative of *purgare*. He merely says that those in the third category "are neither damned nor immediately saved, but punished in the expectation of salvation."[28]

A *Summa* against the heretics from the early thirteenth century, erroneously attributed to Praepositivus of Cremona (d. c. 1210), chancellor of Paris, accuses a group of heretics known as Passagins of refusing to pray for the dead. The pseudo-Praepositivus begins by refuting their interpretation of the story of Lazarus and the rich man and by arguing that the bosom of Abraham, "or limbo of hell," located above both the lower hell and the middle hell, existed only in the past, prior to Christ's descent into the underworld. He then takes up the question of the value of prayer for the dead. Prayers must be said "for the medium good, who are in Purgatory, not to make them better but to set them free sooner, and for the medium bad, not to save them but to lessen their punishment." Pseudo-Praepositivus thus remains largely Augustinian in outlook, distinguishing between purgation in Purgatory, which exists, and "more tolerable damnation," which probably takes place in Hell. He invokes the following authorities in support of the Catholic doctrine of suffrages: 2 Maccabees 12, Proverbs 11:7 (on which Bede commented by saying, "When the righteous man dies, his hope does not perish"—cf. *PL* 91.971), and above all Matthew 12:32, where it is "plainly demonstrated that certain sins are forgiven in the life to come." Thus one must pray for the dead.[29]

Alan of Lille (d. 1203) presents a rather different case. To begin with, he is a master of the first rank. As a teacher at the new university of Montpellier,[30] he took part in the battle against the Waldensian and Catharist heretics, but in his treatise *Against the Heretics* (*Contra Haereticos*), he "dropped the question of Purgatory."[31] But he did treat the question in his treatises on penance and preaching.

In discussing penance in his *Summa on the Art of Preaching* (*Summa de arte praedicatoria*), Alan makes the following assertion: "There is a triple fire: purgatorial, probative, peremptory. The purgatorial fire is the satisfaction [of sins], the probative fire is the examination [*tentatio*], and the peremptory is eternal damnation." The purgatorial fire is twofold: it takes place in part along the way (i.e., in this world), through penance, and in part after this life, through purgatorial punishment. "If we purge ourselves in the first, we are exempted from the second and third; if we have not undergone the first, we will feel the second. . . . The first, Purgatory, excludes the other two. . . . Purgatorial fire is merely the shadow and the picture of the second, and just as the shadow and picture of material fire causes no pain . . . the fire of repentance is not bitter in comparison with the second purgatorial fire." Augustine is then cited.[32] What interests Alan of Lille, then, is penance. This was a time when the whole idea of penance was undergoing considerable change, and Alan identifies what Augustine called "earthly tribulation" with penance in this world.

In his treatise on penance, the *Liber poenitentialis*, which was composed after 1191 and of which several versions are extant, including one long version written between 1199 and 1203, Alan asks whether the Church, through the mediation of the bishop or priest, can absolve from penance. Alan's ideas may seem disconcerting: he believes that what is properly called purgatorial fire is the "fire" of penance in this world, and he limits the power of the priest or bishop to offer exemption from purgatorial punishment, i.e., from penance. After death, however, the Church is powerless: this view was not shared by the clerics of the thirteenth century.[33]

In these texts, Alan of Lille, whose vocabulary is at once traditional and innovative, speaks of purgatorial fire (*ignis purgatorius*) and purgatorial pain (*poena purgatoria*) in addition to Purgatory as such. It is worthy of note that he uses the substantive in a very interesting "question" on which I shall comment later, when we are ready to discuss the "time of purgatory": "The question has been raised, whether one who is required to complete [a penance in this world of] seven years and who does not complete it will be in Purgatory for seven years. We answer: beyond any doubt he will complete this satisfaction in Purgatory, but how long he will be there, only he who weighs the punishments in the balance can tell."[34] This raises the issue of the apportionment of punishments in Purgatory and the whole matter of penitential bookkeeping.

THE BACKWARDNESS OF THE CANON LAWYERS

Contemporary with the theological spurt centered in Paris was another intellectual movement of the second half of the twelfth century, the new developments in canon law that stirred excitement throughout Christendom. The intellectual, institutional, and political center of this movement was Bologna, as was mentioned earlier when we briefly considered that key text, the *Decretum* of Gratian (which dates from around 1140). But with respect to the inception of Purgatory the legal movement is conspicuous by its absence. As Landgraf wrote in 1948 in a more general context, "We cannot hide the fact that, in general, the canonists were far from fostering progress in systematic theology; indeed, they usually tried to impede it."[35] So much is admitted by one canonist, the author of one of the earliest commentaries on the *Decretum* of Gratian, the *Summa coloniensis* (*Summa of Cologne*), who in 1169 said in regard to the issue of suffrages for the dead, and hence of Purgatory, that "I never discussed the question, which is of interest to theologians more than to canonists."[36] So it should come as no surprise that the great late-twelfth-century canonist, Uguccione (or Huguccio) of Pisa, in his *Summa Decretorum*, completed sometime between 1188 and 1192, allows that, whereas the time of purgation extends from the moment of death until the Last Judgment, the location in which purgation occurs is another matter. Augustine, in a text reproduced in the *Decretum* of Gratian, spoke of secret, hidden places, and Uguccione for his part confesses that he can add nothing to this: "*Ignoro et ego.*"[37]

But this silence on the question was not to last, because the canonists soon perceived that this was an important topical issue of direct concern to themselves. In the first few years of the thirteenth century, Sicard of Cremona (d. 1215), commented on Gratian, i.e., Augustine, as follows: "This, we must understand, means those who are in Purgatory, but some think that it means those who are tormented in purgatory, all of whose punishments may be mitigated."[38] It is interesting to note that, on the manuscript of the *Summa Coloniensis* mentioned above, there is a note of Sicard's remarks in a thirteenth-century hand, as if correcting the indifference of the author of the *Summa*. Purgatory is also discussed, for example, in the gloss on the *Decretum* of Gratian prepared shortly after 1215 by John the Teuton (d. 1245). John subscribes to Augustine's remarks on the secret places, reproduced in the *Decretum*, but maintains that suffrages can help the medium good obtain release from the fire of Purgatory sooner than they otherwise would.[39]

THE TURN OF THE THIRTEENTH CENTURY: PURGATORY TAKES HOLD

Three authors from the early thirteenth century epitomize, in my view, the new way of looking at the other world that came into fashion once Purgatory had become an established place.

Innocent III: A Letter and a Sermon

The first champion of the new scheme was Pope Innocent III (1198–1216). It is noteworthy that the pontiff was so quick to accept the new ideas. In a letter sent to the archbishop of Lyons in 1202 he is still circumspect. As for the conclusions to be drawn from Augustine's division of the dead into four categories (copied by Gratian), Innocent leaves these up to the prelate's discretion.[40] But in a sermon for All Saints' Day on the subject of the two seraphim, the three armies, and the five dwelling places of the spirits of the dead, the pope is a good deal more explicit.[41]

The two seraphim are the two testaments. The three armies are the Church triumphant in Heaven, the Church militant on earth, and the Church "abiding in Purgatory." The first acts through praise, the second through combat, and the third through fire. It is the third to which Paul alludes in the First Epistle to the Corinthians. There are also five places in which human spirits reside. Of these one is supreme and reserved for the supremely good, and one base, reserved for the supremely bad. The middle place is for those who are both good and bad. Between the supreme place and the middle place is a place for those who are medium good, and between the middle place and the base place is a place for those who are medium bad. The supreme place is Heaven, in which the blessed reside. The base place is Hell, for the damned. The middle place is the world, where both sinners and the righteous are found. Between the supreme place and the middle place is the earthly paradise, in which Enoch and Elijah, who will eventually die, are still living. Between the middle place and the base place is Purgatory, where those who have not done penance in this world or who have carried with them into the grave the taint of some venial sin are punished. Though there are five places, there are only three armies. Those who are in paradise, though they belong to the army of God, do not in themselves constitute an army, for there are only two of them. The army in the middle place extols the triumphant army in Heaven and on the following day prays for those who are in Purgatory. At this point Innocent III includes a psychological observation: "Who indeed would not willingly praise the saints to the indivisible Trinity, when we believe that by the prayers and merits of the saints we too will one day be helped to reach their side? And who would not willingly pray to the indivisible Trinity for the dead, when he himself must die; who would not do in this life for another what he wishes to be done for him after his death?" To conclude his remarks, the pope emphasizes the solemnity of All Saints' Day.

This is an astonishing passage: Innocent III mentions Purgatory several times and, using traditional symbolism, gives a full, clear, and most carefully constructed account of both this world and the other, a perfect plan in which every man has his place from birth until the end of time, the earthly portion of which is subject to the strict control of the Church. The Church itself is divided in three. Where Augustine had distinguished between the "peregrinating" Church and the "celestial" Church, the twelfth century introduced a new distinction, one between the "militant" Church—the expression was first used by Peter Comestor[42]—and the "triumphant" Church. Innocent III adds the Church of Purgatory, introducing a third element which later would complete the triad under the name, "the suffering Church." Rationalized, the system of five places introduced by pseudo-Peter Damian and pseudo-Bernard emerged victorious. The pontiff expresses his wonderment at the system's perfect order: "O, how reasonable and salutary is the institution of this observance!"[43]

Purgatory and Confession: Thomas of Chobham

The second text is an excerpt from the *Confessors' Summa* by the English cleric Thomas of Chobham, who was trained in Paris in the circle around Peter the Chanter. I shall have more to say later on about confession and its connection with the inception of Purgatory, as well as about the influence of the decisions taken by the Fourth Lateran Council (1215); I shall also discuss the confessors' manuals as evidence for the upheaval in spiritual life that was taking place in this period, as men confronted new problems of conscience and began to ask ever more insistent questions about both this world and the next, and as the Church took steps to maintain its control over the new society.

Thomas of Chobham began writing the *Summa confessorum* shortly before the opening of the Fourth Lateran Council and finished it just after the council terminated its labors. Purgatory is discussed in connection with masses for the dead. The *Summa* states that "mass is celebrated for the living and for the dead, but for the dead doubly, because the sacraments of the altar are petitions for the living, thanksgivings for the saints, and propitiations for those in Purgatory, and result in remission of their punishment. And to signify this the host is divided into three parts, one of which is for the saints and another for those to be sanctified. The former is a thanksgiving, the latter a supplication."[44]

The *Summa* then takes up the question whether the mass for the dead has any efficacy for the damned in Hell, basing itself on the authority of chapter 110 of Augustine's *Enchiridion*, which speaks of "more tolerable damnation." Thomas of Chobham reports the opinion that "damnation" should be understood to mean "the punishment of Purgatory, because nothing can be done for the damned in Hell."[45]

Clearly, Purgatory is here being taken as an accepted fact and integrated into both penitential discipline and the liturgy. The bonds between the living and the dead were being tightened.

THE OLD AND NEW VOCABULARY OF THE OTHER WORLD

Finally, the old terminology had to be adapted to fit the new geography of the otherworld. Some people began to ask what the meaning of such biblical expressions as "the mouth of the lion," "the hand of hell," "the lake of hell," "the place of darkness," and "Tartarus" might be in relation to Purgatory. In a work composed around 1200 (which mentions the names of both Peter the Chanter and Praepositivus), perhaps by Paganus of Corbeil, the author writes that when it is stated that prayer "frees their souls from the mouth of the lion, from the hand of hell, and from the lake of hell," what is meant is purgatorial fire itself, according as it is stronger or weaker.[46] Geoffrey of Poitiers (d. 1231) gives another explanation in his *Summa*: "It is better to say that there are various abodes in Purgatory: some are called dark and obscure places, others the hand of hell, others the mouth of the lion, and still others Tartarus. And from these punishments the Church asks that the souls of the dead be liberated."[47]

Now it is Purgatory's turn to be divided up. The words of John 14:2, "In my Father's house are many mansions," once applied to the other world in its entirety, were now applied to the new region, Purgatory. What we are beginning to witness might be called, begging the reader's indulgence, the "subdividing" of Purgatory.

SIX

Purgatory between Sicily and Ireland

FROM the time of Drythelm to the time of Charles the Fat, living voyagers traveled to the hereafter, leaving their bodies behind on earth to be returned to at journey's end. These journeys were considered to be "real" by the men of the Middle Ages, even if they depicted them as "dreams" (*somnia*). Visions of this kind continued throughout the twelfth century, and the last of them, the Purgatory of Saint Patrick, marks the beginning of a significant new phase in the rise of Purgatory and the development of a dual geography: a geography of this world coupled with a geography of the next.

The same period also saw the emergence of a new type of story, a genre that helped to popularize Purgatory in the thirteenth century. In these tales the souls of the dead undergoing punishment in Purgatory appeared to the living and asked for suffrages or warned them to mend their ways before it was too late. In substance these stories were modeled on Book 4 of the *Dialogues* of Gregory the Great, except that now the ghosts returned to earth not to purge what remained of their sins but rather to be on special furlough for a brief period, usually no longer than the duration of a dream.

MONASTIC VISIONS: GHOST STORIES

Apparitions occurred most frequently in the monasteries, which should come as no surprise, since it was in the monasteries that Gregory the Great was most assiduously read, not only his *Moralia* but also his *Dialogues*, the second book of which was instrumental in fashioning Saint Benedict's "image." Furthermore, in a time when people were suspicious of dreams (as Gregory the Great counseled them to be, backed up by Peter Damian in the eleventh century), monks, who were better able than other people to withstand the temptations of the Devil (as Saint Anthony had done) and more worthy of receiving the authentic and edifying word of God, were the primary beneficiaries of apparitions and visions.

So, for example, in tract 34, part 2, of *De diversis apparitionibus et miraculis*, written between 1063 and 1072, Peter Damian of Ravenna, one of the leading figures of Italian eremitism who became a cardinal around 1060 and who was quite conscious of the importance of the remembrance of the dead in the devotions of eremetical groups or "communities of prayer,"[1] reports on two apparitions of souls undergoing purgatorial punishments.[2] The first, according to Peter's informant, a priest named John, took place in Rome a few years before Peter wrote. During the night of the Feast of the Assumption of Mary, while the people of Rome were busy praying and chanting litanies in the churches, a woman in the basilica of Santa Maria in Campitello saw her godmother, who had died a year earlier.

> Since the crowd prevented them from speaking, the woman decided to wait at a street corner which her godmother would have to pass on her way out of the basilica. When the godmother passed by, the woman immediately asked her, "Aren't you my godmother, Marozia, who is dead?" The other woman answered, "I am." "How can you be here then?" She said: "Until today I was in the grip of no slight punishment, for when I was still of tender age I gave in to indecent lust and committed shameful acts with girls of my age, and alas! having forgotten them, even though I confessed to a priest, I did not submit to the judgment [of penance]. But today the queen of the world has poured forth prayers for us and liberated me from the places of punishment [de locis poenalibus] and by her intervention a multitude greater than the population of Rome has been plucked from torment. We are therefore visiting the holy places dedicated to our glorious lady to thank her for so great a boon." When the woman doubted the truth of this story, her godmother added: "To verify the truth of what I say, know that one year from now, on the very day of this feast, you are certain to die. If you continue to live, which will not happen, you can then accuse me of lying." With these words she vanished from sight. Preoccupied with the prediction of her death, the woman thereafter led a cautious life. Almost a year later, on the eve of the holiday, she fell ill, and on the very day of the feast she died, as predicted. The moral of the story, frightening as it is, is this: for the sin she had forgotten this woman was tortured until the immaculate Mother of God intervened on her behalf.

This remarkably evocative tale marks the first appearance of the Virgin Mary in purgatorial places. As Marian devotion, late to develop in the West, began its astonishing rise to popularity, the Virgin came to the fore as the mainstay of souls consigned to what would later be known as Purgatory.

Peter Damian claimed to have heard the other edifying story from Rainaud, the bishop of Cumae, who had himself heard it from Bishop Umberto of Saint Ruffina, now dead. "A priest who was asleep in the dead of night was called to a vision by his godfather, who was dead:

"Come see a spectacle that cannot fail to move you." And he led him to the basilica of Saint Cecilia in the atrium of which he saw Saints Agnes, Agatha, and Cecilia herself in a choir of numerous resplendent holy virgins. They were preparing a magnificent throne which stood on a higher plane than those around it, and there the Holy Virgin Mary with Peter, Paul, and David, surrounded by a brilliant assemblage of martyrs and saints, came to take her place. While silence reigned in this holiest of gatherings and all respectfully remained standing, a woman who, though a pauper, wore a fur cloak, prostrated herself at the feet of the immaculate Virgin and implored her to have pity on the dead patrician, John. When she had repeated her prayer three times and received no answer, she added, "You know, my lady, queen of the world, that I am that unfortunate woman who lay naked and trembling in the atrium of your great basilica [Santa Maria Maggiore]. That man [the patrician John] saw me and immediately took pity on me and covered me with the fur that I am wearing." Where-upon Mary, blessed of God, said: "The man for whom you are pleading was crushed by a great weight of crimes. But he had two good points: charity toward the poor and devotion, in all humility, to the holy places. In fact he often carried oil and kindling on his own shoulders for the lights of my Church." The other saints testified that he did the same for their churches. The queen of the world ordered that the patrician be brought before the assembly. At once he was dragged in, bound and chained, by a horde of demons.[3] Whereupon Our Lady ordered that he be delivered, and he went to swell the ranks of the saints [the elect]. But she ordered that the bonds from which he had just been set free be kept for another man, still living.

There follows a ceremony in St. Peter's Basilica, presided over by the saint himself, whereupon "the priest who was having the vision awoke and the dream terminated."

It is clear that the places of punishment (*loca poenalia*) and instruments of torture (*lora poenalia*) in this story belong to what would later be called Purgatory, since no one returns from Hell. But their character here is infernal, as is made clear by the presence of demons rather than angels.

In one of his letters Peter Damian recounts another ghost story told to him by one Martin, a very religious person from the hermitage of the Camaldolese. In the monastery *ad Pinum*, near the sea, there was a monk who, weighed down by sin, had been given a long, hard penance. He asked a brother who was a close friend of his to help him and share his penitential burden. The latter, whose life was beyond reproach, accepted, and though he thought he had a great deal of time remaining in which to carry out his promise, he soon died. A few days after his death, he appeared in a dream to the penitent monk, who asked about his condition. The dead monk told him that on his account he had suffered a fate hard and cruel. Delivered from his own sins, he was still laden down with those of his companion. He asked for help from his living brother and from the entire convent. All the monks submitted to penance, and the dead man reappeared, this time with a serene and even happy look. Thanks, he said, to the prayers of his brothers he had not only been delivered from the pain of punishment but by a miraculous decision of the right hand of the Most High he had recently been transported among the elect. Peter Damian ends his account with these words: "Thus does divine clemency instruct the living by means of the dead."[4]

Almost a century later, Peter the Venerable, abbot of Cluny, recorded in his treatise *De miraculis* (written between 1145 and 1156) "visions or revelations of the dead" that he has gathered and seeks to explain. He feels that in his day there has been an increase in the number of apparitions, and what they have revealed has, he says, turned out to be true. In any case this is what he has heard from many people worthy of being believed.[5]

Among these frightening and curious ghosts is a dead knight, who appears to a priest named Stephen and asks him to repair two wrongs that he, the knight, had committed and forgotten to confess. The knight then returns a second time to thank Stephen for freeing him from the punishment he had been subjected to.[6] A devoted reader of Gregory the Great, Peter the Venerable does not seek to localize the place of purgation any more than Gregory. Some souls return to complete their penance at the spot where their sins were committed, whereas other souls, guilty of worse sins, are consigned to Hell.[7]

By the end of the century, with Purgatory now in existence, visions, particularly those originating in Cistercian monasteries, had begun describing this new region of the other world. This should come as no surprise in view of the role played by Cîteaux in the inception of Purgatory. One manuscript of Cistercian origin, a collection of *exempla*, or edifying stories, of a sort soon to become extremely popular, recounts a number of visions involving punishments to which souls are subjected after death. Following the vision of Saint Fursy in Bede's *Historia ecclesiastica Anglorum*, one "monk's vision" tells of the torture of a knight who had taken an excessive interest in birds of prey during this life and was on that account subjected to a horrible torture in the next: a buzzard perched on his fist constantly tore at his flesh with its beak and claws. This despite the fact that he had apparently led quite a virtuous life: the harshest punishments are inflicted in Purgatory (*in purgatorio*) for excesses we tend to look upon with indulgence. Thus our monk sees dead souls who, while alive, had used herbs and berries not as medicines but as drugs and aphrodisiacs; they are condemned to roll live coals in their mouths without respite. Others guilty of excessive laughter are seen being whipped. Those guilty of gossip are slapped repeatedly. Others who made obscene gestures are chained in the midst of flames. And so on.[8] Even saints must spend short periods of time in Purgatory for what appear to be slight faults. One of the first to pay his dues to the new belief was none other than the great Cistercian Saint Bernard himself, who, as we saw earlier, spent a brief period in Purgatory for his failure to believe in the Immaculate Conception.[9]

FOUR MONASTIC JOURNEYS TO THE OTHER WORLD

I have selected four twelfth-century journeys to the hereafter, to my mind the most important of any we have, for closer scrutiny. The first of these is worthy of note, I think, because it concerns the vision of a laywoman, the mother of Guibert of Nogent, and an experience of a quite intimate kind. The visions of Alberic of Settefrati and Tnugdal are included for their wealth of detail and also because their authors come from areas that are noted for otherworldly fantasy: southern Italy and Ireland. Finally, Saint Patrick's Purgatory is in a sense the doctrine's literary birth certificate. For our purposes these visions are of interest because they show how the idea of Purgatory as a separate region of the other world made its way into a traditional genre, tentatively at first and later in the form of an image which, despite its hazy outlines, is clear enough. They will also enable us to appreciate the role of the monastic imagination in the inception of Purgatory.

A Woman in the Other World: The Mother of
Guibert of Nogent

The first vision is recounted by a monk who lived in the early part of the twelfth century and who has left us several highly original works, particularly the treatise On the Relics of the Saints (De pignoribus sanctorum), which some scholars have read as heralding the dawn of critical thought, and the autobiography De vita sua, the first work of its kind and one that was to have many successors after the close of the Middle Ages.[10] Guibert of Nogent's account of his life has yielded two kinds of information of great interest to historians. In the first place the work contains an account of the political and social upheaval in the northeastern corner of France and a description of the beginnings of the communal movement in the story of the dramatic events that overtook the commune of Laon in 1116. It also contains an extraordinary wealth of psychological observations, for the interpretation of which historians have either turned to psychoanalysts or attempted to play psychoanalyst themselves.[11]

Here is Guibert of Nogent's account of his mother's vision:*

One summer night, for instance, on a Sunday after matins, after she had stretched out on her narrow bench and had begun to sink into sleep, her soul seemed to leave her body without her losing her senses. After being led, as it were, through a certain gallery, at last she issued from it and began to approach the edge of a pit. After she was brought close to it, suddenly from the depths of the abyss men with the appearance of ghosts leaped forth, their hair seemingly eaten by worms, trying to seize her with their hands and to drag her inside. From behind the frightened woman, who was terribly distressed by their attack, suddenly a voice cried out to them, saying, "Touch her not." Compelled by that forbidding voice, they leaped back into the pit. Now I forgot to say that as she passed through the gallery, as she knew she had left her mortal being, her one prayer to God was to be allowed to return to her body. After she was rescued from the dwellers in the pit and was standing by its edge, suddenly she saw that my father was there, appearing as he did when he was young. When she looked hard at him and piteously asked of him whether he was called Evrard (for that had been his name), he denied that he was.

Now, it is no wonder that a spirit should refuse to be called by the name which he had as a man, for spirit should give no reply to a spirit which is inconsistent with its spiritual nature. Moreover, that spirits should recognize each other by their names is too absurd to be believed; otherwise in the next world it would be rare to know anyone except those close to us. Clearly it is not necessary for spirits to have names, since all their vision, or rather their knowledge of vision, is internal.

Although he denied that he was called by that name, and yet nonetheless she felt that it was he, she then asked him where he was staying. He indicated that the place was located not far away, and that he was detained there. She also asked how he was. Baring his arm and his side, he showed both of them so torn, so cut up with many wounds, that she felt great horror and emotional distress as she looked. The figure of a little child was also there, crying so bitterly that it troubled her greatly when she saw it. Moved by its cries, she said to him, "My lord, how can you endure the wailing of this child?" "Whether I like it or not" said he, "I endure it." Now, the crying of the child and the wounds on his arm and side have this meaning. When my father in his youth was separated from lawful intercourse with my mother through the witchcraft of certain persons, some evil counselors appealed to his youthful spirit with the

*Cited here after C. C. Swinton Bland's English translation, revised by John F. Benton, ed., *Self and Society in Medieval France: The Memoirs of Abbot Guibert of Nogent*, Harper & Row, 1970, pp. 93–96.—Trans.

vile advice to find out if he could have intercourse with other women. In youthful fashion he took their advice, and, having wickedly attempted intercourse with some loose woman unknown to me, he begat a child which at once died before baptism. The rending of his side is the breaking of his marriage vow; the cries of that distressed voice indicate the damnation of that evilly begotten child. Such, O Lord, O Inexhaustible Goodness, was Thy retribution on the soul of Thy sinner, who yet lives by faith. But let us return to the orderly narrative of the vision.

When she asked him whether prayer, almsgiving, or the mass gave him any relief (for he was aware that she frequently provided these things for him), he replied that they did, adding, "But among you there lives a certain Liégearde." My mother understood that he named this woman so that she would ask her what memory of him she had. This Liégearde was very poor in spirt, a woman who lived for God alone apart from the customs of the world.

Meanwhile, bringing her talk with my father to an end, my mother looked toward the pit, above which was a picture, and in the picture she saw a certain knight named Renaud, of no mean reputation among his countrymen. After dinner on that very day, which as I said before was a Sunday, this Renaud was treacherously killed at Beauvais by those close to him. In that picture he was kneeling with his neck bent down, puffing to blow up a fire in a heap of fuel. This vision was seen in the early morning, whereas he perished at midday, doomed to descend into those flames which he had kindled by his deserts. In the same picture she saw a brother of mine who was helping, but he died long afterward. He was taking a dreadful oath by the sacrament of God's body and blood. The significance of this is precisely that by false swearing and by taking the holy name of God and His sacred mysteries in vain, he earned both his punishment and the place of his punishment.

In the course of the same vision, she also saw that old woman who, as I said, lived with her at the beginning of her conversion, a woman who clearly was always mortifying her body with crosses on the outside, but, it was said, was not enough on her guard against a hunger for vainglory. She saw this woman carried off by two coal-black spirits, her form a mere shadow. Moreover, while that old woman was alive and the two were living together, when they were talking of the state of their souls and the coming of death, they once took a mutual pledge that the one who died first should, through the grace of God, appear to the survivor and make known to her the nature of her condition, whether good or bad. They confirmed this by prayer, earnestly beseeching God that after the death of either the other should be allowed to discover by the revelation of some vision her happy or unhappy state. When the old woman was about to die, she had seen herself in a vision deprived of her body and going with others like her to a certain temple, and, as she went, she seemed to be carrying a cross on her shoulders. Coming to the temple with that company, she was compelled to stay outside, the doors being barred against her. Finally, after her death she appeared to someone else in the midst of a great stench to express her gratitude for giving prayers which had saved her from decay and pain. While the old woman was dying, at the foot of the bed she saw standing a horrible devil with eyes of dreadful and monstrous size. When she adjured him by the holy sacraments to flee in confusion from her and seek nothing of her, with that frightful charge she drove him off.

My mother drew her conclusions about the cries of the infant, of whose existence she had been aware, from the exact way in which the vision agreed with the facts, when she put them together, and from the immediate prophecy of the impending slaying of the knight, whom she had seen assigned to the place of punishment below. Having no doubt about these things, she devoted herself wholly to bringing help to my father. Setting like against like, she chose to take on the raising of a little child only a few months old that had lost its parents. But since the Devil hates good intentions no less than faithful actions, the baby so harassed my mother and all her servants by the madness of its wailing and crying at night—although by day it was very good, by turns playing and sleeping—that anyone in the room could get scarcely any sleep. I have heard the nurses whom she hired say that night after night they could not stop shaking the child's rattle, so naughty was he, not through his own fault, but made so by the Devil within, and that a woman's craft failed entirely to drive him out. The good woman was tormented by extreme pain; amid those shrill cried no contrivance relieved her aching brow, nor could any sleep steal over her sorely tried and exhausted head, since the frenzy of the child goaded from within and by the Enemy's presence caused continual disturbance. Although she passed her sleepless nights in this way, she never appeared listless at the performance of the night offices. Since she knew that these troubles were to purge away those of her husband, which she had seen in her vision, she bore them gladly, because she rightly thought that by sharing his suffering herself she was lessening the pains of the other sufferer. Yet she never shut the child out of her house, never appeared less careful of him. Indeed, the more she perceived that the Devil was cruelly blazing against her to destroy her resolve, the more she chose to submit with equanimity to any inconvenience rising from it; and the more she happened to experience the eagerness of the Devil in the irritation of the child, the more she was assured that his evil sway over the soul of her husband was being countered.

Comparing what she saw with what she knew convinced Guibert's mother that her vision was true, and she thereupon gave herself over entirely to the task of aiding her husband. She understood that in her vision she had seen the "penal regions of the underworld" (*poenales locos apud inferos*) to which the knight whose image she had seen shortly before his death had been condemned.

She adopted an orphan child, whose nighttime crying tortured her and her servants. But she held firm despite the efforts of the Devil, who made the child's screams unbearable, and despite the complaints of her entourage, who urged her to give the child up. She knew that her sufferings would help to purge those of her husband, which she had seen in her vision.

Sadly, we must pass over the questions of family and personal relations raised by this passage. Nor can we pause to consider the digression on the matter of names, those emblems of medieval man. And we will say nothing of the way in which this story combines themes that are usually kept distinct: the vision of places of punishment in the other world, the pact between living individuals who agree that the first one to die will return to tell the survivor of his experiences beyond the grave, the child who disturbs sleep,[12] and the very "modern" dreamlike or nightmarish atmosphere of the tale. Instead we shall concentrate on those elements that recur constantly in other stories of travels through or sojourns in Purgatory and that ultimately became part of the "system."

To begin with, there is the infernal character of the place in which Guibert's father is being kept and to which his mother is in danger, according to her vision, of being dragged down. This is a sort of place or square located near a well or, in another vision, near a temple from which diabolical creatures emerge: black devils,[13] specters whose hair is crawling with vermin, monsters with huge black eyes, a world in which horrors of sight, sound, and smell—monstrous visions, unbearable noises, fetid odors—combine with physical pains. It is a world of torture, a penal colony, in which fire stands out among the various instruments of torture. It is a world of nameless spirits forced to undergo torture in order to expiate their sins. It is a world of suffering from which the living can snatch the dead by means of prayer, alms, and sacrifice, according to the traditional theory of suffrages, as well as by sharing in trials whose nature is related to the nature of the sin committed. Two features predominate above all others: first of all, this is a place, even if it is not yet clearly distinguished from other regions of the underworld (described variously as a square, a well, a temple, a penal colony—*poenarum locos, poenales locos*; Guibert's mother asks her husband's ghost *ubi commaneret*, where he has been living); and second, great stress is laid on solidarity between the living and the dead. This solidarity is of two kinds: one based on family or blood ties or, even more, on the marital bond (at a time when the Church is placing particular emphasis on the words of Paul according to which husband and wife are of the same flesh), and the other based on spiritual ties, like the bond formed between the convert and the old woman who helps her in her conversion. Finally, the key element of the system is the expiation of sins by suffering, which constitutes both punishment and purgation. This suffering is purgative of man's suffering (*molestias istas molestiarum hominis . . . purgatrices*).

Let us turn now to two other texts, which are more literary and traditional than Guibert's account of his mother's vision but still show powerful imaginations at work: the visions of Alberic and Tnugdal.

Alberic of Settefrati at Monte Cassino

Alberic of Settefrati, born around 1100, had a vision when he was ten, during the course of an illness which left him in a coma for nine days and nine nights. After entering the famous Benedictine monastery at Monte Cassino during the period when Gerard was abbot (1111–23), Alberic recounted his vision to the monk Guidone, who wrote it down. Passed on from hand to hand and by word of mouth, the story suffered alteration, however, and Senioretto, abbot from 1127 to 1137, advised Alberic to rewrite it with the help of Pietro Diacono. It is this version of the story that has survived.[14] It bears earmarks of other visions familiar to the monks of Monte Cassino: The Passion of Perpetua and Felicitas, the Vision of Wetti, the Vision of Saint Fursy, and the Life of Saint Brandon. Some authorities claim that they can also detect signs of Muslim influence, but this can have been limited at best, since Hell, according to Muslim eschatology, is reserved for infidels and polytheists and there seems to be nothing in Muslim doctrine that might correspond to Purgatory.[15]

Saint Peter, accompanied by two angels, Emmanuel and Eligius, appeared to the young Alberic, who had been wafted into the sky by a white dove, and took him off to see the penal and infernal places (*loca poenarum et inferni*). The account of the vision seems interminable.[16] Here I can only summarize it, but I have tried to remain as close to the original text as possible in order to preserve the precision of its imagery and the impression that, despite the guidance of Saint Peter, the monk's wanderings are in fact quite aimless. It is against this aimlessness that we will be able to measure the gradual increase in order that occurs as Purgatory becomes more and more sharply defined.

Alberic first comes upon a place where he sees burning balls of fire and flaming clouds of gas, in which children who died during their first year of life are being purged. Their punishment is light because they did not have time to commit very many sins. The curve measuring the degree of sinfulness in fact parallels the ages of man. It rises through youth and maturity and declines with old age. The time spent in places of purgation is proportional to the quantity of sin and therefore to the age at which death occurs. Children who die before the age of one spend seven days in these places; those who die before the age of two spend fourteen days; and so on (Alberic does not go into any more detail, no doubt because continuing this arithmetic progression would have raised delicate issues).

He then comes upon a frozen valley in which adulterers, fornicators, participants in incest, and others guilty of crimes of lust are being tortured. Next comes another valley thick with thorny shrubbery in which women who refused to suckle their infants hang by their breasts, sucked by serpents, and women guilty of adultery hang by their hair, in flames. Next is an iron ladder with fiery rungs at the foot of which is a basin of boiling pitch: climbing up and down this ladder are men who had sexual relations with their wives on days when the sexual act is prohibited (Sundays and holy days). There follows an oven with sulphurous flames in which rulers who acted as tyrants toward their subjects are consumed, along with women guilty of abortion and infanticide. After this oven comes a burning lake which resembles a lake of blood. Into this lake are plunged unrepentant murderers, after spending three years with an effigy of their victim hung around their necks. Nearby is a huge burning basin filled with bronze, tin, lead, sulphur, and boiling resin, in which bishops, patrons, and other church officials must remain for periods ranging from three to eighty years for allowing their ministries to be carried out by perjuring, adulterous, or excommunicated priests.

Alberic is subsequently taken close to Hell, a pit filled with horrible shadows from which cries, moans, and fetid odors spill forth. Nearby stands an enormous chained dragon, in whose fiery throat countless souls are being swallowed like flies. Because of the thick darkness, it is impossible to make out whether these souls are disappearing into the shadows or going into Hell itself. Alberic's guides tell him that this is the place where Judas, Ananias, Caiaphas, Herod, and other sinners condemned without judgment are kept.

In another valley the sacrilegious are being burned in a lake of fire and simoniacs in a hole through which flames pass up and down. In another horrible place, dark and rank, filled with sizzling flames, serpents, dragons, shrill cries and terrifying moans, purgation is being carried out on souls that have abandoned the clerical or monastic state, failed to do penance, committed perjury, adultery, or sacrilege, borne false witness, or perpetrated other "crimes." They are purged in proportion to their sins, like gold, lead, tin, or other substances, just as Paul said in his First Epistle to the Corinthians.

Then a great bird comes, carrying a small, old monk on its wings. The bird drops the monk into the shadowy pit of Hell, where he is immediately surrounded by demons. But the bird then returns and plucks the monk from their grasp.

At this point Saint Peter announces to Alberic that he is leaving him with the two angels: Alberic, scared to death, is attacked by a horrible demon that tries to drag him down into Hell, but Saint Peter comes back to deliver him and propels him into a place of paradise.

Before going on to describe Paradise, Alberic gives a few additional details about what he has seen in the places of punishment. He says that he saw thieves and plunderers chained naked, unable to stand erect and bound by chains of fire fastened to their necks, hands, and feet. He saw a great river of fire flowing out of Hell, and spanning this river a bridge of fire which quickly and readily broadened when the souls of the righteous passed over it but which shrank to a filament's breadth when the souls of sinners crossed, thus casting them down into the river where they remained until, purged and roasted like meat, they were finally able to cross the bridge. Saint Peter reveals to him that this river and this bridge are called purgatories.[17]

Saint Peter then tells Alberic that a man must not despair, no matter how great his crimes, because any sin can be expiated through penance. Finally, the apostle shows Alberic a field so huge that it would take three days and three nights to cross it, and covered with a dense growth of thorns. In this field is a gigantic dragon ridden by a devil with the appearance of a knight, who holds a great serpent in his hand. This devil chases after any soul that falls into the field and strikes it with his serpent. When the soul has run around enough to unburden itself of all its sins, its way becomes less obstructed and it is able to escape.

Leaving these purgatorial places, Alberic moves on to happier locales. Souls finally made worthy to reach *refrigerium* come to a very agreeable place, which smells of lilies and roses. In the middle of this field is Paradise, to which most souls will gain entry only after the Last Judgment, except for the angels and the saints who are accepted without judgment into the sixth heaven. The most glorious of all the saints in this place is Benedict, and the most glorious of all the souls in the field are those of the monks. Alberic's guides heap praise upon the monks and describe the program of life they must follow in order to be worthy of glory. They must always love God and their neighbor. Beyond that, most of the prescriptions are negative: to withstand insult and persecution, resist the temptations of the Devil, work with the hands without desiring wealth, resist vice, and live in fear of God. After pointing out that the three most dangerous sins are gluttony (*gula*), avarice (*cupidas*), and pride (*superbia*), Saint Peter takes Alberic to visit the seven heavens, about which few details are offered, except that the sixth heaven is the abode of the angels, the archangels, and the saints, and that the seventh is where the throne of God is located. The dove then takes him to a place surrounded by a high wall. Looking over this wall, he is able to see what is inside but this he is forbidden, as are all men, to reveal.[18]

In considering this account, I will say nothing about the mosaic of literary sources from which it draws its inspiration, nor will I discuss the Benedictine loyalties that lie behind it. As far as the inception of Purgatory is concerned, the interest of the story is limited but not negligible, in part because of what it does not say and the boundaries it does not trespass.

There is no doubt that the account is extremely confused and that the picture it gives of the geography of the hereafter is still more confused. Alberic is a long way indeed from forming a clear concept of a third realm of the other world. The other world that he describes is extraordinarily compartmentalized. With Saint Peter's help we move at will from the penal places to the pits of Hell or to Paradise or to the surface of the earth. But considerable importance is attached to the "penal places," from which one ultimately escapes into salvation. Any accounting must remain approximate, because of the extreme redundancy of the description, but the figures I come up with are the following: out of fifty "chapters," sixteen are devoted to what will become Purgatory, compared with twelve to Paradise and its immediate surroundings and only one to Hell in the proper sense of the word.

The vision has practically nothing to say about the "theory" of purgatorial places, at best proposing a rather crude theology. Any sin can consign a soul to these places, and all sins can be expiated. The role of penance is exalted, but nothing is said about the relative importance of penance on earth compared with expiation in the places of suffering. No distinction is made between serious sins and lesser sins (the dividing line between mortal and venial sins had not yet been drawn). Apparently, the sins that are here expiated in temporary but infernal punishments are primarily the *scelera*, or crimes, which according to Augustine lead straight to Hell. Finally, after expiation souls do not enter directly into Paradise but must wait in an antechamber or vestibule of Paradise as such: the field of happiness.

Still, post-mortem purgation occupies an important place in this account. In describing the river and the bridge, Alberic uses the word "purgatory" in such a way that the epithet seems quite close to the substantive. Furthermore, he shows a clear tendency to introduce a system of bookkeeping or accounting, even if in this case a confused numerological symbolism is involved, and to establish a proportion between the sin committed on earth and the time of expiation in the other world.

Reading this vision leaves one with the impression that its author or authors, living in an old-fashioned monastic environment, felt the pressure to make room for purgation in the other world but were unable to give order to their thinking, which draws heavily on the traditional culture of their world for many features of the vision, including the old idea of *refrigerium*.

A similar impression results from reading yet another vision, this one drawn from Ireland, at the opposite end of the world of Benedictine monasticism.[19]

Ireland: Tnugdal's Vision of an Other World without Purgatory

Tnugdal's other world—his voyage includes no earthly episode—is somewhat better organized than Alberic's. Like the Cassinian monk, Tnugdal first passes through a series of places in which various categories of sinners are being tormented: murderers, traitors, misers, thieves, abductors, gluttons, and fornicators. The places where they are being punished are of unusual dimensions: deep valleys, a very high mountain, an enormous lake, a huge house. Later on Dante was to give the theme of the mountain a special treatment of his own. Here, the souls on the mountain are subjected alternately to extremes of heat and cold. Darkness and stench are everywhere. Monstrous beasts add to the horror. One of these beasts sits on a frozen lake and devours souls in its fiery gullet, digests them, and then vomits them up (an old Indo-European theme). The souls thus reincarnated have sharply pointed beaks with which they tear at their own bodies. The victims of this beast are fornicators, particularly fornicating monks. In Piranesi-like images Tnugdal sees the souls of gluttons cook like bread in an immense oven. Those who have accumulated sin upon sin are tortured in a valley full of noisy forges by a blacksmith-torturer named Vulcan. Along with the distinctive treatment of various sins and vices, prominence is given to the notion of the quantity of sin. Furthermore—a sign of the times in the justice-smitten twelfth century—the angel makes clear that God is, despite the variety of tortures, nonetheless merciful and, above all, just: "Here each person suffers according to his deserts, in keeping with the verdict of justice."

Then follows a long descent down a steep precipice into the lower regions of Hell, where Tnugdal faces horrors, cold, stench, and darkness greater than anything he has endured previously. He sees a rectangular trench like a cistern from which there emerges a smoky, fetid flame full of demons and souls that resemble sparks, rising for a time, vanishing into nothingness, and falling back into the depths. He then comes to the very gate of Hell and has the privilege to witness, as a living person, what the souls of the damned, plunged in darkness, cannot see, any more than they can see Tnugdal himself. Finally, he sees the prince of darkness himself, a beast larger than all those he has seen previously.

Then the stench and darkness lift and Tnugdal and his angel discover, at the base of a huge wall, a multitude of sad men and women beleaguered by wind and rain. The angel explains that these are the souls of those who are not entirely wicked, who tried to live honorably but who did not dispense their temporal wealth to the poor and who must spend several years out in the rain before being shown the way to a good rest (*requies bona*). Passing through a gate in the wall, Tnugdal and his companion come upon a beautiful, sweet-smelling field, full of flowers and brightly lit, a pleasant place in which crowds of men and women frolic gaily. These are the not entirely good, those worthy of being plucked out of the tortures of Hell but not yet ready to join the saints. In the middle of the field stands the fountain of youth, whose water bestows the gift of eternal life.

At this point in the story we come upon a very curious account of the legendary kings of Ireland—whom Tnugdal evidently considers to have been real historical figures. Those who were wicked have repented, and those who were good were nevertheless guilty of certain sins, and so they are here either in the midst or at the end of a period of expiation. Just as Benedictine patriotism inspired Alberic's vision, so Irish "nationalism" makes its appearance here. This is also another instance of the tradition of the hereafter that we encountered earlier in the vision of Charles the Fat. The existence of a purgatorial place (the word purgatory is not actually uttered here) makes it possible to level moderate criticism at the monarchy, which is both honored and rebuked.

Thus we find kings Domachus and Conchobar, both extremely cruel and violently hostile to one another, turned gentle and reconciled in friendship, having repented before they died. Should this be read as a call for unity of the Irish clans? Even more important is the vision of King Cormachus (Cormac), who is seated on a throne in a very beautiful house whose walls, made of gold and silver, have neither doors nor windows but can be penetrated at any point. He is served by paupers and pilgrims, to whom he distributed his property while still alive. After a short while, however, the house becomes dark, all the inhabitants turn sad, the king begins to cry, gets up, and leaves the room. All the souls stand and reach out their hands to heaven, begging God to "have pity on they servant." Then we see the king plunged into fire up to his navel, his entire body covered with a hair shirt. The angel explains that the king suffers for three hours each day and rests for twenty-one hours. He suffers up to his navel because he was an adulterer and over his entire body because he was responsible for the death of a count who was close to Saint Patrick and because he committed perjury. All his other sins have been forgiven.

At length Tnugdal and the angel reach Paradise, which consists of three regions surrounded by walls. A wall of silver encloses the place reserved for righteous couples; a wall of gold surrounds the place set aside for the martyrs and the chaste, monks and nuns, and defenders and builders of churches; and finally, a wall of precious stones surrounds the virgins and the nine orders of angels, the saint-confessor Ruadan, Saint Patrick, and four (Irish!) bishops. With this final vision Tnugdal's soul returns to his body.

What Tnugdal's vision clearly shows is this: while the geography of the other world is still fragmented, with Hell as such appearing to be unified only because it cannot be visited, three principles are beginning to govern the organization of the various purgatorial places. The first of these principles is geographical: we pass from one area to another, the transition being marked by contrasts of terrain and temperature. The second is moral: those undergoing purgation are distributed among the various places according to the nature of their vices. The third is, properly speaking, religious, not to say theological: men are classified into four categories, namely, the entirely good, who go directly to Paradise after death; the entirely wicked, who are individually judged immediately after death (Tnugdal stresses that the damned "have already been judged") and sent to Hell; the not entirely good; and the not entirely wicked. But Tnugdal is not entirely clear about the last two categories. If we read him literally, it would seem that the souls in these two groups are distinct from the generality of sinners being tortured in the upper region of Hell. In speaking of the not entirely wicked Tnugdal makes no allusion to their having passed through penal places and limits himself to saying that they spend a "few years" in wind and rain, suffering from hunger and thirst. As for the not entirely good, the angel tells Tnugdal that "they have been plucked from the torments of Hell" but are not yet worthy of entering into true Paradise.

Given the date, it is rather suprising, too, that the idea of purgation does not figure in the account (nor is the word mentioned). Tnugdal has made a clumsy attempt to organize a whole range of elements from literary and theological tradition into a vision that he is incapable of unifying. For one thing, he mentions the existence of two Hells, but he is unable to indicate the precise function of the upper Hell. For another, he clearly subscribes to Augustine's theory of the four categories, ranging men on a scale of good and evil from best to worst. But since he does not know what categories to consign to the upper Hell, he has created new regions to accommodate those for whom he has no other place and winds up with something like five regions in his other world. This fivefold division was in fact one of the ways proposed in the twelfth century for solving the problem of how to reshape the other world. The weakest point in Tnugdal's conception (I allow myself to make this value judgment because I believe that the coherence of the system of Purgatory was an important factor in its success with both clergy and the masses in an "age of rationalization") is that Tnugdal does not establish any connection between the places of waiting (and expiation in one degree or another of severity) and the lower regions of Hell. If he had provided for passage first through the one and then through the other, he would have given a concrete solution to the issues raised by Augustine's categorization. He did not do so probably in part because his conception of space was still confused but, even more, because his conception of time did not allow a solution (it bears repeating that space and time cannot be separated). For Tnugdal, the time of the other world was an eschatological time that had little or no similarity to time on earth, historical time. Here and there, it is true, he does slip in references to periods of "a few years" in the other world, but these periods do not follow one another in any orderly succession. The time of the other world had not yet been unified, and a fortiori there was a great gulf between the conceptualization of time in this world and time in the next.

Discovery in Ireland: "Saint Patrick's Purgatory"

Although the fourth imaginary voyage, to which we now turn, was the work of a monk (a Cistercian, however), it introduces into the usual traditional context certain important novelties. One of these is of particular importance: Purgatory is named as one of three regions of the other world. This brief work occupies an essential place in the history of Purgatory, in whose success it played an important, if not decisive, role. The work I have in mind is the celebrated *Purgatorium Sancti Patricii*, "Saint Patrick's Purgatory."[20]

The author is a monk named "H" (an initial which Matthew Paris in the thirteenth century expanded for no good reason to Henricus, or Henry) who at the time of writing lived in the Cistercian monastery of Saltrey in Huntingdonshire. He was asked to write the story by a Cistercian abbot, the abbot of Sartis (today Wardon in Bedfordshire). He had first heard the tale from another monk, Gilbert, who was sent to Ireland by Abbot Gervase of the Cistercian monastery of Luda (today Louthpark in Huntingdonshire) to look for a site suitable for the founding of a monastery. Since Gilbert did not speak Gaelic, he took with him the knight Owein as interpreter and bodyguard, and Owein tells him the adventure story in which he figures as the hero in Saint Patrick's Purgatory.

In the preamble to his work H of Saltrey invokes Augustine and especially Gregory the Great to remind his readers how much the living stand to profit from edifying visions and revelations concerning the hereafter. This is particularly true of the various forms of punishment that are called "purgatorial" (*que purgatoria vocatur*), in which those who may have committed sins during their lives but who nevertheless remained righteous are purged and thereby enabled to achieve the eternal life to which they are predestined. The punishments are proportioned to the seriousness of the sins committed and to the degree of goodness or wickedness of the sinners. Corresponding to the range of different sins and punishments is a gradation in the places of punishment, in the subterranean Hell which, according to some, is a dark prison. The places in which the worst tortures are inflicted are at the bottom, and the places of maximum joy are at the top. The middling good and middling bad receive their just deserts in the middle (*media autem bona et mala in medio*). From this it is clear that H of Saltrey has adopted the system of three categories (rather than Augustine's four) and the idea of an intermediary place.

Furthermore, souls receive purgatorial punishment according to their merits, and those souls that God allows to return to their earthly bodies after being punished exhibit marks similar to corporeal marks as reminders, proofs, and warnings.[21]

While Patrick was preaching the Gospel, without much success, to the recalcitrant Irish and seeking to convert them by the fear of Hell and the allure of Paradise, Jesus showed him in a foresaken place a round, dark hole (*fossa*) and told him that if a person animated by a true spirit of penitence and faith spent a day and a night in this hole, he would be purged of all his sins and would see the tortures of the wicked and the joys of the good. Patrick hastened to build a church beside this hole, installed regular canons in the church, had a wall built around the hole, and entrusted the gate key to the prior of the church. Numerous penitents were supposed to have entered this place since the time of Patrick, who, it is said, ordered that their accounts be recorded. The name given to the place was Purgatory, and since Patrick was the first to have tasted its fruits, it became known as Saint Patrick's Purgatory (*sancti Patricii purgatorium*).[22]

According to custom, those who wished to enter Saint Patrick's Purgatory were required to obtain authorization from the bishop of the diocese, who was supposed to attempt to dissuade them. If he could not do so, he sent the applicant together with his authorization to the prior of the church, who also tried to persuade the person to choose another form of penance with the warning that many had died after passing through the gate. If he too failed, the prior then ordered the candidate to begin his ordeal with two weeks of prayer. At the end of this time the candidate attended a mass, during which he took communion and was exorcised with holy water. He was then taken, in a procession of chanting priests, to Purgatory. The prior opened the gate, reminding the candidate that there were demons about and that many previous visitors had vanished. If the candidate persisted, he was blessed by all the priests and then, making the sign of the cross, passed through the gate into Purgatory. The prior shut the gate behind him. On the following day at the same hour, the procession returned to the hole. If the penitent emerged, he returned to the church and spent another two weeks in prayer. If the gate remained closed, it was assumed that the penitent had died, and the procession withdrew. This was a particular kind of ordeal, or judgment of God, a type that may have been typical of Celtic tradition.

At this point in his account, H of Saltrey skips to his own time (*hiis nostris temporibus*), which he further specifies as the time of King Stephen (1135–54). In the thirteenth century Matthew Paris was even more explicit about the date: without the slightest evidence he says that the adventure of Owein the knight took place in 1153. Heavily weighed down with sins of unspecified nature, Owein, having successfully negotiated the preliminary phases of the ordeal, enters the hole cheerfully and with confidence. He looks upon his undertaking as essentially a knightly adventure, which he confronts by himself, intrepidly (*novam gitur miliciam aggressus miles noster, licet solus, intrepidus tamen*).[23] Advancing through thickening shadows, he comes to a sort of monastery, inhabited by twelve figures clad in white robes, rather like monks. Their leader explains the rules of the trial to him. He is to be surrounded by demons, who will try either to frighten him with the sight of terrible tortures or to seduce him with false words. If he gives in to the fear or the seduction and retraces his steps, he is lost, body and soul. If he feels he is about to give in, he is instructed to invoke the name of Jesus.

At this moment the demons burst in, and from now until the end of his infernal journey they do not leave him for a moment, as he glimpses countless frightening visions by the light of torturing flames and in the midst of fetid ordors and shrill cries. From each of the trials he is about to undergo the knight will emerge victorious by invoking the name of Jesus, and after each trial he will refuse to quit and turn back. I shall therefore omit mention of the denouement of each episode. The devils first build a pyre in a room of the house from which his journey begins and attempt to throw him upon it. After passing through a dark desert and being whipped by a cutting wind with an edge as sharp as a sword's he comes to a limitless field in which men and women are lying naked on the earth, to which they are fastened by burning nails through their hands and feet. He then enters a second field in which people of every age, sex, and condition are lying on their backs or their stomachs, preyed upon by fiery dragons, serpents, and toads; a third field in which men and women with burning nails piercing all their limbs are whipped by demons; and finally a fourth field, a real chamber of horrors of the most diverse kinds, where he sees men and women suspended by iron hooks stuck in the sockets of their eyes or in their ears, throats, hands, breasts, or genitals, while others have fallen victim to hell's kitchen and are being baked in ovens, roasted over open fires, or turned on spits—and so on. Next he sees a great wheel of fire, with men fastened to it being spun at high speed through the flames. This is followed by a huge bathhouse, in which a multitude of men and women, young and old alike, are plunged into vats of boiling metals, some completely submerged, others immersed up to their eyelids or lips or necks or chests or navels or knees, while some have only a single hand or foot in the cauldron. Owein then comes to a mountain and to a river of fire flowing in a deep gorge with sheer walls. On the summit a crowd of people is lashed by a violent, glacial wind which blows some of them into the river, from which they attempt to escape only to be pushed back in by demons equipped with iron hooks.

Finally, he comes upon a horribly foul black flame escaping from a well, in which innumerable souls rise like sparks and fall back again. The demons accompanying the knight tell him that "this is the gate of Hell, the entrance of Gehenna, the broad highway that leads to death. He who enters here will never leave again, for there is no redemption in Hell. This is the eternal fire prepared for the Devil and his fiends, and you cannot deny being of their number." As he feels himself being caught up and carried down into the well, Owein once more utters the name of God and finds himself at some distance from the pit facing a very broad river of fire traversed by what seems to be an impassable bridge, since it is so high as to induce vertigo, so narrow that it is impossible to set foot on it, and so slippery that it would be impossible in any case to maintain one's footing. In the river below, demons are waiting with iron hooks. Once again Owein invokes the name of Jesus and advances onto the bridge. The further he advances, the wider and more stable the bridge becomes, and half-way across he can no longer see the river to the right or the left. He escapes one last infuriated attempt by the demons and, climbing down from the bridge, finds himself facing a very splendid high wall whose gates, made of pure gold set off by precious gems, give off a delightful odor. He enters and finds himself in a city of marvels.

At the head of a procession are two figures resembling archbishops, who address Owein in the following terms:[24]

> We are going to explain to you the meaning [rationem] of what you have seen. This is the earthly Paradise. We have come here because we have expiated our sins—we had not completed our penance on earth prior to death—in the tortures you saw along the way, in which we remained for a more or less lengthy period depending on the quantity of our sins. All whom you have seen in the various penal places, except those below the mouth of Hell, will come, after their purgation is complete, to the rest in which we find ourselves, and ultimately they will be saved. There is no way for those who are being tortured to know how long they will remain in the penal palaces, because their trials can be alleviated or abridged by means of masses, psalms, prayers, and alms given in their behalf. By the same token, we, who are enjoying this wonderful repose and joy but who have not yet been found worthy to go up to Heaven, will not remain here indefinitely; every day some of us move from the earthly Paradise to the celestial Paradise.

They then have Owein climb a mountain and from there show him the gates of the celestial Paradise. A tongue of flame comes down from these gates and fills them with a delicious sensation. But the "archbishops" bring Owein back to reality: "You have seen part of what you wanted to see: the repose of the blessed and the tortures of sinners. Now you must return by the same path you took to get here. If from now on you live well in the world, you can be sure that you will join us after your death, but if you live badly, you have seen what tortures await you. On your way back you will have nothing more to fear from the demons, because they will not dare to attack you, nor from the tortures, for they will not harm you." In tears, the knight starts back and ultimately rejoins the twelve people he left at the start, who congratulate him and announce that he has been purged of his sins. The prior opens the gate a second time and Owein leaves Saint Patrick's Purgatory to begin a second two-week period of prayer in the church. Following this he takes the cross and leaves on a pilgrimage to Jerusalem. When he returns he goes to the king, his lord, and asks him to designate a religious order in which the knight may live. This happens to be the time when Gilbert of Luda is about to depart on his mission. The king offers Owein the chance to serve as the monk's interpreter. Delighted, the knight accepts "because in the other world I saw no order in glory as great as the Cistercian order." They build an abbey, but Owein, as it turns out, does not want to become either a monk or a lay brother and is content to remain Gilbert's servant.

For our purposes, the imagery of the other world is not the most important thing about this story, though that imagery certainly must have contributed largely to its success. Most of the items traditional since the *Apocalypse of Paul* are included, and the images prefigure those to be found in subsequent visions, the *Divine Comedy* in particular. But the imagery is more the general imagery of Hell than an imagery peculiar to Purgatory. Certain themes are left out, however, and their absence here no doubt contributed to the fact that they all but vanish from later accounts. Cold, for example, has been supplanted almost entirely by fire, whereas previously heat and cold had generally been linked in the penal imagery of the hereafter.

In the vision of Drythelm, for example, the visitor to the other world first comes to a wide, deep valley whose left slope is engulfed in terrible flames while its right slope is whipped by a violent snowstorm. Similarly, Tnugdal, before coming to the lower region of Hell, encounters "a great mountain traversed by a narrow path, one side of which is a stinking, sulphurous, smoky fire while the other is wind-whipped ice."

In the sermon attributed to Saint Bernard we read that "those who are in Purgatory awaiting redemption must first be tormented either by the heat of fire or by the rigors of cold."

But the significance of cold as a punishment had for some time not been clearly perceived. The idea of a beneficent *refrigerium* had more or less supplanted it.

In the vision of the Emperor Charles the Fat, the imperial dreamer transported into the infernal beyond hears his father, Louis the German, standing in boiling water up to his thighs, utter the following words: "Have no fear, I know that your soul will return to your body. If God has allowed you to come here, it was so that you might see the sins for which I am undergoing these and the other torments you have seen. I spend one day in this basin of boiling water, but the next day I am transported into that other basin, in which the water is very cool." The author of this text has failed to grasp the original significance of the rite, since the move into the cold water is described as a favor that the emperor owes to the intercession of Saint Peter and Saint Rémi.

In *Saint Patrick's Purgatory* cold figures only in the passage describing the glacial wind that whips the summit of the mountain at the bottom of Purgatory. Fire, which in the twelfth century represented the very place of purgation, has superseded cold. The birth of Purgatory thus sounded the death knell for the concept of *refrigerium* and paved the way for the eventual disappearance of the bosom of Abraham.[25]

Saint Patrick's Purgatory at once met with considerable success. Shane Leslie has written that the work was "one of the best sellers of the Middle ages." Its date of composition is uncertain. It is generally said to have been written around 1190, since its translation into French by the celebrated English poetess Marie de France presumably cannot have taken place later than the last decade of the twelfth century. In addition, Saint Malachy, who was canonized in 1190, is mentioned in the *Tractatus* in his quality of saint. But other scholars put the date of composition somewhat later, around 1210.[26] While I have tried to situate the time when the word *purgatorium* first appeared and to date the decisive change in the representation of the hereafter as precisely as possible, I do not think it is particularly important for our purposes to say that *Saint Patrick's Purgatory* was written in 1210 rather than 1190. The key point, rather, is this: that the new region of the other world took shape in two phases, first in theological-spiritual literature between 1170 and 1180 at the prompting of Parisian masters and Cistercian monks, and then in visionary literature stemming from the 1180–1215 period. In fact, the *Life of Saint Patrick* by Jocelyn of Furness, composed between 1180 and 1183, mentions Saint Patrick's Purgatory but situates it on Mount Cruachin Aigle in Connaught.[27] The real events in the history of beliefs, mentalities, and sensibilities can rarely be dated to the precise day or year. The birth of Purgatory is a phenomenon that we can associate with the turn of the thirteenth century.

By contrast, it is of considerable importance that a description of Purgatory, explicitly mentioned and associated with a specific place on earth, should have appeared around the year 1200. The composition of the *Tractatus* by H of Saltrey must have been roughly contemporaneous with the rise of the legend and the creation of a pilgrimage. Saint Patrick's Purgatory is mentioned again, omitting the story of Owein the knight, in the *Topographia Hibernica* of Giraldus Cambrensis, the first edition of which dates from 1188, but it is not mentioned in the oldest known manuscript and is found only in a marginal note in a thirteenth-century manuscript. Giraldus travelled in Ireland in 1185–86. In chapter 5 of the second part of the *Topographia Hibernica* he describes a lake in Ulster in which there is an island divided into two parts. One of these parts is pleasant and beautiful, with an official church, and renowned as a place frequented by saints. The other, wild and horrible, is abandoned to demons. There are nine holes in the earth. Those who dare to spend the night in one of these holes are seized by evil spirits and must endure horrible tortures in an unspeakable fire until morning, and when they are found are in an almost inanimate state. It is said that if one does penance by undergoing these tortures, infernal punishments can be escaped after death, unless very grave sins are committed in the meantime.[28]

This island, Station Island, is located in Lough Derg (Red Lake) in County Donegal in the present-day Irish Republic near the border with Northern Ireland. Pilgrims have apparently been making their way to Saint Patrick's Purgatory there ever since the end of the twelfth century. Pope Alexander VI condemned the practice in 1497, but the chapel and the pilgrimage revived in the sixteenth century and have survived several subsequent destructions and interdictions in 1632, 1704, and 1727. Pilgrimages became particularly frequent after 1790 and a large chapel was erected. A huge new church dedicated to Saint Patrick was completed in 1931 and every year some 15,000 pilgrims visit the site between June 1 and August 15.[29]

While Saint Patrick's Purgatory is clearly related to Irish Christianity and the cult of Saint Patrick, it is doubtful whether in the twelfth century it had the same Catholic and Irish nationalist overtones that it acquired subsequently and still carries with it today. Indeed, it seems probable that the pilgrimage was first begun and controlled by English regular clergy.

Following the translation by Marie de France,[30] numerous Latin versions of H of Saltrey's *Tractatus* appeared as well as many translations into vernaculars, especially French and English.[31] The Latin version was included by Roger of Wendover in his *Flores Historiarum*, compiled prior to 1231. Matthew Paris, who continued Roger's work in his *Chronica majora*, repeats the story verbatim. That great popularizer of Purgatory, the German Cistercian Caesarius of Heisterbach, who may or may not have known H's *Tractatus*, in any case has this to say in his *Dialogus miraculorum* 12.38: "Let anyone who doubts the existence of Purgatory go to Ireland and enter the Purgatory of Patrick and he will have no further doubts about the punishments of Purgatory." Five authors of the most influential edifying histories of the thirteenth century made use of the *Purgatorium Sancti Patricii*: James of Vitry in his *Historia orientalis* (chap. 92); the two Dominicans Vincent of Beauvais, in the *Speculum historiale* (bk. 20, chaps. 23–24), and Stephen of Bourbon, in his *Tractatus de diversis materiis praedicabilibus* (see below); Humbert of Romans in *De dono timoris*; and Jacobus da Voragine (Jacopo da Varazze) in his celebrated *Golden Legend*, where we read the following passage. "And

Saint Patrick learned, by revelation, that this well led to a purgatory, and that those who wished to descend there could expiate their sins and would be dispensed from any Purgatory after their death."[32] Gossouin of Metz speaks of it in his *Image of the World*, of which there are verse versions from 1245 and 1248 and a prose version from 1246.[33] Here is an excerpt from one of the verse versions:*

> In Ireland there is a lake
> Which day and night burns like fire,
> And which is called Saint Patrick's
> Purgatory. And even now
> If someone comes
> Who is not genuinely repentant,
> He is immediately carried away and lost,
> And no one knows what has become of him.
> But if he confesses and is repentant,
> He must suffer many a torment
> And purge himself of his sins.
> The more there are of them, the more he suffers.
> And he who from this place has returned,
> Nothing more pleases him
> In this world, and never again
> Will he know laughter but shall live in tears,
> Moaning about the evils that exist
> And the sins that men commit.[34]

This poem the learned Saint Bonaventure had read either in the original or in a summary, and he discusses it in his commentary on the *Sententiae* of Peter Lombard.[35] Froissart asks a noble Englishman, Sir William Lisle, who traveled in Ireland in 1394, if he has visited "Saint Patrick's Purgatory." Lisle answers in the affirmative and allows that he and a companion even spent a night in the famous hole, to which he refers as a cellar. Both of them slept there and had visions in dreams, and Sir William is convinced that "all that is mere fantasy," exhibiting an incredulity rare for the time.[36]

Dante studied the *Tractatus* of H of Saltrey quite closely. The work's renown did not end with what is traditionally considered the Middle Ages. Rabelais and Ariosto allude to it. Shakespeare thought that the story was familiar to the spectators of *Hamlet*[37] and Calderon wrote a play on the theme.[38] The vogue for Saint Patrick's Purgatory in both high and popular literature lasted at least until the eighteenth century.[39]

The essential point about both the cult and the *Tractatus* is this: at last there was a description of Purgatory, a place with a name of its own and an other world consisting of three regions (not counting the antechamber of Paradise that Owein visits). Alongside Hell and Heaven, which Owein is

---

*Here translated literally into English from the slightly modernized French text cited by the author.—Trans.

not permitted to see, there is Purgatory, in which the hardy knight-penitent travels extensively and which he describes at length. Furthermore, the geography of the next world is fitted into the geography of this one, not by means of a clumsy juxtaposition, as was the case with Alberic of Settefrati, but rather by specifying the precise location on earth of one of Purgatory's mouths. What could be more in keeping with the beliefs and the mentality of an age in whch cartography, taking its hesitant first steps, depicted Paradise (strictly speaking, the earthly Paradise) as contiguous with the world of the living? As the process of "spatialization" of Purgatory went forward, it became more and more necessary to find the mouths, to provide means of access for those living souls allowed to enter from earth. For a long time these mouths remained more or less indistinguishable from the mouths of Hell, and here the image of the "hole" (or shaft or well) took hold. The topography of the mouths of Purgatory centered on caves and caverns. The fact that Saint Patrick's Purgatory, situated in a cavern on an Irish isle, became so popular reinforced the image of Purgatory as a hole.

Would Anglo-Irish Christianity impose its Purgatory on Christendom without opposition? At the other end of the Christian world, in southern Italy, on the banks not of the ocean but of the Mediterranean Sea, another Purgatory, which had been taking shape for a long time, now began to sharpen its outlines as well. This second Purgatory was in Sicily.

The Sicilian Effort

Evidence for Anglo-Irish concern with travels in Purgatory dates back, so far as we know, to Bede at the beginning of the eighth century. Evidence for Sicilian concern with the subject dates back even farther, to the seventh century, and continues through the thirteenth century. The most important episode, for our purposes, took place in the eleventh century and was discussed earlier: the vision of a hermit in the Lipari Islands, brought back to the mainland by a Cluniac monk and reported first by Jotsuald and later by Peter Damian in their lives of Saint Odilo, abbot of Cluny (994–1049). Here it is said that the lamentations of the dead can be heard emerging from the crater of a mountain inside which the dead are purged.[40]

A century later, Julian of Vézelay delivered his twenty-first sermon, which is interesting in two respects. To begin with, his words offer us an exceptionally clear insight into a particular sensibility with regard to death. Undoubtedly the sermon draws its inspiration in part from two customary sources: on the one hand the ancient tradition that earthly pleasures must be left behind at death, and on the other the monastic tradition of detachment from the things of this world. But the text also reverberates with echoes of delight in man's sojourn on earth, particularly among the dominant classes, which in this period were much given to enjoying the luxurious surroundings of their rural estates, sumptuous houses, rich clothing and furs, works of art and horses, to say nothing of the pleasures of the body. Taken together, these things stand as the sign of a new state of mind, a psychology that emphasizes the value of this world and that provides a framework for explaining why some men began to take an increasing interest in the survival of the world and hence to ask themselves more insistently than before about the nature of the interval between individual death and the end of the world. Here is what Julian of Vézelay has to say:

> Three things terrify me, and at their mere mention my inner being trembles with fear: death, Hell, and the Judgment to come.
>
> I am therefore frightened by the approach of death, which will take me out of my body and away from the pleasing light, shared by everyone, into I know not what region reserved for the spirits of the faithful. . . . After me the history of mankind will unfold without me. . . .
>
> Farewell, hospitable [hospita] earth, on which I have long worn myself out for futile purposes, on which I have inhabited a house of mud, which, though it be mere mud, I leave unwillingly [invitus]. . . . And yet . . . it is unwillingly [that I go] and I will leave only if I am driven out. Pale death will burst in upon my redoubt and drag me, in spite of my resistance, to the door. . . .
>
> Along with the world, we leave behind everything that is of the world. The glory of the world is left behind on that sad day: farewell to honors, wealth, and property, to broad and charming meadows, to the marble floors and painted ceilings of sumptuous houses! And what about the silks and squirrel furs, the variegated coats, the silver cups and fine, neighing horses on which the wealthy who gave themselves airs once paraded! But even this is as nothing, for we must also abandon a wife so sweet to look at, we must abandon our children, and we must leave behind our own bodies, for which we would willingly pay gold to redeem them from this seizure.[41]

The second point of interest in Julian's sermon is that it once again mentions Sicily as the place on earth from which it is possible to gain access to the other world. Here is his first description of those who are burning in eternal flames and those who are doing penance in purgatorial fire:

> To say nothing of those whom Gehenna is burning, who are called "ethnics" from the word Et(h)na, on account of the eternal fire, and for whom there will never more be repose— leaving them aside . . . there are certainly others who, after the death of their body, must endure very long and painful labors. As long as they lived they refused "to bring forth those fruits

worthy of repentance" (Luke 3:8), and yet at the moment of death they confessed and felt feelings of penitence; that is why, upon the decision of the Priest "unto whom the Father hath committed all judgment" (John 5:22), they shall be allowed to complete in purgatorial fire the penitential satisfaction that they neglected to give in this world. This fire, which consumes "wood, hay, and straw heaped up on the foundation of faith" burns those whom it purges; they "shall be saved; yet so as by fire" (1 Cor. 3:12–13 and 15), for they will surely not go from the purgatorial fire to the eternal fire: "The lord does not judge the same case twice" (Job 33:14).

Then, a little farther on, he gives further details about the fire of Gehenna: "The fire sticks to its fuel without respite but consumes it not. Just as the Salamander, a tiny reptile, walks over hot coals without harm to its body; just as asbestos, once it catches fire, burns continuously and is not diminished by the flames; so Etna has burned ceaselessly since perhaps the beginning of the world without exhausting its flammable material."[42]

These excerpts make it clear how Julian, following the medieval cleric's practice (inaugurated by Isidore of Seville) of concocting fantastic etymologies, is able to prove that Mount Etna is the point of contact between the earth and Gehenna, between the living and the dead. But where is the dividing line between Hell and Purgatory in this account?

A curious bit of evidence is available from the early years of the thirteenth century. The cultivated and curious English cleric Gervase of Tilbury, in his *Otia Imperialia (Imperial Diversions)*, written in 1210 and dedicated to Otto IV of Brunswick, the loser at the battle of Bouvines (1214), discusses the hereafter, partly in a traditional vein which pays no heed to such recent novelties as Purgatory, and partly in the form of a singularly interesting and unprecedented story. In chapter 17 of part 3, Gervase discusses two Paradises and two Hells. Just as there is an earthly Paradise as well as a celestial Paradise, so, he tells us, "there are two Hells: one terrestrial, which is said to be situated in a hole in the earth, and in this Hell there is a place, far removed from the places of punishment, which, because of its calm and remoteness, is called 'bosom,' as one speaks of a bosom [gulf] of the sea, and it is said that this is the bosom of Abraham because of the parable of the rich man and Lazarus. . . . There is another Hell, windy and dark, into which the wicked angels have been hurled in order that they be punished, just as the good angels are in the celestial Paradise [empyrean]."[43] What interests Gervase in this account is apparently the fact that certain of these demons visit the earth in order to couple with mortal women, thereby engendering exceptional men who are referred to as "fatherless" or "sons of virgins," such as Merlin the Magician and the future Antichrist.

Later on, Gervase describes various geographic "marvels," particularly ones found in Sicily, and in so doing tells the following story, gleaned in the course of his own travels in that island (in about 1190):

> There is in Sicily a mountain, Etna, which burns with sulphurous fire, near the city of Catana. . . . The common people call this mountain Mondjibel,[44] and the inhabitants of the region tell that in our own time the great Arthur appeared on its deserted slopes. It happened one day that a groom employed by the bishop of Catana ate too much and so became sleepy. The horse that he was combing escaped and disappeared. The groom searched in vain for the horse on the slopes and precipices of the mountain. Increasingly concerned, he began exploring the dark caves on the mountain. A path, which was very narrow but flat, led him to a large, pleasant meadow filled with delights of every kind.
>   There, in a palace built by magic, he found Arthur asleep on a regal bed. After learning the reason for his visit, the king had the horse led in and returned it to the boy to be given to his bishop. He then told of how he had been wounded some time ago in a battle against his nephew Modred and the duke of the Saxons, Childeric, and how he had lain there for a long time since, trying to heal his wounds, which kept reopening. And according to the natives who told me the tale, he sent gifts to the bishop, who showed them to an admiring crowd of onlookers struck dumb by this extraordinary story.[45]

The great Arturo Graf has treated this text and this legend in an admirable article.[46] Here we shall have to be satisfied with merely indicating the legend's place in the history of Purgatory. Gervase of Tilbury was unaware of Purgatory's existence; not only does he continue to adhere to the image of the bosom of Abraham, but he places Arthur in surroundings that resemble some sort of miraculous pagan other world more than the Christian hereafter. More than anything else the text is astonishing evidence of the encounter between northern and southern, Celtic and Italian traditions. A twelfth-century sculpture in the Modena cathedral also bears witness to the same encounter between the Arthurian legend and Italy.[47] What is more, this encounter throws new light on some of the unpredictable elements that played a role in the localization of Purgatory.

Purgatory was attracted toward two poles: Paradise and Hell. It might have developed into either a near-paradise or a quasi-hell. At a very early date, Purgatory (in various rudimentary forms) veered toward the infernal pole, and it was a long time before it began to differentiate itself from Hell. Not before the thirteenth century—and in some accounts even later—did it become anything other than a shallow region of Hell in which souls were tormented not for eternity but for a specified length of time, an upper

Gehenna. Thus Purgatory took shape in the context of a vision of the other world which was more often than not infernal.

Generally speaking, during Purgatory's long period of incubation, this portion of the other world was situated underground, in close contact with Hell; it was the upper portion of Hell. But during this period, in which a confused geography predominated, the infernal model of Purgatory was contaminated and corrected by two other models. One of these was a quasi-paradisaical model of Purgatory.[48] The other grew out of a desire to find a truly intermediary place between Heaven and Hell.

To these dimly perceived problems various solutions, some more coherent, others less, were proposed prior to the thirteenth century. Sometimes a place resembling Hell is set alongside a second place rather like Paradise. In the very murky vision of Tnugdal, for example, there are two regions, both situated between Heaven and Hell and located on either side of a wall, one beleaguered by wind and rain, the other pleasant and irrigated by the water from a fountain of life. The first region holds the souls of the not entirely wicked, the second the not entirely good. Sometimes the place of purgation seems to be located on the surface of the earth but in a deep, narrow valley plunged in darkness, quite like the valleys of Hell. This is the case with the vision of Drythelm.

The Infernalization of Purgatory and Its Limits

No other text resembles Gervase of Tilbury's in depicting Purgatory as a place of repose. His account describes waiting in what is surely a region of the dead (a mountain filled with fire to which the groom is led by a black horse in the role of conductor of souls, where Arthur's earthly wounds turn out to be incurable, constantly reopening) but where a hero like Arthur lies "on a regal bed . . . in a palace built by magic . . . in the midst of a large, pleasant meadow filled with delights of every kind."

At this decisive moment in the history of Purgatory, then, it seems that Latin Christendom, which could not make up its mind whether the mouth of Purgatory was in Ireland or Sicily, also had difficulty deciding whether Purgatory should be made more like Hell or more like Heaven. In fact, while Gervase was busy gathering stories that reflected ideas from the past more than ideas from the present, the decision had already been made. Burdened with the weight of oriental apocalyptic literature, a literature full of fires, tortures, sound and fury; defined by Augustine as the site of punishments more painful than any earthly pain; and given its finishing touches by a Church that dispensed salvation but only in fear and trembling, Purgatory had already veered in the direction of Hell. In treating the legend of Arthur in Etna, Arturo Graf has magisterially demonstrated how the infernalization and satanization of the episode were consummated between the time of Gervase of Tilbury's account and that of the Dominican Stephen of Bourbon some fifty years later. Arthur's Purgatory was turned into a temporary Hell.[49]

Nor was Sicily, unlike Ireland, destined to become a lasting site for Purgatory. To understand why, we must work our way back to the Christian sources of the other world in Sicily. Now, it is true that the Christian other world drew extensively on a rich, ancient heritage, most brilliantly expressed in the mythology of Etna, the infernal home of Vulcan and his forges. But one of the greatest Purgatory's early medieval founders, Gregory the Great, pitched its foundations in Sicily, as is attested by two stories from his *Dialogues*.

In the first text the monk Peter asks Gregory if the good recognize one another in Paradise (*in regno*) and the wicked in Hell (*in supplicio*), and Gregory answers with the story of Lazarus and the rich man. Then he moves on to accounts of visions seen by the dying, by this time a traditional genre (think, for example, of the visions of Saint Martin in that model of Latin hagiography, the *Vita Martini* of Sulpicius Severus). First, he tells an anecdote about a monk who, at the moment of his death, sees Jonas, Ezechiel, and Daniel. Then comes the story of the young Eumorfius. One day, Eumorfius sends his slave to his friend Stephen to say, "Come quickly because the ship that is to take us to Sicily is ready to leave." While the slave is on his way, both men die. This astonishing tale fascinates Peter, who seeks enlightenment from Gregory:

> PETER: But I ask you, why did a ship appear to the departing soul, and why did he say that after death it would take him to Sicily?
> GREGORY: The soul needs no vehicle [*vehiculum*], but it is not surprising that, to a man still placed within his body, there should appear that which he is used to seeing by means of his body, so that he might in this way comprehend where his soul might be taken spiritually. The fact that he told this man that he would be taken to Sicily can mean only one thing: more than any other place, it is in the isles of that land that the fire-spitting cauldrons have opened up. These, as the experts tell it, expand with each passing day, for, as the end of the world is drawing near, and as the number who shall be gathered there to be burnt, above and beyond the number already there, is uncertain, these places of torment must enlarge themselves to receive them all. It is the will of almighty God that these places be shown as a corrective to the men living in this world, so that increduluous minds [*mentes infidelium*] who do not believe that infernal torments exist may see the place of torments, so that those who refuse to believe on the basis of hearsay alone may see with their own eyes.
> As for those, saved or dammed, who made common cause in their works, they are taken to equally common places, as the

true word should suffice to convince us, even if examples are lacking.[50]

That this astonishing mixture of pagan legends and quite orthodox Christianity, of vulcanology and the theology of the last things, should be found in the work of the great eschatological pope should come as no surprise. The second story that deals with the volcanic isles of Sicily and infernal places is one we are already familiar with, the story of the punishment of Theodoric, who is thrown into the volcano of the Liparis.[51]

The most striking feature of this story is the political use it makes of the other world. It remained current throughout the Middle Ages and was the forerunner of other visions of kings punished in the hereafter, two examples of which have already been encountered: the Carolingian sovereigns in the vision of Charles the Fat and the Irish kings in the vision of Tnugdal. But the fact that the Christian places of punishment are located in Sicily is equally significant. The tales recounted from Jotsuald and Peter Damian are obviously part of the same tradition.

Between the time of Gregory the Great and the texts of the eleventh to thirteenth centuries mentioned above (Jotsuald's and Peter Damian's lives of Odilo and Gervase's story of Arthur on Mount Etna), another text was written, a very interesting document concerning the Lipari Isles as an infernal site. This rare eighth-century text informs us about two things: a volcanic eruption that occurred between 723 and 726 and the continuity of a belief that was linked to an unusual place. It is an account of a stop made in the Liparis by a pilgrim to Jerusalem, Saint Willibald:

> From there he went to the town of Catana, and then to Reggio, a city of Calabria. It is there that Theodoric's hell is found. After arriving, they left their boat to see what this hell was. Willibald, driven by curiosity to see what was inside this hell, wanted to climb to the summit of the mountain below which lay the opening of hell, but he could not. Sparks coming from the depths of the black Tartarus rose to the edge and there spread out and piled up. Just as the snow when it falls from the sky piles up in white hillocks that reach to the aerial arches of the sky, so the sparks accumulated at the summit prevented Willibald from climbing. But he saw a terrible and horrible black flame spitting from the pit amidst the roar of thunder. He looked at the great flame and the vapor of smoke rising terribly, very high into the sky. This lava [*pumex* or *fomex*], of which writers have spoken, he saw rising in flames from hell, from which it was hurled into the sea and then cast back onto the land. Men harvested it and carried it away.[52]

The meaning of this passage is clear. What had been located in Sicily, in the volcanoes of the Liparis as well as in Etna, ever since antiquity (and here again, Christianity was merely giving a new interpretation to old beliefs, which it kept *in situ*), was Hell. For a long time Christianity's purgatorial places would be very similar to Hell or even part of it. But once Purgatory came into existence in its own right (even if the punishments to be endured there were still infernal punishments, though of limited duration), it became necessary to insure its autonomy, and to begin with its topographical autonomy within the geographical system of the other world. In Sicily the deeply rooted infernal tradition did not permit Purgatory to flourish. The ancient Hell stood in the way of the youthful Purgatory.

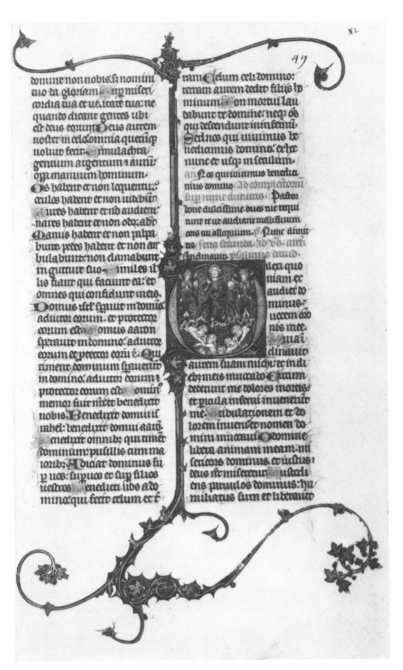

1. Judgment and Rescue from Purgatory (*Breviary of Philip the Fair*). See Appendix 3. Paris BN 10845 Latin MS 1023, fol. 49. Photo © Bibliothèque nationale.

2. The other world: system of receptacles (old cathedral of Salamanca). Leaving the receptacle of Purgatory. See Appendix 3. Photo © "Los Angeles," Salamanca.

3. Leaving Purgatory
(Breviary known as
Breviary of Charles V).
See Appendix 3. Paris BN
2928 Latin MS 1052, fol.
556v. Photo © Biblio-
thèque nationale.

4. Saint Patrick's Purgatory today: the long-term endurance of beliefs and pilgrimage practices (Station Island, Lough Derg, County Donegal, Ireland).

SEVEN

The Logic of Purgatory

THE dead exist only through and for the living. Innocent III said so: the living concern themselves with the dead because they will join them in the future. And in a Christian society, particularly in the Middle Ages, the meaning of the future is not merely chronological but first and foremost eschatological. The natural and the supernatural, this world and the next, yesterday, today, tomorrow, and eternity are conjoined in a seamless fabric, punctuated by events (birth, death, resurrection), qualitative leaps (conversion), and unforeseen occurrences (miracles). The Church was everywhere, playing its ambiguous roles: to discipline and to save, to justify as well as to contest the established order. From the end of the fourth to the middle of the twelfth century, from Augustine to Otto of Freising, the prelate uncle of Frederick Barbarossa, society lived, more or less (actually rather less than more), in accordance with an ideal, the City of God. The essential thing was that the earthly city, despite its imperfections, not take a turn for the worse and drift toward evil and the Devil. The validity of the model extended even beyond the twelfth century, and as long as the feudal world of the powerful and the weak, the good and the wicked, the black and the white continued to survive, Satan continued to launch violent and troubling offensives.

But with the prodigious progress made by Christendom between the end of the eleventh and the middle of the thirteenth century, or, to take intellectual boundary markers, between the time of Anselm and the time of Thomas Aquinas, matters could no longer remain so simple. Between man and man, as between man and God, there are, it was recognized, intermediary states, stages, and transitions; communications were more sophisticated than had been thought; space and time were broken down and reassembled in new ways; the boundaries between life and death, the world and eternity, Heaven and earth all shifted their positions. Even the measuring instruments changed: intellectual equipment, values, technology. The Gregorian reform, which lasted from the mid-eleventh until the mid-twelfth century and which was the Church's response to the challenge laid down by the new structures of Christendom, eventually eliminated the old rhetoric. But in the meantime, even though it was becoming more and more difficult to conceal the changes that had stolen over Christendom, the Church continued to occupy center stage with its old dualistic rhetoric: the two cities, the two powers, the two swords, the clergy and the laity, the pope and the emperor—and the two armies, Christ's and Satan's. Here Innocent III is both irrefutable witness and actor. He was a great pope, not because he was instrumental, as historians used to maintain, in bringing about the triumph of a hypothetical legalistic feudalism [*fèodalitè juridique*] which in fact never existed, but rather because, in spite of his errors (who, in the year 1200, could have imagined that the Cistercians would prove incapable of successfully battling heresy?), he reestablished the power of the Church over the new society, not by opposing that society but by adapting to it. Innocent III laid it down that from his time forward there were to be three churches: between the army of God and the army of Zebulon there was "the army that is in Purgatory."[1]

THE OTHER WORLD AND THE PROGRESS OF JUSTICE

To what does the this emergence of a third society in the other world correspond? Does it correspond to an evolutionary change in the idea of salvation, to which human conceptions of the other world are generally related?

The ideas that living human beings formed about the other world were inspired, I think, more by a need for justice than by a yearning for salvation, except perhaps in brief periods of eschatological fervor. The other world was supposed to correct the inequalities and injustices of this one. But this corrective and compensatory function of the other world was not independent of terrestrial judicial realities. Since, according to Christian doctrine, the eternal destiny of each man is determined by the Last Judgment, the image of judgment assumed a singular importance. The end of time and the beginning of eternity are described in the New Testament: this is the moment of truth when the Lord separates the sheep from the goats, placing the saved on his right and the damned on his left (Matt. 25:31–46). It is the coming of the Holy Spirit: "And when he is come, he will reprove the world of sin, and of righteousness, and of judgment: of sin because they believe not in me; of righteousness, because I go to my Father, and ye see me no more; of judgment, because the prince of this world is judged" (John 16:8–11). And finally, it is the judgment of nations: "And I saw the dead, small and great, stand before God; and the books were opened: and another book was opened, which is the book of life and the dead were judged out of those things which were written in the books, according to their works. . . . And death and hell were cast into the lake of fire. This is the second death. And whosoever was not found written in the book of life was cast into the lake of fire" (Rev. 20:12–15).

But this last, comprehensive judgment allows for only two possibilities: life or death, eternal light or eternal fire, Heaven or Hell. Purgatory would depend on a less solemn verdict, an individual judgment immediately after death, which medieval Christians were inclined to represent in combative imagery: good angels fought bad angels (or demons, as they were sometimes called) for possession of the newly liberated soul. The souls in Purgatory are elect souls, destined ultimately to be saved. Angels therefore have jurisdiction over them, but within a complex judicial process. A soul may win a reprieve or early release from punishment, not by virtue of its own good conduct but thanks to outside intervention in the form of suffrages. The duration of punishment therefore depends not only on God's mercy, symbolized by the zeal of the angels to snatch souls away from the demons, but also on personal merits amassed over a lifetime and on suffrages undertaken by the Church at the behest of friends and relatives of the deceased.

This system was obviously inspired by judicial procedures and legal ideas associated with this world rather than with the next. The twelfth century was a century of justice in two respects: justice, as an ideal, was one of the century's most important values, while at the same time judicial practice was undergoing considerable change. The ambiguous notion of justice evolved within a context circumscribed by this ideal on the one hand and this practice on the other. Feudal lords claimed the right to administer justice and used that right to dominate the inhabitants of their seigneuries and to reap considerable profits. Against them, kings and territorial princes claimed to uphold the ideal of justice and to enforce its reality. Ecclesiastics, for their part, extended the Christian concept of justice, expanded the activities of the episcopal tribunals and officialities, and, most important of all, established a new type of law, canon law, in the hope of casting the Church in the role of champion of mankind's collective aspirations.

Temporal authorities also expanded their judicial role in the twelfth century, frequently issuing resounding appeals to justice as an ideal. This is true of the great feudal monarchies, especially in England, but also in Capetian France, where from Louis VI and Louis VII to Philip Augustus, from Suger to Philip's panegryrists, the image of the just king acquired new importance as the activities of the royal courts expanded.[2] It is also true of the great territorial principalities. One bloody episode, the murder of Charles the Good, count of Flanders, in the count's chapel at Bruges in 1127 by the members of a family of *ministeriales,* provided the occasion for a memorable piece of reportage, which has survived. There, painted against the background of Flander's emerging economic power, we find in the somewhat idealized portrait of the assassinated count a statement of the political ideal to which governments of the twelfth century subscribed. The author of this essay, Galbert of Bruges, a notary and staff member of the count's government, lists justice as the foremost of the virtues of the prince.[3] Charles, the just prince, was surnamed "the Good."

The great initiator of the twelfth-century canon law movement, Bishop

Yves of Chartres, lays out in the prologue to his *Decretum* (1094) a theory of dispensation, that is, a theory of the power of the ecclesiastical authorities to permit nonapplication of the rules of law in certain cases. Here he makes a fundamental distinction between different rules of justice: imperative rules, suggestions, and "tolerances" (*praeceptum, consilium, indulgentia*).[4]

In the early years of the twelfth century, Alger of Liège, a deacon and scholasticus [*écolâtre*] of Saint Lambert's Church and later canon of the cathedral before retiring at the end of his life to Cluny (no star of the nascent intelligentsia, Alger was an average cleric) wrote, under the inspiration of Yves of Chartres, a *Book of Mercy and Justice* (*Liber de misericordia et justitia*).[5] This was a work of political ideology, situated in a religious context. Although the Church played its part in the violence of the century, in Christendom as well as in the crusade against the infidels, it followed its divine model in not separating mercy from justice. Alger laid down the rules of tolerance, which essentially consisted in not bringing accusation without legal proofs. As his point of departure he took the antithesis between strict law and tolerance that had been classical since Augustine, and revised it, spelled it out, and adapted it to the quite different, and agitated, ideological and social climate of the early twelfth century. He specifies the aims which, he says, are the ends of justice: to seek reconciliation, to investigate intentions scrupulously, and to define carefully the role of the will in the offense.

As Abelard and Gratian would do after him, Alger cites contradictory passages from the Bible: there is such "diversity" in Scripture (*tanta diversitas scripturarum*)! Thus he found room to maneuver, as it were, among the various authorities. At the end of the century, drawing the lesson from the interpretive ingenuity of the theologians and canonists, Alan of Lille said that citations have noses of wax—the clever can twist them any way they please.

Alger pushed the idea of tolerance quite far. He wrote that "if the iniquitous cannot be corrected, they must be tolerated. . . . The wicked must be tolerated in order to preserve unity," i.e., peace. He argues that "even a man who is condemned, if he has truly repented, can be reestablished in his rights, because he does not sin who exercises justice" (*non peccat qui exercet justitiam*).

Finally, he comes to the way in which an accused person can exculpate himself, purge himself of his crimes, real or alleged: "An accused can purge himself [*expurgare*] in three ways: by producing irrefutable witnesses, by submitting to a thorough examination, or by confessing prior to any publicity and by repenting" (*confessione et penitentia*). Finally, "if an accused has not wished to purge himself and is subsequently either found guilty or confesses his sins himself, he shall be condemned."[6]

Reflection on sin is encountered in theology as well as in canon law.

Crime (*crimen*), delict (*delictum*), guilt (*culpa*), and sin (*peccatum*) are all words used in the twelfth century by both theologians and canonists, and attempts were made to differentiate these various terms.

In a classic study of the doctrine of guilt in canon law from Gratian to the *Decretals* of Gregory IX,[7] Stephan Kuttner begins by stressing in his preface the magnitude of this great intellectual and social movement: not only was the science of canon law inaugurated in the twelfth century, but the second half of the century saw a steady increase in the literary output of the canonists, which included not only glosses on the *Decretum*, but also the *Summas* as well as the ecclesiastical regulations, or decretals, that were collected by Gregory IX in the corpus of canon law compiled in 1234. Kuttner then begins his study proper with "Abelard and the concept of crime."

NEW CONCEPTS OF SIN AND PENANCE

The words and ideas of Alger of Liège have brought us very close to Purgatory. Citing the authors who inspired him, Alger classifies himself as a descendant of the fathers of Purgatory, of Augustine and Gregory the Great—not the Gregory of the *Dialogues*, however, but the Gregory of the *Moralia in Job* and the *Liber pastoralis*. We actually reach Purgatory when we enter the sphere of penance, on the borderline between spiritual life and material and social life, where during the twelfth century Church and society embarked on a new venture.

Complementing Kuttner's work, Robert Blomme, a historian of theology, also encounters the characteristic twelfth-century notion of justice in his study of "the doctrine of sin in the schools of theology during the first half of the twelfth century."[8]

In the second half of the century, Peter Comestor, who was perhaps the "inventor" of Purgatory, compiled the *Liber Pancrisis*, an anthology, of a type then fashionable, of *sententiae* and *quaestiones* together with citations from the Church Fathers and commented on "by modern masters" (*a modernis magistris*). The masters cited are early twelfth-century theologians belonging to the school of Laon: William of Champeaux, Anselm and Raoul of Laon, and Yves of Chartres.[9] These scholars played an important role in the evolution of ideas concerning sin and penance. There is no need to rehearse here the careful work[10] that has been done on the great intellectual and moral revolution of the twelfth and early thirteenth centuries, a revolution that changed the way men thought about sin and profoundly altered penitential practices. These changes were brought about by exploring the connections between sin and ignorance and by seeking to discover the intentions behind the sinner's behavior.

At the origin of these changes stands Anselm of Canterbury. The great theologian insisted on the essential difference between voluntary sin and sin due to ignorance. In the *Cur Deus homo* (2.15, 2.52, 2.115) he says this: "There is such a difference between the sin committed knowingly and the sin committed through ignorance, that a sin that one would never have been able to commit because of its enormity, had one but known, is merely venial, because it was committed through ignorance."[11] All the major schools of the first half of the twelfth century—the schools of Laon, Abelard, and the Victorines—subscribed to and elaborated upon this fundamental distinction, which later became traditional. Two distinctions assumed special importance later on. First, there was the distinction between vice and sin, the latter implying the assent, or *consensus*, of the sinner. Second was the distinction between guilt and punishment (*culpa* and *poena*), which one of Abelard's disciples glosses in the Cambridge Commentary as follows: "Sin, it must be said at the outset, has two aspects: that which involves guilt [*culpa*], which is the consent [*consensus*] or contempt of God [*contemptus Dei*], as when one says that a small child is without sin, and that which involves the punishment, as when we say we have sinned in Adam, that is, that we have incurred a punishment."[12] For our purposes, the important point is that guilt (*culpa*), which normally leads to damnation, can be pardoned through contrition and confession, while punishment (*poena*), or expiatory castigation, is effaced by "satisfaction," that is, by completing the penance ordered by the Church. If contrition and/or confession have taken place but penance has not been undertaken or completed, whether voluntarily or involuntarily (e.g., because death intervenes), the punishment (*poena*) must be completed in purgatorial fire, i.e., from the end of the century onward, in Purgatory.[13]

Henceforth all spiritual and moral life centered on the search for intentions, on the examination of what was voluntary and what was involuntary, on the deed committed knowingly as opposed to the deed committed out of ignorance. The notion of personal responsibility was thereby considerably expanded and enriched. The pursuit of sin became part of "an internalization and personalization" of moral life, which called for new penitential practices. What was now sought more than internal proof was confession; what counted more than punishment was contrition.[14] All this led to the attribution of fundamental importance to confession—confession whose nature was transformed.

At the turn of the twelfth century, as the old structures tottered on their foundations, there appeared an anonymous, little studied, obscurely dated, and yet fundamentally important work, a treatise *On True and False Penitence* (*De vera et falso poenitentia*).[15] It met with huge success in the twelfth century and was cited by Gratian in his *Decretum* and by Peter Lombard. It is true that its authority did not rest solely on the novelty—in many respects—of its content: it was believed to be the work of Augustine himself. I shall concentrate on just three of its ideas, which became part of Church practice and which left their mark on the system of Purgatory.

The first of these ideas is that, in case of peril and in the absence of a priest, it is legitimate and useful to confess to a lay person. The lay person does not grant absolution, but the desire to confess is proof of contrition and may lead to absolution of the guilt (*culpa*). This practice is scarcely to be recommended except as a last resort in cases where there is imminent danger of death, and, if the potential victim escapes, it is advisable that he confess a second time to a priest, who will be able to grant absolution. If the person dies, he will have only the punishment (*poena*) to undergo: in other words the practice usually leads to Purgatory. What follows is a proof of this assertion.

At the very end of the twelfth century, the Englishman Walter Map in his *De nugis curialium* recounts the story of a nobleman, ardent in battle, who becomes a monk and who is obliged in unusual circumstances to fight. He routs his enemies but shortly thereafter, while accompanied only by a lay brother (*puer*), he is mortally wounded by an enemy soldier lying in ambush in a vineyard: "Sensing that he was on the verge of death, he confessed his sins to his servant, who was alone with him, and asked the servant to impose a penance. This fellow, an incompetent layman, swore that he did not know how. The monk, used to reacting promptly in every situation, and fervently repentant, said: 'By the mercy of God, very dear son, order that my soul do penance in Hell until the day of [final] Judgment, so that the Lord may then have pity on me and so that I will not see along with the impious the face of fury and wrath.' The servant, in tears, then said these words: 'My lord, I impose upon you as penance that which your lips have uttered here before God.' And the other man, acquiescing by word and glance, devoutly accepted this injunction and died."[16] The Hell in question here, from which one can escape on Judgment Day, is of course the upper Hell, or, in other words, Purgatory, of which Walter Map, whose mind was hostile to novelties and who was an enemy of the Cistercians, remained unaware.

The second idea is that penance should not be done only once in a person's life, after the commission of a great sin or on the point of death, but if possible several times.

The third idea is that "secret sins require secret penance, public sins require public penance." This hastened the decline and disappearance of the old public penance. Society was no longer made up of small groups of the faithful in which public penance had its natural place. Even the great "political" penances, modeled after the case of Theodosius, who undertook to do the penance imposed on him by Saint Ambrose, had their swan song in mock battles between pope and emperor: Henry IV at Canossa, Barbarossa at Venice, or, in a rather different vein, that extraordinary mise-en-scène of the Albigensian Crusade in which Raymond VII of Toulouse was brought to humble himself at Notre-Dame in Paris.

What emerged from all this was the practice of auricular confession, which became integrated into spiritual life as a regular if not daily practice;

this was confession in person, sinner to priest, one to one. The "secret of the confessional" developed later, but the groundwork had been laid earlier. The year 1215 saw a major occurrence, one of the greatest events of medieval history. The Fourth Lateran Council, in its twenty-first canon, *Omnis utriusque sexus*, made auricular confession at least once a year compulsory for all adult Christians, male and female. This established, generalized, and extended a practice toward which Christianity had been moving for at least a century. Everyone was required to examine his conscience: the soul was thus plumbed to new depths, and introspective practices previously limited to clerics, especially monks, were now extended to laymen. This decision was the culmination of a long evolution; it sanctioned a need. And yet it came as a considerable surprise in the first half of the thirteenth century. The habit of confession was not easily acquired, either by laymen or by clerics. How to confess and how to hear confession, what to confess and what to ask, and, for the priest, what penance to impose for those avowals of sins that were neither enormous nor extraordinary but generally modest and routine—all these were questions that needed to be answered. Priests, embarrassed and in some cases even frightened by their new responsibilities, particularly if they were not well educated, soon received help from specialists. These men prepared confessors' manuals, often in several versions of varying difficulty, the simplest being intended for the "simple" priests. Thomas of Chobham's manual is a pioneering example of the genre.[17] Among the questions raised and the penitential panoramas viewed was one that was new and that assumed a place of considerable importance: Purgatory. Its importance was only enhanced by the fact that it also accepted sinners whose sins, venial in character, might legitimately fall through the sieve of the confessional.

Venial sins have a lengthy history, part of which is familiar to us. The scriptural basis for the idea consists in two passages from the First Epistle of John: to begin with, these words from 1 John 1:8: "If we say that we have no sin, we deceive ourselves, and the truth is not in us"; and above all, the following passage from 1 John 5:16–17: "If any man see his brother sin a sin which is not unto death, he shall ask, and he shall give him life for them that sin not unto death. There is a sin unto death: I do not say that he shall pray for it. All unrighteousness is sin: and there is a sin not unto death."

First outlined by Tertullian, the idea was fleshed out by Augustine and Gregory the Great. They used a variety of terms to describe these lesser sins: minute (*minuta*), small or smaller (*parva, minora*), slight or slighter (*levia, leviora*), and above all, the felicitous idea of the quotidian (*quotidiana*) or routine sin. The term venial (*veniale, venialia*) did not come into common usage until the twelfth century and, according to A. M. Landgraf, the system in which mortal sins are contrasted to venial sins was fully worked out only in the second half of the twelfth century by the disciples of the theologian Gilbert Porreta (Gilbert de la Porrée), who died in 1154: this group included the anonymous authors of Quaestiones, Simon of Tournai, Alan of Lille, and others.[18] In any case, the expression "venial sin" belongs to that group of notions and words that emerged in the twelfth century along with Purgatory and that together with Purgatory form a system. The word has the further interest of meaning "worthy of *venia*," i.e., of pardon, a meaning of which twelfth-century clerics were well aware. The notion thus carried a legal-spiritual connotation.

A treatise on theology of the school of Laon, dating from the early twelfth century and entitled the *Judgments of Arras (Sententiae Atrebatenses)* states that "different penances are required for criminal sins and for venial sins. Criminal sins, that is, sins subject to damnation, are those that one commits knowingly and deliberately. The others, which come from the invincible weakness of the flesh or from invincible ignorance, are venial, that is, not damnable."[19] Pardon for the latter can be readily obtained by confession, almsgiving, or similar actions. Anselm of Laon (d. 1117) offers the same opinion in his *Sententiae*. Abelard, in his *Ethics*,[20] contrasts criminal sins (*criminalia*) with venial or slight sins (*venialia aut levia*). Hugh of Saint-Victor and the Victorines were the first to raise a question that was destined to receive a variety of answers: Can a venial sin become a mortal sin? The Victorines answered yes, if the sin involved contempt for God. Alan of Lille dwells at length on the distinction between mortal sin and venial sin, laying out the various opinions on the matter and in effect summarizing the evolution of the doctrine over the course of the twelfth century.[21]

I shall not go into the theological subtleties surrounding the notion of venial sin. It is true that discussion of these issues sometimes involves Purgatory. But here, I think, we begin to venture onto ground where thirteenth-century theologians, to say nothing of late medieval scholastics and their modern counterparts, were so at home that they never thought of leaving. Purgatory was thus dragged down into a whirlpool of delirious scholastic ratiocination, which raised the most otiose questions, refined the most sophisticated distinctions, and took delight in the most elaborate solutions. Can a venial sin become mortal? Does an accumulation of several venial sins equal a mortal sin (a question raised earlier by Augustine, but in simple terms)? What is the fate of a person who dies with both a mortal sin and a venial sin on his head (assuming it is possible for this to occur, which some authorities doubted)? And so on. Examination of the documentary evidence of discussions of venial sin and Purgatory, as these issues were lived and debated in thirteenth-century Christendom, has convinced me that the rarefied argumentation of intellectuals cut off from their roots in society had scarcely any influence on the conceptions of Purgatory held by the mass of the faithful. At most, perhaps, echoes of these intellectual meanderings persuaded a few sane and simple spirits that Purgatory was something to be avoided: they rejected Purgatory not because of doctrinal conflict but because of irritation with the intellectual snobbery to which it sometimes gave rise after the end of the twelfth century. The theologians of the twelfth century—a diverse group among whom we must be sure not to forget the monastic theologians—were abstract thinkers, because science is abstract and theology had become a science. But they were generally alert to what was going on in the society around their cathedrals, cloisters, and urban schools, lapped as they were by the rising tide of the new society, and they knew that to think about venial sin or Purgatory was to think about society itself. By contrast, the theologians and canonists of the thirteenth century were products of a corporate movement, mental workers isolated from the manual laborers in the urban workplace. Increasingly, they barricaded themselves behind their academic chairs and their pride as specialists of the spirit.

MATERIAL FOR PURGATORY: VENIAL SINS

But this stage had not yet been reached in the twelfth century. In regard to venial sin two questions arose that are relevant to our concerns: How could one get rid of venial sins? And closely related to this: What is the connection between venial sin and Purgatory?

So long as Purgatory did not truly exist and the definition of venial sin remained unclear, the tendency, as we have seen, was to believe that venial sin could be effaced by prayer, especially the Lord's Prayer, alms, possibly confession, and perhaps, as Augustine himself had suggested, by the purgatorial fire to come. Bernard, who does not use the expression venial but refers to lesser sins as quotidian, smaller (*minora*), or "not unto death" (*quae non sunt ad mortem*) and who believed that the best way to purge such sins was through prayer, went so far as to hold that confession was useless for some of them. The evolution that took place in the twelfth century led to the drawing of a parallel between venial sin and Purgatory. The criterion of ignorance, to which theologians began to attach more and more importance, applied in particular to venial sin. Guilt (*culpa*) thereby being excluded, there remained the punishment to be suffered in Purgatory. Furthermore, exegeses of 1 Corinthians 3:10–15 compared structures of wood, hay, and straw to venial sins, and since traditionally it was these structures that were held to be destroyed by purgatorial fire while allowing those who had constructed them to be saved "through the fire," it was natural that venial sins should lead to Purgatory. This is explicitly argued, for example, by John of God (Johannes de Deo) at the end of the twelfth century in his *Summa* on penances: "Venial sin has three degrees, namely, wood, hay, and straw. Venial sins are purged in fire."[22] Earlier, Peter Lombard had argued in his *Sententiae* that, from Paul's First Epistle to the Corinthians, "it follows that certain venial sins are effaced after this life" and, further, that venial sins "are dissolved in fire."[23] Purgatory thus became the normal receptacle of venial sins, and this opinion was widely popularized in the thirteenth century. At the end of the twelfth century Purgatory was the place of purgation for two kinds of sinful situations: venial sins and sins regretted and confessed but for which penance has yet to be completed. One *quaestio* sums up the system quite well, though in a somewhat archaic vocabulary. According to Landgraf, this originated in the circle of Odo of Ourscamp: "It is true that certain souls, when they are separated from the body, enter at once into purgatorial fire; but they are not all purged there, only some of them. All that enter there are punished. Thus it would be better to call this fire punitive fire rather than purgatorial fire, but it has been given the nobler name. Among the souls that enter there, some are purged and punished, others merely punished. Purged and punished are those that have brought with them wood, hay, or straw. . . . Merely punished are those that, having repented and confessed all their sins, died before completing the penance imposed on them by the priest."[24]

In fact, to ask what kind of sin led to purgatory is to ask the wrong question. Although venial sin and purgatory came into being at almost the same time and there was a close connection between the two, the real point is that the clerks of the late twelfth and early thirteenth centuries were not primarily interested in abstractions such as crime, sin, guilt, and so on, but rather in men: society was their primary preoccupation. Now, of course, they took society as they found it and reconstructed it in accordance with religious criteria, but the essence of the Church's ideological and spiritual activity was to take the society of men, living and dead, and make it into a society of Christians. The Church was concerned to classify men, but only according to Christian categories.

Before we embark on a study of those categories, a remark is in order. Earthly justice, that is, the judicial apparatus of feudal society, was, as I mentioned earlier, frequently used, if not as a model, then at least as a term of reference by twelfth- and early thirteenth-century theologians in constructing theories of justice in the other world. In the light of what has just been said about sin and penance, I should like to discuss two further examples of this. In the early twelfth century, Abelard, in his attempts to develop an ethics based on intentions, discusses the case of a criminal who is judged and sentenced in the same way by two different judges. In both cases the judgment is correct and that required by justice, but one of the judges acts out zeal for justice, the other out of hatred and vengeance. By 1200 this idea had undergone further development paralleling that of the judicial system.

In a question discussed also by William of Auxerre (d. c. 1237) and by the Dominican Hugh of Saint-Cher, the Parisian chancellor Praepositivus of Cremona (d. c. 1210) raises one of those issues that at first sight seems otiose but (as is sometimes the case) actually has a very specific significance. He asks if there is no chance that a simple venial sin will be punished in Hell and not in earthly penance or in Purgatory. And he answers that this may not be impossible, because the sin must not be judged in itself but rather in accordance with various "justices"—in the legal sense of various "jurisdictions"—within whose purview it may happen to fall. From the standpoint of the *for* (jurisdiction) of Hell, the sin may be worthy of eternal punishment, while from the standpoint of the *for* of penance or of Purgatory it may deserve only temporary punishment. So it is, he adds, that a petty theft is punished in Paris merely by the cutting off of an ear but in Chartres by the amputation of a foot. Less concrete, Hugh of Saint-Cher merely says that the same manifest sin is punished severely in Paris, more severely in Orléans, and very severely in Tours.[25] Here we have a case in which scholastic speculation proceeds with quite dizzying speed from the most abstract theological reflection to the most concrete historical reality. And what if the other world were merely a feudal kingdom—with a welter of fragmented jurisdictions, each with its own standards of justice and disparate punishments, an other world modeled after prerevolutionary, preindustrial society? What if this new realm, Purgatory, were merely a mosaic of seigneuries with unclear boundaries, ill protected against encroachments by the infernal kingdom? It happens, sometimes, that at an unexpected place in a document history drops its mask.

FROM TWO (OR FOUR) TO THREE: THREE CATEGORIES OF SINNERS

Now that Purgatory has been born, now that it exists and is beginning to grow, we must look to the way in which men, Christians, were categorized if we want to know how it was populated. Here we touch on one of history's essential mechanisms, the mechanism by which mental frameworks and logical tools are transformed. And among the operations of thought, one is of particular importance for both intellectuals and society at large: classification and its subspecies, categorization.

Here we must focus on logical schemes apart from concrete social realities. At the end of the twelfth century the categories were simple, but a problem had arisen. On the one hand there were four categories of men, categories first defined in the fourth century by Augustine but taken up and revitalized around 1140 by Gratian: the entirely good, the entirely wicked, the not entirely good, and the not entirely wicked. Where do the men in these categories go after death? Three places were now available, if we leave aside the earthly Paradise (in headlong decline by this time and home only to Enoch and Elijah), the bosom of Abraham (also on the way out), and the two Limbos. The latter were unequal in status. Since Christ's descent into Hell, the Limbo of the Patriarchs had been empty and it was supposed to remain empty until the end of time. It survived only as a historical memory. The children's Limbo, which would continue for centuries to be an object of controversy, did not stand on the same plane as the three other regions of the hereafter. It was the place for human beings not weighed down by any personal sin but only by original sin, whereas Hell, Purgatory, and Paradise were reserved for three categories of individuals who had sinned qua individuals with one degree or another of responsibility and for whom different fates lay in store: the wicked would go to Hell, the good to Heaven, and those not entirely good or not entirely bad to Purgatory for a time and then to Heaven. Though it is possible to find, in the theoretical writings of certain thirteenth-century scholastics up to the time of Dante, a system of the other world involving "five regions," the system that began to establish itself at the end of the twelfth century was one involving three regions.

The problem therefore seems to be a simple one: a fourfold categorization of men must be made to correspond to a threefold division of space. Suppose that we continue for a moment to argue in the abstract, independent of any concrete historical context. There are obviously two ways to solve the problem without upsetting both systems at once. Either the set of three can be enlarged to four, or the set of four pared down to three. At this point two factors intervene. In the first place, Augustine, who first defined the set of four, was actually able to define the fate of only three of the four groups, the not entirely wicked being destined, according to the saint, only to the highly hypothetical fate of "more tolerable damnation."

I believe that Augustine was torn between two alternatives. On the one hand, despite his subtlety, he was forced to accept the binary schemes whose grip on men's minds was tightening in late antiquity, as men fell back for the sake of survival on simplified intellectual tools. Though somewhat less vague about the not entirely good and the purgatorial fire that could save them than he was about the not entirely wicked, Augustine did not succeed in giving a clear account of the fate of this other intermediary group either. Still, he basically favored an other world consisting of three parts: Heaven, fire (Purgatory), and Hell, and it was by remaining faithful to the spirit rather then the letter of his writings that twelfth-century thinkers, much imbued with Augustinism, eventually came to propose a ternary model.

A triad of kinds of sinners was thus matched to a triadic other world: this development was encouraged by another change, namely, the general shift from binary to ternary logical schemes that came about in the twelfth century, particularly among clerics. This change was related to the other vast changes then sweeping the Christian world. Switching back and forth between systems involving two categories and systems involving four categories was not a revolutionary matter: in both systems the basic logic remained binary. The real change came when Augustine's four categories of men (viewed from the standpoint of salvation) were pared down to three.

Here I must pause for a moment and ask the reader to reflect. I imagine that anyone who has followed me this far must be either amused or irritated. There are, he is probably thinking, only two possibilities. Is this some sort of abstract game without any relation to historical reality? Or is it something perfectly obvious to anyone: Mankind has always divided and redivided itself in a variety of ways—into two, three, or four categories. What could be more "natural"? But wait. I am wrong. The reader has read Georges Dumézil, Claude Lévi-Strauss, Georges Duby, he has read sociologists like Theodore Caplow,[26] and he has done some thinking of his own. He therefore knows that reality is more complicated than these two simplistic hypotheses would suggest. Hence they must be rejected. From the various simple codes available to them, men in different times and places have had to make a choice, a choice that depends on their culture and history. It is less simple than it might seem to form a group, a class, or a system. Three persons or three things rarely form a triad. When a binary system has been customary for centuries, it is not easy to shift to a ternary system to express a totality. Accordingly, it seems to me that the essential change that occurred in the Christian system of the other world in the twelfth century was this: the binary system consisting of Heaven and Hell (or Paradise and Hell) was replaced by a ternary system consisting of Heaven, Purgatory, and Hell. Of course the change applied only until the end of time, not for all eternity, of which Christian society was not yet ready to change its concept. This is a crucial point, and I shall have more to say about it later on. But the change and the way it came about were, I think, related in a deep sense to changes in feudal society between the eleventh and fourteenth centuries. To clarify what I mean, let me begin by considering the formal change from four categories of sinners to three.

This change took place in two phases in quick succession. The first phase, whose beginnings we have already examined, involved changing an adverb in Augustine's categorization. Rather than speak, as Augustine had done, of the entirely (*valde*) good or wicked, people began to speak of the medium (*mediocriter*) good or medium wicked, thus bringing the two intermediate categories closer together. The crucial moment came when the two were combined into one: medium good and medium bad. This change aroused some indignation, and for good reason. Grammatically and ideologically, the move was a bold one. It amounted to nothing less than combining two opposites—and what opposites (the righteous and the wicked, good and evil)!—in a single category. Once this forceful blow had been struck, it was a relatively routine matter to reduce the new category, eventually, to one whose wickedness was merely "mediocre."

The theologians started things off. Between 1150 and 1160 Peter Lombard made the following pronouncement: "The offices that the Church celebrates for the dead are helpful for the following people and for the following purposes: for the medium wicked suffrages are valid for the mitigation of punishment; for the medium good they are valid for full absolution."[27] The canonists, as we saw earlier, were behind the times. But most of them caught up, and quickly: the new classification was the work of jurists more than of theologians.

Gratian reproduced the passage from Augustine discussing the four categories. One of the first *Summas* to comment on the *Decretum*, the *Summa Lipsiensis*, or Leipzig Summa, composed in about 1186, shows clearly how difficult it was for thinking on this point to progress: "According to others, 'damnation' is the word for the punishment endured by the medium good or medium bad in Purgatory, though it is usual to speak of damnation only in connection with those damned for all eternity. The medium good are those who die after receiving a penance for venial sins, but without having time to complete that penance. The medium bad are those who die with venial sins, although one might call them good, since venial sin, it seems, does no harm. Some understand that what is being discussed here applies only to the medium good, certain of whom are fully pardoned; they receive only a more tolerable damnation, that is, a punishment."[28] Around 1188 the celebrated Uguccio of Pisa vigorously protested in his *Summa* against the evolution then under way: "Certain theologians on their own authority distinguish only three kinds of men [rather than the four of Augustine and Gratian]. Some are entirely good, some entirely bad, some medium good and medium bad. They are saying in effect that the medium good and the medium bad are the same, i.e., those who are in purgatorial fire, and that only these can profit from suffrages by obtaining early release. Their 'damnation,' i.e., punishment [is more tolerable] because, there, they are punished less. But this opinion seems to me almost heretical, for it leads to the identification of good and evil, since in reality one who is medium good is good, and one who is medium bad is bad. Similarly, only the good are in purgatorial fire, since no one with a mortal sin can be there. But with a venial sin no one is bad. Hence in purgatorial fire there is no one who is bad."[29]

The *Summa Coloniensis*, or Summa of Cologne of 1169, did not treat the subject, which it said was one for the theologians. But on the Bamberg manuscript consulted by Landgraf someone has added the schema worked out by Sicard of Cremona (d. 1215), which is quite clear and categorical:

Deceased	entirely good	For them, thanksgiving is made
	entirely bad	For them, consolations for the living
	medium	For them, full pardon or more tolerable damnation

Sicard then added the following words: "In order that their damnation may become more tolerable, this must be understood as being said of those who are in Purgatory."[30]

Finally, a thirteenth-century gloss on the *Sententiae* attempts to recast the thinking of Augustine and Peter Lombard in the light of the recent evolution:

> Here is what the master understood with Augustine: Certain of the dead are entirely good, and the Church does no suffrages for them because they have no need of them. . . . They are glorified beyond a shadow of doubt. Certain of the dead are entirely wicked, and the Church does no suffrages for them either, because they have deserved their fate. They are damned beyond a shadow of doubt. Some are in between, and for them the Church does suffrages, for they have deserved it. On their fate, see [and he refers the reader to another chapter].

The gloss again takes up the explanation by detailing the two components of the intermediary category, and a note of Augustinian doubt creeps in: "Certain of the dead are medium good, and suffrages earn them full absolution; they are beyond a shadow of doubt in Purgatory. Certain are medium bad, and suffrages earn them mitigation of their punishment. And we may hesitate to say whether they are in Purgatory, or in Hell [damned], or in both."[31]

At the end of the twelfth century Raoul Ardent also distinguished between three kinds of dead souls: the entirely good, the medium good, and the entirely damned (*valde boni, mediocriter boni, omnino damnati*):

> Those who are entirely good go directly to repose after death, and they have no need of our prayers and offerings—it is rather we who benefit from theirs. Those who are medium good and who undertake a true confession and penance, since they are not yet perfectly purged, are purged in purgatorial places [*in purgatoriis locis*] and, for them, beyond a shadow of a doubt, prayers, alms, and masses are profitable. It is not through new merits after death that they receive this benefit, but rather as a consequence of their previous merits [from before death]. Those who are entirely damned did not deserve to profit from such boons. But we, brothers, who do not know who has need and who does not, to whom it may profit and to whom it cannot profit, we must offer prayers, alms, and masses for all, including those for whom we have no certainty. For the entirely good these are thanksgiving, for the medium good expiations, and for the reprobate a kind of consolation for the living. Finally, whether or not these offerings are profitable to those for whom they are made, in any case they may be profitable to those who make them with devotion. . . . Thus he who prays for others works for himself (PL 155.1485).

Even though this passage has not yet drawn the places of purgation together into a single, unified Purgatory, the idea that the dead are divided into three groups is clearly established.

LOGICAL MODELS AND SOCIAL REALITIES
A DECENTERED INTERMEDIARY

Two very important aspects of this ternary model's remarkable construction have yet to be noted. The first, on which I place great stress, is that a quaternary model (in fact a binary model of two pairs) was replaced by a ternary model. This was an aspect of a far-reaching change affecting the whole outlook of the Christian intelligentsia beginning in the eleventh century. Broadly speaking, dyads of the inferior/superior type, such as powerful/pauper (*potens/pauper*),[32] cleric/layman, monk/cleric, gave way to more complex triads.

In the early Middle Ages thought naturally organized itself in binary patterns. The powers that ruled the universe were two: God and Satan (though it is important to note that Christianity subordinated the devil to God in rejecting Manichaean dogma). Society naturally divided itself into pairs of opposites: the powerful and the poor, the clergy and the laity. Moral and spiritual life were conceived in terms of the opposition between the virtues and the vices. These were antagonists locked in fierce combat, as suggested by Prudentius's poem *Psychomachia*. The embattled frontier even divided individuals in two, half God's and half Satan's. The pride of the powerful contrasted with the envy of the poor. The attractions of virtue vied with the snares of vice. But from the year 1000, pluralistic models, many of them inherited from Greek and Roman antiquity and even more from early Christianity, began to overtake the dualistic models. In the twelfth century models based on the number seven enjoyed considerable success: the seven sacraments, the seven capital sins, the seven gifts of the Holy Spirit.

But the most important change was the replacement of binary patterns by ternary patterns and the concomitant shift from blunt opposition, bilateral confrontation, to the more complex interplay of three elements.

One such ternary model was that of the three orders: those who pray, those who fight, and those who work (clergy, nobles, and peasant masses). This ternary scheme is of a special type: it pits two elements of the group against the third, the masses, who, though dominated, were able to gain access to ideological representation.[33] This is the kind of model studied by Theodore Caplow: two against one.

The model on which Purgatory was based was no less successful (from the second half of the twelfth century) and no less linked to the evolving structures of feudal society. Its principle was this: to introduce an intermediary category between two extremes. The new category was not made secondary or subordinate to the original two. Rather, the center was raised up. Purgatory is an intermediate place in two senses: the souls there are neither as happy as the souls in Paradise nor as unhappy as the souls in Hell, and Purgatory comes to an end at the time of the Last Judgment. All that remained to make it truly intermediary was to assign it a location between Paradise and Hell.

Here again, the essential application of the model was of a sociological order. The point was to represent—not describe—society as it emerged from the second phase of the feudal revolution, that of the growth of cities, just as the model of the three orders had done for the first phase, that of agricultural advance. In its most general and widespread formulation, the model distinguished between *maiores*, *mediocres*, and *minores*.[34] The Latin captures the meaning and function of the scheme better than French or English. The two groups at either end of the scale are denoted by comparatives: the larger, the smaller. The words express a relationship, a proportion, a social interaction. What is the role of the intermediate group in this mechanism? To enlarge itself at the expense of its neighbors, or one of its neighbors, joining forces with one against the other, or alternately, first with one and then with the other. At the beginning of the thirteenth century Francis of Assisi borrowed a term from this classification to describe the brothers of the order he created: the "Minors."[35] The most common application of the model was to feudal society as it was modified by urban growth: between the great (lay and ecclesiastic) and the small (rural and urban workers) an intermediate category had been born, namely, the "bourgeois," who formed a group so diverse that I prefer not to speak of it as a class (and therefore prefer to avoid the term "the bourgeoisie").

At this point we notice a second characteristic of the model: the intermediate element is not equidistant from the two poles. Theoretically, the position of the intermediate category of the triad is such that it can gain advantage by forging alliances with, or moving closer to, one pole or the other. The bourgeois would take advantage of this situation in their battles against both great and small. In the case of Purgatory, however, freedom of action was blocked on one side, since few were admitted to Paradise. The mobile frontier turned out to be the one between Purgatory and Hell. The center was displaced toward the somber border, as we shall see when we come to descriptions of the other world, descriptions which were hardly brighter than the black visions of the early Middle Ages.[36] It is clear that, as far as the sociological uses of this model were concerned, it was no less important than that of the three orders. The latter created the Third Estate, the former the middle classes.

Let me be clear about my meaning. It would be absurd to argue that the bourgeoisie created Purgatory, or that Purgatory in one way or another derived from the bourgeoisie, assuming a bourgeoisie even existed at the time. What I am proposing as a hypothetical interpretation of Purgatory is this: that Purgatory was one of a group of phenomena associated with the transformation of feudal Christendom, of which one key expression was the creation of ternary logical models through the introduction of an intermediate category.[37] The model, I am quite sure, was firmly rooted in socioeconomic structures. But I am no less sure that the mediation of mental, ideological, and religious structures was a necessary ingredient in the system's functioning. Purgatory was not a product of this system but an element in it.

The reader may also be skeptical about the importance I have attached to certain minor changes of vocabulary. Purgatory went from an adjective to a noun, one adverbial phrase (*non valde*) was replaced by another (*mediocriter*), and somehow I am interpreting both cases as signs of profound change. I do indeed believe that minor linguistic changes, occurring at strategic points in social discourse, can point to important historical phenomena. Furthermore, I believe that these shifts in vocabulary and meaning are all the more significant when they occur within rigid ideological systems. To be sure, medieval Christendom was neither static nor sterile—this much I hope to have shown. On the contrary, it was a period of considerable creativity. But innovation at the ideological level came in tiny steps, or perhaps I should say in insignificant words.

CHANGES IN INTELLECTUAL FRAMEWORKS: NUMBER

Changing along with Purgatory, making the idea possible and making room for it to exist, were habits of thought and intellectual equipment that were part and parcel of the new mental landscape. Together with Purgatory there emerged new attitudes with respect to number, time, and space.

In the realm of number, Purgatory introduced into eschatology a new kind of calculation: not symbolic numerology or the abolition of measure in eternity, but a realistic form of reckoning, the kind used in the courts. Sentences to Purgatory were not indefinite; they had fixed terms. As early as the mid-eleventh century, in reporting on moans that had been heard to rise out of the crater of Stromboli, Jotsuald explained that the souls of sinners were being tortured there *ad tempus statutum*, for the time that had been allotted. At the end of the twelfth century, in a *quaestio* discussed in Odo of Ourscamp's circle, there is talk of those who believe that venial sin is not punished eternally but "for a term in Hell."

The creation of Purgatory combined a process of spatialization of the universe with an arithmetic logic that governed the relationship between human behavior and the situation of the soul in Purgatory. Before long we find discussions of the proportion between the time spent in sin on earth and the time spent in torment in Purgatory, or again, of time in relation to the suffrages offered to the dead and in relation to the acceleration of their liberation from Purgatory. This bookkeeping was further developed in the thirteenth century, the century of the rise of cartography and the unfettering of calculation. Later, Purgatory time became mixed up with the bewildering question of indulgences.

The idea of a "term of sentence" is part of a broader mental outlook, which sprang originally from a concern for justice and eventually led to the institution of a complex system of bookkeeping associated with the world to come. The fundamental idea, handed down from the earliest Fathers, from Augustine, and constantly reiterated over the centuries, was this: that punishment, and specifically, in this instance, the time spent in Purgatory, should be proportioned to the seriousness of the sin. But it was not until the thirteenth century that the idea of proportionality, originally qualitative in nature, became quantitative. This change had to do with progress that had been made in arithmetic and mathematics. Alexander of Hales, a Parisian academic who became a Franciscan in the first half of the thirteenth century, asks in his *Gloss on the Sententiae of Peter Lombard* whether purgatorial punishment can be "unjust and nonproportional" (*injuste et improportionalis*). Here is his answer:

> Although Purgatory punishment [*poena purgatorii*] is not proportional to the pleasure one took in sinning, it is comparable; nor is its bitterness proportional to the bitterness of temporary punishment; it is however proportional to it in this sense: 'Proportionality is in effect the similitude of proportions.' The proportion of temporary punishment due in this world for a sin to the temporary punishment due, also in this world, for a greater sin, is equivalent to the proportion of Purgatory punishment due for a smaller sin compared to the Purgatory punishment due for a greater sin, but the Purgatory punishment is not proportional to the temporary punishment in this world. The reason why it is appropriate that Purgatory punishment should be disproportionately bitter compared with the punishment endured [purged] in this world, even though both are voluntary, is that the punishment endured in this world is the punishment of the soul suffering with the body, while Purgatory punishment is the punishment of the soul itself, immediately. Just as what one suffers [on one side] is not proportional to what one suffers [on the other], so is suffering to suffering. What is more, temporary punishment in this world is voluntary in the proper sense of the word, Purgatory punishment is voluntary in the figurative sense.

This astonishing passage does not stop at explaining the greater intensity of purgatorial punishments by arguing that the soul is more vulnerable without the protection of the body but goes on to introduce mathematical, topological considerations into the discussion of punishments in the other world. The passage cites only one authority: "Proportionality is in fact the similitude of proportions." This citation is not from the Bible, the Fathers, or the Church: it is from Euclid's *Elements*, Book 5, definition 4.[38]

A commentary on the *Sententiae* from the early thirteenth century, in which the question of the quantitative efficacy of suffrages is raised, is, according to Landgraf, probably the first text to use the terms "arithmetic proportion" and "geometric proportion."[39] Purgatory ushered in the "accountancy of the hereafter."[40] Previously there had been only eternity or an indefinite period of waiting. But now time in Purgatory could be calculated according to the magnitude of suffrages; ratios could be established between the time lived in this world and the time endured in the next, for psychological aspects of duration were also taken into account (time apparently moved very slowly in Purgatory). Thirteenth-century documents inform us about the nature of these calculations. They remind us that the thirteenth century was the century of calculation, as Alexander Murray has shown in a very suggestive work,[41] as well as the age of bookkeeping and of merchants and functionaries who prepared the first budgets. What has been called (admittedly not without exaggeration) "the first budget of the French monarchy" dates from the reign of Philip Augustus, the king under whom Purgatory was either born or came or age. The Church and the sinners in its charge began keeping double-entry accounts with respect to earthly time and the time of Purgatory. According to the Book of Revelation, the books would be opened on Judgment Day and the dead judged according to their contents, but now, in the meantime other account books were already being audited: the accounts of Purgatory.

SPACE AND TIME

Purgatory was also associated with new concepts of space and time. It was related to a new geography of the other world, which was no longer made up of tiny receptacles set side by side, like seigneurial monads, but consisted rather of vast territories, kingdoms as Dante would one day call them. Christians had by now begun to explore the world along crusade, missionary, and trade routes. "At the end of the twelfth century," writes George Kish, the leading specialist on the history of maps, "a change took place: the medieval world set itself in motion. In consequence, travelers began bringing back information that by the fourteenth century reshaped medieval maps." The map of the other world was reshaped at the same time, or perhaps even earlier. Terrestrial cartography, previously little more than an assemblage of topographical ideograms, now ventured to introduce realism into topographical representation. Otherworldly cartography, though still heavily charged with symbolism, complemented these efforts to explore space.[42] Time too was affected: indeed, time is the element in the doctrine of Purgatory most susceptible to measurement. This was a great novelty: time could now be measured in the hereafter. It was thus subject to various computations, evaluations, and comparisons. It also figured—"comparably" (*comparative*), to borrow the term used by

Alexander of Hales—in new ways of preaching. Sermons were designed to instruct and to save. At the end of the twelfth century preachers, eager to make their sermons more persuasive, began including anecdotes, or *exempla*, in their texts. These anecdotes were said to be historical, "authentic." Time in the sermon was traditionally the time of eschatology, the time of conversion and salvation: now preachers began introducing segments of historical time, time that was datable and measurable. Such was the effect of Purgatory on the time of the other world. Indeed, Purgatory became one of the favorite themes of the *exempla*.

CONVERSION IN THIS WORLD AND INDIVIDUAL DEATH

In all these changes, in all this turmoil, we sense the effects of two great trends which, at a deeper level, explain the birth of Purgatory.

The first of these was the weakening of that commonplace medieval attitude, *contemptus mundi*, contempt of the world.[43] Fostered primarily by monastic spirituality (which, as Jean Delumeau has shown, continued to encourage contempt of the world at the height of the Renaissance), it gave way before the new devotion to earthly values that was associated with the creative spirit of the time.

Gustavo Vinay has written some impassioned lines on the optimism of the twelfth century: "If there was a joyful century in the Middle Ages, it was this one: this was the century when Western civilization exploded with astonishing vitality, energy, and desire for renewal. Its climate was the best of medieval times. . . . The twelfth century is typically the century of liberation, when men cast aside all that had been born rotten for more than a millennium." And yet, Vinay goes on to say, it was also, paradoxically, a time when in the midst of this "explosion of vitality" the fear of death and suffering also came into being: "The men of the Middle Ages really began to suffer in their happiest period, when they had begun to breathe deeply, when for the first time, it seemed, they became aware that all the future lay ahead, when history took on dimensions it had never before assumed."[44]

Making due allowances for what is exaggerated in this passionate and sensitive account, it remains true that Gustavo Vinay has properly comprehended the conversion to this world that began in the twelfth century and extended into the next. Indeed, the change proved to be a lasting one, despite various torments, doubts, and instances of regression. That the fear of death should have developed simultaneously is paradoxical only in appearance. The value that was now attached to earthly life only made the moment of leaving it that much more awesome. Indeed, what was new was fear of that moment, the hour of death, now added to the fear of Hell: the former even began to replace the latter. Purgatory, representing new hope for the other world and heightened awareness of the moment of passing, has its place in this upheaval of values.

Christians were no longer all convinced that the Last Judgment was imminent. Not yet happy, Christendom had nevertheless finally tasted growth after centuries of mere reproduction or even recession. More "goods" were being produced, and values formerly situated in the life to come were now in one degree or another incarnated here below: justice, peace, wealth, beauty. The Gothic cathedrals, places of "refreshment, light, and peace," seemed to bring Paradise to earth. In mentioning *refrigerium* and capturing echoes of the primitive liturgy in connection with the Gothic church, I am not merely abandoning myself to metaphor. Meyer Schapiro and Erwin Panofsky, commenting on Suger's writings concerning the new architecture of Saint-Denis, point out that "Suger's phraseology is reminiscent of the *tituli* of primitive Christianity in which neo-Platonic doctrines . . . were expressed in a similar way."[45] Mankind had taken up residence on earth. Previously it had not been worth the bother to devote too much attention to the brief moment that was supposed to separate death from resurrection. But now Heaven and Hell by themselves were no longer enough to satisfy society's need for new answers. The intermediate period between individual death and collective judgment became an important matter for reflection. A choice was necessary between the eschatological fanatics, who refused to engage in such reflection, instead concentrating all their hopes on the advent of the millennium or on the Final Day, and those who took up residence on earth and so acquired an interest in the sequel of earthly life, the interval between death and resurrection: the Church came down on the side of the latter. If the wait was to be lengthy, it was imperative to find out what became of the dead in the meantime: What will become of us tomorrow?

Now, it is true that, if a majority of Christians chose to reside on earth, a minority rose up against this choice, clamored more insistently than ever for the Second Coming, and meanwhile looked to the advent of the reign of the just in this world, the millennium. From Joachim of Floris to Celestine V, from the Children's Crusade to the flagellants and the spirituals, the "fanatics of the Apocalypse" were more agitated than ever. I even suspect Saint Louis, king of the penitential crusade, of dreaming that he might carry his kingdom with him into eschatological adventure, even as his officers busied themselves with calculating and measuring, with establishing his realm on a firm footing. I suspect that he may have dreamed of being a king of the last days, as some German emperors, it has been suggested, imagined themselves. And yet it was Saint Louis who said, "No one loves his life as much as I love mine."[46]

Except among a handful of "madmen," the Apocalypse was no longer in vogue. In the eleventh and early twelfth centuries it had been the book of the Bible most commented on.[47] But it had since declined to a secondary position, behind the Song of Songs, which glows with an ardor as much earthly as it is celestial. Apocalypses vanish from Gothic tympana, giving way to Last Judgments in which Purgatory does not yet figure but which use the pretext of depicting remote events in order to portray earthly society and exhort it to mend its ways.

The leading writers on medieval iconography have called attention to the gradual (and relative) effacement of the Apocalypse in favor of the Last Judgment. Emile Mâle has this to say:

> Until the end of the twelfth century this was the accepted mode of representing the avenging God of the Last Day, but it was then superseded by a new conception of the Judgment scene. Magnificent compositions appeared which were inspired not by the Apocalypse, but by St. Matthew's gospel, and representations inspired by the Book of Revelation became comparatively rare. . . . it cannot be said that the Apocalypse was a very fruitful source of inspiration, for from the fourteenth century artists preferred to borrow the picture of the end of the world from St. Matthew's gospel.[48] The evangelist's account is certainly less vivid, but it furnishes material more appropriate for plastic representation. God is no longer seen as a great precious stone whose brilliance no man can suffer, but as the Son of Man, who appears on His throne such as He was on earth, and whose face will be recognized by the people. A few additional features were taken from a chapter on the resurrection of the dead in the first epistle to the Corinthians.

The principle innovation introduced by following Saint Matthew, Mâle tells us, was the "separation of the saved from the lost." In representations of the Apocalypse God was "at once glorious as a sovereign and threatening as a judge." In thirteenth-century judgments God is "the Son of Man," depicted "as redeemer, judge, and living God."[49]

Henri Focillon also considers this question: "The iconography of the twelfth century . . . is dominated by the Apocalypse, from which it borrowed its redoubtable visions as well as the image of Christ the Judge, sitting in glory, surrounded by inhuman figures. . . . The iconography of the thirteenth century did away with the visions, the epics, the Orient, and the monsters. It was evangelical, human, western, and natural. It brought Christ down nearly to the level of the faithful. . . . Of course he still sits enthroned at the top of the tympanum, presiding over the reawakening of the dead and the meting out of eternal punishments: even so, he remains the Christ of the Gospels and preserves his gentle humanity."[50]

If Christ, as portrayed on Gothic tympana, was still an eternal judge, the shift from apocalyptic thunderbolts to realistic representation of the Judgment and of various groups of resurrected human beings made it possible to give prominence to justice, with which the inception of Purgatory is so intimately associated. Increasingly, the saved, whom Christ entrusts to the care of angels to be led to Paradise, were depicted as "saints," souls that had already passed through Purgatory and been purged, purified.

With the establishment of life on earth and the newfound mastery over time, and with the extension of life beyond the grave into Purgatory, the primary concern was for the dead. Not that I believe (and in this I am with Paul Veyne) that death was an object of interest in itself. Concern was shown for the dead, rather, because it was through death and through the dead that the living increased their power here below.[51] The twelfth century saw the enrichment of memory. The great beneficiaries of this were, of course, the aristocratic families, which compiled their genealogies and extended them ever farther back in time.[52] Death was less and less a frontier. Purgatory became an annex of the earth and extended the time of life and of memory. Suffrages became an increasingly active business. And the revival of the last will and testament also helped to push back the frontier of death, even though Purgatory is not mentioned in these documents until quite late.

Though the new solidarity between the living and the dead—incipient in Cluny—strengthened family, corporate, and fraternal ties, Purgatory, caught up in a personalization of spiritual life, actually fostered individualism. It focused attention on individual death and the judgment that followed.

In an institutional and legal perspective, Walter Ullmann has argued that "the turn of the thirteenth century was the time when the seeds of future constitutional development and the emergence of the individual in society were sown."[53] He also shows that this was the time of the "emergence of the citizen." This nascent individualism also affected the sphere of death and the other world. Purgatory gave rise to citizenship of the other world, to citizens of the time between death and the Last Judgment.

These changes were also reflected in the liturgy. While still mute on the subject of Purgatory, the liturgy nevertheless adapted itself to new ways of classifying the dead. The ceremonial changes associated with the new classifications reveal a heightened concern with the fate of the individual. An example may be found in the following excerpt from "On the celebration of the service for the dead," taken from the *Summa on Ecclesiastical Offices* written by Jean Beleth, a canon of Notre-Dame in Paris, prior to 1165: "Before the body is washed or wrapped in a winding-sheet, the priest or his vicar should go to the place where it lies and, with holy water and an outpouring of prayers, invoke the saints and pray to them to receive [the body's] soul and transport it to the place of joy. There are in fact some souls that are perfect, which, as soon as they leave the body, fly at once to the heavens. There are others entirely wicked, which fall immediately to hell. There are others, in the middle [*medie*], for which a recommendation of this sort must be made. This is also done for the wicked, to be prepared for any eventuality. Once washed and shrouded the corpse should be brought to the church and a mass sung."[54] This is followed by the passage from Augustine included by Gratian in his *Decretum*, concerning the four categories of the dead, still ranging from the elect to the damned.

Brandon has written that "in order to bridge the gap between the interests of the individual with his lifespan of three-score years and ten and those of the human race extending over millennia (a gap which the Jewish religion never successfully bridged), the Church invented the idea of Purgatory."[55]

PART THREE

THE TRIUMPH OF PURGATORY

EIGHT

The Scholastic Systematization

THE thirteenth century was the century of organization. Christian society was subjected to ever tighter control. The first treatises on rural economics since antiquity made their appearance. In the towns the crafts, the new building and textile industries, commerce, and banking were often regulated. Labor was subject to control by the guilds and spiritual life to control by the confraternities. The constraints imposed by political institutions became tighter, in the city and even more in the monarchical state, as we see in France and the papal monarchy and to a lesser degree in the Iberian states and in England. Organization also affected the intellectual world, where the universities, the schools run by the mendicant orders, and the urban schools joined forces to tame and redirect the unruly ideological and scholastic forces set loose in the previous century. Summas were written in theology and law in a period that saw the revival of interest in Roman law and the development of canon law. Debate, decision, and implementation, knowledge and its uses, were all systematized.

A TEMPERED TRIUMPH

Purgatory was affected by all these developments and rose to a position of prominence, though under tight ecclesiastical control. Scholasticism, influential in Purgatory's inception, assured its ultimate victory, but the triumph was limited and not unalloyed.

It is beyond the scope of this book to trace the way in which scholasticism adopted and helped to establish Purgatory. The process lasted through the first three quarters of the thirteenth century, up to the time of the Second Council of Lyons (1274), which gave Purgatory official status among the doctrines of the Latin Church. I shall examine what some of the greatest theologians of the period from 1220 to 1280 said about Purgatory: among the men whose work I want to consider are William of Auxerre, William of Auvergne, Alexander of Hales, Saint Bonaventure, Saint Thomas Aquinas, and Albertus Magnus. My intention is not to show how Purgatory relates to each man's thought, but rather to interpret their comments on Purgatory by showing how it figured in their work.

Thirteenth-century theology is probably less abundant in ideas and impassioned debates than is the work of the late twelfth-century masters from Peter Lombard to Peter the Chanter, from Gilbert Porreta to Praepositivus of Cremona. The ardor of thirteenth-century debate at the University of Paris should not be forgotten, however. The atmosphere was indeed quite lively, as *quaestiones* and *quodlibeta* were disputed.[1] Bold assertions were put forward in various intellectual conflicts, such as the great dispute between the regular and secular masters, the Averroist affair, and the debate provoked by the pronouncements of the obscurantist bishop Etienne Tempier in 1270 and 1277.[2]

This is not the place to go into detail about these celebrated episodes, which more often than not merely provide a backdrop for the theology of Purgatory. The young mendicant orders were quick to take an interest in newly discovered power of academic knowledge: the Dominicans immediately jumped into the fray with little soul-searching, while the Franciscans were somewhat more dubious about getting involved. A number of masters from the mendicant orders rose rapidly to the front ranks of scholastic learning and drew large audiences of students, at the expense of the secular masters, who reproached their rivals for their ideal of mendicancy, their thirst for power, and their lack of corporate solidarity, to say nothing of the part played by simple jealousy. In the thirteenth century the great doctors of Purgatory were mendicant masters.

The intellectuals of the thirteenth century read, in Latin translation, the great Greek philosophers of antiquity (Plato and especially Aristotle) and the great Arab philosophers of the Middle Ages (Avicenna, who died in 1037, and Averroes, who died in 1198). Ecclesiastical authorities looked askance at this interest in "pagan" philosophers. A doctrine attributed to Averroës drew a distinction between rational truths and revealed truths. It was admitted that these might conflict or be incompatible, in which case Averroists held that reason should take precedence over faith. That Averroës' writings met with success at the University of Paris in the thirteenth century cannot be denied. That Parisian masters actually professed the doctrine of two truths is less certain. But several of them were accused of having done so and became the objects of vehement polemical attacks. The Averroist controversy and the doctrine of Purgatory were separate matters. But the scholastics were determined to discuss Purgatory on the basis of reason as well as authority.

Finally, it was from Paris itself that the great reaction came. In 1270 Bishop Etienne Tempier condemned thirteen propositions that he declared to be erroneous and inspired by pagan philosophy. In 1277 219 additional propositions were also condemned. The "errors" dealt with in these two syllabi are various in origin, but the primary target in 1270 was Averroism, or at any rate what was called by that name, and in 1277 it was Aristotelianism, including a part of the teaching of Thomas Aquinas. The impact of Etienne Tempier's condemnations is difficult to assess, and it is not my purpose here to do so. If the atmosphere engendered by this brutal censorship was not favorable to theological research in general, the direct consequences for the theology of Purgatory were not very important. This was so in the first place because the problem occupied a marginal position in the Parisian controversies. Only the last two of the articles condemned in 1277 had any bearing on the other world. More important, Latin theological reflection on the subject of Purgatory was essentially complete by 1274, the year in which Purgatory was officially consecrated by the Second Council of Lyons.

Thirteenth-century debates were perhaps even more heated at the faculty of arts (what we would nowadays call the faculty of arts and sciences, where young students received their basic instruction—little is known about these medieval counterparts of our undergraduate institutions) than at the faculty of theology. So far as the universities were concerned, however, Purgatory was primarily a matter for the theologians—hence largely a Parisian affair. By the thirteenth century it had been true for quite some time that law was taught primarily in Bologna, theology primarily in Paris. But the environment in which theology was taught was an international one, for students and masters alike. Along with the Frenchmen William of Auxerre and William of Auvergne we find the Englishman Alexander of Hales, the German Albert of Cologne, and the Italians Bonaventure of Bagnoreggio and Thomas of Aquino, all lending luster to Paris's faculty of theology.[3]

In what ways was the triumph of Purgatory limited, as I said a moment ago? For one thing, the fact that Purgatory was successful in official Latin theology should not be allowed to conceal the equally striking fact that it failed to take hold in large parts of Christendom. It was rejected by the Waldensian and Catharist heretics at a time (the thirteenth century) when the head-on confrontation between Catharism and the Catholic Church was one of the great issues of the day. The Greeks remained hostile to the new doctrine, even if they were obliged for political reasons to keep that hostility under wraps while an ephemeral Union of the Churches was concluded at the Council of Lyons (1274), and Latin theologians were forced to debate with Greeks who did not accept this innovation in the afterlife. As a result of these discussions the Latin Church refined its definition of Purgatory in the thirteenth century, much as it had been led to declare Purgatory's existence by the fight against heresy at the end of the previous century.

Furthermore, Purgatory's triumph was tempered by the fact that Latin intellectuals, who were beginning to play an important role in the Roman curia and the ecclesiastical hierarchy as well as in the universities, were in some degree suspicious of the innovation. This suspicion is difficult to pinpoint and document. But one senses its presence. It crops up here and there in these men's works. The suspicion was twofold. It was no doubt due in part to a certain embarrassment in the face of a belief whose basis in Scripture was so scant and so doubtful, but even more to fear that the belief was being swamped by vulgar and superstitious piety, to fear of an other world so close to popular folklore and to the popular sensibility, an other world defined more by the imagination than by theory, more by the senses than by the spirit. One senses a desire to rationalize Purgatory, to tidy it up, to control it—in a word, to purge it of its offensive popular trappings.

Here, for example, is the way in which one of the first great Parisian theologians of the thirteenth century approached the problem of Purgatory. In his *Summa aurea* (1222–25), William of Auxerre (d. 1231), one of those who introduced Aristotle into scholastic theology, has occasion to discuss Purgatory in two respects, in relation to suffrages and to purgatorial fire.

The questions concerning suffrages ("What good are suffrages for those who are in Purgatory?" and "Can suffrages done for those who are beyond charity be useful to those who are in Purgatory?"[4]) are very interesting from the standpoint of the development of what has been called the "accountancy of the hereafter."

William stands somewhere between the problem of purgatorial fire and the problem of Purgatory itself. As for the way in which purgatorial fire purges souls, William of Auxerre is mainly interested in the theoretical problem of the efficient cause (*causa efficiens purgationis*). He takes a middle-of-the-road position on the question whether there exists "room for acquiring merit" (*locus merendi*) in the other world. Although he seems to agree with the opinion that would later be adopted by the great scholastics, namely, that merits cannot be acquired after death, he challenges those who deny the possibility of amendment by fire, which "purges souls by acting in them without impressing its quality upon them" (*ignis purgatorius purgat animas agendo in eas tamen non intendit eis imprimere qualitatem suam*). This was a theoretical issue of great importance, for upon its resolution depended the answer to the question whether or not merits were reversible. Reversibility was not officially recognized until the fifteenth century. For the time being, the souls of Purgatory were the beneficiaries of the suffrages of the living, who received nothing in return, except the merit of having completed a work of mercy, prayer for the dead, in this life, which could redound to their benefit in the next.

The writings of the great scholastics on Purgatory bear multiple signs of the university's methods. I shall mention two. Teaching in the universities was conducted largely by way of commentary on manuals. In the thirteenth century the most important of these was the *Sententiarum Libri Quatuor* of Peter Lombard. Now, as we saw earlier, Peter Lombard deals in book 4 of this work with purgatorial fire, which by the thirteenth century had become Purgatory. In commenting on the *Sententiae*, therefore, the Parisian masters were led to discuss Purgatory, even though Peter, who died in 1160, had no such concept at his disposal. Paul's First Epistle to the Corinthians remained an important reference and text for commentary, but increasingly Peter Lombard's own text superseded the biblical passage as the fundamental statement on the question.

Academic teaching also revolved around a methodical, rational program, not without relation to the concerns and intellectual fashions of the day, such as Aristotelianism and Averroism. But the questions, even in the system of *quodlibeta*, intended in principle to allow treatment of any question even outside the framework of the regular program, made sense only in relation to a broader interpretation. Purgatory had its place in a system of "last things," under the head *De novissimis*.[5] For the great theologians of the day, it was an accepted idea, professed by the Church and included in academic programs, but not a cause for excitement.

In the twelfth century the intermediate hereafter had been intimately related to a number of major problems of common interest to theologians, mystics, and in less elaborate form to some laymen: biblical exegesis, the nature of sin, penitential practices, the status of visions and dreams. To the questions thus raised, theology, especially Parisian theology, contributed much in the way of answers during the second half of the century, as we have seen.

In the thirteenth century academic theology—again centered in Paris—established Purgatory and incorporated it into the system of Christian thought, but the problem was apparently no longer crucial. At this point we must turn our attention in two different directions, looking first at the intellectuals, then at pastors and at the masses.

Purgatory as a Continuation of Earthly Penance
William of Auvergne

M. de Wulf, one of the best historians of medieval thought, has written that "the line of great speculative theologians begins with William of Auvergne, one of the most original minds of the first half of the century. . . . William was the first great philosopher of the thirteenth century."[6] With respect to Purgatory, I prefer to say that William of Auvergne was the last great theologian of the twelfth century.[7] Etienne Gilson offers the following assessment: "By his whole habit of thought as well as his style, William belongs to the late twelfth century," adding that William was, with Abelard and Bernard of Clairvaux, the last great French theologian of the Middle Ages. I wonder if the fact that William of Auvergne was somewhat "old-fashioned" is due not, as some have argued, to his hostility to Aristotelianism (which was probably not as great as has been claimed) but rather to the fact that this secular clergyman, this pastor, however great a theologian he may have been, nevertheless remained closer to the

concerns and mental habits of his flock than the new academic intellectuals, who outstripped him in scholastic theology at the price of being
somewhat shut up in the Latin Quarter ghetto just then coming into
existence.

Born around 1180 at Aurillac, William of Auvergne was regent and
master of theology at Paris from 1222 to 1228 and bishop of Paris from
1228 until his death in 1249. Between 1223 and 1240 he composed an
immense work, the *Magisterium divinale sive sapientiale*, consisting of
seven treatises, the most important of which, *De universo* (*On the universe
of creatures*) was written between 1231 and 1236.

William begins this work by outlining a system of geography in which
this world and the next are united. The place of the soul's happiness is
situated at the summit of the universe, in the Empyrean; the place of its
unhappiness is located in the depths, in the underground chasm opposite
the heaven of the Empyrean; happiness and unhappiness are mingled in
the world of the living. Following this sketch William turns to the subject
of Purgatory. He considers two classical problems: the location of Purgatory and the nature of purgatorial fire. The bishop of Paris immediately
raises the question of the location of purgation, since the term Purgatory is
by this time an established part of his vocabulary: "If the place of purgation of souls, which is called Purgatory, is a specific place, destined for the
purgation of human souls, distinct from the earthly Paradise, from Hell,
and from the place where we reside, then there is a problem."[8]

That something remains to be purged after death is, for William of
Auvergne, an "obvious fact" (*manifestum est*). He then turns to the main
point of his conception of Purgatory, namely, that it is a continuation of
earthly penance. The idea of Purgatory as a place of penance, never more
clearly expressed than here, is quite in line with twelfth-century tradition,
as I believe I have demonstrated.

William then gives one reason why purgation is an obvious necessity:
those who die suddenly or without warning, for example, "by the sword,
suffocation, or excess of suffering," those whom death takes unawares
before they have had time to complete their penance, must have a place
where they may do so. He also mentions other reasons to believe in the
existence of Purgatory. For instance, there is the difference between mortal
sins and lesser sins. Since sins are not all equal, the compulsory expiation
cannot be the same for the most grave as for the least grave: the penance
for murder or plunder, for example, should be different from the penance
for excessive laughter or overindulgence in food and drink. The former
sins require expiation by punishment (*per poenam*), the latter expiation by
penance (*per poenitentiam*).

As for lesser sins, the soul laden down by them obviously cannot enter
Paradise, nor can it be sent on their account to Hell. These sins must
therefore be expiated before the soul can be transported into celestial

glory. In consequence, there must be a place, in the future, where this expiation can occur. William of Auvergne is in no doubt as to the time of Purgatory: it comprises the interval between death and resurrection.

William also draws a sharp distinction between Hell and Purgatory. Though he does not emphasize the painful nature of purgation after death, as it became common to do later in the thirteenth century, he does draw a parallel between penance in Purgatory and expiation, and between trials in Purgatory and penalties or penitential punishments (*poena purgatoriae et poenitentiales*). This was in fact his most important idea: "purgatorial penalties are penalties that complete the penitential purgation begun in this life." He adds that the frequency of unforeseen death, imperfect repentance prior to death, and death in a state of lesser sin makes these penalties "necessary for many souls" (*necessariae sunt multis animabus*). In other words, Purgatory is quite likely to be heavily populated. Though the point is not spelled out, it is obvious that, on this view, the population of Purgatory has been swelled at the expense of Hell. Furthermore, the existence of Purgatory is not inimical to the practice of a Christian life on earth, nor is it an invitation to laxity in this life—quite the contrary: "Because, out of fear of purgation in the future, in the absence of other motivations, men are more ready and more eager to begin penitential purgation in this life and more likely to continue it with greater zeal and vigor in order to complete it before dying."

Thus William proves by argument that Purgatory exists and relates it to penance. He then gives other proofs. One is drawn from experience. The common experience of apparitions by souls or men engaged in these purgations after death attests to the reality of Purgatory. Aware of the importance of the literature dealing with purgation in the other world, to which I have devoted much of this book, William stresses the concrete details contained in these accounts and tales of apparitions, demands, premonitions, and revelations, which are not only amusing (*quae non solum auditu jocundae sunt*) but also useful and salutary. This is why suffrages for the dead are necessary: prayers, alms, masses, and other pious works.

And then there is one final reason for the existence of Purgatory: justice requires it. "Those who have denied the existence of Purgatory," William writes, "have not been aware of repentance." Repentance "is a spiritual judgment, a judgment in which the sinful soul indicts itself, testifies against itself, pronounces a judgment against itself." But every judgment must satisfy the requirements of justice. Not all sins are equally grave; different sins deserve different punishments. If human justice does not tolerate confusion of penalties, divine justice, which is also divine mercy, tolerates it even less. Here again William of Auvergne is following very much along the trail blazed in the twelfth century, an age that was, as we have seen, hungry for justice as well as repentance.

Now that the existence of Purgatory has been demonstrated, its location remains to be established. On this point William of Auvergne was more perplexed, since "no law, no text states the answer" (*nulla lex, vel alia scriptura determinat*). What is revealed by visions and apparitions must therefore be believed. These tell us that purgation occurs at many places on this earth. William is at pains to provide theoretical, rational justification for this finding as well: "The thing is not surprising, for these purgations are merely supplements of penitential satisfactions, hence it is wrong to assign them to any place other than that of the pentitent. . . . This is the same place that is assigned to the whole and to the parts; where there is a place for man, there is also a place for his hands and feet; these purgations are merely parts of penances." Thus William's doctrine of penitential purgatory leads him to locate Purgatory in this world. Perhaps he was merely a reader of Gregory the Great looking for a rational explanation (*apparere etiam potest ex ratione*). More than that, after setting forth his geographic system of the universe, he could not, I think, have reached any other conclusion. Paradise is above, Hell below, and our earth occupies the intermediate level. Purgatory, that intermediate place par excellence, could not have been placed anywhere else. Nearly a century later, Dante would follow the line laid down by William of Auvergne: Dante's Purgatory is a place closer to Heaven than to Hell, a place where, upon entering, one first encounters the victims of sudden or violent deaths, and even suicides, as in the case of Cato the gatekeeper. But thanks to his conception of the earth as a hemisphere, Dante was able to locate the mountain of Purgatory in a place intermediary yet specific.

The second problem concerning Purgatory that William of Auvergne treats in *De universo* is the problem of fire, which at this time was not only an essential, required accessory of Purgatory but also, in many cases, its very embodiment. Alan E. Bernstein thinks he sees a contradiction in the chapters that William devotes to the fire of Purgatory. According to Bernstein, William seems to incline toward the concept of an immaterial or even purely "metaphorical" fire, even if he does not say so in so many words. But in the end, Bernstein argues, he accepts the idea of a material fire. Bernstein tries to resolve this contradiction by imagining that William of Auvergne elaborated a two-tiered theory: for his students and for intellectuals (including himself), he speculates, so we are told, on the idea of a pseudo-fire, putting forward views similar to those of Origen. For the mass of the faithful, he sets forth, according to Bernstein, a more materialistic, realistic concept of purgatorial fire, one more readily comprehended by ruder minds. Now, it is true that the bishop of Paris was both a theologian working at a high level of abstraction and a pastor deeply concerned about the *cura animarum*, the welfare of his flock. But I think that the duplicitous teaching imputed to him by Alan Bernstein is scarcely credible in a prelate of the first half of the thirteenth century, nor does it provide a satisfactory interpretation of the text of *De universo*.

Remember that this *summa* of William of Auvergne's treats the universe of creatures. In it, he sketches a typology and a phenomenology of fire. Fire, he tells us, comes in many varieties. In Sicily, for example, there are fires with curious properties: a kind of fire, for example, that turns hair phosphorescent without burning it. There are also creatures—animals like the salamander, for instance—that are incorruptible by fire. Such is the scientific truth about fire on earth. Might not God have created a special kind of fire to get rid of slight and incompletely expiated sins? William's first concern, then, is to show that the fire of Purgatory is not a fire like other fires. In particular, it is different from the fire of Gehenna, hellfire. William's point is in fact to distinguish clearly between Purgatory and Hell. Consequently there must be different kinds of fire in the two places. Yet even hellfire is different from the kind of fire we are familiar with on earth, fire that consumes. Hellfire burns without consuming, since the damned are tortured for all eternity. If, then, there is a fire that must burn in perpetuity without consuming, might not God have created a fire that burns while consuming only sins, purifying the sinner? Fires that burn without consuming are nonetheless real, however. Furthermore, William is sensitive to the opinion of those who point out that, according to one possible idea of Purgatory, an idea confirmed by the testimony of its denizens in various apparitions, fire is not the only form of expiation to be endured there. Fire is therfore not a metaphor but a generic term used to designate the whole range of expiatory and purificatory processes to which souls are subjected in Purgatory.

This brings us to the central argument on which Alan Bernstein rests his belief that William of Auvergne holds a metaphorical theory of fire. Fire, according to William, can be efficacious even in the imagination, as in nightmares, for example, where it terrifies without being real. But just as he has already shown elsewhere that belief in Purgatory leads to improved penitential practice in this world, here William is merely trying to prove that purgatorial fire is effective in bringing about eternal salvation. What he wants to say, I think, is that, since fire is efficacious when it exists only in man's imagination, in dreams, for example, it is even more efficacious when it is real. For how can one doubt that William of Auvergne believed and taught that the fire of Purgatory is real, is material? As Alan Bernstein himself points out, William says that purgatorial fire "corporeally and really tortures the bodies of souls" (*corporaliter et vere torqueat corpora animarum*). Did anyone ever offer better or bolder arguments for the view that the theater of Purgatory is not a theater of shadows but a corporeal theater, in which souls suffer in their bodies from the bite of a material flame?

Purgatory and the Mendicant Masters

The great mendicant theologians offer us a coherent body of doctrine, assuming that we are willing to neglect minor variations from individual to individual and order to order.

A. Piolanti does not always get things in the correct proportions but in general he has given a good definition of the overall position of the great scholastics (Alexander of Hales, Saint Bonaventure, Saint Thomas Aquinas, and Albertus Magnus): "In the thirteenth century the great scholastics, in glossing the text of Peter Lombard, constructed a more consistent synthesis: though they debate such secondary issues as the remission of venial sins, the gravity and duration of the penalty, and the location of Purgatory,[9] they hold as a doctrine of faith the existence of Purgatory and the temporal limitation of the penalty and are agreed that the fire is real."[10]

The Views of the Franciscans

From a Commentary on Peter Lombard to a Science of the Hereafter: Alexander of Hales

I had occasion above to cite an excerpt from Alexander of Hales' gloss on Peter Lombard's *Sententiae*, which dwelt in some mathematical detail on the question of "proportionality" in regard to Purgatory. Here I should like to say a bit more about the structure of Alexander's commentary and the main points made there by the great Parisian master.[11]

An Englishman born around 1185, Alexander became master of arts in Paris before 1210 and taught theology there from about 1225 until his death in 1245. In 1236 he joined the Friars Minor and held the first Franciscan chair of theology at the University of Paris. He was one of the first Parisian theologians to explicate Aristotle, despite the repeated prohibitions (the fact that they were repeated shows that they went unheeded) against reading the works of the "prince of philosophers." The *Summa theologica* long attributed to him was not in fact his work but that of Franciscan academics highly influenced by his teaching. On the other hand, he was the author of the *Gloss* on the *Sententiae* of Peter Lombard, which he was the first to use as a basic text for the academic teaching of theology (after the Fourth Lateran Council virtually consecrated Peter Lombard as official theologian in 1215). The *Gloss* was probably written sometime between 1223 and 1229. Alexander was also the author of *Disputed Questions*, similarly composed prior to his joining the Franciscans, which explains the full title of the work (*Quaestiones disputatae antequam esset frater*).

In his gloss on book 4 of Peter Lombard's *Sententiae*, Alexander deals with Purgatory in "distinctions" 18 and, especially, 20 ("On belated penance, purgatorial punishment, and reductions"[12]) and 21 ("On remission and punishment of venial sins, building of gold, hay, and straw, and the seven modes of remission of sin"[13]).

Clearly, he is interested in the problem of Purgatory as a place especially intended for sinners whose belated penance is incomplete and for sinners guilty only of venial sins. And, like others before him, he obviously makes use of Paul's First Epistle to the Corinthians.

Alexander begins with a reflection on the nature of fire. There is, he says, a fire that will purge souls until the end of the world: "There is a double fire: one, purgatorial, which purges souls from now until the day of Judgment [i.e., the Last Judgment], and another, which will precede the Judgment, which will consume this world and purify those who build of gold, etc., if they are then found with something combustible. Mark well that there are three species of fire: light, flame, and coals [lux, flamma, carbo], and that it is divided up into three parts: the superior for the elect, the middle for those who must be purged, and the last for the damned."

Apart from the references to Aristotle, who wrote that "the coals, the flame, and the light are different from one another" (Topics 5.5), and to Paul, it is plain that Alexander is reconciling the opposing traditional opinions on the nature of the fire—that it is active prior to resurrection on the one hand, after resurrection at the time of the Last Judgment on the other—by maintaining that there are two fires: one purgatorial, between death and resurrection, the other consummatory or purificatory between resurrection and judgment. The Aristotelian classification of three kinds of fire enables Alexander to specify the median, intermediary nature of Purgatory, which corresponds to the flame that purges, whereas the light is reserved to the elect and the hot coals to the damned. Here we have a good example of the kind of logical tool that Aristotle provided to thirteenth-century scholastics.

1. The fire of Purgatory purges venial sins (purgans a venialibus): "Sin is remitted and purged in this life by love [charitas] in many ways, as a drop of water in the oven of fire, by the eucharist, confirmation, and extreme unction. After death it is purged in Purgatory.

2. It also purges penalties owed for mortal sins not yet sufficiently expiated (et a poenis debitis mortalibus nondum sufficienter satisfactis).

3. It is a punishment greater than any temporal punishment(poena maior omni temporali). Here Alexander reverts to the Augustinian theme, out of concern to combat the accusation of laxity that might otherwise attach to a view that leaves Hell more or less empty.

4. Is it an unjust, disproportionate punishment (nonne iniusta et improportionalis)? The importance of this question was discussed in the previous chapter.

5. There is faith and hope but as yet no (beatific) vision (ibi fides et spes, nondum visio): Alexander insists, along with many others, that Purgatory is hope, because it is the antechamber of Paradise, but he also

stresses that it is not yet Paradise and that the souls there are deprived of the vision of God.

6. Those who escape or avoid it are few (*illud vitantes seu evolantes pauci*). "Few in number are those in the Church whose merits are sufficient that they need not pass through Purgatory" (*transire per purgatorium*). Purgatory is, for the majority of men, the temporary holding place in the other world. Quantitatively, it is argued here, Purgatory is paramount.

Elsewhere Alexander of Hales treats the relations between the Church and Purgatory. The first problem is that of the jurisdiction of the *for* (tribunal) within whose purview the soul in Purgatory falls. "To the objection that it does not lie within the power of the keys (the power to pardon sins given by Jesus to Peter and, through Peter, to all bishops and priests) to remit purgatorial punishment by commutation as temporary punishment, it must be answered that those who are in Purgatory [*in purgatorio*] fall in some sense within the jurisdiction of the *for* of the militant Church and likewise purgatorial fire insofar as it is appropriate to the satisfactory punishment (which completes the penance). Hence, since all the faithful belong either to the militant Church or to the triumphant Church, those [in Purgatory] are in the middle [*in medio*], and since they belong neither entirely to the militant nor entirely to the triumphant Church, they can be subject to the power of the priest [*potestati sacerdotis*] because of the power of the keys."

This is a text of the utmost importance, which, at a time when the jurisdiction of the Church was being reorganized in canon law both theoretically and practically, asserted the Church's jurisdiction, at least in part, over the new territory just opened up in the other world. Until then the spiritual judicial power, the tribunal (or *for*) of the soul was sharply divided. Death marked the dividing line: on one side, in this world, man fell under the temporal jurisdiction of the Church, within the purview of the ecclesiastical *for*; on the other side, he fell under the jurisdiction of God alone, within the purview of the divine *for*. To be sure, the recent legislation concerning the proclamation and canonization of saints had conferred upon the Church power over certain of the dead, whom it was able to place, from the moment of death, in Paradise and in the ecstasy of the Beatific Vision; but in so doing, "the Church pronounced on the fate of only a tiny number."[14] But ecclesiastical interference in the affairs of Purgatory affected the majority of the faithful. The new territory was probably not entirely annexed by the Church. Owing to its middle position, it fell under the jurisdiction of both God and the Church. Cojurisdictions were at this time an increasingly common feature of the feudal system, and one might say, borrowing a term from feudal law, that God and the Church enjoyed *pariage* (coseigniory) over Purgatory. But what a gain for the Church in its hold over the faithful! At a time when its power was being challenged both mildly by those who had been converted to the pleasures of the earthly life (*insouciants*, as they were called) and harshly by heretics, the Church extended its power over the faithful into the other world.

In doctrine the question pertained to the meaning of the Church, in the fullest and broadest sense of the word, and it fell to Alexander of Hales to give one of the earliest clear statements of the role of the "communion of saints" in relation to Purgatory. The question was, "Are the suffrages of the Chruch useful to the dead in Purgatory?" The answer: "Just as specific pain entails satisfaction for the sin, so the common pain of the universal Church, crying for the sins of dead believers, praying and lamenting for them, is an aid to satisfaction; it does not create satisfaction in itself, but with the pain of the penitent aids in satisfaction, which is the very definition of suffrage. Suffrage is in fact the merit of the Church, capable of diminishing the pain of one of its members."[15] Thus the notion of pain and suffering began to emerge, first as simple expiation and later as the source of merits that would enable the souls in Purgatory not only to complete their purgation with the help of the living but also to become worthy to intervene with God on behalf of the living.

In any case, the Church, in the ecclesiastical, clerical sense, drew considerable power from the new system of the hereafter. It administered or supervised prayers, alms, masses, and offerings of all kinds made by the living on behalf of the dead and reaped the benefits thereof. Thanks to Purgatory the Church developed the system of indulgences, a source of great power and profit until it became a dangerous weapon that was ultimately turned back against the Church.

Here again Alexander of Hales was both observer and theorist of the evolution. He was cautious: "To the objection that the Church cannot by virtue of the perfect obtain satisfaction for the rest, I answered that it can obtain an aid but not full satisfaction. But, it is further objected, how can one obtain this kind of reduction of penalty for one's dead relatives when they have already fallen into the hands of the living God, and the Lord said, 'When I shall receive the congregation, I shall judge uprightly' (Ps. 75:3)? We answer: only the weigher of souls knows the magnitude of the penalty owed for each sin, and it is not meet that man seek to know too much. But those who, in love, go to the aid of the Holy Land may be in such devotion and generosity of alms that, themselves liberated from all their sins, they are able to liberate their relatives from Purgatory, by obtaining satisfaction for them."

In other words, indulgences for the dead were still being dispensed sparingly, and only to members of that exceptional group of Christians, increasingly rare in the thirteenth century, the crusaders. But the apparatus was in place and ready to go into operation. At the end of the century Boniface VIII would use it to fuller advantage on the occasion of the Jubilee of 1300.

In *Quaestiones disputatae "antequam esset frater,"* written between 1216 and 1236, Alexander of Hales makes several further allusions to Purgatory. In question 48, discussing venial sins, he distinguishes between the guilt, which is erased by extreme unction, and the penalty, which must be paid in Purgatory.[16] Elsewhere he refers to the bitter, acerbic nature (*acerbitas*) of purgatorial punishment.[17] To the question whether souls in Purgatory have hope, he answers with a fine metaphor involving passengers on a ship. Their hope comes not from their merit but from the action of others. Travelers may get about either by using their own two feet or by other means, by horse or by boat, for example. The souls in Purgatory are "like passengers on a ship: they acquire no merit but pay for their transportation; similarly, the dead in Purgatory pay the penalty they owe, not like the captain, who can acquire merits on the boat, but merely as cargo."[18]

Bonaventure and the Last Things

Giovanni di Fidanza, who was born about 1217 at Bagnoreggio on the border of Latium and Umbria and who later took the name Bonaventure, came to Paris as a young man, joined the Franciscan order in 1243, became a "bachelor of the Bible" (i.e., one authorized to explain the Holy Scriptures) in 1248, "bachelor of law" (i.e., one qualified to comment on Peter Lombard's *Sententiae*) in 1250, and master of theology in 1253.[19] Thus it was early in his career, between 1250 and 1256, that he composed his *Commentary* on Peter Lombard, before becoming minister general of the Friars Minor in 1257 and cardinal in 1273. The work bears the marks of Augustine's inspiration, characteristic of the Franciscan doctor.[20]

In distinction 20 of book 4 of his *Commentary* on the *Sententiae*, Bonaventure deals with "Purgatorial punishment in itself." He begins by asserting that it is doubtless after this life that this punishment occurs. To the question "whether the punishment of Purgatory is the greatest of temporal puishments" (*utrum poena purgatorii sit maxima poenarum temporalium*), he answers that it is the heaviest penalty "of its kind," heavier than any temporal penalty that the soul can suffer while it is joined to the body. Thus Bonaventure, while following Augustinian tradition in emphasizing the severity of the punishment endured in Purgatory and in recognizing the connection that can be established between this punishments and punishments in this world, nevertheless lays stress on what is unique about Purgatory. His work probably contains echoes of theories on the proportionality of purgatorial penalties earlier proposed by Alexander of Hales, who was his teacher. Bonaventure then turns to a problem that concerned all the great scholastics, in whose systems the category of "will" plays a prominent part: namely, whether or not purgatorial punishment is voluntary. Will was important in Bonaventure's own thinking: in the third of the six degrees of contemplation described in the *Itinerary of the Spirit toward God*, he describes the soul that "sees shining in itself the image of God, because in the three powers, memory, intelligence, and will, the soul itself sees God by itself as in his image" (J.-C. Bougerol).

All the great scholastics, in various formulations depending on their particular systems, accorded only a limited voluntary character to purgatorial punishment, since, as Alexander of Hales established, free will was immobilized after death and merit became impossible to acquire. Accordingly, for these theologians, venial sins are pardoned in Purgatory "as to the penalty" (*quoad poenam*) but not "as to the guilt" (*quoad culpam*), this being pardoned at the very moment of death itself. Thomas Aquinas, who followed the letter of Peter Lombard's text more closely than some others, wrote in his *Commentary* on the *Sententiae* that "in the other life, venial sin is remitted as to the guilt itself by the fire of Purgatory to him who dies in a state of grace, because this punishment, being in some sense voluntary, has the virtue of expiating any guilt compatible with sanctifying grace." He reconsiders this position in *De malo*, where he holds that venial sin no longer exists in Purgatory; as for guilt, it has already been erased by an act of perfect charity at the moment of death.

Bonaventure believed that purgatorial punishment was voluntary only to a minimal degree (*minimam habet rationem voluntarii*), for though the will might "tolerate" it, it desires its opposite," that is, the cessation of punishment and the reward of heaven.[21] The following question bears on the relationship between Purgatory and Paradise: "Is there less certainty of glory in the punishment of Purgatory than there is in the way [*via*]?[22]—that is, in this world in which man is a pilgrim, *viator*? Here is Bonaventure's answer: "There is more certainty of glory in Purgatory than in the way but less than in the homeland [*patria*]." Here Purgatory is seen as hope and in a sense as even more than that, since Bonaventure uses the word "certainty." But he introduces degrees into the notion of certainty. He is following what has become the fundamental concept of Purgatory as a "middle," an intermediate place, distinguishing between two phases if not two places in Paradise: the homeland (the term *patria*[23] construed in this way is also found in the work of other writers), which seems rather close to the idea of the bosom of Abraham, where souls find repose, and glory, which is at once the ecstasy of the beatific vision and a sort of "deification" of man, whose soul, reunited with his resurrected body, is made "glorious."

Here Bonaventure raises a question of great interest to us, because it takes him into the sphere of the imagination, which played so important a role in the actual history of Purgatory. He answers the question, "Is purgatorial punishment inflicted by the office [*ministerio*] of demons?" as follows: "The punishment of Purgatory is not inflicted by the ministry of demons or by the ministry of good angels, but it is probable that souls are taken to Heaven by good angels, and to Hell by bad ones."

Thus Bonaventure views Purgatory as a sort of no-man's-land between the domain of the angels and the domain of the demons. But here again we find that inequality within equality that I said earlier was a fundamental structural feature of the medieval mind: Bonaventure places Purgatory nearer to Paradise than to Hell, at least to the extent that the guides to both of these realms, as Dante would call them, are good angels. In this he contradicts the opinion put forward by most visions of the hereafter, *Saint Patrick's Purgatory* in particular. Purgatory took hold in the thirteenth century in an atmosphere of dramatization of Christian beliefs. In the case of Purgatory this drama stemmed mainly from the conflict between the noninfernal, not to say preparadisaical, view that predominated, as it seems to me, in the late twelfth century, in spite of the prevalence of dark visions, and what Arturo Graf has called the gradual "infernalization" of Purgatory over the course of the thirteeth century. In this respect Bonaventure is fairly traditional.

He was also traditional with respect to the location of Purgatory. "Is the site of Purgatory above, below, or in the middle?" (*superius an inferius an in medio*). His answer is original: "The place of Purgatory is probably, according to the common law, below [*inferius*], but it is in the middle [*medius*] according to the divine economy [*dispensationem divinam*]." Notice, first of all, that, as in the previous question concerning angels and demons, we are in the domain of opinions, probabilities, and not certainties. Whenever the imaginary and the concrete were touched upon, the great scholastics more or less avoided the issue. But Bonaventure's opinion is quite interesting in that it brings together (without concealing the differences, not to say the opposition) a common law, according to which Purgatory is located beneath the earth, and a divine plan that places Purgatory in an intermediate position, in keeping with the new logic of the other world. Bonaventure is thus operating on two levels, one of common law, the other of divine economy, a duality duplicated by the divergence between tradition and the tendencies of theology.

Bonaventure expresses further doubts as to the location of Purgatory in two other passages in the *Commentary* on Book 4 of the *Sententiae*. In discussing the fire of Purgatory and glossing Peter Lombard's own gloss on 1 Corinthians 3:15,[24] he argues against the opinion that purgatorial fire has a spiritual purgative value over and above its punitive value, and that it therefore purges sin (venial or otherwise), that is to say, guilt, in the manner of a sacrament. To support his refusal to view the fire of Purgatory as a new force (*vis nova*) beyond punishment, he calls to witness Gregory the Great's assertion that many souls are purged in diverse locations (*per diversa loca*) and that purification of guilt can be accomplished only by grace. This harks back to the Gregorian tradition that purgation occurs in this world in the places where sin is committed.

Earlier, in the sixth question of distinction 20 Bonaventure discusses another view as to the location of Purgatory, namely, that of *Saint Patrick's Purgatory*. From this vision he drew the conclusion that the site of purgation could depend on the intercession of a saint, for, as he says, "someone" had obtained from Saint Patrick the right to be punished at a certain spot on earth, and it was this that had given rise to the legend that this spot was the location of Purgatory (*in quodam loco in terra, ex quo fabulose ortum est, quod ibi esset purgatorium*). But his own conclusion is merely that there are various places of purgation. Thus, while attesting the popularity of *Saint Patrick's Purgatory*, he takes the view that, while its report of the location of Purgatory may be valid as a special case, in other respects it has merely been a source of "fables." As we shall see, this opinion was not shared by a Cistercian such as Caesarius of Heisterbach. But it is good evidence of the suspicious attitude of one intellectual toward the folkloric literature concerning visions of Purgatory.

Bonaventure again deals with the question of Purgatory's location in discussing the classical idea of the "receptacles of souls" in article 1 of distinction 44 of book 4.[25] He draws a careful distinction between the geography of the other world prior to Christ's coming and its geography after the Incarnation. Before Christ Hell comprised two stories: one at the very bottom (*locus infimus*) in which souls are subjected to both the pain of the senses (*la peine du sens*, material punishments) and the penalty of damnation (*la peine du dam*, or privation of the beatific vision), the second a low place (*locus inferior*) but above the other story, where souls are subjected only to the penalty of damnation. Included in the latter were the Limbos (actually, in the Middle Ages, the singular, *limbus*, was used whether only one Limbo was defined or more than one), the Limbo of small children and the Limbo of the Fathers or bosom of Abraham.

After Christ there are *four* places: Paradise, Hell, Limbo, and Purgatory. Even though the idea is not explicitly mentioned, one has the impression that Purgatory is a consequence of the Incarnation related to the remission of sins accomplished by the coming of Christ. It is also worth noting that of the two Limbos only the children's remains, but this results in a total of four places, because Bonaventure clearly distinguishes between this Limbo and Hell (whereas Albertus Magnus combines Limbo and Hell, as we shall see). Bonaventure continues his account, characteristically, by combining the system of four places with another system, this one ternary and abstract, involving "three states" of the elect: a state of remuneration (in other words, Paradise), a state of tranquil expectation (*quietae expectationis*, i.e., the bosom of Abraham), and a state of purgation (i.e., Purgatory). He then adds the following: "As for the state of purgation, this corresponds to an indeterminate place in relation to us and in itself [*locus indeterminatus et quoad nos et quoad se*], for all are not purged in the same place, although many are probably purged in a certain place." Here he invokes the authority of his favorite author, Augustine.

All in all, then, Bonaventure had no clear idea about the location of Purgatory. But for his clearer awareness of the complexity of the problem, he might be mistaken for a wavering theologian of the twelfth century such as Hugh of Saint-Victor. Yet he is forced to acknowledge that the belief in Purgatory increasingly centers on a specific place, though he himself regards this merely as the place where the majority of souls are purged and continues to allow a variety of other places (including some in this world, just as Gregory the Great had supposed) to be purgatorial sites. Is this a sign of Bonaventure's perplexity in the face of conflicting authorities? More important than that, I think, is his distaste for making Purgatory more a place than a state, a state that to be sure needs to be localized but in an abstract way, dispersed among various real, and what is more, temporary, sites.

When he asks whether one can benefit from "reprieves" (*relaxationes*) while in Purgatory or only while in this world,[26] Bonaventure, following Alexander of Hales, uses the occasion to stress the power over Purgatory of the Church in general and the pope in particular. This passage is an important step in the development of indulgences and papal power over the dead, which Boniface VIII would inaugurate with the Jubilee of 1300.

Bonaventure then returns to the question of the fire of Purgatory.[27] He asks whether this is corporeal or spiritual or even metaphysical, determines that the opinions of the doctors vary and that his master, Augustine, was in doubt, but nevertheless concludes ("concedes") that the fire is "material or corporeal" in nature. This aspect of the problem should properly be studied in relation to contemporary discussions with the Greeks, in which the Franciscans and Bonaventure himself played a very large part.[28]

By contrast, Bonaventure takes a firm, not to say vehement, position on the liberation of souls from Purgatory prior to the Last Judgment (characterizing his opponents as *stulti*, imbeciles).[29] He forcefully argues, notably against the Greeks, that such liberation can occur, leading to the beatific vision. He bases his case both on the authorities and on rational arguments. Among the authorities he first cites the words spoken by Jesus on the Cross to the good thief: "Today thou shalt be with me in Paradise" (Luke 23:43). The three arguments are interesting: (1) After purgation there can be no "delaying element" in Purgatory. The soul takes flight as soon as purgation is complete. (2) To refuse a mercenary his pay is to commit an offense against justice; but God is just par excellence, so that as soon as he finds a man worthy of being rewarded, he rewards him (a suggestive reference to justice, in the tradition of the twelfth century, and to the problem of the just wage, which relates to the social and economic ethics that the scholastics were attempting to work out in conjunction with the rise of wage labor). (3) Finally, a psychological argument: to defer hope unduly is an act of cruelty, and if God were to keep saints far from their reward until Judgment Day, he would be very cruel indeed.

Toward the end of the *Commentary* on the *Sententiae* Bonaventure turns to the question of suffrages.[30] Modifying Augustine's position somewhat, he essentially distinguishes between three categories of the dead: the good (*boni*) who are in Paradise, the medium good (*mediocriter boni*), and the entirely bad. He then gives what became the standard answer, that only the medium good can benefit from the suffrages of the living, but he adds that they are not in "a state to merit" (*in statu merendi*) because after death there is no further merit.

After commenting on Peter Lombard in the course of his university teaching, Bonaventure felt the need to set forth his ideas in a more personal way on the whole range of problems facing the theologian, just as Thomas Aquinas did in his *Summa theologica*. In Bonaventure's case the product of this desire was the *Breviloquium* (1254–56). The modest place that Purgatory occupies in this work shows that Bonaventure believed that his main thoughts on this subject could be read in his *Commentary* on Peter Lombard (it is difficult to determine whether this was written before or after the *Breviloquium*, however). In the *Breviloquium* Bonaventure says that, insofar as the purgatorial penalty is "punitive," it is inflicted by means of material fire, and that insofar as it is "expurgative," it manifests itself in the form of spiritual fire.[31]

As for suffrages,[32] which he does not hesitate to call "ecclesiastic," thus indicating the Church's dominant role in this area, he unequivocally states that these are valid "for the medium good, that is, for those who are in Purgatory," but ineffective "for the entirely bad, that is, for those who are in Hell" and "for the entirely good, that is, for those who are in Heaven," whose merits and prayers procure many boons for the members of the militant Church.[33]

Finally, Bonaventure mentions Purgatory in two sermons for the day of commemoration of the dead, All Souls' Day, November 2. In the first,[34] he distinguishes between the damned, the elect, and those who must be purged (*damnati, beati, purgandi*). He bases his belief in the existence of the latter category, whose members he numbers among the "imperfect," on various citations from the bible.[35] In the second sermon he appeals primarily to prayer and refers to the prayer of Judas Maccabee, which he says is worthwhile for those who "are undergoing tribulations in Purgatory because of their inveterate sins but who will ultimately be transferred to eternal ecstasy"; he further interprets Judas, Jonathan, and Simon allegorically as "the faithful, simple, and humble prayer by means of which those who are in Purgatory are liberated."[36] It is fitting that we should have concluded this brief survey of Bonaventure's views on Purgatory with a discussion of prayer, a subject on which the illustrious Franciscan was one of the greatest teachers of all time.[37]

The Dominicans

Without leaving Paris let us now turn our attention back a few years and examine the teachings on Purgatory of the two greatest Dominican masters, Albertus Magnus and Thomas Aquinas. Chronology is not to be neglected in studying the world of the Parisian theologians, but we must be careful about what sequences we consider. Rather than look at Parisian teaching in general, it is probably better to follow the changes in the doctrinal line laid down independently by each of the two great mendicant orders. Albertus Magnus made his main ideas on Purgatory known between 1240 and 1248. They were popularized in 1268 by one of Albert's disciples, Hugh Ripelin of Strasbourg. They also influenced the original work of another disciple, a great thinker in his own right, Thomas Aquinas, who first expressed his views on Purgatory in the courses he gave in Paris between 1252 and 1256 (he was commenting on Peter Lombard's *Sententiae* at almost the same time as Bonaventure). Thomas's ideas were put into polished form by a group of disciples after his death in 1274. This "coalition" of Dominican thinkers was responsible for the ultimate achievement of scholasticism in establishing a balance between Aristotelian method and Christian tradition, the "optimum" construction of "rational" academic teaching and thought in the thirteenth century. The doctrinal genius of Albert and Thomas was widely disseminated thanks to the *Compendium* of Hugh of Strasbourg and the *Supplement* to the *Summa theologica* by Reginald of Piperno and his collaborators.

The Scholastic Plan of Purgatory: Albertus Magnus

Albert of Lauingen, born about 1207, joined the Dominicans at Padua in 1223 but was trained in Cologne and in other German convents and later in Paris, where he was "bachelor of law" from 1240 to 1242 and then master of theology, the occupant of one of the two Dominican chairs at the University of Paris from 1242 to 1248.[38] It was during this period that Albert, a reader of Aristotle but not yet an "Aristotelian" in the true sense of the word, composed two ponderous works in theology, the *Summa de creaturis*, of which the treatise *De resurrectione* is probably a part (it figures as such in the manuscripts and was composed prior to 1246),[39] and a *Commentary on the Sententiae of Peter Lombard*. Albert deals with Purgatory in both of these works.

De resurrectione is probably the equivalent of a treatise "De novissimis," of the "Last Things," that was supposed to conclude the *Summa de creaturis*. In the manuscripts that contain it, the treatise remains incomplete, concluding with the Last Judgment without going on to treat "eternal beatitude, eternal crowns, and the house and mansions of God" as promised.

After discussing the resurrection in general in the first part and the resurrection of Christ in the second, Albert turns in the third part to the resurrection of the wicked. The "places of punishment," he declares, are "Hell, Purgatory, the Limbo of children, and the Limbo of the Fathers." To the question whether Hell is a place he replies that it is twofold: there is an outer Hell which is a material place and an inner Hell which is the punishment that the damned endure wherever they may be; the location of Hell is "in the earth's core" and punishments there are eternal. The "authorities" cited are as usual Augustine plus Hugh of Saint-Victor and, on the questions of location and the nature of fire, Gregory the Great and *Saint Patrick's Purgatory*. On questions of logic appeal is made to Aristotle.

Purgatory, according to *De resurrectione*, is indeed a place, located near Hell. It is even described as the upper part of Hell. The reason why Gregory and Patrick say that Purgatory is on this earth is that there are cases in which souls from Purgatory appear in this world, by special dispensation, in order to give warning to living humans. Hugh of Saint-Victor and Paul (1 Cor. 3) are cited, the latter with commentary by Augustine, to show that venial sins are dissolved in Purgatory. This demonstration is rather lengthy and it provides Albert with the opportunity to indulge in subtle logical argumentation, backed up by the authority of Aristotle. More briefly, he then discusses the nature and intensity of purgatorial punishments. He is of the opinion that the souls in Purgatory do not suffer from infernal punishments, because they have the benefit of the light of faith and the light of grace; what they lack for the time being is the beatific vision, but this privation is not to be confused with inward darkness. The demons are satisfied to take souls to Purgatory to be purged, but they do not purge them there. Finally, freezing (*gelidicium*) is not a punishment inflicted in Purgatory, because it is used to punish coldness in charity and as such is not applicable to souls in need of purgation. Albert here makes no mention of the principal punishment, fire, having had occasion to discuss this subject previously when, in dealing with Hell, he found it necessary to distinguish Hell from Purgatory. Finally, to those who, with Augustine, believe that purgatorial punishments are marked by more "bitterness" (*acerbitas*) than any punishments in this world, and to others who think that purgatorial punishments are to infernal punishments as the image of fire is to fire itself or as a point is to a line, Albert answers by appealing to logic and raising the debate to a higher plane. He enlists the help of Aristotle (*Physics* 1.3c.6–206b.11–12), who says that one can only compare things that are comparable, to wit, finite with finite. Hence the problem of *acerbitas* cannot be discussed. The difference between Purgatory and Hell is a question not of intensity but of duration. What the soul in Purgatory aspires to, moreover, is not to regain its body but rather to rejoin God. It is in this sense that Augustine, who was not thinking about the fire of purgatory, must be understood. The third part of *De resurrectione* concludes with a comprehensive treatment of all the places of punishment (*De locis poenarum simul*). Albert thereby shows that he was acutely aware of the fact that the various regions of the other world constitute a unified system, whose unity is at once material and spiritual: there is a geography and a theology of the hereafter.

Albert considers the problem of the "receptacles of souls" from three points of view. The first question is whether these receptacles are a final resting place or a stopping place along the way to somewhere else. If a final resting place, are they places of glory or of punishment? There is only one place of glory: the kingdom of heaven, Paradise. As for places of punishment, a distinction must be made between places where the only punishment inflicted is the punishment of damnation, namely, the Limbo of Children, and places where punishment of the senses is inflicted in addition to damnation, namely, Gehenna, Hell. If the receptacles are merely temporary stopping places, the same distinction must be made: damnation only in the Limbo of the Fathers and damnation plus punishment of the senses in Purgatory.

It is also possible to look at the question from the standpoint of the cause of merit. Merit can be either good or bad or both good and bad (*bonum conjunctum malo*). If good, the kingdom of heaven is the appropriate place. If bad, it must be due to the person's own sin or to alien sin (*ex culpa propria aut aliena*). If due to a personal sin, the appropriate place is Gehenna. If due to an alien sin (i.e., original sin), the appropriate place is the Limbo of Children. If due to a mixture of good and evil, it cannot be a question of mortal evil, which would be incompatible with the grace that attaches to the good. Hence it is a venial sin, which can arise either from personal guilt or from alien guilt. In the first case one goes to Purgatory, in the second to the Limbo of the Fathers.

Finally, the question can be looked at from the standpoint of what there is in each place. Four qualities apply: the place can be afflictive, dark, light, or gratifying (*afflictivum, tenebrosum, luminosum, laetificativum*). If the place is light and gratifying, it is the kingdom of heaven. If it is afflictive and dark because the beatific vision is postponed, then it is Purgatory.[40] If it is dark directly but not afflictive, it is the Limbo of Children. If it is dark indirectly but not afflictive, it is the Limbo of the Fathers. Albert is aware that he has not exhausted all possible combinations of these four qualities but demonstrates that the exemplary cases he considers are the only compatible combinations.[41]

If I have dwelt at length on the argument put forward by Albertus

Magnus, my point was in part to show what scholasticism made of Purgatory; in other words, to show the rationalization of a belief which, as we have seen, arose as much from imagery as from reasoning, as much from fantastic tales as from authorities, and which did not develop in any straightforward way but rather through countless meanderings, hesitations, and contradictions, culminating finally in a tightly knit fabric of beliefs. But it was also in part because, in my view, Albertus Magnus, more than other scholastic thinker, was able to provide the system of Purgatory with a theory to account for the largely empirical content it had received at its inception half a century earlier.

This text is interesting for other reasons as well. Better than anyone else, Albert was able to harmonize the imaginary and logical components, the components derived from authority and those derived from reasoning, of beliefs such as the belief in Purgatory. He expelled the devils from Purgatory but let them come as far as its borders. He rejected cold but welcomed heat, fire. He distinguished between interior and exterior space but acknowledged that the other world is a system of material places. Though he may have wished to purify the imagination, it was not a question of principled hostility but one of determining when the imagination stood in contradiction to logic, truth, or the deeper meaning of the belief.

This text also shows that for Albert it was important, if not essential, to draw a careful distinction between Purgatory and Hell. In his view this is another logical consequence of the system. Purgatory corresponds to a certain state of sin, one in which good and evil are mixed. From this it follows, first of all, that the system basically has three parts and not five: *aut est bonum aut est malum aut bonum conjunctum malo* (either good or evil or good combined with evil). The main consequence of this is that Purgatory is an intermediate place, but a decentered one, above rather than below the true median, closer to Heaven, to God, than to Hell. For the evil implicit in it is venial, not mortal, while the good, like all good, is the good of grace. It is therefore wrong to believe that all thirteenth-century thinking in regard to Purgatory tended in the direction of "infernalization." This was indeed, as we shall soon see, the path ultimately taken, but the reason must be sought in an overriding decision by the institutionalized Church in this period to rely on the preaching of fear, to allow its inquisitors to wield instruments of torture in this world as well as in the next.

In the *Commentary on the Sententiae,* which must have been composed shortly after *De resurrectione,* Albertus Magnus gives a fuller, more detailed discussion of Purgatory, which in some respects marks an advance over his earlier position. It is still book 4 of the *Sententiae,* distinctions 21 and 45, that provide the occasion for the discussion of Purgatory. In summarizing the Dominican master's commentary, I shall try to bring out something of Albert's manner of argument and to show by what route he came to hold positions that do not always coincide with those set forth in *De resurrectione*.

In distinction 21,[42] Albert considers the following points. Is it true that there are sins after death, as Christ says in the Gospel: "Whosoever speaketh against the Holy Ghost, it shall not be forgiven him, neither in this world, neither in the world to come" (Matt. 12:32)? Are these sins the venial sins to which Augustine alludes in discussing wood, hay, and straw (1 Cor. 3:12)? Is it possible to believe that this purgation will take place by means of a purgatory and transitory fire, and that this fire will be harsher than any from which man can suffer in this life (Augustine, *City of God* 21.26), since Paul says (1 Cor. 3:15) that man will be saved yet as by fire (*quasi per ignem*), which might lead one to scorn this fire?

Albert considers these questions and sets forth his answers in twelve articles. The question treated in the first article is this: Are certain venial sins forgiven after this life? The answer is affirmative and is based both on authorities, particularly Gregory the Great (Book 4 of the *Dialogues*), and on reason. Here are two of Albert's arguments: (1) After death it is no longer the time to increase one's merit but it is time to use the merit (acquired here below) for appropriate ends; (2) the pain of death itself can erase many sins if it is suffered for that end, as in the case of martyrs, but this is not the case with ordinary deaths (*in aliis communiter morientibus*). Purgatory is closely related to general conduct in this world and is made for the ordinary run of mortals.

Article 2: What is the meaning of building of wood, hay, or straw (1 Cor. 3:12)? Answer: the different materials stand for different kinds of venial sin. Authorities invoked: Saint Jerome and Aristotle.

Article 3: What is the foundation of these structures? It would seem that it cannot be faith, since faith is ordained in view of good works and venial sins are not good works. Answer: the foundation is in fact essentially faith, which causes hope to persist in us. The different materials lend their substance to the edifice, but the walls consist of hope, which reaches out toward things eternal; at the very top of the edifice is love (*charitas*) in the place of perfection. The reflection on Purgatory is thus grafted onto a theology of the cardinal virtues.

Article 4 is crucial for Albert. It is essentially aimed at answering the following question: "Is there a purgatorial fire after death or not?" Now, Peter Lombard knew nothing of Purgatory, so to answer this question was to take a position on the existence of Purgatory as well as on that of purgatorial fire, and to do so was all the more delicate since it was a central issue of contemporary debates with the Greeks and since the "doctors of Purgatory" (the expression is mine, not Albert's), Augustine and Gregory the Great, were dubious about this fire.

After examining a number of authorities and rational objections, Albert answers several times that "this is what we call Purgatory." He mentions Matthew 12:31–32 and 1 Corinthians 3:15 and joins to this scriptural evidence the testimony of an anonymous Greek "expositor," whose services he enlists, in a spirit of ecumenicism, in favor of a consensus on the existence of purgatorial fire after death; he also makes use of Aristotle and, it is worth noting, of Saint Anselm's *Cur Deus homo*, thus tracing an impressive philosophical and theological line from the ancient Greeks to Latin and Greek writers of the twelfth century. Then, as was his wont, and following the custom of scholastics generally, he considers the rational arguments for the necessity of purgation after death.

Albert deals with all objections by skillfully mingling the adjective *purgatorius* ("fire" is understood) and the noun *purgatorium*: "In any case it is necessary, according to all reason and faith, that there be a purgatorial fire [*purgatorius*]. These reasons are principally moral, and from them it follows in a concordant way that there is a Purgatory [*purgatorium*]."

As for Augustine's hesitations, Albert asserts that they did not concern the existence of Purgatory but rather the interpretation of Paul's text. Furthermore, he points out that other saints speak expressly of Purgatory and that to deny its existence would be a heresy. Albert, who would later be followed by his disciple Thomas Aquinas, went farther than any other theologian of his day on this point.

As for the "moral" reasons alluded to above, Albert does not dwell on the subject of fire but turns to the problems of purgation. He demolishes objections to the existence of Purgatory by refuting the parallelism between good and evil: he throws the weight of love into the scales of justice and asserts that God, "after death, rewards only those who resemble him by love and condemns no one who does not turn away from him and hate him. . . . None who are purged will be condemned."

Article 5 deals with a question that is practical as well as theoretical: "Why are there several names for the penalties of Hell and only one for Purgatory, namely, fire?" Albert's answer is that Hell is made to punish and that there are several ways to accomplish this, for example, by cold as well as by heat. Purgatory, on the other hand, is made to purge and this can only be done by an element that has purgative and consumptive powers. Cold does not have these powers but fire does. Here Albert is clearly making use of his predilection for the natural sciences.

After completing his exegesis of the First Epistle to the Corinthians in article 6, where he discusses gold, silver, and precious gems, also with reference to the Aristotelian distinction between light, flame, and coals, Albert takes up the problem of whether purgation is voluntary or involuntary in article 7. He concludes that souls want to be purged and saved, but that they want to be purged in Purgatory only because no other avenue to salvation and liberation is open to them. Their will is conditioned.

Article 8 concerns the venial sins of the damned. This is treated as a school exercise: the damned are condemned eternally not for their venial sins but for their mortal sins.

Article 9 raises the same question that Bonaventure considered: Are the souls in Purgatory punished by demons? Like the Franciscan doctor, Albert thinks that demons do not minister to the sins of Purgatory, but he is not sure. On the other hand one of his speculations is of interest in considering visions of the other world: he believes that demons delight in the sight of souls being tortured in Purgatory and that they sometimes look on these tortures as being inflicted. "This," he says, "is what one sometimes reads," and he goes on to explain a passage from the *Life of Saint Martin* in these terms. Some have argued that since, according to this *Life*, the devil frequently stood at the saint's bedside, even though he knew from his works that the saint would not be damned, it must have been because he, the devil, hoped to drag Martin off to Purgatory when he died. Albert's hypothesis demolishes this interpretation.

Article 10 dwells at some length—a length required by the topical interest of the subject—on "the error of certain Greeks, who say that no one enters Heaven or Hell before Judgment Day and that everyone must wait in intermediate places [*in locis mediis*] to be transferred [after Judgment] to one or the other."

Following a lengthy and objective discussion of Greek views on the question, Albert concludes that there is no doubt that one can go to Heaven or Hell either immediately after death or at some time between death and the Last Judgment, thus giving legitimacy to the time of Purgatory and authorizing the belief that souls can leave Purgatory more or less quickly, which in turn served as justification of suffrages. Albert rests this conclusion—in which he repeats that to believe otherwise is a heresy, even a very wicked heresy (*haeresis pessima*)—on Luke 25:43 and 16:22, Revelation 6:2, and Hebrews 2:40, as well as on rational argument, as usual. Among the arguments he cites, I shall mention one, which is particularly illuminating in regard to the social and ideological context. The Greeks argued that the dead form a community and that, as in urban communities where decisions are made in common (*in urbanitatibus in quibus in communi decertatur*,[43] the decision regarding both the saved and the damned must be taken and executed in a single moment. For his part, Albert maintains that it is unjust to refuse workers (*operarii*) their wages once they have finished their work, and he points out that one sees (*videmus*) employers of agricultural laborers offering a bonus (*consolatio specialis*) to the best workers.[44] This was one of Albert's favorite ideas: if one speaks of a "just wage" (a theoretical and practical issue of the day), it is well to remember that God is supremely just. One might be tempted to call him the most just of patrons, or of "providers of work."

Articles 11 and 12 deal with confession and do not mention Purgatory, but in discussing issues of guilt (*culpa*) and mortal and venial sins the articles involve Purgatory indirectly. Here we find ourselves back in the same penitential context that had surrounded theological debate on the new Purgatory from the time of Peter Lombard to that of Albert the Great.

In article 45 of the first part of distinction 44 of this commentary, Albertus Magnus gives the best account known to me of the thirteenth-century system of otherworldly geography. The question being treated is this: "Are there five receptacles for souls after they have been separated from the body?" The solution is as follows: "To this it must be answered that the receptacles of souls are diverse and that they diversify themselves in this way. They are either a terminal place or a place of passage. Of terminal places there are two: where the merit is bad, Hell, where the merit is good, the Kingdom of Heaven. But the terminus for bad merit, that is, Hell, is twofold, depending on proper merit and on contrary pact with nature, the first case corresponding to the lower Hell of the damned, the second to the Limbo of Children, which is the upper Hell. . . . If a place of passage, it can result from a lack of proper merit or from failure to have paid the price. . . . In the first case it is Purgatory, in the second the Limbo of the Patriarchs before the coming of Christ."[45]

Thus there are actually only three places: Paradise, Hell, which is divided into Gehenna and a Limbo for Children (in place of the old upper Hell, a forerunner of Purgatory), and Purgatory (to which there is also attached a second part, the Limbo of the Fathers, but this has been empty and closed forever since Christ's coming).

This elegant solution to the problem of three versus five places was obtained by purely abstract reasoning, though it is obviously based on Scripture and tradition. Finally, in article 4 of distinction 45, concerning suffrages for the dead, Albert reaffirms that suffrages are effective for souls in Purgatory. He points out that they fall under the jurisdiction of the *for* of the Church and emphasizes that the love of the militant Church (*charitas Ecclesiae militantis*) is the source of suffrages) and that, although the living can perform suffrages to benefit the dead, the reverse is not true.[46]

That this is a considerably more substantial doctrine than that set forth in *De resurrectione* is apparent. Clearly, Albert was led to add to his teaching by the nature of the work: starting with Peter Lombard led him to the theology of sacraments and penance (which formed the context in which Purgatory was born), and the discussion of suffrages forced him to take up the theme of solidarity between the living and the dead. But one cannot help feeling that Albert's thinking has deepened in the meantime. The obligation to give proofs of the existence of Purgatory forced him to develop new arguments. He cites more "authorities," and their range is wider. His exegesis of the texts, in particular of Paul's First Epistle to the Corinthians, delves deeper than before. When he considers what takes place in Purgatory, he focuses more on the process of purgation than on the penalties. He has more to say about the time of Purgatory, considering the variable duration of individual stays, whereas in *De resurrectione* he was satisfied to say that Purgatory would last only until the Last Judgment, not beyond. In discussing suffrages he refers to the communion of saints and makes comparisons that situate his text within an acute vision of the economic, social, political, and ideological realities of his time. Finally, he treats the whole system of otherworldly geography in a single essay, explicitly stating that the Limbo of the Patriarchs existed only until Christ's coming. He reduces the number of regions of the hereafter to four and in fact to three: in other words, his reasoning conforms to the underlying logic that shaped the geography of the Christian other world.

Of all the great scholastics, Albertus Magnus was the one who treated Purgatory in the clearest and firmest manner, the one who gave it, if I may say so, an elevated theological status, at the price perhaps of omitting to discuss a few points while shrewdly circumventing others, and without attacking widespread beliefs or putting forward theses incompatible with such beliefs.

A Manual of Theological Popularization

Albert's influence was spread by a work of theological popularization (vulgarization) composed by one of his disciples, which was mistakenly included in the nineteenth-century edition of Albert's complete works. This was the *Compendium theologicae veritatis* (*Compendium of the True Theology*) by the Dominican Hugh Ripelin, prior of the Dominican monastery at Strasbourg from 1268 to 1296, who is sometimes known as Hugh of Strasbourg. A date of 1268 has been assigned to the *Compendium*.[47]

In book 4 we find a very clear explanation of the geography of the other world and of the disappearance of the bosom of Abraham, in the context of a discussion of Christ's descent into Hell:

> In order to know what hell Christ descended to, we must remember that Hell has two meanings and refers either to the punishment or to the place of punishment. In the first sense we say that demons always carry Hell with them. If Hell designates the place of punishment, a distinction must be drawn between four [places]. There is the Hell of the damned, in which one endures the punishments of the senses and the punishment of damnation [deprivation of the divine presence] and in which there is both inner and outer darkness, i.e., the absence of grace: it is eternal mourning. Above is the Limbo of Children, where one endures the punishment of damnation but not the punishment of the senses, and there is both inner and outer darkness.
>
> Above this place there is Purgatory [Hugh uses the masculine *purgatorius* and not the neuter *purgatorium* implying locus,

place], where there is the punishment of the senses and the punishment of damnation for a certain period, and there is outer darkness but not inner darkness, for by grace one has inner light there, because one sees that one will be saved. The upper place is the Limbo of the Holy Fathers [the Patriarchs], where there was the punishment of damnation and not of the senses, and there was outer darkness, but not the darkness of deprivation of grace. It is into this place that Christ descended and liberated his own and thus "swallowed up" Hell, for he carried away a part of it and left another. But for the elect, God completely destroyed death, as it is written in Hosea 13:14: "O death, I will be thy plague; O grave, I will be thy destruction." This place was also called the bosom of Abraham; it is the heaven of the empyrean, for Abraham is there forevermore. Between these places there is no passage, except in the past from the third to the fourth, that is, from Purgatory to the Limbo of the Holy Fathers [patriarchs].[48]

If this text is reminiscent of Albert the Great's ideas in his *Commentary* on the *Sententiae*, it should be noted that Purgatory is here said to be part of Hell and is not as clearly set apart from the children's Limbo as in Albert's work, where Limbo is first removed from Purgatory and then attached to Hell. Hugh is more conservative in this respect than Albert, and his thinking shows the process by which Purgatory was "infernalized." By contrast, his attempts at rationalization are more deliberately set in a historical perspective, and in this Hugh shows his fidelity to the spirit of Albertus Magnus. The historical decline of the bosom of Abraham is clearly noted; but as we are by this time quite well aware, it was not Christ's descent into Hell—that is, in terms of positive historiography, in the time of the Gospels—that did away with the bosom of Abraham or elevated it to Heaven, but rather the inception of Purgatory, which occurred around the turn of the thirteenth century.

As far as Purgatory is concerned, the essential part of the discussion comes in book 7, *On the End of Time* (*De ultimis temporibus*), where Purgatory occupies chapters 2 through 6, sandwiched between the first chapter, devoted to the end of the world, and the final chapters, which deal with the Antichrist.[49] The *Compendium* begins by asserting that Purgatory is hope, because those who are there "know that they are not in Hell." There are many reasons, moreover, why Purgatory must exist. In the first place, as Augustine said, because there are three kinds of men: the very wicked, the very good, and those who are neither very wicked nor very good, who must get rid of their venial sins by way of purgatorial punishment. The six other reasons cited have to do essentially with justice and the need for baptismal purification before the beatific vision can be enjoyed. But as soon as souls are purged they fly to Paradise, toward glory.

Punishment in Purgatory is twofold: there is the punishment of damnation and the punishment of the senses, which is very harsh (*acerba*). The fire of Purgatory is at once corporeal and incorporeal, not by metaphor but by image, by similitude, "like a real lion and a painted lion": both are real, but as we might say nowadays, a "paper lion" is not a real lion.

As for the location of Purgatory, Hugh refers to what he has said about Christ's descent into Hell and adds that if, according to the common law, Purgatory is located in a compartment of Hell, certain souls may, by special dispensation, purge themselves in certain places where they have sinned, as is revealed by certain apparitions.

The suffrages of the Church (chapter 4) are not good for obtaining eternal life but are good for securing liberation from punishment, whether by mitigation of the punishment or by early release. There are four kinds of suffrages: prayer, fasting, alms, and the sacrament of the altar (the mass). Suffrages can be of benefit only to those who, in this world, showed themselves worthy of benefiting from them after death. In an orginal and curious way, the Compendium adds that suffrages can also be of use to the saved and the damned. They can benefit the saved by "augmentation," for the addition of souls delivered from Purgatory augments the "accidental" glory of all the blessed. And they can affect the damned by "diminution," for the decrease in the number of the damned alleviates the pain of the lost souls. If this argument is specious as regards the saved, it seems to me absurd as regards the damned. Here, the scholastic machine, always intent on finding symmetries, has, I think, gone awry.

Finally, the *Compendium*, like Bonaventure, contends that laymen can benefit the dead by suffrages only through the accomplishment of good works. The beneficiaries of indulgences cannot transfer their indulgences to other living individuals or to the dead. By contrast, the pope—and only the pope—can dispense indulgences to the dead both by the authority and by the suffrage of good works through love (*charitas*). Thus the pontifical monarchy extended its power beyond its temporal realm into the hereafter: from this time forward it could send saints to Paradise by canonization and remove souls from Purgatory.

Purgatory at the Heart of Intellectualism: Thomas Aquinas and Man's Return to God

I have attempted to show how a few of the leading scholastic thinkers discussed Purgatory, forcefully asserting its existence while remaining doubtful as to its location and discreet as to its more concrete manifestations, affording it a relatively minor place in their theological systems. Still, it is a delicate matter to circumscribe in a few pages the place that Purgatory occupied in the most complex theological work of the thirteenth century, that of Thomas Aquinas.

Thomas deals with Purgatory at several points in his work.[50] The son of the count of Aquino, Thomas was born at Roccasecca Castle in southern Italy at the end of 1224 or the beginning of 1225, joined the Dominicans at Naples in 1244, and studied at Naples and Paris, and at Cologne with Albertus Magnus. It was while he was "bachelor of law" at Paris from 1252 to 1256 that Thomas composed not a true commentary on Peter Lombard's *Sententiae* but a *Scriptum*, a series of questions and discussions centered on that work. There he discusses Purgatory in connection with questions 21 and 45 of book 4. The organization of the *Scriptum*, so it has been said, is "totally theocentric." There are three parts: "God and his being, the creatures insofar as they come from God, and the creatures insofar as they return to God."[51] The third part, devoted to the return (*redditus*), is divided into two sections. Purgatory is discussed in the second of these.

Thomas also deals with Purgatory in various polemical attacks on Muslims, Greeks, and Armenians and, more generally, on the "Gentiles," a term that probably embraced Jews and heretics as well. These were written in Italy, mostly at Orvieto in 1263 and 1264. They include the *Contra errores Grecorum* (*Against the Errors of the Greeks*), written at the behest of Pope Urban IV; *De rationibus fidei contra saracenos, Graecos et Armenos ad Cantorem Antiochiae* (*On the Reasons of the Faith against the Saracens, Greeks, and Armenians for the Cantor of Antioch*), and book 4 of the *Summa contra Gentiles* (*Summa against the Gentiles*). I shall disucuss these polemics later on, when I deal with Purgatory in the context of negotiations between Greeks and Latins.

Purgatory also figures in *De malo* (*On Evil*), a compendium of topics debated at Rome in 1266–67. Thomas Aquinas died on March 7, 1274, at the Cistercian abbey in Fossanova while on his way to attend the Second Council of Lyons. He left unfinished his great work *Summa theologica*, in which, following the example of Bonaventure in the *Breviloquium*, Thomas showed his concern to give a more personal (and, unlike Bonaventure, more ample) treatment of problems first taken up in the *Scriptum* with respect to Peter Lombard's *Sententiae*. A group of disciples led by Reginald of Piperno finished the *Summa* by adding a *Supplement* for the most part based on Thomas's earlier writings, especially the *Scriptum*. This is the case for the portion of the text concerned with Purgatory, which figures in the essay on "the last things" near the end of the work.

I shall concentrate my analysis on the *Supplement*, referring when necessary to the *Scriptum*.[52] I understand that this choice may arouse objections. The *Supplement* is not an authentic work of Thomas himself, even if it was composed by conscientious and respectful disciples whose desire was to rely exclusively on Thomas's own texts. This compilation of excerpts distorts Thomas's thought in two ways: by making it more rigid and less inventive than it was originally, and by passing off a relatively early version of Thomas's teachings as the crowning achievement of the entire theological edifice. On the other hand the *Supplement* has the advantages of being coherent and of citing Thomas verbatim; it also represents what late medieval clerics took to be Thomas's definitive position concerning the problems of the hereafter.

Question 69 of the *Supplement* deals with the resurrection and, before that, with "the receptacles of souls after death" (it corresponds to question 1 of distinction 45 of the commentary on book 4 of the *Sententiae*). The authors of the *Supplement* apparently took the view that the plan of the *Summa* was primarily linear, with chronological guideposts of the form "before, during, after."[53] Thomas Aquinas, viewing the whole process from the standpoint of the *redditus*, the creature's return to God, orients it with respect to this end and not along a historical trajectory. In the next chapter I shall try to explain how, in the thirteenth century, the mass of the faithful thought of the time of purgatory as a combination of eschatological time and ordinary linear time [*temps successif*]. Of all the great thirteenth-century scholastics, Thomas seems to me the most remote from the common view of his contemporaries concerning the Last Things. His thought is lofty in the strongest sense of the word. With eternity for its subject, a reality as transitory as Purgatory did not occupy a very important place, all the more so because the creature in Purgatory has no further merit. My impression is that Thomas dealt with Purgatory because the question was obligatory, because, to lapse for a moment into academic jargon, it was "in the syllabus," and not because he thought the issue was a crucial one. To Thomas, Purgatory seemed, to use a word that was not part of his vocabulary, "vulgar."

I feel that it is important to preserve the relatively rigid form given by the *Supplement* to the Thomist doctrine of Purgatory. The exposition of that doctrine begins with a question divided into seven articles on the abode of souls after death. The seven articles are as follows: (1) Are certain abodes assigned to souls after death? (2) Do souls go to these places immediately after death? (3) Can souls leave these places? (4) Does the expression "the bosom of Abraham" designate a limbo of Hell? (5) Is this limbo the same as the Hell of the damned? (6) Is the Limbo of Children the same as the Limbo of the Patriarchs? (7) Is there a fixed number of receptacles?

To the first question Thomas replies in the affirmative, but only after considering the apparently contradictory opinions of his two favorite Christian thinkers, Boethius ("the common opinion of the sages is that incorporeal beings are not in a place") and Augustine (*XII Super Genesim ad litteram*). He defines the location of these abodes abstractly: "To separated souls . . . one can assign certain corporeal places corresponding to their degress of dignity," and they are "as in a place" (*quasi in loco*). Here the word *quasi* is used, harking back to Augustine's *quasi per ignem*.

By contrast, Thomas brings the most elevated and dynamic theological ideas into contact with the most common psychology when he declares that "souls, because they know what place is assigned to them, conceive either joy or sadness therefrom: in this way their abode contributes to their reward or punishment."[54]

In article 2 he draws the following conclusion on the basis of a comparison with the gravitation of bodies: "Since the place that is assigned to a soul corresponds to the reward or punishment that it has deserved, as soon as this soul is separated from the body it is swallowed up in hell or flies to heaven, unless, in the latter case, a debt owed to divine justice delays its flight, making a prior purgation obligatory."[55] In the course of the discussion, in order to justify the emergence of souls from Purgatory prior to the Last Judgment, when all bodies whose souls are worthy will attain glory together, Thomas answers the arguments of the theorists of community (Albertus Magnus's *urbanitates*) and the Greeks as follows: "Simultaneous glorification of all souls is less essential than simultaneous glorification of all bodies."

Article 3 deals with ghosts, the subject matter of an important chapter in the history of social imagination that has until recently been treated by historians with undue contempt.[56] Thomas Aquinas is clearly preoccupied by the nature of apparitions, visions, and dreams, by their manifestation during sleep or wakefulness, and by the question of their character: are they appearance or reality? Medieval Christian society never really came to grips with its dreams or their interpretation.[57] Souls, whether saved, damned, or in Purgatory, can leave the other world and appear to the living, according to Thomas, who takes notice of the literature of visions, though with obvious reluctance. God allows this to happen only to instruct the living or, in the case of the damned and to a lesser extent the souls in Purgatory, to terrify them (*ad terrorem*). The saved may appear at their own discretion, the others only with God's permission. Apparitions of the saved and the damned are, thank God (this is an interpolation but not, I think, a misrepresentation of Thomas's views), rare: "If the dead go to Heaven their union with the divine will is such that nothing seems permissible to them that they do not see to be in compliance with the dispositions of Providence; if they are in Hell, they are so overwhelmed by their pains that they think more of lamenting their fate than of appearing to the living." This leaves souls in Purgatory, of whom Gregory the Great has written. They "come to implore suffrages," but, as we shall see shortly, Thomas is at pains to set limits to the wanderings of these souls too. By contrast, it is normal for souls purged in Purgatory to go to Heaven when the purgation is complete.

Article 4: the bosom of Abraham was indeed a limbo of Hell, but since Christ's descent into Hell it no longer exists. Thomas is here following the teaching of his master, Albertus Magnus. In article 5 he elaborates as follows: "the Limbo of the Patriarchs probably occupied the same place as Hell or a place nearby though more elevated." Article 6 distinguishes between the Limbo of Children and the Limbo of the Patriarchs. The former still exists, but since the children in it are not guilty of anything but original sin, they are liable only to the slightest of punishments, and even Thomas wonders whether it is not so much punishment as mere delay in glorification (*dilatio gloriae*) to which they are subject.

In article 7 Thomas outlines a typology of receptacles in the other world.[58] First hypothesis: "The receptacles correspond to merit or demerit," so that there must be two abodes in the other world, Paradise for merit and another place for demerit. Second hypothesis: "It is in one and the same place that, while alive, men earn merit or demerit." Hence it is possible to envisage that, after death, all are assigned to the same abode. Third hypothesis: these places correspond to sins, which may be of three kinds: original, venial, and mortal. Hence there must be three receptacles. "The dark air which is represented as the prison of demons" and the terrestrial Paradise of Enoch and Elijah may also count. Thus there are more than five receptacles.

There may also be reason to think that a special place is needed for souls that leave the world burdened only with original sin together with venial sins. Such a soul cannot go to Heaven or to the Limbo of the Patriarchs, since it has no grace; nor can it go the Limbo of Children, since there the punishment of the senses, due for the venial sins, is not administered; nor can it go to Purgatory, since souls do not remain in Purgatory forever and an eternal punishment is due; nor can it go to Hell, since only mortal sin can condemn a soul to perdition. Thus, according to this curious scholastic hypothesis, the Limbo of the Patriarchs is to be counted in the typology, even though it has been permanently closed by Christ, and venial sin cannot be pardoned after death and does not fall within the purview of Purgatory.

What is more, since the receptacles correspond to merit and demerit, of which there are infinitely many degrees, the number of receptacles may also be said to be infinite. Nor can it be ruled out that souls are punished in this world in the places where they have sinned. Furthermore, just as souls in a state of grace but burdened with venial sins have their own special abode, Purgatory, which is distinct from Paradise, so too should souls which are in a state of mortal sin but which have accomplished some good works for which they should be rewarded have a separate receptacle, distinct from Hell. Finally, just as the Fathers awaited the glorification of their souls prior to Christ's coming, so they now await the glorification of their bodies. Just as they waited in a specific receptacle prior to the coming of Christ, so they should now wait in a place other than the one they will occupy after the resurrection, namely, Heaven.

After surveying all these hypotheses, Thomas gives his own solution to the problem: The receptacles of the souls correspond to different statuses. The word that Thomas uses, status, was much in vogue in the thirteenth century. It was used not only to designate the various socioprofessional conditions of men in this world but also to refer to the varying legal, spiritual, and moral standings of different individuals. Here we detect the influence of law on theology. If the status of the soul at the time of death was such as to be ready to receive the ultimate reward of righteousness, then the soul went directly to Heaven; if its status deserved the ultimate reward of wickedness, it went directly to Hell. If it bore only the burden of original sin, then it went to the Limbo of Children. If the soul's status was not such as to be ready to receive final retribution, it would go to Purgatory if its status stemmed from a personal cause, to the Limbo of the Patriarchs (nonexistent since Christ's descent into Hell, however) if its status stemmed from nature alone.

Thomas then justifies his answer. Invoking Pseudo-Dionysius and Aristotle (*Ethics* 2.8.14), he asserts that "there is only one way to be good but many ways to be bad." Hence there is only one place to reward good but many for sinners. Demons reside not in the air but in Hell. The terrestrial Paradise is part of this world and does not count as one of the receptacles in the other world. The punishment of sin in this life is out of the question, for it does not change a man's status with respect to merit or demerit. Since evil never occurs in the pure state, unmixed with good, and vice versa, the sovereign good, beatitutde, can only be obtained after all evil has been purged, and if this does not occur at the moment of death, there must be a place where purgation can be completed after death. This place is Purgatory.

Thomas adds, moreover, that those in Hell cannot be deprived of all good, that the good works carried out on earth may be worthy of earning them some mitigation of their pain. Thomas is probably thinking here, even though he does not cite him, of Augustine and his hypothesis that "more tolerable damnation" is available for the "not entirely wicked."

Accordingly, there are four open abodes in the other world: Heaven, the Limbo of Children, Purgatory, and Hell, and one closed abode, the Limbo of the Patriarchs. While Thomas does not doubt the existence of a place of purgation, Purgatory, he is not interested in its intermediary character but only in the fact that its existence is temporary. From the standpoint of eternity, which is his, there are only three genuine regions of the other world: the heavenly Paradise, the Limbo of Children, and Hell. Of all the scholastic systems, the Thomistic has the fullest and richest insight into the problems connected with the places of the other world, but it is also the most "intellectual" of the systems, the farthest removed from the common mental outlook of the era.

Question 70 takes up the question of the condition of the soul separated from its body and of the punishment inflicted on it by corporeal fire. This corresponds to article 3 of question 33 of the *Scriptum*, which concerns distinction 44 of book 4 of Peter Lombard's *Sententiae*. Here Thomas defends the idea of a corporeal fire.

At this point the *Supplement* poses a question concerning the punishment due for originial sin alone, that is, for souls in the Limbo of Children, as well as a question concerning Purgatory that the editors of the Leonine edition[59] of Thomas's works placed in an appendix. They were probably right to have done so, since Thomas's plan for the *Summa* does not seem to require interrupting the flow of the discussion of the Last Things at this point for a digression. At the same time they are emphasizing the fact that Purgatory was not an essential part of the *Summa*'s system. But I shall pause to deal with this digression now, since my own work centers on Purgatory.

The question on Purgatory has eight parts:[60] (1) Is there a Purgatory after this life? (2) Is it in the same place that souls are purged and the damned punished? (3) Does the punishment of Purgatory exceed any temporal punishment in this life? (4) Is this punishment voluntary? (5) Are the souls in Purgatory punished by demons? (6) By the punishment of Purgatory is venial sin expiated as to guilt? (7) Does purgatorial fire eliminate the application of the punishment? (8) Is one person set free from this punishment more quickly than another?

God's justice, as Thomas answers in the first of these questions, requires that a person who dies after repenting of his sins and receiving absolution but before completing his penance must be punished after death. Hence "those who deny Purgatory speak against divine justice: this is an error, which separates them from the faith." The fact that the authority invoked here is Gregory of Nyssa may be seen as a shrewd maneuver in the polemic against the Greeks. Thomas adds that, "since the Church orders us 'to pray for the dead, that they may be delivered from their sins,' which can only apply to those who are in Purgatory, those who deny Purgatory are resisting the authority of the Church: they are heretics." Here Thomas is in agreement with Albertus Magnus.

To the second question Thomas responds by describing the geography of the other world in a manner somewhat at odds with the topography and arguments given in question 69, which we examined a moment ago. This difference does not seem to have bothered the authors of the *Supplement*, but it is one more reason to relegate the whole question to the appendix, as the editors of the Leonine edition did. Nevertheless, we must take a closer look at this second account of Purgatory's location. "Scripture says nothing definite about the location of Purgatory," Thomas notes, and no rational argument is decisive.[61] But, from statements of the saints and revelations vouchsafed to many of the living, it is probable that the location of Purgatory is twofold. According to "the common law," the site of Purgatory is a low (subterranean) place contiguous to Hell, and it is the same fire that burns the just in Purgatory and the damned below. According to "the dispensation," it is clear that some are punished in various places in this world, "either for the instruction of the living or for the relief of the dead, so that by making their suffering known to the living, the latter may temper it through suffrages of the Church." Thomas is hostile, however, to the idea that purgation occurs at the place where the sin was committed. Once again he is plainly concerned to minimize the presence of ghosts on earth as much as possible.[62] Finally, Thomas rejects the opinion of those who believe that, according to the common law, Purgatory is located above us (i.e., in the sky), on the grounds that the souls in Purgatory are between us and God in status. This is impossible, he argues, because they are being punished not for what is superior in them but for what is inferior. A specious argument indeed, one reminiscent of a play on words or of the false etymologies that so pleased medieval clerics. However that may be, the remark is interesting because it shows that Thomas played a part in the "infernalization" of Purgatory in the thirteenth century and also that there were clerics who believed that Purgatory was not subterranean but almost celestial. These were precursors of Dante, who set the mountain of Purgatory on earth but allowed it to rise toward Heaven.

As for the third question, which concerns the harshness of punishment, Thomas holds that for both the punishment of damnation and the punishment of the senses "the least degree of either one or the other surpasses the greatest pain that one can endure in this world." The harshness (*acerbitas*) of purgatorial punishment comes not from the quantity of sin punished but from the situation of the person being punished, since sin is punished more heavily in Purgatory than in this world. Thomas plainly does not wish to lend his support to the idea that there may be a quantitative relationship between the sin committed here below and the punishments endured in Purgatory. Though he insists on God's justice in these matters, he does not speak of proportionality. He does not take the least step in the direction of an "accountancy of the hereafter."

In maintaining, in response to the fourth question, that the punishment of Purgatory is voluntary not because souls desire it but because they know that it is the way to be saved, Thomas is refuting the opinion that the souls in Purgatory are so absorbed in their pain that they do not know that they are being purged by it and believe that they are damned. The souls in Purgatory, Thomas insists, know that they will be saved.

Like Albertus Magnus, Thomas thinks that it is not demons that torment souls in Purgatory but that demons may possibly accompany souls to Purgatory and take pleasure in seeing their suffering. This is his answer to the fifth question. To the sixth and seventh questions he responds that purgatorial fire purges venial sins, but here he gives the appearance of conceiving this fire in a metaphorical sense. On this point he seems to have shared some of Augustine's doubts.

Finally, if Thomas argues that certain souls can indeed be delivered from Purgatory more quickly than others (which leads him to sketch a commentary on 1 Corinthians 3:10–15) and if he does on this occasion use the word "proportion," his purpose is to bring out the intensity and duration of purgatorial punishment in order to make clear the nature of its harshness (*acerbitas*). There is no doubt that he wished to avoid establishing any sort of vulgar arithmetical accounting of the time spent in Purgatory.

Returning to the main line of the essay on the Last Things, the authors of the *Supplement* have Thomas take up the problem of suffrages for the dead in question 71, making use of the second question of distinction 45 of the *Scriptum* on Peter Lombard's *Sententiae*. This is the most thorough treatment of this question that I know of prior to the nineteenth century.[63] Thomas responds to the fourteen following questions: (1) Can suffrages done for one soul benefit another? (2) Can the dead be helped by the works of the living? (3) Can suffrages done by sinners benefit the dead? (4) Are suffrages done for the dead useful to those who do them? (5) Are suffrages useful to the damned? (6) Are suffrages useful to those who are in Purgatory? (7) Are they useful to the children who are in Limbo? (8) Are they useful to the blessed? (9) Are the prayers of the Church, the sacrifice of the altar, and alms useful to the dead? (10) Are the indulgences granted by the Church useful? (11) Are funeral ceremonies useful? (12) Are suffrages more useful for the one for whom they are intended than for others of the dead? (13) Are suffrages done for many souls at once as useful to each one as if they were destined solely for that one? (14) Are common suffrages as useful to those who have no others as are the special suffrages and common suffrages together for those who benefit from both?

I feel bound to reproduce the essential outlines of Thomas's answers in the order in which they were given by his disciples, lest I distort his thought even further. I am particularly interested in his answers as they relate to Purgatory. Here, then, is the way Thomas responded to the above questions:

1. Our acts may have two effects: they may acquire a status or they may acquire a good as a consequence of a status, such as an accidental reward or the remission of a punishment. The acquisition of a status can only be obtained by one's own merit. So it is for eternal life. By contrast, because of the "communion of saints" (*sanctorum communio*) one can offer good works to others as a sort of donation: prayers procure grace for them, and the correct use of this grace can yield eternal life, provided that they have deserved as much by themselves—an admirable balance is struck between individual merit and collective solidarity or charity.

2. "The bond of charity that links the members of the Church is valuable not only to the living but also to the dead who have died in a state of love [charitas]. . . . The dead live on in the memory of the living . . . and so the suffrages of the living can be useful to the dead." Thomas is hereby refuting Aristotle's opinon (*Ethics* 1.11) that "no communication is possible between the living and the dead." This holds good only for the relations of civil life and not for those of spiritual love, which are based on charity, on the love of God "for whom the spirits of the dead are alive." Of all the expressions of the bonds between the living and the dead that I have come across in my research on Purgatory, this is the most beautiful.

3. Yes, even the suffrages of sinners are useful to the dead, because the value of suffrages depends on the condition of the deceased and not on that of the living. Thus suffrages are similar to sacraments in that both are effective by themselves, independent of the person performing the act.

4. As "satisfactory acts" (expiations of penalties), suffrages become the property of the deceased, who alone can benefit from them, but as "meritorious acts" deserving of eternal life they may be useful both to him who gives and to him who receives, by reason of the charity from which they proceed.

5. Yes, according to certain texts (particularly 2 Macc. 12:40), suffrages can be useful to the damned, but Thomas thinks that by damnation is meant condemnation in the broadest possible sense, and the assertion holds good particularly for the punishment of Purgatory. In any case such benefits fall under the head of miracles and can only occur rarely (this may have been the fate of the emperor Trajan). In passing Thomas refutes the opinions of Origen, Praepositivus, and the disciples of Gilbert de la Porrée and William of Auxerre. And he again refutes, this time quite explicitly, any idea of proportionality, even if supported by a citation from Gregory the Great.

6. Suffrages are useful to souls in Purgatory and are even specially intended for the them, because Augustine said that that suffrages are addressed to those who are neither entirely good nor entirely bad. The accumulation of many suffrages, moreover, can even wipe out purgatorial punishment.

7. These suffrages are useless for children who have died without baptism, who are not in a state of grace, because suffrages cannot change the status of the dead.

8. They are also useless to the blessed, since suffrages are an aid and aid is inappropriate to those who want for nothing.

9. Suffrages can be useful on condition that there is union in love [*charitas*] between "the living and the dead." The three most effective suffrages are alms (as the main effect of charity), prayer (the best suffrage according to the intention), and the mass (for the Eucharist is the source of

charity and is the only sacrament whose efficacy is communicable). The most effective masses are those that contain special prayers for the dead, but the intensity of devotion of the person celebrating the mass or causing it to be celebrated is essential. Fasting is also useful but less so than the mass, because it is more external. The same is true of the gift of candles or oil recommended by Saint John of Damascus.

10. Yes, indulgences are applicable to the dead, because "there is no reason why the Church should be able to transfer common merits, the source of indulgences, to the living and not to the dead." On this point Thomas's vigilance failed him. He was too much a "man of the Church."

11. In regard to the usefulness of funeral rites, Thomas is again more liberal than Augustine, whose authority he invokes. Augustine said that "everything that one does for the bodies of the deceased accomplishes nothing in regard to eternal life but is merely a duty of humanity."[64] For Thomas ceremonial burial may be indirectly useful to the dead by providing an occasion for good works for the benefit of the Church and of the poor as well as a stimulus to prayers for the dead. More than that, burial in a sanctuary or holy place, provided it is not done for vainglory, may help by securing the aid of the saint in whose proximity the body is buried. Here Thomas shows himself to have been a man of his time and order. Dominicans (and Franciscans) welcomed and even solicited the tombs of laymen (especially powerful and wealthy laymen) in their churches and cemeteries, and laymen were increasingly eager to obtain the benefit of church burial, previously limited to monks and clerks. Perhaps the most interesting point in this article, however, is the fact that Thomas, citing Paul (Eph. 5:29: "For no man ever yet hated his own flesh"), makes the following statement: "Since the body is part of human nature, it is natural for man to love it." This is a far cry indeed from the traditional monastic contempt for the body, "that abominable vestment of the soul."[65]

12. In spite of the communion of saints, Thomas believes that suffrages are more useful to their intended recipients than to others, since his view is that what counts is above all the intention of the living person doing the suffrage, since the dead soul can no longer acquire merit. He is not persuaded by the argument that this individualized system favors the wealthy in Purgatory more than the poor. The expiation of penalties, he argues, is as nothing compared with the possession of the kingdom of heaven, and there the poor are favored.

13. "He who prays is not capable of providing, by a single prayer, as much satisfaction for many as for one." Thomas here is decidedly on the side of the individual, not to say of individualism.

14. "We may believe that, through an effect of divine mercy, the surplus of particular suffrages, overabundant with respect to their intended recipients, is applied to other souls who are deprived of such suffrages and who have need of assistance."

In all his answers Thomas shows that he was aware of the problems of debt and the transfer of property. His vocabulary is consciously borrowed from legal and economic terminology. Thomas rejects the accountancy of the hereafter but does not rule out certain transactions more reminiscent of the indebted petty nobility than of the merchant class. Need I add that his thinking remains essentially religious? He continues to be preoccupied more by statuses than by things, more by conditions than by places, more by being than by possessing.

Now that we have completed our survey of Thomas's views as set forth in the *Supplement*, it remains to complete our study by looking at a couple of passages from authentic works of Thomas's own hand, which will help us to see how his thinking on various points changed after he wrote the *Scriptum* as a commentary on Peter Lombard's *Sententiae*.

In the portion of the *Summa theologica* written by Thomas himself, larger in bulk than the *Supplement* written by his disciples, there are two passages that deal with Purgatory. In article 8 of question 89 of the first part of the *Summa*, Thomas deals with apparitions of the dead, or ghosts. He points out that these apparitions are to be classed among the miracles of God, who allows them to occur through the agency of either good angels or demons. Thomas compares these apparitions with apparitions that occur in dreams and stresses that in both cases they can occur without the knowledge of the dead who nevertheless constitute their content. Actually, Thomas does not mention Purgatory at this point—even though he is discussing suffrages for the dead—and, curiously enough, he makes no allusion to those ghosts who are quite obviously conscious of their fate and of the fact that they have returned to earth as ghosts, since they come to implore the suffrages of the living. Here again we sense Thomas's uneasiness concerning these vagabonds from the other world, whose number and independence he tries as much as he can to minimize. They are manipulated by God in every respect, he says, and can gain permission to leave their receptacle or prison only "by a special dispensation of God" (*per specialem Dei dispensationem*). In fact, the most interesting point for our purposes is that here Thomas situates his theories on the separated soul in the context of a discussion of places and distances (*distantia localis*, question 89, article 7). Is remoteness an obstacle to knowledge? Are demons favored by their speed and agility of motion (*celeritas motus*, *agilitas motus*)? Spatial distance is especially important with respect to the divine light, but temporal distance is also important: Can separated souls know the future? Thus Thomas, reticent though he may be about constructing any "vulgar" spatial equivalent of situations in the hereafter, is nevertheless aware of the importance of abstract reflection on space and time, which are related to one another but governed by different "reasons."[66]

In article 11 of question 7 of *De malo* (1266–67), Thomas again wonders if venial sins are forgiven after death in Purgatory. His response is of course that they are, but what interests him is to demonstrate that the difference between mortal and venial sin is one of kind rather than degree. He also considers the question of guilt as opposed to punishment. In the *Scriptum* on the *Sententiae*, he had thought, along with Peter Lombard, that "in the other life, venial sin is pardoned even as to guilt by the fire of purgatory to anyone who dies in a state of grace, because this punishment, being in a certain sense voluntary, has the virtue of expiating any guilt compatible with sanctifying grace." But in *De malo* he says this: "Venial sin no longer exists in Purgatory as to the guilt; as soon as the just soul is freed from the bonds of the body, an act of perfect charity erases its guilt, so that only the punishment remains to be expiated, the soul being in a state where it is impossible for it to deserve a reduction or remission of this penalty."[67]

What interests Thomas throughout is the sin, the condition of the soul, and not the contingencies of a transitory place of which he is content merely to affirm the existence, since it is within the faith and the authority of the Church and in conformity with the rational demonstration of the relations between God and man.

The Refusal of Purgatory

The Heretics

Against the scholastic approval of Purgatory we must weigh its rejection by Greeks and heretics. The opposition of heretics persisted at the theoretical as well as the practical level, as we shall see presently. It was rooted in a long-standing, stubborn refusal to accept prayers for the dead, or suffrages, which as we saw earlier played a part in the orthodox decision to sharpen the doctrine of Purgatory at the end of the twelfth century. Rejected by the Arras heretics in 1025, suffrages were again rejected in 1143–44 by the Cologne heretics, against whom prior Eberwin of Steinfeld appealed to Saint Bernard for help: "They do not admit that there is a purgatorial fire after death but teach that souls go immediately either to eternal rest or eternal punishment at the moment they leave the earth, according to the words of Solomon: 'If the tree fall toward the south, or toward the north, in the place where the tree falleth, there shall it be' (Eccl. 11:3)."[68]

Probably at about the time when, as we saw earlier, Bernard of Fontcaude was asserting the new structure of the hereafter against the Waldensians, a *Summa against the Heretics*, which was falsely attributed to Praepositivus of Cremona but which must, according to its editors, date from the end of the twelfth century, mentioned the hostility to prayers for the dead of heretics known as "Passagins" and in this connection discussed Purgatory. Since Purgatory exists in this text but the souls of the dead are still divided into four rather than three categories, the suggestion that it dates from the final years of the twelfth century seems reasonable.[69]

In response to the Passagins' refusal of prayers for the dead, the *Summa* suggests the following solution, closely in line with the ideas of Augustine:

> We pray for the living, indifferently, regardless of how wicked they may be, because we do not know who will be damned and who will be saved. But we pray above all for our brothers and for the dead; not for the entirely good, because they have no need of our prayers, and not for the entirely bad, because to them our prayers would not be useful, but for the medium good who are in Purgatory, not to make them better but so that they may be liberated sooner, and for the medium bad, not so that they may be saved but so that they may be punished less.[70]

The chronicle of Ralph, abbot of the Cistercian monastery of Coggeshall in England between 1207 and 1218, in recounting a youthful adventure of Gervase of Tilbury discusses the ideas of heretics known as Publicans,[71] prevalent in several parts of France, particularly the area around Rheims, where they figured prominently in an outbreak of witchcraft in 1176–80: "They maintain that children should not be baptized before reaching the age of reason. They add that prayers should not be said for the dead and that intercession should not be asked of the saints. They condemn marriage and preach virginity to conceal their lasciviousness. They detest milk and any food derived from it as well as all food that is the product of coitus. They do not believe in purgatorial fire after death but hold that as soon as the soul is delivered it goes immediately either to rest or damnation."[72]

Almost all thirteenth-century treatises on heresies and heretics number the rejection of Purgatory among the errors of the majority of heretical sects (sects that "orthodox" authors often found it hard to tell apart), particularly the Waldensians. In a treatise destined for use by preachers— about which I shall have more to say later on—written by Stephen of Bourbon in the years prior to his death in 1261, we find the following statement about the Waldensians of the Valence region in Dauphiné around the year 1235: "They also state that there is no purgatorial punishment other than in this life. For the dead, neither the good offices of the Church nor anything else that can be done has any effect."[73] Anselm of Alexandria (in northern Italy), a Dominican inquisitor, wrote a treatise some time between 1266 and 1270 in which he attempts to distinguish between Waldensians and Cathari and, among the Waldensians, between those of Lombardy and their ultramontane counterparts, the Poor of Lyons. Among the common beliefs of the two Waldensian groups he includes the denial of Purgatory: "Like the Ultramontanes, the Lombards do not believe in Purgatory, in the oath, in the right of justice. . . . And also [for both] there is no Purgatory. Nothing is gained by visiting the tombs of the saints, adoring the cross, building churches, saying prayers and masses, or giving alms for the dead."[74]

The same note is struck in the famous *Manual of the Inquisitor* by the Dominican Bernard Gui, the fruit of a lifetime's experience written down near the end of his life early in the fourteenth century: "The Waldensians also deny that there is a Purgatory for souls after this life, and, in consequence, assert that prayers, alms, masses, and other pious suffrages of the faithful on behalf of the dead do no good." Moreover, "they also say and teach their adepts that true penance and purgatory for sins can only take place in this life, not in the other. . . . Similarly, according to them, souls, when they leave the body, go immediately either to Paradise, if they are supposed to be saved, or to Hell, if they are supposed to be damned, and there is no other place [abode] for souls after this life except Heaven or Hell. They also say that prayers for the dead no not help them at all, since those who are in Paradise do not need them, while for those who are in Hell there is no rest."[75]

The attitude of the Cathari toward Purgatory seems to have been more complex. I shall come back to it. Documents concerned with concrete beliefs, especially at Montaillou, indicate that their position was both subtle and confused. The theoretical writings examined here generally accentuate a negative attitude to Purgatory. In 1250 a *Summa on the Cathari and the Poor of Lyons* (*Summa de Catharis et Pauperibus de Lunduno*) was written by Rainerius Sacconi, a heretic who was converted by Peter of Verona. Like Peter, Rainerius became a Dominican inquisitor, but he escaped the assassination attempt that cost Peter his life (and immediately made him Saint Peter Martyr in the eyes of the Church). In this *Summa* we find the following statement: "Their second error is to say that God inflicts no purgatorial punishment, for they totally deny Purgatory, and no temporary punishment, for that is inflicted by the devil in this life."[76]

Further information about certain Cathari, again Italians, dubbed "Albaniens" or "Albanais" (a term frequently corrupted into "Albigeois," or Albigensians), is provided by a brief summa probably composed by a Franciscan between 1250 and 1260, which says that they disbelieve not only in Purgatory but also in Hell, since Hell was not created by the God who, according to Genesis, created this world, that is to say, Lucifer. Accordingly, "they say there is no purgatorial fire and no Purgatory."[77]

The Greeks

If, on the level of preaching and polemic, it was the Church's battle against heretics contemptuous of the idea of redemption after death that led it, in the late twelfth century, to accept and refine the belief that there is a place to which souls go to be purged aftr death, it was theological controversy and negotiation between members of the Latin and Greek eccleasiastical hierarchies that led the Latin Church in the thirteenth century to utter its first dogmatic pronouncements on Purgatory. Theory at the summit of the Church hierarchy crowned practice at the grass roots. Purgatory developed partly out of Christian aspirations and partly out of conflict among Christians.

Ever since the split between the two churches in 1054, the culmination of the gradually widening breach that had first opened no later than the fourth century,[78] there had been no lack of discussions and talks aimed at reunion. The question of the other world had played no role in these talks. The Greek Church had sown the first doctrinal seeds that eventually led to Purgatory, but it had not cultivated them. It was content with a vague belief in the possibility of redemption after death, coupled with a practice that differed little from Latin practice, involving prayers and suffrages. But when the Latin belief took hold, leading to a thorough revision of the geography of the other world, the problem of Purgatory pushed its way to the forefront of discussion and controversy. The first phase of debate revolved largely around the issue of purgatorial fire.

During the first half of the thirteenth century the talks between the two churches encountered not only religious obstacles per se but, even more important, political obstacles. The papacy supported the Latin empire established at Constantinople in 1204 by the Fourth Crusade, whereas the Greeks recognized only the Byzantine emperor, who had retreated to Nicaea.

In the midst of the negotiations Purgatory burst upon the scene. Here is Daniel Stiernon's humorous as well as accurate account: "Fire! Alas, yes, there was also the fire of Purgatory, which kindled spirits one year later. From Apulia, where the first sparks flew in November 1235, the conflagration spread to the patriarchal throne, if it is indeed true that Germanus II, challenged in the new debate, composed a treatise on this theme, this burning topic—oh, how burning—which was destined to leave lasting traces."[79]

Actually, the oldest significant evidence of the Greco-Latin debate over Purgatory is slightly earlier in date. It is. a report of a controversy in the Greek monastery at Casole, near Otranto, at the end of 1231, which pitted George Bardanes, metropolitan of Corfu, against one of the pope's envoys, the Franciscan Bartholomew. The report, probably incomplete, was prepared by the Greek prelate. George Bardanes begins by stating that the Franciscans "approve the false doctrine that there exists a purgatorial fire [πῦρ καθαρτήριογ] to which souls are sent if they die after confession but before completing penance for their sins, where they are purified and delivered from punishment prior to the Last Judgment."[80] The authority invoked by the Franciscans is "Saint Gregory the Dialogue," that is, Gregory the Great, who was so called by the Greeks in order to distinguish him from the many other Gregorys.

This is how the debate is supposed to have unfolded:

The question put by the Latin, who was named Bartholomew, was approximately as follows:

"I want to learn from you Greeks where souls go when they die without doing penance and have not had time to complete the *epitimies*[81] their confessors have ordered."

Our response for the Greeks:

"The souls of sinners do not go from here to Hell everlasting, for he who is to judge the whole universe has not yet come with his glory to distinguish the just from the sinners, but they go to dark places which give a foretaste of the tortures that sinners must undergo. For, since several places and several rests have been prepared for the just in the house of the Father, according to the words of the Savior,[82] so too do various punishments exist for the sinners."

The Latin:

"We do not have this belief, but we believe that there is a special purgatorial fire, that is to say,[83] a fire that purifies, and that through this fire, those who pass from this world without repenting, such as thieves, adulterers, murderers, and all who commit venial sins, suffer in this (purificatory) fire for a certain time and purify themselves of the taint of their sins, and are then delivered from punishment."

"But, my excellent friend," said I, "anyone who believes such things and teaches them seems to me to be a perfect disciple of Origen. Indeed, Origen and his followers approved the doctrine of the end of Hell, and even demons are supposed to obtain their pardon after several years and be delivered from eternal punishment. Then you have only to appeal to your wisdom by referring to the words of the Gospel given by God, since the Lord summons the just to resurrection of life, whereas sinners are summoned to the resurrection of judgment.[84] And further: "Depart from me, ye cursed, into everlasting fire, prepared for the devil and his angels."[85] And elsewhere: "There shall be weeping and gnashing of teeth,"[86] and "where their worm dieth not and the fire is not quenched."[87]

Since the Lord holds so many threats of this kind over those who leave this life with wicked actions and crimes unpurified (by penance), who will dare to signify that there is a purificatory fire and a so-called end to punishment prior to the decision of the Judge? But if it were possible by any means whatsoever prior (to the Last Judgment) to pluck from torture those who leave this world guilty of whatever sins, what would have prevented the very faithful Abraham, most beloved of God, from releasing from the fire the rich man without mercy, when he begged, with words capable of moving the depths of one's heart, for a mere drop of water from the tip of one finger to cool his tongue; but he was told: "Remember that thou in thy lifetime receivedst thy good things, and likewise Lazarus evil things: but now he is comforted, and thou art tormented."[88] And he learned that there was a deep and unbreachable gulf between him and Lazarus the poor man.

But since the Minorite heard all of this without being persuaded and stopped up his ears, we set before his eyes the texts of the Fathers, which bear God (i.e., which are inspired by God), concerning the Holy Scriptures, so that, seized by respect before the authority of the greatest masters, he might give up his objection.

The authorities did not shake the Franciscan's convictions, however, and both sides held on to their respective positions.

THE FIRST PONTIFICAL DEFINITION OF PURGATORY (1254)

In the last years of the pontificate of Innocent IV, there was a change in the atmosphere of the discussions between the Greeks and the Latins, and there is reason to think that the two sides were headed for agreement when the pope died in 1254. A few weeks before his death, on March 6, 1254, the pontiff sent to Cardinal Eudes of Châteauroux, his legate to the Greeks on Cyprus, an official letter (*sub catholicae*), which marks a major turning point in the history of Purgatory. Judging that the number of points of accord between the Greeks and Latins was sufficient, and choosing to leave in obscurity the thorny question of when the passage through purgatorial fire takes place, before or after the resurrection of the dead, the pope asked the Greeks to accept a definition of Purgatory which in point of fact remains authoritative to this day:

> Since the Truth asserts in the Gospel that, if anyone blasphemes against the Holy Spirit, this sin will not be forgiven either in this world or in the next: by which we are given to understand that certain faults are pardoned in the present time, and others in the other life; since the Apostle also declares that the work of each man, whatever it may be, shall be tried by fire and that if it burns the worker will suffer the loss, but he himself will be saved yet as by fire; since the Greeks themselves, it is said, believe and profess truly and without hesitation that the souls of those who die after receiving penance but without having had the time to complete it, or who die without mortal sin but guilty of venial (sins) or minor faults, are purged after death and may be helped by the suffrages of the Church; we, considering that the Greeks assert that they cannot find in the works of their doctors any certain and proper name to desig-

nate the place of this purgation, and that, moreover, according to the traditions and authority of the Holy Fathers, this name is Purgatory, we wish that in the future this expression be also accepted by them. For, in this temporary fire, sins, not of course crimes and capital errors, which could not previously have been forgiven through penance, but slight and minor sins, are purged; if they have not been forgiven during existence, they weigh down the soul after death.[89]

This letter is the birth certificate of Purgatory as a doctrinally defined place.

THE SECOND COUNCIL OF LYONS AND PURGATORY (1274)

A further step was taken by the Second Council of Lyons in 1274. But before we see what this was, it may be in order to look at various episodes that marked the negotiations, mixed with polemics, carried on by the Greeks and Latins in the third quarter of the thirteenth century.

In 1263 Thomas Aquinas was called to give his expert opinion in a polemic against the Greeks. Nicholas of Durazzo, bishop of Crotona, "learned in Latin and Greek," had written a *Libellus on the Procession of the Holy Spirit and the Trinity against the Errors of the Greeks* (*Libellus de processione spiritus sancti et de fide trinitatis contra errores Graecorum*), a Latin copy of which was sent in 1262 to Pope Urban IV, who solicited the advice of Thomas Aquinas. The *Libellus*, which was interested primarily in the *filioque*, aimed to prove that the Greeks of the thirteenth century were not even faithful to the Fathers of the Greek Church, who, it was argued, professed the same doctrines as the Latins. It was in fact a helter-skelter collection[90] of errors, falsifications, and false attributions. The papacy nevertheless conceived the idea of using this document as the basis of its negotiations with the Greeks. Thomas Aquinas apparently felt "a sense of uneasiness" upon reading the *Libellus*. He did not challenge the authenticity of the texts cited in it but did attack the validity of some of them and frequently preferred to recur to other authorities. In any case the influence of the *Libellus* did not diminish the importance of *Contra errores Graecorum* (*Against the Errors of the Greeks*), which Thomas wrote during the summer of 1263 at Orvieto and which provided the Latins with an arsenal of arguments to use against their Greek adversaries.[91] The bulk of the text, thirty-two chapters, deals with the procession of the Holy Spirit in the Trinity, while five brief chapters are devoted to the primacy of the Roman papacy and two remaining short chapters to the consecration of the unleavened bread for the Eucharist and to Purgatory. In these last chapters Thomas argues for the existence of Purgatory along the lines he later took up in the *Supplement* to the *Summa theologica*, discussed above.

The political situation created by the Greek recapture of Constantinople in 1261 and the apparent restoration of the integrity of the Byzantine Empire led, however, to an attempted reconciliation of the Latin and Greek Churches, for which purpose the Second Council of Lyons was convoked in 1274.[92]

Union between the Latins and Greeks was desired for political reasons by Pope Gregory X, who saw union as a prerequisite for the success of the crusade he wanted to organize, as well as by Emperor Michael VIII Paleologus, who wished not only to ward off a possible attack by Charles of Anjou but also, as Gilbert Dagron has amply demonstrated, to resume along traditional lines a grand policy of "organic liaison between the West and the East."

Discussions of union remained shrouded in ambiguity and never touched the heart of the matter until the basileus forced the hand of the Greek hierarchy; on January 16, 1275, union was proclaimed after the Patriarch Joseph I, who had refused to go along, was deposed. Nothing came of this union, but it did allow Purgatory to consolidate its position within the Latin Church. The formula adopted was a compromise proposed by Pope Clement IV in a letter sent on March 4, 1267, to Emperor Michael VIII. This was reiterated in a letter from Gregory X to Michael on October 24, 1272, and in the profession of faith that the emperor sent in response on March 1274. It was incorporated in an appendix to the constitution *Cum sacrosancta* of the council, promulgated with slight changes in phrasing on November 1, 1274.

Here is the gist of the text:

> However, owing to various errors that have been introduced by the ignorance of some and the malice of others, (the Roman Church) states and proclaims that those who fall into sin after baptism must not be rebaptized, but that through a genuine penitence they obtain pardon for their sins. That if, truly penitent, they die in charity before having, by worthy fruits of penance, rendered satisfaction for what they have done by commission or omission, their souls, as brother John has explained to us, are purged after their death, by purgatorial or purificatory penalties, and that, for the alleviation of these penalties, they are served by the suffrages of the living faithful, to wit, the sacrifice of the mass, prayers, alms, and other works of piety that the faithful customarily offer on behalf of others of the faithful according to the institutions of the Church. The souls of those who, after receiving baptism, have contracted absolutely no taint of sin, as well as those who, after contracting the taint of sin, have been purified either while they remained in their bodies or after being stripped of their bodies are, as was stated above, immediately received into heaven.[93]

This text is less advanced than that of Innocent IV's letter, written twenty years before. It mentions *poenis purgatoriis seu catharteriis,* the Latinized Greek word echoing the Latin word that the Greeks had already Hellenized. But the word *purgatorium,* purgatory, does not appear. There is no mention of either a place or a fire. Was this backpedaling due solely to the hostility of the Greeks, or did it also reflect the doubts of some Western theologians? The latter is not out of the question, particularly in light of the fact that some documents suggest that the Byzantine imperial chancellery, at any rate, was prepared to accept the word "purgatory." In the professions of faith sent by Michael VIII in 1277 to Pope John XXI and later to Pope Nicholas III, both the Greek and Latin versions speak of the penalties "of purgatory" or "of purification" (*poenis purgatorii seu catharterii* in Latin, ποιναισ πουργατορίον ήτοι καθαρτηρίου in Greek. The same is true of the profession of Andronicus II a few years later. It is also possible that the Second Council of Lyons proposed a formula, since lost, that followed the terms of Innocent IV's letter of 1254 rather than Clement IV's letter 1267.[94]

PURGATORY AND MENTALITIES: THE EAST AND THE WEST

But the important point lies elsewhere. In the first place, as A. Michel was well aware, "from the dogmatic standpoint, the text imposed on the Greeks indubitably represented the Catholic doctrine. It is the equivalent of a definition *ex cathedra.*"[95] It was the first proclamation of belief in the purgatorial process, if not in Purgatory itself, as a dogma.

The second interesting fact is that, at the dogmatic level, Purgatory was not defined as a specific place or as a fire in either of the two Church assemblies that definitively established the dogma of Purgatory as part of Roman Christianity: the Council of Ferrara-Florence in 1438–39, once again in opposition to the Greeks,[96] and the Council of Trent in 1563, this time in opposition to the Protestants.

Notwithstanding the hesitation of the theologians and the prudence of the Church, I remain convinced that Purgatory succeeded because it was given a concrete spatial embodiment and because it provided ample room for the exercise of the imagination.

Before we turn to the examination of Purgatory's "popular" appeal in the thirteenth century, however, I should like first to say a word or two about a document connected with the debate between the Greeks and the Latins, which contains a confession that sheds light on the underlying attitudes of Western Christians at the time of Purgatory's inception and popularization. Following the Second Council of Lyons (1274), Michael VIII Paleologus attempted to enforce respect for the union among the Byzantine clergy. The monasteries of Mount Athos became one of the leading centers of resistance. In May 1276 the imperial police made a "sweep" of Athos, expelled and dispersed most of the monks, and took two prisoners, Nicephorus and Clement, whom the emperor, out of deference to the Latins, ordered put on a Venetian boat and taken to Saint John of Acre, where they were handed over to the papal legate. The legate was no mere nonentity but Thomas of Lentini, a Dominican, who forty years earlier had received Thomas Aquinas into the Dominican order.

Thomas of Lentini, who besides being papal legate was also bishop of Acre and patriarch of Jerusalem, had a frank discussion with the two Greek monks and ultimately decided to have them placed under house arrest in Cyprus.[97] In the course of the discussion the question of Purgatory came up—and it was indeed the Purgatory (τὸ πθρκατὸριον) that was in question.

> THE LATIN: And Purgatory, what do you say about that?
> THE GREEKS: What is Purgatory, and what Scripture did you learn it from?
> THE LATIN: From Paul, when he says that [men] are tried by fire: "If a man's work be consumed, he shall suffer the damage, but he shall in this way be saved, as by fire."
> THE GREEKS: In truth he is punished without end.
> THE LATIN: Here is what we say. If someone, after having sinned, goes to confess, receives a penance for the guilt, and dies before completing this penance, the angels cast his soul into the purificatory fire, that is, into the river of fire, until it has completed the time that remains of what has been set by the spiritual [father], the time it was unable to complete owing to the unpredictable suddenness of death. It is after completing the time that remains, we say, that it goes purified into this eternal life. Do you believe this too: Is this the way it is, or not?
> THE GREEKS: Look, we not only do not accept this, we anathematize it, as do the fathers in council. According to the words of the Lord, "You go astray, knowing neither the Scriptures nor the power of God."

The Greek view is that the Latins, faced with the Scriptures, which do not mention Purgatory, can only cite visions of souls allegedly saved from torment in the hereafter. But, they add, "these facts, contained in dreams and reveries that people tell, are full of ravings and hence offer no certainty." Therefore, "do good during your lifetime, for everything is inert after death, and because of that prayer for those who have not done good during their own life is not granted."

At this point Thomas of Lentini rekindles the debate:

> THE LATIN: In what place do the souls of the righteous currently repose, and in what place are the sinners?

THE GREEKS: According to the word of the Lord, the righteous such as Lazarus are in the bosom of Abraham, and the sinners such as the rich man without pity are in the fire of Gehenna.

THE LATIN: Many simple believers in our Church have difficulty accepting this. The restoration [apokatastasis], they say, has not yet come, and for this reason souls experience neither punishment nor rest. Therefore, if this is the way it is.

. . .

Here, just at the point where information of great importance to us is to be given, there is a gap in the manuscript. My interpretation is therefore partly hypothetical.

To begin with, note the Latin churchman's paradoxical recourse to the Origenist notion of *apokatastasis*. However, the crucial point has to do, I think, not with doctrine but with the mental dispositions of the Latins to which Thomas of Lentini alludes. Many simple believers were no longer content with the contrast between Gehenna and the bosom of Abraham, the stark division between Hell and Paradise from the moment of individual death. The need for Purgatory, for a final episode between death and resurrection, for a continuation of the process of penitence and salvation beyond the bogus boundary of death was a requirement rooted in the masses, a need voiced—in the West, at any rate—by the *vox populi.*

NINE

Social Victory: Purgatory and the Cure of Souls

PURGATORY triumphed in the thirteenth century both in theology and in dogma. Doubts about its existence were silenced: it became a truth of faith and of the Church. In one form or another, concretely or in varying degrees of abstraction, it was accepted as a place. It took on an official character. It enriched the meaning of a very old Christian practice, suffrages for the dead. But it was controlled by the theologians and the Church hierarchy, who refused to allow the imagination of the faithful to run riot.

At this point I would like to consider how Purgatory was received by the mass of the faithful, by the various social and occupational groups that made up medieval society, insofar as a question of this kind is open to historical investigation. Broadly speaking, Purgatory made even more impressive headway with the populace than it did with the theologians and clergy.

When the Church brought Purgatory down from the heights of theological controversy into the realm of daily teaching and pastoral practice, mobilizing the resources of the imagination in the process, it apparently scored a tremendous success. By the end of the thirteenth century Purgatory is ubiquitous: we find it mentioned in sermons, in wills (still hesitantly), and in vernacular literature. The Jubilee of 1300 signals the triumph of Purgatory, which seems to have provided a meeting ground where the aspirations of the Christian masses could find their accommodation with the prescriptions of the Church. Opposition among intellectuals and even heretics collapsed. Only the imagery associated with Purgatory resisted change in the wake of victory: Was this due to conservatism in iconography or to the difficulty of representing an intermediary, temporary, ephemeral world? Or was it because the Church tried hard to insure that Purgatory would stay close to Hell or even to "infernalize" it, and tried to keep it from being depicted as reassuring rather than frightening?[1] The inception of Purgatory required that a place be found for it, that a site be set aside for purgatorial punishment, because the wandering of suffering souls could no longer be tolerated. But space and time are inseparable, even when the space involved has a complex structure, as Thomas Aquinas pointed out in the case of Purgatory.

ACCOUNTING FOR TIME

Purgatory is a place, but it is also a time, since one definition of Purgatory is that it is a Hell of limited duration. Hence there is a time of Purgatory, which like the place also took shape at the turn of the thirteenth century. Men were then reconsidering the nature of time in general, and it is in relation to this that Purgatory time is best understood.

Previously, man's thinking about time had been dominated by religious ideology; time was accordingly conceived of in a variety of ways. The Church taught that there were six ages and that mankind had come to the sixth and last of these, the age of debility and decline. Two great events dominated the history of the universe: the Creation and the Incarnation of Christ. Together these determined the orientation of time. For the Creation was followed by the Fall, whereas the Incarnation raised the promise of redemption, pointing toward the Last Judgment, which would abolish time and usher in eternity. The Church believed and preached that the end was near. One notable consequence of this was a lack of concern about the presumably brief interval between the death of any individual and the resurrection of all bodies at the time of the final judgment. This picture did not please everyone: various individuals and groups put a stricter construction on the texts or rebelled against authority or did both. Two changes were suggested in the received view.

Some people wished to see a rejuvenation of the world, a return to the primitive Church—a Christian form of the myth of the Golden Age. Others, sometimes the same individuals, believed or hoped that, in keeping with the Book of Revelation, the end of the world would be preceded not only by the trials of the Antichrist but, before that, by an extended period of justice, the millennium. At the beginning of the thirteenth century, millenarianism, long condemned by the Church, found a new prophet, the abbot Joachim of Floris, whose ideas inflamed the minds of many followers throughout the century, particularly among the Franciscans.[2]

Human life, moreover, was regulated by a variety of time schemes: liturgical time, calendar time, which the Church controlled, the daily routine marked by the ringing of bells, rural time, largely determined by natural rhythms but punctuated by partially Christianized annual rites, such as the twelve-day cycle at the beginning of the traditional year from Christmas to Epiphany, Carnival and Lent, Rogation Days and Saint John's Day during the harvest, feudal time punctuated by the springtime *ost* and the dates when rents fell due, and the great assemblies of Pentecost. Time was repetitive, not to say circular.

Nevertheless, segments of linear time, intervals that had been given a direction, did take shape. These were associated with a new way of using individual and collective memory. Direct memories of the past can scarcely date back more than a hundred years, as Bernard Guénée has shown.[3]

Among the nobility direct memory is combined with written memory, with dates recorded more or less by chance in charters, with legends concerning ancestors and family founders gathered together for the compilation of a family genealogy.[4] Particularly significant for our purposes is memory of the dead, so vital a concern of Cluny in the eleventh and twelfth centuries, even before the location of Purgatory was established. This concern was expressed in the obituary books or *Libri memoriales* and in the establishment of November 2, the day after All Saints' Day, as a day for the commemoration of the dead, as well as in the liturgy aimed at seeking salvation for the dead beyond the grave.[5]

The combination of eschatological time and terrestrial time was characteristic of new attitudes toward time in the thirteenth century. Time in this world was increasingly conceived in terms of significant events, events that served as milestones measuring mankind's forward progress.

This was of course a linear time, a succession of intervals, quite like the time of narrative. So it is noteworthy that an extraordinary outpouring of narrative literature began around 1150 and even more after 1200: the narrative lay, the fabliau, and the romance became fashionable genres within the space of a few decades.[6] The success of Purgatory was contemporary with the rise of the narrative. More than that, the two phenomena are related. Purgatory introduced a plot into the story of individual salvation. Most important of all, the plot continued after death.

At death all souls must enter time that is essentially eschatological in character, whether they go directly to Hell or Paradise or whether they wait, for the duration of the interval between death and the Last Judgment, in either a neutral but rather gray and somber place like the Jewish *sheol* or in a receptacle such as the bosom of Abraham. But the theory of receptacles, which had essentially enjoyed the favor of Christianity until the twelfth century, was transformed to such an extent as to become a pedantic affectation. The Limbo of the Fathers, the Patriarchs, was permanently shut down; the bosom of Abraham was emptied; Enoch and Elijah remained alone in the earthly Paradise. Only the Limbo of Children and Purgatory were left.

Despite some lingering doubts, for the most part traceable back to Augustine, the temporal boundaries of Purgatory were, by the thirteenth century, clearly marked. Entrance into Purgatory occurs only after death. Purgation does not begin on earth. The development of penitential beliefs and practices undoubtedly helped to encourage the birth of Purgatory. But William of Auvergne's "penitential" conception of Purgatory was not shared by anyone after him to the same degree. Thomas Aquinas gave the theoretical explanation by pointing out that penance can occur only during life; after death there is only punishment. Therefore entrance into Purgatory occurs only at the moment of death. Just as Purgatory has ceased to encroach on terrestrial time, so too it ceases to intrude upon eschatological time as such, namely, the time after the resurrection. The "fire" does not puge during the Last Judgment, only before.

The most important thing is that, for individual souls, the time of Purgatory no longer extends over the whole interval between death and resurrection. Indeed, it is more likely that the soul in Purgatory will be delivered prior to the Last Judgment, the exact time of deliverance depending on the quantity and quality of sins remaining to be purged and the intensity of suffrages offered by the living. Thus there came to be established in the hereafter a variable, measurable, and, even more important, manipulable time-scale. This accounts for the precision with which the narrators of apparitions of souls from Purgatory, not to mention souls themselves in their speeches to the living, discuss the time elapsed since death, the time already served in Purgatory, sometimes even predicting the time left to serve,[7] and above all the exact moment when the soul may leave Purgatory for Paradise at the end of its term of punishment.

It was in this connection that calculation, "accountancy," of the relationship between the quantity of sin committed on earth, the quantity of suffrages proffered as reparations, and the length of time spent in Purgatory, first established itself. Alexander of Hales, with his considerations of proportionality, had given a sort of theoretical justification of this kind of calculation, which Thomas Aquinas sought to head off. The development of the system of indulgences opened the door to every sort of excess with respect to this system of accountancy. In any case a relationship was established between the time of this world and the time of the next, the time of sin and the time of purgation.

Two further consequences of the system of Purgatory were also of major importance. First, the period prior to death took on a new importance. To be sure, sinners had always been warned of the danger of sudden death and urged to prepare themselves in time to escape the torments of Hell. But in order to avoid so heavy a damnation strong measures had to be taken: scandal and the worst sins had to be avoided, or, if they were not, exemplary penance had to be done as quickly as possibly, preferably in the form of a long pilgrimage. For those with realtively easy access to a monastic order—secular clerics, nobles, powerful leaders—taking vows when old age and decay set in provided a good guarantee against damnation. Now the system of Purgatory made it possible to define more subtly differentiated forms of practice that could prove equally decisive if the goal was merely to avoid Purgatory. The best way to do this, apart from leading a holy life, was penance—preceded, increasingly, by confession—but there was still hope of escaping Hell *in extremis* and reducing one's risk to mere Purgatory if one had at least begun to repent. Final contrition increasingly became the last resort for those who wished to take advantage of Purgatory. Life's final moments accordingly took on a new intensity: even though it was long since too late for most sinners to hope for direct admission to Heaven, there was still time to be saved by way of Purgatory. In *L'Homme devant la mort*, Philippe Ariès writes that in the fourteenth and fifteenth centuries "the fate of the immortal soul was decided at the moment of physical death." It seems to me that this was already true of the thirteenth century and, further, that Purgatory was one of the main reasons for the dramatization of the moment of death.[8]

As a matter of fact, Ariès also says that as time went by "there was less and less room for ghosts and their manifestations." I agree, but I would add that the change had already begun in the thirteenth century, the only exceptions being the small number of souls in Purgatory and the still smaller number of the saved and the damned to whom God granted "special permission" to make brief appearances on earth for the edification of the living, though they were no longer allowed to wander. If one compares Jacobus da Voragine's *Golden Legend*, written about 1260, to the testimony given by the residents of Montaillou to the inquisitors a half-century later, one is struck by the contrast between the great bustle of souls around the heretical villagers reluctant to accept Purgatory and the virtual absence of ghosts in the book of the Dominican preacher eager to spread the belief in Purgatory.[9]

Ghosts made a comeback in the Renaissance, however, for although Purgatory continued to play its role of forging a link between the dead and the living, even adding new forms of devotion for the purpose, it apparently ceased to fulfill the function of a prison for suffering souls. Historians of the sixteenth century have shown how ghosts once again began to roam the earth and how escapees from Purgatory danced in earthly cemeteries.[10]

It therefore seems to me that Philippe Ariès is not correct when he adds that "the belief in Purgatory, a place of waiting, long reserved to scholars and theologians or to poets, ultimately became truly popular, but not before the middle of the seventeenth century." In fact, at least one writer has raised the question whether in certain regions such as the area around Toulouse the vogue for Purgatory had not come to an end by the eighteenth century.[11]

Implicit in the system of Purgatory, moreover, was a fairly precise definition of the bonds between the living and the dead and of the way these could be turned to account in suffrages. When souls from Purgatory appealed for assistance, to whom did they turn? First to their blood relatives, forebears and descendants alike. Second, to their spouses; in the thirteenth century, in particular, the role of widows was especially important. Finally, to their superiors: this is clear, for example, in the case of a monk who returns to ask help of a prior or an abbot, but we also find cases of a vassal, a domestic, or a servant addressing his lord or master, as though the lord's obligation to protect his inferiors, as established by the feudo-vassalic contract [*contrat féodo-vassalique*], continued beyond the grave into the time of Purgatory, different from and supplementary to ordinary time. Little by little, between the thirteenth and sixteenth centuries, the solidarity of Purgatory would become involved in the new forms of sociability associated with the confraternities. Here, one must be careful, however, and Ariès, even if he places the date of the change too late, has rightly understood that Purgatory altered the significance of death's frontier. In one sense it lowered the barriers by extending the possiblity of pardon into the other world, but at the same time it put an end to the idea that life and death constitute a seamless fabric and that one crosses from this life to eternity, whether for glory or damnation, promptly and directly. Now an increasing number of souls were required to do a "stint" (to paraphrase Gabriel Le Bras) in a region of the other world between earthly life and its eternal reward.

The temporal pattern of Purgatory, as expressed in apparitions and revealed in the relations between the living and the dead, can be described in this way: shortly after death (a few days or months afterward, seldom later), a soul in Purgatory appears to a living person to whom it was related on this earth, informs that person more or less fully about its situation and about the other world in general and Purgatory in particular, and then urges the person to perform, or to have performed by a relative or friend or by a community, suffrages (fasts, prayers, alms, and especially masses) in its behalf. The soul then promises to inform the person in a subsequent apparition whether or not these suffrages have proved effective. This second apparition can occur in one or two stages. If the latter, the soul usually informs its benefactor upon its first reappearance what portion of its punishment has already been redeemed. Usually this is some simple fraction, such as a half or a third, symbolized by the fact that the ghost's "body" (or "clothing") is half or one-third or two-thirds black (representing the portion yet to be redeemed).

It may come as a surprise (and people in the thirteenth century, not yet accustomed to Purgatory as a commonplace, show their surprise quite plainly) that the time spent in Purgatory is usually very short, on the order of a few days or months, although in one of the most interesting early cases, involving a usurer from Liège, purgation lasted fourteen years, divided into two seven-year periods.[12] The reason for this is that time seems to pass very slowly in Purgatory, owing to the harshness (*acerbitas*) of the punishment. As we shall see, one day seemed as long as a year to some inmates. That purgatorial time should have this intensity is noteworthy in several respects. To begin with, it was a way, admittedly rather crude, of solving the problem of establishing proportionality between earthly time and time in Purgatory, a proportionality that related two quantities unequal in magnitude and different in kind. Furthermore, it involved recourse to a psychological notion (the subjective sense of duration) that accords well with the increasing "psychologization" that we find in literature of the same era. Last but not least surprising or least important, it represents an inversion of the traditional way of experiencing time in the other world as conveyed by folklore. Consider, for instance, countertype 470 in the Aarne-Thompson classification of popular tales:[13] "Years experienced as days: years spent in the other world seem like days because of forgetfulness" and, even more, because life there is so pleasant. The shift from the pleasant Celtic other world to the very harsh other world of Purgatory occasioned a reversal of the sense of time. A remarkable development: in the relations between high culture and folklore, a play of inversions, it is generally folklore that imagines a topsy-turvy world. Here, the idea of an other world from which souls return was borrowed by high culture from folklore, and high culture introduced an inversion for reasons of its own. The reciprocal borrowings and symmetrical approaches of high culture and folklore are clearly in evidence. I view this as one proof that folklore played a role in the inception of Purgatory.[14] Think, for example, of the end of the *Voyage of Bran*, when Bran and his companions want to return to earth after their journey through the marvelous isles that are in fact nothing less than the other world. One of them jumps from the boat to the bank and turns into a pile of ashes, "as if he had been on the earth for hundreds of years." In the thirteenth century visionary literature had not yet exhausted its capacity to beguile its listeners and readers. From this time on, accounts of travels in the other world would make room for Purgatory, openly discussed and mentioned by name.

NEW VOYAGES IN THE OTHER WORLD

In the first years of the century, a German Cistercian, Conrad, who had been a monk at Clairvaux and later abbot of Eberbach in the Taunus, described a series of miracles and told anecdotes to trace the beginnings of his order in *The Great Cistercian Exordium* or the *Account of the Beginnings of the Cistercian Order* (*Exordium Magnum Cisterciense Sive Narratio de Initio Cisterciensis Ordinis*). This work contains several ghost stories. Purgatory is seldom mentioned, because the work purports to be the history of a time, the twelfth century, until the last two decades of which Purgatory did not yet exist. One of the stories is borrowed from the *Book of Miracles* written in 1178 by Herbert of Clairvaux. In this story, Baudouin of Guise, a castellan from the region of Rheims much given to violence and plunder who nevertheless venerates Pierre, the abbot of Igny, dies repentant but before he has time to complete his penance. On the very night of his death he appears to a monk, calling upon the help of Saint Benedict, while at the same time an angel appears to Pierre of Igny to ask the Cistercian community to do suffrages for the fallen castellan. Some time later, two angels bring the dead man before Pierre, present at the altar of the abbey church at Igny. He is dressed in black but handsome clothes made of good fabric. The abbot understands that the black clothing is a sign of penance and that the apparition before the altar is a sign that the man will be saved. Since he makes no further appearance, everyone is certain that he has been received into the purgatorial places (*in locis purgatoriis*), a promise of future salvation. It is clear that here the system is not yet fully perfected, since the dead man does not return to inform the living of his passage from Purgatory to Paradise.[15]

Another story has Augustine appearing in a vision to a monk of Clairvaux to lead him through innumerable places of punishment up to the very entrance of the pit of Gehenna.[16]

In still another story Conrad sets himself the task of showing just how frightening and terrifying the trial by purgatorial fire (*examen ignis purgatorii*) is: he tells the story of a monk who, before dying, is led in spirit into the infernal places (*ad loca infernalia*), where he has a brief vision reminiscent of *Saint Patrick's Purgatory* (as well as the *Apocalypse of Paul*), and then to a place of refreshment (*ad quemdam refrigerii locum*). Conrad explains that the dead are welcomed into this place after their guilt has been purged, the time required depending on the quantity and quality of their sins; he cites Bernard's sermon on the occasion of the death of Humbert, prior of Clairvaux, in which the saint stated that sins committed in this world have to be paid down to the last penny a hundred times over in the purgatorial places (*in purgatoriis locis*).[17]

Souvenirs of a time when Purgatory was still on the verge of being born, the visions and apparitions of the *Magnum Exordium Cisterciense* have an archaic flavor. By contrast, Purgatory's presence is clear in the visions reported at a slightly later date by two English Benedictines, heirs of the great Celtic and Anglo-Saxon tradition established by Bede. The first of these, Roger of Wendover, a monk of the great Abbey of Saint Albans who died in 1236, tells in his *Flowers of History* (*Flores historiarum*) written in 1206 of the voyage of Thurchill in the other world.[18]

While working in a field, Thurchill, a peasant of the village of Tidstude in the bishopric of London, witnessed the apparition of a man who claimed to be Saint Julian the Hospitaller. The apparition announced that he would return the following night to take the peasant to his patron, Saint James, whom the peasant venerated, and to show him, with God's permission, secrets hidden from men. The next night, the saint comes and awakens the peasant in his bed. He causes his soul to leave his body, which remains lying in bed but not inanimate. The guide takes the peasant to a great, splendid basilica with only one, not very high, wall on the north side. Saint Julian and Saint Domnius, guardians of the basilica, show it to Thurchill. Here are the places assigned by God to the dead who are either damned or destined to be saved by the punishments of Purgatory (*per purgatorii poenas*). Near the wall Thurchill sees souls splotched with black and white. The whitest souls are closest to the wall and the blackest farthest away. Beside the wall gapes the pit of Hell, and Thurchill sniffs its fetid odor. This stench should be as a warning to him, Julian says, because he is remiss in paying the Church his tithe. Julian then shows him the east end of the church, where there is a great purgatorial fire, through which souls pass before being purged in another Purgatory, this one consisting of a very cold lake through which passage is controlled by Saint Nicholas (whom we have already encountered as a saint of Purgatory). Finally the souls pass more or less quickly across a bridge of pointed stakes and sharp nails which leads to the mountain of Paradise (the mount of joy, *mons gaudii*). Back at the center of the basilica, Julian and Domnius show Thurchill how the souls are sorted and weighed. Saint Michael the archangel, Saint Peter, and Saint Paul represent God. Saint Michael leads the completely white souls through the flames of the purgatorial fire and the other places of punishment without harm and then takes them to the mount of Paradise. Those who are stained black and white are directed into the purgatorial fire by Saint Peter, there to be purged by the flames. The entirely black souls are weighed by Saint Paul and the Devil. If the scales tip toward Paul, he takes the soul to be purged in purgatorial fire. If they tip toward the Devil, he carries the soul off to Hell. Accompanied by Saint Domnius, Thurchill then takes a lengthy tour of Hell with Satan as a guide. They do not visit the lower Hell. As they draw near the vestibule of the mount of joy, Thurchill remarks that Saint Michael moves the souls forward more or less quickly depending on the number of masses said on behalf of their release by their friends and the universal Church. Thurchill then rapidly tours the many mansions of the paradisaical mountain with Saint Michael as his guide and ends his tour with a visit to the Earthly Paradise. Saint Julian then appears once more to order him to tell what he has seen. Every year on All Saint's Day, Thurchill tells his story. He does so of course in the vernacular but everyone admires the way this previously uncultivated and thick-tongued peasant now exhibits such fine eloquence.[19]

Archaic in many of its details, this account does divide the other world into three main regions, Paradise, Hell, and Purgatory, but the geographic division is not perfect. Hell still has an upper and a lower portion, Paradise contains many mansions and is situated on a mountain that resembles the tower of Babel, and Purgatory consists of three pieces joined together in makeshift fashion: the fire, the cold lake, and the bridge.

PREACHING PURGATORY: THE *EXEMPLA*

The stories described in the preceding section were still addressed to a narrow audience, inside the monasteries. The lay masses had not yet been touched. Purgatory was popularized mainly through sermons, in particular through anecdotes that preachers included to add savor to their homilies, to amuse while teaching. For the Church the use of short narratives was a primary means of adjusting its apostolate to contemporary taste as well as a continuation of a long tradition. These edifying anecdotes, or *exempla*, are reminiscent, despite some differences, of the stories that Gregory the Great included in his *Dialogues*. As we saw earlier, these tales were a milestone along the road to Purgatory. The crucial encounter of Purgatory and the *exemplum* in the thirteenth century provides a spectacular climax to a story that begins six and a half centuries earlier with Gregory the Great.[20]

Sermons always occupied an important place in the Church's mission, but the thirteenth century witnessed a renaissance of the sermon, as preaching found a new language and became more direct and realistic. The mendicant friars quickly took the lead in bringing about this change.[21] Sermons together with their embedded *exempla* were the "mass media" of the thirteenth century. They carried the message to all the faithful, except for a few who preferred the tavern to masses and sermons. Besides being an eagerly anticipated part of the service, the sermon together with its *exempla* developed as a genre in its own right, independent of the regular ritual. Sermons were preached in public squares as well as in the churches; they were forerunners of the public speech or lecture. In contrast to the *jongleurs*, whose audience consisted primarily of nobles, popular preachers became the "idols" of the Christian crowd. Through them the masses gazed upon and learned about Purgatory.

A Precursor: James of Vitry

James of Vitry was one of the first preachers to use the later popular device of spicing his sermons with *exempla*. Trained at the University of Paris in the first few years of the thirteenth century and later curate of Oignies in northern France, James had contacts with the Beguines, women who went into retreat in the midst of cities, where they lived a cloistered existence midway between that of lay women and nuns. He was a preacher renowned throughout much of Christendom, especially France, and eventually became bishop of Acre in Palestine and finally cardinal-bishop of Tusculum (he died in 1240): a considerable figure.[22] Not much attention is paid to Purgatory in his collected sermons, but the new system of the hereafter is already fully accredited in them, and we do find a few interesting details. To understand them, we must consider his *exempla* in conjunction with the more theoretical portions of the sermons in which James gave expression to his thinking on the subject.

Two passages are particularly significant. The first occurs in a standard sermon, *To Spouses* (*Ad conjugatos*): "Contrition changes the punishment of Hell into punishment of Purgatory, confession [changes it] into temporal punishment, appropriate satisfaction [changes it] into nothingness. In contrition sin dies, in confession it is removed from the house, in satisfaction, it is buried."[23] The logic here is worthy of note: Purgatory is associated with contrition and with the penitential process, and stress is laid on the decisive step away from Hell when the soul enters Purgatory.

In a standard Sunday sermon James of Vitry refers to the idea that Sunday is a day of rest in Purgatory: "It is pious to believe, as many saints attest, that on the Lord's Day the souls of the dead in Purgatory rest or at least are subjected to less harsh punishment until Monday, when the Church in its compassion habitually helps them by celebrating a mass for the dead. Accordingly, it is right that the Sunday rest in Purgatory should not be enjoyed by those who did not honor the Lord's Day in this world, because they refused to refrain from servile labor and secular business, or, worse still, because they gave themselves to carousal and revelry and other desires of the flesh, or danced and sang lasciviously, or because they did not fear to stain and dishonor Sundays with quarrelling and disputation, with vain and idle talk, with brazen and slandering words."[24]

Here the Sabbath rest in Hell has been converted into Sunday relaxation in Purgatory, and a link has been established between Sunday behavior in this world and Sunday punishment in the next. The Church has established a definite connection between earthly behavior and Purgatory in an edifying parallelism.

In James of Vitry's standard sermons addressed to various audiences (*sermones vulgares* or *ad status*) I have found only two *exempla* in which Purgatory plays an essential role. The first, which may have been borrowed from the Cistercian Helinand of Froimont and which is possibly derived from the legends surrounding the figure of Charlemagne, is addressed to "those in tears over the death of relatives or friends"—in other words, the sermon is concerned with the new forms of sociability that link the living and the dead. A knight in Charlemagne's entourage, engaged in an expedition against the Saracens in Spain, leaves a will asking a relative to sell his horse for the benefit of the poor. The unscrupulous relative keeps the horse. After eight days the dead knight appears and reproaches the relative for delaying his release from Purgatory; the knight further makes it known that the relative will expiate his sin by dying a miserable death on the following day. The day comes and the hapless relative is carried off by black crows and dropped onto a rock, where he dies of a broken neck.[25] The responsibility of the living to the dead in Purgatory is thus evoked fairly subtly, and the distinction between venial sin and mortal sin is illustrated. The purpose of the sermon was of course to induce executors to carry out the terms of wills, particularly where reparations were involved. The range of threats hanging over the heads of those who failed to do so was increased by the addition of Purgatory to the danger of damnation in Hell.

The second *exemplum* scarcely mentions Purgatory but is important nonetheless. It comes from a sermon on the crusade. A woman prevents her husband from going to hear a crusading sermon preached by James of Vitry himself. But the man manages to listen through a window. When he hears the preacher say that through the penance of the crusade a man can avoid punishment in Purgatory and Gehenna and gain the Kingdom of Heaven, he foils his wife's surveillance, jumps through the window, and is the first to go and take the cross.[26] Crusade, indulgence, Purgatory—a reminder of the threefold system of the hereafter: another model is here established, a model in which Purgatory played an increasingly important intermediary role.

TWO IMPORTANT POPULARIZERS OF PURGATORY

It was the regular clergy, the preaching friars most intimately involved with the urban environment, that took the lead in the use of sermons and *exempla* to disseminate belief in Purgatory. I have chosen to look at two among many. They are quite different both from James of Vitry and from each other. Both were regulars, but one was a Cistercian monk, the other a Dominican friar. Both lived in the first two-thirds of the thirteenth century, but one died in 1240, the other in 1261. One was a German, and his geographical and cultural roots were in Cologne. The other was French, and his experience ranged from an education at the University of Paris to activity as an inquisitor over a broad territory centering on the Dominican monastery in Lyons. Both wrote works intended directly or indirectly for use by preachers, and both filled their treatises with *exempla* to the point that their works have been considered by some (wrongly) as collections of *exempla*. Above all, both men attached very great importance to Purgatory, both in the *exempla* and in the theoretical works on which they based their preaching. Their writings reveal an other world consisting of three fairly equal parts: Hell, Purgatory, and Heaven. Thus begins the vision of the afterlife that would eventually culminate in Dante's Divine Comedy.

The Cistercian Caesarius of Heisterbach

In a dialogue form deliberately reminiscent of Gregory the Great, the Cistercian Caesarius of Heisterbach produced, between 1219 and 1223, a work entitled *Dialogus miraculorum* (*Dialogue on Miracles*), which is actually a collection of anecdotes, told by a monk to a novice, in which we can see the traditional genre of the miracle story being transformed into the *exemplum*, or edifying tale.[27] The collection is arranged as a pilgrimage of the Christian toward the Last Things, that is, toward the other world. This pilgrimage takes place in twelve stages, which constitute the twelve books (*distinctiones*) of the *Dialogus miraculorum*: conversion, contrition, confession, temptation, demons, simplicity, the Virgin Mary, vision, the Eucharist, miracles, the dying, and the reward of the dead.[28] Obviously it is in this final chapter that Purgatory is most fully in evidence, both in the number and detail of the *exempla* and in the structure of the work.

The structure of the twelfth and final distinction is simple. The dead are rewarded in three ways. Some receive the glory of Heaven (the Celestial Paradise), others receive the eternal punishments of Hell, still others receive the temporary punishments of Purgatory. Of fifty-five *exempla*, twenty-five are devoted to Hell, sixteen to Purgatory, and fourteen to Paradise. From this simple enumeration, it is clear that, even though Caesarius was of a generous and merciful disposition and the infernalization of Purgatory had not yet reached the heights it would attain later in the century, Hell is still the place from which the largest number of lessons is drawn. To frighten was, if not the preacher's first concern, then at least one of his primary preoccupations.[29] Still, Purgatory commands attention almost equal to that accorded to Hell and Heaven.

Purgatory did not wait until the final distinction of the *Dialogus miraculorum* to make its appearance, however. Andrée Duby has found eight "*exempla* of Purgatory" in the first eleven books of the *Dialogus*, several of which shed considerable light on Caesarius's views concerning the doctrine of Purgatory.[30] Indeed, if Purgatory was by this time a standard part of the last chapter of Christian *summas*, devoted to the Last Things, or *novissima*, it was also encountered along the way, looming on the horizon of each stage of the spiritual life.

I shall begin by discussing four important *exempla* drawn from the first eleven books before turning to the last "distinction," which contains a group of *exempla* concerned with Purgatory. In the first chapter, which deals with conversion, Caesarius of Heisterbach tells the story of an untalented student who, in order to succeed in his studies, takes the Devil's advice to resort to magic. Holding in his hand a talisman that Satan has given him, he succeeds brilliantly in his examinations. But he then falls ill and on the brink of death confesses to a priest, who tells him to throw the talisman away. He dies and his soul is transported into a horrible valley, where spirits with long, pointed fingernails toss him about like a ball and cruelly wound him. God takes pity on him and orders the demons to cease their torture. The student's soul rejoins his body, which comes back to life. Frightened by what he has seen and felt, he converts and joins the Cistercian order. Ultimately he becomes the abbot of Morimond. At this point a dialogue begins between the novice and the monk, i.e., Caesarius. The novice asks if the place where the student was tormented was Hell or Purgatory. Caesarius answers that, if the valley of punishment were part of Hell, it would mean that the student's confession had not been accompanied by contrition. The student did agree to keep the magic stone, but he refused to swear allegiance to the demon. Nevertheless, Caesarius is reluctant to say explicitly that the abbot's vision was of Purgatory, because it contains not angels but demons. Caesarius's master in the schools of Cologne, Rudolph, taught that demons never touch saved souls, which are brought to Purgatory, "if they are worthy," by good angels—the phraseology suggests that Purgatory is a promise of Paradise, hope, a grant of God's merciful justice.[31]

In chapter 2, on contrition, Caesarius tells the story of a young monk who leaves his monastery, sets himself up as a highway bandit, and is mortally wounded while laying siege to a castle. Before dying, however, he confesses. To his confessor the enormity of his sins seems so great that no penance suggests itself. The dying man suggests two thousand years of Purgatory at the end of which he hopes to receive God's mercy, and before dying he asks the priest to transmit to a certain bishop a letter asking the bishop to pray for his soul. He dies and is carried off to Purgatory. The bishop, who has never ceased to love the former monk, despite his apostasy, prays for him and for an entire year has all the clergy of the diocese pray for him also. At the end of the year the dead man appears to him, "pale, emaciated, shriveled, clad in black." But he thanks the bishop, for this year of suffrages has, he says, spared him a thousand years of Purgatory and another year of aid will free him altogether. The bishop and his clergy renew their efforts. At the end of the second year the dead man again appears to the bishop "in a white cowl and with a serene look about him"—in other words, dressed as a Cistercian. He announces that he is about to leave for Paradise and thanks the bishop for these two years, the equivalent of two thousand years in Purgatory. The novice marvels at the power of the dead man's contrition and of the prayers that set him free. Caesarius emphasizes that contrition is more effective than suffrages, which can reduce punishment but not increase glory.[32]

In the last book of the *Dialogus miraculorum* we find the story of Christian, a young Cistercian monk of Heisterbach, which is also instructive about Caesarius's views concerning the bookkeeping of Purgatory. Christian was a very pious monk, who during his lifetime gave off a fragrance similar to the odor of sanctity but who was feebleminded and privy to visions of the Virgin, angels, and even Jesus himself, as well as afflicted with trials and temptations, such as losing the gift of tears acquired by kissing a crucifix. His final trial is a cruel illness. Saint Agatha appears to him and exhorts him to bear the disease piously, for sixty days of suffering will be counted as sixty years. Sixty days after this apparition, on Saint Agatha's feast day, the monk died. According to Caesarius, Saint Agatha's words can be interpreted in two ways: either the sixty days of sickness have purged the monk of sins equal to sixty years in Purgatory, or else the way in which he has borne up under his sixty days' suffering have earned him merit worth sixty years.[33] Thus Caesarius gave a positive connotation to merits acquired in this world. As in the previous case he rates man's active will as more important than his passive virtues.

The story of the monk Christian of Hemmenrode aims to highlight the power of the Virgin Mary. This Christian, also rather naive, while a student and then a priest even before becoming a monk, resists various temptations and is favored with visions by Saint Mary Magdalene and above all by the Virgin Mary. After becoming a monk of Hemmenrode, he is dreaming one day about the punishments of Purgatory and has a vision of the Virgin in the midst of other virgins accompanied by the dead emperor Frederick Barbarossa. The Virgin is presiding at Christian's burial and she takes his soul with her into heaven, while troops of demons breathing walls of fire clamor in vain after it. Angels take the soul into a great fire and instruct it that after death it will return to this place and be required to pass through this fire. After coming back to life, Christian continues to lead a holy and humble life, filled with visions, in the monastery. The reason for his humility is that in his youth he not only lost his virginity but had two natural sons, both of whom have entered the Cistercian order. Hence he has all the more need of the Virgin's assistance. But this is so unfailing that when he dies, the Virgin and the infant Jesus appear to him dressed in the Cistercian cowl and receive him into Paradise. Thus the vision prophesying that he will pass through purgatorial fire does not come true.[34]

With the stories of the two Christians, Caesarius intends to show that the worst is never certain: the first Christian escapes Hell and goes to Purgatory, and the second is spared Purgatory and rewarded with Paradise.

The *exempla* of the twelfth and final "distinction" having to do with Purgatory can at first sight be divided into three groups. The grouping is based on traditional ideas together with more recent innovations. It was in keeping with the new spirit of the times to relate the geography of the other world to the various categories of sin. By contrast, it was traditional to enumerate the various types of suffrages. It was characteristic of the thirteenth century to emphasize the severity of purgatorial punishments, and this is reflected even in so indulgent a spirit as Caesarius of Heisterbach.

The first group, then, which consists of eight exempla numbered 24–31, deals with the following categories of sin: avarice, lust, magic, disobedience, perverse obstinacy, levity, and sloth.

The Usurer of Liège: Purgatory and Capitalism

The first *exemplum* of the series seems to me to be of particular importance. Here is the story of the usurer of Liège:

> THE MONK: A usurer of Liège died in our time. The bishop expelled him from the cemetery. His wife then went to the apostolic see to beg that he be allowed burial in hallowed ground. The pope refused. She then pleaded for her husband: "I have been told, my Lord, that man and woman are but one and that, according to the Apostle, an unbelieving man can be saved by his believing wife. What my husband forgot to do, I,

who am a part of his body, shall willingly do in his place. I am ready to become a recluse for him and to redeem his sins from God." Giving in to the prayers of the cardinals, the pope had the dead man moved to the cemetery. His wife moved near his tomb, shut herself up as a recluse, and strove night and day to appease God for the salvation of his soul through alms, fasts, prayers, and vigils. After seven years her husband appeared to her clad in black and thanked her: "May God reward you, for, thanks to your trials, I have been plucked from the depths of Hell and the most terrible punishments. If you render me further services of this kind for seven years, I shall be completely delivered." And she did. He again appeared to her after seven more years, but this time clad in white and with a happy look about him. "Thank God and you, for today I have been set free."

THE NOVICE: How can he say that today he is being set free from Hell, a place from which no redemption is possible?

THE MONK: "The depths of Hell" means from the harshness of Purgatory. Similarly, when the Church prays for the dead with the words, "Lord Jesus Christ, King of Glory, free the souls of all the faithful from the hand of Hell and from the depths of the abyss, etc." it is not praying for the damned but for those who can be saved. The hand of Hell, the depths of the abyss—here these mean from the harshness of Purgatory. As for our usurer, he would not have been set free from his punishments if he had not expressed contrition in the end.[35]

The main points in this passage are obvious. For one thing, there is the emphasis on the marital tie at a time when the Church was trying to impose a model of monogamous marriage based on equality between husband and wife, as against a male-centered aristocratic model that revolved around the preservation of patrimony and showed little concern for the unique and indissoluble character of the marital bond.[36] The system of suffrages for souls in Purgatory generally involved aristocratic kinship structures, in which the wife's role was secondary. By contrast, here, in an urban bourgeois context, the marital tie becomes paramount in the next world as well as in this one. Attention is also focused on the proportionality between the time of suffrages on earth and the time of punishment in Purgatory; the apparitions are orchestrated to emphasize this proportionality, with the total time divided into two periods of seven earthly years, completion of the first marked by the apparition of the soul in black, of the second by its apparition in white. The whole range of suffrages is described: alms, fasts, prayers, and vigils. Only masses are lacking, but this is partially compensated by an extreme form of the communion of saints: penance in the form of substitution of the living for the dead, a penitential hermit's existence in the middle of the city, as the wife assumes the life of a recluse. Finally, there is the terminological precision regarding the relationship between Purgatory and Hell, the shift from the biblical vocabulary of Hell to the new vocabulary of Purgatory, which preserves the harshness of Hell but for a limited duration only.

But the most astonishing aspect of this passage has yet to be mentioned. The big surprise—probably felt as such by those who heard and read this *exemplum*—is that its hero is a usurer. This was a time when the Church was redoubling its efforts to combat usury, a practice severely condemned by the Second, Third, and Fourth Lateran Councils (in 1139, 1179,[37] and 1215, respectively), condemned again by the Second Council of Lyons (in 1274), and yet again by the Council of Vienna (1311). It was also a time when a great campaign was being organized throughout Christendom against usury, which flourished at the beginning of the thirteenth century in northern Italy and in Toulouse and which was in the process of replacing pride as the foremost of mortal sins.[38] That favorite theme of Romanesque imagery, the usurer dragged down to Gehenna by the swollen purse hanging from his neck, was constantly before the eyes of the faithful. And yet, despite all this, here we have a soul, saved by a hypothetical final contrition and by his wife's devotion, and despite the opposition of the Church personified by the highest official in its hierarchy, and the soul is that of a usurer.

I have shown elsewhere[39] how, as in this *exemplum*, usurers in the thirteenth century were under certain conditions plucked from Hell and saved by and through Purgatory. I have also ventured the controversial opinion that Purgatory, by making the salvation of the usurer possible, contributed to the birth of capitalism. Here I want to emphasize Purgatory's sociological contribution. One of Purgatory's functions was in fact to save from Hell sinners belonging to specific social groups. Previously, members of these groups had had but little hope of escaping perdition, either because their activities involved them in certain grave sins or because their occupations were traditionally viewed with hostility.

For one thing, extremely serious sins, such as apostasy or lust, especially when committed by monks, no longer stood in the way of ultimate salvation, though the sinner had to pay the price of a more or less extended stay in Purgatory. But previously he would have been without hope. Now, particularly at Cîteaux, he could count on the then flourishing cult of the Virgin—what better intercessor could there be in apparently hopeless cases?—and on the solid ties of community binding the members of the order to one another. For another, occupational groups hitherto condemned and held in contempt—those whose work involved spilling blood, handling money, or trading in unclean commodities—now had hope, provided they were clever enough to forge sufficiently close ties with their friends and relatives in this world (could ill-gotten gains be used for the purpose?). Here it was not the Virgin but the wife who could work miracles. It is worth noting too that thirteenth-century anti-usury legislation and jurisprudence show a keen interest in the widows of usurers.

Purgatory Is Hope

A second *exemplum* concerned with greed has a recently deceased prior, pale and soft in appearance, his cowl threadbare, appear to a Cistercian nun and reveal to her that he is about to be delivered from Purgatory on the occasion of a celebration in honor of the Virgin Mary, thanks to the suffrages of one of his monks. The nun is dumbfounded: everyone believed this prior to have been such a "saint!" The reason for his passage through Purgatory was that, driven by greed, he had expanded his monastery's possessions beyond reasonable limits. In this story involving a prior, a monk, and a nun, we see the influence of a three-cornered system that governed relations within the Cistercian community. Women have an important role to play in the functioning of Purgatory, particularly at Cîteaux and more especially in the work of Caesarius of Heisterbach.[40]

A nun of Zion in Friesland commits a very grave sin. She is seduced by a priest and dies in childbirth. Before dying she entrusts herself to the care of her blood relations: her father, her mother, her two married sisters, and a cousin. But these relatives, despairing of being able to save the nun's soul, since her case seems so clear-cut, do not undertake any suffrages. The soul therefore seeks out a Cistercian abbot, who is quite astonished by the apparitions since he does not know the woman. Shamefaced, she asks timidly "for at least a psalter and a few masses," not daring to reveal to the abbot either the nature of her sin or her full identity. Eventually he runs into an aunt of the dead woman, also a Cistercian nun, who explains the whole story. The relatives are alerted and their hope is rekindled. At the same time all the monks and nuns of the province are involved. We are not told the results of this mobilization beyond the indubitable fact that the sinner is quickly saved. The Virgin does not intervene directly in the case, but the heroine's first name, the only detail she confides to the abbot, is Mary. Told with great tact and psychological verisimilitude, this brief story highlights Purgatory's essential function in the early thirteenth century. The relatives of the unfortunate girl, we are told, were at first desperate but then regained hope (*de animae ejus salute desesperantes . . . spe concepta*). Purgatory is hope.[41]

Another *exemplum* depicts a husband praying for his dead wife, who has appeared to her sister-in-law, a recluse, to let her know about the very harsh punishment that she, the dead woman, is undergoing in Purgatory. This woman, by all appearances good and decent, had used magic to hold on to her husband's love. The novice, neglecting the superstitious aspect of this behavior, is surprised by God's severity toward sins that he thinks of as peccadilloes. Beware, the text seems to say, our point of view is not necessarily the same as God's.[42] Caesarius goes even further. God is very strict, even exacting. When monks do not obey all the orders of their superiors and resist stubbornly even in little things, God is not indifferent: he overlooks nothing.[43]

Besides negligence, its opposite, stubbornness, is also punished in Purgatory. Indeed, stubbornness is another form of disobedience. A schoolmaster who has become a monk of the monastery at Pruilly behaved with such strictness that his abbot had tried in vain to exert a moderating influence. The monk dies, and one night, when the abbot is in the church stalls for lauds, three figures resembling burning candles appear to him in the choir. He recognizes them: the figure in the center is the schoolmaster, and he is flanked by two lay brothers who had died a short while before. The abbot asks the dead monk how he is. "I am well," the monk responds. The abbot, remembering his stubbornness, is surprised: "You're not suffering because of your disobedience?" The apparition answers, "Oh, yes, I am suffering from many very severe torments. But since my intention was good, the Lord has not damned me." As for the lay brothers, the abbot is surprised that the one who was an apostate shines more brightly than the other, against whom no one had the slightest reproach. The monk explains that the first had repented after committing his sin and had surpassed the other in fervor, the second brother being only lukewarm. At this point we encounter an interesting detail: in order to leave irrefutable evidence of his apparition and proof both that Purgatory exists and that souls can briefly return from it, the dead monk kicks the choristers' podium so hard that it splits. In this way a "relic" of Purgatory was born. Many such "relics," the oldest dating from the end of the thirteenth century, the most recent from the present century, are collected in the Museum of Purgatory in Rome. What lesson is to be drawn from this *exemplum*? Caesarius and the novice agree that it upholds the Benedictine value system, which reproves those who are too strict as well as those who are too lax in their duties.[44] Thus Purgatory is being used to confirm the Benedictine exaltation of moderation. The allusion to laxity is also a skillful way of managing the transition to the case of the sacristan John of the monastery of Villers, a religious man who was, however, lax in word and deed (*in verbis et signis*). Condemned to Purgatory, he appears to his abbot, who is terrified by the vision.[45]

Finally, to complete the survey of monastic sins punished in Purgatory, we come to sloth. An abbot of Hemmenrode respected the discipline of the order in all respects except one: he balked at doing manual labor with the other brothers. Before dying, this monk had promised another monk, whom he loved above all others, that he would appear to him thirty days after his death to inform him of his condition. On the appointed day he appeared, glowing above the waist, completely black beneath. He asked the monks to pray for him and appeared once more to announce that he had been released from Purgatory.[46] At this point in the dialogue the novice asks for information about the hierarchy of suffrages. Are prayers more effective than alms? The answer is contained in a series of *exempla*.

First comes the case of a dead man who appears to a friend and indicates that the order of suffrages is as follows: first prayers, actually a rather lukewarm suffrage, then alms, and finally masses. In the mass Christ prays, and his body and blood are alms.[47]

Next, an adolescent of noble birth who has become a lay brother at Clairvaux is tending sheep in a barn. A dead cousin appears to him and asks that three masses be said to enable him to escape some very severe torments. The masses are said and the cousin reappears to give thanks and says that the virtues of the Eucharist should not come as a surprise, for a brief absolution may be enough to liberate certain souls.[48]

This is followed by the apparition of the monk Christian of Heisterbach, who was discussed above. He died while the abbot was away. When the abbot returns seven days later, he merely says, "May he rest in peace," and this is enough to deliver Christian from Purgatory.[49]

Here again, the intercession, modest as it is, must be made by a valid intermediary. Another story: a Benedictine nun from the monastery of Rindorp near Bonn was fervently devoted to Saint John the Baptist. After her death she appeared to another nun, who was also her sister by blood and who had been praying for her, to announce that she was leaving Purgatory. But she reveals that her intercessor was not Saint John but Saint Benedict, who agreed to kneel before God on her behalf. This story is a reminder to monks and nuns that it is to their advantage to honor the founders of their orders.[50]

The final *exempla* on Purgatory in Caesarius's *Dialogues* are designed to bring out the harshness of purgatorial punishments. The novice asks Caesarius if it is true that the least punishment in Purgatory is greater than any imaginable punishment in this world. Caesarius answers by giving the opinion of a theologian whom he has consulted on this question: "This is not true, unless we are speaking of punishments of the same kind. For example, purgatorial fire is stronger than any earthly fire, purgatorial cold more bitter than any cold in this world, and so forth." But there can be punishments in Purgatory less severe than certain earthly punishments. Though he admits the harshness of purgatorial punishments, Caesarius, a man of moderate spirit concerned to show how flexible the system of Purgatory can be, stresses the wide range of purgatorial pains, the very broad spectrum of punishments available.

Thus a nun of the monastery of Mont-Saint-Sauveur near Aix-la-Chapelle, Sister Gertrude, appears to another nun of her own age, Sister Marguerite, with whom she had been in the habit of chatting during services. Condemned to purge her sin in the place where it was committed, Gertrude is required to return four times to participate in the services of her convent, unseen except by her friend. The novice voices the opinion that this punishment is relatively minor compared with certain earthly punishments.[51] Finally, Caesarius gives an *exemplum* that shows what one might call the "degree zero" of Purgatory. A young and very pure child, William, joins the order only to die at the end of his year's probation. He appears to a monk and says that he is undergoing punishment. The monk is terrified by the news: "If you, so innocent, if you are punished, what will happen to a poor sinner like me?" To this the young person replies, "Take heart. My only suffering is that I am still deprived of the vision of God." A few prayers said over the course of a week are enough to bring the soul back, this time protected by the cloak of the Virgin and on its way to Paradise.

Caesarius is here describing a Purgatory that is very like the Limbo of Children, and he emphasizes that little William's case is not exceptional: a theologian has told him that a certain number of the just, who have only venial sins to expiate, are not punished in Purgatory beyond being deprived of the vision of God for a certain length of time.[52]

Caesarius here touches one extreme of the doctrine of Purgatory. Not only has he made the range of punishments as broad as possible, but he is explicitly linking theological reflection on Purgatory to another concern, which, though not explicitly mentioned, must often have been associated with it, namely, reflection on the beatific vision. To comprehend the full range of medieval theological thinking about the intermediate time of Purgatory, the time between the moment of death and the moment of resurrection and judgment, it must be understood that Purgatory was hemmed in from below by Hell and from above by Heaven: purged souls that escaped the horrors of Hell were drawn upward by the summons of Paradise, tending to reduce Purgatory to a single yet crucial lack, the absence of the beatific vision. In fact, it was among the great theologians of the thirteenth century that the doctrine of the beatific vision (granted to the just immediately after their individual judgment) took on its definitive form.[53] Purgatory, in its upper reaches, may be nothing less than evidence of the reality of a beatific vision prior to the Last Judgment.

Caesarius's survey concludes with a reminder: certain visions, he tells us, show that there are a number of places in this world where purgatory may be located. Gregory the Great provided examples. But the most convincing account is that of *Saint Patrick's Purgatory*. Listen to Caesarius: "Let him who doubts the existence of Purgatory go to Ireland and let him enter into Saint Patrick's Purgatory. He will then have no more doubts about the reality of purgatorial punishments."[54]

Caesarius of Heisterbach was a well-placed observer: as an influential actor in the process, he gives a first-hand account of the way in which the men of the Middle Ages came to believe that Pugatory was a concrete place. Behind the particular features of his thinking, we can make out the main elements in the system of Purgatory. To begin with, Purgatory was seen as the culmination of a penitential process. Final contrition was the necessary and sufficient condition for this process to take place, as we saw in the case of the usurer of Liège, but it normally proceeded through the stages of contrition, confession, and penitence. Second, Purgatory came into being only after its location had been specified and the nature of purgatorial punishment decided on. At the time Caesarius was writing, these questions had not yet been entirely resolved. Nevertheless, Purgatory had become increasingly distinct from the earth, Limbo, Paradise, and, above all, Hell. To distinguish clearly between Purgatory and Hell was one of Caesarius's main concerns.

We also find in Caesarius's writings a rather simplistic bookkeeping. He draws in part on old monastic traditions of numerical symbolism and in part on new accounting practices, which were just then extending their influence from commerce into the realm of penance.

Above all, Caesarius insists on solidarity between the living and the dead, solidarity that for him is based primarily on the Cistercian family, which combines the blood kinship of the nobility with the artificial kinship of the religious community, but also partly on new forms of marital and professional bonds as exemplified most clearly in the case of the usurer of Liège.

The Dominican Stephen of Bourbon and the Infernalization of Purgatory

When we turn from the *Dialogue on Miracles* written around 1220 by the Cistercian Caesarius of Heisterbach to the *Treatise on Preaching* (*Tractatus de diversis materiis praedicabilibus*) composed by the Dominican Stephen of Bourbon between approximately 1250 and 1261, when death interrupted his unfinished labors, we find that the climate has changed dramatically. Purgatory now represents not hope but fear.

The author, born at Belleville-sur-Saône around 1195, studied at Saint-Vincent of Mâcon and then at the University of Paris before joining the Dominican order. The center of his activities was the Dominican monastery at Lyons, which he often left to visit Auvergne, Forez, Burgundy, and the Alpine regions in his capacity as preacher and inquisitor. At the end of his life Stephen began work on a great treatise intended for use by preachers, in which he, like Caesarius, included a large number of *exempla*. But unlike Caesarius, who drew primarily on his own experience and based the majority of his *exempla* on anecdotes of recent events known to him by hearsay, Stephen drew equally on contemporary tradition and written sources. Hence his narratives do not follow a rule unto themselves, as do those of Caesarius, but are tailored to fit a plan based on the seven gifts of the Holy Spirit.[55] Stephen of Bourbon allows himself to be carried away by the scholastic spirit and multiplies, frequently in a highly artificial way, division and subdivisions. Purgatory is the subject of chapter 5 of the first gift of the Holy Spirit, the gift of fear (*De dono timoris*).[56]

The book on the gift of fear has ten chapters: (1) on the seven kinds of fear; (2) on the effects of fear of the Lord; (3) that God is to be feared; (4) on Hell; (5) that the future Purgatory is to be feared; (6) on the fear of the Last Judgment; (7) on the fear of death; (8) on the fear of sin; (9) that the present peril is to be feared; (10) on the nature of the enemies of the human race (demons).

From the beginning, Stephen of Bourbon plunges us into a Christianity of fear. Purgatory is set in a context of eschatological fear where it occupies a position quite close to that of Hell.

Purgatory is the subject of the fifth chapter. This chapter is in turn subdivided into seven sections, a quite artificial choice dictated by the fact that the Lyons Dominican liked to organize his work in accordance with a numerical symbolism (using sevens, tens, twelves, etc.). The seven sections treat the present Purgatory, the future Purgatory, the nature of the sinners and sins with which Purgatory is connected, the seven reasons to fear Purgatory (grouped under three heads), and finally the twelve types of suffrage that can help souls in Purgatory.

Following traditional concepts abandoned by most of his contemporaries, Stephen of Bourbon held that earthly life could be viewed as a preliminary Purgatory in which sins could be purged in twelve ways, of which I shall spare the reader the enumeration. Here, no argument is given, only biblical authorities cited one after another. The second chapter is intended to prove the existence of a Purgatory of souls stripped of their bodies in the future. The proof is by appeal to authority, both from the New Testament (Matthew 12, Gregory the Great's *Dialogues* 4, and 1 Corinthians 3) and the Old (the Old Testament sources speak of fire and trials in the future). Since there must be remission of sins after death, there has to be an appropriate place for the ultimate purgation to occur, and this cannot be either Hell or Paradise. Stephen condemns heretics, particularly Waldensians, "who say that there is no purgatorial punishment in the future" and reject suffrages for the dead. In one of those quick shifts habitual with him, Stephen then describes the eight kinds of punishment discussed in the book of *Laws*, without explaining what these have to do with Purgatory, and he then declares that those who reject Purgatory sin against God and against all the sacraments.

Who is punished in Purgatory? At the beginning of chapter 3, Stephen lists three categories of sinners destined for Purgatory: those who have "converted" too late, those who have only venial sins on their heads when they die, and those who have not done sufficient penance in this world. This is followed by another short section, which amounts to little more than a brief commentary on 1 Corinthians 3:10–15.

Chapters 4, 5, and 6 are devoted to the reasons man has to fear punishment in Purgatory. There are seven such reasons: harshness (*acerbitas*), diversity (*diversitas*), duration (*diuturnitas*), sterility (*sterilitas*), noxiousness (*dampnositas*), the quality of the torments (*tormentorum qualitas*), and the small number of aids (*subveniencium paucitas*).

These negative characteristics of purgatorial punishment are illustrated primarily by means of *exempla*. There is a lengthy description of Saint Patrick's Purgatory and its tortures, borrowed from the *Apocalypse of Paul*, for the purpose of showing how harsh and various the punishments are. As for duration, reference is made to the feeling of the soul undergoing punishment that time is passing very slowly, because of the suffering it must endure. An equivalence is established between this world and the next by way of redemption. Stephen suggests, with some hesitation (with much hesitation, he might say), that a year of Purgatory can probably be redeemed in one day. Sterility refers to the impossibility of acquiring merit after death. The noxiousness of Purgatory is due to the absence of the vision of God. Unlike Caesarius of Heisterbach, for example, who seems to believe that this deprivation is the least of the punishments that one can endure in Purgatory, Stephen maintains that to be deprived of the vision of God, even for a single day, is no small harm. He turns this nice phrase: if need be, a saint would rather be in Hell in the sight of God than in Paradise and out of his sight. From these rather obscurantist pages this glimpse of the beatific vision shines forth as a ray of sunlight.

When he comes to discuss the "quality of torments," Stephen refers, significantly, to what he has already said about the punishments of Hell. The small number of aids has to do with Stephen's pessimism. In his view, "the living quickly forget the dead," and the souls in Hell cry out like Job, "Have pity on me, have pity on me, you at least, my friends, for the hand of the Lord has touched me." He goes on: "Friends in good fortune, the friends of the world are like a dog which, as long as the pilgrim is seated at table with a bone in hand, wags its tail as a sign of affection, but as soon as his hands are empty no longer recognizes him." Once again, Purgatory is being likened to Hell, "for Hell is oblivious."

In conclusion, Stephen of Bourbon goes into considerable detail concerning the twelve types of suffrages that can aid souls in Purgatory. Here again *exempla* are used as illustrations. The Dominican's writing in this section is rather confused, but the list of twelve suffrages runs as follows: mass, pious offerings, prayer, alms, penance, pilgrimage, crusade, execution of a pious will, restitution of ill-gotten gains, intercession of the saints, faith, and general suffrages of the Church based on the communion of saints. Stephen is apparently moved by three concerns: to emphasize the role of close relatives and friends of the dead person, "his own" (*sui*) family and "friends" (*amici*); to underscore the value of suffrages executed by those who are good, the righteous; and finally to remind his readers of the Church's role in dispensing and controlling suffrages.

There is no need for a detailed account of Stephen's thirty-nine *"exempla* of Purgatory,"* and in any case many of them are borrowed from older sources reviewed or cited earlier, such as Gregory the Great, Bede, Peter the Venerable, James of Vitry, and others.

I shall, however, consider three *exempla* that Stephen claims to have been told directly and that he introduces with the word *audivi*, "I have heard." In spite of this it seems likely that the first such case has a written source, since it occurs in Gervase of Tilbury's *Otia imperialia* (c. 1210), unless Stephen's informant himself read it there. In any case it is interesting to compare Gervase's version to Stephen's. Here is the way Gervase tells the story:

> In Sicily there is a mountain, Etna, ablaze with sulphurous flames, near the city of Catana. . . . The ordinary people call this mountain Mondjibel and the inhabitants of the region say that on its deserted slopes the great Arthur appeared in our own time. One day it came to pass that a groom employed by the bishop of Catana, who had overeaten, was overcome by lassitude. The horse that he was combing escaped and disappeared. The groom searched in vain along the slopes and precipices of the mountain. His worry increasing, he began to explore the dark caves of the mountain. A very narrow but flat path led him to a vast and charming meadow, full of delights.
>
> There, in a palace built by magic, he found Arthur lying on a regal bed. The king, upon learning why he had come, had the horse brought in and returned it to the boy so that he could take it back to the bishop. He told him how, wounded in a battle against his nephew Modred and the duke of the Saxons, Childeric, he had been lying there for a long time, waiting for his wounds to heal, but they constantly reopened. And, according to the natives who told me the story, he sent gifts to the bishop, who showed them off to a large crowd of people, who were struck dumb by this extraordinary story.[57]

And here is Stephen of Bourbon's version:

> I heard from a certain Apulian friar, named John, who said he came from the region where the event occurred, that a man was one day looking for his master's horse on Mount Etna, where they say Purgatory is located, near the city of Catana. He came to a city which he entered through a small iron gate. He asked the gatekeeper about the horse he was looking for. The gatekeeper answered that it must have gone to the court of his master, who would either return the horse or tell him what had become of it. The man begged the gatekeeper to tell him what he ought to do. The gatekeeper told him that he had better not eat a dish that would be offered to him. In this city he saw a crowd the size of the whole population of the earth, of all kinds

and all occupations. After crossing many courts he came to one in which he saw a great prince in the midst of his entourage. Many dishes were offered to him and he refused to eat. He was shown four beds and told that one of them had been prepared for his master and three others for usurers. And this prince told him that he would set a compulsory date for his master and the three usurers to appear or they would be brought by force, and he gave him a golden vessel with a golden cover. He was told not to remove the cover but to carry it to his lord as a sign that he should drink the contents. The horse was returned to the man. He returned and carried out his mission. The vessel was opened and a boiling flame surged forth. It was thrown into the sea along with the vessel and the sea caught fire. The other men, although they had confessed, had done so only out of fear and not out of true repentance, and on the appointed day they were carried off on four black horses.[58]

The differences between Gervase's account and Stephen's are these: Purgatory is not named in the former but is in the latter; the city has lost its charm; the fire of Purgatory is foreshadowed by the fire in the vessel; the prepared beds are no longer places of rest but suggest beds of torture; the horse prefigures the four black horses that carry souls to the other world, harbingers of death. Between one version and the other the story has been "infernalized," to borrow Arturo Graf's apt expression.[59]

Stephen claims to have heard another story from a friar, an old and pious priest. Once upon a time there was a provost who feared neither God nor man. God took pity on him and afflicted him with a serious illness. The man spent all that he possessed on drugs and other remedies, all to no avail. After five years, still as sick as ever, unable to stand up and without anything to live on, he became desperate because of his poverty, his miserable condition, and his suffering and began murmuring against God, who had kept him living for so long in such misery. An angel was sent to reproach him for murmuring in this way, to exhort him to be patient, and to promise that, if he withstood these ills for another two years, he would be fully purged and would go to Paradise. The man answered that he could not, that he would rather die. The angel told him that he had to choose between two years of suffering or two days of purgatorial punishment before God would allow him to go to Paradise. He chose two days in Purgatory and was carried off by the angel and sent to Purgatory. The harshness (*acerbitas*) of the punishment seemed so severe that before half a day had elapsed he felt he had been there forever. He began to cry, to moan, to call the angel a liar, to say that he was not an angel but a devil. The angel came, exhorted him to be patient, reproached him for murmuring, and told him he had been there only a short while. The man begged the angel to return him to his former state and said that, if this was permitted, he would be ready to endure patiently his afflictions not merely for two years but until the Last Judgment. The angel agreed and the provost patiently endured all his ills for the remainder of the two years.[60]

This story clearly, not to say simplistically, depicts the elementary proportionality between days in Purgatory and years on earth and shows that the harshness of purgatorial punishment is infinitely greater than that of any earthly punishment.

One final *exemplum*: "I have heard," Stephen of Bourbon tells us, "that a child of a great family died when he was nearly nine years of age. In order to engage in gambling he had accepted a loan at interest from the family of his father and of his mother [*sic*]. He did not think of this at the moment of death and, though he had confessed, he had not made restitution." Shortly thereafter, the child's soul appears to a member of his family and says that he is being severely punished for not having paid what he owed. The person to whom he appears inquires about the debts and pays them all off. The child then reappears to him and announces that he has been set free of all punishment. He looks very happy. "This child was the son of the Duke of Burgundy, Hugh, and the person to whom he appeared was the duke's own mother, the child's grandmother, who told me the story herself."[61] This story is a schematic reminder of the mechanics governing the apparitions of souls from Purgatory and it emphasizes the importance of the restitution of property for the liberation from Purgatory. Restitution has become an instrument of salvation as well as a regulatory principle of economic life in this world.

Stephen of Bourbon's treatise seems to have been highly successful, and his *exempla* were frequently cited. Their use helped to popularize the image of a vulgarized, infernalized Purgatory, which became an object of simplistic calculation.

For one last look at the *exempla* of Purgatory, let us turn next to an anthology of *exempla* classified in alphabetical order under various headings in the *Alphabetum narrationum*, which was compiled in the early years of the fourteenth century by the Dominican Arnold of Liège and of which there are many more or less faithful copies in the vernacular (English, Catalan, and French) as well as Latin dating from the fourteenth and fifteenth centuries. Under the heading "Purgatory" we find fourteen *exempla* grouped according to eight themes. Four deal with the punishments of Purgatory, their intensity, their duration, and the fear they inspire: "The punishments of Purgatory are diverse" (no. 676), which means that purgatorial fire is not the only one; "the punishment of purgatory is harsh (*acerba*) and long," as Augustine taught; "the punishment of Purgatory, even if it does not last very long, seems to last for a long time," suggesting the inverted time scheme of folklore; and finally, "Purgatory is more feared by the good than by the wicked," which locates Purgatory closer to Paradise than to Hell but also attests to its severity.

Two *exempla* are concerned with the location of Purgatory and acknowledge that purgation can take place on earth: "Some are purged among the living" and "some do their Purgatory among the people in whose midst they sinned." Finally, two of the *exempla* deal with suffrages: "The punishment of Purgatory is alleviated by prayer," and "the punishment of Purgatory is effaced by the mass." The *exempla* are borrowed from Gregory the Great, Peter the Venerable, *Saint Patrick's Purgatory*, the Cistercians Helinand of Froimont and Caesarius of Heisterbach, James of Vitry, and the Dominican Humbert of Romans, the author of a "gift of fear" (*De dono timoris*) very similar to that of Stephen of Bourbon.[62]

To conclude this study of the use of the sermon and the *exemplum* to popularize Purgatory in the thirteenth century, I shall first discuss the biographical background of the first Dominicans, then consider preaching among the Beguines, and finally turn to the exploitation of visions of Purgatory for political ends.

DOMINICANS IN PURGATORY

In the mid-thirteenth century the mendicant orders supplanted the Cistercians in the spiritual administration of society. But some Dominicans and Franciscans remained in large part faithful to monastic traditions. A contemporary of Stephen of Bourbon, for example, one Gerard of Frachet, suggest a view of the Dominicans' interest in Purgatory rather different from Stephen's.

Gerard of Frachet provides us with invaluable evidence about the diffusion of the belief in Purgatory within the Dominican order. A Limousin born in Chalus (Haute-Vienne), Gerard joined the Dominicans in Paris in 1225, became prior of Limoges and then provincial for Provence, and died at Limoges in 1271. He wrote a history of the Dominican order between 1203 and 1254, based on his memorabilia. It consists of five parts. The first is devoted to the beginnings of the order, the second to Saint Dominic, the third to the master-general Jordan of Saxony, Dominic's successor as the head of the order, the fourth to the progress of the order (*de progressu ordinis*), and the fifth to the death of friars.

The structure of the work is significant. The fifth and last part aptly expresses the attitudes of a religious milieu that is representative of both tradition and innovation in the Church. Death gives meaning to life; it is situated at the point where earthly existence joins eschatological destiny. Gerard of Frachet attests to the focusing of attention on the moment of death in its relation to what lies beyond death, a development that partly accounts for the success of Purgatory.

Let us take a closer look at part five of the "Lives of the Brothers of the Order of Preachers" or "Chronicle of the Order from 1203 to 1254." What we find is a description of all the possible ways in which friars can die and all the possible conditions in which they may find themselves in the hereafter. First to be discussed are the martyrs of the order, the happy dead, and visions and revelations that accompany death. Then comes a discussion of the situations of souls after death. Here we find, first of all, a description of the friars in Purgatory, followed by remarks on the snares of the Devil, ways of helping the dead, the unhappy fate of apostates, and the glory of those who win renown after death by working miracles. Thus, like Purgatory itself, the *exempla* concerning the friars in Purgatory occupy a pivotal, intermediary position.

The fourteen *exempla* or stories of Purgatory proposed by Gerard of Frachet do not form a treatise as in the case of Caesarius of Heisterbach or Stephen of Bourbon. Their purpose is to serve the glory of the order, to meet its internal needs. Stories showing happy friars in glory alternate with other stories designed to make the brothers think. They are reminiscent of the *Exordium magnum* written by Conrad of Eberbach for the Cistercian order at the beginning of the century, and compared with the work of Caesarius in particular they seem rather traditional.

The first story goes like this: An old preacher and a novice die on the same day at the Cologne monastery. After three days the novice appears. Because of his fervor his stay in Purgatory has been short. By contrast the preacher does not appear until a month has gone by. His stay has been longer because of his compromises with the secular clergy. Yet his destiny is more brilliant than that of the novice, as is symbolized by his garments, which are decorated with precious gems and a gold crown, rewards for the converts he has made.

The next four stories are set in England. At Derby a young friar on the brink of death passes from joy to anguish. He experiences joy because first Saint Edmund and then the Virgin appear to him. He experiences anguish because, though he is virtually certain of being saved, he fears that the venial (*modica*) sins that weigh him down may nevertheless consign him to perdition. The story is a reminder that a thin line separates venial from mortal sins, Purgatory from Hell.

Friar Richard, a lector in an English monastery on his deathbed, at first has terrible apparitions and then a revelation that he will be saved thanks to the aid of the Dominican friars as well as the Franciscans, whom he has always loved. The story is clearly a call for collaboration between the two orders.

Friar Alan, prior of York, also assailed by frightening visions at the moment of death, would rather endure terrifying fire until the Last Judgment than see again the devils that appeared to him. Thus Purgatory, even in its most painful form, is more easily endured than even the external aspects of hell.

A curate, terrified by a vision that Hell lies in store, joins the Dominicans and after his death appears to his confessor to reveal that he has been saved and that the confessor will be too.

The next two stories take place "in Spain," at Santarem (today in Portugal). In one we see a friar go to Purgatory because he receives help from the secular clergy at the moment of death, and in the other a second friar suffers the same fate for the conceit of believing himself a good singer.

An Italian friar from Bologna suffers Purgatory for having been overly passionate about architecture. A Portuguese friar from Lisbon is punished, also in Purgatory, for taking an undue interest in manuscripts. The friar Gaillard of Orthez sees his breast and flanks burned in an apparition because he took too great an interest in the construction of new monasteries; he asks the friars to pray for him. Friar John Ballestier of Limoges spends seven days in Purgatory for his sins and attests to the fact that the punishment for venial sins is very severe. He adds that angels came to lead him to Paradise.

This detail is quite interesting because it prefigures the iconography of Purgatory: before long we begin to see angels reaching out to the dead to help them out of the new place and up to Heaven.

Friar Peter of Toulouse, devoted as he is to his order, and despite all the converts he has made, reveals in a dream that he has spent several months in Purgatory for unspecified sins.

In another story, an excellent friar dies with a look of terror on his face. When he appears a few days later, he is asked why he had this frightened look. His answer is from Job: "*Quia territi purgabuntur*," for they shall be purged in terror. Another friar undergoes torture because he loved wine so much that he drank it undiluted.

These *exempla* illustrate certain features of the system of Purgatory: namely, the duration of the stay and the importance of apparitions. They are particularly instructive for what they reveal about their use within the Dominican order. In part they offer a whole casuistry of venial sins. Beyond that they paint a picture of life in the order in which the friars' concerns are shown to be closer to the traditional concerns of monks than to the intellectual concerns some writers have ascribed to them, based on the example of a few major figures.

At this point I would like to turn from the Dominican friars to the Beguines, women inspired like the Dominicans by the desire to lead a new kind of religious life, for whom meditation on Purgatory was prescribed.

PURGATORY AND THE BEGUINES

The world of the Beguines in the thirteenth century was a highly interesting one. They were women who withdrew from the world to live a religious life either singly or in groups in houses set apart in special quarters of certain cities. Their status was midway between that of a laywoman and that of a nun. They aroused both interest and anxiety on the part of the Church and were made the object of a special apostolate.

In studying the sermons delivered in 1272–73 by preachers, for the most part Dominicans and Franciscans, at the Sainte-Catherine chapel of the beguinage of Paris, which was founded by Saint Louis around 1260, Nicole Beriou frequently encountered mention of Purgatory.[63] One sermon depicted the glorious souls in Paradise, represented by Jerusalem, exhorting their brothers in Purgatory, represented by Egypt. We read that the punishments of Purgatory are harsh and that we must concern ourselves with the fate of our relatives, tormented and powerless in Purgatory.[64]

Another sermon exhorts the Beguines to pray for "those in Purgatory" that God may set free "his prisoners from the prison of Purgatory."[65]

The idea that can be seen taking shape here is the following: it is advantageous to pray for souls in Purgatory, because, once they reach Paradise, they will pray for those who have helped them out. "They will not be ungrateful," a second preacher maintains. Yet another exhorts the Beguines to pray for those who are in Purgatory, not for those in Hell but rather those who are in the Lord's prison and who, as one says in the vernacular, "cry and bawl," whom the living must set free by means of alms, fasts, and prayers.[66]

We must not wait for Purgatory or Hell to complete our penance, one preacher insists,[67] while another, a Franciscan, lists the six categories of individual for whom one must regularly pray (*pro quibus solet orari*) and includes those who are in Purgatory in his list.[68] A third preacher indicates that prayers must be said especially "for relatives and friends."[69] He indicates that the first fruit of penance is to deliver the soul from punishment in Purgatory,[70] and the Franciscan warns that "those who say 'Bah! I'll do my penance in Purgatory' are crazy, because there is no comparison between the severity of punishment in Purgatory and any kind of punishment in this world."[71] Of particular interest is the declaration made by one Franciscan preacher on Palm Sunday. He has no wish to be one of those "great weighers of souls" (*non consuevi esse de illis magnis ponderatoribus*) who consign some to Hell and others to Heaven. "The middle way," he says, "seems the safest to me. Thus, since I cannot see into the hearts of different men, I would rather send them to Purgatory than to Hell out of despair, and the rest I leave to the supreme master, the Holy Spirit, who instructs our hearts from within."[72] Is there a more beautiful expression of Purgatory's function?

This little corpus of sermons to the Beguines in Paris accentuates three important aspects of Purgatory: (1) Purgatory is God's prison. This vast incarceration of souls imposes on the living the duty to pray for the liberation of the imprisoned, a duty that harks back to the ancient tradition of praying for prisoners in the early days when Christians were the victims of persecution, a tradition that has been sharpened by sentiments of justice and love. (2) Purgatory establishes solidarity between the living and the dead, a point stressed by almost all the preachers. And finally, (3) Purgatory is closely related to penance: either penance delivers the soul from Purgatory, or Purgatory completes the penitential process.

PURGATORY AND POLITICS

In a chronicle composed at the Dominican monastery at Colmar in the early fourteenth century we find a story which shows that Purgatory was from the beginning a political weapon in the hands of the Church. It is the story of a mime who sees in Purgatory Rudolph of Habsburg (1271–90), the son of Rudolph, king of the Romans.

The story, recounted by the Dominican Otto, is supposed to have taken place in Lucerne. In this city lived two friends, a blacksmith and a mime by the name of Zalchart. One day the mime goes to perform at a spot where a wedding is being held. While he is gone the blacksmith dies. Mounted on a large horse he then appears to Zalchart and takes him and his hurdy-gurdy to a mountain, which opens to allow them to enter. There they meet many great personages who have died, including Rudolph, duke of Alsace, the son of Rudolph, king of the Romans. The dead approach Zalchart and ask him to tell their wives and friends that they have been suffering very harsh punishments, one for having pillaged, the other for having practiced usury; they beg their living relatives to restore what they have taken. Rudolph also confides a message for his heirs to Zalchart, instructing them to make restitution of certain usurped property. He also tells Zalchart to inform his father, the king of the Romans, that he is going to die soon and come to this place of torment. As a seal of authenticity he makes two painful marks on Zalchart's neck. The mountain then opens to allow Zalchart to make his way back to the world of the living and he delivers the messages entrusted to him, but the "sign of recognition" (*intersignum*) on his neck becomes infected and he dies ten days later.

The whole story is permeated with the atmosphere of folklore: the blacksmith is a demonic guide and the mime one of the Devil's fiddlers. Purgatory in the tale is so "infernalized" that when Zalchart asks Rudolph, "Where are you?" Rudolph answers, "In Hell."[73]

Purgatory also infiltrated the world of saints and hagiography. By the thirteenth century sainthood had come under the control of the papacy: saints were no longer made by the *vox populi* (warranted by miracles) but by the *vox Ecclesiae*, the voice of the Church. The concept of sainthood evolved, moreover: for recognition of sanctity miracles were still necessary, but beyond that a virtuous life and spiritual aura acquired ever increasing importance. A new type of saint, different from the martyrs, confessors, and miracle workers of old, was incarnated in Saint Francis of Assisi, whose model was Christ himself.[74] But intellectuals and common folk alike were affected by popular forms of piety, mass devotion, that drew sustenance from traditional hagiographic sources. In addition to individual lives of saints there grew up anthologies of hagiographic legends written in a new spirit; even in medieval catalogues these are referred to as *legenda nova* or "new legends." To be sure, the primary audience for these anthologies was "the small world of clerics living in community," and the "mass audience" was not directly affected. But the new spirit did filter down to the masses through preachers and artists, who drew extensively on the legends for frescos, miniatures, and sculpture. More than that, a vast effort was made to translate, adapt, and abridge the legends, making them available in the vernacular. This put them within reach of those inmates of monasteries and convents who spoke no Latin, the lay brothers and the nuns, and also made the legends available to lay society generally.[75]

PURGATORY IN THE "GOLDEN LEGEND"

Italy was rather slow to contribute to this outpouring of hagiography but by 1260 or so it gave the world the legendarian who, despite his mediocrity, enjoyed the most spectacular success: Jacopo da Varazze (Jacobus da Voragine), the author of the *Golden Legend* (*Legenda aurea*). A potpourri of material drawn from diverse sources, the *Golden Legend* nevertheless welcomed "modern" devotional themes. Purgatory was accepted.[76] It figures prominently in two chapters, one devoted to Saint Patrick, the other dealing with the Commemoration of Souls.

The *Golden Legend* attributes the following origin to Saint Patrick's Purgatory: "Since Saint Patrick was preaching in Ireland and not harvesting much fruit, he prayed to the Lord to give a sign that would frighten the Irish and induce them to repent. Following the Lord's orders, he drew with his stick a large circle at a certain spot; the earth opened up inside the circle and a very large, very deep pit appeared. It was revealed to Saint Patrick that here was a location of Purgatory. If anyone wished to descend into it, he would have no further penance to accomplish and would undergo no other purgatory for his sins. Many did not come back, and those who did come back were supposed to stay from one morning until the following morning. But many entered who did not come back." Jacopo da Varazze then summarizes the pamphlet by H of Saltrey (who is not named), but he changes the name of the hero, substituting a noble named Nicolas for the knight Owein.[77]

The collection of legends parallels the liturgical calendar, giving summary accounts of the doctrines associated with the major events and seasons of the liturgical year. Purgatory is mentioned in connection with the Commemoration of Souls on November 2.[78] The discussion immediately takes up the problem of Purgatory. The commemoration is described as a day whose purpose is to bring suffrages to the dead who are not the beneficiaries of specific assistance. On Peter Damian's authority the practice is said to have been begun by Odilo, abbot of Cluny. The text we encountered earlier has here been modified so as to make Odilo not the auditor of the story of the monk returned from his pilgrimage but rather the direct witness of the cries and screams not of the dead undergoing torture but of demons infuriated at the sight of souls being wrested from their grasp by alms and prayers.

Jacopo da Varraze then answers two questions: (1) Who is in Purgatory? (2) What can be done for those who are there?

The Ligurian Dominican, a devoted adept of the scholastic practice of numbered subdivisions, breaks the first question down into three parts: (1) Who must be purged? (2) By whom? (3) Where? In answer to subquestion one, there are three categories of the purged: (1) those who die without fully completing their penance; (2) those who descend into Purgatory (*qui in purgatorium descendunt*) because the penance imposed on them by their confessor was less than it should have been (Jacopo also allows for the case in which penance is greater than it should have been, thus affording the soul a supplementary glory); and (3) those who "carry with them wood, hay, and straw," a reference to Paul's First Epistle to the Corinthians, which Jacopo uses to discuss venial sins.

In developing these principles Jacopo outlines an arithmetic of Purgatory. For example, he says that "if one was supposed to endure a punishment of two months in Purgatory, one could be aided [by suffrages] in such a way as to be set free at the end of just one month." Following Augustine, he points out that the punishment of purgatorial fire, though not eternal, is very harsh and exceeds every terrestrial punishment, even the torments of martyrs. Jacopo carries the infernalization of Purgatory rather far, holding, for example, that it is demons, wicked angels, that are responsible for tormenting the dead in Purgatory. Where other writers maintained that Satan and the demons looked on with pleasure at the torments of souls being purged, Jacopo argues the opposite, namely, that it is the good angels that (may) come to watch and console. The dead in Purgatory also have another consolation: they await "the future glory [Heaven] in certitude." With respect to this future glory they have a certitude "of the middle type" (*medio modo*), emphasizing the importance of the "intermediate" as a category. The living wait in uncertainty; the elect are certain and do not wait; souls in Purgatory wait but in certainty. On the other hand, Jacopo da Varazze, who has at bottom no ideas of his own but merely sets the opinions of others side by side, concludes his discussion of this question by saying that it may be better to believe that punishment in Purgatory is carried out not by demons but by the commandment of God alone.

On the next question, the location of Purgatory, after examining what had by this time become the prevailing opinion, Jacopo lists a series of other views that he believes to be compatible with it. The common view, he says, is this: "Purgation is accomplished in a place near Hell called Purgatory."[79] He adds, however, that "this is the opinion [*positio*] of most learned men [*sapientes*], but that others believe that it is situated in the air and in the torrid zone." Furthermore, "by divine dispensation, various places are sometimes assigned to certain souls either to alleviate their punishment or with an eye to their more rapid liberation or in order to edify us or, again, so that the punishment may be completed at the site of the sin or, yet again, thanks to the prayer of a saint." In support of the latter hypothesis he cites several authorities and *exempla*, mainly drawn from Gregory the Great but also including the story of master Silo, originally from Peter the Chanter but also found in James of Vitry and Stephen of Bourbon; for the intervention of a saint he refers to *Saint Patrick's Purgatory*.

As for suffrages, Jacopo adheres to the standard view that four kinds are particularly effective: the prayer of friends, alms, masses, and fasting. He invokes the authority of Gregory the Great (the story of Paschasius and several others), Peter the Venerable, Peter the Chanter, the last two books of the Maccabees, and Henry of Ghent, a celebrated Parisian master of the second half of the century, as well as a story that is interesting because it mentions indulgences offered in connection with the Crusades, in this case the crusade against the Albigensians: "The indulgences of the Church are equally effective. For example, a papal legate once asked a valiant warrior to fight the Albigensians on behalf of the Church and awarded him an indulgence for his dead father; he served the Church for forty years, at the end of which his father appeared to him in splendor and thanked him for his liberation."[80]

Finally, Jacopo indicates that it is the "medium good" who benefit from suffrages. In a final palinode he retracts his idea that the suffrages of the wicked are of no use to the souls in Purgatory and says that this is not true of either the celebration of masses, which are always valuable, or the carrying out of good works that the dead person orders the living person to do, even if the latter is wicked.

This lengthy section concludes with an *exemplum* taken from the *Chronicle* of the Cistercian Helinand of Froimont from the beginning of the thirteenth century, the action of which is set in the time of Charlemagne, in the year 807 to be precise. "A knight on his way to Charlemagne's war against the Moors asks a relative to sell his horse and give the money to the poor if he should die in battle. The knight dies and this relative keeps the horse, which pleases him greatly. Shortly thereafter the dead knight appears to him, shining as brightly as the sun, and says: 'Good kinsman, for eight days you have made me suffer punishments in Purgatory because you did not sell the horse and give the money to the poor; but you shall not take it with you to Paradise [*impune non feres*] for on this very day the demons are going to take your soul off to Hell, while I, purged, am on my way to the kingdom of God.' Suddenly there were heard in the air sounds like the roaring of lions, bears, and wolves, and he was removed from earth."[81] This is a version of one of the two *exempla* on Purgatory contained in the James of Vitry's *sermones vulgares* as well as in the works of Odo of Cheriton and Thomas of Cantimpré. It is a classic from the collections of *exempla*. As recounted in the *Golden Legend*, it became more or less the *vade mecum* of Purgatory in the thirteenth century. It contains most of the essential items of information about Purgatory from the time of Augustine on, with several more recent texts added in order to make further theoretical points or provide illustrations.

A SAINT OF PURGATORY: LUTGARD

Hagiographic literature provides surprising support for the contention that Purgatory enjoyed wide popularity. The souls in Purgatory are in need of assistance. They get it primarily from their relatives, their friends, and their communities. But what about saints? Are not certain saints obliged to serve as intercessors, helpers? Naturally the Virgin, the mediatrix par excellence, plays a particularly active role. Saint Nicholas, already patron of many things, was at this time adding Purgatory to the list, so to speak. But one case is especially worthy of note. This is the rise, in the thirteenth century, of the cult of Saint Lutgard, who was nothing less than the saint of Purgatory. She was a Cistercian, educated in the Benedictine monastery of Saint-Frond, and may have been no more than a lay sister. She died blind in 1246 at the monastery of Aywières in the diocese of Namur in Brabant. She seems to have been associated in some way with the Beguines and had connections with James of Vitry, from whom she received at least one letter, and with Mary of Oignies, a celebrated Beguine, whose life was written by James of Vitry. She made a name for herself in the history of mysticism and along with certain Beguines helped to promote worship of the Heart of Christ.[82]

Immediately after Lutgard's death, a well-known Dominican, Thomas of Cantimpré, wrote a *Life*, sometime between 1246 and 1248. But Lutgard was not officially canonized. She never, Thomas tells us, learned to speak French (perhaps because she wished to stay close to the laity by holding on to her native Flemish culture) and seems to have been regarded as somewhat suspect by the official Church. Innocent IV instructed Thomas of Cantimpré to correct his first version of her biography. The Dominican refers to Lutgard as "pious" (*pia*) and not as saintly (*sancta* or *beata*), but she was regarded and honored as a saint "in the old way." According to Thomas's *Life*, she specialized in liberating souls from Purgatory. Some of those she helped were notorious not to say famous personages.

The first we hear about was Simon, abbot of Fouilly, "a fervent man but hard on those under him." He died prematurely. He was particularly fond of the pious Lutgard, who was greatly upset by his death. She did special penances (*afflictiones*) and fasted on his behalf, asking the Lord to free his soul. The Lord answered, "Thanks to you I shall be benevolent towards the one you are praying for." A determined militant when it came to releasing souls from Purgatory, Lutgard then said, "Lord, I shall not stop crying and I shall not be satisfied by your promises until I have seen the one whom I implore you to set free." Then the Lord appeared to her and showed her the soul in person, now set free from Purgatory. "After this Simon frequently appeared to Lutgard and told her that he would have spent forty years in Purgatory if her prayer had not helped him to secure God's mercy."[83]

At the moment of her death the blessed Mary of Oignies attested to the fact that Lutgard's prayers, fasts, and other activities had great power. She made the following prophecy: "Beneath heaven, the world has no intercessor more faithful and more effective in liberating souls from Purgatory by her prayers than dame Lutgard. During her life she will now accomplish spiritual miracles, and after her death she will accomplish corporeal miracles."[84]

Cardinal James of Vitry himself may have benefited from Lutgard's intercession. Four days after his death, Lutgard, who did not know he had died, was transported to Heaven and saw James's soul being taken by angels to Paradise. "The spirit of Lutgard congratulated him and said, 'Most Reverend Father, I did not know of your death. When did you leave your body?' He answered, 'Four days ago, and I spent three nights and two days in Purgatory.' She was astonished: 'Why did you not let me know immediately after death, so that as a survivor I could deliver you from punishment with the help of the sisters' prayers?' 'The Lord,' he answered, 'did not want to sadden you with my suffering, he preferred to console you with my liberation, with my completed Purgatory, and my glorification. But you will soon follow me.' With these words the pious Lutgard returned to herself and with great joy forecast to the sisters her coming death, her Purgatory, and her glorification." According to Thomas of Cantimpré, there was a second witness to James of Vitry's passage through Purgatory, a friar from the Dominican monastery in Rome where James was originally buried, to whom God also revealed on the fourth day after James's death that he had been purged and glorified.[85]

Finally, the blessed Mary of Oignies appears to Lutgard and asks her to intervene on behalf of their friend Baldwin of Barbenzon, the prior of Oignies and former chaplain of Aywières, whom she had promised to help at the moment of death.[86]

Thomas of Cantimpré ends with the following words: "O venerable Mary, truthful in testimony and faithful in promise, you who were kind enough to ask the pious Lutgard for the suffrage of her prayers for all mortals, you who, when you were still on this earth, prayed to her who was the most powerful for liberating souls from Purgatory, now exalted in heavenly joy you have again come to ask her help for a dead friend."

THE LIVING AND THE DEAD: WILLS AND OBITUARIES

Purgatory also figures among the principal manifestations of the new forms of solidarity between the living and the dead that emerged in the thirteenth century. Documentary evidence of the change is contained, for example, in wills. Purgatory makes only a timid appearance in thirteenth-century wills and does not really catch on until the fourteenth century, and even then there are regional differences.[87] Consider the will of Renaud of Burgundy, count of Montbeliard, which dates from 1296 (with a codicil added in 1314). The will does endeavor to disburden the soul of the future deceased by arranging for payment of his debts and for masses to be celebrated on the anniversary of his death "for the remedy of the soul" (the expression *pro remedio animae* was traditionally used in deeds of gift and later in wills, a usage revived in the twelfth century) and thus adverts to suffrages for the dead in Purgatory. But the word Purgatory is not used.[88] What is needed is a thorough study of the the attitude of the mendicant orders, which are known to have been eager "legacy hunters" as well as popularizers of Purgatory (through the preaching of sermons and *exempla*). Had they not by the end of the thirteenth century supplanted the Cistercians as popularizers of Purgatory?

Religious establishments always kept books of remembrance of the dead. But the death rolls of the preceding period now gave way to new remembrances known as "obituaries," and though Purgatory does not figure in them directly, its growing importance played a great role in the change, according to one specialist in the subject, Jean-Loup Lemaître:

> By the end of the twelfth century, with the rediscovery of the will, the increase in the number of pious legacies, and the spread of the belief in Purgatory, necrological documentation underwent a considerable change. Simple inscriptions honored by a commemoration and suffrages were supplanted by inscriptions accompanied by indications of an office to be celebrated. The *officium plenum*, once an exception, now became the rule. Since the office for the dead, whether solemn or not, was a supererogatory service, it was important to ensure that it would be celebrated by means of a foundation, which led to a change in the character of the notices. In addition to the name of the deceased and his rank or office these now included mention of the elements that made up the foundation, generally in the form of rent: details included the property serving as the basis of the rent, a list of debtors and their heirs, and sometimes even instructions as to distribution, so much to the celebrant, so much to his assistants, for lighting, for bell-ringers, etc. In some cases even the type of service to be cele-

brated was mentioned. Sometimes the foundation was made while the beneficiary was still alive, and the service founded in such cases was a mass, usually for the Virgin or the Holy Spirit; after the death of the founder this was to be converted to a mass on the anniversary of death.

The inscription process thus varied and evolved over time. Initially, the obits of members of the community, spiritual associates, and anniversary foundations for which modalities of execution were indicated were listed side by side. Gradually, the inscription of the foundations came to predominate and supplanted the automatic, complimentary inscription of mere names to commemorate. To be sure, it was still laudable to remind the chapter or refectory of the names of the deceased for whom the suffrages of the community were required, but the essential thing was to know which offices had to be celebrated, on whose behalf they were to be said, and what pittance (food allowance) or sum of money, as the case may be, was attached to the celebration. The book therefore had a double use but was hardly used any longer to record obits founded in the community.

This is why, beginning in the thirteenth century, we witness the gradual disappearance from these compilations of the names of members of the community (particularly in monastic communities) in favor of laymen, bourgeois or nobles concerned about securing salvation and abbreviating their stay in Purgatory by means of pious foundations.[89]

Finally, we come across at least one explicit piece of evidence concerning the place of Purgatory in the preoccupations of the members of one confraternity. The confraternities, like the funerary associations of antiquity, were associations one of whose primary concerns was to supervise funerals and suffrages for dead members. Specifically, I want to look at the charter of the confraternity of barbers in Arras, which dates from 1247.

This text (originally written in Old French, since one of the parties, the barbers, was a group of laymen who knew no Latin) is of great significance. Purgatory was central to this association, which was a type of sworn society specific to the new urban environment. Such an association linked the members, male and female, of a profession governed by elected officials of a communal type (mayor and aldermen) to the community of one of the new mendicant religious orders, the Dominicans, whose apostolate was closely bound up with the new urban society.

Be it known, to all who are or shall be, that the prior of the Preaching Friars of Arras and the convent of aforesaid Friars have granted, by the authority of the master of the Order, to the barbers of Arras a *charité* [confraternity] to be made in the honor of God and of Our Lady and Our Lord Saint Dominic.

And to them are granted three masses each year in perpetuity to all the brothers and sisters who shall join the confraternity, remain members, and die members. The first mass is the day of the translation of Monsignor Saint Dominic and the two others are the anniversary of their father and mother passed away. And to them are granted full association [*compaignie*] and full participation in all the goods that have been done and will be done day and night in their convent of Arras and by all their order in holy Christendom for all the living who in the Confraternity shall maintain themselves in grace, and, for those who shall die, to abbreviate their punishments in Purgatory and hasten their eternal rest. To all the aforementioned things the prior and friars associate [*acompaigne*] all the men and all the women who will enter into this Confraternity through the mediation of the mayor and aldermen whom the barbers shall choose. And in order to certify this deed and render it established [*estande*—stable, fixed] and provable, the prior and convent of the aforementioned friars have sealed this charter with their seal. This was done in the year of the Incarnation of Our Lord MCC and XLVII, in the month of April.[90]

About this text—to my knowledge the only one of its kind to have survived—I should like to offer two hypotheses. First, that the mendicants, promoters of new attitudes toward death, played a major role in the popularization of Purgatory. And second, that Purgatory was of particular interest to the members of certain professions, those that were held in contempt, regarded as suspect, such as the barber-surgeons who worked in daily contact with the body and with blood and whose livelihood was classed among the disreputable occupations, the *inhonesta mercimonia*. Is it not likely that the barbers, like the usurers, saw Purgatory as their best chance of escaping Hell? And is it not possible that one of the consequences of Purgatory's progress was to rehabilitate professions the spiritual position of whose members had been precarious, restoring their prospect of salvation and thus giving religious sanction to their increased social status?

Purgatory in the Vernacular: The Case of French

A study of literature in the vernacular remains to be done. Its interest would lie in what we might learn about the propagation of the new hereafter in literary works "consumed" directly by the lay public. Of course we encounter Purgatory in collections of *exempla* in the vernacular or in "catchall" chronicles such as the *Ménéstrel de Reims*. But by the thirteenth century literary production in, say, French was so abundant that the best we can do is take a representative sampling. On the basis of samples produced by a number of scholars,[91] I think that Purgatory had a secondary part in various literary genres. From Tobler-Lommatzch's *Vocabulaire de l'ancien français* we learn that Purgatory never figured in epics (a genre that antedates Purgatory, though *chansons de geste* were composed in the thirteenth century) and that the first literary work in French to mention Purgatory was Marie de France's *Espurgatoire saint Patriz.*

Philip of Novare, an Italian knight, was a jurist and writer involved in affairs in the Holy Land and Cyprus. In his retirement, sometime after 1260, when he was more than sixty years of age, he began to write in French, the literary language of Christendom, a treatise in which he sums up the experience of a lifetime: *Les quatre temps d'âge d'homme* (*The Four Ages of Man*). The young, Philip tells us, are guilty of many acts of imprudence and even of folly. As they do little penance in this world, they must pay a rather heavy and lengthy penalty in Purgatory.[92]

In the *Roman de Baudouin de Sebourc* we read the lines,

> He goes straight to paradise . . .
> Without passing through Purgatory.[93]

These lines recall the intermediate role of Purgatory, its position as a way station on the road to Paradise.

Gautier of Coincy, canon of Soissons and author of the richest and best-known collection of *Miracles of Our Lady* in verse (1223), speaks of Purgatory as a place of punishment:

> In Purgatory is the sum.
> Led there he was for the misdeeds
> He committed in this life.[94]

Jehan of Journi, a lord of Picardy, wrote the following words in his *Dîme de pénitence* (*Penitential Tithe*) composed in Cyprus in 1288:

> And a wise man should moderate his behavior
> As much as he can.
> Let him give alms while he is alive
> So that at his death these may help
> Him to go to Purgatory,
> To make himself pure for paradise.[95]

Doubtless the most interesting of all these literary texts is this passage from the fabliau *La Cour de paradis* (*The Court of Paradise*):

> It is told that the Day of Souls
> Is after All Saints' Day
> Of that may all be certain;
> She tells us this story,
> Tha the souls in Purgatory
> Are these days long at rest;
> But that those who will not be forgiven
> Who will be damned for their sins
> Take it as certain
> That they will have neither rest nor sojourn.

The connection between All Saints' and the Commemoration of Souls (the first and second of November, respectively) is strongly emphasized, and the connection of both solemnities with Purgatory is clearly indicated. The novelty of these verses lies above all in the fact that, whereas the idea of an infernal Sabbath, a weekly respite for the damned, is denied, the notion of a two-day respite in Purgatory has supplanted James of Vitry's notion of Sunday rest. Infernalization must have progressed considerably to allow the transfer to Purgatory of the theme of respite for the damned.

At the turn of the fourteenth century there occurred a great event that enhanced the status of Purgatory in response to both the aims of the Church and the aspirations of the faithful. This was the Jubilee of 1300.[96]

INDULGENCES FOR PURGATORY: THE JUBILEE OF 1300

In that year Pope Boniface VIII, already locked in combat with the king of France, Philip the Fair, and through him with all of lay Christian society, increasingly restive under the pontifical yoke, for the first time invited all Christians to come to Rome for the celebration of the jubilee in remembrance of the Mosaic law set forth in chapter 25 of Leviticus. The year was to be set aside as a sort of super-sabbatical, a year of expiation and rest, of liberation and return to the roots; this was to be repeated henceforth at intervals of seven times seven years, i.e., every fiftieth year. These symbolic year of jubilee were probably never effectively realized. Here again Christianity continued Jewish practice; Luke 4:19 foretold "a Lord's year of grace." Ever since the early Middle Ages, the idea of the jubilee, though not put into practice by the Church, was interpreted by certain ecclesiastical authors in the light of new Christian concepts of penance and forgiveness. Hence it is not surprising that the revival of the jubilee should have been linked to the recent rise of Purgatory, which was also associated, historically and theoretically, with penance.

Isidore of Seville defined the jubilee in his *Etymologies* as a year of remission (*remissionis annus*).[97] The promoters of the Jubilee of 1300 emphasized not only that it was a year of absolution but also that it marked the beginning of a new century. Thus the jubilee was held out to the faithful as a culmination of penance, a sort of substitute millenium tightly controlled by the Church and the Holy See.

The pope granted pilgrims who came to Rome for the jubilee year a plenary indulgence (*plenissima venia peccatorum*) complete pardon of all sins, a favor hitherto bestowed only on crusaders. The benefit of this indulgence was extended, moreover, to include the dead, that is, to souls in Purgatory. This unprecedented extension came about late in the year and in a rather indirect way.

It was on Christmas Day in the year 1300 that Boniface VIII granted a plenary indulgence to all pilgrims who had died while on pilgrimage, either en route or in Rome, as well as to all those who, having had the firm intention to embark on a pilgrimage, were prevented from doing so.[98] The measure nevertheless proved to be of the utmost importance.

What the pope appeared to have decided on was "the immediate liberation from all punishment of certain souls in Purgatory."[99] To be sure, the theoretical powers of the pope in this domain had already been delineated, most notably by Bonaventure and Thomas Aquinas, as we saw earlier. But apparently those powers had never before been put to use. The living had hitherto been able to free the dead from Purgatory only *per modum suffragii*, that is, by the transfer to the dead of meits acquired by the living through good works.

It seems that, after the thunderbolt of 1300, the pope's power to free souls from Purgatory remained purely theoretical until the fifteenth century. It did not matter, for example, that the canonist Alessandro Lombardo (d. 1314) asserted that the pope could aid those in Purgatory with indulgences either indirectly or "by accident," and that he could accord indulgences to all "who pray or do good for the dead who are in Purgatory." Boniface's successors in the fourteenth century did not, so far as we know, make use of this exorbitant power over the other world. But the first step, however limited in scope, had already been taken. A new phase in the inclusion of indulgences in the system of Purgatory had begun.

Persistent Hostility to Purgatory

Boniface's decision concerning the highly successful Jubilee of 1300 was in a sense the climactic moment in Purgatory's thirteenth-century triumph. But as we leave that triumphal century we would do well to bear in mind that not all Christians approved of Purgatory's victory.

To begin with there were the heretics. In 1335, for example, at Giaveno in the Piedmont, a number of Waldensians stated to the Dominican inquisitor that "in the other life there are only Heaven and Hell, and Purgatory exists only in this world."[100]

Other cases involve either out-and-out or suspected heretics who nevertheless seem to have been able to accommodate Purgatory to their beliefs, either by integrating it with notions about the other world drawn from folklore or by succumbing to Purgatory's imaginary appeal. One such case concerns a woman, Rixenda, who was interrogated by the Inquisition at Narbonne in 1288. She seems to have been a Beguine connected with the Franciscans. Her testimony indicates that, eight years earlier, "she was carried off to Heaven and there saw Jesus both standing and seated and his mother Mary right next to him and nearby Saint Francis." She adds that "she saw her father and mother in Purgatory in the process of expiating their sins, and they told her that in order to save them [here there is a gap in the manuscript] . . . and they said that thanks to her prayers many souls are taken from Purgatory, especially her father and mother and a cousin, Aucradis. She also said that in her flight she saw a woman, Feralguière of

Béziers, overburdened with punishments in Purgatory, thrashed and beaten for three days. . . . She saw her father and mother at the Gate of Heaven, and shortly thereafter they were received into their mansion." In the following day's testimony she adds that the souls that leave Purgatory do not go directly to Heaven but wait a while in their mansion. Thus, her father and mother, whom she liberated from Purgatory by her prayers and by making restitution of a debt in kind owed by them, had to wait one day and one night at the Gate of Heaven.[101]

The same is true of some of the Cathari villagers of Montaillou. Here I think some modifications of Emmanuel Le Roy Ladurie's conclusions are in order: "In all these stories," Le Roy Ladurie maintains, "one important thing is missing—Purgatory." In the trial of Raimond Vaissière of Ax, Jean Barra testifies under oath that "when we were both at Encastel, he told me to join the sect of the late Pierre Authié, the heretic, because if I did so, my soul, upon leaving my body, would immediately go to or enter Heaven and would never see Hell, the abyss, or Purgatory."[102]

In the most fully documented case studied by Le Roy Ladurie, that of Arnaud Gélis alias Bouteiller of Mas-Saint-Antonin, we encounter ghosts as well as Purgatory. To the soul of the late Pierre Durand, which appears in the Saint-Antonin Church, Arnaud asks the usual question in a rather familiar way: "I asked him how things were going, and he said, 'All right now, but I was in a bad spot for a while.' I asked him where. He answered, 'I passed through the fire of Purgatory, which was harsh and evil. But I just passed through.' He also asked me to pray for him. . . . I saw him one other time in the cloister and after that I never saw him again, for I believe he was at rest."[103]

Arnaud Gélis also tells us that Purgatory was in some degree taking the place of Hell: "All those who preceded me said that eternal damnation was not to be feared, for one had only to be a faithful Christian, to confess and repent, in order not to be damned."

Pierre Durand was an exception, however. According to the revelations vouchsafed to Arnaud Gélis, the souls of the dead normally wandered about visiting churches: "They do penance by visiting various churches. Some go more quickly than others, in the sense that those who have the greatest penance to do go the fastest. So in other words usurers run like the wind; but those who have a smaller penance walk slowly. I never heard any of them say that they had to undergo any punishment other than this motion, except for Piere Durand, who passed through the fire of Purgatory. When they're done visiting churches in this way, they go to the place of rest, in which they remain until Judgment Day, according to what the dead have told me."[104]

Accordingly, when Arnaud Gélis abjures, he is required to acknowledge that he now has a higher estimate of Purgatory's importance: "On the first article, retracting the error there contained, that although he did believe as stated, he now firmly believes that the souls of dead men and women go to Purgatory, in which they complete the penance not done in this world. That done, they go to the heavenly Paradise where they find the Lord Christ, the Holy Virgin, the angels, and the saints."[105]

We come across another form of opposition to Purgatory among certain monastic poets, particularly in Italy. Some of these men were conservatives and traditionalists who preferred to stick to the old couple, Heaven and Hell, and to close their eyes to the newer Purgatory, the brainchild of theologian-intellectuals. Bonvesino dalla Riva,[106] a Milanese who lived in the second half of the thirteenth century, was a tertiary of the order of Umiliati and the author of a *Libro delle Tre Scritture*. There, between the "black" scripture that describes the twelve punishments of Hell and the "golden" scripture that depicts the twelve glories of Paradise, we find not Purgatory but the Incarnation, the passion of the Redeemer, which constitutes the "red" scripture, composed of the blood of Christ.

At about the sme time another poet, the Franciscan Giacomino da Verona borrows from Bonvesino the black and gold "scriptures" for use in a poem entitled *On the Celestial Jerusalem and the Infernal Babylon*, where, between the joys of Paradise and the punishments of Hell, no allowance is made for intermediate purgations. Allusion is made, however, to the "subtleties" of the theologians (v. 19) and to the sharp distinction between good and evil: "Evil leads to death with the lost angel/Good gives life with the good Jesus" (vv. 331–32); the intention is apparently to rule out Purgatory as an intermediary.[107]

For others the hostility, if not to Purgatory then at least to certain pious exaggerations involving Purgatory, is apparently related to the fear of falling into pagan superstitions. Thus the Dominican Jacopo Passavanti, in a passage of his celebrated *Specchio di vera penitenza* in which he denounces "the false and idle opinions left over from paganism or introduced by the false doctrine of the demon," attacks "the vanity and cupidity of mortals who want to lord it over divine justice and who, by their works, their words, and their offerings, claim to pluck souls from Purgatory after a certain period of time. This is a great presumption and a dangerous error."[108]

Bonvesino dalla Riva and Giacomino da Verona have been regarded as precursors of Dante. The comparison only serves to accentuate the audacious genius of the author of the *Divine Comedy*, to which we turn next.

TEN

The Poetic Triumph
The *Divina Commedia*

ALITTLE more than a hundred years after its inception, Purgatory
benefited from an extraordinary stroke of luck: the poetic genius
of Dante Alighieri, born in Florence in 1265, carved out for it an
enduring place in human memory. Between his exile from Florence in
1302 and his death at Ravenna in 1321, Dante composed the *Divina
Commedia*, of which the first two books, that is, the *Inferno* and the
Purgatorio, were completed in 1319, as is shown by a letter from the
Bolognese scholar Giovanni del Virgilio.

It is not merely to give one more proof of the importance of historical
accidents that I have chosen to complete this study of Purgatory with a
chapter on the *Divine Comedy*. Nor is it merely to leave Purgatory on the
heights to which Dante raised it. A more important reason for my choice is
that Dante's extraordinary work makes a vast symphony out of the
fragmentary themes whose history I have attempted to trace. *Il Purgatorio*
is the sublime product of a lengthy gestation. It is also the noblest representation of Purgatory ever conceived by the mind of man, an enduring
selection from among the possible and at times competing images whose
choice the Church, while affirming the essence of the dogma, left to the
sensibilty and imagination of individual Christians.

It would be absurd for me to presume to add my meager contribution to
the already dense commentaries on the *Divine Comedy* by specialists in
Dante. Instead I have chosen to read the poem naively, guided only by my
awareness of the many writers who preceded Dante in the quest for
Purgatory.[1] Let me begin by retracing the progress of the narrative.

DANTE'S SYSTEM OF PURGATORY

Already in the last verse of the *Inferno* Dante had said a great deal about
Purgatory. The poet and his guide, Vergil, have emerged from Hell and
"beheld again the stars." Purgatory, therefore, is not underground. It is
situated on the earth, beneath the starry firmament. The poet and his guide
are welcomed by an old man, a sage of antiquity, Cato of Utica, the
guardian of Purgatory. Purgatory is a mountain whose lower portion
serves as an antechamber, a place of waiting for the dead not yet worthy to
enter Purgatory in the narrow sense. The mountain is situated in the

334

southern hemisphere, which according to Dante's authority, Ptolemy, is the site of a forsaken ocean imaccessible to living men. The location of the mountain is diametrically opposite Jerusalem (*Purgatorio* 2.3 and 4.68ff.).* We reach Purgatory, properly so called, in the ninth canto, when Vergil announces to his companion that:

> You are now at Purgatory. See the great
> encircling rampart there ahead. And see
> that opening—it contains the Golden Gate.
> (9.49–51)

Purgatory comprises seven circles or cornices (*cerchi, cerchie, cinghi, cornici, giri, gironi*) ranged one above the other, their circumferences diminishing as one moves closer to the summit. In each of these circles souls are purged of one of the seven deadly sins: in order, these are pride, envy, wrath, sloth, avarice, gluttony, and lust. At the summit of the mountain Vergil and Dante enter the Earthly Paradise, in which the last six cantos (cantos 28 to 33) of the *Purgatorio* are set. On the threshhold of this paradise Vergil relinquishes his office as guide and says to Dante, for whom he has hitherto led the way:

> Expect no more of me in word or deed:
> here your will is upright, free, and whole,
> and you would be in error not to heed
> whatever your own impulse prompts you to:
> lord of yourself I crown and mitre you.
> (27:139–43)

The poet vanishes, leaving Dante in tears (30.49–54). Soon Beatrice appears to act as his guide in the final phase of his pilgrimage, the journey to the third kingdom, Paradise.

No one has expressed better than Dante the relationship between this world and the next in the system of Creation. Emerging from Hell, one comes next to the intermediate and temporary level of the earth, from which the mountain of Purgatory rises toward Heaven. At its summit is situated the Earthly Paradise, no longer relegated to a forgotten corner of the universe but placed at its proper ideological level, the level of innocence, situated between the peak of purification in Purgatory and the beginning of glorification in Heaven. The two limbos have apparently been eliminated in this discussion; thirteenth-century theologians complacently expatiated on these marginal places, but they do not seem to have been deeply rooted in either belief or practice. The other world in which the mass of the faithful actually believed contained not five regions

---

*Unless otherwise indicated, all subsequent parenthetical references in this chapter are to the *Purgatorio*, canto and verse; I have followed John Ciardi's English translation.—Trans.

but three. The two limbos do make an appearance elsewhere in the *Divine Comedy*: the limbo of the sages of the ancient world, the patriarchs, and the limbo of unbaptized children of the Christian world. We feel how Dante must have been torn: on the one hand there was his admiration of, his gratitude and affection toward, the great pagan spirits—to which the choice of Vergil as a guide bears eloquent witness—and his tender pity for infants who have died an early death; on the other there was his strict Christian orthodoxy. No one can be saved who has not been baptized. But the denizens of the two limbos obsess Dante throughout his long pilgrimage. For the sages and the righteous who lived before Christ he envisions two different fates. Those who lived under the old law are saved, because Christ has descended into the Limbo of the Patriarchs and chosen some "for elevation among the elect" (*Inferno* 4.61); he then closed this part of Hell forever. The pagans must remain at this level of darkness, but God has provided the upper reaches of Hell, the first circle, with a noble castle (*nobile castello*) in which the pagan sages live in "a green meadow blooming round" bordered by "a luminous and open height" (*Inferno* 4.106ff.) Throughout his journey Dante continues to hark back to the sages of old. Among those mentioned explicitly in *Il Purgatorio* are Aristotle and Plato, together with many others whose fruitless yearning for the true God Dante recalls (3.40–45). Juvenal and Vergil are described in "our court in the Infernal Limbo" (22.14). Statius anxiously asks his master Vergil if the great Roman writers are damned, and Vergil replies that they all "walk the first ledge of the dark of Hell and . . . speak often of the glorious mountain [Purgatory] on which the Nine who suckled us [i.e., the Muses] still dwell" (22.97ff.) Furthermore, one of them has been placed by God as the guardian of the mount: Cato of Utica. Some commentators find it surprising that this role was entrusted to one who is not merely a pagan but also a suicide. But Dante's admiration for a man whose championing of liberty cost him his life was intense (1.70–75). In the *Banquet*, Vergil made Cato the symbol of the citizen, the hero of civic life, who describes himself as having been born "not for himself but for my country and for the world."[2]

As for young children who died unbaptized, bearing only the taint of original sin, their place is with the pagan sages in the castle placed in the first circle of Hell. This Vergil reveals to the troubadour Sordello whom he meets in ante-Purgatory:

> There is a place below where sorrow lies
>   in untormented gloom. Its lamentations
>   are not the shrieks of pain, but hopeless sighs.
> There do I dwell with souls of babes whom death
>   bit off in their first innocence before
>   baptism washed them of their taint of earth.
>   (7.28–33)

Dante again mentions the infants who are kept in the limbo of Hell in *Il Paradiso*:*

> But since the Christian age such things were vain;
> For then, without true baptism in Christ
> Such innocence in Limbo must remain.

Dante knew how to give Purgatory its full dimensions because he understood its role as an active intermediary and because he was able to relate its spatial representation to its underlying spiritual logic. He bridged the gap between cosmogony and theology. Certain commentators have suggested that Dante included in the *Divine Comedy*—almost as padding—knowledge that he acquired in his frequentation, as he put it, of the "schools of the religious and the disputes of the philosophers," to which he gave himself body and soul after the death of Beatrice in 1290. Can it be that anyone fails to see that Dante's cosmogony, philosophy, and theology are the very substance—or, rather, the substance and the spirit—of his poem?

Purgatory is clearly a "second kingdom" between Hell and Heaven. But Dante's idea of this intermediate zone is dynamic and imbued with spirituality. Purgatory is not a neutral intermediary but an intermediary with an orientation. It points from the earth, where the future elect are when they die, to Heaven, their eternal abode. As they proceed on their way, they are purged and become more and more pure as they come closer and closer to the summit, to the spiritual heights to which they are destined. From the abundance of geographical imagery of the other world bequeathed him by earlier centuries, Dante chose the one image that expresses Purgatory's true logic, that of the climb: a mountain. Dante's eschatology is a synthesis of the most traditional ideas (fear of Hell and desire of Heaven) and the most recent (Purgatory). His feelings about the Last Things are not crystallized in the moment of death. This he is content to evoke in a significant way in the second canto of the *Purgatorio*, where the souls in the boat of the angel-pilot of the Lord sing "as if they raised a single voice 'In exitu Israel de Aegypto,'" a psalm commonly sung in the Middle Ages when a body was moved from its home to the church and then to the cemetery (2.46–48). The essential thing is the climbing of the mountain, which is constantly referred to ("climbing" is mentioned repeatedly throughout the *Purgatorio*).[3] At times the mountain itself is called the "sacred mount" (*il sacro monte*—19.38) or the "holy mount" (*il santo monte*—28.12). In two verses in which Dante demonstrates his gift for conveying several meanings at once, he refers to the mountain as a *poggio* or volcano and as pointed upward toward the heavenly destination:

*Here cited after the English translation by Dorothy Sayers and Barbara Reynolds.—Trans.

> I raised my eyes in wonder to that mountain
> that soars highest to Heaven from the sea.
> (*e diedi il viso mio incontro al poggio*
> *che'inverso il ciel piu alto si dislaga*)
> (3.14–15)

The mountain of Purgatory is very high, very steep, very difficult to climb. Vergil literally pulls Dante along, and they climb on all fours:

> Squeezed in between two walls that almost meet
> we labor upward through the riven rock:
> a climb that calls for both our hands and feet.
> Above the cliff's last rise we reached in time
> an open slope. "Do we go right or left?"
> I asked my Master, "Or do we still climb?"
> And he: "Take not one step to either side,
> but follow yet, and make way up the mountain
> till we meet someone who may serve as guide."
> Higher than sight the peak soared to the sky. . . .
> (4.31–40)

The "second kingdom," a world unto itself, is divided into regions that Dante also calls kingdoms, the "seven kingdoms" through which Vergil asks Cato the gatekeeper to let him and Dante pass: "Grant us permission to pursue our quest/across your seven kingdoms" (1.82).

From one kingdom to the next, from one cornice to the next, the travelers climb by steep stairways or steps (*scale, scaglioni, scallo, gradi,* etc.). In the description of the ascent from the fourth to the fifth cornice we are told that they are "summoned up between the walls of rock" (19.48).

THE MOUNTAIN OF PURGATION

But this mountain is the mountain of purgation, and purgation is the essence of what goes on there. Dante states this theme at the outset:

> Now shall I sing that second kingdom given
> the soul of man wherein to purge its guilt
> and so grow worthy to ascend to Heaven.
> (1.4–6)

Vergil, speaking to Cato, points out that the purpose of this portion of their journey is to show Dante what this purgation is:

> . . . Now I mean
> to lead him through the spirits in your keeping,
> to show him those whose suffering makes them clean.
> (1.65–66)

While surveying purgation in general, Dante pauses from time to time to attend to the purgation of particular individuals. For example, he stops to

338

view the purgation of the poet Guido Guinizelli in the seventh cornice, reserved for the lustful: "I am Guido Guinizelli, here so soon/because I repented before I died" (26.92).

Purgation is accomplished on the mountain in three ways. First, by material punishment that mortifies the wicked passions and instills virtue. Second, by meditation on the sin to be purged and its correlative virtue: in a sense the *Purgatorio* incorporates a treatise on the vices and virtues. The meditation in question is encouraged by the example of the illustrious or familiar souls encountered on the various cornices. Here Dante is adapting the traditional political uses of Purgatory (and what poet was more political than Dante?) to the purposes of a higher spiritual lesson. Third and last, purgation is accomplished through prayer, which purifies the soul, strengthens it by the grace of God, and expresses its hope.[4]

Love is the principle that governs the assignment of souls to the various cornices of Purgatory. Half-way up the mountain, between the third cornice, reserved for the wrathful, and the fourth, reserved for the indolent, Vergil explains the workings of this principle to Dante.

During a pause in the climb that does not interrupt the spiritual lesson he is receiving by degrees, Dante puts a question to his guide:

> I said: "Dear Father, what impurity
> is washed in pain here? Though our feet must stay,
> I beg you not to stay your speech."

All sins have in common absence of the love of God, that is to say, of the good. Love may "turn to evil" or "show less zeal than it ought for what is good," or it may "turn on its Creator": this is the true nature of sin. On the mountain of Purgatory the true love of God is restored. The soul climbs to regain its love, to find its way back to God after being delayed by sin. Dante here combines metaphors of the mountain and the ocean in this place where the mountain looms up out of the sea. Here is Vergil's answer:

> That love of good which in the life before
> lay idle in the soul is paid for now.
> Here Sloth strains at the once-neglected oar.
> (17.85–87).[5]

THE LAW OF PROGRESS

The whole logic of the mountainous Purgatory lies in the progress that the soul makes while climbing: with each step upward it becomes more pure. The ascent is twofold, spiritual as well as physical. As a sign of this progress the punishment is alleviated as the soul rises, as if the climb becomes easier, the mountain less steep, as the soul sheds its burden of sins.

As Vergil tells Dante while they are still in the ante-Purgatory:

And he: "Such is this Mount that when a soul
  begins the lower slopes it most must labor;
  then less and less the more it nears its goal.
    (4.88–90)

Again, mixing metaphors of climbing and sailing:

Thus when we reach the point where the slopes seem
  so smooth and gentle that the climb becomes
  as easy as to float a skiff downstream
  then will this road be run, and not before . . .
    (4.91–94)

By the first cornice the difficulty has already lessened, the narrow paths
have been replaced by stairs:

"Come," he said, "the stairs are near, and now
  the way is easy up the mountainside."
    (12.92–93)

At the top of this first staircase Dante again draws a parallel between
progress in the climb and spiritual progress:

We climbed the stairs and stood, now, on the track
  where, for a second time, the mount that heals
  all who ascend it, had been terraced back.
    (13.1–3)

At the following cornice, an angel tells the mountaineers that things
have gotten even easier:

We stand before the Blessed Angel now.
  With joyous voice he cries: "Enter. The stair
  is far less steep than were the two below."
    (15.34–36)

When the travelers reach the fifth cornice, where souls are lying face
down and crying, they call out to them for help, alluding as they do to the
principle of progressive improvement as they rise:

"O Chosen of God, spirits whose mournful rites
  both Hope and Justice make less hard to bear,
  show us the passage to the further heights."
    (19.76–78)

Again, a number of essential attributes of Purgatory are here com-
pressed in a brief synthesis: the souls in Purgatory are destined to be saved
in Heaven, they are the souls of the elect, they are suffering, but God's
justice which is perfect and mingled here with mercy and hope alleviates
their suffering and decreases it by degrees as they rise toward Heaven.

At the sixth cornice Dante reminds his friend Forese Donati that Purgatory, to which Vergil has brought him, is a place that straightens a man out and makes him righteous:

> From there with many a sweet encouragement
> he led me upward and around the mountain
> which straightens in you what the world has bent.
> (23.124–26)

PURGATORY AND SINS

This Purgatory is indeed the place where sins are expiated, but Dante seems at least partly to have neglected the teachings of the theologians on this score. The sins expiated in Dante's Purgatory are not venial sins, about which the poet has little to say save perhaps for an allusion to excessive love for one's own kin, one of the "slight" sins mentioned by Augustine. Essentially the sins purged on the seven cornices of Dante's Purgatory are the seven capital sins, the same sins punished in Hell. Dante, who always kept the underlying logic of Purgatory in view, clearly saw it as a Hell of limited duration. It is a reprise, in a minor key, of the infernal torments appropriate to each class of sin, with this difference: the sinners in Purgatory have sinned less gravely than those in Hell, whether because they have partly effaced their sin by repentance and penance, or because they were less inveterate sinners, or because their sins were mere blemishes on lives otherwise animated by the love of God.

The seven categories of sin are symbolically engraved on Dante's forehead by an angel, who seven times marks the letter P (*peccato*, sin) with the tip of his sword:

> Seven P's, the seven scars of sin,
> his sword point cut into my brow. He said:
> "Scrub off these wounds when you have passed within."
> (9.112–14)

As Dante leaves each cornice, an angel comes and wipes away one of the wounds or sins engraved on his brow.

In the seventeenth canto, after Vergil explains the list of infractions against love, he goes on to explain in terms of the principle of love the system of seven capital sins. The first three perversions of the love of good into the love of evil are the three kinds of hatred that one can feel toward one's neighbor, or as Dante puts it, the three evils with which one may like to see one's neighbor afflicted (*'l mal che s'ama è del prossimo*). These are the desire to see him "cast down from his eminence" in order to further one's own advance, the desire to see "his ruin and shame," and the desire for vengeance against him. Thus the first three capital sins are pride, envy, and wrath (17.112–23).

Then there are three kinds of love that "seeks good but without measure." Vergil tells Dante that he may learn for himself what these three forms of corrupt love are as they continue on. They turn out to be avarice, gluttony, and lust.

At the midpont of the system is "lax love," tepid love, "slow" love (*lento amore*). This is the sin that is expiated half-way up the mountain: indolence, disgust for life, a sin engendered by the monastic environment and called in Latin *accedia* (from which the Italian *accidia*). This is the sin being purged by the "sad" (*tristi*) souls on the fourth cornice.

Clearly, this list of seven deadly sins is a hierarchical one, since it is said that the souls progress as they move up from one cornice to the next. Here again Dante reveals that he was both a traditionalist and an innovator. A traditionalist because he puts pride at the head of the list of sins, whereas by the thirteenth century it had become more common for avarice to occupy the first place.[6] An innovator because he considers the sins of the spirit committed against one's neighbor—pride, envy, and wrath—to be more grave than the sins of the flesh, committed in large part against oneself—avarice, gluttony, and lust. For this latter vice Dante offers the benefits of Purgatory, just as he had offered the torments of Hell, to homosexuals as well as heterosexuals (canto 26).

As for the mechanics of getting to Purgatory, Dante seems to have paid particular attention to tardy repentance. He brings up the subject at several points. In ante-Purgatory, for example, Belacqua asks what good it is to climb, "for I delayed the good sighs till the last" (4.132). And in the next canto Dante encounters souls who died by violence, "all sinners to our final hour" (5.52–53).

When we come to the first cornice we are reminded that a soul that waits until the end of life to repent cannot be admitted to Purgatory without aid (11.127–29). Dante is therefore surprised to meet Forese Donati in Purgatory less than five months after his death, for Donati, slow to repent, should have been in ante-Purgatory, "still below, with those who sit and wait, repaying time for time" (23.83–84).

ANTE-PURGATORY

Dante's originality in fact lies in his having imagined that, before entering the area in which the actual progress of purgation takes place, many sinners wait for a time in an ante-Purgatory at the base of the mountain. It may be that, as Purgatory was increasingly promised to those who merely made an act of contrition in extremis (a trend apparent even earlier, in the work of Caesarius of Heisterbach), Dante, inclined though he was to believe that God's mercy is bountiful, felt it necessary to establish this period of waiting as an additional trial to be endured before admission could be gained to Purgatory proper.

It is a troubled crowd of "new souls" ignorant of the road to Purgatory that asks Vergil and Dante to "show us the road that climbs the mountain-side" (2.59–60). When Dante asks his friend Casella, whom he meets in ante-Purgatory, "But why has so much time been taken from you?" Casella answers

> . . . "I am not wronged if he whose usage
> accepts the soul at his own time and pleasure
> has many times refused to give me passage:
> "his will moves in the image and perfection
> of a Just Will. . . ."
> (2.94–98)

Casella tells as if it were true the old legend that the souls of the dead who are not damned but who must purge themselves gather at Ostia near the mouth of the Tiber:

> "And so it was that in my turn I stood
> upon that shore where Tiber's stream grows salt,
> and there was gathered to my present good.
> "It is back to the Tiber's mouth he has just flown,
> for there forever is the gathering place
> of all who do not sink to Acheron."
> (2.100–105)

The proud Sienese Provenzano Galvani avoided spending time in ante-Purgatory only by dint of a pious work which for him was a humiliation. In order to pay a friend's ransom he begged publicly on the town square: "It was this good work spared him his delay" (11.142). And Guido Guinizelli tells Dante that he is in Purgatory "so soon because I repented full before I died" (26.93).

At the time Dante was making his journey to the other world, however, the obstacles standing before the gate of Purgatory were removed and a large crowd of waiting souls was hastened on its way toward the mountain thanks to the decision of Pope Boniface VIII to grant indulgences in the Jubilee of 1300. This decision is alluded to by Casella when he tells Dante and Vergil that Cato the boatman has "for three months now taken all who asked, without exception" (2.98–99). There is no better evidence of the upheaval in Purgatory-related practices occasioned by Boniface's innovative gesture.

It is not up to the individual soul, then, to decide if or when it may enter Purgatory. Nor is Dante's Purgatory to be thought of as a foretaste of Paradise. His cornices reverberate with the sound of tears and moans. As Dante draws near in a dream, he is seized by fear. He wakes with a start and turns white, like "one whose blood is turned to ice by dread" (9.42). Vergil has to calm him.

The mountain is plainly a place of punishment. On the second cornice, for example, the envious are whipped, even if the lash is plaited with love:

> . . . This circle purges
> the guilt of Envious spirits, and for these
> who failed in Love, Love is the lash that scourges.
> (13.37–39)

And later we learn that the shades of the envious endure still worse tortures:

> for each soul has its eyelids pierced and sewn
> with iron wires, as men sew new-caught falcons,
> sealing their eyes to make them settle down.
> (13:70–72)

Between the sins committed on earth and the intensity and duration of punishment in Purgatory, including the time of waiting in ante-Purgatory, there is a proportionality (beyond the correspondence between particular sins and a particular level of the mountain) which I have already described as one of the essential features of the system of Purgatory.

In ante-Purgatory Frederick II's legitimated bastard Manfred, who died excommunicate, declares:

> "Those who die contumacious, it is true,
> though they repent their feud with Holy Church,
> must wait outside here on the bank, as we do,
> "for thirty times as long as they refused
> to be obedient . . ."
> (3.136–40)

And Belacqua says this:

> "I must wait here until the heavens wheel past
> as many times as they passed me in my life,
> for I delayed the good sighs till the last."
> (4.130–32)

Vergil's great admirer Statius turns this rule of proportionality upside down when he asserts that he would gladly spend another year in Purgatory if only he could have lived in Vergil's time (21.100–102).

Nevertheless, Dante agrees with Augustine that the punishments of Purgatory are worse than the worst punishments on earth. He makes this point in his own imaginative way, making use of Purgatory's rugged terrain:

> Meanwhile we reached the mountain's foot; and there
> we found so sheer a cliff, the nimblest legs
> would not have served, unless they walked on air.
> The most forsaken and most broken goat-trace
> in the mountains between Lerici and Turbia
> compared to this would seem a gracious staircase.
> (3.46–51)

FIRE

Dante frequently alludes to the one feature that before his time was more or less identified with Purgatory: fire. In the nightmare that torments him as he draws near the mountain, he sees a fire:

> It seemed that we were swept in a great blaze,
> and the imaginary fire so scorched me
> my sleep broke and I wakened in a daze.
> (9.31–32)

Later he imagines that he has returned to Hell:

> No gloom of Hell, nor of a night allowed
> no planet under its impoverished sky,
> the deepest dark that may be drawn by cloud
> ever drew such a veil across my face,
> nor one whose texture rasped my senses so,
> as did the smoke that wrapped us in that place.
> (16.1–5)

On the seventh and last cornice fire burns the lustful (25:137):

> Here, from the inner wall, flames blast the ledge,
> while from the floor an air-blast bends them back,
> leaving one narrow path along the edge.
> This path we were forced to take as best we might,
> in single file. And there I was—the flames
> to the left of me, and the abyss to the right.
> (25.112–17)

The fire is so hot that it prevents Dante from throwing himself into the arms of his master, Guido Guinizelli: "the flames prevent my drawing near" (26.102). A little later on the troubadour Arnaut Daniel also "hid himself within the fire that makes those spirits ready to go higher" (26.148).

Finally, there is a wall of fire that must be traversed in order to pass from Purgatory into the Earthly Paradise. The angel of the last cornice tells Dante that "till by flame purified no soul may pass this point. Enter the fire . . ." (27:10–11). Dante stares apprehensively at the flames:

> I lean forward over my clasped hands and stare
> into the fire, thinking of human bodies
> I once saw burned, and once more see them there.
> (27:16–18)

Vergil reassures him:

> Believe this past all doubt: were you to stay
> within that womb of flame a thousand years,
> it would not burn a single hair away.
> (27:25–27)

345

The trial is painful, however, even though Vergil goes first into the flames:

> Once in the flame, I gladly would have cast
> my body into boiling glass to cool it
> against the measureless fury of the blast.
> (27:49–51)

To help Dante endure the trial Vergil speaks to him constantly about Beatrice, and a singing voice calls out to him from the other side.

Reminiscent of the fires of Hell, this fire is nevertheless a thing apart. Vergil reminds Dante of this fact as he prepares to take his leave: "My son, you now have seen the torment of the temporal and the eternal fires" (27:127–28).

PURGATORY AND HELL: REPENTANCE

Purgatory does, to be sure, remind Dante of Hell at numerous points. If the mountain with its nine regions—ante-Purgatory, the seven cornices, and the Earthly Paradise—prefigures the nine spheres of Heaven, it is even more a reminder to Dante, as he climbs, of the nine circles of Hell. Still, the poet is careful to point out the fundamental difference between Hell and Purgatory, which he makes apparent to our senses. In the first place the gate of Purgatory is narrow (9.75–76), which contrasts with the broad portal of Hell and is reminiscent of the words of the Gospel: "Enter ye at the strait gate: for wide is the gate, and broad is the way, that leadeth to destruction, and many there be which go in thereat: Because strait is the gate, and narrow is the way, which leadeth unto life, and few there be that find it" (Matt. 7:13–14). Or again: "Strive to enter in at the strait gate: for many, I say unto you, will seek to enter in, and shall not be able" (Luke 13:24).

Dante is even more explicit:

> Ah, what a difference between these trails
> and those of Hell: here every entrance fills
> with joyous song, and there with savage wails.
> (12.112–14)

If I am right in thinking that Dante more than anyone else made Purgatory the intermediate region of the other world, then it follows that he rescued Purgatory from the infernalization to which the Church subjected it in the thirteenth century. Dante was in a sense more orthodox than the Church, more faithful to Purgatory's underlying logic. He depicts Purgatory as a place between two extremes, but closer to one of them, straining in the direction of Paradise. For him it is a place of hope, of initiation into joy, of gradual emergence into the light.

The reason for this is that Dante, more than most of the great scholastics, was faithful, as previously William of Auvergne had been faithful—almost to excess—to the great tradition of twelfth-century theology, which had rooted Purgatory in penance. We see evidence of this, for example, in the Miserere, the song of humility required for expiation and purification (5:22–24). We see it also in the exquisite and subtle symbolism of the three steps that lead to Purgatory:

> I saw a great gate fixed in place above
> three steps, each its own color; and a guard
> who did not say a word and did not move.
> . . .
> We came to the first step: white marble gleaming
> so polished and so smooth that in its mirror
> I saw my true reflection past all seeming.
> The second was stained darker than blue-black
> and of a rough-grained and fire-flaked stone,
> its length and breadth crisscrossed by many a crack.
> The third and topmost was of porphyry,
> or so it seemed, but of a red as flaming
> as blood that spurts out of an artery.
> . . .
> With great good will my Master guided me
> up the three steps and whispered in my ear:
> "Now beg him humbly that he turn the key."
>   (9:76–108)

"This scene," as one commentary explains, "is a representation of penance: the angel represents the priest, who is silent, because it is the sinner who must take the first step. The three stairs of different colors represent the three acts of the sacrament: contrition, confession, and satisfaction, acts different in themselves but together constituting the sacrament, just as the three stairs together lead to a single threshhold."[7]

The first step symbolizes contrition (*contritio cordis*), which is supposed to make the penitent as white as marble. The second represents confession (*confessio oris*), which causes the penitent to turn deep purple with shame. The third embodies penance in the proper sense (*satisfactio operis*), which is flaming red like the ardor of charity, of love, by which the penitent is now motivated.

Once past the threshhold of purgation, the repentant soul, even though it has now entered "this world in which the very power to sin is lost" (26.131–32), must still, as a human being invested with free will, manifest its desire for purgation. Dante follows Vergil "with good will" (*di buona voglia*).

In the heart of Purgatory Statius reminds Vergil and Dante that the soul must want to purify itself:

The soul, surprised, becomes entirely free
　to change its cloister, moved by its own will,
　which is its only proof of purity.
　Before purgation it does wish to climb. . . .
　　　　(21.61–64)[8]

This is Dante's reading of the abstract scholastic discussion as to whether purgatorial punishment is or is not "voluntary."

The soul's penance includes its portion of bitterness (the *acerbitas* of the theologians and the pastors). Thus, in the description of misers and wastrels in the fifth cornice, we read

The nature of avarice is here made plain
　in the nature of its penalty; there is not
　a harsher forfeit paid on the whole mountain.
　　　　(19.115–17)

Again, in the Earthly Paradise, the fair Matilda, dancing and singing, welcomes Dante, still accompanied by Vergil, and sings Psalm 32, a psalm of penitence:

Beati, quorum tecta sant peccata!
　　　　(28.80)

Remorse is especially important in the penitential process, and it is fitting that it should be expressed by tears. In ante-Purgatory are the victims of violent deaths who in the little time left them before expiring were able not only to repent but also to pardon their murderers and torturers:

Thus from the brink of death,
　repenting all our sins, forgiving those
　who sinned against us, with our final breath
we offered up our souls at peace with Him
　who saddens us with longing to behold
　His glory on the throne of Seraphim.
　　　　(5.55–60)

Also in ante-Purgatory Buonconte di Montefeltro tells how he repented on the brink of death and thus landed in the hands of God's angel, to the great consternation of one of Hell's angels, the devil who watched his prey snatched from him thanks to a single tear, *per una lacrimetta*:

God's angel took me up,
　and Hell's cried out: 'Why do you steal my game?
If his immortal part is your catch, brother,
　for one squeezed tear that makes me turn it loose. . . .
　　　　(5.104–7)

When Dante discovers on the misers' cornice Pope Adrian V, who, shamefaced, tries to hide, he addresses him thus:

> O Soul in whom these tears prepare
> that without which no soul can turn to God . . .
> (19.91–92)

Along the edge of this fifth cornice are "they who drain slow, tear by tear, the sin that eats the race" (20:5–6).

Upon entering the Earthly Paradise, finally, Dante reminds us one last time that in order to taste this happiness a soul must first pay the price of repentance, which causes tears to flow (30.145).

HOPE

Dante insists, however, that in Purgatory hope reigns supreme. The souls in Purgatory, which are endowed with immaterial bodies (evoked by a leitmotif, the shades that one seeks in vain to embrace),[9] are delivered souls, already saved.

Hope is frequently expressed through prayer. The *Purgatorio* is punctuated throughout with prayer and hymn. Dante had the secret of integrating into his poem the liturgy that the scholastics usually kept out of their writings. And it was the image of souls in prayer that late medieval artists chose to distinguish Purgatory from Hell. In the latter place, where there is no hope, what is the use of prayer? By contrast, in the former, the certainty of salvation has to be embodied in prayer, which not only represents the certain end but actually brings it nearer. The joyful expectation is symbolized by white and green, the colors of purity and hope.

From the moment the travelers first set foot in ante-Purgatory they see the color white:

> Then from each side of it came into view
> an unknown something-white; and from beneath it,
> bit by bit, another whiteness grew.
> (2.22–24)

Vergil encourages Dante and urges him to seek the light: "And you, dear son, believe as you have believed" (3.66). When the pilgrims begin their climb they are again driven on by desire and hope toward the light:

> here nothing but swift wings will answer wholly.
> The swift wings and the feathers, I mean to say,
> of great desire led onward by that Guide
> who was my hope and light along the way.
> (4.27–30)

They pass by praying souls in ante-Purgatory: "There, hands outstretched to me as I pushed through, was Federico Novello; and the Pisan" (6.16–17). The watching angels have robes and wings the color of hope:

> I saw two angels issue and descend
>   from Heaven's height, bearing two flaming swords
>   without a point, snapped off to a stub end.
> Green as a leaf is at its first unfurling,
>   their robes; and green the wings that beat and blew
>   the flowing folds back, fluttering and whirling.
>   (8.25–30)

> Hearing their green wings beating through the night,
>   the serpent fled . . .
>   (8.106–7)

And on the first cornice there is the great episode in which those guilty of the sin of pride recite the Pater, saying the last verse calling for deliverance from evil only for the sake of form, since they are now free of sin and no longer have need of it.

> This last petition, Lord, with grateful mind,
>   we pray not for ourselves who have no need,
>   but for the souls of those we left behind.
>   (11.22–24)

The first souls that Dante sees in ante-Purgatory are already "fortunate souls" (2.74), souls of the elect: "O well-concluded lives! O souls thus met among the already chosen," Vergil says, addressing them (3.73).

To the envious on the second Cornice Dante also says, "O souls afire with hope of seeing Heaven's Light" (13.85–86).

The salvation of souls in Purgatory is a product of God's justice, which punishes but which is also a source of mercy and grace. Salvation is also helped by the soul's own remaining will. On the misers' cornice Hugh Capet makes this clear:

> We wail or mutter in our long remorse
>   according to the inner spur that drives us,
>   at times with more, at others with less force.
>   (20.118–20)

HELP FROM THE LIVING

Above all, the progress of purgation and the ascent to heaven are dependent on help from the living. Dante here subscribes fully to the belief in suffrages. Most of the souls in Purgatory seek the aid of a relative or friend, but some appeal more broadly to the communion of saints.

Manfred, who is waiting to enter Purgatory, asks the poet to go, on his return to earth, and let his daughter, "my good Constance," know how matters stand, since Constance, knowing that her father has been excommunicated, may think that he is damned: "For here, from those beyond, great good may come" (3.145).

Belacqua has lost all hope of quickly entering Purgatory, unless someone prays for him: "Prayer could help me, if a heart God's love has filled with Grace should offer it" (4.133–34).

Jacopo del Cassero solicits the aid of all the residents of Fano:

> I, then, who am no more than first to plead,
>   beg that if ever you see that land that lies
>   between Romagna and Naples, you speak my need
> Most graciously in Fano, that they to Heaven
>   send holy prayers to intercede for me;
>   so may great offenses be forgiven.
>   (5.68–72)

Buonconte of Montefeltro complains that his wife Giovanna and his family have forgotten him: "Because Giovanna and the rest forget me I go among these souls with head bowed low" (5.89–90).

Dante is nearly overwhelemed by the demands of the souls waiting before the gate of Purgatory:

> When I had won my way free of that press
>   of shades whose one prayer was that others pray,
>   and so advance them toward their blessedness. . . .
>   (6.25–27)

Dante is also asked by Nino Visconti to urge his little daughter Giovanna to help him:

> When you have once more crossed the enormous tide,
>   tell my Giovanna to cry out my name
>   there where the innocent are gratified.
>   (8.70–72)

The proud who recite the Pater call upon the living to help them, because for their part they pray for those on earth as much as they are able. Dante, who seems here to be moving toward a belief in the reciprocity of merits, joins in their appeal:

> If they forever speak our good above,
>   what can be done for their good here below
>   by those whose will is rooted in God's love?
> Surely, we should help those souls grow clear
>   of time's deep stain, that each at last may issue
>   spotless and weightless to his starry sphere.

Some souls, then, are forgotten in Purgatory; others are helped. Sapia of Siena, who repented too late, has been helped by his compatriot Pier Pettinaio, a Franciscan tertiary:

> Not till my final hour had all but set
>   did I turn back to God, longing for peace.
> Penance would not yet have reduced my debt
> Had not Pier Pettinaio in saintly love
>   grieved for my soul and offered holy prayers
>   that interceded for me there above.
> (13.124–29)

Certain souls ask Dante to seek the prayers not of a living person but of God. On the cornice of the wrathful, for example, Marco the Lombard says, "I pray you to pray for me when you have mounted there," that is, to Heaven (16.50–51).

And Statius invokes God's help for the souls on the fifth cornice: "May He call them soon to go above!" (21.72).

But the suffering souls in Purgatory naturally seek even more the intercession of the Virgin and the saints. For example, among the envious on the second cornice, Dante hears "prayers and plaints. 'O Mary, pray for us,' I heard them cry; and to Michael, and to Peter, and all Saints" (13.50–51).

THE TIME OF PURGATORY

Dante and Vergil travel in Purgatory for four days during the Easter season, the season of the resurrection, of the victory over death, of the promise of salvation. They spend one day, Easter Sunday, in ante-Purgatory, the two following days on the mountain of Purgatory, and the fourth day, Wednesday, in the Earthly Paradise. Throughout his journey Dante carefully notes the movement of the sun and the stars that light their way as they climb and symbolize the grace of God, which accompanies the travelers and leads the souls in Purgatory on toward Heaven.

Beyond this, the entire *Purgatorio* is larded with indications concerning time. In the *Inferno* the only indications of time had to do with the progress made by Vergil and Dante on their travels. By contrast, Purgatory is a realm that subsists in time.[10] Dante points out how Purgatory's time relates to historical time. The maximum length of a stay in Purgatory is the interval between death and the Last Judgment. Here the poet is addressing the reader:

> Reader, I would not have you be afraid,
>   nor turn from your intention to repent
>   through hearing how God wills the debt be paid.
> Do not think of the torments: think, I say,
>   of what comes after them: think that at worst
>   they cannot last beyond the Judgment Day.
> (10.107–11)

In the *Purgatorio* time is a symphony: the time of Dante's journey is superimposed upon time as it is experienced by the souls in whose midst he is traveling. Time is a congeries of various tempi, a composite of the experience of each of the souls undergoing trial in the space between earth and Heaven and in the interval between earthly life and eternity. Time is speeded up and slowed down, it shuttles back and forth between the memory of the living and the anxiety of the dead. It is a time still attached to history and yet already absorbed by eschatology.

In Purgatory time is marked out by the progress made by souls. Along the boundary between human time and divine eternity, miracles occur. These are the only events that can take place in Purgatory.

When Vergil and Dante are on the fifth cornice, where the misers are, the mountain shudders:

> We . . .
>> were expending every ounce of strength
>> on the reamining distance to the stairs,
> when suddenly I felt the mountain shake
>> as if it tottered. Such a numb dread seized me
>> as a man feels when marching to the stake.
>> (20:125–29)

But then a strange thing happens: shouts of joy are heard all around:

> Then there went up a cry on every side,
>> so loud that the sweet Master, bending close
>> said: "Do not fear, for I am still your Guide.
> "Glory to God in the Highest!" rang a shout
>> from every throat—as I could understand
>> from those nearby, whose words I could make out.
>> (20.133–38)

In the next canto Statius explains the meaning of this earthquake to the two pilgrims:

> [The mountain] trembles whenever a soul feels
>> so healed and purified that it gets up
>> or moves to climb; and then the great hymn peals.
>> (21.58–60)

Thus the shock of events in Purgatory is due to the flight of souls that have become worthy of climbing toward Heaven. The resulting earthquake and clamor are produced by the passage of a soul from time to eternity.

Dante's Purgatory is of course also a time of suffering and trial. In any case the souls in Purgatory are deprived of the true joy, that of the beatific vision, since, as Pope Adrian V sadly puts it,

We would not raise our eyes to the shining spheres
but kept them turned to mundane things: so Justice
bends them to earth here in this place of tears.
(19.18–20)

Toward the Light

But all of Purgatory aspires toward the heights. Beatrice will not replace
Vergil as Dante's guide to Paradise until he reaches the Earthly Paradise in
the thirty-first canto, but Vergil predicts her coming while they are still in
ante-Purgatory:

Do you understand me? I mean Beatrice.
She will appear above here, at the summit
of this same mountain, smiling in her bliss.
(6.46–48)

The scholastics wondered whether demons or angels attend to the souls in
Purgatory. Dante is in no doubt as to the answer: it is the good angels, the
angels of Heaven, God's angels who are responsible for souls purging their
sins. At the very gateway to Purgatory one of those angels marks Dante's
forehead with the seven P's representing the seven deadly sins. And at the
entrance to each cornice there is another angel to show the pilgrims the
way and yet another angel at the exit to wipe away one of the P's.

What is more, despite occasional encounters with darkness, smoke, and
the night (but always under the stars), the travelers find that the mountain
of Purgatory gradually becomes enveloped in light as they climb. Their
ascent is a climb toward the light. Between the darkness of Hell and the
illumination of Heaven, Purgatory is a study in chiaroscuro in which the
light steadily drives out the dark.[11]

At the very beginning, while the travelers are still at the water's edge, the
sun rises and restores color to both the landscape and to Dante's face:

I lifted my tear-stained cheeks to him, and there
he made me clean, revealing my true color
under the residue's of Hell's black air.
(1.127–29)

Light also comes from the angels who reflect the light of Heaven from their
faces: "I could see clearly that their hair was gold, but my eyes drew back
bedazzled from their faces" (8.34–35).

As they are about to enter the second cornice, Vergil looks at the sun:

O Blessed Lamp, we face the road ahead
placing our faith in you. . . .
You are the warmth of the world, you are its light,
. . .your rays alone should serve to lead us right.
(13.16–21)

Upon climbing up from the second to the third cornice, Dante is even dazzled:

> I felt my brow weighed down
> by a much greater splendor than the first.
> I was left dazzled by some cause unknown.
> (15.10–12)

Vergil explains to him thus:

> "Do not be astonished," answered my sweet Friend
> "if those of the Heavenly Father still blind you.
> He has been sent to bid us to ascend."
> (15.28–30)

Finally, the Earthly Paradise already bathes in the light of Heaven: "And the shadows fled on every side . . ." (27.112).

The final purification takes place. From a fountain flow two rivers, one of which, the Lethe, washes away all memory of sin while the other, the Eunoe (an invention of Dante's), restores the memory of all the good one has done (28.127–32). This is Dante's last word on the process of penitence and purgation, in which memory plays so large a part. It is the final metamorphosis of memory, it too cleansed of sin. Evil is forgotten and all that remains in memory is that which is immortal in man, the good. Memory, too, has crossed the eschatological threshhold.

Dante then comes upon the true light: "O splendor of the eternal living light!" (*O isplendor di viva luce eterna*, 31.139). The poet, having completed his journey through Purgatory, drinks the waters of the Eunoe and, like a purged soul, comes to the final verse of the Purgatorio, "pure and ready to climb up to the stars" (*puro e disposto a salire alle stelle*).

Why Purgatory?

THE history of Purgatory did not end with the beginning of the fourteenth century. Purgatory insinuated itself into the deepest recesses of Christian and later Catholic belief. The most fervent, most "glorious" moments in the history of Purgatory belong to the period between the fifteenth and nineteenth centuries. Besides the traditional means of publicity, such as sermons and pamphlets and, later, books, images played an important part in propagating the new doctrine.[1] Frescoes, miniatures, engravings, chapel and altar decorations all served to crystallize the images surrounding the idea of Purgatory. Deprived of the possibilities inherent in the literary frenzy that all but overwhelmed certain visions of the other world, architecture, sculpture, and painting provided Purgatory with the means to entice the onlooker with a direct vision, culminating the process that had evolved for Purgatory a location, a substance, and a content of its own.[2]

Developments in the realm of doctrine and practice were no less important. Purgatory had begun to be mentioned in wills, but only to a limited degree. Starting in the fourteenth century, however, the new place begins to make greater and greater inroads, at different dates and with different intensities in different regions—in some areas we witness a veritable floodtide of testamentary references to Purgatory.[3] At times institutions make up for a want of bequests or, by appealing to the generosity of the faithful, compensate for a shortfall. In southern France, for example, where Christians continued to harbor doubts, not to say hostility, with regard to the third region of the hereafter, it became common practice to circulate a "bowl [*bassin*] for souls in Purgatory" during mass in order to collect "the money of the faithful" for a special fund, the "Purgatory charity" (*oeuvre du Purgatoire*), which is the subject of an admirable study by Michelle Bastard-Fournié. This was the petty cash of the communion of saints. Together with sculpture, practices such as this reveal changes in the beliefs associated with Purgatory, an expansion of their range, so to speak. The devotion to the souls in Purgatory that we can see in the altarpieces and ex-votos shows that at some point these souls begin to acquire not only merit but also the power to transfer their merit to the living, to return service for service, to give assistance to men and women on earth. Thus the reversibility of merits, in doubt in the twelfth and thirteenth centuries and usually denied, eventually won a place in doctrine. The system of solidarity between the living and the dead instituted an unending circular flow, a full circuit of reciprocity. The two extremes were knit together. Furthermore, an institution such as the "bowl for souls in Purgatory" proves that suffrages other than the special day set aside on November 2 could be applied to all the dead supposedly in Purgatory, even if the givers believed that their offerings were destined primarily to shorten the suffering of "their" dead. The communion of saints manifested itself to the full. Its application became general.

In the thirteenth century Purgatory gave rise to at best limited forms of spirituality—leaving aside Dante's great poem. Saint Lutgard was an ardent helper of souls in Purgatory, but she seems not to have established any explicit link between her devotion to those souls and the deeper current of spirituality of which she was one of the earliest promoters, namely, worship of the Sacred Heart. First developed among the Beguines, this form of devotion was spread by Hadewijch and Mechtilde of Magdeburg and later by the Benedictine nuns Mechtilde and Gertrude of Hackeborn. In the late thirteenth century it exerted a powerful influence over the nuns of Helfta in Saxony. With Gertrude the Great (d. 1301 or 1302) Purgatory entered the highest realms of mysticism, and later attained the pinnacle (or, if you prefer, the depths) of mystical devotion with Saint Catherine of Genoa (1447–1510), the author of a *Treatise on Purgatory*.

In the area of dogma and theology, Purgatory was ultimately enshrined in the doctrine of the Catholic Church between the middle of the fifteenth and the beginning of the seventeenth century, first being affirmed against the Greeks at the Council of Florence (1439) and later against the Protestants at the Council of Trent (1562). Trent, an affair of theologians and rulers more than of pastors, established Purgatory in dogma once and for all but, like its thirteenth century predecessors, remained noncommittal as to Purgatory's imaginary content. Nor does the imagination play much of a role in the two great syntheses by the Jesuits Bellarmino and Suarez, in which Purgatory is rooted in the theology of the post-Tridentine catechism.

Purgatory enjoyed a more ample existence, however, in the leading Catholic styles of the fifteenth to nineteenth centuries. There is a flamboyant gothic Purgatory and a Purgatory of the *devotio moderna*. There is not only a Counter Reformation Purgatory but also—more important perhaps—a classical Purgatory, a baroque Purgatory, a romantic Purgatory, and a Sulpician Purgatory. The leading historians of attitudes toward death in the period from the sixteenth century to the present, Philippe Ariès, Pierre Chaunu, François Lebrun, Alberto Tenenti, and Michel Vovelle, all discuss Purgatory in their books. These discussions are not always as clear as one might wish, however.[4] The historians in question have focused their research primarily on what is enduring in mankind's attitudes toward death, and Purgatory, though a prominent if elusive feature of Christian thinking about the afterlife, seems to have been a perishable rather than an enduring idea. Still, I hope to have shown that, as early as the thirteenth century, Purgatory did begin to change the attitude of Christians toward the final moments of life on this earth. Purgatory dramatized the end of earthly existence and charged it with an intensity compounded of mingled fear and hope. The essential choice between Heaven and Hell could still be played out at the last moment, since Purgatory was the antechamber of Paradise. The last instants of life became man's last chance. In consequence, I feel that further work remains to be done before we can hope to understand how death and Purgatory were related from the fourteenth century to date.

In this book I have attempted to trace the way in which Christian ideas about the other world were formed in the period between the fourth and fourteenth century. Taken together, these ideas constitute an ideological and imaginary system. As I sat down to write my conclusion, however, I found that I was nagged by anxiety. For my purpose was to suggest that the key component of this system of ideas was its centerpiece, Purgatory, which came for a time to occupy a tenuous position between Heaven and Hell. But what if it isn't so?

Isn't it possible that the real energizing and organizing force of the system lay not in Purgatory but in Heaven? Paradise has aroused surprisingly little interest among historians, even though, when I look at the evidence I have amassed, it becomes clear that it was not nearly so monotonous and insipid as has been said. This plain of Paradise—watered by powerful rivers, transfigured by light, resounding with song in perfect harmony, bathed in exquisite fragrances, and suffused with the ineffable presence of the divine unfolded in the infinitude of the empyrean—this is a world that has yet to be discovered.[5] Beyond Purgatory and its hope and certainty of salvation, its response to the need for a more refined and precise justice, its intensified attentiveness to the need for complete purification in the final stage of the soul's return, might it not have been the promise of Christ on the cross to the crucified thief that animated the entire system: "Today shalt thou be with me in paradise" (Luke 23:43)?

Despite all the infernal imagery, Purgatory's center of gravity may have shifted so far toward Paradise as to make the desire for Heaven the energizing force of Christian doctrine—that desire for Heaven which, according to the *Divine Comedy*, causes souls to fly constantly toward God, causing the mountain of Purgatory to tremble with each joyful thunderclap that marks the arrival in Heaven of yet another soul.

If so, then I have not fully penetrated the virtual silence of the sources to discover the true nature of the beatific vision, the absence of which would represent not Purgatory's "degree zero" but the last bleak stretch to be traversed on the road to eternity. On this view the key to the spatial and temporal organization of Purgatory should be sought not by studying what Pierre Chaunu calls "extended duration" (*surdurée*) or what Philippe Ariès calls "the biographical postscript" (*supplément de biographie*) but rather by concentrating on what comes just prior to the beatific vision, just before eternity. Was John XXII right? Was Purgatory more a pre-eternity than a post-existence?

This is not the real source of my anxiety, however. Throughout the history we have been studying, was it not the principal concern of the Church to preserve the belief in Hell everlasting? Wasn't the point of introducing a temporary Purgatory mainly to throw the inextinguishable fires of Hell into sharp relief? Wasn't the second kingdom merely a protective buffer for the infernal realms? Wasn't Purgatory the price that the Church had to pay to hold onto the ultimate weapon, damnation? This is the view taken by Jean Delumeau, whose work has shed sulphurous light on "the Christianity of fear."

Perhaps a view of this kind would help us to understand the attitude toward Purgatory of most Catholics today. The Catholic attitude is concerned with the afterlife in general, but Purgatory is an especially important concern. The problem faced by the Church today is one that it has faced many times before: How to bring about an *aggiornamento* that some will regard as a stage in the slow but steady progress toward an "ideal" Christianity, a progress that is both a return to the roots and the culmination of an advance, and that others, of different belief, will see as nothing more than an attempt by a backward institution to catch up with history's halting march. No matter: once again it is the imaginary content of the afterlife that is being sacrificed for the sake of purification, in order to eradicate "primitive" beliefs. At best, a few individuals, informed about the past, respectful of others, and concerned to strike a proper balance, will agree with Father Y. M. Congar that "here again we are going to have to purify our thinking and eliminate not all of our imagery—for without images thought is impossible, and some of these images are valid and a few of them quite beautiful—but at least some of our wilder fancies."[6] And who indeed would quarrel with the idea of getting rid of certain tortures, infernal in the true sense of the word (even if they are alleged to be purgatorial) and all too obviously copied from practices that unfortunately have not yet vanished from this world? One point made by the great Dominican theologian is surely well taken, namely, that a way must be found to adapt man's beliefs to his changing social and intellectual circumstances but without excising man's imagination—that essential part of his memory and being. All too often in history, progress toward adaptation has come at the expense of the imagination. But man's reason is sustained by images. History at its deepest level shows this to be true.

My concern is that the desire to purify will prove especially costly to Purgatory. For I hope to have shown that the inception, elaboration, and dissemination of this doctrine depended crucially on the imagination, so crucially that Father Congar has to make himself sound almost like an Origenist in order to save Purgatory in a manner that today's Catholic hierarchy, with its current outlook, can approve.

As for the rank-and-file of the faith, it seems to me that the causes of disaffection with Purgatory are not the same and may even be contrary to the causes at work within the hierarchy. The clergy has been moving toward a less infernal, less material conception of Purgatory. Among the rank-and-file, on the other hand, there is growing indifference to the idea of an intermediate interval in the afterlife. In our own time, particularly in the so-called developed societies, man's questioning, his hopes and fears, have concentrated on two polar extremes. As for this world, if we leave out of account the large number of people who really "don't care," it is the image of death looming on the horizon that has tended to draw man's gaze. The question is how to die. For Catholics as well as adherents of other religions and people who for one reason or another must face the issue of death, the decision again seems to have narrowed to a choice between various paradises and various hells: paradises that are projections of this-wordly dreams and hells that are projections of fears for which a new kind of imagery has been invented. *Our* apocalypse is nuclear destruction, and a part of mankind has already endured the terrifying experience.[7]

Yet there will always, I hope, be a place in man's dreams for subtlety, justice, accuracy, and measure in every sense of the word, for reason (O reasonable Purgatory!) and hope. I hope that it will be a long while before it can truly be said of Purgatory that its time is past.

APPENDIX ONE
Bibliography of Purgatory

AN up-to-date bibliography of works about Purgatory would run to considerable length. Many books about Purgatory are the work of ill-informed authors interested more in polemic (among both Protestants and Catholics) or apology (among Catholics) than in dispassionate historiography. All too often one has the impression that Catholic scholarship concerning Purgatory made only scant progress from the time of Bellarmine and Suarez until the first half of the twentieth century. A. Michel's substantial article on "Purgatory" in the *Dictionnaire de Théologie catholique*, ed. E. Vacant, E. Mangenot, and E. Amann (1936), vol. 13, cols. 1163–1326, remains fundamental. It is written in a traditional and anti-Protestant spirit. The best brief overview of the subject, in my opinion, is that of A. Piolanti, "Il dogma del purgatorio," in *Euntes docete* 6(1953):287–311. The article "Fegfeuer" in the *Lexicon für Theologie und Kirche* (1960), vol. 4, cols. 49–55, is superficial. The work of the Protestant E. Fleischhak, *Fegfeuer. Die christlichen Vorstellungen vom Geschick der Verstorbenen geschichtlich dargestellt* (1969), is intended to inform Protestants about Catholic views on the subject; it is sympathetic but the information it contains is secondhand, incomplete, and not always accurate.

The work most abounding in fruitful suggestions is by the ethnologist and historian Marcus Landau, *Hölle und Fegfeuer in Volksglaube, Dichtung und Kirchenlehre* (Heidelberg, 1909). Unfortunately the information it contains is out of date and incomplete, and the book suffers from the ethnologist's disregard of chronology.

Concerning medieval exegesis of a biblical passage that played a key role in the development of Purgatory, the reader will wish to consult J. Gnilka, *Ist 1 Kor. 3:10 ein Schriftzeugnis für das Fegfeuer? Eine exegetsich-historische Untersuchung* (Düsseldorf, 1955).

The history of Purgatory in the ancient world has been revitalized by the excellent works of Joseph Ntedika, *Evolution de la doctrine du Purgatoire chez saint Augustin*, (Paris: Etudes augustiniennes, 1966), and *L'Evolution de l'au-delà dans la prière pour les morts. Etudes de patristique et de liturgie latines* (Louvain-Paris, 1971).

In J. Goubert and L. Cristiani, *Les plus beaux textes sur l'au-delà*, the reader will find texts of varying value and pitched on different levels; still, there are a few significant texts concerning Purgatory.

"Purgatorium"
The History of a Word

THE crucial moment came in the second half of the twelfth century when the noun *purgatorium* was added to the vocabulary alongside the adjective *purgatorius* (*purgatoria, purgatorium*). Curiously enough, this linguistic event, which in my view is the sign of an important evolution in beliefs about the other world, has until now escaped notice by historians of Purgatory or at any rate claimed their attention only briefly. Even Joseph Ntedika errs when he accords to either Hildebert of Lavardin or Hildebert of Le Mans (d. 1133) the honor of having been the first to use the word *purgatorium* (*Evolution de la doctrine du Purgatoire chez saint Augustin*, p. 11 n. 17). The same error occurs in the article on "Fegfeuer" in the *Lexicon für Theologie und Kirche*, vol. 4, col. 51. A. Piolanti ("Il dogma del Purgatorio," *Euntes Docete* 6[1953]:300) says merely that "in this century [the twelfth] the first drafts of the treatise *De purgatorio* appeared (from this point on the adjective became a noun)." E. Fleischhak claims, without giving any references (for good reason!), that "the word *purgatorium* had been in use since Carolingian times" (*Fegfeuer* [1969], p. 64).

In order to maintain, as I have done, that the term very probably made its first appearance between 1170 and 1180, certain false attributions have to be corrected and certain emendations made in the published editions of texts from before 1170. The emendations involve mainly expressions such as *ignis purgatorius*, *poena(e) purgatoria(e)*, *loca purgatoria*, or *in [locis] purgatoriis*. *Purgatorium* appears in the published versions as a substantive only because the publications were based on manuscripts prepared after 1170, in which the copyist must have replaced, say, *ignem purgatorium* by plain *purgatorium*, a natural thing to do given the fact that by this time the use of the noun was current.

Peter Damian (d. 1072), in his fifty-ninth sermon for the feast of Saint Nicholas, did not use the word *purgatorium* but, we are told, did single out Purgatory as one of the five regions in which the souls of men can be received: (1) *regio dissimilitudinis* (this world); (2) *paradisus claustralis* (paradise on earth, i.e., the cloister); (3) *regio expiationis*, the place of expiation—Purgatory; (4) *regio gehennalis*, Hell; and (5) *paradisus supercoelestis*, the heavenly paradise.

In describing the region of expiation this sermon uses the expression *loca purgatoria* (PL 144.838). But it is now acknowledged that this text is the work not of Peter Damian but rather of that notorious forger Nicholas of Clairvaux (d. after 1176), who was Saint Bernard's secretary. For example, F. Dressler, *Petrus Damiani. Leben und Werk* (Anselmiana 34) Rome (1954), appendix 3, pp. 234–35, lists nineteen sermons which in all likelihood are not the work of Peter Damian, including sermon 59, and adds that these are "probably" the work of Nicholas of Clairvaux, "einem gerissenen Fälscher." Cf. J. Ryan, "Saint Peter Damiani and the Sermons of Nicholas of Clairvaux: A Clarification," *Medieval Studies* 9(1947):151–61. Furthermore, in the *Patrologia latina* Migne published the same sermon (no. 59) twice, once under the name Peter Damian (*PL* 144.835–39) and a second time under the name Nicholas of Clairvaux (*PL* 184.1055–60). Nicholas of Clairvaux is probably also the author of sermon 42, "De quinque negotiationibus et quinque regionibus," which is attributed to Saint Bernard and which takes a line very similar to that of Peter Damian but in which the system of three regions (within the five) and the word Purgatory (*purgatorium*) appear with a clarity that I do not think could have been achieved prior to 1153, the date of Saint Bernard's death: *Tria sunt loca, quae mortuorum animae pro diversis meritis sortiuntur: infernus, purgatorium, caelum* (Saint Bernard, *Opera Omnia*, ed. J. Leclercq and H. M. Rochais, vol. 6, 1, p. 259). Dom Jean Leclercq and H. M. Rochais have been kind enough to confirm to me in writing as well as in conversation what they have already written in various articles (J. Leclercq, "Les collections de sermons de Nicolas de Clairvaux," *Revue benedictine* [1956], and H. M. Rochais, "Enquête sur les sermons divers et les sentences de saint Bernard," *Analecta SOC* [1962]), namely, that the evidence neither confirms nor refutes the attribution to Saint Bernard of sermon 42: "We have maintained the attribution of *De diversis* 42 to Saint Bernard . . . which does not mean that our judgment is not subject to change. I believe that the text is one of which there exist several versions due not to Saint Bernard himself but to Nicholas of Clairvaux and others, which would explain the introduction of anachronistic terminology" (J. Leclercq, letter of October 5, 1979). Madame Monique-Cecile Garand, who was kind enough to examine for me Latin manuscripts 2571 of the Bibliothèque nationale of Paris and 169 of Cambrai—probably the earliest manuscripts—argues cautiously on the basis of paleographic evidence that the former must be from the third quarter of the twelfth century (but perhaps prior to the canonization of Saint Bernard in 1174, since the word *sanctus* does not figure in the title and has been added in the *ex-libris*) and the latter from the second half of the century. A date of around 1170 therefore seems reasonable. I am convinced that the sermon is not by Saint Bernard and that it was written at the earliest some twenty years after his death. On Nicholas of Clairvaux, compare also the comments of G.

Constable, *The Letters of Peter the Venerable II, Nicholas of Montieramey, and Peter the Venerable* (Cambridge, Mass., 1967), pp. 316–30.

Before Saint Bernard, the word *purgatorium* is supposed to have occurred in a text by Hildebert of Lavardin, bishop of Le Mans and archbishop of Tours (d. 1133), and even so careful a scholar as Ntedika accepted this erroneous attribution, as I mentioned a moment ago. Sermon 85, "Jerusalem quae aedificatur," which was published with Hildebert's sermons by Beaugendre in 1708 and reproduced by Migne in *Patrologia latina* 171.741 (*hi, qui in purgatorio poliuntur*), was long ago restored to its true author, Peter Comestor, by Hauréau, "Notice sur les sermons attribués à Hildebert de Lavardin," in *Notices et extraits des manuscrits . . .*, 32(2)(1888), p. 143. Compare A. Wilmart, "Les sermons d'Hildebert," in *Revue Bénédictine* 47(1935):12–51. The attribution to Peter Comestor was confirmed by M. M. Lebreton, "Recherches sur les manuscrits contenant des sermons de Pierre le Mangeur," in *Bulletin d'Information tions de L'I.R.H.T.* 2(1953):25–44. François Dolbeau has kindly informed me that in the oldest manuscripts of these sermons, which he too confirms to have been the work of Peter Comestor, one does in fact find the phrase *in purgatorio* (MSS 312 [303] and 247 [238] of Angers, from the end of the twelfth century), but that the whole clause in which this phrase occurs is missing from an older manuscript, MS 227 [218] from the Bibliothèque municipale of Valenciennes, which dates from the middle of the twelfth century.

It seems that the noun *purgatorium* does occur in a letter sent in 1176 by the English Benedictine Nicholas of Saint Albans to the Cistercian Peter of Celle (in 1180–82 according to information generously provided by A.-M. Bautier): "Porro facto levi per purgatorium transitu intravit in gaudium Domini sui" (*PL* 202.624). Furthermore, Peter Comestor, who died in 1179 and who may have used the noun *purgatorium* in the sermon "Jerusalem quae aedificatur," apparently never used it in *De sacramentis*, which was written between 1165 and 1170. Accordingly, it would seem that the earliest use of *purgatorium* as a noun occurred shortly after 1170 in the writings of several men: the Cistercian Nicholas of Clairvaux, the Benedictine Nicholas of Saint Albans, and Peter Comestor, a secular master in the school of Notre Dame of Paris.

This leaves one problem that I have been unable to resolve satisfactorily. In Migne there is an anonymous treatise, *De vera et falsa poenitentia*, which was attributed in the Middle Ages to Augustine but which actually dates from the late eleventh century or, more likely, from the first half of the twelfth century and in which the term *purgatorium* is used as a noun: *ita quod nec purgatorium sentiunt qui in fine baptizantur* (*PL* 40.1127). The fact that a few lines further on the text speaks of *ignis purgationis* proves nothing but leaves the word *purgatorium* isolated. I am convinced that it was simply left in the manuscripts from the end of the twelfth century on and that the original text must have read *ignem purgatorium*. There is no doubt the *De vera et falsa poenitentia* is from before the middle of the twelfth century, since it was cited not only by Peter Lombard, who died in 1160 (*PL* 192.883), but also in Gratian's *Decretum*, which was written around 1140 (*PL* 187.1559, 1561, and 1637). Unfortunately, despite my research, carried out with the assistance of François Dolbeau, Agostino Paravicini Bagliani, and Madame Marie-Claire Gasnault, I was unable to consult any manuscript of *De vera et falsa poenitentia* from before the end of the twelfth century, and my conviction remains a hypothesis to be verified. I can only add that I hope one day to see a scholarly edition of this text, which is so important for the history of penance, a central theme of twelfth-century theology and religious practice. Compare A. Teetaert, *La Confession aux laïques dans l'Eglise latine depuis le VIIIe jusqu'au XIVe siècle* (Paris, 1926), pp. 50–56, and C. Fantini, "Il tratatto ps. agostiniano De vera et falso poenitentia," in *Ricerche di storia religiosa* (1954), pp. 200–209.

For a significant example of the way in which the expression *ignis purgatorius* was transformed, from the end of the twelfth century on, into the noun *purgatorium*, particularly where the noun in the more recent text and the adjective in the original text are in the same grammatical case, consider the following. Alexander of Hales, in his *Gloss on the Sententiae of Peter Lombard* (written between 1223 and 1229) cites the *De potestate legandi et solvendi* of Richard of Saint Victor (d. 1173) as follows: "per incendium purgatorii scoria peccati excoquitur" (*Glossa in IV libros Sentiarum Petri Lombardi*, lib. IV, dist. XX, ed. Quaracchi, vol. 4, p. 354). But Richard of Saint Victor's original text reads "per incendium purgatorii ignis scoria peccati excoquitur" (*PL* 196.1177).

At the end of the twelfth and the beginning of the thirteenth century we find *purgatorium* and *ignis purgatorius* being used as virtual synonyms, sometimes by the same author. Peter of Celle, to whom Nicholas of Saint Albans wrote around 1180 on the subject of *purgatorium* (in connection with Saint Bernard), uses only the expression *ignis purgatorius* in his treatise *De disciplina claustrali* (composed in 1179; see *PL* 202.1133). Since the earliest manuscripts of several twelfth-century works have not survived, it will be difficult to pinpoint with any degree of certainty the earliest usage of the word *purgatorium*.

Madame Anne-Marie Bautier has kindly called my attention to one of the earliest definitions of Purgatory, which is found in a life of Saint Victor, martyr of Mauzon, recently published by F. Dolbeau (*Revue historique ardennaise*, vol. 9, p. 61): "Purgatorium ergo, locum conflationis, ergastulum purgationis, iste sanctus repperit in gremio ecclesiae in qua conflari injuriis et passionibus meruit, quibus ad remunerationem victoriae laureatus pervenit." This shows that some saints (including Bernard himself) were thought not to go directly to Paradise but to pass first through Purgatory.

Finally, when we turn to dictionaries and glossaries of medieval Latin, it appears that the earliest example of the word *purgatorium* cited by Du Cange is the letter sent in 1254 by Innocent IV to Eudes of Châteauroux. J. F. Niermeyer, *Mediae Latinitatis Lexicon Minus* (Leyden, 1976), says this: "subst. neutre purgatorium le Purgatoire, the Purgatory, S. XIII." A. Blaise, in his *Dictionnaire latin-français des auteurs du Moyen Age*, Corpus christianorum, Continuatio Maedievalis (Turnhout, 1975), pp. 754–55, says that the word first appeared in the twelfth century, prior to which a periphrasis such as *purgatorius ignis* was used; he cites the pseudo-Augustine (of *De vera et falsa poenitentia*), the letter of Innocent III from the beginning of the thirteenth century, and the sermon of Hildebert of Lavardin, which should actually be attributed to Peter Comestor (d. 1179). As a definition he gives "séjour penitentiel situé dans une île et appelé 'purgatoire de S. Patrice' ou Patrick."

J. H. Baxter and C. Johnson (*Medieval Latin Word-List from British and Irish Sources* [Oxford, 1934]) simply gives "purgatorium, purgatory (eccl.), c. 1200." R. E. Latham, in his *Revised Medieval Latin Word-List from British and Irish Sources* (London, 1965), distinguishes between "purgatorium (theol.) c. 1150" and "purgatorium Sancti Patricii (in Lough Derg) c. 1188." I think that the date "circa 1150" comes from the date 1153 assigned by the tradition surrounding Saint Patrick's Purgatory to the knight Owein's adventure. The date (and probably the story) is pure fantasy.

As for the vernacular languages, the earliest mention of Purgatory in French probably occurs in the form "espurgatoire" in the *Espurgatoire Saint Patriz* by Marie de France around 1190 (or possibly later, between 1208 and 1215, according to the hypothesis put forward by F. W. Locke in *Speculum* [1965], pp. 641–46).

My friend Josef Macek informs me that the Czech word for Purgatory, *Očistec*, first occurs between 1350 and 1380 in translations of Latin works. But this Purgatory seems not to have been clearly distinguished from Limbo or even Hell. For Jan Hus Purgatory was "the third hell" (*třetie pehlo in Vyhlad viery*, MS M, Library of the University of Brno, MK, fol. 16a.). At the beginning of the fifteenth century the Taborites refused to believe in Purgatory and punned on the words *očistec* and *ošistec* (deceit) or referred to Purgatory as *purgáč*, meaning purgative. Concerning the rejection of Purgatory by the Waldensians and Hussites, see Romolo Cegna, "Le De reliquiis et de veneratione sanctorum: De purgatorio de Nicola della Rosa Nera detto da Dresda (di Cerruc), maître a Prague de 1412 a 1415," *Mediaevalia Philosophica Polonorum*, vol. 23 (Wroclaw-Warsaw-Krakow-Gdansk, 1977).

Earliest Images

I N THE article entitled "Fegfeuer" (Purgatory) in the excellent *Lexicon der christlichen Ikonographie*, ed. E. Kirschbaum (1970), vol. 2, col. 17, W. Braunfels writes: "We find no representation of Purgatory in the figurative art of either early Christian times or of the Middle Ages up to the end of the fourteenth century."

While it does seem to be the case that the iconography of Purgatory does not begin to spread until the end of the fourteenth century, representations of Purgatory are found in the previous century, and it seems likely that careful iconographic investigation would turn up an even greater abundance of images of Purgatory of earlier date.

Here I want to describe three such representations (see the illustrations accompanying the text).

1. The earliest, to which my attention was called by Father Gy, is a miniature found on folio 49 of the so-called Breviary of Philip the Fair (Paris, Bibliothèque nationale, Latin MS 1023). This manuscript, which dates from the period 1253–96 and which on formal grounds probably requires a date close to the end of this period, i.e., 1296, is very probably the breviary that Philip the Fair ordered to be illustrated by a celebrated Parisian painter, Master Honoré, in 1296, as we know from the account books of the Louvre treasury for that year.

The small (3.5 cm × 4 cm) miniature on folio 49 of that breviary probably represents a judgment of souls. Christ in majesty together with two flanking seraphim occupies about two-thirds of the frame's height. In the lower portion we see four souls in Purgatory, two of them still immersed in flames while the other two are being pulled out of the fire by two angels that have broken through the ceiling of clouds. The figure comprises four levels: a golden Heaven, an area of clouds, a sublunary region ruled as a grid, and the fire. (Cf. V. Leroquais, *Les Bréviaires manuscrits des bibliothèques publiques de France* [Paris, 1934], vol. 2, no. 487, pp. 465–85.)

2. A miniature in some respects similar to the foregoing and in other respects different is found in the so-called Breviary of Charles V, which was probably commissioned by a lady of the French royal family between 1347 and 1380, the date by which it is known to have been included in

Charles V's library (Paris, Bibliothèque nationale, Latin MS 1052, fol. 556v., cf. Leroquais, *Les Bréviaires manuscrits*, vol. 3, pp. 49–56). This miniature, also small, is placed "in commemoration of the dead," that is to say, on November 2, whereas the preceding one was used to illustrate Psalm 114, *Dilexi*, in which the psalmist thanks Yahweh for having delivered him from the snares of *Sheol*. Christ does not figure in this second miniature, in contrast to the first. Two large angels are pulling two souls up toward Heaven, and only the feet of these souls remain in the fire. Eleven heads represent a host of souls in Purgatory of varying social conditions (we recognize a pope, a bishop, etc.), all immersed in the flames. There are three levels in the composition: a very thin blue sky (filling perhaps a tenth of the frame's height), an intermediate grid that occupies about half the height of the frame, and an infernal region featuring rocks and a large hole filled with fire. I am indebted to Mr. François Avril for bringing this miniature and its reproduction to my attention.

3. The third representation of Purgatory is a fresco in the old cathedral at Salamanca, which shows the four regions comprising the early fourteenth-century conception of the other world. On the left (as we look at the composition) is Heaven, and on the right Hell. In the center there are receptacles with souls in them. Those on the left represent Purgatory, those on the right the limbos. An angel has come to one of the upper receptacles of Purgatory to take a soul to Heaven. According to an inscription, the date of the painting is 1300 by the Spanish calendar, which would correspond to 1262, but François Avril believes on stylistic grounds that the fresco cannot be earlier than the first half of the fourteenth century. For the reproduction I am indebted to Professor Luis Cortès. Cf. Jose Guidol Ricart, *Ars Hispanica* (Madrid, 1955), vol. 9, *Pintura Gotica*, p. 47.

APPENDIX FOUR
Recent Works

S INCE completing this work in January 1981, I have learned of various other studies that touch more or less directly on Purgatory. Paolo Santarcangeli, in *NEKYIA, La discesa dei poeti agli Inferni* (Milan, 1980), p. 72, describes Saint Patrick's Purgatory in the course of a discussion of the symbolic geography involved in the location of Hell on various islands.

Three important studies treat visions of and journeys to the other world. Michel Aubrun's "Caractères et portée religieuse et sociale des Visiones en Occident du VIe au XIe siècle," was published in *Cahiers de civilisation médiévale* (April-June 1980), pp. 109–30. Aubrun gives a very shrewd analysis of the religious and psychological climate surrounding these visions. He is perceptive about the attitude of the ecclesiastical hierarchy, which wavered from reserve to out-and-out cooptation, in keeping with the medieval Church's distrust of dreams. Aubrun does not really touch on the "problem" of Purgatory, since his study ends with the beginning of the twelfth century, but he rightly notes the presence in Bede's "Vision of Drythelm" of a sort of "penitential Purgatory in the northeast" and a "Purgatory of waiting in the southeast." This two-part Purgatory has affinities with the dual hereafter of Celtic tradition, one part of which was quasi-infernal, the other quasi-paradisaical, and is a forerunner of Dante's *Purgatorio* with its ante-Purgatory.

The great Soviet medievalist Aaron J. Gurjewitsch (whose work on the *Categories of Medieval Culture*, first published in 1972, has appeared in German translation as *Das Weltbild des mittelälterlichen Menschen* [Dresden, 1978], and is soon to appear in French in Gallimard's Bibliothèque des Histoires), sent a paper to be read in March 1981 at a colloquium on "Christian Time" (fourth century to ninth century) organized by the French Centre national de la Recherche scientifique, which the author was unable to attend in person. This important paper will soon be published in *Annales E.S.C.* under the title "L'individu et l'imagination de l'au-delà." Gurjewitsch criticizes Pierre Chaunu and especially Philippe Ariès for having based their ideas concerning Purgatory on such evidence as wills and, even more, iconographic sources, which were slow to accept the new doctrine, whereas other evidence suggests that the inception and propagation of Purgatory occurred much earlier than these authors think. I agree that these other sources—visions of the other world and *exempla*, of which I have made extensive use in this book—are indispensable and give us a different view of the history of Purgatory. Gurjewitch and I both argue that the crucial period came at the end of the twelfth century and the beginning of the thirteenth. In my view, however, Gurjewitsch himself has neglected valuable evidence from the areas of theology, liturgy, and religious practice. I agree with him that Purgatory and the whole system of beliefs concerning the other world revealed by the sources suggest that death was becoming an increasingly individualized affair and that the idea of an individual judgment immediately after death was taking on increasing importance. But if all the sources are taken into account, particularly those that speak of suffrages, it becomes clear, as I hope to have shown, that the increased importance of individual salvation went hand in hand with action by the communities of which the individual was a member, whether these were kinship groups or artificial communities on earth or a supernatural, spiritual community, the communion of saints.

In April 1981 Claude Carozzi presented to the XXIXe Settimana di Storia del Centro Italiano di studi sull'Alto Medioevo at Spoleto, devoted to the theme "Popoli e paesi nella cultura altomedievale," a remarkable paper entitled "La géographie de l'au-delà et sa signification pendant le haut Moyen Age," which will be published in the conference proceedings. The paper is an outline of the thesis he is preparing on the visionary literature of the sixth to the thirteenth century. Purgatory was the central theme of Carozzi's paper. I agree with him as to the importance of geography in the development of beliefs about the other world and have no quarrel with his identification of the main phases in the process: Gregory the Great's *Dialogues*, Bede's "Vision of Drythelm," the politicization of the other world in Carolingian times, and the decisive evolution toward greater concreteness in the major texts of the twelfth and early thirteenth centuries. But we differ on a point I regard as essential. Claude Carozzi speaks of Purgatory as early as the eighth century, perhaps even as early as the sixth century. He is a "realist" where I am a "nominalist" who believes in the fundamental significance of changes in vocabulary. He is therefore inclined to view the end of the twelfth century as the time of the birth of Hell—that is, of a distinct place of eternal punishment—rather than as the birth of Purgatory. As a provocative and witty remark, this suggestion is a fertile one. But I do not believe that it accords with the historical reality. Claude Carozzi has brought great erudition and intelligence to the study of a literary genre. A historical phenomenon such as the birth of Purgatory has to be explained in terms of a whole range of sources, analyzed in their full historical context. My summary greatly simplifies Carozzi's argument, however. Further comment must await the final publication of his thesis, which I am sure will be of great interest.

In light of these recent studies I should point out that I have not studied all the extant visions of the hereafter for the period from the eighth to the thirteenth century. The texts left out are, I trust, only those that did not affect my argument one way or the other, notwithstanding their intrinsic interest. It goes without saying that the word *purgatorium* does not occur in any of them. Below I summarize briefly my reasons for omitting certain visions analyzed by the three authors just cited and, before them (although in less detail and from a less historical point of view), by authors such as Becker, Dods, MacCullogh, Seymour, Patch, and, more recently, Dinzelbacher.

Seventh Century: The Vision of Bonellus
(*PL* 87.433–35).

The Spanish abbot Valera, who died in the last decade of the seventh century, recounts the travels of the monk Bonellus in the other world. While in an ecstatic trance, he is taken by an angel to a habitation, a gleaming cell made of precious gems, which is to be his future dwelling place provided he perseveres in his ascetic practices. In another trance a demon drags him down into the pit of Hell. No allusion is made to any sort of purgation, but certain details suggest the future system of Purgatory. The location is in the depths of the earth, where demons are tossing souls into a terrible fire. Bonellus sees a horrible chained devil, but this is apparently not Satan, since the monk is simply shown "the lower pit of the abyss in which the punishments are even harsher and more cruel." A poor man whom he has helped on earth tries to come to his aid—an allusion to the system of suffrages. The monk manages to hold out by making the sign of the cross, a gesture that recurs in Saint Patrick's Purgatory. Ultimately he returns to earth. It bears repeating that the idea of purgation is not mentioned, only a hierarchy of sites and punishments. The system is dualistic: one place, unnamed, is very pleasant, the other is an abyss (*abyssus*) called Hell (*infernus*).

Seventh Century: The Vision of Barontus (678/79)
(*MGH, SRM*, vol. 5, pp. 377–94).

Barontus, a monk of the monastery of Longoretus (Saint-Cyran near Bourges) is carried off during a severe illness by two demons but receives help from the archangel Raphael and Saint Peter, who show him the four gates of Paradise and allow him to glimpse Hell, in which crowds of men and women grouped by category of sin are tortured by devils. There is no mention of purgation.

Eighth Century: The Vision of the Monk of Wenlock (c. 717)
(*MGH*, Epistolae, vol. 3, pp. 252–57).

In a letter to the abbess Eadburge of Tenet, Saint Boniface recounts the vision of a monk of the English abbey of Wenlock in Shropshire. Angels take him around the world and then show him the fiery pit of Hell, and he hears the moans and tears of souls in the lower inferno. They also show him a very pleasant place that he is told is called the paradise of God. The only interesting point as far as the prehistory of Purgatory is concerned is that there is a bridge that crosses a river of fire, from which some souls fall into the river and become either fully immersed or immersed as far as the knees or armpits. These, the monk is told, "are the souls that left mortal life without having rid themselves completely of certain slight sins and who had need of some pious punishment from the merciful God in order to become worthy of him." Thus the idea of purgation is present, though the word is not used. But this text is quite backward compared with Bede's "Vision of Drythelm," which is almost contemporary with it.

Eleventh Century: Otloh of Saint-Emmeran

Otloh of Saint-Emmeran and Fulda (1010–70), the author of the first medieval autobiography, which some commentators have gone so far as to compare to Augustine's *Confessions*, also wrote a *Book of Visions* (*PL* 146.341–88), a book well within the monastic tradition that tells of Otloh's own visions as well as visions culled from various other sources, primarily the *Dialogues* of Gregory the Great. Among the visions taken from other sources is that of the monk of Wenlock as reported by Saint Boniface (col. 375–80) and that of Drythelm as recounted by Bede (col. 380–83). Given the age of Otloh's sources, we not only fail to find any mention of Purgatory in these visions but even the expressions *ignis purgatorius* and *poenae purgatoriae* occur only rarely.[1] For example, in vision 14, a monk from a Bohemian monastery, one Isaac, finds himself in a lovely meadow in which he sees Saints Gunther, Maurice, and Adalbert, who tell him that they had to "pass through purgatorial fire" before coming to this *refrigerium*. Otloh thus contributed nothing new to the future Purgatory. His visions are interesting for some of the incidental matter they contain. For example, he frequently suggests that spoliation of monastic property by laymen is a prime cause of their punishment in the hereafter (in vision 7 a lord guilty of this crime appears to his two sons in an aerial cavalcade that must be one of the earliest evocations of the so-called "Wild Hunt" [*mesnie Hellequin*]. Furthermore, he is much given to the use of visions for political ends. For example, the vision of the monk Isaac is intended to show the supremacy of the episcopal see of Regensburg over that of Prague. Vision 17 shows the empress Theophano, wife of Otto II and mother of Otto III, appearing to a nun to ask for help in escaping the torments she is suffering in the other world for having succumbed, as oriental women will, to a taste for excessively sumptuous ornament and dress. A fine example of the way the other world was used to express the cultural divide between East and West.

Early Thirteenth Century: Thurchill's Vision

I shall say a little more about the vision of Thurchill, which is literally astonishing. I discussed this vision at length some years ago in my seminar but gave it relatively short shrift above because, though roughly contemporary with Saint Patrick's Purgatory, which was probably slightly earlier in date, Thurchill's vision did little to bring about the success of Purgatory compared to H of Saltrey's famous little work. Thurchill's vision, which has been assigned the date 1206, was probably the work of the English Cistercian Ralph of Coggeshall. Two Benedictines, Roger of Wendover and Matthew Paris (d. 1259), inserted the vision in their works, the former in his *Flores historiarum* and the latter in his *Chronica Majora*. At the behest of Saint James, Thurchill, a simple peasant from the London area, is taken while asleep to the other world, where his guides are Saint Julian the Hospitaller and Saint Domnius. Inside a great basilica without walls similar to the cloister of a monastery he visits "the places where the wicked are punished and the abodes of the just." As was common in the early thirteenth century, we find Purgatory referred to by such archaic terms as *loca poenalia* and *ignis purgatorius* as well as the new noun *purgatorium* (*per purgatorii poenas*). The geography of Thurchill's other world is still rather confused, and Purgatory, in keeping with the old image of multiple *receptacula animarum*, is not yet fully unified. Thus, in addition to a variety of other purgatorial places, there is a Purgatory presided over by Saint Nicholas (*qui huic purgatorio praeerat*). Two particular features of Thurchill's vision are typical of the early thirteenth-century mentality: great importance is attached to the weighing of souls, a feature also found in Gothic sculpture, and there is associated with Purgatory a typology of sins in which the deadly sins (in this case pride) are mixed with sins specific to certain social groups (we are told of the punishments endured by a priest, a knight, and a legist—an interesting version of the trifunctional scheme of classification). What has most struck exegetes of Thurchill's vision is its theatrical character, culminating in the astonishing scene in which the pilgrim looks on as the demons make a spectacle or game (*ludos vestros*) of torturing the denizens of Purgatory (p. 503). Henri Rey-Flaud, *Pour une dramaturgie du Moyen Age* (Paris, 1980), pp. 82–83, draws a parallel between Thurchill's vision and the theatrical movement of the time, particularly the exactly contemporary Game of Saint Nicholas by the Arrageois Jean Bodel. As in the case of iconography, however, the theatricalization of Purgatory apparently proved abortive, and the mysteries continued to be governed by the dualistic system of Heaven and Hell.

Finally, there is, along with Saint Patrick's Purgatory and Thurchill's vision, a third major vision of the other world from the turn of the thirteenth century, that of the monk of Eynsham (Evesham), which is also found in Ralph of Coggeshall's *Chronicon Anglicanum* (ed. J. Stevenson

[1875], pp. 71–72) as well as in Roger of Wendover's *Flores historiarum* and Matthew Paris's *Chronica Majora* (vol. 2, pp. 243–44). I decided not to consider it because it is too close to the "Vision of Drythelm" and its picture of Purgatory is still extremely fragmentary.

Francois Dolbeau has kindly called my attention to an article by Brian Grogan, "Eschatological Teaching of the Early Irish Church," published in *Biblical Studies, The Medieval Irish Contributions*, ed. M. McNamara, Proceedings of the Irish Biblical Association, no. 1 (Dublin, 1976), pp. 46–58. Purgatory is discussed here at some length. Though he does not say so clearly because he uses the term Purgatory prematurely, Grogan confirms that Hell was not distinguished from the *ignis purgatorius* until the end of the twelfth century and that the *Purgatorium Sancti Patricii* is the first text pertaining to Ireland in which the word *purgatorium* occurs.

I have received but have not had time to make use of an article by Gilbert Dagron entitled "La perception d'une différence: les débuts de la 'Querelle du Purgatoire,' " *Actes du XVe congrès international d'Etudes byzantines*, IV, History (Athens, 1980), pp. 84–92.

Notes

THE THIRD PLACE

1. On Luther and Purgatory, see P. Althaus, "Luthers Gedanken über die letzten Dinge," in *Luther Jarhbuch* 23(1941):22–28.

2. M. Gourgues, *A la Droite de Dieu—Résurrection de Jésus et actualisation du Psaume CX, 1, dans le Nouveau Testament* (Paris, 1978), argues that the New Testament evinces little interest in Christ's place at the right hand of God.

3. See Carlo Ginzburg, "High and Low: The Theme of Forbidden Knowledge in the XVIth and XVIIth century," *Past and Present* 73(1976):28–41.

4. Before then, texts referring to the kinds of situations that led to the creation of Purgatory used only the adjective *purgatorius, purgatoria*—meaning "capable of purging"—and then only in what came to be standard expressions: *ignis purgatorius*, or purgatorial fire, *poena purgatoria*, or purgatorial pain (or punishment), sometimes given in the plural as *poenae purgatoriae*, and more rarely, *flamma, forna, locus, flumen* (flame, oven, place, river). This usage probably encouraged the use of the expression *in purgatorio*, with *igne* understood, i.e., in purgatorial fire. It is probable that the neuter substantive *purgatorium*, often used in the phrase *in purgatorio*, benefited originally from the similarity with *in (igne) purgatorio*. When one encounters *in purgatorio* in a late twelfth- or early thirteenth-century text, it is often difficult to know whether it should be read as "in purgatory" or "in purgatorial fire," with the noun implied. But by this date it scarcely matters, since the substantive purgatory—Purgatory the place—exists, and both expressions refer to it.

5. The few authors of studies on Purgatory who have noticed the problem generally mention it in a brief and usually mistaken note. Joseph Ntedika, the author of two excellent studies of fundamental importance, says of Hildebert of Le Mans that "he was probably the first to use the word purgatorium" (*L'Evolution de la doctrine du purgatoire chez saint Augustin*, p. 11 n. 17). The sermon once attributed to Hildebert of Le Mans has long been known to be the work of another man (see Appendix 2). A. Piolanti, "Il dogma del Purgatorio," *Euntes Docete* 6(1953):287–311, a remarkable essay, leaves it at this: "In this century (the twelfth) the first versions of the treatise *De purgatorio* appeared (the adjective had by this time been transformed into a noun)." As for Erich Fleischhak, *Fegfeuer, Die christlichen Vorstellungen vom Geschick der Verstorbenen geschichtlich dargestellt* (1969), we find the following on p. 64: "The word *purgatorium* was used from Carolingian times to denote both the act of purification and the place of purification." No reference is given—for good reason.

6. From a geographical point of view, see for example J. Jakle et al., *Human Spatial Behavior: A Social Geography* (North Scituate, Mass., 1976); and J. Kolars and J. Nystuen, *Human Geography: Spatial Design in World Society* (New York, 1974). From a zoological standpoint: H. E. Howard, *Territory in Bird Life* (London, 1920). From a linguistic standpoint: B. L. Whorf, *Language, Thought, and Reality* (New York, 1956). And from an interdisciplinary standpoint, C. R. Carpenter, "Territoriality: A Review of Concepts and Problems," in A. Roe and C. G. Simpson, eds., *Behavior and Evolution* (New Haven, 1958); H. Hediger, "The Evolution of Territorial Behavior," in S. L. Washburn, ed., *Social Life of Early Man* (New York, 1961); A. Buttimer, "Social Space in Interdisciplinary Perspective," in E. Jones, ed., *Readings in Social Geography* (Oxford, 1975); and not to be overlooked, A. Jammer, *Concepts of Space* (New York, 1960), with a preface by Albert Einstein.

7. E. T. Hall, *The Hidden Dimension* (New York, 1966).

8. *Le Jugement des morts* (in Egypt, Assyria, Babylonia, Israel, Iran, Islamic India, China, and Japan), vol. 4 in Collections des Sources Orientales (Paris, 1961), p. 9.

9. Thomas Aquinas was particularly sensitive to the difficulties involved in making spiritual souls feel the pain caused by material fire. He called upon biblical authority (Matt. 25:41) and on the analogy between souls separated from their bodies and demons to make the following assertion: "Separated souls can therefore suffer from a corporeal cause" (*Summa theologica*, Suppl., 70,3). The question of the corporeality of the soul may have worried Johannes Scotus Erigena in the ninth century and his disciple Honorius Augustodunensis in the twelfth: see Claude Carozzi, "Structure et fonction de la vision de Tnugdal," in A. Vauchez, ed., *Faire Croire*, proceedings of the colloquium of the French School in Rome, 1979, published in 1980. Though I will not follow Claude Carozzi here, I do wish to thank him for sending me a copy of his paper prior to publication.

10. Claude Lévi-Strauss, "Les organisations dualistes existent-elles?" *Anthropologie structurale*, vol. 1 (Paris, 1958), especially p. 168.

11. G. Van der Leeuw, *La Religion dans son essence et ses manifestations* (Paris, 1955), p. 53 (originally published in Dutch).

12. C.-M. Edsmann, *Ignis Divinus: Le feu comme moyen de rajeunissement et d'immortalité: contes, légendes, mythes et rites* (Lund, 1949). Let us pay tribute to that now outdated classic and pioneering work, J. G. Frazer's *Myths of the Origin of Fire* (London, 1930), as well as to the beautiful essay by Gaston Bachelard, *Psychanalyse du feu*. On sacred fire in Iran, see K. Erdmann, *Das iranische Feuerheiligtum* (Leipzig, 1941). Encyclopedia articles on "Feuer" by A. Closs in *Lexikon für Theologie und Kirche*, 4 (1960), pp. 106–7, and especially "Feu de l'Enfer," "Feu du Jugement," and "Feu du Purgatoire," by A. Michel in *Dictionnaire de théologie catholique*, vol. 2 (Paris, 1939), and "Feu" by J. Gaillard in *Dictionnaire de spiritualité*, vol. 5 (Paris, 1964), are worth consulting, though they tell us little about the archaic forms of the religion of fire. In the aprocryphal gospels baptism by fire is found in various forms. In the *Two Books of the Game*, based on a Greek original (from Egypt) dating from the first half of the third century, Jesus, after the resurrection, gives one of the apostles a triple baptism, by water, fire, and the Holy Spirit: see E. Hennecke and W. Schneemelcher, *Neutestatmentliche Apokryphen*, 3d ed., vol. 1 (Tübingen, 1959), p. 185. In the Gospel of

Philip, used by the Gnostics and Manichaeans and probably originating in Egypt in the second century, we find baptism by water and by fire (ibid., p. 198).

13. Cicero, *Tusculanes*, 5, 77.

14. Valerius Maximus, *Factorum et dictorum memorabilium libri novem*, III, 3, ext. 6. As Edsmann remarks, in Mozart's *Magic Flute* "Tamino and Pamina pass through two caves, the first of which contains a waterfall and the second of which is filled with fire."

15. As an example of a "pure" but narrow theological view, I cite the following opinion: "Because of the way Our Lord, in speaking of the finger of Lazarus and the tongue of the wicked rich man, must comply with the requirements of the language of the common people, some people used to thinking of the soul and body as inseparable may have felt it warranted to assert that separated souls are equipped with bodies *sui generis*, as the imagination requires. But to make such an assertion is to place an obstacle in the path of the true philosophy of the dogma." See J. Bainvel, "Ame," in *Dictionnaire de théologie catholique*, vol. 1 (Paris, 1909), p. 1001. To argue in this way is to cut oneself off from historical understanding.

16. Heinrich Günter states that "visions of the hereafter became a popular motif of folklore of which we find examples in every era and which is as old as mystical speculation." See *Die christliche Legende des Abendlandes* (Heidelberg, 1910), p. 111.

17. See Jacques Le Goff, "Culture cléricale et traditions folkloriques dans la civilisation mérovingienne," and "Culture ecclésiastique et culture folklorique au Moyen Age: Saint Marcel de Paris et le dragon," *Pour un Autre Moyen Age* (Paris, 1977), pp. 223–35 and 236–79; translated as *Time, Work, and Culture in the Middle Ages* (Chicago, 1980). See also Jean-Claude Schmitt, "Religion populaire et culture folklorique," *Annales Economies. Sociétés. Civilisations* (1976), pp. 941–53.

CHAPTER 1

1. These excerpts are taken from Chandogya Upanishad and are cited and interpreted by Jean Varenne, "Le jugement des morts dans l'Inde," in *Le Jugement des morts*, Sources orientales, vol. 4 (Paris, 1961), pp. 225–26.

2. Ibid., pp. 215–16. See also L. Scherman, "Eine Art visionärer Hollenschilderung aus dem indischen Mittelalter. Nebst einigen Bemerkungen über die älteren Vorstellungen der Inder von einer strafenden Vergeltung nach dem Tode," in "Festschrift Konrad Hofmann," *Romanische Forschungen* 5(1890):539–82.

3. Cf. J. D. C. Pavry, *The Zoroastrian Doctrine of a Future Life* (New York, 1926); J. Duchesne-Guillemin, *La Religion de l'Iran ancien* (Paris, 1962).

4. See the article entitled "Bridge" by G. A. Frank Knight in "ERE," vol. 2.

5. Duchesne-Guillemin, *La Religion de l'Iran ancien*, p. 335.

6. J. Yoyotte, "Le Jugement des morts dans l'Egypte ancienne," in *Le Jugement des morts*, p. 69.

7. E. Hornung, Altägyptische Höllenvorstellungen, *Abhändlungen der sächsischen Akademie der Wissenschaften zu Leipzig, Philologisch-historische Klasse*, Band 59, Heft 3 (Berlin, 1968).

8. Ibid., pp. 9–10.

9. E. A. W. Budge, *The Egyptian Heaven and Hell*, vol. 3 (London, 1906), p. xii.

10. See, for example, Victor Berard, *Les Navigations d'Ulysse*, vol. 4: *Circe et*

les morts (Paris, 1929), pp. 281–372, which is overly concerned with locating real geographical sites. This "geographical realism" sometimes obscures the essential point, which is the way structures of the imagination and cultural traditions combine. Attempts have even been made to attribute descriptions of cold places in Purgatory to Nordic authors and descriptions of hot places to Mediterranean authors. In the beginning hot and cold were paired, as we have seen, and this pairing is probably Indo-European in origin. There is no reason to regard it as the reflection of the climate of Tibet or the Caucasus.

11. Victor Goldschmidt, *La Religion de Platon* (Paris, 1949), pp. 75–84.

12. A. Boulanger, *Orphée: Rapports de l'orphisme et du christianisme* (Paris, 1925).

13. Ibid., p. 128.

14. Pindar, vol. 1, Aimé Puech trans., Collection G. Budé, Les Belles Lettres (Paris, 1922), p. 45.

15. Brooks Otis, *Virgil: A Study in Civilized Poetry* (Oxford, 1964).

16. E. Norden, *P. Vergilius Maro. Aneis, Buch VI*, 4th ed. (Darmstadt, 1957), pp. 207–349. Concerning Christian reactions, see P. Courcelle, "Les Pères de l'Eglise devant les enfers virgiliens," *Archives d'histoire doctrinale et littéraire du Moyen Age* 22(1955).

17.
> Hinc exaudiri gemitus, et saeva sonare
> verbera, tam stridor ferri tractae catenae
> constitit Aneas, strepituque exterritus haesit.
> (vv. 557–59)

The translation given here is from Patric Dickinson's version of *The Aeneid* (New York, 1961), p. 136.–Trans.

18.
> Ahi quanto son diverse quelle foci
> dall'infernali! che quivi per canti
> s'entra, e la giu per lamenti feroce.
> (*Purgatorio* 12.112–14)

19.
> . . . camposque nitentis
> desuper ostentat.
> (*Aeneid* 6.677–78)

20. The translation is Dickinson's, p. 141.—Trans.

21. Cf. E. Ebeling, *Tod und Leben nach den Vorstellungen der Babylonier* (Berlin-Leipzig, 1931). Concerning the ambiguous "sacred" quality of darkness in Greek writings, see Maja Reemda Svilar, *Denn das Dunkel ist heilig. Ein Streifzug durch die Psyche der archäischen Griechen* (Berne-Frankfurt, 1976).

22. Cf. J.-M. Aynard, "Le Jugement des morts chez les Assyro-Babyloniens," in *Le Jugement des morts*, Sources orientales, vol. 4, pp. 83–102.

23. Cf. P. Dhorme, "Le Séjour des morts chez les Babyloniens et les Hébreux," *Revue biblique* (1907), pp. 59–78.

24. The snares of *sheol* are also mentioned in 2 Samuel 22:6 and in Job 18:7–10. A similar theme is found in Egyptian writings. Cf. M. Eliade, *Images et Symboles: Essais sur le symbolisme magico-religieux* (Paris, 1952), pp. 124–52.

25. Beyond reading the Old Testament, I have consulted J. Pedersen, *Israel, Its Life and Culture*, vols. 1 and 2 (London-Copenhagen, 1926), pp. 460ff.; R. Martin-Achard, *De la mort à la Resurrection d'après l'Ancien Testament* (Neuchâtel-Paris, 1956); and N. J. Tromp, *Primitive Conceptions of Death and the*

Other World in the Old Testament, Biblia et Orientalia, vol. 21 (Rome, 1969). This last study illuminates the Old Testament by drawing on material from Ugaritic texts found at Ras Shamra.

26. Cf. Znadef, *Death as an Enemy According to Ancient Egyptian Conceptions* (Leyden, 1960).

27. See also Job 12:22, 15:22, 17:13, 18:18, 19:8, 28:3, and 38:16–17.

28. I am following the translation of this version, together with commentary, by François Martin, *Le Livre d'Henoch traduit sur le texte ethiopien* (Paris, 1906).

29. R. L. Bensly, ed., *The Fourth Book of Ezra: The Latin Version,* with an introduction by M. R. James (Cambridge, 1895).

30. "Si inveni gratiam coram te, domine, demonstra et hoc servo tuo, si post mortem vel nunc quando reddimus unusquisque animam suam, si conservati conservabimur in requie, donec veniant temopra illa in quibus incipies creaturam renovare aut amodo cruciamur" (7.75).

31. "in habitationes non ingredientur, sed vagantes errent amodo in cruciamentis, dolentes semper et tristes per septem vias" (7.79–80).

32. "Quinta via, videntes aliorum habitacula ab angelis conservari cum silentio magno" (7.82).

33. "Habitacula sanitatis et securitatis" (7.121).

34. "Septem diebus erit libertas earum ut videant septem diebus qui predicti sunt sermones, et postea conjugabuntur in habitaculis suis" (7.199–201).

35. "Quintus ordo, exultantes quomodo corruptibile effugerint nunc et futurum quomodo hereditatem possidebunt, adhuc autem videntes angustum et (labore) plenum, a quo liberati sunt, et spatiosum incipient recipere, fruniscentes et immortales" (7.96).

36. "Animarum autem superiora esse habitacula" (*De bono mortis* 19.44: Migne, *Patrologia latina,* vol. 14., col. 560).

37. "Eo quod spatium, inquit (Ezra) incipiunt recipere fruentes et immortales" (ibid., col. 562).

38. Concerning the Judeo-Christian apocalypse, see J. Daniélou, *Théologie du judéo-christianisme,* vol. 1 (Paris-Tournai, 1958), pp. 131–64.

39. Ethiopian and Greek versions exist. There is also an excellent German translation: E. Hennecke and W. Schneemelcher, *Neutestamentlich Apokryphen in deutscher Übersetzung,* vol. 3, part 2 (Tübingen, 1964), pp. 468–83.

40. A. Harnack, "Die Petrusapokalypse in der älten abendländischen Kirche," in *Texte und Untersuchungen zur Geschichte der altchristlichen Literatur,* vol. 13 (1895), pp. 71–73.

41. See O. Wahl, ed., *Apocalypsis Esdrae. Apocalypsis Sedrach. Visio Beati Esdrae* (Leyden, 1977).

42. The long version was published by M. R. James in Apocrypha anecdota, Texts and Studies, vol. 2, part 3, (1893), pp. 11–42. The best known of the shorter versions, version 4, was published by H. Brandes in *Visio S. Pauli: Ein Beitrag zur Visionlitteratur, mit einem deutschen und zwei lateinischen Texten* (Halle, 1885), pp. 75–80. A version in old French was published by P. Meyer, "La descente de saint Paul en Enfer," *Romania* 24(1895):365–75. The other short versions have been published by Theodore Silverstein, *Visio Sancti Pauli. The History of the Apocalypse in Latin, together with Nine Texts* (London, 1935), which contains a remarkable, fundamental introduction.

43. Augustine, *Tractatus in Joannem* 98.8.

44. The idea of a Sabbath rest was a widespread popular belief among the Jews, from whom the Christians took it over. See Israël Lévi, "Le repos sabbatique des âmes damnées," *Revue des Etudes juives* (1892), pp. 1–13. See also the introduction by Theodore Silverstein to *Visio Sancti Pauli*, pp. 79–81: "The Sunday Respite."

45. In particular I have read the works of H.-C. Puech: "La Ténèbre mystique chez le pseudo-Denys l'Aréopagite et dans la tradition patristique" (1938), reprinted in *En quête de la Gnose*, vol. 1 (Paris, 1978), pp. 119–41; and "Le Prince des Ténèbres en son royaume," *Etudes carmélitaines* (1948), pp. 136–74 (special issue on Satan). Concerning the anguish of time in Hell, see *En quête de la Gnose*, vol. 1, pp. 247ff.

46. See J. Bonsirven, *Eschatologie rabbinique d'après les Targums, Talmuds, Midraschs. Les éléments communs avec le Nouveau Testament* (Rome, 1910).

47. J. Bonsirven, *Textes Rabbiniques des deux premiers siècles chrétiens pour servir à l'intelligence du Nouveau Testament* (Rome, 1955), pp. 272 and 524. René Gutman informs me that "the Talmudic treatise 'Principles of Rabbi Nathan' asserts that the souls of the impious wander through the world, ceaselessly humming. Angels stand at either end of the world tossing the souls back and forth. The rabbis imagined nothing less than an aerial Purgatory in which sinful souls were tossed and rolled about by violent currents whose purpose was to purify them and thus prepare the way for entry into heaven."

48. Concerning the context of these rabbinical writings, see the classic work of P. Volz, *Die Eschatologie der jüdischen Gemeinde im neutestamentlicher Zeitalter* (Tübingen, 1934).

49. I say "story" rather than "parable" deliberately, following Peter Comestor who said, in the twelfth century, that this was not a parable but an *exemplum*.

50. M. Eliade, *Traité d'histoire des religions* (Paris, 1953), pp. 175–77.

51. Two excellent studies are available which analyze patristic and medieval commentaries on this text: A. Landgraf, "I Cor. 3:10–17, bei den lateinischen Vätern und in der Frühscholastik," *Biblica* 5(1924):140–72; and J. Gnilka, *Ist 1 Kor. 3:10–15 en Schriftzeugnis fur das Fegfeuer? Eine exegetisch-historische Untersuchung* (Düsseldorf, 1955). See also Edsmann, *Ignis Divinus*.

52. J. Kroll, *Gott und Hölle. Der mythos vom Descensuskämpfe* (Leipzig-Berlin, 1932); W. Bieder, *Die Vorstellung von der Höllenfahrt Jesu Christi* (Zurich, 1949).

53. S. Reinach, "De l'origine des prières pour les morts," *Revue des Etudes juives* 41(1900):164.

54. O. Kern, ed., *Orphicorum Fragmenta* (Berlin, 1922), p. 245, cited by J. Ntedika, *L'Evocation de l'au-delà dans la prière pour les morts. Etude de patristique et de liturgie latines, IVe-VIIIe siècles* (Louvain-Paris, 1971), p. 11.

55. Diodorus of Sicily 1.91, cited by Reinach, "De l'origine," p. 169.

56. See above.

57. See, for example, H. Leclercq, "Défunts," in *Dictionnaire d'Histoire et d'Archéologie ecclésiastiques*, vol. 4, cols. 427–56, and "Purgatoire," ibid., vol. 14/2 (1948), cols. 1978–81. See also F. Bracha, *De existentia Purgatorii in antiquitate christiana* (Krakow, 1946).

58. *Dictionnaire d'Histoire et d'Archéologie ecclésiastiques*, vol. 14/2, cols. 1980–81.

59. Ibid., vol. 4, col. 447.

60. C. Mohrmann, "Locus refrigerii," in B. Botte and C. Morhmann, eds., *L'Ordinaire de la messe. Texte critique, traduction et études* (Paris-Louvain, 1953), p. 127; and, by the same author, "Locus refrigerii, lucis et pacis," in *Questions liturgiques et paroissiales* 39(1958):196–214.

61. "Eam itaque regionem, sinum dico Abrahae, etsi non caelestem, sublimiorem tamen inferis, interim refrigerium praebere animabus iustorum, donec consummatio rerum resurrectionem omnium plenitudine mercedis expungat . . ."

62. "Temporale aliquos animarum fidelium receptaculum . . ."

63. "Herodis tormenta et Iohannis refrigeria; mercedem . . . sive tormenti sive refrigerii" (*Adversus Marcionem* 4.34); "per sententiam aeternam tam supplicii quam refrigerii" (*De anima* 33.11); "supplicia iam illic et refrigeria" (*De anima* 58.1); "metu aeterni supplicii et spe aeterni refrigerii" (*Apologeticum* 49.2); "aut cruciatui destinari aut refrigerio, utroque sempiterno." Cf. H. Fine, *Die Terminologie der Jenseitsvorstellungen bis Tertullian* (Bonn, 1958).

64. J. Goubert and L. Cristiani, trans., *Les plus beaux textes sur l'au-delà* (Paris, 1950), pp. 183ff.

65. A. Stuiber, *Refrigerium interim. Die Vorstellungen vom Zwischenzustand und die frühchristliche Grabekunst* (Bonn, 1957); de Bruyne, "Refrigerium interim," *Rivista di archeologia cristiana* 34(1958):87–118, and 35(1959):183–86.

66. De Bruyne, 1959, p. 183.

67. E. R. Dodds, *Pagan and Christian in an Age of Anxiety* (Cambridge, 1965).

68. C. van Beek, ed., *Passio sanctarum Perpetuae et Felicitatis* (1936). The article by F. J. Dolger, "Antike Parallelen zum leidenden Dinocrates in der Passio Perpetuae," *Antike und Christentum* 2(1930):1–40, tells us a good deal about the general atmosphere surrounding this text but does nothing to alter our contention that its significance was profoundly new. Dodds, *Pagan and Christian in an Age of Anxiety*, pp. 47–53, gives an interesting commentary on the *Passio Perpetuae*, but his concern is not with the adumbration of Purgatory.

69. Van Beek edition, p. 20.

70. Ibid., p. 22.

71. L. Vouaux, *Les Apocryphes du Nouveau Testament. Les Actes de Paul et ses lettres apocryphes* (Paris, 1913).

72. "Enimvero et pro anima eius orat, et refrigerium interim adpostulat ei" (*De monogamia* 10.4).

73. Concerning "the thirst of the dead," see Mircea Eliade, *Traité d'Histoire des religions* (Paris, 1953), pp. 175–77. I do not accept the argument that various concepts of Hell correlate with the local climate, that thirst and fire go along with "Asiatic" visions of Hell and "low temperatures" (cold, ice, frozen marshes, etc.) with "Nordic" visions. Dodds, *Pagan and Christian in an Age of Anxiety*, pp. 47–53, rightly notes that the basin in the *Passion of Perpetua* is reminiscent of baptism. The question whether Dinocratus was or was not baptized interested early Christian authors, especially Augustine.

74. Shortly before his death, H.-I. Marrou cited P. A. Fevrier, "Le culte des martyrs en Afrique et ses plus anciens monuments," *Corsi di cultura sull'arte*

ravennate e bizantina (Ravenna, 1970), p. 199, in order to draw attention to an African inscription that sheds new light on the notion of *refrigerium*: "A new and curious detail is added by the tombs at Tipasa, namely, that cisterns and wells are present and that importance is attached to water. Water is not merely a part of the meal but flows over the tomb, and it is reasonable to ask if water is not a necessary ingredient of the *refrigerium* mentioned in the texts. It is well known that, in its earliest sense, the term *refrigerium* evoked one of the most pregnant images of the good life after death, first for the pagans and later for the Christians (Acts 3:20). By extension the word came to refer to the final meal, interpreted more or less straightforwardly as a symbol of the hoped-for happiness. A monument such as the one that concerns us here suggests that the image of a layer of water flowing over a background scene of sea life was a concrete way of picturing the 'refreshment,' or *refrigerium*, associated with the funeral banquet." See H.-I. Marrou, "Une inscription chrétienne de Tipasa et le *refrigerium*," *Antiquités africaines* 14(1979):269.

CHAPTER TWO

1. On Clement of Alexandria in relation to the inception of Purgatory, the essential work is still G. Anrich, "Clemens und Origenes als Begründer der Lehre vom Fegfeuer," in *Theologische Abhandlungen, Festgabe fur H. H. Holtzmann* (Tübingen-Leipzig, 1902), pp. 95–120. A good treatment from a Catholic point of view may be found in A. Michel, "Origène et le dogme du Purgatoire," in *Questions ecclésiastiques* (Lille, 1913), summarized by the author in his article "Purgatoire" in the *Dictionnaire de Théologie catholique*, cols. 1192–96. Brief but judicious remarks on the prehistory of Purgatory are made by A. Piolanti, "Il Dogma del Purgatorio," in *Euntes Docete* 6(1953); concerning the baptism by fire, see C.-M. Edsman, *Le Baptême de feu*, pp. 3–4; and for an exegesis of Paul's First Epistle to the Corinthians, see J. Gnilka, *Ist 1 Kor. 3, 10–15 ein Schriftzeugnis fur das Fegfeuer?*, especially p. 115.

2. The main texts cited by Anrich, "Clemens und Origenes," p. 99 n. 7 and p. 100 n. 1, are the following: *Gorgias* 34.478 and 81.525; *Phaedo* 62.113d; *Protagoras* 13.324b; and *Laws* 5.728c.

3. Clement of Alexandria, *Stromata* 5.14 and 7.12.

4. Origen, *De principiis* 2.10.6 and *De oratione* 29.

5.　　　　aliis sub gurgite vasto
　　　　infectum eluitur scelus, aut exuritur igni
　　　　. . .
　　　　donec longa dies perfecto temporis orbe
　　　　concretam exemit labem, purumque relingquit
　　　　aetherium sensum . . .

6. Clement of Alexandria, *Stromata* 4.24.

7. Ibid., 8.6.

8. Origen, *In Exodum*, homily 6, in J.-P. Migne, *Patrologiae cursus completus, series graeca*, 162 vols. (Paris, 1857–66; hereafter cited as *PG*), 13.334–35; *In Leviticum*, homily 9, *PG*, 12.519.

9. For example, *In Jeremiam*, homily 2; *In Leviticum*, homily 8; *In Exodum*, homily 6; *In Lucam*, homily 14; etc.

10. *De principiis* 2.11 n. 6; *In Ezechielem*, homily 13 n. 2; *In Numeros*, homily 26.

11. Cf. K. Rahner, "La doctrine d'Origène sur la pénitence," *Recherches de Science religieuse* 37(1950).

12. "Aliud pro peccatis longo dolore cruciatum emundari et purgari diu igne, aliud peccata omnia passione purgasse, aliud denique pendere in die judicii ad sententiam Domini, aliud statim a Domino coronari."

13. A. Michel, "Purgatoire" in *Dictionnaire de théologie catholique*, col. 1214.

14. P. Jay, "Saint Cyprien et la doctrine du Purgatoire," in *Recherches de théologie ancienne et médiévale* 27(1960), pp. 133–36.

15. "emundatio puritatis . . . qua iudicii igni nos decoquat" (in J.-P. Migne, *Patrologiae cursus completus, series latina*, 221 vols. [Paris, 1844–64], 9.519A]; hereafter cited as *PL*).

16. In *In Psalmum CXVIII*, sermo 20, *PL*, 15.1487–88. On trial by fire, see also *In Psalmum CXVIII*, sermo 3, *PL*, 15.1227–28, and *In Psalmum XXVI*, *PL* 14.980–81.

17. "et si salvos faciet Dominus servos suos, salvi erimus per fidem, sic tamen salvi quasi per ignem" (*Explanatio Psalmi XXXVI*, n. 26, *Corpus Scriptorum Ecclesiaticorum Latinorum*, hereafter cited as *CSEL*, 64.92.

18. *De obitu Theodosi*, 25, *CSEL* 73.383–84.

19. *De excessu Satyri* 1.29, *CSEL* 73.225.

20. "Et sicut diaboli et omnium negatorum atque impiorum qui dixerunt in corde suo: Non est Deus, credimus aeterna tormenta; sic peccatorum et tamen christianorum, quorum opera in igne probanda sunt atque purganda, moderatam arbitramur et mixtam clementiae sententiam iudicis" (*In Isaiam* 46.24, *PL*, 24.704b).

21. "Qui enim tota mente in Christo confidit, etiam si ut homo lapsus mortuus fuerit in peccato, fide sua vivit in perpetuum."

22. "Ideo autem dixit: sic tamen quasi per ignem, ut salus haec non sine poena sit; quia non dixit: salvus erit per ignem; sed cum dicit: sic tamen quasi per ignem, ostendit salvum illum quidem futurum, sed poenas ignis passurum; ut per ignem purgatus fiat salvus, et non sicut perfidi aeterno igne in perpetuum torqueati ut ex aliqua parte operae pretium sit, credidisse in Christum" (*PL* 17.211).

23. "Transivimus per ignem et aquam et induxisti nos in refrigerium."

24. *Epist.* 28 (*CSEL* 29.242–44); and *Carmen* 7.32–43 (*CSEL*, 30.19–20).

25. We also find *ignis purgationis*, the fire of purgation (*De Genesi contra Manicheos* 2.20.30), and *ignis emendatorius*, corrective fire (*Enarrationes in Psalmos* 37.3). In the *City of God* 21.13, where the expression *poenae purgatoriae* occurs three times in twelve lines, Augustine also uses *poenae expiatoriae*, expiatory punishments, as a synonym, one reason among others that convinces me that *purgatoriae* should not be translated as "purificatory."

26. See *Bibliothèque augustinienne*, vol. 37, pp. 817–18.

27. "nec usque adeo vita in corpore male gesta est, ut tali misericordia iudicentur digni non esse, nec usque adeo bene, ut talem misericordiam reperiantur necessariam non habere." (I have used the English translation by Henry Bettenson [London: Penguin Books, 1967], in which the cited passage may be found on p. 1004.—Trans.).

28. Matthew 25:34 and 41–46.

29. "et post hanc vitam habebit vel ignem purgationis vel poenam aeternam."

30. "Quanquam illa receptio, utrum statim post istam vitam fiat, an in fine

saeculi in resurrectione mortuorum atque ultima retributione judicii, non minima quaestio est sed quandolibet fiat, certe de talibus qualis ille dives insinuatur, nulla scriptura fiere pollicetur."

31. "Ita plane quamuis salui per ignem, gravior tamen erit ille ignis, quam quidquid potest homo pati in hac vita" (*Enarrationes in Psalmos* 38.3 CCL, 38.384).

32. See note 45, "Les miséricordieux," by G. Bardy in Bibliothèque augustinienne, vol. 37 (Paris, 1960), pp. 806–9.

33. "Porro si utraque regio et dolentium et requiscentium, id est et ubi dives ille torquebatur et ubi pauper ille laetabatur, in inferno esse credenda est, quis audeat dicere dominum Iesum ad poenales inferni partes venisse tantum modo nec fuisse apud eos qui in Abrahae sinum requiescunt? ubi si fuit, ipse est intellegendus paradisus, quem latronis animae illo die dignatus est polliceri. Quae si ita sunt, generale paradisi nomen est, ubi feliciter vivitur. Neque enim quia paradisus est appellatus, ubi Adam fuit ante peccatum, propterea scriptura prohibita est etiam ecclesiam vocare paradisum cum fructu pomorum."

34. *Enchiridion* is Greek for "manual," a term which, from the sixteenth century on, came into popular usage, as is well known.

35. I have given an outline of an approach for studying dreams and dream interpretation in the medieval West in "Les rêves dans la culture et la psychologie collective de l'Occident médiéval," *Scolies* 1(1971):123–30, reprinted in *Pour un autre Moyen Age*, pp. 299–306 (and translated as "Dreams in the Culture and Collective Psychology of the Medieval West," *Time, Work, And Culture in the Middle Ages*, trans. Arthur Goldhammer (Chicago, 1980), pp. 201–4).

36. On millenarianism, see the note by G. Bardy in Saint Augustine, *Cité de Dieu*, 19–22, Bibliothèque augustinienne, vol. 37 (Paris, 1960), pp. 768–71; and Jacques Le Goff, "Millénarisme," *Encyclopedia Universalis*, vol. 11 (1971), pp. 30–32.

37. The text from Ambrose may be found in *PL* 14.950–51: "Et ideo quoniam et Salvator duo genera resurrectionis posuit, et Joannes in Apocalypsi dixit: Beatus qui habet partem in prima resurrectione (Apocalypse 20:6) isti enim sine judicio veniunt ad gratiam, qui autem non veniunt ad primam resurrectionem, sed ad secundam reservantur, isti urentur, donec impleant tempora inter primam et secundam resurrectionem, aut si non impleverint, diutius in supplicio permanebunt. Ideo ergo rogemus ut in prima resurrectione partem habere mereamur."

38. The author notes that, in the French edition of this work, he took citations from Augustine from the French translations of the *Confessions, Enchiridion, City of God,* and *De cura gerenda pro mortis* contained in various volumes of the Bibliothèque augustinienne, but that he corrected certain terms that he felt were incorrectly translated from Latin into French: in particular he used "*purgatoire*" rather than "*purificatoire*" in translating the expression *ignis purgatorius*, and "*temporaires*" rather than "*temporelles*" in translating the expression *poenae temporariae*. I have made corresponding changes in the English translations of Augustine's works cited above.—Trans.

39. Pierre Jay, "Le Purgatoire dans la prédication de saint Césaire d'Arles," *Recherches de théologie ancienne et médiévale* 24(1957):5–14.

40. Caesarius of Arles, *Sermones*, ed. G. Morin and C. Lambot, Corpus Christianorum (Turnhout, 1953), vol. 104, pp. 682–87 and 723–29.

41. "non pertinet ad me quamdiu moras habeam, si tamen ad vitam aeternam perrexero": "The time I shall wait does not matter to me if ultimately I come to eternal life." The text does not specify where the waiting is to take place, but it is clear from the previous sentence that purgatorial fire is meant (*in illo purgatorio igne*). Pierre Jay astutely notes that when Thomas Aquinas later took up Augustine's commentary on Psalm 37, he wrote *ille ignis purgatorii*, the fire "of" purgatory—but this was in the thirteenth century!

42. Concerning Gregory the Great, see C. Dagens, *Saint Grégoire le Grand, Culture et expérience chrétiennes* (Paris, 1977), part 3, "Eschatology," pp. 345–429. Concerning Gregory's eschatology, see also N. Hill, *Die Eschatologie Gregors des Grossen* (Freiburg-im-Breisgau, 1942); and R. Manselli, "L'eschatologia di S. Gregorio Magno," *Ricerche di storia religiosa* 1(1954):72–83.

43. Gregory the Great, *Moralia in Job*, ed. A. Bocognano, part 3, Sources chrétiennes (Paris, 1974), p. 167 (here cited after *Morals in the Book of Job*, A Library of Fathers of the Holy Catholic Church [Oxford, 1845].—Trans.)

44. Ibid., pp. 315–17.

45. "Discere vellim, si post mortem purgatorius ignis esse credendus est." Since I made these translations (The author translated the cited passages from the edition of U. Moricca, Gregory the Great, *Dialogi*; [Rome, 1924], and I have rendered his translations into English.—Trans.) the third volume in the fine edition of Gregory's *Dialogues*, together with their French translations, has been published under the editorship of A. de Vogüé and P. Autin in the Sources chrétiennes series (Paris: Editions du Cerf, 1980). The passage commented on here (4.41) is found on pp. 146–51 of this edition. The story of Paschasius (4.42) is found on pp. 150–55.

46. Revelation 12:55; Isaiah 49:8; 2 Corinthians 6:2; Ecclesiastes 9:10; Psalm 117:1; Matthew 12:32).

47. "sed tamen de quibusdam levis culpis esse ante judicium purgatorius ignis credendus est," "hoc de parvis minimisque peccatis fieri posse credendum est, sicut est assiduus otiosus sermo, immoderatus risus, vel peccatum curae rei familiaris." At the end of the chapter Gregory speaks of the fire of the future purgation, "de igne futurae purgationis," of the possibility of being saved by fire, "per ignem posse salvari," and again of the "peccata minima atque levissima quae ignis facile consumat" (*Dialogi* 6.41).

48. Gregory the Great, *Dialogi* 4.57.1–7 (Vogüé-Antin ed., vol. 3, pp. 184–89).

49. Ibid., 4.57.8 and 17 (Vogüé-Antin ed., pp. 188–95). There is no mention of fire in this story.

CHAPTER THREE

1. "et quodam purgatorio igne purganda" (*PL* 83.757).

2. Julian of Toledo, *Prognosticon*, book 2, *PL* 96.474–98. The *ignis purgatorius* is discussed in columns 483–86. The influence of Julian of Toledo on those who shaped the doctrine of Purgatory in the twelfth century, especially Peter Lombard, has been studied by N. Wicki, *Das "Prognosticon futuri saeculi," Julians von Toledo als Quellenwerk der Sentenzen des Petrus Lombardus.*

3. M. C. Diaz y Diaz, ed., *Liber de ordine creaturarum. Un anonimo irlandes*

del siglo VII (Santiago de Compostella, 1972). One regret: Manuel Diaz y Diaz's excellent edition has a tendency to present the work in a slightly anachronistic way. For example, on page 29 of the structural analysis, it is forcing the text to say: *infierno* (cap. XIII) *purgatorio* (cap. XIV) *y gloria* (cap. XV–XVI). The same can be said about the translation of chapter XIV, of which the title, in those manuscripts that have one, is *De igne purgatorio,* "On Purgatorial Fire," translated in Spanish as *Del purgatorio,* "Of Purgatory." This is misleading in two respects: first, five centuries had yet to pass before there was any such place as "Purgatory," and second, this text marks a clear step backward when compared with the overall evolution of the doctrine that would culminate in the concept of Purgatory.

4. As Manuel Diaz y Diaz rightly remarks, these "sins" make sense primarily in a monastic setting.

5. Saint Columban, *Instructiones,* Instructio 9. De extremo judicio, PL 246–47: "Videte ordinem miseriae humanae vitae de terra, super terram, in terram, a terra in ignem, de igne in judicium, de judicio aut in gehennam, aut in vitam: de terra enim creatus es, terram calcas, in terram ibis, a terra surges, in igne probaberis, judicium expectabis, aeternum autem post haec supplicium aut regnum possidebis, qui judicium expectabis, qui de terra creati, paululum super eam stantes, in eamdem paulo post intraturi, eadem nos iterum, jussu Dei, reddente ac projiciente, novissime per ignem probabimur, ut quadam arte terram et lutum ignis dissolvat, et si quid auri aut argenti habuerit, aut caeterorum terrae utilium paracarassimo (paracaximo) liquefacto demonstret.

6. *PL* 87.618–19.

7. *PL* 89.577.

8. *PL* 94.30.

9. *De fide Sanctae Trinitatis* 3.21, *PL* 101.52.

10. *Enarrationes in epistolas Pauli, PL* 112.35–39.

11. *Expositio in Mattheum* 2.3, *PL* 120.162–66.

12. *De varietate librorum* 3.1–8, *PL* 118.933–36. The commentary on 1 Corinthians 3:10–13 is found in *PL* 117.525–27.

13. *Expositio in epistolas Pauli, PL*.134.319–21. The passage concerning the contrasting sins reads as follows: "attamen sciendum quia si per ligna, fenum et stipulam, ut beatus Augustinus dicit, mundanae cogitationes, et rerum saecularium cupiditates, apte etiam per eadem designantur levia, et venialia, et quaedam minuta peccata, sine quibus homo in hac vita esse non potest. Unde notandum quia, cum dixisset aurum, argentem, lapides pretiosos, non intulit ferum, aes et plumbum, per quae capitalia et criminalia peccata designantur" (col. 321).

14. Ratherius of Verona, *Sermo II De Quadragesima, PL* 136.701–2: "Mortui enim nihil omnino faciemus, sed quod fecimus recipiemus. Quod et si aliquis pro nobis aliquid fecerit boni, et si non proderit nobis, proderit illi. De illis vero purgatoriis post obitum poenis, nemo sibi blandiatur, monemus, quia non sunt statutae criminimus, sed peccatis levioribus, quae utique per ligna, ferum et stipula indesignatur." On Ratherius, an astonishing personality and an author more Liegeois than Veronese, see *Raterio di Verona, Convegni del Centro di Studi sulla spiritualità medievale* 10 (Todi, 1973).

15. *PL* 150.165–66.

16. *Periphyseon* 5, *PL* 122.977.

17. *De praedestinatione,* chap. 19, *"De igni aeterno," PL* 122.436.

18. Burchard of Worms, *Decretorum libri* 20.20.68–74, *PL* 140.1042–45.

19. *Acta synodi Atrebatensis Gerardi I Cameracensis Episcopi*, chap. 9, *PL* 142.1298–99.

20. I am summarizing the vision of Thespesios on the basis of the account given in E. J. Becker, *A Contribution to the Comparative Study of the Medieval Visions of Heaven and Hell, with Special Reference to the Middle English Versions* (Baltimore, 1899), pp. 27–29; for the vision of Timarchos, I have used H. R. Patch, *The Other World According to Descriptions in Medieval Literature* (Cambridge, Mass., 1950), pp. 82–83.

21. P. Dinzelbacher, "Die Visionen des Mittelalters," *Zeitschrift für Religions- und Geistesgeschichte* 30(1978):116–18 (summarizing an unpublished Habilitationschrift entitled "Vision und Visionsliteratur im Mittelalter" [Stuttgart, 1978]). See also idem, "Klassen und Hierarchien im Jenseits," *Miscellanea Medievalia*, vol. 12, 1, and idem, *Soziale Ordnungen im Selbstverständnis des Mittelalters* (Berlin-New York, 1979), pp. 20–40. Claude Carozzi is currently working on a thesis on "Voyages dans l'Au-delà dans le haut Moyen Age."

22. See Kuno Meyer, ed. and trans., *The Voyage of Bran, Son of Febal, to the Land of the Living*, 2 vols. (London, 1895–87). This work includes a study by Alfred Nutt, "The Happy Other-World in the Mythico-Romantic Literature of the Irish: The Celtic Doctrine of Re-birth," which shows the Celtic roots of a possible "heavenlike" Purgatory.

23. Cf. Maurer, "Die Hölle auf Island," *Zeitschrift des Vereins für Volkskunde* 4(1894):256ff. See also H. R. Ellis, *The Road to Hell: A Study of the Conception of the Dead in Old Norse Literature* (Cambridge, 1943). On "Valhole" (Valhalla), see Georges Dumézil, *Les Dieux des Germains* (1959), p. 45. From the standpoint of modern German folklore studies, cf. H. Siuts, *Jenseitsmotive deutschen Volksmärchen* (Leipzig, 1911).

24. J. H. Waszink, ed., *Carmen ad Flavium Felicem de resurrectione mortuorum et de iudicio Domini* (Bonn, 1937).

25. On Bede as a historian, see P. H. Blair, "The Historical Writings of Bede," and Charles N. L. Brooke, "Historical Writing in England between 850 and 1150," in the anthology *La Storiografia altomedievale*, 1969 Spoleto Conference (1970), pp. 197–221 and 224–47. See also J. M. Wallace-Hadrill, *Early Germanic Kingship in England and on the Continent* (Oxford, 1971), chap. 4: "Bede," pp. 72–97.

26. *Historia ecclesiastica gentis Anglorum* 3.19. The first *Vita Fursei*, which Bede virtually copied, was published by B. Krusch in *MGH, SRM*, vol. 4, pp. 423–51.

27. "Vallis illa quam aspexisti flammis ferventibus et frigoribus horrenda ridis, ipse est locus in quo examinandae et castigandae sunt animae illorum, qui differentes confiteri et emendare scelera quae fecerunt, in ipso tandem articulo ad poenitentiam confugiunt, et sic de corpore exeunt: qui tamen quia confessionem et poenitentiam vel in morte habuerunt, omnes in die iudicii ad regnum caelorum perveniunt. Multos autem preces viventium et ellemosynae et jejunia et maxime celebratio missarum, ut etiam ante diem judicii liberentur, adjuvant." (I have followed the English translation by Leo Sherley-Price: Bede, *A History of the English Church and People* [Penguin, 1955, rev. ed. 1968], pp. 292–93.—Trans.)

28. The vision of Drythelm was repeated in the eleventh and twelfth centuries

by authors of the first rank: Alfric in his homilies (see B. Thorpe's 1846 edition, vol. 2, pp. 348ff.), Otloh of Saint-Emmeran in his *Liber Visionun* (*PL* 146.380ff.), and the Cistercian Helinand of Froimont at the turn of the thirteenth century (*PL* 212.1059–60).

29. *Visio Guetini* in *PL* 105.771–80; also in *MGH, Poetae latini*, vol. 2. Walahfrid Strabo's poetic version has been published in translation and commented on in an excellent study by David A. Traill, *Walahfrid Strabo's Visio Wettini: Text, Translation, and Commentary* (Frankfurt, 1974).

30. Psalm 118, according to the numbering used in the Greek Bible and the Vulgate (which was the Bible used in the Middle Ages) is, according to the Hebraic numbering usually used today, Psalm 119, of which the editors of the Jerusalem Bible had this to say: "a litany of ardent and tireless fidelity . . . [in which] all the emotions of the heart find expression; God who speaks, who gives his meditated, beloved, and treasured law, is the source of life, of security, of true and complete happiness."

31. B. de Gaiffier, "La légende de Charlemagne: Le péché de l'empereur et son pardon," *Etudes critiques d'hagiographie et d'iconologie* (Brussels, 1967), pp. 260–75.

32. See W. Levison, "Die Politik in den Jenseitsvisionen des frühen Mittelalters," *Aus rheinischer und fränkischer Frühzeit* (Düsseldorf, 1948). In about 1100 this text was inserted by Hariulf into his *Chronicle of Saint Riquier*, F. Lot, ed. (Paris, 1901), pp. 144–48; in the twelfth century it was inserted by William of Malmesbury in his *De Gestis regnum Anglorum*, W. Stubbs, ed., pp. 112–16; and in the thirteenth century, by Vincent of Beauvais in his *Speculum*. It is found in a great many other scattered manuscripts. The monks of Saint-Denis attributed it to their benefactor Charles the Bald. This was one of many falsifications executed in this abbey. It was Abelard who, in the early twelfth century, compounded his problems by denouncing another fraud, involving the pseudo-Dionysius, Paul's convert and the supposed founder of the monastery.

33. Emperor Louis II the German.

34. (Here translated from the French translation cited by Le Goff, that of R. Latouche, from *Textes d'histoire médiévale du Ve au XIe siècle* [Paris, 1951], pp. 144ff.—Trans.) Concerning Louis the Blind, see R. Pupardin, *Le Royaume de Provence sous les Carolingiens* (Paris, 1901), app. 6, "La Visio Karoli Crassi," pp. 324–32. In the "Vision of Rotcharius," which, like the "Vision of Wetti," dates from the early ninth century (see W. Wattenbach, ed., *Auszeigen für Kunderer deutschen Vorzeit* 12[1875], cols. 72–74), and in which sinners are purged by being immersed in fire up to their chests while boiling water is poured over their heads, Charlemagne is among the elect, having been rescued from punishment by the prayers of the faithful.

35. Egbert of Liège, *Fecunda Ratis*, ed. Voigt (Halle, 1889).

36. Cf. D. Sicard, *La Liturgie de la mort dans l'Eglise latine des origines à la réforme carolingienne, Liturgiewisssenschäftliche Quellen und Forschungen*, Veröffentlichungen des Abt-Herwegen-Instituts der Abtei Maria Laach, vol. 63 (Munster, 1978). The Latin text of the three prayers is on pp. 89–91. The Gallican prayer speaks of three patriarchs, not just of Abraham. "Thy friend Abraham" is joined by "the chosen Isaac" and "thy beloved Jacob." Similarly, the Gelasian Sacramentary refers to the "bosoms" (*in sinibus*) of the three patriarchs.

37. See the excellent study by J. Ntedika, *L'Evocation de l'au-delà dans la prière pour les morts. Etude de patristique et de liturgie latines: IVe–VIIIe siècle* (Louvain-Paris, 1971), esp. pp. 118–20.

38. B. Capelle, "L'intercession dans la messe romaine," *Revue benedictine* (1955), pp. 181–91. Reprinted in *Travaux liturgiques*, vol. 2 (1962), pp. 248–57.

39. D. Sicard, *La Liturgie de la mort*, p. 412. Concerning the first resurrection, see D. B. Botte, "Prima resurrectio, Un vestige de millénarisme dans les liturgies occidentales," *Recherches de théologie ancienne et médiévale* 15(1948):5–17. The idea endured, bolstered by the Book of Revelation. Traces of it may be found, for example, in a pamphlet on the confession of Guy of Southwick at the end of the twelfth century, published by Dom. A. Wilmart in *Recherches de théologie ancienne et médiévale* 7(1935):343.

40. J. Leclercq, "Documents sur la mort des moines," *Revue Mabillon* 45(1955):167.

41. Cf. N. Huyghebaert, *Les Documents nécrologiques*, in Typologie des Sources du Moyen Age occidental, fasc. 4 (Turnhout, 1972); J.-L. Lemaître, "Les obituaires français. Perspectives nouvelles," *Revue d'Histoire de l'Eglise de France* 44(1978):69–81. Only seven *libri vitae* are still extant. One of these, that of Remiremont, has been published in an exemplary edition by E. Hladwitschka, K. Schmid, and G. Tellenbach, "Der liber memorialis von Remiremont. Zur kritischen Erforschung und zum Quellenwert liturgischer Gedenkbücher," in *Deutscher Archiv für Erforschung des Mittelalters* 35(1969):64–110.

42. A bibliography pertaining to the "dead rolls" may be found in two articles by J. Dufour, "Le rouleau mortuaire de Bosson, abbé de Suse (v. 1130)," *Journal des savants*, pp. 237–54, and "Les rouleaux et encycliques mortuaires de Catalogne (1008-1102)," *Cahiers de civilisation médiévale* 20(1977):13–48.

43. K. Schmid and J. Wollasch, "Die Gemeinschaft der Lebenden und Verstorbenen in Zeugnissen des Mittelalters," in *Frühmittelälterliche Studien* 1(1967):365–405.

44. W. Jorden, *Das cluniazenische Totengedächtniswesen* (Munster, 1930). J.-L. Lemaître, "L'inscription dans les nécrologies clunisiens," in *La Mort au Moyen Age*, colloquium of the Société des historiens médiévistes de l'enseignement supérieur public, 1975 (Strasbourg, 1977), pp. 153–67.

45. Jotsuald's text is in *PL* 142.888–91 and Peter Damian's in *PL* 144.925–44.

PART TWO

1. See Georges Duby's great book, *Les Trois Ordres, ou l'imaginaire du féodalisme* (Paris: Gallimard, 1979), available in English as *The Three Orders: Feudal Society Imagined*, trans. Arthur Goldhammer (Chicago 1980). The Indo-European roots of tripartite ideology have been laid bare in magisterial fashion by Georges Dumézil. The current state of the question is discussed in my article "Les trois fonctions indo-européennes, l'historien et l'Europe féodale," *Annales Economies. Sociétés. Civilisations* (1979), pp. 1187–1215.

CHAPTER FOUR

1. See Appendix 2 on *purgatorium*.

2. See Claude Carozzi, "Structure et Fonction de la Vision de Tnugdal," in the collection entitled *Faire croire*, soon to be published by the Ecole française de

Rome. In my opinion Carozzi exaggerates the importance of a supposed controversy between "materialists" and "immaterialists" in the twelfth century and dates the emergence of Purgatory too early, but his contribution is quite stimulating. Carozzi may be right in thinking that there was in some twelfth-century writers, such as Honorius Augustodunensis, a tendency to see all otherworldly occurrences as *spiritualia*, spiritual phenomena, but this tendency had scarcely any influence on the genesis of Purgatory, a still rather vague notion whose development might at this point have been blocked. When Honorius Augustodunensis has occasion to describe the places in which souls are found in the other world, as he does in the *Elucidarium*, he is forced to concede that in some degree their nature is material, as we shall see. The debate as to whether the fire most frequently indicated as the instrument of purgation was material or spiritual did not last much beyond the first few centuries of the Christian era. The idea that the soul has no body and cannot therefore occupy any material space, put forward by Johannes Scotus Erigena in the ninth century, had little influence, no more than most other teachings of this isolated thinker. See M. Cappuyns, *Jean Scot Erigène. Sa vie, son oeuvre, sa pensée* (Louvain-Paris, 1933). In the first half of the thirteenth century Alexander of Hales expressed the opinion of most theologians, which confirmed the widespread belief: "Sin is not remitted without a double penalty: the remission has no value if there is no suffering on the part of the body" (Non ergo dimittitur peccatum sine duplici poena; non ergo valet relaxati cum nulla sit poena ex parte corporis), *Glossa in IV Libros Sententiarum* 4, dist. 20. No doubt the essential point is to notice that "spiritual" does not mean "disembodied."

3. *PL* 172.1237–38. Claude Carozzi is probably right to be suspicious of this edition.

4. *PL* 40.1029.

5. See Y. Lefèvre, *L'Elucidarium et les Lucidaires* (Paris, 1954).

6. *PL* 153.139.

7. See J. Morson and H. Costello, eds., *Les Sermons de Guerric d'Igny*, vol. 1, trans. P. Deseille, Sources Chrétiennes, vol. 166 (1970). I have followed this translation, merely replacing, as I have done throughout this work, the words "purify," "purification," and "purificatory" by "purge," "purgation," and "purgatorial" wherever the Latin reads *purgare*, *purgatio*, or *purgatorius*. Actually, Guerric also uses the word *purificare*. But for him it seems that the two terms were virtually synonymous. The Bible authorized this interpretation. Compare the theme of his Fourth Sermon with Luke 2:22: "Postiquam impleti sunt dies purgationis eius (Mariae)." The two sermons from which I have cited excerpts are on pages 356–85 of the volume cited. On Guerric d'Igny and "Purgatory," see D. de Wilde, *De beato Guerrico abbate Igniacensi ejusque doctrina de formatione Christi in nobis* (Westmalle, 1935), pp. 117–18.

8. See below.

9. *PL* 157.1035–36. See P. Glorieux, "Les Deflorationes de Werner de Saint-Blaise," *Mélanges Joseph de Ghellinck*, vol. 2 (Gembloux, 1951), pp. 699–721.

10. Studied by A. M. Landgraf, *Commentarius Porretanus in primam epistolam ad Corinthios*, Studi e Testi, 177, (Vatican City, 1945).

11. Achard de Saint-Victor, *Sermons*, ed. J. Chatillon (Paris, 1970), p. 156.

12. See J. Longère, *Oeuvres oratoires de maîtres parisiens au XIIe siècle* (Paris, 1975). Interesting remarks on the other world may be found in vol. 1, pp. 190–91,

and vol. 2, pp. 144–45, though the author fails to note the "birth of Purgatory." Concerning the beginnings of homiletic literature in French, see M. Zink, *La Prédication en langue romane avant 1300* (Paris, 1976).

13. W. Foerster, ed., *Li Dialoge Gregoire lo Pape*, a twelfth-century French translation of the Dialogues of Pope Gregory, accompanied by the Latin text (Paris, 1876), pp. 254–55. The expressions "purgatorial fire" and "fire of purgation" are worthy of note. I remind the reader that I have used these terms systematically (instead of the usual "purification") to translate texts written prior to the first appearance of the noun *purgatorium*, whose meaning is not exactly the same. In this I am reverting to the medieval lexicon not out of antiquarian affectation but rather out of a concern for accuracy.

14. Cited by Charles-V. Langlois, *La Vie en France au Moyen Age*, vol. 4 (Paris, 1928), p. 114.

15. *Recueil des historiens des croisades*, vol. 1, bk. 1 (1884), p. 44.

16. See R. Baron, *Science et sagesse chez Hugues de Saint-Victor* (Paris, 1957), and the bibliography to the French edition of A. M. Landgraf, *L'Introduction à l'histoire de la littérature théologique de la scolastique naissante* (Montreal-Paris, 1973), revised and completed by A.-M. Landry and P. Goblioni, pp. 93–97 as well as pp. 43–44. With respect to the doctrine of salvation, see H. Koster, *Die Heilslehre des Hugo von St. Victor, Grundlage und Grundzüge* (Emsdetten, 1940).

17. O. Lottin, "Questions inédites de Hugues de Saint-Victor," *Recherches de théologie ancienne et médiévale* (1960), pp. 59–60.

18. *PL* 176.586–96. The passage cited literally in translation is found in column 586, CD.

19. See Appendix 2 on *purgatorium*. For the time being I shall pass over another text which, though important, adds nothing about Bernard's own position. But it does lay out the views of heretics who were opposed to the idea of purgation after death, and I shall discuss it later on in connection with the relationship between heresy and Purgatory.

20. Saint Bernard, *Sermon XVI De diversis*, in *Opera*, ed. J. Leclercq and H. Rochais, vol. 6, bk. 1, pp. 144 and 147.

21. The sermon *In obitu Domni Humberti, monachi Clarae-Vallensis*, is found in ibid., vol. 5, p. 447.

22. Ibid., vol. 6, bk. 1, pp. 11–12.

23. *Decretum Magistri Gratiani*, ed. A. Friedberg (Leipzig, 1879), vol. 1, col. 728.

24. Ibid., pp. 1066ff.

25. "Ergo ubi sunt poenitentes post mortem? in purgatoriis. Ubi sunt ea? nondum scio."

26. "Unde peracta purgatione poenitentes, tam nostri, ex purgatoriis (quae extra infernum) ad coelos, quam veteres ex purgatoriis (quae in inferno) ad sinum Abrahae refrigerandi, jugiter conscendere videntur."

27. This text may be found in *PL* 186.823–30, specifically columns 826 and 827.

28. *PL* 202.201–2 and 224–26.

29. R. M. Martin, *Oeuvres de Robert de Melun*, vol. 2, *Questiones (theologia) de Epistolis Pauli* (Louvain, 1938), pp. 174 and 308.

30. Pierre de Celle, *L'Ecole du cloître*, ed. G. de Martel, Sources chrétiennes,

vol. 240 (1977), pp. 268–69. I have replaced "fire of purgatory" in the translation with "purgatorial fire," which is closer to the Latin text: *in igne purgatorio.*

31. *Conflictus Helveticus De Limbo Patrum,* ed. F. Stegmuller, in *Mélanges Joseph de Ghellinck,* vol. 2 (Gembloux, 1951), pp. 723–44. The sentence cited occurs on page 737.

32. *Homiliae de tempore* 1.43, *PL* 155.1484. Rather than "places" *(loca),* one might understand "pains" *(poenae).* Since the expression *loca purgatoria* does occur in the same time period, I prefer this interpretation of the expression *in purgatoriis,* which in any case suggests a desire to find a specific location for the process of purgation.

33. *PL* 211.1064.

34. "Quia vero sunt quidam qui in purgatoriis poliantur, ideo de eis tanquam de indignioribus hodierna die agimus, pro eis orantes, oblationes et elemosinas facientes." See J. Longère, *Oeuvres oratoires de maîtres parisiens au XIIe siècle,*" vol. 2 (Paris, 1975), p. 144 n.

Chapter Five

1. For details, see Appendix 2.

2. *PL* 171.739ff. The most interesting part of the passage reads as follows in the original Latin: "Ad hunc modum in aedificatione coelestis Jerusalem tria considerantur, separatio, politio, positio. Separatio est violenta; politio purgatoria, positio aeterna. Primum est in augustia et afflictione; secundum, in patientia et expectatione; tertium in gloria et exsultatione. Per primum (cribratur) homo sicut triticum; in secundo examinatur homo sicut argentum; in tertio reponitur in thesaurum" (col. 740).

3. "Tertio, memoria mortuorum agitur, ut hi qui in purgatorio poliuntur, plenam consequantur absolutionem, vel poenae mitigationem" *(PL* 171.741).

4. Haureau, "Notice sur les sermons attribués a Hildebert de Lavardin," *Notices et Extraits des manuscrits de la Bibliothèque nationale et autres bibliothèques* 23(2)1888:143; R. M. Martin, "Notes sur l'oeuvre littéraire de Pierre le Mangeur," *Recherches de théologie ancienne et médiévale* 3(1932):54–66; A. Landgraf, "Recherches sur les écrits de Pierre le Mangeur," *Recherches de théologie ancienne et médiévale* 3(1932):292–306 and 341–72; A. Wilmart, "Les sermons d'Hildebert," *Revue bénédictine* 47(1935):12–51; M. M. Lebreton, "Recherches sur les manuscrits contenant des sermons de Pierre le Mangeur," *Bulletin d'information de l'Institut de Recherche et d'Histoire des Textes* 2(1953):25–44. J. B. Schneyer, *Repertorium der lateinischen sermones des Mittelalters für die Zeit von 1150–1350* (1972), vol. 4, p. 641, accepts the attribution to Peter Comestor of Sermon 85 (*Jerusalem quae aedificatur*) from the old edition of Beaugendre (1708), where it is attributed to Hildebert, an attribution also accepted by Migne (PL 171.739ff). F. Dolbeau was kind enough to examine for me what were thought to be the two oldest known manuscripts. He confirms the attribution to Peter Manducator and the reading *in purgatorio* (MS Angers 312(303), fol. 122v and Angers 247(238) fol. 76v, both from the late twelfth century). But he has located an even older manuscript (Valenciennes, Bibliothèque municipale 227(218) fol. 49) in which the phrase *in purgatorio poliuntur* does not appear. It is surprising that Joseph Ntedika, generally quite well informed, should have written of Hildebert that "he is probably the first to use the word *purgatorium*": *L'Evolu-*

tion de la doctrine du purgatoire chez saint Augustin (Paris, 1966), p. 11, n. 17. Concerning Peter Manducator, the reader may also wish to consult I. Brady, "Peter Manducator and the Oral Teachings of Peter Lombard," *Antonianum* 41(1966):454–90.

5. Peter Manducator, *De Sacramentis, De penitentia*, chaps. 25–31, ed. R. M. Martin, in *Spicilegium sacrum Lovaniense* (Louvain, 1937), vol. 17, pp. 81–82.

6. *PL* 198.1589–90.

7. Things are not made any clearer by the fact that there were several Odo's and Master Odo's in Paris in the second half of the twelfth century. One of them was chancellor from 1164 to 1168. See M. M. Lebreton, "Recherches sur les manuscrits des sermons de différents personnages du XIIe siècle nommés Odon," *Bulletin de l'Institut de Recherche et d'Histoire des Textes* 3(1955):33–54.

8. "Cum materialis poena sit ille ignis, in loco est. Ubi ergo sit, quarendum relinquo." The *Quaestiones magistri Odonis* were published by J. B. Pitra, *Analecta novissima spicilegii Solesmensis altera continuatio* (Tusculum, 1888), vol. 2, pp. 137–38.

9. A. M. Landgraf, "Quelques collections de *Quaestiones* de la seconde moitié du XIIe siècle," *Recherches de théologie ancienne et médiévale* 6(1934):368–93 and 7(1935):113–28. On p. 117 of the latter Landgraf expresses his doubts as to the questions published by Pitra and cites the works of M. Chossat, "La Somme des Sentences," *Spicilegium Sacrum Lovaniense* 5 (Louvain, 1923), and J. Warichez, "Les disputationes de Simon de Tournai," ibid., 12 (Louvain, 1932).

10. O. J. Blum, *St. Peter Damian: His Teaching on the Spiritual Life* (Washington, 1947); J. Ryan, "Saint Peter Damiani and the Sermons of Nicolas of Clairvaux," *Medieval Studies* 9(1947):151–61; and especially F. Dressler, *Petrus Damiani. Leben und Werk*, Studia Anselmiana, vol. 34 (Rome, 1954), particularly Anhang 3, pp. 234–35.

11. This sermon is attributed to Nicolas of Clairvaux in the *Patrologia Latina* 184.1055–60, though it is also found under the name of Peter Damian in *PL* 144.835–40. The sermon is for the feast day of Saint Nicolas, who was one of the "patron saints of Purgatory." The sermon attributed to Saint Bernard may be found in the complete works edited by J. Leclercq and H.-M. Rochais: Bernard, *Opera*, vol. 6, pt. 1, pp. 255–61. Concerning the sermons *De diversis* attributed to Saint Bernard, especially sermon 42, see H.-M. Rochais, "Enquête sur les sermons divers et les sentences de Saint Bernard," *Analecta SOC*, 1962, pp. 16–17, and *Revue bénédictine* 72(1962).

12. On Nicolas of Clairvaux, see Ryan, "Saint Peter Damiani and the Sermons of Nicolas of Clairvaux"; A. Steiger, "Nikolaus, Monch in Clairvaux, Sekretär des heiligen Bernhards," *Studien und Mitteilungen zur Geschichte des Benediktinerordens und seiner Zweige*, N. F. 7(1917):41–50; and J. Leclercq, "Les collections de sermons de Nicolas de Clairvaux," *Revue bénédictine* 66(1956), especially p. 275 n. 39.

13. Madame M.-C. Garand was kind enough to examine two of the oldest manuscripts (Paris, Bibliothèque nationale, Latin MS 2571 and Cambrai 169). She writes me the following: "The fact that the sainthood of Saint Bernard is not mentioned in the title and is the subject of a correction in the *ex-libris* undoubtedly places the date of the manuscript prior to his canonization in 1174. But it may be that it was not much prior to that time, because the handwriting is already rather

broken and could well be from the third quarter of the twelfth century. As for the Cambrai manuscript, the handwriting and special characters again suggest the second half of the century."

14. Saint Bernard, *Opera*, ed. J. Leclercq and H. Rochais, vol. 5, pp. 383–88, especially p. 386. Sermon 78, *De diversis*, on the same subject seems to me a forced and simplified plagiarism of Bernard rather than a wholly genuine text. But this is merely an impression. I have not conducted any research into the matter. See B. de Vregille, "L'attente des saints d'après saint Bernard," *Nouvelle Revue Théologique*, 1948, pp. 224–44.

15. The manuscript is Latin MS 15912 of the Bibliothèque Nationale of Paris. Madame Georgette Lagarde was kind enough to transcribe the passages summarized here. The expression *in purgatorio* is found in folio 64b, and the *exemplum* drawn from the life of Saint Bernard in folios 65c–66a.

16. See J. Baldwin, *Masters, Princes and Merchants: The Social Views of Peter the Chanter and His Circle*, 2 vols. (Princeton, 1970).

17. Peter the Chanter, *Summa de Sacramentis et Animae Consiliis*, J. A. Dugauquier, ed., in *Analecta mediaevalia Namurcensia* 7(1957):103–4.

18. Ibid., pp. 125–26.

19. Peter the Chanter, *Summa de Sacramentis*, pt. 3, 3.2a: *Liber casuum conscientiae*, ed. J. A. Dugauquier, in *Analecta Mediaevalia Namurcensia* 16(1963):264.

20. *PL* 205.350–51. The date 1192 was proposed by D. van den Eynde, "Précisions chronologiques sur quelques ouvrages théologiques du XIIe siècle," *Antonianum* 26(1951):237–39.

21. J. Warichez, "Les Disputationes de Simon de Tournai," manuscript, Louvain, 1932. Disputes 40, 55, and 73 are found on pp. 118–20, 157–58, and 208–11, respectively.

22. *PL* 211.1054. See P. S. Moore, *The Works of Peter of Poitiers, Master in Theology and Chancellor of Paris (1193–1205)*, Publications in Medieval Studies, vol. 1, (Notre Dame, Ind., 1936).

23. "Vie de saint Victor, martyr de Mouzon," ed. F. Dolbeau, *Revue historique ardennaise*, vol. 9, p. 61.

24. R. Manselli, "Il monaco Enrico e la sua eresia," *Bolletino dell'istituto Storico Italiano per il Medio Evo e Archivo Muratoriano* 65(1953):62–63. On heresies in the twelfth century, see the fundamental work of R. Manselli, *Studi sulle eresie del secolo XII* (Rome, 1953).

25. Saint Bernard, *Opera*, vol. 2, p. 185. See the editor's introduction, vol. 1, p. ix.

26. *PL* 204.795–840 (chapters 10 and 11 are in columns 833–35). Cf. A. Paschowsk and K. V. Selge, *Quellen zur Geschichte der Waldenses* (Göttingen, 1973), and L. Verrees, "Le traité de l'abbé Bernard de Fontcaude contre les vaudois et les ariens," *Analecta praemonstratensia* (1955), pp. 5–35. G. Connet thinks that these ideas "were professed, at least at the outset, by sects other than the Waldensians." See his "Le cheminement des vaudois vers le schisme et l'hérésie (1174–1218)," *Cahiers de civilisation médiévale* (1976), pp. 309–45.

27. "Tria quippe sunt loca quae spiritus a carne solutos recipiunt. Paradisus recipit spiritus perfectorum. Infernus valde malos. Ignis purgatorionis eos, qui nec

valde boni sunt nec valde mali. Et sic, valde bonos suscepit locus valde bonus; valde malos locus summe malus; mediocriter malos locus medocriter malus, id est levior inferno sec pejor mundo" (*PL* 204.834–35).

28. "Et hic non damnantur, nec statim salvantur, sed puniuntur sub exspectatione percipiendae salutis" (*PL* 204.1268).

29. The *Summa contra haereticos* ascribed to Praepositivus of Cremona, ed. J. N. Garvin and J. A. Corbett (Notre Dame, Ind., 1958), especially pp. 210–11.

30. See the fundamental study of M.-T. d'Alverny, *Alain de Lille. Textes inédits avec une introduction sur sa vie et ses oeuvres* (Paris, 1965).

31. G. Connet in *Cahiers de civilisation médiévale* (1976), p. 323.

32. *Summa de arte praedicatoria*, PL 210.174–75.

33. *Liber poenitentialis*, ed. J. Longère, (Louvain-Lille, 1965), vol. 2, pp. 174–77.

34. Ibid., p. 177: "Item quaeritur si iste debebat implere septem annos et non implevit, utrum per septem annos sit in purgatorio? Respondemus: procul dubio implebit illam satisfactionem in purgatorio, sed quamdiu ibi sit, ille novit qui est librator poenarum."

35. A. M. Landgraf, *Einführung in die Geschichte der theologischen Literatur der Frühscholastik* (Ratisbon, 1948). An updated, more complete French translation was published in 1973: see p. 58 of that version.

36. Cited by A. M. Landgraf, *Dogmengeschichte der Frühscholastik* (Ratisbon, 1956), vol. 4, bk. 2, p. 260 n.3.

37. Based on Latin MS 3891 of the Bibliothèque Nationale in Paris, fol. 183v (of which I was graciously informed by Father P. M. Gy).

38. Cited by Landgraf, *Dogmengeschichte*, 4/2, p. 261 n. 6.

39. Johannes Teutonicus, fols. 335v, 336.

40. *PL* 214.1123.

41. *PL* 217.578–90. Here is the crucial passage: "Deus enim trinus et unus, tres tribus locis habet exercitus. Unum, qui triumphat in coelo; alterum, qui pugnat in mundo; tertium, qui jacet in purgatorio. De his tribus exercitibus inquit Apostolus: 'In nomine Jesu omne genu flectatur, coelestium, terrestrium et infernorum' (Phil. 2). Hi tres exercitus distincte clamant cum seraphim, Sanctus Peter, sanctus Filius, sanctus Spiritus. Patri namque attribuitur potentia, quae convenit exercitui, qui pugnat in via; Filio sapientia, quae competit exercitui, qui triumphat in patria; Spiritui sancto misericordia, quae congruit exercitui, qui jacet in poena. Primus exercitus in laude, secundus in agone, tertius autem in igne. De primo legitur: 'Beati qui habitant in domo tua, Domine, in saecula saeculorum laudabunt te' (Ps. 83); de secundo dicitur: 'Militia est vita hominis super terram; et sicut dies mercenarii, dies ejus' (Job 7). De tertio vero inquit Apostolus: 'Uniuscujusque opus quale sit, ignis probabit' (1 Cor. 3). Sane quinque loca sunt, in quibus humani spiritus commorantur. Supremus, qui est summe bonorum; infimus, qui est summe malorum; medius, qui est bonorum et malorum: et inter supremum et medium unus, qui est mediocriter bonorum; et inter medium et infimum alter, qui est mediocriter malorum. Supremus, qui est summe bonorum, est coelum, in quo sunt beati. Infimus, qui est summe malorum, est infernus, in quo sunt damnati. Medius, qui est bonorum et malorum, est mundus, in quo justi et peccatores. Et inter supremum et medium, qui est mediocriter bonorum, est paradisus; in quo sunt Enoch et Elias, vivi quidem,

sed adhuc morituri. Et inter medium et infimum, qui est mediocriter malorum, in quo puniuntur qui poenitentiam non egerunt in via; vel aliquam maculam venialem portaverunt in morte."

42. Charles Thouzellier, "Ecclesia militans," *Etudes d'histoire du droit canonique* (Paris, 1965), vol. 2, pp. 1407–24.

43. "O quam rationabilis et salubris est hujus observantiae institutio" (*PL* 217.590).

44. Thomas of Chobham, *Summa Confessorum*, ed. F. Broomfield (Louvain-Paris, 1958), pp. 125–26.

45. Ibid., p. 127.

46. Latin MS 14883, fol. 114, Bibliothèque Nationale, Paris, cited by A. M. Landgraf, *Dogmengeschichte*, vol 4/2, p. 281 n. 61.

47. "Melius est, ut dicatur, quod diverse mansiones sunt in purgatorio: alia appelantur obscura tenebrarum loca, alia manus inferni, alia os leonis, alia tartarus. Et ab istis poenis petit Ecclesia animas mortuorum liberari" (ibid., p. 281 n. 61).

CHAPTER SIX

1. The text of the pamphlet may be found in *PL* 145.584–90 with chapter titles added by the editor that are frequently anachronistic (e.g., "liberat a poenis purgatorii"). Concerning Peter Damian and the memory of the dead, see F. Dressler, *Petrus Damiani: Leben und Werk* (Rome, 1954). Concerning death in monastic circles, see Leclercq, "Documents sur la mort des moines," *Revue Mabillon* 45(1955):165–80.

2. *PL* 145.186, 188.

3. The Latin text is explicit in a sustained and realistic manner: "poenalibus undique loris astrictum et ambeintium catenarum squaloribus vehementer attritum."

4. *PL* 144.403.

5. *De miraculis* 1.9, *PL* 189.871.

6. *De miraculis* 1.23, *PL* 189.891–94.

7. *De miraculis* 1.18, *PL* 189.903–8.

8. The manuscript in question is Latin MS 15912, which was partially transcribed by Georgette Lagarde in conjunction with the work on the *exemplum* of the group studying the historical anthropology of the medieval West at the Ecole des Hautes Etudes en sciences sociales. The visions reported occur on folio 64.

9. This anecdote about Saint Bernard's brief stay in Purgatory (see above) was not used by Jacobus da Voragine in the *Golden Legend*. Bear in mind that Mary's Immaculate Conception did not become Catholic dogma until 1854.

10. Guibert de Nogent's *De vita sua* (originally entitled *Monodiae*, "poems for one voice," memoirs) is found in volume 156 of *Patrologia latina*. Its place in the history of autobiography is discussed by G. Kisch, *Geschichte der Autobiographie* (Frankfurt, 1959). See J. Paul, "Le démoniaque et l'imaginaire dans le *De vita sua* de Guibert de Nogent," in *Le Diable au Moyen Age*, Senefiance no. 6, Aix-en-Provence (Paris, 1979), pp. 371–99.

11. See John F. Benton's introduction to the English translation of Guibert's memoirs by C. C. Swinton Bland, *Self and Society in Medieval France: The Memoirs of Abbot Guibert of Nogent* (New York, 1970), and the suggestive article

by Mary M. McLaughlin, "Survivors and Surrogates: Children and Parents from the Ninth to the Twelfth Centuries," in *The History of Childhood*, ed. Lloyd de Mause (New York, 1975), pp. 105-6.

12. Cf. Jean-Claude Schmitt, *Le saint lévrier: Guinefort, guérisseur d'enfant depuis le XIIIe siècle* (Paris, 1979).

13. Concerning the connection between the color black and the Devil in the Middle Ages, see J. Devisse and M. Mollat, *L'Image du noir dans l'art occidental*, 2 vols. (Freiburg, 1979), vol. 2: *Des premiers siècles chrétiens aux grandes découvertes*.

14. Text published by Dom Mauro Inguanez in *Miscellanea Cassinese* 11(1932):83-103, preceded by an essay by Dom Antonia Mirra, "La visione di Alberico," ibid., pp. 34-79.

15. Regarding Muslim influences, see the somewhat exaggerated claims put forward by M. Asin Palacio in *La Escatologia musulmana en la "Divina Commedia"* (Madrid, 1919) and *Dante y el Islam* (Madrid, 1929), as well as the more moderate ones of E. Cerulli, *Il "libro della Scala" et la questione delle fonti arabo-spagnole della Divina Commedia* (Rome, 1949). Concerning the absence of Purgatory in Islam, see especially E. Blochet, "Etude sur l'histoire religieuse de l'Iran," *Revue de l'histoire des religions* 20, no. 40 (1899), p. 12. See also M. Arkoun, J. Le Goff, T. Fahd, and M. Rodinson, *L'Etrange et le Merveilleux dans l'Islam médiéval* (Paris, 1978), pp. 100-101.

16. It covers twenty printed pages.

17. The published text (p. 93) reads as follows: Hoc autem insinuante apostolo, purgatorii nomen habere cognovi. Assuming that the word "fluminis" is implicit, I read this as follows: "I learned that it bore the name of purgatory (river)." In fact, the chapter heading, which according to the editor is transcribed from the manuscript, is *De flumine purgatorio* (on the purgatorial river). It is as an adjective in the genitive, with reference to this passage, that the word *purgatorii* (*purgatorius*) figures in the catalogue of the new *Du Cange Glossary*, as A.-M. Bautier has kindly informed me.

18. Though no reference is given, this interdiction obviously comes from Paul, 2 Corinthians 12:2-4. Here is the end of the journey: Saint Peter ultimately leads Alberic through fifty-one earthly provinces—the provinces of the ancient Roman Empire—where he shows him the sanctuaries of the saints and various edifying *mirabilia*. The story ends with a description of Saint Peter, various sayings of the apostle, the return of Alberic's soul to his body, the vision of his mother praying to an icon representing Saint Paul for his recovery, and his entry into the monastery at Monte Cassino.

19. *Visio Tnugdali*, ed. Albrecht Wagner (Erlangen, 1882). I remind the reader of Claude Carozzi's recent study, "Structure et fonction de la vision de Tnugdal," cited previously.

20. The *Purgatorium Sancti Patricii* was published twice in the seventeenth century, by Messingham in his *Florilegium Insulae Sanctorum* in 1624, which is reproduced in *PL* 180.975-1004, and by the Jesuit John Colgan in his *Triadis thaumaturgae . . . acta* (Louvain, 1647). Modern versions have been provided by S. Eckleben, *Die älteste Schilderung vom Fegfeuer des heiligen Patricius* (Halle, 1885); by E. Mall, who gives, opposite the text published by Colgan, the manuscript that may be regarded as being closest to the original text (MS E VII 59 of

Bamberg, from the fourteenth century) and variants from a manuscript from the British Museum, Arundel 292 (end of the thirteenth century): "Zur Geschichte der Legende vom Purgatorium des heiligen Patricius," in *Romanische Forschungen*, ed. K. Vollmoller (1891), vol. 6, pp. 139–97; by U. M. van der Zanden, *Etude sur le Purgatoire de saint Patrice* (Amsterdam, 1927), who published the text of a manuscript from Utrecht from the fifteenth century, together with an appendix consisting of a corrected version of the Arundel 292 manuscript; and by Warncke in 1938. I used the Mall edition. The *Purgatorium Sancti Patricii* has frequently been studied, in both its Latin and vernacular versions (especially English and French—with Marie de France's *L'Espurgatoire saint Patriz* in a class by itself). Several of these studies, though dated, are still valuable. Most situate the text either in the context of age-old beliefs about the other world or in relation to folklore. Though frequently not sufficiently critical and nowadays out of date, these studies remain a model of historical openmindedness. Among those worth citing are the following: Theodore Wright, *St. Patrick's Purgatory: An Essay on the Legends of Purgatory, Hell and Paradise, Current During the Middle Ages* (London, 1844); Baring-Gould, *Curious Myths of the Middle Ages* (1884, reprint ed. Leyden, 1975): "St. Patrick's Purgatory," pp. 230–49; G. P. Krapp, *The Legend of St. Patrick's Purgatory, Its Later Literary History* (Baltimore, 1900; Philippe de Felice, *L'autre monde. Mythes et légendes: le Purgatoire de saint Patrice* (Paris, 1906). The study that is considered to be most complete, Shane Leslie's *St. Patrick's Purgatory: A Record from History and Literature* (London, 1932), is not the most interesting. V. and E. Turner have given a very suggestive anthropological interpretation of the pilgrimage to Saint Patrick's Purgatory in modern times, which unfortunately contributes nothing to our subject: *Image and Pilgrimage in Christian Culture* (Oxford, 1978), chap. 3: "St. Patrick's Purgatory: Religion and Nationalism in an Archaic Pilgrimage," pp. 104–39.

21. In Rome, in the church of the Sacro Cuore del Suffragio, there is a small "museum of Purgatory," which contains a dozen signs (generally burn marks made with a hand, indicating the fire of Purgatory) of the apparition of souls from Purgatory to the living. These occurred at intervals from the end of the eighteenth century to the beginning of the twentieth. The system of Purgatory proved long-lived indeed.

22. The details about Patrick, who lived in the fifth century, are invented. The older lives of Patrick are silent on the subject. As far as we can tell from the current state of the documentary evidence, Saint Patrick's Purgatory is mentioned for the first time in the new life of the saint written by Jocelyn of Furness between 1180 and 1183. Since the knight Owein is not mentioned there, the 1180–83 period is generally regarded as the terminus a quo for the dating of the *Tractatus* of H of Saltrey.

23. See Erich Köhler, *L'Aventure chevaleresque. Idéal et réalité dans le roman courtois* (Paris, 1974).

24. Although I have enclosed the archbishops' story in quotation marks, I have abridged and paraphrased it.

25. These images of the other world are still prevalent today among the descendants of the Mayas, the Lacandons of southern Mexico: "The 'sage' Tchank'in Maasch . . . was an inexhaustible source of stories about this realm of shadow in

which frozen streams and rivers of fire run side by side." J. Soustelle, *Les Quatre Soleils* (Paris, 1967), p. 52.

26. F. W. Locke, "A New Date for the Composition of the Tractatus de Purgatorio Sancti Patricii," *Speculum*, 1965, pp. 641–46, rejects the traditional date of around 1189 in favor of the 1208–15 period as the time when the *Tractatus* was written. This means that the date of the *Espurgatoire Saint Patriz* must also be pushed ahead by some twenty years. Richard Baum, "Recherches sur les oeuvres attribuées à Marie de France," *Annales Universitatis Saraviensis* 9(1968), has recently argued not only that the *Espurgatoire* was later than the last decade of the twelfth century but also that it was not the work of Marie de France. As we shall see later on, Giraldus Cambrensis's *Topographia Hibernica* and Jocelyn of Furness's *Life of Saint Patrick* do not provide decisive information concerning the dating of the *Tractatus*.

27. The *Life of Saint Patrick* by Jocelyn of Furness was published in the seventeenth century in the same collections as H of Saltrey's *Purgatorium*, by Messigham (*Florilegium insulae sanctorum* [Paris, 1624], pp. 1–85) and Colgan (*Triadis thaumaturgae* [Louvain, 1647]). The passage concerning the Purgatory on Mount Cruachan Aigle occurs on page 1027. It has been republished in the *Acta Sanctorum*, entry for March 17, vol. 2, p. 540–80.

28. Giraldus Cambrensis, *Opera*, ed. J. F. Dimock (London, 1867), vol. 5: *Rerum Britannicarum medii aevi scriptores*, pp. 82–83. It was immediately after this passage in the manuscript from the first half of the thirteenth century that the words, "This place was called Patrick's Purgatory by the inhabitants," were added, and it is told how Saint Patrick obtained its creation. Cf. C. M. van der Zanden, "Un chapitre intéressant de la *Topographia Hibernica* et le *Tractatus de purgatorio sancti Patricii*," *Neophilologus* (1927). Giraldus Cambrensis seems to have written the *Topographia* at the time when a pentitential pilgrimage—doubtless something in the nature of an ordeal—was shifted from the largest island, Saints' Island, in the northwestern corner of Lough Dergh, to the smaller Station Island, which explains the synthesis in a single island divided between saints and demons.

29. Apart from the very interesting study by V. and E. Turner cited in n. 20 above, the available studies of the pilgrimage are either mediocre or summary. Cf. John Seymour, *Saint Patrick's Purgatory. A Mediaeval Pilgrimage in Ireland* (Dundald, 1918); J. Ryan, *New Catholic Encyclopedia* (1967), vol. 11, p. 1039. The fourth chapter of Philippe de Felice's *L'Autre Monde, Mythes et Légendes, Le Purgatoire de saint Patrice* (Paris, 1906), which is entitled "Histoire du Sanctuaire du Lough Derg" is not without interest and concludes with this judicious remark: "The persistence of Saint Patrick's Purgatory over the centuries is a clear, incontrovertible fact, the importance of which deserves to be called to the attention of sociologists." On pp. 9ff., he tells how, together with a cousin, he made his way with some difficulty to Lough Derg and the isle of Purgatory in 1905. In 1913 Cardinal Logue, the primate of Ireland, made the following declaration after visiting Station Island: "I believe that any person who here at Lough Derg completes the traditional pilgrimage, the penitential exercises, the fast, and the prayers that are the equivalent of so many indulgences, and who subsequently dies, will have to suffer very little in the other world" (cited by V. and E. Turner, p. 133). Anne Lombard-Jourdan, who visited Lough Derg and Saint Patrick's Purgatory in

1972, was kind enough to provide me with a copy of the official program, which bears the seal of the local bishop, the bishop of Clogher. During the Middle Ages the length of the penance was reduced from fifteen days to nine days, the nine-day period being more standard with the Church. In more recent times the period was still further reduced, to three days, which is the rule today, but the heart of the pilgrimage is still a trial of twenty-four hours. The 1970 program states that "the Vigil is the principal spiritual exercise of the pilgrimage and means that one goes entirely without sleep for a full twenty-four hours without interruption." An extraordinary continuity of beliefs and practices! See plate 4.

30. *L'Espurgatoire Saint Patriz* by Marie de France was published by Thomas Atkinson Jenkins in Philadelphia in 1894. See L. Foulet, "Marie de France et la Légende du Purgatoire de saint Patgrice," *Romanische Forschungen* 22(1908):599–627.

31. Paul Meyer mentions seven French verse versions of *Saint Patrick's Purgatory* in his *Histoire littéraire de la France*, vol. 33, pp. 371–72, and *Notices et Extraits des manuscrits de la Bibliothèque nationale* (Paris, 1891), vol. 34: Marie de France's version; four anonymous thirteenth-century versions; Beroul's version; the version of Geoffroy de Paris introduced by the Fourth Book of the *Bible des sept états du diable*. One of these was published by Johan Vising, *Le Purgatoire de saint Patrice des manuscrits Harleien 273 et Fonds français 2198* (Göteborg, 1916). The noun "purgatory" is used there several times. For example:

> Par la grant hounte qu'il aveit
> Dist qe mout bonnement irreit
> En purgatoire, qe assez
> Peust espener ses pechiez (vv. 91–94).
>
> . . . .
>
> Com celui qe ne velt lesser
> En purgatoire de entrer (vv. 101–2)

There are also several French prose versions. One of these was published by Prosper Tarbe, *Le Purgatoire de saint Patrice. Légende du XIIIe siècle, publiée d'après un manuscrit de la Bibliothèque de Reims* (Reims, 1842). The oldest English versions (thirteenth century) were published by Hortsmann in *Alten Englische Legenden* (Paderborn, 1875), pp. 149–211; Koelbing in *Englische Studien* (Breslau, 1876), vol. 1, pp. 98–121; and L. T. Smith, *Englische Studien* (Breslau, 1886), vol. 9, pp. 3–12.

An edition in Occitan was published at the beginning of the fifteenth century by A. Jeanroy and A. Vignaux, *Raimon de Perlhos. Voyage au purgatoire de saint Patrice, Textes languedociens du XVe siècle* (Toulouse, 1903). This edition also contains Occitanian versions of the vision of Tindal (Tnugdal) and the vision of Saint Paul, which Raymond of Perelhos attributes to himself as he does the voyage to Saint Patrick's Purgatory. All of these texts come from manuscript 894 of the Bibliothèque municipale of Toulouse, illustrating the fifteenth-century taste for visions of the hereafter and Purgatory. In this small group of texts the vision of Tindal (Tnugdal) is converted into a vision of Purgatory. The title (fol. 48) is "Ayssi commensa lo libre de Tindal tractan de las penas de purgatori." On the fortunes of Saint Patrick Purgatory in Spain, see J. Perez de Montalban, *Vida y Purgatorio de San Patricio*, ed. M. G. Profeti (Pisa, 1972).

32. (Here translated into English from the French translation of the *Légende*

dorée by T. de Wyzewa (Paris, 1920), p. 182.—Trans.) Concerning Stephen of Bourbon and Humbert of Romans, see L. Frati, "Il Purgatorio di S. Patrizio secondo Stefano di Bourbon e Umberto de Romans," in *Giornale storico della letteratura italiana* 8(1886):140–79.

33. The prose version by Gossouin of Metz was published by O. H. Prior, *L'Image du monde de maître Gossouin. Rédaction en prose* (Lausanne-Paris, 1913).

34. This excerpt from the *Image du monde* by Gossouin of Metz is from the slightly modernized French version of the text given by the Count of Douhet in the *Dictionnaire des légendes du christianisme*, ed. Migne (Paris, 1855), col. 950–1035.

35. Quaracchi edition, vol. 4, p. 526. The great Franciscan master says that this was his source for the legend that Purgatory is found in these regions ("ex quo fabulose ortum est, quod ibi esset purgatorium").

36. Froissart, *Chroniques*, ed. Kervyn de Lettenhove (Brussels, 1871), vol. 15, pp. 145–46.

37. Shakespeare, *Hamlet*. When the ghost of his father appears to Hamlet (act 1 scene 5), this is what the ghost says:

> I am thy father's spirit
> Doom'd for a certain term to walk the night
> And, for the day, confin'd to fast in fires,
> Till the foul crimes, done in my days of nature,
> Are burnt and purg'd away.

Later, Hamlet's father says that his murder at the hands of his brother was all the more foul because he had no time to confess and do penance before dying. When the ghost has disappeared, Hamlet, without telling Horatio and Marcellus what the ghost has said, invokes Saint Patrick:

> HORATIO: There's no offence, my lord.
> HAMLET: Yes, by Saint Patrick, but there is, Horatio,
> And much offence, too. Touching this vision
> It is an honest ghost.

38. Calderon's *El Purgatorio de San Patricio* was first published in 1636.

39. The Count of Douhet, in his very interesting article, "Saint Patrice, son purgatoire et son voyage," published a version still thought highly of in the eighteenth century. He writes (col. 951): "Of the thousands of versions available, we have chosen a recent one, still popular in the last century, which fully renders the intentions of the Middle Ages."

40. Jotsuald (whose name is also found spelled Jotsald, Jotaud, and Jotswald), *Vita Odilonis*, PL 142.926–27; Peter Damian, *Vita Ordiolonis*, PL 144.935–37. See above. On popular beliefs associated with the volcanoes in the Lipari Isles and the cult of Saint Bartholomew, whose relics appeared in Lipari in about 580, as well as the cult of Saint Calogero, a Sicilian hermit who lived for a time in the Liparis and who appears in the odes of the monk of Sergio in the ninth century (he was canonized in the sixteenth century), see G. Cozza Luzi, "Le eruzioni di Lipari e del Vesuvio nell'anno 787" in *Nuovo Giornale Arcadico*, 3 (Milan, 1890); and G. Iacolino, "Quando le Eolie diventarono colonie dell'Inferno. Calogero un uomo solo contro mille diavoli," *Arcipelago*, anno 2, no. 4 (Lipari, 1977). Bernabo Brea is preparing a study on these traditions from antiquity to the present.

41. Julien of Vézelay, *Sermons*, ed. D. Vorreux, vol. 2, Collections sources chrétiennes, vol. 13 (Paris, 1972), pp. 450–55. Julien gives the same etymology for *ethnici*, derived from Etna, in sermon I x, vol. 1, p. 224.

42. Ibid., pp. 456–59 and 460–63.

43. Gervase of Tilbury, *Otia Imperialia*, in *Scriptores Rerum Brunsvicensium* (Hanover, 1707), vol. 1, p. 921 (the edition of Leibniz who, in his preface, shows his deep aversion, as a man of the Enlightenment, for the Middle Ages).

44. Here we see the influence of the Arabic word "Djebel" (mountain), a sign of the Muslim presence in Sicily and of the prestige of Etna, which is referred to as "the" mountain.

45. *Otia Imperialia*, ed. Leibniz, p. 921.

46. Arturo Graf, "Artù nell'Etna," in *Miti, leggende e superstizioni del Medio Evo* (Turin, 1893), vol. 2, pp. 303–35.

47. See R. S. Loomis, "The Oral Diffusion of the Arthurian Legend," in R. S. Loomis, ed., *Arthurian Literature in the Middle Ages: A Collaborative History* (Oxford, 1959), pp. 61–62, and, in the same volume, A. Viscardi, "Arthurian Influences in Italian Literature from 1200 to 1500," p. 419.

48. See Alfred Nutt's essay *The Happy Otherworld in the Mythico-Romantic Literature of the Irish, The Celtic Doctrine of Rebirth*, which follows Kuno Meyer's edition of the voyage of Bran, a saga written in the seventh century and recast in the tenth century, of which the earliest manuscripts date from the beginning of the twelfth century: *The Voyage of Bran, Son of Febal, to the Land of the Living. An Old Irish Saga* (London, 1895).

49. I shall have more to say later on about Stephen of Bourbon.

50. Gregory the Great, *Dialogi* 4.33–37, ed. V. Moricca, pp. 278–85.

51. Ibid., 4.30.

52. *Hodoeporicon S. Willibaldi*, in *Itinera hierosolymitana*, ed. T. Tobler and A. Molinier (Geneva, 1879), pp. 272–73. I am indebted to my friend Anne Lombard-Jourdan for my knowledge of this text.

CHAPTER SEVEN

1. "pro exercitu qui jacet in purgatorio" (*PL* 217.590).

2. Suger, *Vie de Louis VI le Gros*, ed. and trans. H. Waquet, Les classiques de l'Histoire de France au Moyen Age (Paris, 1964). Suger began a life of Louis VII but left it unfinished: it was published by J. Lair in the Bibliothèque de l'école des chartes (1875), pp. 583–96. The *Gesta Philippi Augusti* by Rigord and the *Philipis* by William the Breton were published by F. Delaborde, *Société de l'Histoire de France* (Paris, 1882–85).

3. See Galbert de Bruges, *Le meurtre de Charles le Bon*, trans. J. Gengoux, under the direction of R. C. Van Caeneghem, who also provides an introduction (Antwerp, 1977). (There is also a convenient English translation, *The Murder of Charles the Good, Count of Flanders*, ed. and trans. James Bruce Ross [New York, 1959].—Trans.).

4. Yves of Chartres, *Prologus in Decretum*, PL 161.47–60. On suffrages Yves reproduces the texts of Gregory the Great, *Dialogues* 4.39 and 4.55, PL 161.993–95 and 999–1000.

5. G. Le Bras, "Le Liber de misericordia et justitia d'Alger de Liège," *Nouvelle*

Revue historique de droit français et étranger (1921), pp. 80–118. The text of the *Liber* is found in Migne, *PL* 180.859–968.

6. See Alger of Liège, *Liber*, chaps. 28, 43–44, 83, 93. The passage on purgation occurs in chapts. 61–62 (*PL* 80.929–30).

7. Stephan Kuttner, *Kanonistische Schuldlehre von Gratian bis auf die Dekretalen Gregors IX* (Vatican City, 1935).

8. R. Blomme, *La Doctrine du péché dans les écoles théologiques de la première moitié du XIIe siècle* (Louvain: Gembloux, 1958).

9. O. Lottin, "Pour une édition critique du *Liber Pancrisis*," *Recherches de théologie ancienne et médiévale* 13(1946):185–201.

10. Beside Blomme, *La Doctrine*, see P. Delahaye et al., *Théologie du péché* (Paris, 1960), vol. 1.

11. Anselm of Canterbury, *Cur Deus Homo* (Why God Became Man), Latin text, with introduction, notes, and translation by R. Roques (Paris, 1943).

12. *Commentarius Cantabrigiensis in Epistolas Pauli e Schola Petri Abaelardi vol. 2: In epistolam ad Corinthias Iam et IIam, Ad Galatas et Ad Ephesos*, ed. A. Landgraf (Notre Dame, Ind., 1939), p. 429, cited by Blomme, *La Doctrine*, p. 250 n. 2.

13. This point was recognized and underscored by H. C. Lea, *A History of Auricular Confession and Indulgences in the Latin Church* (Philadelphia, 1896), vol. 3: *Indulgences*, p. 250 n. 2.

14. See Blomme, *La Doctrine*, p. 340. The importance of the confession has been well described by Michel Foucault, *Histoire de la sexualité* (Paris: 1976), vol. 1: *La volonté de savoir*, pp. 78ff.

15. The text published in *PL* 40.1127–28 cannot possibly be the original one, or so it seems to me (see Appendix 2). On the import of the treatise, see A. Teetaert, *La confession aux laïques dan l'Eglise latine depuis le VIIIe jusqu'au XIVe siècle* (Paris, 1926), pp. 50–56.

16. Walter Map, *De nugis curialium*, ed. M. R. James (Oxford, 1914). Cited by J. C. Payen, *Le Motif du repentir dans la littérature française médiévale (des origines à 1230)* (Geneva, 1968), p. 109, in which the author sees clearly that it is Purgatory that is involved but fails to say that Walter Map calls it Hell.

17. See C. Vogel, *Les "Libri poenitentiales,"* Typologie des sources du Moyen Age occidental, fasc. 27 (Turnhout, 1978). See also J. Le Goff, "Métier et profession d'après les manuels de confesseurs du Moyen Age," *Miscellanea Mediaevalii* (Berlin, 1964), vol. 3: *Beiträge zum Berufsbewusstsein des mittelälterlichen Menschen*, pp. 44–60, reprinted in *Pour un Autre Moyen Age* (Paris, 1977), pp. 162–80 (and in English translation in *Time, Work and Culture in the Middle Ages*, trans. Arthur Goldhammer [Chicago, 1980], pp. 107–21).

18. The essential works are those of A. M. Landgraf: *Das Wesen der lässlichen Sunde in der Scholastik bis Thomas von Aquin* (Bamberg, 1923), and *Dogmengeschichte der Frühscholastik* (Ratisbon, 1956), pt. 4: *Die Lehre von der Sunde und ihren Folgen*, especially chap. 3: "Die Nachlassung der lässlichen Sunde," pp. 100–202. See also T. Deman, s. v. "Péché," *Dictionnaire de théologie catholique*, vol. 12, pt. 1 (1933), cols. 225–55; M. Huftier, "Péché mortel et péché véniel," chap. 7, and P. Delahaye et al., *Théologie du Péché*, pp. 363–451 (unfortunately marred by erroneous citations, e.g., one from Augustine in which *quotidiana* is

replaced by *venialia*); J. J. O'Brien, *The Remission of Venialia* (Washington, 1959) (an abstract Thomist who manages to avoid mentioning Purgatory); F. Blaton, "De peccato veniali. Doctrina scolasticorum ante S. Thomas," *Collationes Gandavenses* (1928), pp. 134–42.

19. O. Lottin, "Les Sententiae Atrebatenses," *Recherches de théologie ancienne et médiévale*, vol. 10 (1938), pp. 344. Cited by R. Blomme, *La Doctrine*, p. 61 n. 1.

20. Abelard, ed. V. Cousin, vol. 2, p. 621.

21. See Landgraf, *Dogmengeschichte*, vol. 4, pt. 2, pp. 102ff.

22. Cited in ibid., p. 116.

23. *Libri Sententiarum*, Quaracchi, vol. 2 (1916), pp. 881–82.

24. Landgraf, *Dogmengeschichte*, vol. 4, pt. 2, p. 165 n. 34: "verum est quo quaedam animae, cum soluuntur a corporibus, statim intrant purgatorium quemdam ignem; in quo tamen non omnes purgantur, sed quaedam. Omnes vero quotquot intrant, in eo puniuntur. Unde videretur magis dicendus punitorius quam purgatorius, sed a digniori nomen accepit. Earum enim, quae intrant, aliae purgantur et puniuntur, aliae puniuntur tantum. Illae purgantur et puniuntur, quae secum detulerunt ligna, fenum, stipulam. Illi puniuntur tantum qui confitentes et poenitentes de omnibus peccatis suis decesserunt, antequam iniunctam a sacerdote poenitentiam peregissent."

25. Landgraf, *Dogmengeschichte*, vol. 4, pt. 2, p. 234.

26. Theodore Caplow, *Two against One: Coalitions in Triads* (1969).

27. *Libri IV Sententiarum*, Quaracchi, vol. 2 (1916), pp. 1006–7.

28. Landgraf, *Dogmengeschichte*, vol. 4, pt. 1, p. 262 n. 7.

29. Ibid., p. 262 n. 9.

30. Ibid., p. 262 n. 6.

31. Ibid., pp. 270–71.

32. K. Bosl, "Potens und pauper. Begriffsgeschichtliche Studien zur gesellschäftlicher Differenzierung im frühen Mittelalter und zum Pauperismus des Hochmittelalters," in *Frühformen der Gesellschaft im mittelälterlichen Europa* (Munich-Vienna, 1964), pp. 106–34.

33. Duby, *Les Trois Ordres*; Le Goff, "Les trois fonctions indo-européennes."

34. On the *mediocres*, see D. Luscombe, "Conceptions of Hierarchy before the XIIIth C.," in *Miscellanea Mediaevalia* 12/1. *Soziale Ordnungen im Selbstverständnis des Mittelalters* (Berlin-New York, 1979), pp. 17–18.

35. See Jacques Le Goff, "Le vocabulaire des catégories sociales chez François d'Assise et ses biographes du XIIIe siècle," in *Ordres et classes*, Colloque d'histoire sociale Saint-Cloud, 1967 (Paris-The Hague, 1973), pp. 93–124.

36. By contrast, from an eschatological standpoint it was shifted toward Paradise, since souls automatically go from one to the other.

37. The concept of inequality within equality, e.g., in equidistance, is typical of the "feudal" mentality. See my remarks on the relations between lord and vassal in *Pour un Autre Moyen Age*, pp. 365–84 (English trans. p. 237–87).

38. Alexander of Hales, *Glossa in IV libros sentiarum Petri Lombardi*, Bibliotecca Franciscana scholastica Medii Aevi, vol. 15, Quaracchi (1957), pp. 352–53: "Cum enim proportionalis esset poena temporalis culpae temporali poena autem purgatorii improportionaliter habeat acerbitatem respectu poenae hic temporalis, punit supra condignum, non citra. Respondemus quod . . . licet autem poena purgatorii non sit proportionalis delectationi peccati, est tamen

comparabilis; et licet non sit proportionalis secundum proportionem poenae hic temporali quoad acerbitatem, est tamen proportionalis secundum proportionalitatem. 'Est autem proportinalitas similitudo proportionum' [Euclid, Element 5, definition 4]. Quae enim est proportio poenae temporalis hic debitae alicui peccato ad poenam temporalem debitam hic maiori peccato, ea est proportio poenae purgatorii debitae minori peccato ad poenam purgatorii debitam maiori peccato; non tamen est proportio poenae purgatorii ad poenam hic temporalem. Ratio autem propter quam convenit poenam purgatorii esse acerbiorem improportionaliter poena purganti hic, licet utraque sit voluntaria, est quia poena purgans hic est poena animae per compassionem ad corpus, poena vero purgatorii est poena ipsius animae immediate. Sicut ergo passibile improportionale passibili, ita passio passioni. Praeterea, poena temporalis hic simpliciter voluntaria, poena purgatorii voluntaria comparative."

I should like to thank Georges Guilbaud and Father P. M. Gy, who were kind enough to help me read this exciting but difficult text, M. Guilbaud with his skills as a mathematician and student of scholasticism, Father Gy with his knowledge as a theologian.

39. A. M. Landgraf, *Dogmengeschichte*, vol. 4, pt. 2., p. 294 n. 2. This is a commentary on the *Sententiae* from the thirteenth century: "sciendum quod secundum quosdam suffragia prosunt damnatis (purgatorio) quantum ad proportionem arithmeticam, non geometricam."

40. I borrow this expression from the title of a remarkable study by J. Chiffoleau, *La comptabilité de l'au-delà. Les hommes, la mort et la religion en Comtat Venaissin à la fin du Moyen Age* (Rome: Ecole française de Rome, 1980).

41. A. Murray, *Reason and Society in the Middle Ages* (Oxford, 1978). J. Murdoch speaks of a "frenzy to measure" among the academics at Oxford in the fourteenth century: J. E. Murdoch and E. D. Sylla, eds., *The Cultural Context of Medieval Learning* (Dordrecht, 1975), pp. 187–89 and 340–43. This frenzy began at least a century earlier and was not confined to Oxford.

42. On medieval cartography, see, among other works, J. K. Wright, *The Geographical Lore of the Times of the Crusades* (New York, 1925); G. H. T. Kimble, *Geography in the Middle Ages* (London, 1938); L. Bagrow, *Die Geschichte der Kartographie* (Berlin, 1951); M. Mollat, "Le Moyen Age," in *Histoire Universelle des explorations*, ed. L. H. Parias, (Paris, 1955), vol. 1; G. Kish, *La carte, image des civilisations* (Paris, 1980).

43. On contempt of the world, see R. Bultot, *La doctrine du mépris du monde en Occident, de saint Ambroise à Innocent III* (Louvain, 1963).

44. G. Vinay, *Il dolore e la morte nella spiritualità dei secoli XII e XIII* (Todi, 1967), pp. 13–14.

45. Meyer Schapiro, cited by Erwin Panofsky, *Gothic Architecture and Scholasticism* (New York, 1957), p. 000.

46. Joinville, *La Vie de Saint Louis*, ed. N. L. Corbett (Sherbrooke, 1977), pp. 85–86 and 214.

47. See G. Lobrichon, "L'Apocalypse des théologiens au XIIe siècle," thesis for the Ecole des Hautes Etudes en sciences sociales University of Paris X (Nanterre), 1979.

48. Matthew 25:31–46 and 1 Corinthians 15:52.

49. Emile Mâle, *L'Art religieux du XIIIe siècle en France*, 9th ed. (Paris, 1958),

pp. 369–74. (Here cited after the translation by Dora Nussey, *The Gothic Image* (New York, 1958), pp. 356–64.—Trans.)

50. H. Focillon, *Art d'Occident* (Paris, 1965), vol. 2: *Le Moyen Age gothique*, pp. 164–65.

51. See the works of the German historians at Freiburg and Munster (G. Tellenbach, K. Schmid, J. Wollasch) cited by J. Wollasch, "Les obituaires, temoins de la vie clunisienne," *Cahiers de Civilisation Médiévale* (1979), pp. 139–71; Paul Veyne, *Le Pain et le Cirque* (Paris, 1976).

52. See especially Georges Duby, "Remarques sur la littérature généalogique en France aux XIe et XII siècles," *Comptes rendus de l'Académie des Inscriptions et Belles lettres* (1967), pp. 334–45, reprinted in *Hommes et Structures du Moyen Age* (Paris-The Hague, 1973), pp. 287–98. (Available in English translation in *The Chivalrous Society*, trans. Cynthia Postan [Berkeley, Cal., 1977], pp. 149–57.—Trans.).

53. W. Ullmann, *The Individual and Society in the Middle Ages* (Baltimore, 1966), p. 69.

54. Jean Beleth, *Summa de ecclesiasticis officiis*, ed. H. Duteil, Corpus Christianorum Continuatio Mediaevalis 41 A (Turnhout, 1971), pp. 317ff.

55. S. G. F. Brandon, *Man and His Destiny in the Great Religions* (Manchester, 1962), p. 234.

CHAPTER EIGHT

1. Among the *quodlibeta* compiled by P. Glorieux, *La littérature quodlibétique de 1260 à 1320* (1925), only one deals with Purgatory. It is from Thomas Aquinas and dates from Christmas 1269: "Whether one can be released more or less quickly than another from a similar punishment in Purgatory" (utrum aequali poena puniendi in purgatorio, unus citius possit liberari quam alius (quod. II, 14), p. 278).

2. The two hundred–nineteenth and final proposition condemned in 1277 pertains to the fire of the hereafter, not further defined: "That the soul separated [from the body] can in no way suffer in fire" (quod anima separata nullo modo patitur in igne). The teaching in question was given at the faculty of arts, not the faculty of theology. Cf. R. Hissette, *Enquête sur les 219 articles condamnés à Paris le 7 mars 1277* (Louvain-Paris, 1977), pp. 311–12.

3. The bibliography of thirteenth-century scholasticism is enormous. Most of the comprehensive syntheses are more interested in philosophy than in theology. For an overview one may wish to consult the classics: Etienne Gilson, *La Philosophie au Moyen Age*, 3d ed. (Paris, 1947); M. de Wulf, *Histoire de la philosophie médiévale*, 6th ed. (Louvain, 1936), vol. 2; and F. van Steenberghen, *La Philosophie au XIIIe siècle* (Louvain-Paris, 1966). The great scholastics of the thirteenth century did distinguish between philosophy and theology. The boundary line is not always easy to establish and depends on how these two fields of knowledge are defined. Generally speaking—and I am referring here to the best of cases—it seems to me that these syntheses do not pay enough attention to the distinction between the two disciplines. A brief but suggestive sketch of medieval philosophy as it relates to medieval society has been given by F. Alessio, "Il pensiero dell'Occidente feudale," *Filosofía e Società* (Bologna, 1975), vol. 1. An original interpretation may be found in C. Tresmontant, *La Métaphysique du christianisme et la crise du treizième siècle* (Paris, 1964).

4. Guilielmus Altissiodorensis, *Summa aurea*, ed. Pigouchet (Paris, 1500; reprint ed. by Minerva, Frankfurt-on-Main, 1964), bk. 4, fol. 304v. and 305v.

5. One still finds it under this heading in the methodical catalogue of the excellent library of the Gregorian University in Rome.

6. Concerning William of Auvergne, see the dated work by Noel Valois, *Guillaume d'Auvergne, sa vie et ses ouvrages* (Paris, 1880); the study by J. Kramp, "Des Wilhelm von Auvergne Magisterium Divinale," in *Gregorianum* (1920), pp. 538–84 and ibid., (1921), pp. 42–78, 174–87; and especially A. Masnovo, *Da Guglielmo d'Auvergne a San Tommaso d'Aquino*, 2 vols. (milan, 1930–34).

7. In February of 1979 Alan E. Bernstein presented to the Medieval Association of the Pacific a paper on "William of Auvergne on Punishment after Death," the text of which he was kind enough to send me. I am largely in agreement with his interpretation. I think that he has somewhat exaggerated, as Arno Borst did before him, the influence of the battle against Catharism on William's ideas concerning Purgatory as well as the alleged contradictions in William's doctrine of purgatorial fire. Bernstein is currently engaged in work on "Hell, Purgatory, and Community in Thirteenth-Century France."

8. "De loco vero purgationis animarum, quem purgatorium vocant, an sit proprius, et deputatus purgationi animarum humanarum, seorsum a paradiso terrestri, et inferno, atque habitatione nostra, quaestionem habet" (*De universo*, chap. 60). Guilielmus Parisiensis, *Opera Omnia* (Paris, 1674), vol 1, p. 676. Chapters 60, 61, and 62 (pp. 676–79) of this edition deal with the location of Purgatory. Purgatorial fire is treated in chapters 63, 64, and 65 (pp. 680–82).

9. These points, in my own opinion, are not to be regarded as secondary.

10. A. Piolanti, "Il dogma del Purgatorio," in *Euntes Docete* 6(1953), p. 301.

11. Concerning the life and works of Alexander of Hales, see the *Prolegomena* (pp. 7–75) of volume 1 of the edition of his gloss on Peter Lombard, *Magistri Alexandri de Hales Glossa in quatuor libros sententiarum Petri Lombardi*, Quaracchi (1951).

12. "De sera poenitentia, de poena purgatorii et de relaxationibus," (*Glossa in quatuor libros sententiarum Petri Lombardi*, vol. 4, Quaracchi (1957), pp. 349–65).

13. "De remissione et punitione venialium, de aedificandis aurum foenum, stipulam, de septem modis remissionis peccati" (ibid., pp. 363–75).

14. G. Le Bras, *Institutions ecclésiastiques de la chretienté médiévale* (Paris, 1959), vol. 1, p. 146.

15. "Respondemus: sicut dolor communis Ecclesiae universalis, plangentis peccata fidelium mortuorum et orantis pro ipsis cum genitu, est adiutorius in satisfactione: non quod per se plene satisfaciat, sed (quod) cum poena poenitentis iuvet ad satisfactionem, sicut ex ratione suffragii potest haberi. Suffragium enim est meritum Ecclesiae, poenae alicuius diminutivum" (*Glossa*, vol. 4, p. 354).

16. Alexander of Hales, *Quaestiones disputatae "antequam esset frater,"* Biblioteca franciscana scholastica medii aevi, 3 vols., Quaracchi (1960), vols. 19–21. The passage cited from question 48 occurs on pages 855–56.

17. Ibid., p. 1069.

18. Ibid., p. 1548.

19. Dead in 1274, Bonaventure was not canonized until 1482 and not proclaimed doctor of the Church until 1588. On him, see J.-C. Bougerol, *Introduction*

à l'étude de saint Bonaventure (Paris, 1961) and the five volumes of *S. Bonaventura, 1274–1974* published at Grottaferrata in 1973–74. There is a useful study in Latin of Saint Bonaventure and Purgatory: T. V. Gerster a Zeil, *Purgatorium iuxta doctrinam seraphici doctoris S. Bonaventurae* (Turin, 1932).

20. Bonaventure's *Commentary* on Peter Lombard's *Sententiae* was published in the first four volumes of the monumental edition begun by the Franciscans of Quaracchi in 1882. The commentary on book 4 is found in volume 4, distinction 20, in folios 517–38; articles 2 and 3 of part 1 of distinction 21, in folios 551–56; article 2 of distinction 44, in folios 943–44. A more manageable edition has been provided by the brothers of Quaracchi: *S. Bonaventurae Opera Theologica, editio minor*, vol. 4, *Liber IV Sententiarum* (Quaracchi, 1949).

21. Concerning all these problems, see A. Michel, s.v. "Purgatoire," *Dictionnaire de Théologie catholique*, col. 1239–40.

22. "Utrum in poena purgatorii sit minor certitudo de gloria quam in via . . .," the conclusion of which is, "in purgatorio est maior certitudo de gloria quam in via, minor quam in patria" (*Opera*, vol. 4, fols. 522–24).

23. *Patria* comes from Saint Paul, Hebrews 11:14: "For they that say such things declare plainly that they seek a country [patria]."

24. Second question of article 2 of part 1 of distinction 21.

25. Ibid., fols. 939–42.

26. Second part of distinction 20.

27. Article 2 of part 1 of distinction 21.

28. At the Council of Lyons in 1274, a few days before his death, Bonaventure delivered the solemn speech at the session that made official the union between the Greeks and Latins.

29. Article 3 of this same question.

30. Article 2 of distinction 44.

31. Chapter 2 of the part 7.

32. Chapter 3 of part 7.

33. Bonaventure, *Opera*, vol. 5, fols. 282–83. The brothers of Quaracchi have since provided a more manageable edition of the *Breviloquium* as in the case of the *Commentary on the Sententiae*.

34. *Opera*, vol. 9, pp. 606–7.

35. 1 Corinthians 3:10–15 along with Old Testament authorities (Job 2:18, Prov. 13:12) and other passages from Paul (2 Timothy 4:7–8, Hebrews 9:15), whose relation to Purgatory seems remote.

36. Ibid., p. 608.

37. Concerning the importance of prayer in Bonaventure's theology, which gave Purgatory deep roots in his thought, see Zelina Zafarana, "Pietà e devozione in San Bonaventura," in *S. Bonaventura Francescano*, Convegni del Centro di Studi sulla spiritualità medievale, 14, Todi (1974), pp. 129–57.

38. On Albertus Magnus see O. Lottin, "Ouvrages théologiques de saint Albert le Grand," in *Psychologie et morale aux XIIe et XIIIe siècles* (Gembloux, 1960), vol. 6, pp. 237–97, and *Albertus Magnus, Doctor Universalis, 1280/1980*, ed. G. Meyer and A. Zimmermann, (Mainz, 1980).

39. *De Resurrectione*, ed. W. Kubel, in *Alberti Magni Opera Omnia*, vol. 26 (Munster/W, 1958). Question 6, "De purgatorio," is found on pages 315–18 and question 9, "De locis poenarum simul," on pp. 320–21.

40. Note that Albert, who in this text usually uses the substantive *purgatorium*, here uses the epithet *purgatorius* (*ignis* understood). On this usage see below, the discussion of the *Commentary on the Sententiae*.

41. Albert refutes one last objection: "Many distinctions of merits can be made, alike for those who must be saved, damned, or purged; so there must be more than five receptacles." Response: "The general distinctions must be separated from the paticular distinctions. There may be 'houses' within the 'receptacles.' " This logical refinement also harks back to the Gospel of John.

42. This distinction 21 of the *Commentary on the Four Books of Sententiae of Peter Lombard* is found in Auguste Borgnet's edition of the works of Albertus Magnus, *B. Alberti Magni . . . opera omnia*, (Paris, 1894), vol. 29, pp. 861–82.

43. Pierre Michaud-Quantin, in his great book *Universitas: Expressions du mouvement communautaire dans le Moyen Age latin* (Paris, 1970), pp. 105 and 119, observes that Albertus Magnus, "in studying the action of collectivities, draws a distinction between the *urbanitates* of civil society and the *congregationes* in the Church." Albert first uses the word "congregationes" in this way in a theological discussion concerning Pope Innocent IV's interdiction excommunicating certain collectivities, an important decision taken by this Genoan pontiff. Albert dealt with this problem slightly earlier in his commentary on Peter Lombard (distinction 19, article 7 [*Opera*, vol. 29, p. 808]; our text occurs on page 876 of the same volume). Pierre Michaud-Quantin notes that "in the same context, Bonaventure uses *congregatio* for any civil or religious grouping."

44. Ibid., vol. 29, pp. 877 and 878.

45. Alberti Magni, *Opera Omnia*, ed. A. Borgnet, vol. 30, pp. 603–4.

46. Ibid., vol. 30, p. 612.

47. The *Compendium theologicae veritatis* (hereafter cited as *Compendium*) was published by Borgnet in volume 34 of the *Opera omnia* of Albertus Magnus (Paris, 1895). Concerning Hugh of Strasbourg, see G. Boner, *Über den Dominikaner Theologen Hugo von Strassburg*, 1954.

48. *Compendium* 4.22, vol. 34, p. 147.

49. Ibid., pp. 237–41.

50. Concerning Thomas Aquinas, see M.-D. Chenu, *Introduction a l'étude de saint Thomas d'Aquin* (Montreal-Paris, 1950); J. A. Weisheipl, *Friar Thomas d'Aquino, His Life, Thought, and Works* (Oxford, 1974); *Thomas von Aquino. Interpretation und Rezeption. Studien und Texte*, ed. W. P. Eckert (Mainz, 1974).

51. M. Corbin, *Le chemin de la théologie chez Thomas d'Aquin* (Paris, 1974), p. 267.

52. I have used the edition of the *Summa theologiae* published with a translation and notes by the *Revue des Jeunes* (Paris: Desclée). Purgatory is mentioned in the pamphlet *L'Au-Delà*, 2d ed. (Paris, 1951), which contains questions 69–74 of the *Supplement*, with a translation by J. D. Folghera and notes and appendices by J. Webert. The word *purgatorium* fills six columns in the *Index Thomisticus*, Sectio II, concordantia prima, ed. R. Busa, (1974), vol. 18, pp. 961–62.

53. See the notes by J. Webert in the pamphlet *L'Au-Delà*.

54. Ibid., p. 13.

55. Ibid., p. 17.

56. But see the pathbreaking pages of J. Delumeau, *La Peur en Occident: XIVe–XVIIIe siècles* (Paris, 1978) (see index s.v. *revenants*), and H. Neveux, "Les

lendemains de la mort dans les croyances occidentales (vers 1250–vers 1300)," in *Annales E.S.C.* (1979), pp. 245–63. Jean-Claude Schmitt and Jacques Chiffoleau are engaged in research into medieval ghosts.

57. See Jacques Le Goff, "Les rêves dans la culture et la psychologie collective de l'Occident médiéval," in *Scolies* 1(1971):123–30, reprinted in *Pour un Autre Moyen Age* (Paris: 1977), pp. 299–306, and translated into English as "Dreams in the Culture and Collective Psychology of the Medieval West," *Time, Work, and Culture*, pp. 201–5. Albertus Magnus confronted the problem resolutely in his treatise *De somno et vigilia*.

58. Thomas Aquinas, *L'Au-Delà*, pp. 38–46.

59. The edition destined to become the standard, if not official, edition of Thomas's works, so called because it was begun in 1882 at the behest of Pope Leo XIII, the promoter of neo-Thomism. This edition is not yet complete.

60. Thomas Aquinas, *L'Au-Delà*, pp. 97–128. This question includes bits of distinction 21 of Peter Lombard's *Sententiae* commented on by Thomas in the *Scriptum*.

61. "de loco purgatorii non inuenitur aliquid expresse determinatum in scriptura nec rationes possunt ad hoc efficaces induci" (ibid., p. 105).

62. The commentator on our edition of the *Supplement*, Father J. Webert, is nevertheless scandalized by the attention that Thomas pays to ghost stories: "It is curious," he writes, "that Thomas considers tales about dead individuals who expiate their sins in certain terrestrial locations. This is reminiscent of the 'suffering souls' of fantastic stories" (pp. 304–5). I am astonished, for my part, at the modern commentator's lack of familiarity with medieval visionary literature and with the common mentality of the thirteenth century, which Saint Thomas, intellectual as he was, had to take into account and which he partly shared.

63. Question 71 is found on pages 129–203 of our edition (see n. 52 above).

64. *De cura pro mortuis gerenda*, chap. 18.

65. This contempt for the body, particularly prevalent among monks, did not prevent medieval Christian thinkers (including monks) from believing that salvation could only be "body and soul," indeed, that it could only come about by means of the body.

66. *Summa theologica*, 1, 89, 7, 2d. Roman ed. (Rome, 1920), p. 695: "non est eadem ratio de distantia loci, et de distantia temporis."

67. A. Michel, s.v. "Purgatoire," *Dictionnaire de théologie catholique*, col. 1240. The text of the *Scriptum in IVum Sententiarum*, dist. 21, q. 1, a. 1, is found on pages 1045–52 of the Moos edition. The text of *De malo*, q. 7, a. 11, is found on pp. 587–90 of the Marietti edition of *Quaestiones disputatae*.

68. The original text is among the letters of Saint Bernard (ep. 472) in *PL* 182.676–80. An English translation, with an introduction, of *Everwini Steinfeldensis praepositi ad S. Bernardum* may be found in W. L. Wakefield and A. P. Evans, *Heresies of the High Middle Ages* (New York-London, 1969), pp. 126ff. (the passage on purgatorial fire occurs on p. 131).

69. The Passagins professed strict observance of the Old Testament, including the practice of circumcision. They were classed as a "Judaizing sect." The first mention of them occurs in 1184, the last in 1291. They seem to have been confined to Lombardy and not to have been very active after 1200. See R. Manselli, "I Passagini," in *Bollettino dell'Istituto storico italiano per il medio evo e Archivio*

Muratoriano 85(1963):189–210. They are mentioned together with, but distinct from, the Cathari in the *Summa contra haereticos* ascribed to Preapositivus of Cremona, ed. J. N. Garvin and J. A. Corbett (Notre Dame, Ind., 1958), partially translated into English in Wakefield and Evans, *Heresies of the High Middle Ages*, pp. 173 ff.

70. *Summa contra Haereticos*, pp. 210–11.

71. This name, a distortion of the eastern Paulicians, was applied in the West to any sort of heretic.

72. The original Latin text is found in *Radulphi de Coggeshall, Chronicon anglicanum*, ed. J. Stevenson (London, 1875), pp. 121–25, and is translated into English in Wakefield and Evans, *Heresies of the High Middle Ages*, p. 251.

73. The original Latin text was published with excerpts from the *Tractatus de diversis materiis praedicabilibus*, ed. A. Lecoy de la Marche, *Anecdotes historiques, légendes et apologues tirées du recueil inédit d'Etienne de Bourbon, dominicain du XIIIe siècle* (Paris, 1877), pp. 202–99. An English translation is given in Wakefield and Evans, *Heresies of the High Middle Ages*, p. 347.

74. The Latin text was published by A. Dondaine, "La hiérarchie cathare en Italie, II Le Tractatus de Hereticis d'Anselme d'Alexandrie, O.P.," in *Archivum fratrum praedicatorum* 20(1950):310–24. An English translation is given in Wakefield and Evans, *Heresies of the High Middle Ages*, pp. 371–72.

75. Bernard Gui, born in Limousin in 1261 or 1262, joined the Dominicans in 1279, was trained at Montpellier, and was active as an inquisitor, particularly in the diocese of Toulouse. At the end of his life he was bishop of Lodeve. The *Manual of the Inquisitor* was probably completed in 1323–24. It was published with a French translation by G. Mollat in the series Classiques de l'histoire de France au Moyen Age, vols. 8 and 9 (Paris, 1926–27). The texts cited are found in chapter 2 of part 5.

76. Sacconi's *Summa* was published by A. Dondaine in the preface to his work *Un Traité néo-manichéen du XIIIe siècle: le Liber de duobus principiis, suivi d'un fragment de rituel cathare* (Rome, 1939), pp. 64–78. An English translation is given in Wakefield and Evans, *Heresies of the High Middle Ages*, pp. 333–34.

77. The *Brevis summula contra errores notatos hereticorum* was published by Celestin Douais in *La Somme des autorités à l'usage des prédicateurs méridionaux au XIIIe siècle* (Paris, 1896), pp. 125–33. An English translation is given in Wakefield and Evans, *Heresies of the High Middle Ages*, pp. 355–56.

78. For an overview, see Y. M. J. Congar, "Neuf cents ans après. Notes sur le Schisme oriental," in *L'Eglise et les Eglises: neuf siècles de douloureuse séparation entre l'Orient et l'Occident. Etudes et travaux offerts à dom Lambert Beaudoin* (Chevetogne, 1954), vol. 1. For a less expansive view, see the studies of D. M. Nicol collected in *Byzantium: Its Ecclesiastical History and Relations with the Western World* (London, 1972).

79. D. Stiernon, "Le problème de l'union greco-latine vu de Byzance: de Germain II a Joseph Ier (1232–1273)," in *1274. Année charnière, Mutations et Continuités*, Lyons-Paris colloquium, 1974 (Paris: Centre National de Recherche Scientifique, 1977), p. 147.

80. P. Roncaglia, *Georges Bardanès métropolite de Corfou et Barthélemy de l'ordre franciscain. Les discussions sur le Purgatoire (15 octobre–17 novembre 1231). Etude critique avec texte inédit* (Rome, 1953), pp. 57ff.

81. *Epitimies* are acts of penance and mortification.

82. John 14:3.

83. Bardanes here uses the Greek word ποργτȣ́ριον, a neologism, to translate the Latin.

84. John 5:29.

85. Matthew 25:41.

86. Matthew 24:51.

87. Mark 9:43–48.

88. Luke 16:25.

89. (Here translated into English from Le Goff's French version, incorporating slight corrections of the French translation contained in the article "Purgatoire" in the *Dictionnaire de théologie catholique*, col. 1248.—Trans.) Du Cange cited this letter in his famous glossary s.v. "Purgatorium." Here is the original Latin of the passage most important for our purposes: "Nos, quia locum purgationis hujus modi dicunt (Graeci) non fuisse sibi ab eorum doctoribus certo et proprio nomine indicatum, illum quidem juxta traditiones et auctoritates sanctorum patrum purgatorium nominantes volumus, quod de caetero apud illos isto nomine appeletur."

90. See J. A. Weisheipl, *Friar Thomas d'Aquino*, pp. 168–70.

91. See A. Dondaine, "Nicolas de Crotone et les sources du *Contra errores Graecorum* de saint Thomas," in *Divus Thomas* (1950), pp. 313–40.

92. See the section of the previously cited work *1274. Annee charnière* devoted to *Byzance et l'Union* (pp. 139–207), which includes articles by D. Stiernon (see n. 79 above), J. Darrouzes, J. Gouillard, and G. Dagron. See also B. Roberg, *Die Union zwischen der griechischen und der lateinischen Kirche auf den II. Konzil von Lyon, 1274* (Bonn, 1964). Concerning Byzantine attitudes toward the other world, see the forthcoming book by Gilbert Dagron. I wish to thank Evelyne Patlagean for sending me her paper "Byzance et son autre monde. Observations sur quelques récits," to be published in *Faire croire* (report of colloquium held at the Ecole française de Rome, 1979).

93. Taken from the article "Purgatoire" in the *Dictionnaire de théologie catholique*, cols. 1249–50.

94. Ibid.

95. Ibid.

96. See especially *De Purgatorio Disputationes in Concilio Florentino Habitae*, ed. L. Petit and G. Hofmann (Rome, 1969).

97. See J. Darrouzes, "Les documents grecs concernant le concile de Lyon," in *1274. Annee charnière*, pp. 175–76. The cited text, excerpted from the *Procès de Niciphore* (1277), was published by V. Laurent and J. Darrouzes, *Dossier grec de l'Union de Lyon (1273–1277)*, Archives de l'Orient chrétien, 16 (Paris, 1976), pp. 496–501.

CHAPTER NINE

1. Careful research may perhaps lead to the discovery that the iconography of Purgatory developed earlier than is usually thought (see appendix 3).

2. Concerning Joachim of Floris and millenarianism, see the scholarly work of M. Reeves, *The Influence of Prophecy in the Later Middle Ages. A Study in Joachimism* (Oxford, 1969), and the beautiful book of Henry Mottu, *La Mani-*

festation de l'Esprit selon Joachim de Fiore (Neuchâtel-Paris, 1977). Though open to challenge in places, the inspired work of Norman Cohn, *The Pursuit of the Millennium* (London, 1957) has made a wide public aware of millenarianist movements in the eleventh to sixteenth centuries.

3. B. Guénée, "Temps de l'histoire et temps de la mémoire au Moyen Age," *Bulletin de la Société de l'Histoire de France* 487(1976–77):25–36.

4. See K. Hauck, "Haus- und Sippenbegundene Literatur mittelälterlicher Adelsgeschlechter," *Mitteilungen des Instituts für Österreichische Geschichtsforschung* 62(1954):121–45, reprinted in *Geschichtsdenken und Geschichtsbild im Mittelalter*, Wege der Forschung 21, 1961; Georges Duby, "Remarques sur la littérature généalogique en France aux XIe et XIIe siècles," *Comptes rendus de l'Académie des Inscriptions et Belles-Lettres* (1967), pp. 123–31; idem, "Structures de parenté et noblesse. France du Nord XIe–XIIe siècles," *Miscellanea Mediaevalia in memoriam J. F. Niermeyer* (1967), pp. 149–65. Both of these essays of Duby's are reprinted in *Hommes et Structures du Moyen Age* (Paris, 1973), pp. 267–98. (They have been translated into English by Cynthia Postan and collected in *The Chivalrous Society* [Berkeley, 1977], pp. 134–57.—Trans.). See also L. Génicot, *Les Généalogies*, Typologie des sources du Moyen Age occidental, pamphlet no. 15 (Turnhout, 1975).

5. See the works cited in chapter 3, notes 41–44.

6. On the success of narrative genres in this period see pamphlet no. 12 in the series Typologie des sources du Moyen Age occidental, J.-C. Payen and F. N. M. Diekstra, *Le Roman* (1975), as well as pamphlet no. 13 in the same series, which contains both O. Jodogne's *Le Fabliau* and J.-C. Payen's *Le Lai narratif* (1975). See also the proceedings of the 1959 Strasbourg Colloquium, *La littérature narrative d'imagination: des genres littéraires aux techniques d'expression* (Paris, 1961). There is no comprehensive study of the "narrative phenomenon" in the Middle Ages and of the rise of the narrative in the thirteenth century.

7. In French it is common to say that a convict is sent to prison to "purger sa peine," to "purge" his penalty (as we would say in English, "he is paying the penalty"—trans.); the French locution of course derives from the belief in Purgatory.

8. Philippe Ariès, *L'Homme devant la mort* (Paris, 1977), p. 110.

9. H. Neveux, "Les lendemains de la mort au Moyen Age," *Annales E.S.C.* (1979), pp. 245–63.

10. Jean Delumeau in the first portion of his great synthesis, *La peur en Occident du XIV au XVIII siècle* (1978), and Jean Wirth in his admirable study of *La jeune fille et la mort: Recherches sur les thèses macabres dans l'art germanique de la Renaissance* (1979).

11. Michelle Bastard-Fournié, "Le Purgatoire dans la region toulousaine au XIVe siècle et au début du XVe siècle," *Annales du Midi*, pp. 5–34: "Measured against the scale of historical time, Purgatory's success was fleeting. It seems no longer to have been a central religious concern of the people of Toulouse in the eighteenth century, if testamentary evidence alone is a reliable indication" (p. 5 n. 2).

12. See below, pp. 303–306.

13. A. Aarne and S. Thompson, *The Types of the Folktale*, 2d rev. ed. (Helsinki, 1964), p. 161.

14. Jean-Claude Schmitt takes particular interest in this aspect of the question in his research on ghosts.

15. Conrad of Eberbach, *Exordium Magnum Cisterciense* 2.23, ed. B. Grieser (Rome, 1961), pp. 143–47. I wish to thank Mr. Philippe Dautrey, who is preparing a thesis on *La mort cistercienne*, for calling my attention to these texts.

16. Still taken from the *Liber miraculorum* of Herbert, ibid., p. 229.

17. Ibid., pp. 332–34.

18. See Appendix 4.

19. *Chronica Rogeri de Wendover, Flores Historiarum*, vol. 2, (London, 1887), pp. 16–35. Matthew Paris, who was also a monk of Saint-Albans and who died in 1259, continues Roger of Wendover's work in his *Chronica Majora*, in which he copies Thurchill's story word for word as he found it in the *Flowers of History*. Matthaei Parisiensis, Monachi Sancti Albani, *Chronica Majora*, vol. 2 (London, 1874), pp. 497–511.

20. On the *exemplum*, see the forthcoming pamphlet in the series Typologie des sources du Moyen Age occidental entitled *L'exemplum*, by C. Bremond, J. Le Goff, and J.-C. Schmitt.

21. On preaching, the old work by A. Lecoy de la Marche, *La chaire française au Moyen Age, spécialement au XIIIe siècle* (Paris, 1886, reprint ed. Geneva, 1974), is still a useful source of ideas and information. See also the sketch by J. Le Goff and J.-C. Schmitt, "Au XIIIe siècle: une parole nouvelle," in *Histoire vécue du peuple chrétien* (under the general editorship of J. Delumeau) (Toulouse, 1978), vol. 1, pp. 257–79.

22. On James of Vitry, see Alberto Forni, "Giacomo da Vitry, Predicatore e sociologo," *La Cultura* 17, no. 1 (1980): 34–89.

23. James of Vitry, "Sermones vulgares, Sermo 68 Ad conjugatos," unpublished transcription by Marie-Claire Gasnault based mainly on two manuscripts, Cambrai 534 and Paris Bibliothèque nationale, Latin MS 17509.

24. Unpublished sermon "Sermo communis omni die dominica" (1) based on manuscript 455 of Liège, folio 2–2v. I wish to thank Marie-Claire Gasnault for providing me with the contents of this sermon.

25. *The Exempla or Illustrative Stories from the Sermones vulgares of Jacques de Vitry*, ed. T. F. Crane (London, 1890, reprint ed. Nendeln, 1967). This edition is invaluable for its notes but the text is mediocre and the *exempla* are separated from their context in the sermon, which makes it impossible to gauge their full significance. The *exemplum* cited is no. 114, pp. 52–53.

26. Ibid., no. 122, p. 56.

27. See Fritz Wagner, "Studien zu Caesarius von Heisterbach," *Analecta Cistercensia* 29(1973):79–95.

28. Caesarius of Heisterbach, *Dialogus miraculorum*, ed. J. Strange (Cologne-Bonn-Brussels, 1951). In the article cited in n. 27 above, Fritz Wagner states that a new critical edition is forthcoming. Andrée Duby, whom I wish to thank for her information and suggestions, is preparing an important work on the *Dialogus miraculorum*.

29. In a remarkable paper, a copy of which he was kind enough to send me, Alberto Forni notes that for those who heard sermons preached, the theme of Purgatory "was a source of terror." This is true, but in other contexts the infernalization of Purgatory was not carried so far. A. Forni, "Kerigma e adattamento.

Aspetti della predicazione nella cattolicà nei secoli XII–XIV," to appear in *Bollettino dell'Istituto Storico Italiano per il Medio Evo.*

30. These *exempla* are as follows: chap. 1, no. 32 (conversion of an abbot of Morimond, who returns to life); 2.2 (apostate monk who became highway robber converts at moment of death and chooses two thousand years of Purgatory); 3.24 (a confessor who commits the sin of sodomy with an adolescent and who has done harsh penance but who does not dare confess before his death appears afterward to the adolescent, recounts his punishments in Purgatory, and urges the youth to confess); 3.25 (a Cistercian novice who dies before he can make a general confession escapes Purgatory by confessing to an abbot to whom he appears in a dream); 4.30 (temptations and visions of Christian, a young monk of Heisterbach, who is informed by Saint Agatha that sixty days of painful illness here below will be counted as sixty years in Purgatory); 7.16 (Christian, monk of Hemmenrode, a devotee of the Virgin, has a vision in which he sees his soul pass through a huge fire ultimately to arrive in Paradise); 7.58 (a bandit agress, in honor of the Virgin, to commit no crime on Saturdays and allows himself to be hanged and decapitated: he thus escapes Purgatory); 11.11 (the lay brother Mengoz, brought back to life by the abbot Gilbert, tells that in the other world he saw souls who were due to be liberated from Purgatory in thirty days).

31. 1.32: Strange edition, vol. 1, pp. 36–39.

32. 2.2: ibid., pp. 58–61.

33. 4.30: ibid., pp. 198–202.

34. 7.16: ibid., vol. 2, pp. 17–23.

35. 12.24: ibid., pp. 335–36.

36. See Georges Duby, *Le Chevalier, la femme et le prêtre. Le mariage dans la France féodale* (Paris, 1981).

37. In particular, Christian burial was refused to usurers.

38. Lester K. Little, "Pride Goes before Avarice: Social Change and the Vices in Latin Christendom," *American Historical Review* 76(1971):16–49.

39. Jacques Le Goff, "The Usurer and Purgatory," *The Dawn of Modern Banking,* Center for Medieval and Renaissance Studies, University of California at Los Angeles (New Haven,), pp. 25–52.

40. *Dialogus miraculorum* 12.25, Strange edition, vol. 2, pp. 336–37.

41. 12.26: ibid., pp. 337–38.

42. 12.27: ibid., pp. 338–39.

43. 12.28: ibid., p. 339.

44. 12.29, ibid., pp. 339–40.

45. 12.30, ibid., pp. 340–41.

46. 12.31, ibid., pp. 341–42.

47. 12.32, ibid., p. 342.

48. 12.33, ibid., pp. 342–43.

49. 12.34, ibid., p. 343.

50. 12.35, ibid., pp. 343–44.

51. 12.36, ibid., pp. 344–45.

52. 12.37, ibid., pp. 346–47.

53. See H. Dondaine, "L'objet et le médium de la vision béatifique chez les théologiens du XIIIe siècle," *Revue de théologie antique et médiévale* 19(1952):60–130. Concerning the crisis created in the fourteenth century by Pope

John XXII's denial of the beatific vision, see M. Dykmans, *Les sermons de Jean XXII sur la vision béatifique* (Rome, 1973).

54. *Dialogus miraculorum* 12.38 and 12.39, Strange edition, pp. 347–48.

55. On the theme of the seven gifts of the Holy Spirit in the twelfth and thirteenth centuries (sevens, incidentally, were in vogue: seven sacraments, seven deadly sins, seven liberal arts, etc.), see O. Lottin, *Psychologie et Morale aux XIIe and XIIIe siècles*: vol. 3, *Problèmes de morale* (Louvain, 1949), chap. 16: "Les dons du Saint-Esprit du XIIe siècle à l'époque de saint Thomas d'Aquin," pp. 327–456.

56. An edition of Stephen of Bourbon's treatise is now being prepared in a collaborative effort involving the Ecole nationale des chartes (Paris), the Group for the Historical Anthropology of the Medieval West at the Ecole des Hautes Etudes en sciences sociales (Paris), and the Istituto Storico Italiano per il Medio Evo (Rome). The transcription of *De dono timoris* was done by Georgette Lagarde, to whom I express warm thanks; she used Latin MS 15970 of the Bibliothèque nationale (Paris), in which Purgatory figures on folios 156–64. An anthology of *exempla* drawn from Stephen of Bourbon's compilation was published in the last century by A. Lecoy de la Marche, *Anecdotes historiques, légendes et apologues tirés du recueil inédit d'Etienne de Bourbon, dominicain du XIIIe siècle* (Paris, 1877). The author excerpts fourteen *exempla* dealing with Purgatory on pp. 30–49. Madame Lagarde has transcribed all thirty-nine of the exempla dealing with Purgatory. Humbert of Romans, master-general of the Dominicans, compiled a collection of *exempla* while in retirement at the Dominican monastery in Lyons between 1263 and his death in 1277. This is known as the *Liber de dono timoris* or *Tractatus de habundancia exemplorum*, and it still awaits a critical edition and thorough study. It is very similar to Stephen of Bourbon's treatise.

57. Gervase of Tilbury, *Scriptores rerum brunsvicensium*, ed. Leibniz, 1.921, and Liebrecht, *Des Gervasius von Tilbury Otia imperialia* (Hanover, 1856), p. 12.

58. Latin text in Lecoy de la Marche, *Anecdotes historiques*, p. 32.

59. Arturo Graf, "Artù nell'Etna," in *Miti, leggende e superstizioni del Medio Evo*.

60. Lecoy de la Marche, *Anecdotes historiques*, pp. 30–31.

61. Ibid., p. 43.

62. I wish to thank Colette Ribaucourt, who transcribed an unpublished manuscript of *Alphabetum narrationum*, for sending me the "*exempla* of Purgatory." Concerning the *Alphabetum narrationum*, see Jacques Le Goff, "Le vocabulaire des exempla d'après l'*Alphabetum narrationum*," in the proceedings of the 1978 Paris colloquium, *La lexicographie du latin médiéval* (Paris, 1981). For a rough idea of the place of Purgatory in medieval *exempla*, the reader may wish to consult F. C. Tubach's *Index exemplorum. A Handbook of Medieval Religious Tales*, FF Comunications no. 204 (Helsinki, 1969), which is based primarily on the most important thirteenth- and fourteenth-century collections of *exempla*. The forthcoming pamphlet on the *exemplum* (see n. 20 above) in the Typologie des sources du Moyen Age occidental series comments on the merits and defects of this research tool.

63. Nicole Bériou, "La prédication au beguinage de Paris pendant l'année liturgique 1272–1273," *Extrait des Recherches augustiniennes* 23(1978): 105–229.

64. Ibid., p. 124.

65. Ibid.

66. Ibid., p. 129.

67. Ibid., p. 138.

68. Ibid., p. 143.

69. Ibid., p. 154.

70. Ibid., p. 160.

71. Ibid., p. 185 n. 253.

72. Ibid., p. 221.

73. E. Kleinschmidt, "Die Colmarer Dominikaner Geschictsschreibung im 13. und 14. Jahrhundert," *Deutsches Archiv für Erforschung des Mittelalters* 28(2)1872:484–86.

74. See the fine book by Andre Vauchez, *La Sainteté en Occident aux derniers siècles du Moyen Age (1198–1431). Recherches sur les mentalités religieuses médiévales* (Rome, 1981).

75. On the Latin legendaries see the excellent introduction by Guy Philippart, *Les légendiers latins et autres manuscrits hagiographiques*, Typologie des sources du Moyen Age occidental (Turnhout, 1977). In 1980 Jean-Pierre Perrot defended an interesting thesis at the University of Paris-III on a collection of French thirteenth-century *légendiers*. Research on legendaries in English and German is under way.

76. The edition of the Latin text of the *Golden Legend* edited by Theodor Graese (Dresden-Leipzig, 1846) was based on a single manuscript. The 1900 French translation by Roze (republished in 1967) is mediocre and that of Teodor de Wyzewa (Paris, 1902) is to be preferred, though it is harder to find.

77. *Legenda aurea*, ed. Graese, pp. 213–16.

78. Ibid., pp. 728–39.

79. "Purgantur in quodam loco juxta infernum posito qui purgatorium dicitur" (ibid., p. 730).

80. Ibid., p. 736.

81. Ibid., p. 739.

82. On Lutgard, see S. Roisin, "Sainte Lutgarde d'Aywières dans son ordre et son temps," *Collectanea Ordenis Cistercensium reformatorum* 8(1946):161–72; and L. Reypens, "Sin Lutgarts mysticke opgang," *Ons geest Erf.* 20(1946).

83. *Vita* 2.4, *Acta Sanctorum*, 16 June, vol. 4 (Paris-Rome, 1867).

84. *Vita* 2.9, ibid., p. 198.

85. *Vita* 3.5, ibid., p. 205.

86. *Vita* 3.8, ibid., p. 206.

87. Cf. J. Chiffoleau, *La comptabilité de l'Au-delà, les hommes, la mort et la religion dans la région comtadine á la fin du Moyen Age* (Rome, 1981); and M. Bastard-Fournié, "Le Purgatoire dans la région toulousaine au XIVe et au début du XVe siècle," *Annales du Midi* 5(34)1980, especially pp. 14–17 (and n. 65).

88. J.-P. Redoutey, "Le testament de Renaud de Bourgogne, Comte de Monteliard," *Société d'émulation de Montbeliard*, 75, no. 102 (1979): 27–57. See the short note by P. C. Timbal, "Les legs pieux au Moyen Age," in the proceedings of the 1975 colloquium of the Society of Medieval Historians at Strasbourg, *La Mort au Moyen Age* (Strasbourg, 1977), pp. 23–26.

89. J.-L. Lemaître, *Répertoire des documents nécrologiques français*, under the

direction of P. Marot, Recueil des historiens de la France, 2 vols. (Paris, 1980), pp. 23–24.

90. The original text was published by G. Fagniez, Documents pour servir à l'histoire de l'industrie en France, vol. 1 (Paris, 1898).

91. I have used the examples given by Tobler-Lommatzch, Altfranzösisches Wörterbuch 7 (1969), col. 2096–97, s.v. purgatoire, and the references given by J.-C. Payen in Le motif du repentir dans la littérature française médiévale (des origines à 1230) (Geneva, 1968), s.v. purgatoire, excluding all but those texts in which Purgatory is explicitly mentioned, which means, for example, that the "pious story" of "le chevalier au barisel" is not included.

92. Philippe de Novare, IV ages d'omes, ed. M. de Fréville (Paris, 1888), p. 32: "Si fait li jones po de penitance ou siècle; si estuet qu'il la face grant et longue en purgatoire."

93. Li Romans de Baudouin de Sebourc, XVI, 843, in Tobler-Lommatzch, 7, col. 2097.

94.　　　　　　　En purgatoire c'est la somme
　　　　　　　　　Menez en fu por les meffaix
　　　　　　　　　Qu'en sa vie out ouvrez et fait.
　　　　　　　　　　　　　　(Ibid.)

95.　　　　　　　Et sages home amesurer
　　　　　　　　　Se doit si ke puisse durer
　　　　　　　　　S'aumosne tant qu'il iert en vie
　　　　　　　　　Si qu'a la mort li fache aïe
　　　　　　　　　De li mener en purgatoire
　　　　　　　　　Pour lui poser net en la gloire.

La Dîme de pénitence 2885 (cited by Tobler-Lommatzch, 7, col. 2097).

96. Arsenio Frugoni, "Il Guibileo di Bonifacio VIII," Bolletino dell'Istituto Storico Italiano per il Medioevo e Archivio Muratoriano, 1950, pp. 1–121, reprinted in Incontri nel Medio Evo (Bologna, 1979), pp. 73–177.

97. PL 72.222.

98. Bullarium Anni Sancti, ed. H. Schmidt (Rome, 1949), p. 35.

99. A. Frugoni, Incontri nel Medioevo, p. 106.

100. G. G. Merlo, Eretici e inquisitori nella società piemontese del trecento (Turin, 1977), pp. 167, 176, 178, 185, 192, 196, 198.

101. Inquisitio in Rixendin fanaticam, in I. von Dollinger, Beiträge zur Sektengeschichte des Mittelalters (Munich, 1890), vol. 2, pp. 706–11.

102. J. Duvernoy, Le Registre d'Inquisition de Jacques Fournier (Paris-The Hague, 1978), 1.354.

103. Ibid., p. 160.

104. Ibid., p. 163.

105. Ibid., p. 167.

106. Bonvesino dalla Riva, Le opere volgari, ed. G. Contini, vol. 1 (Rome, 1941). I have consulted the edition of Leandro Biadene, Il libro delle Tre Scritture de Bonvesino dalla Riva (Pisa, 1902). I am indebted to my friends Girolamo Arnaldi and Raoul Manselli for my familiarity with the writings of Bonvesino dalla Riva and Giacomino da Verona.

107. Giacomino da Verona, La Gerusalemme celeste e la Babilonia infernale, ed.

E. Barana (Verona, 1921). I have used the edition of R. Broggini and G. Contini in *Poeti del Duecento*, vol. 1 (Naples, 1960), pp. 627–52.

108. Jacopo Passavanti, *Lo Specchio di vera penitenza*, ed. M. Lenardon, pp. 387–91.

CHAPTER TEN

1. In preparing this chapter, the author used the bilingual French-Italian edition of the *Divina Commedia* published in honor of the seventh centenary of Dante's birth by Les Libraires associés (Paris, 1965). The Italian text of this edition was based on the most recent edition published by the Società Dantesca Italiana; the French translation was that of L. Espinasse-Mongenet, revised by Louise Cohen and Claude Ambroise, with an introduction by Paul Renucci. Also profitable to consult was the translation with abundant original commentary by Andre Pezard, published in the Bibliothèque de la Pléiade, also in 1965. A convenient outline of the structure of the *Purgatorio* is found in the Edizione del Centenario of *Tutte le Opere di Dante*, ed. Fredi Chiapelli (Milan: U. Marsia, 1965). The brief article "Purgatorio" in the *Dante Dictionary* is useful for its topographical as well as ideological characterization of Dante's Purgatory. Interesting information concerning the location and description of Purgatory may be found in the old essay by Edoardo Coli, *Il paradiso terrestre dantesco* (Florence, 1897). As for commentaries, that of G. A. Scartazzini is reprinted with revisions by Giuseppe Vandelli in the critical edition published by the Società Dantesca Italiana, 2d ed. (Milan, 1960); Andre Pezard recommends that of G. Troccoli, *Il Purgatorio dantesco*. I have also used Charles S. Singleton, *Dante Alighieri, The Divine Comedy, Purgatorio, vol. 2: Commentary* (Princeton, 1973) and the notes to the edition edited by Natalino Sapegno (Florence, 1956). For a theological viewpoint, important for my interpretation, the classic study by Father Mandonnet, *Dante, le théologien* (Paris, 1935) can still be read in conjunction with Etienne Gilson's *Dante et la philosophie* (Paris, 1939).

On the subject of Dante's forerunners in visions and descriptions of the other world, I mention the following: H. R. Patch, *The Other World According to Descriptions in Medieval Literature* (1950); A. d'Ancona, *I precursori di Dante* (Florence, 1874); M. Dods, *Forerunners of Dante* (Edinburgh, 1903); Diels, "Himmels und Höllenfahrten von Homer bis Dante," *Neues Jahrbuch* 49(1922):239ff.; A. Ruegg, *Die Jenseitsvorstellungen vor Dante* (Einsiedeln and Cologne, 1945); and especially Giosue Musca, "Dante e Beda," *Studi Storici in onore di Ottorino Bertolini*, vol 2. (1972), pp. 497–524. I am indebted to my friend Girolamo Arnaldi for the opportunity to consult, in excellent circumstances, older commentaries on the *Divina Commedia* published by G. Biagi, G. L. Passerini, and E. Rostagno, *La Divina Commedia nella figurazione artistica e nel secolare commento* (Turin, 1931). The oldest commentaries, namely those of the fourteenth century, in which I was exclusively interested, are mainly philological.

2. "Onde si legge [Cicero's *De Senectute*] di Catone che non a se, ma a la patria e a tutto lo mondo nato esser credea" (*Convivio* 4.27.3).

3. *Il Purgatorio* 1.108; 2.60, 122; 3.46; 4.38, 39; 6.48; 7.4, 65; 8.57; 10.18; 12.24, 73; 14.1; 15.8; 19.117; 20, 114, 128; 21.35, 71; 22.123; 25.105; 27.74; 28.101; and 30.74. And, in the *Paradiso* 15.93 and 17.113, 137.

4. Cf. *Dante Dictionary*, p. 534.

5.   Ed elli a me: "L'amor del bene scemo
             del suo dever quiritta si ristora,
             qui si ribatte il mal tardato remo."
These beautiful lines are difficult to translate.

6. Cf. L. K. Little, "Pride Goes before Avarice: Social Change and the Vices in Latin Christendom," *American Historical Review* 57(1971).

7. This commentary is taken from the translation by L. Espinasse-Mongenet mentioned in note 1 above. The cited passage occurs on page 604.

8.   Della mondizia sol voler fa prova
             che, tutto libero a mutar convento,
             l'alma sorprende, e di voler le giova.

9.   Oi ombre vane, fuor che nell'aspetto!
             Tre volte dietro a lei le mani avvinsi,
             tante mi tornai con esse al petto (2.79–81).

10. See the suggestive article by Luigi Blasucci, "La dimensione del tempo nel Purgatorio," *Approdo Letterario* (1967), pp. 40–57. Concerning the translation into psychological terms of this theological material, see A. Momigliano's shrewd observations in his commentary on the *Purgatorio* (Florence, 1946), especially on the "nostalgia insieme terrena e celeste, che unisce in una medesima malinconia le anime che aspirano alla patria celeste e il pellegrino che ha in cuore la lontana patria terrena."

11. See M. Marti, "Simbologie luministiche nel Purgatorio," *Realismo dantesco e altri studi* (Milan-Naples, 1961).

WHY PURGATORY?

1. See appendix 3.

2. Concerning the various forms taken by Purgatory's "success," see Michelle Bastard-Fournié, "Le Purgatoire dans la region toulousaine au XIVe at au debut du XVe siecle," *Annales du Midi* (1980), pp. 5–7. On the iconography of Purgatory, a vast subject still largely unexplored, the pioneering study by Gaby and Michel Vovelle, *Vision de la mort et de l'au-delà en Provence d'après les autels des âmes du purgatoire: XVe–XXe siècles* (Paris, 1970) should be mentioned, though it does not deal with our period. I was unable to make use of the dissertation, as far as I know unpublished, by Mme A.-M. Vaurillon-Cervoni, "L'iconographie du Purgatoire au Moyen Age dans le Sud-Ouest, le centre de la France, et en Espagne" (Toulouse, 1978), which seems to focus on the late Middle Ages and the sixteenth century.

3. I refer the reader to M. Bastard-Fournié's remarks, especially those concerning Jacques Chiffoleau's fine work on Avignon and the Comtat Venaissin, particularly p. 17 n. 65 and, more generally, p. 7.

4. Philippe Ariès, *L'Homme devant la mort* (Paris, 1977); Pierre Chaunu, *La Mort à Paris—XVIe, XVIIe, XVIIIe siècles* (Paris, 1978); F. Lebrun, *Les Hommes et la mort en Anjou* (Paris, 1973); idem, *Mourir autrefois. Attitudes collectives devant la mort aux XVIIe et XVIIIe siècles* (Paris, 1974); idem, "Les attitudes devant la mort: problèmes de méthodes, approches et lectures différentes," *Annales E.S.C.* (1976). In a recent book that I received as I was writing this conclusion, Pierre Chaunu gives a remarkable characterization of Purgatory in the

sixteenth century that confirms the results of my investigations: see his *L'Eglise, culture et société. Essais sur Réforme et contre-Réforme, 1517–1620* (Paris, 1981), especially pp. 378–80 on the Council of Trent. There he repeats an assertion made in his 1978 book (p. 131) based in part on an outline proposal I made in 1975: Jacques Le Goff, "La naissance du Purgatoire (XIIe–XIIIe siècles)," in the proceedings of the 1975 Strasbourg colloquium, *La Mort au Moyen Age*, with a preface by Pierre Chaunu (Paris, 1977), p. 710. "The explosion of Purgatory," Chaunu writes (p. 64), "and the 'substantiation' of purgatorial punishment can be dated quite precisely. These came about between 1170 and 1180, so far as we can judge from the heterogeneous sources available. Purgatory exploded like an atomic bomb once the critical mass had been assembled." I hope that my statement of the case has been somewhat more careful than this.

5. See R. R. Grimm, *Paradisus Coelestis, Paradisus Terrestris. Zur Auslegungsgeschichte des Paradises im Abendland bis um 1200* (Munich, 1977).

6. Y. Congar, *Vaste monde, ma paroisse. Vérité et dimensions du salut* (Paris, 1966), chap. 7: "Que savons-nous du Purgatoire," p. 76. See also idem, "Le Purgatoire," in *Le mystère de la mort et sa célébration*, Lex orandi, 12 (Paris, 1956), pp. 279–336.

7. In the etymological sense of apocalypse: unveiling, revelation.

Appendix Four

1. The modern editor has in several places made improper use of the term *purgatorium* in his titles for the various visions.

Index